12.00
E6

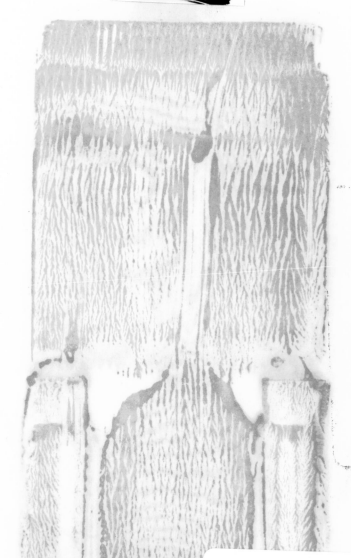

D1249387

WOMEN IN
THE SOVIET ECONOMY

WOMEN IN THE SOVIET ECONOMY

Their Role in Economic, Scientific, and Technical Development

A study sponsored by the Foreign Studies Group, Office of Economic and Manpower Studies, National Science Foundation, and prepared under the supervision of the Department of Economics, University of Maryland

NORTON T. DODGE

THE JOHNS HOPKINS PRESS
Baltimore

TO MY MOTHER AND FATHER

PREFACE

CONCERN IN recent years for the waste of women's talent and labor potential led to the appointment of The President's Commission on the Status of Women, which has issued a series of reports on various problems affecting women and their participation in economic, political, and social life.[1] For any formulation of policy directed toward the better use of our woman power, it is important to know the experience of other nations in utilizing the capabilities of women. For this reason as well as others, the Soviet experience is of particular interest at this time.

Although the lack of reported data on some of the topics under consideration resulted in many unanswered questions, during the past decade there has been a significant improvement in the flow of both statistical and descriptive materials from the Soviet Union. A great variety of statistical handbooks and other materials presenting figures on the country's economic, social, and cultural developments has been screened and analyzed for this study. Because so many of these statistics had to be related to data on population and its characteristics, the pivotal years for analysis in the present study are 1926, 1939, and 1959—the years in which national censuses

for the U.S.S.R. were made. Bench marks so widely separated are of limited use, however, unless one can fill in the gaps with additional information. Thus, intercensal comparisons are supplemented when possible by other published statistics and by estimates of births, deaths, size and structure of the population according to educational attainment, employment, and so forth. Projections of the population by broad age groups are made for 1970 and 1980. As in most studies lacking a strong historical focus, the reader will find that greater attention is devoted—with a few exceptions, when current data are deficient—to more recent materials.

A somewhat analogous progression is attempted in the emphasis by topics, the greatest emphasis being placed on professional women in the field of science and technology. Four chapters do not deal specifically with the labor force but with more general aspects of women, their number, age structure, and education—Chapter 2 on population questions, Chapter 6 on educational trends, Chapter 7 on training in science and technology, and Chapter 8 on educational attainment. Chapters 7 and 8 are, of course, crucial to an understanding of the contribution of women to the scientific and technical achievements of the Soviet Union. Primary emphasis, however, is placed on the role of women in the Soviet labor force. The extent to which

---

[1] The President's Commission on the Status of Women, *American Women* (Washington, D.C., 1963), and other specialized reports.

women participate in the economy as a whole is discussed in Chapter 3. Some of the factors affecting this participation are examined in Chapters 4 and 5. In Chapters 9 and 10, the role of women in the two most important categories of the Soviet labor force is described—the less skilled occupations in agriculture and industry (Chapter 9) and the more highly skilled semiprofessional and professional occupations (Chapter 10). In Chapter 11, I examine and attempt to assess the contribution of women to Soviet science and technology.

The sources used in this study are mainly published Soviet materials. In addition, first-hand information and impressions were gathered in the Soviet Union during a month in the spring of 1955, two months in the summer of 1962, and five weeks in the spring of 1965. During the two latter visits, which took me from Leningrad to Alma-Ata, I had both formal and informal conferences and interviews with several-score Soviet officials, administrators, scientists, engineers, teachers, physicians, economists, and others concerned with problems related to the training and employment of women. Many of those interviewed were women.

Intourist and the Institute of Soviet-American Relations were helpful in arranging my visits to nurseries, kindergartens, schools, higher educational institutions, research institutes, farms, factories, and other institutions and enterprises.

I should like to thank the National Science Foundation for its financial support of this research and to express special thanks to Mr. Joseph P. Kozlowski of the Office of Economic and Manpower Studies for his encouragement and help. This study was initiated by Mr. Michael Roof, but because of other commitments he withdrew from the project. His contribution, particularly in the early stages of the study, was helpful. Mr. Charles West was also very helpful in the initial stages, and his loyal assistance is gratefully acknowledged. Special thanks are due Mrs. Elizabeth Marbury Bass for assistance on the legal sections of Chapter 4, Mr. James Brackett of the Bureau of the Census for invaluable help on Chapter 2, and Mr. Murray Feshbach, also of the Bureau of the Census, for assistance and advice on Chapters 9 and 10, as well as on bibliographic matters. The excellent collection of materials in the library of the Foreign Demographic Analysis Division of the Bureau of the Census, which was made available to me by Mr. Feshbach, yielded much valuable data.

Mrs. May Spiro ably and loyally edited and prepared the initial draft of the manuscript. Imaginative editorial assistance was given by Mrs. Mary Knight. Mrs. Janet Lugo was also of assistance in the final throes of completing the manuscript.

I should also like to thank the staff of the Slavic Room of the Library of Congress, particularly Dr. Gisela Weinfeld, for its generous help over many months. Professor Dudley Dillard, chairman of the Department of Economics, and the departmental secretary, Mrs. Helen Jenkins, have facilitated my work in many ways. Finally, I should like to acknowledge my great debt and gratitude to my old friend and former colleague, Professor Nicholas DeWitt, whose important and fundamental work in the areas of Soviet education and professional manpower has made my task easier.

NORTON T. DODGE

College Park, Maryland
September, 1965

CONTENTS

LIST OF FIGURES

Appendix VII

LIST OF TABLES

Appendix I

Appendix II

Appendix III

DEFINITIONS

Able-bodied age group	Officially 16 to 59 years for men and 16 to 54 years for women
Age-specific birth rate	Number of children born to a thousand women of a given age
Aspirant	Graduate student
Birth rate or crude birth rate	Number of children born per thousand of the total population
CPSU	Communist Party of the Soviet Union
Candidate degree	First Soviet advanced degree; roughly comparable to the Ph.D.
Doctoral degree	Highest Soviet advanced degree; senior to the Ph.D.
Dotsent	Associate professor
Dvor	Traditional peasant household
Feldsher	Assistant physician or medic; term originated in the army
Gosplan	State Planning Committee (Commission)
Gross reproduction rate (GRR)	The maternal gross reproduction rate is the number of female children who will be born per 100 women who will survive through the reproductive ages, if a constant set of age-specific birth rates prevails throughout the period
Internat	Boarding school
Kafedra	Academic department or chair in a higher educational institution
Komsomol	Young Communist League
Kulak	Rich peasant
MTS	Machine Tractor Station
NEP	New Economic Policy (1921–28), under which a wide range of private economic activity was legalized

xvii

Nomenklatura	Appointments list controlled by the party
Oblast	Governmental administrative unit subordinated to a republic; province
Philology	In Soviet usage, the field of languages and literature
Polytechnical institute	General engineering school offering several specialties
Private subsidiary agriculture	Cultivation of private garden plots
R.S.F.S.R.	Russian Soviet Federated Socialist Republic, or Russia proper
Scientific worker (*nauchnyi rabotnik*)	Specialist working not only in a natural science field but in any field of knowledge
Technicum	Specialized secondary school
Trudoden	Labor day; a work-day unit on a collective farm
Working age group	Men and women 16 to 59 years of age
Yasli	Nursery or crèche

WOMEN IN
THE SOVIET ECONOMY

chapter
1

INTRODUCTION

A MAJOR resource of any nation is its people, and the effective utilization of this resource is the precondition for social, economic, or technical development. This study examines Soviet utilization of human resources—specifically, the resources of women—and attempts to present a broad survey of the part played by women in the Soviet economy, particularly in science and technology. Certain other relevant aspects of the life of Soviet women are touched on. The period from the Revolution (1917) to the present, with emphasis on the recent past, is the primary focus, but on occasion it is necessary to examine conditions in pre-Communist Russia in order to gain perspective on the Communist period. This study is intended to provide a foundation for an understanding of the forces which have shaped the role of women in the Soviet economy as well as an appreciation of their contribution to Soviet economic development. Hopefully, it will stimulate further investigation into the many controversial questions which it raises but does not resolve.

In any comparison of Soviet and American manpower resources, one is immediately struck by the differences in the utilization of women. The restricted role of women in the American economy contrasts sharply with their broad role in the Soviet economy. This difference is most striking in the areas of science and technology, where women have come to occupy an extremely significant position in the Soviet Union, particularly at the semiprofessional and intermediate professional levels.

In the chapters ahead it will soon become apparent that the difference in the utilization of women in the two economies stems largely from the fundamental differences in the underlying philosophies and aims of the two societies. The importance of women in the Soviet economy is primarily the result of the profound transformation in the political, economic, and social organization under the Soviet regime. These changes, which have been compressed into a period of fewer than fifty years, are the result of policies deliberately formulated and vigorously, even ruthlessly, pursued by the party and the government. Through the mobilization of the entire society, Soviet totalitarianism has sought to reconstruct not only the economic and social institutions, but also the attitudes and minds of the people. To this end, the regime has exerted absolute control over the various means of mass communication and education and has used them to inspire, manipulate, or drive the public into supporting, or acquiescing in, the regime's programs.

There are limits, of course, to the power of the Soviet regime, even when supported by the modern devices which so facilitate the wielding of centralized power. Formidable restraints are imposed by a society's previous cultural pattern. As the Soviets discovered in Central Asia, long-established beliefs, customs, and practices can be extremely difficult to eradicate. Institutions supporting the *status quo*—the family, school, and church—may show surprising resilience. Some institutions,

1

particularly the school, were soon reorganized to further the objectives of the Soviet regime. Others, such as the church, were eventually tolerated after they had survived in a much-weakened condition a period of vigorous attack. The family, however, as a primary social unit, has remained a constant challenge to the state by virtue of its resistance to outside influences and its tendency to harbor traditional values.

Marxist doctrine held that women were no less subjugated under capitalism than was the proletariat. The family was considered to be founded upon the domestic enslavement of the wife. Not only did the Soviet leadership feel bound to eliminate exploitation in the home, but it also believed that the family perpetuated the outmoded bourgeois ideology. Nikolai Bukharin, a leading party theoretician, stated at the Thirteenth Party Congress in 1924 that the family remained "a formidable stronghold of all the turpitudes of the old regime."[1] For this reason, early legislation aimed not only at improving the status of women, but also at undermining the strength of the family. Women were granted full equality with men under the law. Measures facilitating divorce, legalizing unregistered marriages, legitimizing children born out of wedlock, and legalizing abortion were designed to loosen the bonds which tied the family together.

The attitude of the regime toward the family changed as the regime gained confidence. By the mid-1930's the family was no longer considered a threat to the political control of the younger generation, and the Soviet leadership had become more clearly aware of the family's positive function in preparing children for their future roles in society. Modern industry called for the virtues of promptness, reliability, co-operativeness, and receptivity to direction on the part of workers—all virtues which the family can inculcate better than the state. As a result, much of the early legislation easing divorce and weakening family ties

was modified. Soviet theoretical discussions of the dissolution of the family and the transfer of its functions to the state are now much less frequent; and they refer, not to the near, but to a distant utopian future when the transition from socialism to full communism will be finally achieved.

The family now forms a social unit which preserves much independence from the state; it also competes with the state for the time and energy of women workers. Family demands may prevent some women from participating in the labor force and some women from giving their work sufficient attention, but the government has nevertheless been remarkably successful in maintaining a high level of participation in the labor force by all age groups, even by those in the principal years of child-bearing and child rearing. On the other hand, the double burden of family and work which many women bear has had the unintended social consequence of contributing to a reduction in the birth rate, which in turn may adversely affect future economic growth. It is clear from the complexity of these interrelationships that one cannot properly study women as participants in the labor force without considering how their roles as wives and mothers are affected, and vice versa. In the early chapters of this study, we shall attempt to discover the most important factors encouraging or inhibiting the participation of women in the Soviet economy.

As will be shown, the most important circumstance underlying the high level of participation by women in the labor force has been the forced-draft industrialization of the Soviet Union. The willingness of the regime to sacrifice human welfare for higher rates of economic growth has had a decisive impact on almost every policy affecting women in their economic role. For example, the large relative loss of male population caused by the two World Wars, the Civil War, and the vicissitudes of the 1920's and 1930's would not necessarily of itself have led to an increase in the participation of women in the labor force. However, the regime's determination to maintain the high rate of economic

---

[1] Quoted in Alex Inkeles and Raymond A. Bauer, *The Soviet Citizen* (Cambridge, Mass., 1959), p. 190.

growth necessitated that more women be drawn into and retained in the labor force. This determination also explains the ambivalence of the regime toward the provision of more adequate child-care facilities, cafeterias, and household durables. These would have been provided, even at the expense of investment in producers' goods, if the regime had been less preoccupied with economic growth and more with human welfare. The regime chose, however, to provide only the minimum necessary to keep a large proportion of women in the labor force. As a result, most Soviet women continue to carry heavy domestic burdens in addition to their work responsibilities. The resulting conflict between family and work is found to have important consequences for the productivity of women, especially in the more demanding and creative occupations.

The chapters on education are intended, in part, to show the rapid increase under Soviet rule in the breadth and scope of the education of women. After the Revolution, increasing numbers of girls entered the secondary specialized schools and higher educational institutions. The relative proportion of women in all fields of study increased. As the industrialization drive gained momentum, both the number and the proportion of girls enrolled in the sciences and technology, where the shortages of manpower were greatest, increased impressively. This study examines how young women in the Soviet Union are influenced in their choice of fields and shows why some professions traditionally followed by men—the medical profession, for example —are now largely the province of women. An attempt is made to explain why the relative proportion of female students shrinks as the level of education increases and why, in recent years, there has been a general reduction in the proportion of women enrolled in higher education—a reduction to a level substantially below that which would be expected from the proportion of women in the college-age population. An explanation is called for, since equal access to higher education continues to

be proclaimed as one of the cornerstones of Soviet policy.

The employment of women in unskilled and semiskilled jobs in agriculture, industry, and other sectors of the economy is discussed primarily for the purpose of presenting a background against which the employment of women in semiprofessional and professional occupations can be seen in proper perspective. Although the utilization of women in the professions, particularly in science and technology, is our primary focus of interest, it is important to realize that the bulk of Soviet working women are employed in relatively unskilled work. The largest single group of women is to be found in unskilled field work in agriculture.

With this background, the final chapters turn to our central interest—the employment of women in semiprofessional and professional occupations, especially in the fields of science and technology. The role of women in the various professions and their participation as executives and administrators in various sectors of the economy are examined. As in other countries, the proportion of women in a profession declines as the level of responsibility increases. Notwithstanding this, the proportion of women in a number of professions is so large that their representation in the top echelons is substantial. The present study also assesses the contribution of women to scholarship and research in a wide variety of scientific, technical, and other fields. A number of indirect measures of scholarly productivity are devised and applied. An explanation of the apparent lower scholarly productivity of women is then developed.

The lower productivity of women—particularly in creative scholarly work—has evident implications for the determination of the optimal allocation of scarce educational resources between men and women. The hypothesis is offered that recent trends in the enrollment of women reflect the awareness of planners that women offer the nation a lower average return on investment in their education than men. Similarly, it is concluded that the relatively small proportion of women in jobs with the greatest responsibility is far more a reflection of their lower productivity than the result of discrimination. Indeed, outstanding women are often actively sought by the regime for prominent positions.

For the most part Soviet women appear to have won the battle for equality. However, the reader may feel that for many women equality in work has actually led to inequality, since they must also bear the burden of family responsibilities. For professional women, the stimulation of their work often provides compensation for this extra burden, but for the vast numbers engaged in heavy, monotonous toil there is no compensation.

The overriding aim of the Soviet regime has been rapid economic growth, and from this standpoint the policies of the regime toward women, although sometimes contradictory, have proved successful. Perhaps more than any other, Soviet society has developed and put to use both the strength and the genius of its women.

chapter 2

DEMOGRAPHIC FACTORS AFFECTING EMPLOYMENT

FUNDAMENTAL TO any study of the role of women in the Soviet labor force is an analysis of the underlying demographic data. Information on the age-sex composition of the population and other data from the recent census help to clarify the special pressures which affect the utilization of women. By comparing these data with earlier information and projecting them forward, we may discover much about several of the fundamental forces which have shaped Soviet employment policy in the past and which will influence it in the future. For example, it is sometimes difficult to determine the extent to which the high rate of participation of women in the labor force has been dictated by economic necessity rather than by ideological principles. Although demography may not provide a final answer to this question, it can provide such basic information as the extent of the male deficit and the rate at which this deficit is being dissipated, the present and probable future size of the population group from which workers are drawn, the number of husbandless women who must work, and the family composition and its relationship to the availability of women workers.

Our analysis is centered on the Soviet period, but it will not be limited to it. In almost fifty years of Soviet rule, only three national censuses have been published. Of necessity, then, 1926, 1939, and 1959 are pivotal years

in this analysis.[1] Because each of these censuses was preceded by a period of violent change, estimates are presented for various intercensal years, and references are made to the census of 1897. In order to determine the extent of the irregularities in the age-sex structure which resulted from the many wars and civil disorders over the last half century and to gain some insight into the demographic factors which might shape future policy on the employment of women, projections of the population for 1970 and 1980 are also presented.

AGE-SEX COMPOSITION OF THE SOVIET POPULATION

Sex Ratios. For the Soviet Union, the legacy of the wars, revolutions, and coercive government policies in the first half of the twentieth century is a predominantly female population. According to the 1959 census, females comprised 54.9 per cent of the total population and 63.4 per cent of the population

---

[1]The All-Union Census of 1920, although published, was conducted during the Civil War; the results are consequently incomplete and generally of poor quality. The Urban Census of 1923 was published in full. The results of the National Census of 1937 were repudiated and not published.

in the age group 35 years and over. In comparison, females comprise 50.8 per cent of the total population of the United States and 51.9 per cent of the population in the age group 35 years and over.

Although there may have been occasions during the early Tsarist era when the male population was as heavily decimated as it was during the Communist period, the census of 1897 does not show an abnormal preponderance of females. Females comprised 50.3 per cent of the total population and between 49.8 and 51.1 per cent of the population in the four broad age groups shown in Table 1. Measured in terms of the sex ratios (males per 100 females), the age group 35 to 59 years had the highest ratio, 100.7 males per 100 females, while the age group 60 years and over had the lowest, 95.5 males per 100 females (see Table 2).

By 1926, however, the effects of World War I, the Revolution, and the Civil War were reflected in the sex ratio for the age group 16 years and over, which was markedly lower than it had been twenty-nine years earlier. There were only approximately 90 males per

100 females in the age groups 16 to 34 years and 35 to 59 years, while the sex ratio for the age group 60 years and over was only about 79 males per 100 females. Between 1926 and 1939, a span of years which saw the collectivization of agriculture and the political purges, the numerical predominance of females increased further. Females comprised 52.1 per cent of the Soviet Union's total population in 1939 and 55.5 to 60.2 per cent of the population in the age group 35 years and over. Estimates for 1946, seven years later, show the result of the tremendous loss of males during World War II; they indicate that females comprised 57.4 per cent of the total population and more than 60 per cent of the population in the age group 16 years and over. However, the normal balance of the sexes is gradually being attained for the various age groups. In 1946, females comprised 58.1 per cent of the population in the age group 16 to 34 years, but this proportion dropped to 55.7 per cent in 1950 and to 51.6 per cent in 1959. By 1970 only about 50 per cent of this age group is expected to be

TABLE 1. Females as percentage of total population, 1897–1980.[a]

Age Group	1897	1926	1939	1946	1950	1959	1970	1980
All ages.....................	50.3	51.7	52.1	57.4	56.7	54.9	53.4	52.2
Under 16...................	50.0	49.7	49.7	49.9	49.8	49.1	48.8	48.6
16 to 34....................	50.8	52.7	51.0	58.1	55.7	51.6	49.7	49.1
35 to 59....................	49.8	52.5	55.5	62.8	62.8	62.3	57.1	53.3
60 and over................	51.1	55.9	60.2	65.8	66.8	66.3	67.1	66.9

[a]This table is based on figures from Appendix I, Tables 1 and 2. For 1970 and 1980, series B projections were used.

TABLE 2.　Sex ratios, 1897–1980.[a]

Age Group	1897	1926	1939	1946	1950	1959	1970	1980
All ages..............	98.9	93.5	91.9	74.3	76.2	81.9	87.3	91.7
Under 16.............	100.1	101.2	101.3	99.5	100.8	103.6	105.1	105.6
16 to 34..............	96.9	89.8	96.1	72.0	79.5	93.8	101.0	103.7
35 to 59..............	100.7	90.4	80.1	59.1	59.1	60.6	75.1	87.7
60 and over..........	95.5	78.8	66.1	51.9	49.7	50.8	49.0	49.5

[a]Number of males per 100 females. This table is based on figures from Appendix I, Tables 1 and 2. For 1970 and 1980, series B projections were used.

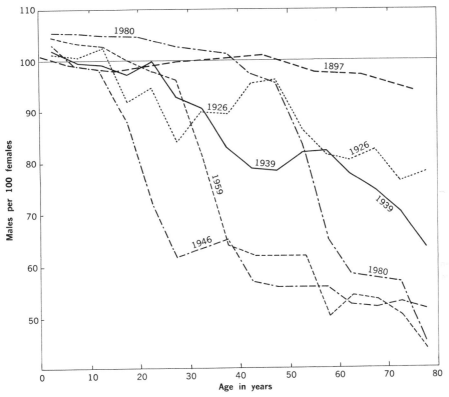

Fig. 1. Sex ratios, 1897–1980 (based on data in Appendix I, Tables 1 and 2).

female. Women comprised the same proportion of the population in the age group 35 to 59 years in 1959 as in 1946—62.3 per cent. By 1970, however, this proportion is expected to drop to about 57 per cent, and by 1980, to 53 per cent. About 67 per cent of the population in the age group 60 years and over still will be female by 1980, almost the same proportion established for 1946. Not until the beginning of the next century, when most persons who were of military age during World War II will have died, can the sex ratio for the older age groups become normal.

Figure 1 provides a graphic representation of the changing pattern of sex ratios by age between 1897 and 1980. Because the data for 1897 display extreme signs of age "heaping," or a tendency for people to express their ages in round numbers, sex ratios for ten-year age

groups were plotted for that year.[2] The sex ratios for 1897 fall reasonably close to the line representing numerical equality of the sexes. The curve for 1926 displays a dip beginning at ages 15 to 19 and a further dip beginning at ages 25 to 29. Lorimer attributes the low sex ratio at ages 15 to 19 to biased reporting,[3]

[2] The data for 1897 show a marked preference for ages ending in the digits 0 and 5, the preference for the digit 0 being much greater. Of the 5.9 million males in the age group 40 to 49 years, for example, 21 per cent gave their ages as 40 years, 16 per cent as 45 years, and only about 5 per cent as 49 years. Data for females show an even greater bias.

[3] Frank Lorimer, *The Population of the Soviet Union: History and Prospects* (Geneva, 1946), p. 42. He reports a tendency to crowd girls "into this most marriageable class in reporting the ages of those slightly younger or those older than 15–19 years."

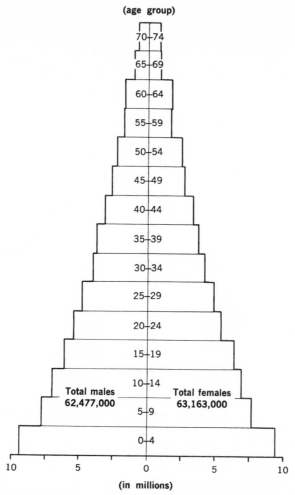

FIG. 2. Population pyramid, Russian Empire, January 28, 1897
(based on figures presented in Appendix I, Table 1).

but the low sex ratios for later years presumably reflect the heavy losses during World War I, the Revolution, and the Civil War. The curve recovers somewhat at ages 40 to 49 and then trails off sharply. The curve for 1939 exhibits roughly the same outline as that for 1926, but the curve is advanced about twelve years. The curve for 1939, however, shows lower dips, presumably reflecting losses due to the collectivization of agriculture and the forced industrialization. The curve for 1946, as might be expected, falls below all the others. The curve for 1980, exhibiting a sharp

drop beginning with the age group 40 to 44, demonstrates the long-term effect of wars on sex ratios.

Age Structure. The population pyramids for selected years from 1897 to 1980 (Figs. 2–9) trace the demographic history of the U.S.S.R.

The population structure of the Russian Empire in 1897 (Fig. 2) is typical of high-fertility, high-mortality countries which have not been markedly affected by such catastrophic events as major wars and severe famines. Populations of this type characteristically have a relatively large number of young people and relatively few old people. More than 41 per cent of the Russian population in 1897 was under age 16, in contrast to 30 per cent in 1959; and only 6.8 per cent of the population was in the age group 60 years and over in 1897, in contrast to 9.4 per cent in 1959. This population structure, altered somewhat by World War I, was inherited by the Bolsheviki in 1917.

Although the basic structure of the population in 1926 (Fig. 3) was still that of a country with high birth and mortality rates, it had been noticeably altered by the events of the preceding dozen years. The bar for the age group 5 to 9 years, representing survivors born during the period 1917 to 1921, is shorter than those immediately above and below; it reflects the depressed birth rate and sharply increased child mortality of the period. The shorter bars for the adult males on the left side of the pyramid reflect, of course, the military losses in World War I and the Civil War.

The Soviet Union entered World War II with a population structure marked by nearly a quarter century of war, famine, and civil strife (Fig. 4). As a result of the widespread practice of abortion during the early 1930's and the chaotic conditions caused by the collectivization drive during that period, the population in the age group 5 to 9 years in 1939 fell far short of that represented in the two adjacent five-year age groups. The population in age groups 15 to 19 and 20 to 24 years, representing survivors born between 1914 and 1923, was also reduced. Finally, the entire male population 25 years and over showed considerable depletion.

The pyramid for 1946 (Fig. 5) shows the structure of the Soviet Union's population at the culmination of the most devastating of the

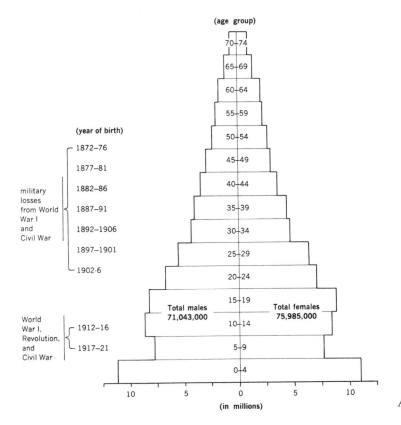

FIG. 3. Population pyramid, December 17, 1926 (based on figures presented in Appendix I, Table 1).

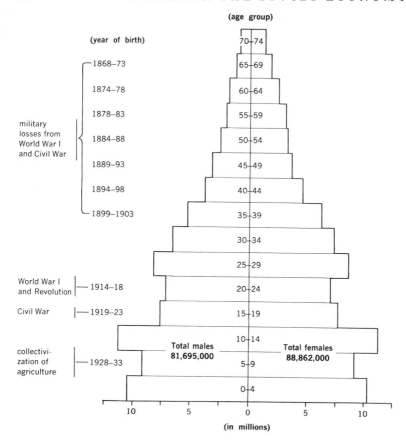

FIG. 4. Estimated population pyramid, January 17, 1939 (based on figures presented in Appendix I, Table 1).

many catastrophes experienced by the Russian people during this century. There were only about three fifths as many children in the age group under 5 years as in the age group 5 to 9 years, which reflects the substantial drop in the birth rate during World War II. The markedly shorter bars on the left side of the pyramid show the cumulative effects of the military losses in the various wars. Thus, in a little less than half a century, the structure of the Russian population was transformed from the rather regular form illustrated by the pyramid for 1897 (Fig. 2) to the highly irregular, skewed configuration represented by this pyramid for 1946.

The pyramid for 1950 (Fig. 6) shows the first signs of the recovery. The bar representing the age group 0 to 4 years is significantly longer than that for ages 5 to 9 years and is an indication of the upswing in the birth rate

after World War II. The bar for the age group 0 to 4 years, because it includes those born during the final year of the war (1945) as well as those born during the famine following the war, and because the postwar birth rate did not recover its prewar level, is shorter than that for ages 10 to 14 years, that is, for those born during the period 1935 to 1939.

The pyramid for 1959 (Fig. 7) shows the structure of the Soviet Union's population a little less than fourteen years after the end of World War II. A somewhat higher birth rate during the 1950's than that during the late 1940's provides relatively longer bars for ages 0 to 4 and 5 to 9 years. Because the years in which the wartime birth rate was at its lowest happened to fall into two of the five-year age groups, the bars for these two groups—10 to 14 and 15 to 19 years—are shorter than the bars immediately above and below, but neither

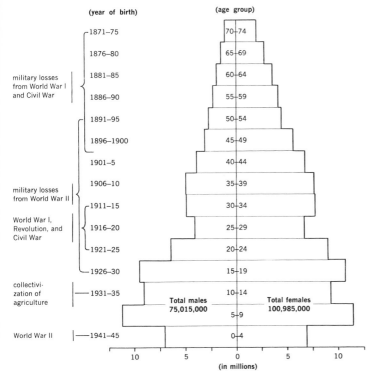

FIG. 5. Estimated population pyramid, January 1, 1946 (based on figures presented in Appendix I, Table 1).

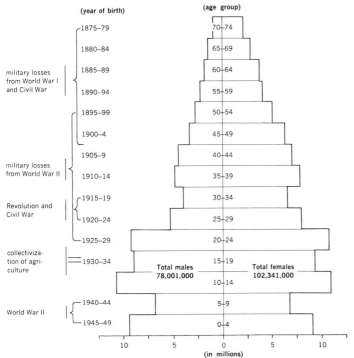

FIG. 6. Estimated population pyramid, January 1, 1950 (based on figures presented in Appendix I, Table 1).

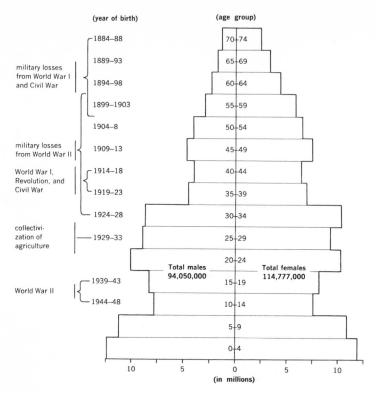

(year of birth)   (age group)

military losses
from World War I
and Civil War

military losses
from World War II

World War I,
Revolution, and
Civil War

collectivi-
zation of
agriculture

Total males
94,050,000

Total females
114,777,000

World War II

FIG. 7. Population
pyramid, January 15,
1959 (based on figures
presented in Appendix
I, Table 1).

bar is so short as that for ages 5 to 9 years in the pyramid for 1950.[4] Although the shape of the pyramid is as irregular as those for other years, the bars on the left side are about the same length as those on the right side for the ages under 30 years. For ages 30 years and over, however, the bars on the left side continue to show the effects of the large military losses.

---

[4]Unpublished estimates of the Soviet population for 1959 by single ages (prepared by the U. S. Bureau of the Census) point to 1943 as the lowest point in the World War II birth curve. The estimates show that there were only about one third as many survivors born during 1943 as during 1938. The Soviet birth rate actually started to decline as early as 1939, but the really sharp drop apparently came in 1942. The estimates show that there were only about half as many survivors born during that year as during 1938. The birth rate began its gradual recovery after 1943, but it may have been as late as 1949 before the Soviet birth rate reached its postwar recovery level, a level significantly lower than that before World War II.

The length of the bars for ages 0 to 4 and 5 to 9 years in 1970 (Fig. 8) is estimated on the basis of the probable birth rate during the 1960's. Since those born during World War II, when birth rates were low, will reach the childbearing ages during the 1960's, the number of births is expected to decline. Only a sharp increase in the size of Soviet families could reverse this trend, and no such increase seems likely.

None of the age groups from which military personnel were drawn during World War I and the Civil War are represented on the pyramid for 1980 (Fig. 9), and the age groups from which military personnel were drawn during World War II are near the top of the pyramid. Persons born during World War II are in the age group 35 to 39 years, where there is a distinct pinching of the pyramid.

When a population structure becomes as irregular as the Soviet Union's, there is a built-in tendency to perpetuate that irregularity. As indicated above, the number of

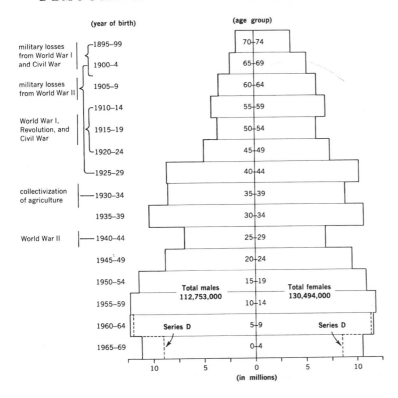

Fig. 8. Projected population pyramid, January 1, 1970 (based on figures presented in Appendix I, Table 2, Series B projection).

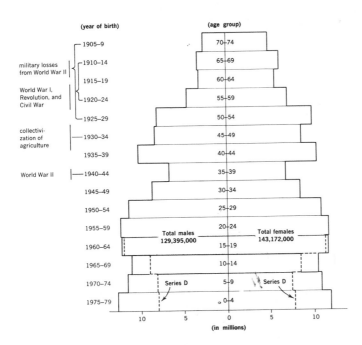

Fig. 9. Projected population pyramid, January 1, 1980 (based on figures presented in Appendix I, Table 2, Series B projection).

births during the 1960's is expected to be lower than the number recorded during the 1950's. The pyramid for 1980 shows the expected indentation in age groups 5 to 19 years as a result of these declining birth rates. It also reflects the expected rise in the number of births during the late 1970's, as persons born in the 1950's—when birth rates were at their postwar peak—replace those born during World War II in the age groups with the highest fertility rates. Had the population projections been carried beyond 1980 to the time when persons born during the 1960's begin to have children, they would indicate that the Soviet birth rate may once again decline as a result of a decreasing number of potential parents. Thus, the indirect effects of World War II will be felt for several generations to come.

A review of the eight population pyramids shows a progressive growth until 1946 in the importance of women as a Soviet manpower resource. During the intermittent upheavals of several wars and the forced government programs in agriculture and industry, the male population was decimated; and although the periods between these holocausts permitted some restoration of the normal population pyramid, the recovery period was never sufficiently long to permit the population to regain a balanced sex ratio. Hence, the catastrophes tended to be cumulative, and by 1946 women outnumbered men by more than 25 million. Only slight improvement had been made by 1959; then the wartime birth deficit began to reduce greatly the number of persons in the working-age groups. Thus, from the standpoint both of the individual woman, who had no husband upon whom she might depend for her economic well-being, and of society, which had too few men available to perform the tasks required by the economy, the increased importance of women as a manpower source appears to have been inevitable, and, as we shall presently see, the pressures to utilize women extensively in the economy can be expected to persist.

Population of Working Age.[5] Throughout the Soviet period, females have been numerically predominant in the age groups from which most of the labor force is drawn. In the Russian Empire of 1897, the division between men and women was about equal in the 66 million persons of working age. By 1926, however, women comprised 52.6 per cent of the 79 million persons of working age—in the somewhat smaller territory occupied by the Soviet Union during this period between wars. This means, as Table 3 shows, that females

TABLE 3.   Population of working age, 1897–1980.[a]

Year	Both Sexes	Male	Female	Difference	Percentage
1897....	66,056	32,772	33,823	1,051	51.2
1926....	78,813	37,334	41,479	4,145	52.6
1939....	94,265	44,482	49,783	5,301	52.8
1946....	100,928	40,102	60,826	20,724	60.3
1950....	106,710	43,820	62,890	19,070	58.9
1959....	125,615	55,089	70,526	15,437	56.1
1970....	139,496	64,979	74,517	9,538	53.4
1980....	164,023	80,104	83,919	3,815	51.2

[a]I.e., age group 16 to 59 years. Population figures are expressed in thousands. This table is compiled from data presented in Appendix I, Tables 1 and 2.

outnumbered males by over 4.1 million. Of the net increase of 15.5 million in the age group 16 to 59 years between 1926 and 1939, 8.3 million, or 53.7 per cent, were females. Thus, on the eve of the World War II, there were, in the prewar territory of the Soviet Union, 94.3 million persons in the age group 16 to 59 years, of whom 49.8 million, or 52.8 per cent, were women.

Between 1939 and 1946, the Soviet population underwent a number of profound changes. First, territory with a prewar population of about 20.1 million—about 12 per cent of the Soviet prewar population—was annexed to the Soviet Union. Secondly, more than three

---

[5]Instead of using the Soviet concept of "able-bodied," usually ages 16 to 54 for women and 16 to 59 for men, in this discussion we adopt, largely for convenience, the concept of "working age," i.e., ages 16 to 59 for both sexes. A substantial proportion of males continues to work until ages 65 or 70.

million persons, many of whom were from the annexed territory, left the Soviet Union. Finally, a very substantial number of persons died as a result of the war. It is impossible to fix precisely the number of war deaths, but since the absolute decline in the population of the present territory is believed to have been about 25 million between June 22, 1941, when the Soviet Union was attacked, and the end of the war in Europe, the number of war deaths must have exceeded this figure in order to have offset the natural increment of population through births.[6]

The net effect of these changes on the working-age population was that there were only an estimated 6.7 million more persons in the age group 16 to 59 years in the postwar territory of 1946 than there were in the prewar territory of 1939. Changes in the sex ratio of this age group, however, were quite significant. The female population of working age increased from 50 million in 1939 to an estimated 61 million in 1946, an increase of some 11 million, whereas the male population of working age decreased from 44.5 million to 40.1 million, a loss of more than 4 million. Thus, in 1946, slightly over 60 per cent of the population of working age was comprised of women, on whom the Soviet Union had to depend for the monumental task of rebuilding the war-torn country. Moreover, since the war which had cost perhaps 15 million military deaths also maimed a substantial part of the surviving male population, the burden on Soviet womanhood was even greater than the population figures imply.

The population of working age rose to 106.7 million in 1950 and to 125.6 million in 1959, a total increase during the thirteen-year period from 1946 to 1959 of 24.7 million. The male population of working age, however, has been increasing more rapidly than the female, because the proportion of males entering the working-age group has been substantially higher than the proportion leaving it. Males comprised 15.0 million, or 61 per cent, and females only 9.7 million of the increase. By 1959, females comprised 56 per cent of the working-age population, a smaller proportion than that immediately after the war, but nevertheless still a significant one.

A great deal has been written during the past few years about a labor shortage in the Soviet Union. The basis for this is that in 1957 persons born during World War II, when birth rates were low, began reaching working age. As a result, the annual number added to the working-age population fell from an estimated increase of 2.2 million in 1956 to an increase of only 0.4 million in 1958 and to an absolute decrease of 0.2 million in 1959. The recovery after 1959 will not be sufficient to match the increase in 1956 until sometime after 1970.

Again, the female population of working age does not fare so well as the male. For example, as shown in Table 4, females accounted for the entire 0.2 million decline from 1959 to 1960. Moreover, by 1965 the projected increase in the male population of working age is 88 per cent of the 1957 increase, while that in the female population is only 71 per cent. By 1970 the projections show that 53.4 per cent of the working-age population will be female. By 1980 numerical equality is expected to be very nearly attained for the population 16 to 59 years of age. Thus, the pressure to utilize women in the labor force as a replacement for the deficit of men is being gradually reduced.

Dependency Ratios. One measure frequently used to determine the economic implications of the age structure is the dependency ratio, or the ratio of the population of dependent age, those under age 16 years and those aged 60 years and over, to the population of working age. Although the measure is imperfect, because some persons of dependent age are actually in the labor force while some of working age are not, it does provide at least a rough measure of the dependency burden.

[6]Both Warren Eason and Michael Roof have estimated 25 million war deaths. See Warren W. Eason, "The Soviet Population Today," *Foreign Affairs* (July, 1959), 601, and Michael K. Roof, "Soviet Population Trends," *Eugenics Quarterly* (Sept., 1961), 129.

TABLE 4.   Annual changes in the sex ratio of the working-age population, 1955–70.[a]

Year	Both Sexes		Male		Female	
	Population	Net Change	Population	Net Change	Population	Net Change
1955............	118,418		50,587		67,831	
1956............	121,028	2,610	52,089	1,502	68,939	1,108
1957............	123,251	2,223	53,410	1,321	69,841	902
1958............	125,095	1,844	54,562	1,152	70,533	692
1959............	125,520	425	55,046	484	70,474	− 59
1960............	125,318	−202	55,183	137	70,135	−339
1961............	125,331	13	55,460	277	69,871	−264
1962............	125,726	395	55,944	484	69,782	− 89
1963............	126,668	942	56,695	751	69,973	191
1964............	127,973	1,305	57,618	923	70,355	382
1965............	129,750	1,777	58,766	1,148	70,984	629
1966............	131,674	1,924	59,971	1,205	71,703	719
1967............	133,705	2,031	61,224	1,253	72,481	778
1968............	135,782	2,077	62,511	1,287	73,271	790
1969............	137,805	2,023	63,794	1,283	74,011	740
1970............	139,596	1,791	64,979	1,185	74,617	606

[a]I.e., population in the age group 16 to 59 years. Population figures are expressed in thousands. This table is based on data from U.S. Department of Commerce, Bureau of the Census, Foreign Demographic Analysis Division, *Estimates and Projec-* *tions of the Population of the U.S.S.R. and of the Communist Countries of Eastern Europe by Age and Sex* (Washington, D.C., April, 1964), pp. 1–10.

In 1897, the Russian Empire had 90.1 persons of dependent age per 100 persons of working age (see Table 5). This ratio had

TABLE 5.   Dependency ratios, 1897–1980.[a]

Year	Ratio	Year	Series	Ratio	Year	Series	Ratio
1897	90.1	1970	A	75.4	1980	A	70.4
1926	86.4		B	74.3		B	66.2
1939	80.9		C	72.2		C	59.1
1946	74.4		D	70.9		D	53.6
1950	69.0						
1959	66.2						

[a]Number of persons of dependent age (those under age 16 and those age 60 and over) per 100 persons of working age (16–59). This table is based on figures presented in Appendix I, Tables 1 and 2.

declined only slightly by 1926 despite the heavy military losses of the World War I and the ensuing Revolution and Civil War. Because the birth rate declined between 1926 and 1939, however, by 1939 there were only an estimated 80.9 persons of dependent age per 100 persons of working age. This drop in the ratio must be attributed to a decline in the proportion of the population under age 16 years, as shown in Table 6. The population of working age comprised 53.6 per cent of the total population in 1926 and 55.3 per cent in

1939, an increase of nearly 4 per cent. During this same period, the population under age 16 dropped from 39.7 to 38.2 per cent of the total population, and the population in the age group 60 years and over remained about the same. Between 1946 and 1959 the population under age 16 years dropped from 33.5 to 30.4 per cent of the total population. On the other hand, the population in the age group 60 years and over increased only slightly, from 9.2 per cent in 1946 to 9.4 per cent in 1959.

Future dependency ratios will hinge on the number of births. If the fertility of Soviet women remains constant at a gross reproduction rate (GRR) of 125, the dependency ratio will increase to about 74.3 by 1970 and then decrease to about 66.2 by 1980.[7] The increase

[7]The terms "fertility" and "birth rate" are used here and elsewhere in this chapter to refer to two rather different concepts. The crude birth rate is a statistical measure which relates total births to the total population. It does not take into account the age-sex structure of the population. Fertility, on the other hand, is not a statistical measure, but rather a nonquantitative concept which takes into account various characteristics of the population which might influence

TABLE 6. Percentage distribution of the population by age and sex, 1897–1980.[a]

Age	January 28, 1897			December 17, 1926			January 17, 1939			January 1, 1946			January 1, 1950		
	Both Sexes	Male	Female	Both Sexes	Male	Female	Both Sexes	Male	Female	Both Sexes	Male	Female	Both Sexes	Male	Female
Under 16.............	40.5	40.8	40.3	39.7	41.3	38.1	38.2	40.1	36.4	33.5	39.2	29.5	31.8	36.9	27.8
16 to 34.............	30.6	30.3	31.0	32.8	32.1	33.5	33.1	33.9	32.4	31.5	30.9	31.9	32.5	32.2	31.9
35 to 59.............	21.9	22.1	21.7	20.8	20.4	21.1	22.2	20.6	23.6	25.9	22.5	28.3	26.7	22.9	29.6
60 and over...........	6.9	6.7	7.0	6.7	6.1	7.2	6.6	5.5	7.6	9.2	7.4	10.5	9.1	7.0	10.7
16 to 59.............	52.6	52.5	52.7	53.6	52.6	54.6	55.3	54.4	56.0	57.3	54.4	60.2	59.2	56.2	61.5

| Age | January 15, 1959 | | | January 1, 1970 | | | | | | | | | | | |
				Series A			Series B			Series C			Series D		
	Both Sexes	Male	Female	Both Sexes	Male	Female	Both Sexes	Male	Female	Both Sexes	Male	Female	Both Sexes	Male	Female
Under 16.............	30.4	34.4	27.2	31.1	34.4	28.3	30.6	33.9	27.9	28.9	33.0	27.1	29.3	32.4	26.6
16 to 34.............	34.6	37.2	32.5	28.6	30.9	26.5	28.8	31.1	26.6	29.1	31.5	26.9	29.3	31.8	27.1
35 to 59.............	25.6	21.4	29.0	28.5	26.3	30.3	28.6	26.5	30.5	29.0	26.9	30.8	29.2	27.1	31.0
60 and over...........	9.4	7.1	11.4	11.9	8.4	14.9	12.0	8.5	15.0	12.1	8.6	15.1	12.2	8.7	15.2
16 to 59.............	60.2	58.6	61.4	57.0	57.2	56.8	57.3	57.6	57.1	58.0	58.4	57.7	58.5	58.9	58.1

| Age | January 1, 1980 | | | | | | | | | | | |
	Series A			Series B			Series C			Series D		
	Both Sexes	Male	Female	Both Sexes	Male	Female	Both Sexes	Male	Female	Both Sexes	Male	Female
Under 16.............	28.6	30.9	26.6	26.8	29.0	24.9	23.6	25.6	21.7	20.9	22.7	19.2
16 to 34.............	29.7	31.7	27.8	27.8	32.6	28.4	31.8	34.2	29.6	32.9	35.5	30.5
35 to 59.............	29.0	28.5	29.5	29.5	29.3	30.2	31.1	30.7	31.5	32.2	31.9	32.5
60 and over...........	12.7	8.8	16.1	13.0	9.1	16.5	13.6	9.5	17.2	14.0	9.9	17.8
16 to 59.............	58.7	60.3	57.3	60.2	61.9	58.6	62.9	64.9	61.1	65.1	67.4	63.0

[a]All ages, 100 per cent in each column except for discrepancies due to rounding. This table is based on figures presented in Appendix I, Tables 1 and 2.

between 1959 and 1970 (see Table 5) will occur because the low birth rate during World War II will limit the number reaching the working age. A lower birth rate is expected, but the decline should not be so sharp as that in the number of entrants to the working-age groups.

the number of births. Several statistical measures are used, however, to quantify the concept. One such measure is the maternal gross reproduction rate (GRR), which may be defined as the number of female children who will be born per 100 women and who will survive through the reproductive ages, if a constant set of age-specific birth rates prevails throughout the period. Age-specific birth rates are the ratios of the number of children born to women of a specific age to the number of women in that age group.

The estimated decrease between 1970 and 1980 is attributed to a drop in the proportion of the population under age 16 years which more than offsets a slight rise in the proportion of age group 60 years and over. The drop in the population under age 16 years will result from a continuation of the generally lower birth rates caused by the decrease in the female population of reproductive age. Should the GRR decline, as postulated in the Series C and D projections,[8] the dependency ratio would nevertheless rise between 1959 and 1970 because of the decrease in the number entering the working age as a result of the low birth rate during World War II. A decline

[8]See Appendix I, Table 2, n.

in the GRR between 1970 and 1980, however, would place the ratio far below that derived for 1959, almost 13 per cent below 1959 in Series D.

THE MARRIED POPULATION

According to data from the 1959 census, almost 70 per cent of the males in the age groups 16 years and over were married in contrast to the females, only a little over half of whom in the same age range were married —a disparity which stems, of course, from the war-inflicted shortage of males in the marriageable ages. However, there was a larger proportion of married females than of married males under age 25 years. Above age 25 years, the proportion of married females fell progressively lower than that of married males (see Table 7). Because of the much larger number of females than of males in the older age groups, it is not surprising to find that 74 per cent of the males age 70 and over were reportedly married as compared with only 17 per cent of the females in the same age group. Although the disparity in the proportion of

married males and females was greater in 1959 than in either 1926 or 1939, large numbers of unmarried women are not a novelty in the Soviet Union.[9] The 1926 census reports that 68 per cent of the males age 16 years and over were married as compared with 62 per cent of the females. The 1939 census reports 69 and 60 per cent, respectively. The tendency for the disparity in marriage ratios to become progressively greater with increased age also shows up in 1926 and 1939.

Data for 1959 show that a higher proportion of rural men than of urban men were married. However, the proportion of married women in the rural part of the country was higher for ages under 25 years and 55 years and over, but lower for ages 25 to 54 (see Table 8). That a greater proportion of the males in rural areas were married seems to be related partly to the tendency for men in such areas to marry at a younger age, since the

[9]The term "married" as used here means "presently married." "Unmarried," consequently, is not intended to mean "never married," but rather "not presently married."

TABLE 7.   The married population, 1926, 1939, and 1959.[a]

Age	Males			Change			Females			Change			Difference (males minus females)		
	1926	1939	1959	1926 to 1939	1939 to 1959	1926 to 1959	1926	1939	1959	1926 to 1939	1939 to 1959	1926 to 1959	1926	1939	1959
16 and over...	683	690	695	7	5	12	616	605	522	−11	−83	−94	−67	−85	−173
16 to 17......	8	4	5	−4	1	−3	54	40	29	−14	−11	−25	46	36	24
18 to 19......	122	53	41	−69	−12	−81	289	250	171	−39	−79	−118	167	197	130
20 to 24......	474	336	274	−138	−62	−200	686	614	501	−72	−113	−185	212	278	227
25 to 29......	808	738	800	−70	62	−8	850	787	759	−63	−28	−91	42	49	−41
30 to 34......	793	891	922	98	31	129	852	818	776	−34	−42	−76	59	−73	−146
35 to 39......	939	929	953	−10	24	14	818	800	725	−18	−75	−93	−121	−129	−228
40 to 44......	944	940	962	−4	22	18	763	759	623	−4	−136	−140	−181	−181	−339
45 to 49......	937	935	963	−2	28	26	702	688	549	−14	−139	−153	−235	−247	−414
50 to 54......	914	921	956	7	35	42	614	593	485	−21	−108	−129	−300	−328	−471
55 to 59......	885	900	943	15	43	58	550	497	433	−53	−64	−117	−335	−403	−510
60 to 69......	791	823	908	32	85	117	408	363	361	−45	−2	−47	−383	−460	−547
70 and over...	552	611	739	59	128	187	202	168	169	−34	1	−33	−350	−443	−570

[a]Number married per 1,000 of total population. This table was compiled from figures in Gosplan SSSR, *Vsesoiuznaia perepisi naseleniia 1926 goda:* tom LI, *Soiuz Sovetskikh Sotsialisticheskikh Respublik* (Moscow, Leningrad, 1931), p. 2; and Tsentral'noe statisticheskoe upravlenie pri Sovete ministrov SSSR, *Itogi vsesoiuznoi perepisi naseleniia 1959 goda: SSSR* (Moscow, 1962), p. 73 (hereafter cited as *Itogi . . . 1959 goda: SSSR*).

greatest differences are found in the age groups 20 to 29 years. An explanation for the differences in the upper ages is not readily apparent. It may be that the more intimate social life in rural areas provides an environment more conducive to marriage, particularly for widowed men. The pattern of urban-rural differences for women seems also to stem from more than one cause, an important one again being the tendency for rural people to marry sooner. For those in the age groups 25 years and over, however, opportunity may be an important variable. Within the age range 25 to 59 years, the number of males per 100 females is lower in rural than in urban areas, except in the age group 35 to 39 years. In a country with so large a deficit of males—if all the males in the most depleted age groups married, no more than 50 to 60 per cent of the unwed females in those age groups could marry—opportunity must play a very significant role for the woman.

For the national economy, the significance of the low proportion of married women is that about 24 million women in the age range 20 to 59 years—a figure equal to half the number of women reported by the census as being in the labor force—do not have husbands upon whom they may depend for their livelihood. The implications of this for female employment cannot be overemphasized, for it is reasonable to assume that virtually all these women are in the labor force. As the ratio of men to women becomes more balanced, the proportion of unmarried women will probably decline; and, although marriage provides the Soviet woman with no immunity from employment, married women are not so likely to be in the labor force.

TRENDS IN THE BIRTH RATE

During the Soviet period, the U.S.S.R. has undergone a demographic transition from a country of relatively high fertility and mortality to one marked by the lower fertility and mortality characteristic of the industrially advanced Western nations. According to recent statistics (see Table 9), the crude birth rate declined from 47.0 per 1,000 of total population in 1913 to 19.7 per 1,000 of total population in 1964. The mortality rate during the same period is reported to have declined from 30.2 to 7.0 per 1,000 of total population.

The combined effect of the Revolution, the Civil War, the collectivization of agriculture, changes in laws governing abortion and fam-

TABLE 8. The urban and rural married population, 1959.[a]

	Males			Females		
Age	Urban	Rural	Difference (rural minus urban)	Urban	Rural	Difference (rural minus urban)
16 and over	686	704	18	531	514	−17
16 to 17	3	7	4	20	37	17
18 to 19	33	50	17	126	221	95
20 to 24	253	298	45	461	550	89
25 to 29	776	827	51	762	756	− 6
30 to 34	912	934	22	786	764	−22
35 to 39	947	959	12	745	704	−41
40 to 44	960	965	5	656	588	−68
45 to 49	961	966	5	580	520	−60
50 to 54	953	959	6	496	476	−20
55 to 59	940	946	6	420	443	23
60 to 69	904	910	6	320	390	70
70 and over	735	741	6	135	190	55

[a]Number married per 1,000 of total population. This table was compiled from figures in *Itogi . . . 1959 goda: SSSR*, p. 72.

TABLE 9. Crude birth, mortality, and natural increase rates, 1913–64.[a]

Year	Crude Birth Rate	Mortality Rate	Natural Increase Rate
1913........	47.0	30.2	16.8
1926........	44.0	20.3	23.7
1928........	44.3	23.3	21.0
1937........	38.7	18.9	19.8
1938........	37.5	17.5	20.0
1939........	36.5	17.3	19.2
1940........	31.3	18.1	13.2
1950........	26.7	9.7	17.0
1951........	27.0	9.7	17.3
1952........	26.5	9.4	17.1
1953........	25.1	9.1	16.0
1954........	26.6	8.9	17.7
1955........	25.7	8.2	17.5
1956........	25.2	7.6	17.6
1957........	25.4	7.8	17.6
1958........	25.3	7.2	18.1
1959........	25.0	7.6	17.4
1960........	24.9	7.1	17.8
1961........	23.8	7.2	16.6
1962........	22.4	7.5	14.9
1963........	21.2	7.2	14.0
1964........	19.7	7.0	12.7

[a]Number per 1,000 of total population. These figures are compiled from statistics in Tsentral'noe statisticheskoe upravlenie pri Sovete ministrov SSSR, *Narodnoe khoziaistvo SSSR v 1962 godu* (Moscow, 1963), p. 30, and *SSSR v tsifrakh v 1964 godu* (Moscow, 1965), p. 14.

ily allowances in the mid-1930's, and World War II on the birth and mortality rates is not known with precision. The Russian demographer Volkov estimates that the annual population losses (excess of deaths over births) were as high as 2.8 million during the period of the Revolution and Civil War.[10] Lorimer found that net losses during collectivization may have been as high as 5.5 million.[11] The legal changes making abortions more difficult to obtain reportedly brought about a decline in their number, and presumably a rise in the birth rate, but this decline appears to have been short-lived.[12] The birth rate in 1943 may have been as low as 8 or 10 per 1,000 of total population, or less than one third of the 1940

level.[13] The absolute decline in population during World War II, between 1941 and 1946, is estimated to have been 25 million.

By 1950, the first postwar year for which official statistics are available, the birth rate had recovered from its wartime low, but it had hardly returned to the prewar level. The crude birth rate of 26.7 for 1950 was almost 10 per 1,000 of total population lower than the 1939 rate. The 1950 mortality rate was also lower than that for 1939, but the decline was less marked. The birth rate remained relatively constant for most of the 1950's, while the mortality rate declined somewhat. During the past several years, however, the birth rate has been declining and the mortality rate has been either stationary or rising.

Birth Rates—Urban, Rural, and Regional Differences. Statistics recently released on birth rates in urban and rural areas indicate that the birth rate in cities is substantially lower than that in rural areas. The 1962 urban birth rate, according to the official figures, was 20.0, in contrast to a rural rate of 24.9.[14]

Birth rates in the Union republics for 1961 and 1962 are given in Table 10, where the republics are listed in the order of descending birth rates. Perhaps the most striking feature is that the republics with the highest birth rates tend to be those with a relatively low Slavic population, while, with the exception of the Baltic States, the lowest birth rates are reported for republics with predominantly Slavic populations. The highest birth rates in the Soviet Union are to be found in Transcaucasia, Central Asia, and Kazakhstan, whose native populations are the least assimilated and probably least capable of assimilation.

If birth rates for the Russian,[15] Ukrainian,

[10]See Frank Lorimer, *op. cit.,* pp. 29–30.

[11]*Ibid.,* p. 135.

[12]See James W. Brackett, "Demographic Trends and Population Policy in the Soviet Union," in Joint Economic Committee of the United States Congress, *Dimensions of Soviet Economic Power* (Washington, D.C., 1962), p. 550.

[13]No specific data are available on the birth rate in 1943, but the birth rate given is based on the estimated persons age 15 in 1959 plus some allowance for mortality in this group. Because of the great uncertainty as to the infant mortality, the estimate is only an approximation.

[14]"Statisticheskie materialy," *Vestnik statistiki,* No. 8 (Aug., 1963), 91.

[15]Officially called Russian Soviet Federated Socialist Republic (R.S.F.S.R.).

TABLE 10. Birth rates in Union republics, 1961 and 1962.[a]

Republic	Slavic Population[b]	Birth Rate[c]	
		1961	1962
Azerbaidzhan S.S.R.....	14.3	42.1	40.3
Turkmen S.S.R.........	18.7	41.0	40.1
Uzbek S.S.R...........	14.7	38.5	37.2
Armenian S.S.R........	3.2	37.6	35.1
Kirgiz S.S.R...........	36.8	35.5	33.6
Kazakh S.S.R..........	52.7	35.3	32.9
Tadzhik S.S.R.........	14.7	34.4	34.1
Moldavian S.S.R.......	27.3	28.2	25.6
Georgian S.S.R........	11.5	24.7	23.6
U.S.S.R...............	77.1	23.8	22.4
Belorussian S.S.R......	97.7	23.5	22.2
Lithuanian S.S.R.......	18.8	22.2	20.8
R.S.F.S.R.............	87.0	21.9	20.2
Ukrainian S.S.R........	95.8	19.5	18.8
Latvian S.S.R..........	33.8	16.7	16.1
Estonian S.S.R.........	22.3	16.5	16.1

[a]Based on figures given in *Itogi . . . 1959 goda: SSSR*, pp. 184, 202–8; and in "Statisticheskie materialy," *Vestnik statistiki*, No. 8 (Aug., 1963), 92.
[b]Per cent of total population; Slavic population includes Russians, Ukrainians, Belorussians, Poles, and Bulgarians.
[c]Per 1,000 of total population in Union republics.

and Belorussian republics are taken as measures of the birth rate for the Slavic population, and the birth rates for the other republics as indicative of the birth rate for the non-Slavic populations, it would appear that the birth rate for Slavs as a group would be about 20 or 21 per 1,000 of total population, and that for non-Slavs about 31 or higher per 1,000 of total population.[16] Stated differently, the Slavic population, a little more than three fourths of the total population of the Soviet Union, accounts for only a little more than two thirds of the births, while the remaining non-Slavic portion of the population accounts for almost one third of the births.

The divergence of the birth rates for the Slavic and non-Slavic populations of the Soviet Union has probably increased since World War II. Data for 1959 on the age composition of the population by nationality groups

show that Slavs comprise 76.4 per cent of the population in the age group 10 to 19 years, 77.0 per cent in the age group 20 to 24 years, but only 72.1 per cent in the age group 0 to 9 years. Data presented above suggest that Slavs currently account for only two thirds of the births.

The significance of the declining birth rate among Slavs is that future entrants into the work force will have to be drawn more extensively from the minority nationality groups. Since several of the larger minority nationalities are Moslem, the Soviet Union will be faced with the problem of overcoming some of the traditional Moslem taboos concerning women in order to ensure as high a level of participation by women in the labor force as in the past.

Recent Trends and Prospects for the Future. Although the crude birth rate has declined since 1950, the maternal gross reproduction rate (GRR),[17] a more refined measure of fertility, because it takes into account the age structure of the population, has remained amazingly stable. The paternal GRR, on the other hand, has declined steadily since 1950, and in 1961 it was only 72 per cent of the 1950 level (see Table 11). This

[17]For definition, see above, n. 7. For a more detailed discussion, see James W. Brackett, *op. cit.*, pp. 528–30.

TABLE 11. Estimated maternal and paternal gross reproduction rates, 1950–61.[a]

Year	GRR		Index (1950 = 100)	
	Maternal	Paternal	Maternal	Paternal
1950.......	131	256	100	100
1951.......	133	253	102	99
1952.......	132	242	101	95
1953.......	127	224	97	88
1954.......	136	231	104	90
1955.......	132	219	101	86
1956.......	130	211	99	82
1957.......	132	209	101	82
1958.......	132	203	101	79
1959.......	131	197	100	77
1960.......	133	193	102	75
1961.......	130	184	99	72

[a]Based on figures from James W. Brackett, "Demographic Trends and Population Policy in the Soviet Union," in Joint Economic Committee of the United States Congress, *Dimensions of Soviet Economic Power* (Washington, D.C., 1962), p. 530.

[16]The birth rates in the non-Slavic republics probably are lower than those in the non-Slavic ethnic groups, because large numbers of Russians, Ukrainians, and Belorussians reside in these republics, particularly in the Kazakh S.S.R.

paradox stems, of course, from the war-induced paucity of males. That the maternal GRR has remained constant—despite an increasing ratio of males to females in the reproductive ages and the consequent increase in the proportion of women married—suggests that married couples are having fewer children.

Although in any society there are countervailing forces which tend to raise or lower fertility, in the Soviet Union the prospects appear to be more conducive to a declining rather than a stable or rising fertility.[18] Recently published age-specific fertility rates show that women in the age group under 35 years, for which the sex ratio has already become normal, have 85 per cent of the babies.[19] Thus, further increases in the ratio of males to females will probably have only a minor influence on fertility. Moreover, at least for the foreseeable future, economic considerations are expected to keep a large percentage of Soviet women in the labor force. The colossal manpower demands of the current and future economic plans call for substantially greater increments to the labor force than can be provided by persons reaching the working age. The only course seems to be even higher participation rates in the labor force by women. Further, despite efforts by the government to alleviate the housing shortage which plagues all Soviet cities, the average family has faint hope of seeing its housing situation materially improved in the near future. Only the elite have any real prospect of obtaining an entire apartment for a single family. Surveys have shown that crowded housing is a major factor restricting family size.

The situation is more serious in certain areas. In Evgenii Ratner's documentary novel *The Long Steppe*, a woman worker, a party activist, referring to a workers' barracks, says:

There are 68 families in the 28 rooms of the "London." I came to this notorious "London" and the women got a grip on me! "We are fed up," they shouted, "with having abortions; we want to have children! But we already have two or three families in every room."[20]

Because of the poor quality and poor distribution of contraceptives in the Soviet Union, abortion is often resorted to as a means of limiting family size.[21] Although no comprehensive figures have been published, the abortion rate appears to be high. Data from a large-scale survey, reported by E. A. Sadvokasova, suggest that the annual number of abortions exceeds that of live births and that the abortion rate for working women is 2.5 times higher than that of nonworking women.[22] It was my impression from conversations with young professional women that the rate was particularly high in this group. Because of the many disadvantages of abortion as a method of limiting births and because of the government's desire to increase the birth rate, a decrease in the number of abortions is a major aim of the state.

Whether fertility declines or not, the Soviet birth rate seems destined to continue its decline. The recent drop can be traced to decreases in the proportion of the population in the reproductive ages. As women born during World War II—when birth rates were quite low—pass through the reproductive ages, only an extremely sharp rise in fertility can prevent this decline. Even if fertility remains constant, the annual number of births is expected to decrease from a postwar high of 5.3 million in 1960 to a low of perhaps 4.5 million by

---

[18]Recently revised estimates by the U. S. Bureau of the Census of the GRR for the period 1960 to 1963 indicate that fertility has been declining.

[19]A. M. Voztrikova, "A Születési Mozgalom, a Házasságkötések és a Család Vizsgálata a Szovjetunióban," *Demografia,* No. 4 (1962), 537–45.

[20]Evgenii Ratner, "Step' shirokaia," *Znamia,* No. 7 (1963), 118.

[21]On the inadequacies of contraceptives, see *Meditsinskiy rabotnik,* Jan. 14 and Apr. 25, 1958.

[22]E. A. Sadvokasova, "Nekotorye sotsial'no-gigienicheskie aspekty izucheniia aborta (po materialam spetsial'nogo issledovaniia v riade gorodov i sel'skikh mestnostei RSFSR za 1958–59 gg.)," *Sovetskoe zdravookhranenie,* No. 3 (Mar., 1963), 45–50.

1967 or 1968. If fertility declines, the Soviet Union may be faced with the prospect of as few as 3.5 million births in the late 1960's.[23]

Are the Soviet authorities concerned about the declining birth rate, and, if so, what can they do to reverse the downward trend? Although several articles about the declining birth rate have appeared in recent issues of Soviet journals,[24] the authors seem to be expressing personal concern rather than official policy. This decline, however, started only recently, and the sharpest drops are expected in the future. Official concern may come later.

In 1936 and 1944, the Soviet Union instigated programs which have been construed as favorable to a higher birth rate. In June, 1936, after a gradual tightening of the regulations governing abortion, the Soviet government issued a decree forbidding abortions for other than medical reasons.[25] At the same time, the first major family-allowance program was introduced. Annual stipends of 2,000 rubles for five years, the first stipend payable at birth, were awarded for the seventh and each successive child until the eleventh. For the eleventh and each successive child, single grants of 5,000 rubles payable at birth plus annual stipends of 3,000 rubles for four following years were awarded. Whether the intent of this program was to effect a rise in the birth rate or merely to provide welfare assistance to financially pressed families is not clear. The measure would appear to be a doubtful incentive for larger families, since payments began only with the seventh child and very few families have more than three or four children.

An extensive program to raise the war-depressed birth rate was promulgated in the decree of July 8, 1944. Among its many provisions were single grants, payable at birth, for the third and fourth children; monthly stipends, payable after the first year,[26] for four years for the fourth and fifth children; monthly payments to unwed mothers; a special tax on unmarried persons and childless couples; sizable reductions in income taxes for parents;[27] paid maternity leave for working mothers; and a series of medals awarded to women with large families. In addition, the 1944 decree attempted to curb abortions by re-emphasizing the criminal responsibility for them. Although abortions had been outlawed in 1936, large numbers of women reportedly had obtained illegal operations.

The various financial programs set forth in the 1944 decree were not new—some actually date from the reign of Lenin—but they were vastly expanded, to the point that they could make a substantial difference in the net income of families with children. When the tax exemption was added to the outright grant, the amount received at the birth of the fourth child was 30 per cent of the estimated average annual wage in 1944; with the tax deduction, the amount received at the birth of the eleventh child was 98 per cent of the average annual wage. Monthly payments received during the second year totaled from 25 per cent of the average annual wage for the fourth child to 70 per cent for the eleventh. Moreover, since allowances were often received for more than one child, the total payments were sometimes substantially more than the average wage.[28] For example, if a woman's fifth, sixth, and seventh children were between ages 1 and 5 years, she received three monthly payments, ranging from 120 to 200 rubles.

The 1944 policy lasted a little more than three years. By the decree of November 25, 1947, the family allowances were cut in half. The rise in the average annual wage, coupled with income-tax reductions, has further diminished the significance of these allowances. The

[23]James W. Brackett, *op. cit.,* p. 533.

[24]E.g., O. E. Chernetskii, "Organizatsiia raboty po snizheniiu abortov," *Sovetskoe zdravookhranenie,* No. 6 (1961), 20–22; and E. A. Sadvokasova, *op. cit.*

[25]Ministerstvo zdravookhraneniia SSR, Institut organizatsii zdravookhraneniia i istorii meditsiny imeni N. A. Semashko, *Postanovleniia KPSS i Sovetskogo pravitel'stva ob okhrane zdorov'ia naroda* (Moscow, 1958), pp. 256, 266.

[26]The grant awarded at birth was considered sufficient for the first year.

[27]The income-tax reductions were actually introduced on April 30, 1943.

[28]James W. Brackett, *op. cit.,* pp. 551–52.

schedule of the family allowances established by the 1936, 1944, and 1947 decrees is given in Table 12.

With these historical precedents for an official population policy and with the general practice of Soviet authorities to pursue any course of action deemed necessary to accomplish their goals, programs to reverse the decline in the birth rate cannot be ruled out. The Soviet authorities, however, will be faced with the dilemma of deciding whether the official policy should be to increase the birth rate now, in order to provide a more adequate labor supply some twenty to twenty-five years hence, or to accept the declining birth rate as a necessary consequence of keeping sorely needed women in the present labor force.

Should the former policy be adopted, specific programs must be designed to encourage women to have more children. The measures of 1944 were of three main types: financial assistance, including maternity leave, the prevention of abortion, and the granting of medals to mothers with large families. Other possibilities are: restrictions on the sale of contraceptives, increased nursery facilities, and preferential treatment of parents in the allocation of housing and scarce consumers' goods. Not all these means are practicable, however, and some are very costly. The reason given for the liberalization of the abortion law in 1955 was the high incidence of illegal abortion. If the restrictions on legal abortion

are restored, women may again resort to illegal abortionists. The cost of financial assistance can be substantial. Had the 1944 family-allowance schedule been in effect in 1961, for example, the payments at birth would have amounted to about 220 million rubles, and the monthly payments, about 630 million rubles, a total cost of about 850 million rubles—double the cost of the present program.[29] Had the schedule of payments then been adjusted to take into account the increase in the average annual wage, the costs would have approached 2 billion rubles.[30] These expenditures, of course, would cover only those children already born. If an extended program should succeed in increasing the annual number of births by, let us say, 500,000, these additional births would cost, on the 1944 schedule, as much as 200 to 250 million additional rubles.

The cost of failure would be high, and success or failure could not be determined for some time after the program had started. Even if the progress of such a program could be judged from the data on pregnancies from the medical service, some months would necessarily elapse before women who had become

[29]The amounts are quoted in new rubles; one should assume that the 1944 schedule of payments would be converted to new rubles on the basis of 1 new for 10 old rubles.

[30]The ruble is now worth $1.10 at the official rate of exchange.

TABLE 12. Family allowances, by decrees of 1936, 1944, and 1947.[a]

	1936 Allowance		1944 Allowance		1947 Allowance	
Child	At Birth	Annually[b]	At Birth	Monthly[c]	At Birth	Monthly[c]
3...................	–	–	400	–	200	–
4...................	–	–	1,300	80	650	40
5...................	–	–	1,700	120	850	60
6...................	–	–	2,000	140	1,000	70
7...................	–	2,000	2,500	200	1,250	100
8...................	–	2,000	2,500	200	1,250	100
9...................	–	2,000	3,500	250	1,750	125
10.................	–	2,000	3,500	250	1,750	125
11, etc.............	5,000	3,000	5,000	300	2,500	150

[a]June 27, 1936; July 8, 1944; and Nov. 25, 1947. Amounts are in old rubles. This table was compiled from figures in Ministerstvo zdravookhraneniia SSSR, Institut organizatsii zdravookhraneniia i istorii meditsiny imeni N. A. Semashko, Postanovleniia KPSS i Sovetskogo pravitel'stva ob okhrane zdorov'ia naroda (Moscow, 1958), pp. 266, 310–12, 323–24.
[b]For five years, from birth; for the 11th and each subsequent child, however, only for four years, the 5,000 rubles paid at birth being considered adequate for the first year.
[c]For four years, from the child's first birthday.

pregnant after the program was initiated began to report to the medical center; and data would probably have to be collected for several more months before a reliable statistical basis would be available for an evaluation of even the initial reaction to the program. Moreover, such a program might require a period of prolonged and intensive propaganda. Thus, a minimum period of eighteen months to two years might be needed for a reasonable test, and the cost during that period could amount to as much as 4 billion rubles, a substantial sum which would necessarily be spent at the expense of other Soviet programs.

FAMILY SIZE AND COMPOSITION

Important influences on the participation of women in the labor force are family size and composition. According to Soviet usage, a family consists of persons "living under a common budget." Of the 208.2 million persons listed as "permanent" population by the 1959 census, 186.9 million, or 89.7 per cent, were family members living together; 12 million persons were family members living separately. The latter group includes students, servicemen, and persons working away from home. As shown in Table 13, about 9.4 million persons, or 4.5 per cent of the total permanent population, were classified as single persons living alone.

The 1959 census lists only 83.1 million males as family members living together as compared with 103.7 million females. Males are numerically predominant among family members living apart, while females are predominant among single persons living alone. Males comprise about two thirds of the family members living apart, but only a little more than one fourth of the single persons living alone.

About 46 per cent of the family members living together and about 61 per cent of those living separately and of single persons living alone are classified as urban. The urban concentration of persons living alone is probably attributable in part to the large number of young persons who leave the farm to work in cities. It is probably also partly related to the acute housing shortage in cities. Because of this shortage, many couples reportedly postpone marriage, and some live apart for some time after marriage. Accommodations for single persons in dormitories or barracks are often provided by an institution or enterprise.

Average Family Size. As expected, rural families tend to be larger than urban families. Table 14 shows that in 1959 the average rural family consisted of 3.9 persons and that the average urban family consisted of only 3.5 persons. When the population was classified according to the traditional broad occupational groups—workers, employees, and col-

TABLE 13. Family composition, by urban and rural residence and by sex, 1959.[a]

Residence and Sex	Total Permanent Population	Family Members			Single Persons Living Alone
		Total	Living Together	Living Separately	
Urban and rural					
Both sexes............	208,247	198,871	186,881	11,989	9,376
Males...............	93,784	91,263	83,147	8,115	2,521
Females..............	114,463	107,608	103,734	3,874	6,855
Urban					
Both sexes............	99,099	93,334	86,045	7,289	5,765
Males...............	44,847	43,078	38,222	4,856	1,769
Females..............	54,252	50,256	47,823	2,433	3,996
Rural					
Both sexes............	109,147	105,536	100,836	4,700	3,611
Males...............	48,936	48,184	44,925	3,259	752
Females..............	60,211	57,352	55,911	1,441	2,859

[a]Figures are expressed in thousands. This table is based on the figures from the national census of Jan. 15, 1959, published in *Itogi . . . 1959 goda: SSSR*, pp. 240–41.

TABLE 14. Family composition, average size, by occupation and by urban and rural residence, 1959.[a]

Occupation	Average Number of Family Members		
	Total	Urban	Rural
All occupations......	3.7	3.5	3.9
Workers...........	3.6	3.6	3.8
Employees.........	3.5	3.4	3.9
Collective farmers....	3.9	3.8	3.9

[a]Information for this table was taken from figures in the national census of Jan. 15, 1959, published in *Itogi . . . 1959 goda: SSSR*, p. 251.

lective farmers—rural families were found to be larger in each category. The difference between urban and rural collective farmers is very small, probably because urban collective farmers live in small towns where conditions are not very different from those in rural villages. The explanation for the lack of major discrepancies in the average family size for the three groups in rural areas probably is that most rural workers and employees work on state farms.

Of the fifteen nationality groups for which Union republics have been established, those indigenous to Central Asia and Transcaucasia are found to have the largest families, and those from the Baltic republics, the smallest. The average family size among the major Slavic groups—Russians, Ukrainians, and Belorussians—is slightly larger than that among the Baltic peoples, but substantially smaller than that among the Asiatic groups. The nationality groups with the largest families—Tadzhiks, Uzbeks, and Turkmen—average 5 or more persons per family; those with the smallest families—Estonians and Latvians—average only 3.0 to 3.1 persons per family. The Slavic groups range from 3.5 (Ukrainians) to 3.7 (Belorussians) persons per family (see Table 15).

An examination of the data for the nationality groups suggests that the urban-rural differences for the country as a whole may be a function of the tendency for nationality groups with large families to be concentrated in rural areas rather than a function of intrinsic urban-rural differences within the groups. The largest urban-rural differences are to be found among the Armenian, Turkmen, and Moldavian peoples. Each of these three groups displays an urban-rural difference equal to or greater than that for the country as a whole. Together they constitute only 2.9 per cent of the total population, however, and could not

TABLE 15. Family composition, average size, by nationality and by urban and rural residence, 1959.[a]

Nationality	Percentage of Population Urban	Average Number of Family Members			Difference (rural minus urban)
		Total	Urban	Rural	
U.S.S.R.................	48	3.7	3.5	3.9	0.4
Tadzhik................	21	5.2	5.1	5.2	0.1
Uzbek.................	22	5.0	4.9	5.0	0.1
Turkmen...............	25	5.0	4.7	5.1	0.4
Azerbaidzhan...........	35	4.8	4.6	4.9	0.3
Armenian..............	57	4.7	4.4	5.0	0.6
Kazakh................	24	4.6	4.7	4.5	−0.2
Kirgiz.................	11	4.5	4.3	4.6	0.3
Georgian...............	36	4.0	3.8	4.1	0.3
Moldavian.............	13	3.9	3.6	4.0	0.4
Belorussian............	32	3.7	3.4	3.7	0.3
Russian................	58	3.6	3.5	3.7	0.2
Lithuanian.............	35	3.6	3.4	3.6	0.2
Ukrainian..............	39	3.5	3.3	3.6	0.3
Latvian................	48	3.1	3.0	3.2	0.2
Estonian...............	47	3.0	3.1	3.0	−0.1

[a]Nationalities are listed in the order of the total average number of family members. This table was compiled from figures in the national census of Jan. 15, 1959, published in *Itogi . . . 1959 goda: SSSR*, pp. 184, 190, 252.

significantly influence the urban-rural differences for the country as a whole. Urban-rural differences are minimal for the Tadzhiks, Uzbeks, and Estonians (0.1 person per family) and for the Russians, Lithuanians, Latvians, and Kazakhs (0.2 person per family). For two of these groups—the Estonians and the Kazakhs—average family size is actually larger in the urban areas. Thus, the family size of the seven nationality groups which constitute more than 60 per cent of the total Soviet population does not differ significantly in urban and rural areas.

Unfortunately, comprehensive information about the relationship between employment status or occupation and family size is not available. Sample data for Siberia have shown, as might be expected, a negative correlation between family size and desire to work.[31] The high participation rate of women in the Soviet labor force indicates, however, that many women with sizable families work. Personal interviews with several-score professional women, who were asked about their own families as well as those of their colleagues, led to the impression that professional women usually have only one child, but, at most, only two. None of the younger women who were preparing for a professional career expressed a desire for more than two children, and the majority wanted only one.

Age-Sex Composition of the Population by Family Size. The summary volume of the 1959 Soviet census provides a series of relative age-sex distributions by family size.[32] These distributions, which are based on a 5 per cent sample, show characteristics of 100 families in each family size, from two to ten or more persons per family. Since the total numbers of families of each size are also reported, the relative age-sex distributions can

be converted to absolute distributions by multiplying the relative number by the total number of families for each class of family size. For purposes of the present study, the relative numbers used were rounded; the absolute numbers therefore display a repetitive pattern which does not exist in the original data. For the same reason, the derived figures for the urban and rural families do not always equal those derived independently for the whole country. These data nevertheless provide some interesting insights into the characteristics of Soviet families.[33]

The data for 1959 show that although females constitute a majority of the members in all family sizes, they tend to be especially predominant in smaller families—more than 62 per cent of the family members in two-member families and almost 57 per cent in three-member families. The proportion of females declines as the family size increases. In families of ten persons or more, as shown in Table 16, only 51.8 per cent of the members are females.

TABLE 16.   Percentage of females in each family size, 1959.[a]

Number of Members per Family	Females	Number of Members per Family	Females
All families	55.5		
2	62.5	7	52.7
3	56.7	8	52.5
4	54.3	9	52.1
5	53.8	10 or more	51.8
6	53.2		

[a]This table is based on figures presented in Appendix I, Table 3.

As would be expected, members of two- and three-member families tend to be older than those of large families. The median age for two-member families is 44.6 years, as compared with a median age of 26.9 years for all families.[34] The median age for three-member families drops to 28.9 years—the influence of young married couples with one child.

[31]A. N. Gladyshev, "Reservy rabochei sily v gorodakh Sibiri," *Izvestiia Sibirskogo otdeleniia Akademii nauk SSSR*, No. 11 (1962), 16–17.

[32]Tsentral'noe statisticheskoe upravlenie pri Sovete ministrov SSSR, *Itogi Vsesoiuznoi perepisi naseleniia 1959 goda: SSSR* (Moscow, 1962), pp. 242–47. (Hereafter cited as *Itogi . . . 1959 goda: SSSR.*)

[33]See Appendix I, Table 3.
[34]*Ibid.*

Two-member families are generally of three basic types: young couples who have not yet had children, older couples whose children have moved away, and older persons living with a relative. Young children are usually found in two-member families only when they are living with just one of their parents or when they are the illegitimate children of single women living alone.

Most older persons live in small families.[35] Almost one third of all persons age 60 years and over were members of two-member families, and more than 53 per cent were members of two- or three-member families. Only 14 per cent of all family members lived in two-member families, and only 35 per cent in two- or three-member families.

Although both older men and older women are more likely to be members of small families, a distinctly smaller proportion of the older women are members of small families. Almost 39 per cent of all male family members age 60 years and over were in two-member families, as compared with only 29 per cent of female family members in this age group. About the same proportion, one fifth, of older men and older women were in three-member families. That a larger proportion of the older males were in two-member families is probably related to the tendency for women to live longer. Many older couples continue to maintain their households after their children move away; and when the husband dies, the wife either lives with a relative or lives alone.

Most children and adolescents belonged to families with three to five members. A little less than 25 per cent of the family members in the age group under 20 years were in four-member families, 21 per cent were in five-member families, and 16 per cent were in three-member families. About one fourth of the family members in the working ages lived in three-member families, and one fourth in four-member families. About one fourth of the women of working age were in three- or four-member families. Since most women of

working age in the Soviet Union are employed—and efforts are being made to employ many of those who are not—the large proportion of women with children entails a number of problems for the economic planners as well as for the families themselves. Many working mothers are able to leave their young children with a grandmother. But as the family statistics suggest, older women are more likely to be members of families without children. Child-care facilities are available, but they are reportedly insufficient.[36]

Family Members Living Apart from Their Families. The 1959 Soviet census reported that almost 12 million persons were family members living apart from their families. Most of these persons probably worked or attended school in other localities or lived alone, but were financially dependent on their families. That most of these 12 million persons were males (67.7 per cent), many in the age group 20 to 29 years (45.6 per cent), tends to strengthen the probability that some members of the armed forces were included, as well as young workers and students of higher education.

The summary volume of the 1959 Soviet census also gives distributions by sex and by urban and rural residence for the 12 million persons living apart from their families (see Table 17). Data by urban and rural residence and by age, but not by sex, are also reported (see Table 18). These data show that urban males constituted the largest component of this group (40.5 per cent), and rural males, the next largest (27.2 per cent). Urban females, on the other hand, comprised only about 20 per cent of the group, and rural females, only 12 per cent. Almost 29 per cent of these 12 million people were in the age group 20 to 29 years and in urban areas; about 17 per cent were urban dwellers under age 20. Of the latter, most were probably age 18 or 19. Older persons, age 60 and over, comprised a relatively small proportion of this group (4.9 per cent).

---

[35]See Appendix I, Tables 4 and 5.

[36]See Chapter 5.

TABLE 17. Family members living apart from their families, by urban and rural residence and by sex, 1959.[a]

Sex	Absolute Number (in thousands)			Percentage		
	Urban and Rural	Urban	Rural	Urban and Rural	Urban	Rural
Both sexes..........	11,989	7,289	4,700	100.0	60.8	39.2
Males..............	8,115	4,856	3,259	67.7	40.5	27.2
Females............	3,874	2,433	1,441	32.3	20.3	12.0

[a]This table was compiled from figures in the national census of Jan. 15, 1959, published in *Itogi . . . 1959 goda: SSSR*, p. 241.

TABLE 18. Family members living apart from their families, by urban and rural residence and by age, 1959.[a]

Age	Absolute Number (in thousands)			Percentage		
	Urban and Rural	Urban	Rural	Urban and Rural	Urban	Rural
All ages............	11,989	7,289	4,700	100.0	60.8	39.2
Under 20...........	3,378	2,065	1,313	28.2	17.2	11.0
20 to 29............	5,470	3,450	2,020	45.6	28.8	16.8
30 to 39............	1,251	796	455	10.4	6.6	3.8
40 to 49............	744	441	303	6.2	3.7	2.5
50 to 59............	557	291	266	4.6	2.4	2.2
60 and over.........	590	245	344	4.9	2.0	2.9
20 to 59............	8,022	4,978	3,044	66.9	41.5	25.4

[a]This table was compiled from figures in the national census of Jan. 15, 1959, published in *Itogi . . . 1959 goda: SSSR*, p. 248.

Nonfamily Members. In addition to the 198.9 million family members in 1959, there were almost 9.4 million single persons living alone. This group displays characteristics both different from and similar to those of the family members living alone. For example, more than 73 per cent of the nonfamily members were females, whereas family members living alone were predominantly males (see Table 19); and about 60 per cent of both groups lived in urban areas. The data by age show two modal groups—one for ages 20 to 29 years, the other for ages 60 years and over (see Table 20). The younger modal group, however, was more prominent in urban areas, and the older, in rural areas.

TABLE 19. Nonfamily members, by urban and rural residence and by sex, 1959.[a]

Sex	Absolute Number (in thousands)			Percentage		
	Urban and Rural	Urban	Rural	Urban and Rural	Urban	Rural
Both sexes..........	9,376	5,765	3,611	100.0	61.5	38.5
Males..............	2,521	1,769	752	26.9	18.9	8.0
Females............	6,855	3,996	2,859	73.1	42.6	30.5

[a]This table is based on figures from the national census of Jan. 15, 1959; see *Itogi . . . 1959 goda: SSSR*, p. 241.

TABLE 20. Nonfamily members, by urban and rural residence and by age, 1959.[a]

Age	Absolute Number (in thousands)			Percentage		
	Urban and Rural	Urban	Rural	Urban and Rural	Urban	Rural
All ages.............	9,376	5,765	3,611	100.0	61.5	38.5
Under 20...........	1,259	935	324	13.4	10.0	3.5
20 to 29.............	2,550	1,924	627	27.2	20.5	6.7
30 to 39.............	976	677	299	10.4	7.2	3.2
40 to 49.............	1,139	639	500	12.1	6.8	5.3
50 to 59.............	1,390	731	659	14.8	7.8	7.0
60 and over.........	2,062	860	1,203	22.0	9.2	12.8
20 to 59.............	6,055	3,971	2,085	64.6	42.4	22.2

[a]This table is based on figures from the national census of Jan. 15, 1959; see *Itogi . . . 1959 goda: SSSR*, p. 248.

Although data by sex and by age are not available, it seems probable that most of the 2 million nonfamily members age 60 years and over were women and that most of the 2.5 million male nonfamily members were under age 30. That the older group was very largely composed of women tends to be supported by the marriage statistics. According to the 1959 census, only about 1 million males but more than 9 million females age 60 years and over were unmarried.[37]

CONCLUSIONS

We have traced the transformation of the Soviet population from a model population structure—equal ratio of males to females, with the number of persons in each age group slightly smaller than that in the group preceding it—to a highly irregular population structure, in which females outnumber males by many millions, and in which the number of persons in each age group bears no natural relationship to that in the adjacent groups. By 1946 there was a deficit of 20.7 million males in the age group 16 to 59 years. By 1959, after more than a decade of relative stability, the male deficit in the working ages had dropped to 15.4 million.

In spite of this narrowing disparity, 24 million women in the age group 20 to 59 years

[37]See above, n. 9.

are unmarried and thus very likely to be in the labor force. This figure is more than two fifths of the number of women in the labor force in 1959 (56.6 million, comprising about 52 per cent of the labor force). Because data by family status to some degree overlap those based on marital status, they provide further insights into the problems which must be faced by individual women as well as by the economy when women comprise 48 per cent of a nation's work force.

Data cross-classified by age and sex for persons living alone are not reported, but there were about 8.8 million women age 20 to 59 in the two categories of persons living alone according to the definitions employed by the 1959 census (nonfamily members and family members living alone). If most of these women worked, they made up a maximum of 18.5 per cent of the 47.6 million employed women of all ages. This means, of course, that most of the other 38.8 million had to be drawn from the women age 20 to 59 years who were living with their families—along with some from the age groups under 20 and over 60 years—or that a minimum of 69 per cent of all women in this age group who have families or are living with their families must be employed.

Determining which 39 million women of the 56 million family members age 20 to 59 were employed is not a simple task. Since working-age women in two-member families either do not have children living with them or, if they do, do not generally have husbands upon whom to rely for their livelihood, most of the 11 million women in these small families were probably in the labor force. But even if 10 million women in two-member families are assumed to have been employed, they would constitute only a little over a quarter of the estimated 38.8 million; the other 29 million had to be drawn from families of three or more persons—that is, from families in which children are probably present.

With about 30 per cent of the Soviet labor force apparently supplied by women likely to have resident children, there inevitably arises a conflict between the role of the woman as wife and mother and her role as a member of the work force. This conflict has apparently contributed to a drop in the birth rate and a rise in the abortion rate. Age-specific birth rates would show an even sharper decline than the statistics on the crude birth rates published by the Soviets. Substantial regional differences in the birth rate reflect nationality differences. The rates in republics with a predominantly Moslem population are approximately twice those of the Baltic republics, the Ukraine, and the R.S.F.S.R.

Data on the marital status of the population suggest that married women must comprise about half of the nearly 48 million working-age women in the Soviet Union. Many of these women work because two incomes are necessary. For many families, a pregnancy poses a catastrophe which has to be averted by abortion. Currently, abortions are performed legally by medically qualified persons at public hospitals under sanitary conditions. Prior to 1955, when the abortion laws were liberalized, abortions were obtained illegally, often under conditions detrimental to the health of the women. The risk was, nevertheless, looked on by many women as preferable to the bearing of a child.

The declining birth rate which the Soviet Union is now experiencing presents a dilemma for the Soviet planners. A low birth rate for an extended period could result in a very severe labor shortage in the future. On the other hand, a reversal of the downward trend in the birth rate—if it is reversible—would require Soviet women to have larger families at a time when their services are needed in the labor force. Moreover, even if the Soviet planners decided to increase the birth rate, they would then have to find a way to implement that decision. A program designed to induce women to have more children could cost as much as 4 billion rubles annually. Moreover, there is considerable doubt whether Soviet women could be persuaded to have larger families unless the standard of living is markedly raised. The required investment in consumers' goods—particularly housing—is probably impossible for the foreseeable future, even if the policy makers adopt an all-out program to provide these incentives.

chapter
3

PARTICIPATION IN THE LABOR FORCE

A LARGE percentage of the population of the Soviet Union has always been engaged in productive economic activity, in contrast to the pattern of manpower utilization in other developed countries. In the pre-Soviet and early Soviet periods, when the country was primarily agricultural, virtually all able-bodied persons, whether male or female, contributed at least part of the year to some form of eco-nomic production for the market. Despite the increased imbalance of the sex ratio, particu-larly in the prime working-age groups, which should have encouraged more women to work, the average participation rate of women in the labor force has actually declined during the past few decades of Soviet rule—from 51 per cent in 1926 to 47 per cent in 1959 (see Table 21). These figures must be interpreted

TABLE 21. Population and labor force, by age and by sex, 1926, 1939, and 1959.[a]

Age and Sex	1926			1939			1959		
	Population	Labor Force		Population	Labor Force		Population	Labor Force	
Both sexes			%			%			%
10 to 15..........	20,800	12,200	59	25,600	6,000	23	17,200	2,000	12
16 to 59..........	78,800	67,000	85	94,000	78,600	84	125,700	98,800	79
60 and over.......	9,800	5,300	54	11,200	5,400	49	19,700	8,200	43
10 and over.......	109,400	84,500	77	130,800	90,100	69	162,600	109,000	67
Total..........	147,000	84,500	58	170,600	90,100	53	208,800	109,000	52
Males									
10 to 15..........	10,500	6,400	61	12,800	3,100	24	8,600	1,000	12
16 to 59..........	37,300	35,700	96	44,700	43,700	98	55,300	50,200	91
60 and over.......	4,300	3,200	74	4,300	3,100	72	6,600	4,000	61
10 and over.......	52,100	45,300	87	61,800	49,900	81	70,500	55,200	78
Total..........	71,000	45,300	64	81,700	49,600	61	94,000	55,200	59
Females									
10 to 15..........	10,300	5,800	56	12,800	2,900	23	8,600	1,000	11
16 to 59..........	41,500	31,300	75	49,400	34,900	71	70,400	48,600	69
60 and over.......	5,500	2,100	38	6,900	2,400	35	13,100	4,200	32
10 and over.......	57,300	39,200	69	69,100	40,200	58	92,100	53,800	58
Total..........	76,000	39,200	51	88,900	40,200	45	114,800	53,800	47

[a]Figures are expressed in thousands, and the percentages are rounded. This table is based on figures from Warren W. Eason, "Labor Force," in *Economic Trends in the Soviet Union*, ed. by A. Bergson and S. Kuznets (Cambridge, Mass., 1963), p. 54.

32

carefully, however, since the slight decline in the average participation rate was the result of two developments, which had opposite effects. On the one hand, the shift of women from rural to urban employment tended to reduce the over-all participation rate. On the other hand, the participation rate of urban women rose substantially and thus tended to offset the decline.

It is the upward trend in the urban participation rate which shows most clearly the effect of the various factors which have drawn women into the main stream of economic activity in the past four decades. A relatively modest increase in the participation rate of women in the age group 16 to 59 years between 1926 and 1939 was followed by a substantial increase from 45.1 per cent to an estimated 67.0 per cent between 1939 and 1959 (see Table 22). Over the entire period from 1926 to 1959 there has been a simultaneous decline in the participation rates of younger and older women. In the younger

group, the decline reflects more years of schooling, and in the older group, an earlier withdrawal or retirement from the labor force.

THE PARTICIPATION PATTERNS BEFORE WORLD WAR II

The high rate of participation by women of all ages in the Soviet labor force in the year 1926 may be readily demonstrated by the superimposition of an employment pyramid on the population pyramid for that year (Fig. 10).[1] The employment pyramid includes, in each five-year age group, all persons classified by the census as economically active, including employed and self-employed persons, family helpers, the military, institutionalized persons, and the unemployed. Although not working at the time of the census, the unemployed might properly be considered a part of the labor force; only 1.3 per cent of the males and 1.0 per cent of the economically active population were unemployed.

In the primarily rural economy of 1926, very high participation rates are reported for women in all age groups. If these rates could be converted to man-year equivalents, they would, of course, be much reduced, particularly for the younger and older women, whose activity in the labor force was often seasonal. On the basis of the sample data presented by L. E. Mints for 2,744 households in eleven regions of the Soviet Union in 1924 and 1925, it is estimated that in terms of man-years the contribution of adult women to agricultural labor was 30 per cent less than that of men in the mid-1920's.[2]

No estimate of variations due to age is possible. Nevertheless, it is clear that productive

TABLE 22. Participation rates of urban women in the labor force, 1926, 1939, and 1959.[a]

Age	Percentage		
	1926	1939	1959
10 to 15.............	13.3	n.a.[b]	3.6
16 to 59.............	40.1	45.1	67.0
60 and over..........	28.1	8.6	13.0

[a]The sources for this table were: for 1926, Gosplan SSSR, *Vsesoiuznaia perepisi naseleniia 1926 goda*, tom XXXIV, *SSSR* (Moscow, 1930), p. 9; for 1939, estimates of Warren W. Eason, *Soviet Manpower, the Population and Labor Force of the U.S.S.R.* (unpublished doctoral dissertation, Columbia University, 1959), p. 449; and for 1959, *Itogi . . . 1959 goda: SSSR*, pp. 64, 97, 106, 107. For 1959, only estimates could be made from the census data, which showed the female urban population by age group and by type of employment; the totals for each type of employment were divided among the younger, the working-age, and the older groups by the percentages given in Figs. 28 and 29 (the age distribution of "physical" occupations in agriculture, except private subsidiary agriculture, and the age distribution of "physical" occupations other than in agriculture). It is assumed that the first distribution applies to collective farmers and private peasants and the second, to workers and employees. For the younger groups it is assumed that a tenth of the persons under age 20 fall in the 10–15 age range. In the case of women employed in private subsidiary agriculture, it is assumed that 2 per cent of the urban women are under age 16. Also, a third of those over 55 (*ibid.*, p. 97) are assumed to fall in the 55–59 age group. Many of these assumptions are only informed guesses, but the resulting participation rates, particularly the rate for the 16–59 age group, are believed to be fairly accurate.

[b]No data available.

---

[1]See also Table 23.

[2]L. E. Mints, *Agrarnoe perenaselenie i rynok truda v SSSR* (Moscow, 1929), pp. 22–23, 28–29. Mints gives the labor contribution of males and females in "grown-man-days." These must be adjusted to subtract the contribution of males and females to production for home consumption and to housework and then reconverted by the appropriate coefficients to calendar man-days of work.

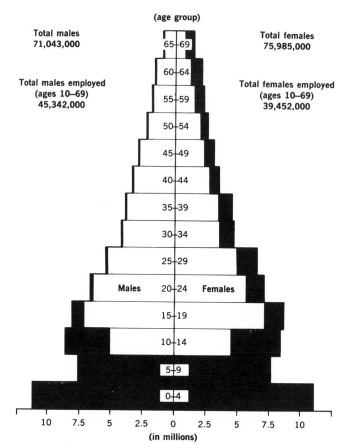

Fig. 10. Population and employment pyramids, 1926 (see Table 23). *Shaded portion,* not employed; *unshaded portion,* employed The population pyramid is identical to that in Fig. 3. The superimposed employment pyramid is based on Gosplan SSSR, *Vsesoiuznaia perepisi naseleniia 1926 goda: SSSR* (Moscow, 1930), tom XXXIV, pp. 8–12.

economic activity was engaged in, for at least part of the year, by almost all men and women from their early teens until old age. The participation rate of women rises rapidly to a peak of 93 per cent for women in their early twenties and then declines sharply to 75 per cent for those in their late twenties, as a result of the increased family responsibilities falling on most women in that age group. It hovers close to the 75 per cent level for the next two decades of age before entering into a more rapid decline in the older age groups.

As the industrialization and urbanization of the Soviet Union progressed during the 1930's, the participation rate for women declined in all age groups, particularly in the older and younger (see Table 21). The decline of the rate for the age group 10 to 15 from 59 per cent in 1926 to 23 per cent in 1939 and to 12 per cent in 1959 is especially striking. This decline, which affected boys and girls equally, is primarily a reflection of the increase in school attendance in the upper grades. By 1959, even children in the rural areas were normally completing seven years of schooling, which carried them up to age

TABLE 23. Population and employment, by sex and by age, 1926.[a]

	Males			Females		
Age	Total	Employed	Partici-pation Rate	Total	Employed	Partici-pation Rate
			%			%
0 to 4	11,238	–	–	11,085	–	–
5 to 9	7,650	–	–	7,620	–	–
10 to 14	8,643	5,015	58	8,448	4,477	53
15 to 19	8,133	7,193	88	8,844	7,070	80
20 to 24	6,712	6,556	98	7,101	5,578	93
25 to 29	5,490	5,429	99	6,547	4,913	75
30 to 34	4,297	4,259	99	4,768	3,565	75
35 to 39	3,994	3,965	99	4,458	3,440	77
40 to 44	3,393	3,365	99	3,562	2,750	77
45 to 49	2,893	2,867	99	3,015	2,327	77
50 to 54	2,343	2,307	98	2,698	1,944	72
55 to 59	1,887	1,838	97	2,318	1,576	68
60 to 64	1,709	1,575	92	2,126	1,158	55
65 to 69	1,157	973	84	1,407	654	47
All ages	71,043	45,342	64	75,985	39,452	52

[a]Figures are expressed in thousands. See pyramids based on this table (Fig. 10). The source of this table was census figures from Gosplan SSSR, *Vsesoiuznaia perepis naseleniia 1926 goda: tom XXXIV, SSSR* (Moscow, 1930), pp. 8-12.

15, and the number of students who continued for eight or more years also rose sharply. Even if these children worked on a collective farm or in private subsidiary agriculture during the summer months, they would be counted in the census returns, not as members of the labor force, but as dependent students. Hence the decline in work actually performed by youths in the 10 to 15 year age group is less than the decline in participation rates might suggest.

THE PRESENT PARTICIPATION PATTERNS

A detailed picture of the participation of women in the labor force in 1959 is given by a population-employment pyramid based on 1959 census data (Fig. 11).[3] The age distribution of the population employed in the socialized and private independent sector, including those employed in the military, is given in the 1959 census not for five-year age groups, but for seven age groups of varying length: age group 0 to 20; three ten-year age groups for ages 20 to 49; age groups 50 to 54 and 55 to 59; and age group 60 and above. The age group 50 to 59 was divided into two five-year groups because women workers and employees in the Soviet Union normally may retire on a state pension at age 55, five years earlier than men.

To convert the broader age groups into five-year groups for purposes of this study, the participation rate for each ten-year age group was calculated, and the intervening rates for five-year periods were interpolated. It was assumed that all employed persons under age 20 fell in the age group 15 to 19. Since the census reported only 600,000 employed persons under age 16, this assumption would not be far from reality, for a large share of these would be in their fifteenth year, and the re-

[3]See also Table 24. For an illuminating critique of census employment data as compared with annual employment data, see Murray S. Weitzman, Murray Feshbach, and Lydia Kulchycka, "Employment in the U.S.S.R.: Comparative U.S.S.R.-U.S. Data," in Joint Economic Committee of the United States Congress, *Dimensions of Soviet Economic Power* (Washington, D.C., 1962), pp. 612–14. For details of the methods of estimating this pyramid, see Appendix II.

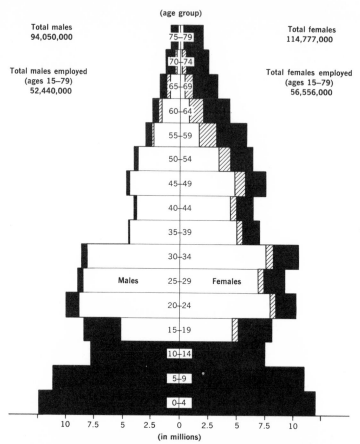

Fig. 11. Population and employment pyramids, 1959 (see Table 23). *Shaded portion* not employed; *unshaded portion,* employed. in the socialized or private independent sector; *crosshatched portion,* occupied in the private subsidiary sector. The military (3.6 million) is included in the unshaded portion. The population pyramid is identical to that in Fig. 7. For the source of the superimposed employment pyramid, see Appendix II.

mainder, under age 15, would be negligible.[4] Employment in the age group 60 and over is distributed among the five-year groups up to age 80 as follows: 60, 25, 10, and 5 per cent.

This distribution is reasonable, and since the numbers involved are small, the over-all picture can only be improved by the use of such a distribution, even though it may not be entirely accurate.

[4]The census figure of 600,000 is, however, an understatement. The 1959 annual employment report lists 2.5 million persons under age 16 as participating in collective farm work alone; see *Trudovye resursy SSSR,* ed. by N. I. Shishkin (Moscow, 1961), pp. 98–99. Their participation in the labor force was limited, averaging only fifty-six days in 1959. Eason (*op. cit.,* p. 54,

Table 21) estimates that 2 million persons in the age group 10 to 15 were employed in the labor force in 1959. Again, if we assume that the bulk of these were in their fifteenth year, the number under age 15 would be negligible and hardly worth estimating for inclusion in the employment pyramids.

TABLE 24. Population and employment, by sex and by age, 1959.[a]

	Males			Females		
Age	Total	Employed	Partici- pation Rate	Total	Employed	Partici- pation Rate
			%			%
0 to 4.............	12,417	–	–	11,906	–	–
5 to 9.............	11,191	–	–	10,848	–	–
10 to 14...........	7,941	–	–	7,649	–	–
15 to 19...........	8,125	5,116	63	8,093	5,055	63
20 to 24...........	10,056	8,877	88	10,287	8,351	81
25 to 29...........	8,917	8,386	94	9,273	7,381	80
30 to 34...........	8,611	8,138	95	10,388	8,138	78
35 to 39...........	4,528	4,375	97	7,062	5,452	77
40 to 44...........	3,998	3,767	94	6,410	4,881	76
45 to 49...........	4,706	4,342	92	7,558	5,665	75
50 to 54...........	4,010	3,594	90	6,437	4,445	69
55 to 59...........	2,905	2,395	82	5,793	3,161	55
60 to 64...........	2,348	1,845	79	4,349	2,069	48
65 to 69...........	1,751	942	54	3,289	1,172	35
70 to 74...........	1,220	454	37	2,645	552	21
75 to 79...........	801	209	26	1,503	234	16
All ages.........	94,050	52,440	56	114,776	56,556	49

[a]Figures are expressed in thousands. See pyramids based on these figures (Fig. 11). The military (3.6 million) is included among males employed. For the source of and method of estimating the figures in this table, see Appendix II.

A more difficult problem is the distribution of persons employed in private subsidiary agriculture, that is, those engaged in the cultivation of private garden plots. The number of males involved is relatively small (914,000), so that errors in the estimates cannot seriously affect the employment pyramid, but the number of females is substantial (8,951,000), and inappropriate distribution might result in significant errors. Since it would be misleading to omit this important category of employment, it was included despite the rather rough estimates of the age distribution. Fortunately, a breakdown of those in the able-bodied age group and those in the older group is given in the 1959 census. This breakdown clearly shows the concentration of persons employed in private subsidiary agriculture in the age group 60 and above.

In a word, the general outline of the employment pyramid for 1959 is firmly based on census data; but the details of its configuration, especially in the upper age levels, are based on necessarily rough estimates. It is believed, however, that these estimates make possible a truer and more meaningful picture of participation in the Soviet labor force than could be given with no estimates at all.

A close examination of Figure 11 immediately reveals a strikingly high participation rate for men in all relevant age groups—so high as to preclude effectively the possibility of there having been more men in the labor force. Almost every able-bodied man who had completed his education and was below age 50 was already employed. In the older age groups, the participation rate begins to drop off fairly rapidly, declining to 90 per cent in the age group 50 to 54 and to 82 per cent in the age group 55 to 59. It may be presumed that the proportion of those who were physically able to work also declined more sharply in these age groups, not only because of age, but also because of the relatively high incidence of war disabilities.

Since men are so fully employed throughout the most important working-age groups, it is not surprising to find that the participation of women in the labor force is also very high. What is most striking is the high rate of their participation in all the most important working-age groups, especially in the age groups 20 to 39, which cover almost the entire childbearing and child-rearing span of a woman's life. The average participation rate in 1959 for this broad age group was almost 80 per cent, a phenomenally high rate for a country as industrially advanced as the Soviet Union. In the United States, by comparison, the rate in 1960 declined from an initial peak of 45 per cent in the age group 20 to 24 to a low of 33 per cent in the next five-year group before rising to 36, 40, and 45 per cent in the next three groups, until a peak of 47 per cent was reached in the age group 45 to 49.[5] This pattern of withdrawal from the labor force and later re-entry is not paralleled in the Soviet Union, where the participation rate begins at a high level and remains high until the older age groups are reached.

Substantial numbers of Soviet women begin to withdraw from employment in the socialized sector as they approach the minimum retirement age—age 55 for most occupations, age 50 for hot, heavy, or hazardous work. But the over-all rate of participation in the labor force remains high, because many of the women who retire from regular employment shift to private subsidiary agriculture. Although a woman's contribution to the economy drops sharply by her withdrawal from a regular full-time job, she continues to appear statistically as a full-fledged member of the labor force; but her work in the private subsidiary sector is, in fact, seasonal, and her contribution is, most probably, much less significant. It is for this reason that the 9 million women engaged in private subsidiary agriculture are considered by the government as a pool of manpower which could ultimately be drawn into the socialized sector.

REGIONAL DIFFERENCES

Population and employment pyramids for 1959 were also prepared from the census data on the fifteen republics of the U.S.S.R.[6] Un-like the employment pyramid for the country as a whole, these do not distinguish employment in the private subsidiary economy. Otherwise, the procedure was the same, except for a few variations in the methods of estimation.[7]

The population and employment pyramids for the republics conform only very generally to the pattern for the whole Soviet Union. The republic which most closely resembles that of the entire country is the R.S.F.S.R., which, because of its size, cannot deviate greatly from the average. Ukraine and Belorussia also conform closely to the average. But sharp contrasts are found between the Baltic republics and the republics of Transcaucasia and of Central Asia.

The Baltic republics, as exemplified by Latvia (Fig. 12),[8] have relatively mature populations, which are growing slowly. Both mortality and birth rates have been relatively low for many years. As a result, the sides of the pyramids are nearly vertical until the older age groups make the pyramids plump in the middle and full at the top. The eight republics of Transcaucasia and Central Asia, as exemplified by Uzbekistan (Fig. 13),[9] present population pyramids which are very broad at the base and spindly at the top. The top parts of these pyramids, age 40 and above, have nearly vertical sides, reflecting the near balance of the high mortality rates, particularly infant mortality rates, and the high birth rates which characterized these populations at an earlier time. As the infant mortality rate declined, successively larger bars were added to the population pyramid, which would have shown a regular stair-step effect at the base if the reduced wartime birth rate had not produced a pronounced indrawn waist. These populations are now growing quite rapidly, as large numbers of children are being added to a population which has a relatively small proportion of older people.

---

[5]U.S. Department of Commerce, Bureau of the Census, *United States Census of Population, 1960: Detailed Characteristics* (Washington, D.C., 1963), p. 487.

[6]See Tables 25 and 26 and Appendix II, Tables 1–13.

[7]Described in Appendix II.

[8]See Table 25 and Appendix II, Tables 7 and 13.

[9]See Table 26 and Appendix II, Tables 4, 9, 10, and 12 (Central Asian republics) and 5, 6, and 11 (Transcaucasian republics).

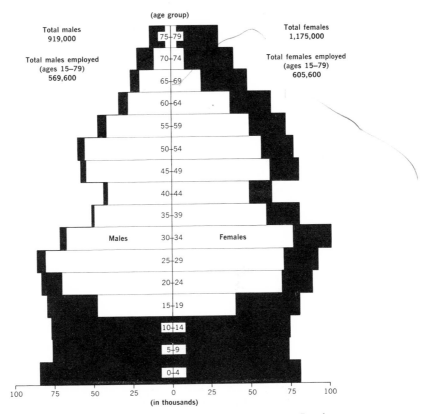

Fig. 12. Population and employment pyramids, 1959, Latvian
S.S.R. *Shaded portion,* not employed; *unshaded portion,* employed,
For the source of these pyramids, see Table 25.

All the population pyramids for the republics reflect the demographic vicissitudes
which the Soviet Union as a whole has suffered. Characteristic are the double waists,
one reflecting the deaths suffered during
World War II, and the other, the wartime
reduction in population which was due to the
lower birth rate and higher infant mortality
rate. The greater loss of males is also clearly
evident in the populations of each republic.
As a result of these underlying demographic
factors which govern manpower potentials,
the pressures are very great in each republic
and in the Soviet Union as a whole to employ
not only every able-bodied male, but also as
many women as possible in order to compensate for the deficit in males and the reduced increments to the working-age group.

The employment pyramids enclosed within
the population pyramids follow much the
same pattern in the individual republics as in
the Soviet Union as a whole. The participation rate of males in the labor force is uni-
formly and substantially higher than that of
females and tends to be close to 90 per cent
or higher in the age groups from 20 to 54
years. Typically, the male participation rate
reaches a peak of from 96 to 99 per cent in
the age group 35 to 39, which suffered severe
losses in the war, but most of whose surviving members are physically able to work. The
participation rate of men in the older age
groups remains higher than that of women. In
ten republics—the Belorussian, Georgian,
Lithuanian, Moldavian, Latvian, Armenian,
Kirgiz, Tadzhik, Azerbaidzhan, and Turkmen—the participation rate of men remains
above 75 per cent up to age 70. It is

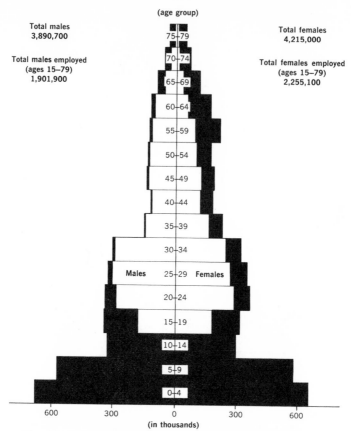

Fig. 13. Population and employment pyramids, 1959, Uzbek S.S.R. *Shaded portion,* not employed; *unshaded portion* employed. For the source of these pyramids, see Table 26.

the R.S.F.S.R., with a participation rate of only 45 per cent for men in the age group 65 to 69, which is primarily responsible for bringing the average for the U.S.S.R. down to 54 per cent.

Of particular interest to us, of course, are the high participation rates for women in all republics and the differences observed among them. A close examination of the employment pyramids shows that the pattern for women in the R.S.F.S.R. and in the Ukrainian, Georgian, Latvian, Kirgiz, and Tadzhik republics conforms closely to that for women in the entire country. Unusually high participation rates are found in Belorussia and Moldavia and, in the older age groups, in

Lithuania, while the Uzbek, Kazakh, and Azerbaidzhan republics show unusually low rates. Participation rates are also low for the younger age groups in the Armenian, Turkmen, and Estonian republics.

Three variables seem to explain most, if not all, of these differences: the degree of urbanization, the extent of the deficit of males in the working-age groups, and the influence of Moslem customs and traditions. In most parts of the Soviet Union the degree of urbanization is the most important variable in the participation rates of women. When the degree of urbanization is low and the rural tradition prevails of most women working seasonally on private plots or on collective farms during

TABLE 25. Population and employment, by sex and by age, 1959, Latvian S.S.R.[a]

	Males			Females		
Age	Total	Employed	Partici-pation Rate	Total	Employed	Partici-pation Rate
			%			%
0 to 4...............	84.6	–	–	81.1	–	–
5 to 9...............	76.3	–	–	73.9	–	–
10 to 14.............	76.8	–	–	74.4	–	–
15 to 19.............	79.3	47.7	60	80.7	40.4	50
20 to 24.............	82.3	72.1	88	88.7	70.0	79
25 to 29.............	85.4	80.5	94	92.1	70.9	77
30 to 34.............	71.1	67.6	95	101.4	77.1	76
35 to 39.............	50.8	48.9	96	81.1	61.0	75
40 to 44.............	43.2	41.0	95	63.4	49.0	77
45 to 49.............	57.6	53.9	94	80.5	62.5	78
50 to 54.............	59.5	54.7	92	77.1	57.0	74
55 to 59.............	46.2	41.2	89	72.1	49.0	68
60 to 64.............	32.8	27.3	80	61.0	37.2	59
65 to 69.............	27.0	20.1	79	50.6	19.1	40
70 to 74.............	22.0	10.8	49	39.7	8.6	22
75 to 79.............	13.2	3.8	29	29.9	3.8	13
All ages...........	919.0	569.6	62	1,174.5	605.6	52

[a]Figures are expressed in thousands. See pyramids based on these figures (Fig. 12). For the source of this table, see Appendix II.

TABLE 26. Population and employment, by sex and by age, 1959, Uzbek S.S.R.[a]

	Males			Females		
Age	Total	Employed	Partici-pation Rate	Total	Employed	Partici-pation Rate
			%			%
0 to 4...............	675.8	–	–	650.3	–	–
5 to 9...............	568.7	–	–	573.4	–	–
10 to 14.............	323.0	–	–	287.5	–	–
15 to 19.............	338.9	175.7	52	311.4	178.9	58
20 to 24.............	333.2	282.9	85	362.2	285.2	79
25 to 29.............	323.6	306.2	95	348.0	264.6	76
30 to 34.............	306.8	293.5	96	317.1	238.1	75
35 to 39.............	155.1	152.5	98	222.6	161.0	72
40 to 44.............	118.5	113.3	96	177.7	124.1	70
45 to 49.............	140.4	131.6	94	181.5	124.2	68
50 to 54.............	138.5	127.8	92	167.3	98.8	59
55 to 59.............	132.3	117.1	89	207.8	95.2	46
60 to 64.............	123.3	103.7	85	167.0	54.8	35
65 to 69.............	89.5	56.4	62	109.8	31.7	27
70 to 74.............	61.7	28.4	46	66.2	15.0	23
75 to 79.............	37.0	12.8	35	50.0	6.3	13
All ages...........	3,890.7	1,901.9	49	4,215.0	2,255.1	54

[a]Figures are expressed in thousands. See pyramids based on these figures (Fig. 13). For the source of this table, see Appendix II.

the peak periods of labor demand, one may expect the participation rate to be high.[10] When the deficit of males and the resultant pressure to utilize female labor are high, the participation rate is also high. In the republics on the southern perimeter of the Soviet Union, Moslem traditions account to a large extent for variations in participation rates. Where these traditions are strong, women tend to marry early, stay in the home, and have more children than women in other cultural environments. As a result, the participation rate of women in the labor force tends to vary inversely with the strength of Moslem custom.

The highest participation rates are found in Moldavia, Belorussia, and, in the older age groups, Lithuania. In Moldavia, 78 per cent of the population is rural, and in Belorussia, 69 per cent—the highest percentages among the fifteen republics. Lithuania also has a large rural population (61 per cent). In these three republics, as in the U.S.S.R. in 1926, women usually work at least part of the year in agriculture, and they are counted as full-fledged participants in the labor force even though their participation is often limited. The deficit of males in these republics is also greater than that in many others and reflects their direct involvement in World War II. The percentage of males in the Moldavian and Lithuanian populations (46 per cent) is the median figure for the fifteen republics, while the percentage in Belorussia (44 per cent) is among the lowest. None of these republics has Moslem elements of any numerical significance in its population.[11]

The lowest participation rates are found in the Kazakh, Uzbek, and Azerbaidzhan republics, where, particularly in the last two,

Moslem traditions are still a potent force limiting the employment of women. These three republics are also among the more urbanized of those in which a Moslem influence exists. In Azerbaidzhan 48 per cent of the population is urban, which is the average for the Soviet Union as a whole. The percentage is slightly lower in Kazakhstan (44 per cent) and considerably lower in Uzbekistan (34 per cent).

Areas in which one might expect a low participation rate because of cultural backwardness and a strong Moslem influence are the Kirgiz and Tadzhik republics. However, Slavic and other non-Moslem elements comprise over 37 per cent of the population in Kirgizia, and in Tadzhikistan only 67 per cent of the population is rural, with many women working part-time in agriculture. These particular circumstances counterbalance influences which might otherwise lead to a low participation rate for women.[12]

The percentage of males in all the republics along the southern perimeter of the Soviet Union is, as one might expect, relatively high, and the pressure to employ women is therefore not so strong as it is in the areas which suffered directly from World War II, such as Belorussia. In the Uzbek, Kazakh, and Azerbaidzhan republics, males make up 48 per cent of the population, a figure exceeded only in the Tadzhik and Turkmen republics (49 per cent). It may be noted that Kazakhstan is unique in having a substantial excess of males in the age group 20 to 29. Most republics have a deficit in this age group, and only a few show a near balance.

THE IMPORTANCE OF WOMEN IN THE LABOR FORCE

The share of women in the labor force is a function both of the proportion of men and women in the able-bodied age group of the population and of the rate of participation of men and women in this age group in the labor

---

[10] Because the women who work only part-time are included, the participation rates in the more rural republics are higher than they would be if they were calculated on a full-time basis.

[11] See *Itogi . . . 1959 goda: SSSR* (Moscow, 1962), pp. 20–27, 202–8; and *Zhenshchiny i deti v SSSR, statisticheskii sbornik* (2d ed.; Moscow, 1963), p. 34.

[12] *Ibid.*

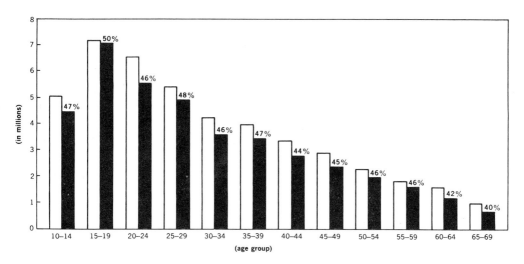

F<small>IG</small>. 14. Age-sex distribution of the labor force, 1926. *Shaded bars,* females; *unshaded bars,* males. For the exact number represented by each bar and for the source of these data, see Table 23.

force. In other words, a comparison of the left and right sides of the employment pyramids will reveal the proportion of males and females among all those employed.

Historically, women have been an important element in the Soviet labor force. Their share in the labor force was 46.4 per cent in 1926, 45.1 per cent in 1939, and 49.4 per cent in 1959. Changes in the total proportion of women in the labor force have been the product both of economic development and of varying percentages of women in the age groups from which the labor force is drawn. As the Soviet Union has become more industrialized and consequently urbanized, there has been a tendency for the participation rate of women to decline. However, there has been a counteracting increase in the deficit of males, which assumed serious proportions as a result of World War II. This deficit has had the dual effect of preventing a further decline in the participation rate after 1939 and of increasing the percentage of women in the age groups from which the labor force is drawn. The balance of these forces was such that the share of women in the labor force declined only slightly from 1926 to 1939, but increased

significantly between 1939 and 1959 (see Table 27).

It is essential to examine the sex distribution of the labor force by age group, since the average percentage of employed women may conceal wide variations within certain age groups. Such was not the case in 1926, when the distribution of employment was very even between men and women among the different age groups, and the proportion of employed women differed very little from the average of 46.4 per cent. A substantial deviation from the average is seen (Fig. 14) only in the age groups 60 to 69; in the age groups 10 to 59, the variations lie between 44 and 50 per cent.

The 1959 census, on the other hand, presents a dramatically different picture (Fig. 15). In the older age groups, the deficit of males is so great that women make up a clear majority of the labor force. Among the five-year age groups from 35 to 59, the percentage of women maintains a level of from 55 to 57 per cent. Only in the age groups under 35 is there a balance or near balance of the sexes. Thus, in the crucial age groups from 35 to 59, from which much of the leadership of the Soviet Union must come, women constitute the preponderant element.

TABLE 27. Total labor force, by major occupational group and by sex, 1926, 1939, and 1959.[a]

Occupational Group	1926				1939				1959			
	Both Sexes	Males	Females	Females %	Both Sexes	Males	Females	Females %	Both Sexes	Males	Females	Females %
Workers and employees	9,600	6,600	3,000	31.3	34,900	23,000	11,900	34.1	63,000	33,600	29,400	46.0
Nonagricultural	(8,400)	(5,800)	(2,600)	(31.0)	(28,800)	(18,600)	(10,200)	(35.4)	(56,400)	(29,700)	(26,700)	(47.3)
Agricultural	(1,200)	(800)	(400)	(33.3)	(6,100)	(4,400)	(1,700)	(27.9)	(6,600)	(3,900)	(2,700)	(40.9)
Co-op. handicraftsmen	n.a.[b]	n.a.	n.a.	n.a.	2,200	1,700	500	22.7	1,400	1,300	100	71.4
Nonco-op. handicraftsmen	1,500	1,100	400	26.7	400	200	200	50.0	200	100	100	50.0
Collective farmers	n.a.	n.a.	n.a.	n.a.	36,300	16,600	19,700	54.3	32,300	14,200	18,100	56.0
Private farmers[c]	70,500	35,300	35,200	49.9	12,600	4,400	8,200	65.1	10,000	3,500	6,500	90.0
"Bourgeoisie"	1,300	1,100	200	15.4	n.a.	n.a.	n.a.	n.a.	n.a.	n.a.	n.a.	n.a.
Employed labor force	82,900	44,100	38,800	46.8	86,400	45,900	40,500	46.9	105,400	48,800	56,600	53.7
Unemployed	1,000	600	400	40.0	n.a.	n.a.	n.a.	n.a.	n.a.	n.a.	n.a.	n.a.
Civilian labor force	83,900	44,700	39,200	46.7	86,400	45,900	40,500	46.9	105,400	48,800	56,600	53.7
Military	600	600	0	0.0	3,400	3,400	0	0.0	3,600	3,600	0	0.0
Total labor force	84,500	45,300	39,200	46.4	89,800	49,300	40,500	45.1	109,000	52,400	56,600	51.9
Nonagricultural labor force	12,800	9,200	3,600	28.1	34,800	23,900	10,900	31.2	60,700	33,900	26,800	44.2
Agricultural labor force	71,700	36,100	35,600	49.7	55,000	25,400	29,600	53.8	48,300	18,600	29,700	61.5

[a]Figures are expressed in thousands. This table is based on figures from Warren W. Eason, "Labor Force," in Economic Trends in the Soviet Union, ed. by A. Bergson and S. Kuznets (Cambridge, Mass., 1963), p. 84. The 1959 figures have been corrected on the basis of the final census returns.

[b]No data available.

[c]Includes individual farmers and persons occupied solely in subsidiary agriculture.

44

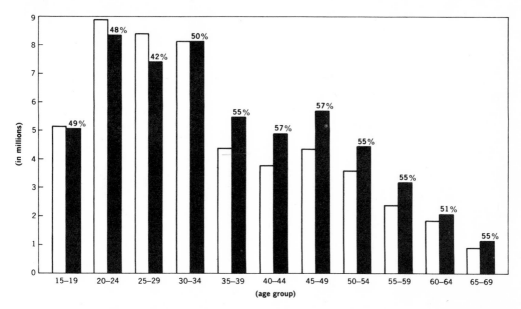

FIG. 15. Age-sex distribution of the labor force, 1959. *Shaded bars,* females; *unshaded bars,* males. For the exact number represented by each bar and for the source of these data, see Table 24.

CHANGING PATTERNS OF FEMALE EMPLOYMENT

Changes in the importance of women within the different occupational groups have not all followed a uniform pattern. The largest increase in the proportion of employed women —from 31.0 per cent in 1926, to 35.4 per cent in 1939, and to 46.9 per cent in 1959— has been among the nonagricultural wage and salary workers (see Table 27). The share of women in the agricultural labor force as a whole was already high (49.7 per cent) in 1926 and increased only slightly (56.4 per cent) by 1959.

Table 28 shows some very important shifts in the basic employment pattern for Soviet women. In 1926, only 9.2 per cent of the women in the labor force were employed in the nonagricultural sector; thus, 90.8 per cent were engaged in agriculture, which at that time meant private agriculture. Males also worked primarily in agriculture, although the proportion (79.7 per cent) was somewhat smaller. By 1939, as a result of the labor de-

mands of industrialization, the proportion of women in the nonagricultural labor force had increased to 26.9 per cent, and the proportion in agriculture had declined to 73.1 per cent. Further industrialization and the effects of World War II continued the trend. In 1959, 44.7 per cent of employed women were in the nonagricultural labor force and only 55.3 per cent were in agriculture. Again, the proportion of males in the agricultural labor force declined to 42.7 per cent in 1959.

Thus, the great transformation in the position of women was the shift from predominantly agricultural employment to a rough balance between agricultural and nonagricultural employment. This shift reflects, of course, the vast economic and cultural transformation which has converted the Soviet Union from a largely backward agricultural society into a much more developed and complex industrial society. However, a large proportion of its population is still engaged in agriculture and in many ways remains isolated from modern industrial civilization. This transformation has meant new ways of gaining a livelihood for

TABLE 28.   Percentage distribution of the total labor force, by major occupational group and by sex, 1926, 1939, and 1959.[a]

Occupational Group	1926			1939			1959		
	Both Sexes	Males	Females	Both Sexes	Males	Females	Both Sexes	Males	Females
Workers and Employees...............	11.4	14.6	7.6	38.9	46.6	29.4	55.5	60.0	50.9
Nonagricultural....................	(10.0)	(12.8)	(6.6)	(32.1)	(37.3)	(25.2)	(46.8)	(49.1)	(44.4)
Agricultural.....................	(1.4)	(1.8)	(1.0)	(6.8)	(8.9)	(4.2)	(8.7)	(10.9)	(6.5)
Co-op. handicraftsmen...............	1.8	2.4	1.0	2.5	3.5	1.3	1.2	2.4	0.2
Nonco-op. handicraftsmen.............	n.a.[b]	n.a.	n.a.	0.4	0.4	0.5	0.2	0.2	0.2
Collective farmers...................	n.a.	n.a.	n.a.	40.4	33.7	48.6	30.6	24.6	36.7
Private farmers[c]....................	83.4	77.9	89.8	14.0	8.9	20.2	9.2	6.3	12.0
"Bourgeoisie"......................	1.5	2.5	0.6	n.a.	n.a.	n.a.	n.a.	n.a.	n.a.
Employed labor force.................	98.1	97.4	99.0	96.2	93.1	100.0	96.7	93.5	100.0
Unemployed........................	1.2	1.3	1.0	n.a.	n.a.	n.a.	n.a.	n.a.	n.a.
Civilian labor force...................	99.3	98.7	100.0	96.2	93.0	100.0	96.7	93.5	100.0
Military...........................	0.7	0.3	0.0	3.8	6.9	0.0	3.3	6.5	0.0
Total labor force.....................	100.0	100.0	100.0	100.0	100.0	100.0	100.0	100.0	100.0
Nonagricultural labor force...........	15.1	20.3	9.2	38.8	48.5	26.9	51.6	57.3	44.7
Agricultural labor force..............	84.9	79.7	90.8	61.2	51.5	73.1	48.4	42.7	55.3

[a]For the source of these figures, see Table 27, n.
[b]No data available.

[c]Includes individual farmers and persons occupied solely in subsidiary agriculture.

many women, but, for a strikingly large proportion, the past four decades of Soviet rule have meant only a continuation of unskilled, backbreaking work in the fields.

POPULATION AND EMPLOYMENT IN 1959

The population and employment data for 1959 are consolidated in a comprehensive balance in Table 29. In later chapters, these data form the basis for a more detailed analysis of the role of women in the labor force. Here, it is sufficient to point out some of the most significant relationships which they reveal (as summarized in Table 30). Females made up 49.1 per cent of the underage population, 54 per cent of the able-bodied population, and 74 per cent of the overage population. Women comprised 58.3 per cent of the entire population outside the labor force. Males and females outside the labor force were almost equal in number in the underage group, but women made up 71.1 per cent of the able-bodied and 78.7 per cent of the overage categories. Among those in the labor force (including the armed forces), women made up 51.9 per cent of the total, 50.2 per cent of

the able-bodied group, and 67.5 per cent of the overage group. In the nonmilitary labor force, the percentages were 53.7, 52.1, and 67.5. Of the entire female population, 49.3 per cent were in the labor force, and 50.7 per cent were unemployed. Almost all the underage girls were in the dependent category. Of the able-bodied women, 75.8 per cent were in the labor force, and the bulk of the remainder were in the dependent or pensioner categories. Of the overage women, 38.3 per cent still participated in the labor force, while the remainder were almost equally divided between the dependent and pensioner categories.

In evaluating Soviet policies regarding the employment of women as revealed in these data and in later chapters, a theoretical framework is desirable. This cannot, however, be found in the Soviet economic literature. With few exceptions, Soviet authors tend to view the employment of more women as desirable under all circumstances. The concept of an optimal proportion of employed women is nowhere formally expressed even though Soviet practice implies the application, either consciously or unconsciously, of some such concept. For a better understanding of what is meant by an optimal proportion, in an economic sense, a simple model is presented here

TABLE 29. Distribution of the labor-force and nonlabor-force population by socioeconomic category, sex, and age group, 1959.[a]

Socioeconomic Category	Both Sexes				Males				Females			
	All Ages	Underage	Able-bodied	Overage	All Ages	Underage	Able-bodied	Overage	All Ages	Underage	Able-bodied	Overage
Total population	208,827[b]	(63,496)[b]	(119,822)[b]	(25,501)[b]	94,050[c]	32,331[d]	(55,079)[e]	6,640[f]	114,776[c]	31,165[d]	(64,751)[e]	18,861[f]
Total labor force	108,995[c]	(496)[e]	(97,793)[g]	10,706[e]	52,440[h]	(258)[e]	(48,699)[e]	(3,483)[e]	56,556[h]	(238)[e]	(49,094)[e]	(7,223)[e]
Armed forces	3,623[h]	—	3,623[h]	—	3,622[h]	—	(3,622)[h]	—	1[h]	—	1[h]	—
Civilian labor force	105,372[c]	(496)[e]	(94,170)[b]	10,706[e]	48,817[c]	(258)[e]	(45,077)[e]	(3,483)[e]	56,555[c]	(238)[e]	(49,093)[e]	(7,223)[e]
Socialized sector	95,241[h]	(495)[e]	88,925[h]	5,820[e]	47,739[h]	258[i]	44,722[h]	2,759[e]	47,503[h]	237[i]	44,203[h]	3,061[i]
Workers and employees	62,961[h]	(123)[e]	(60,774)[e]	(2,063)[e]	33,570[h]	(66)[e]	(32,380)[e]	(1,125)[e]	29,391[h]	(57)[e]	(28,394)[e]	(938)[e]
Nonagricultural branches	56,350[h]	(59)[e]	(54,532)[e]	(1,758)[e]	29,672[h]	(29)[e]	(28,691)[e]	(953)[e]	26,678[h]	(30)[e]	(25,841)[e]	(805)[e]
Agricultural branches	6,611[h]	(64)[e]	(6,242)[e]	(305)[e]	3,898[h]	37[i]	3,689[i]	172[i]	2,713[h]	27[i]	2,553[i]	133[i]
Collective farmers	32,280[c]	(372)[e]	(28,151)[e]	(3,757)[e]	14,169[c]	(192)[e]	(12,342)[e]	(1,634)[e]	18,111[c]	(180)[e]	(15,809)[e]	(2,123)[e]
Nonagricultural branches	557[i]	—	(557)[j]	—	437[h]	—	(437)[h]	—	120[h]	—	120[h]	—
Agricultural branches	31,723[i]	(372)[e]	(27,594)[e]	(3,757)[e]	13,731[h]	192[i]	11,905[i]	1,634[i]	17,992[i]	180[i]	15,689[i]	2,123[i]
Private independent sector	266[h]	(1)[e]	(210)[e]	(56)[e]	165[h]	(0.4)[e]	(142)[e]	(23)[e]	101[e]	(1)[e]	(68)[e]	(33)[e]
Independent artisans	174[h]	—	(160)[e]	(15)[e]	133[h]	—	(123)[e]	(10)[e]	42[h]	—	(37)[i]	(5)[k]
Individual peasants	92[h]	1[i]	(50)[e]	(41)[e]	32[h]	0.4[i]	19[i]	13[i]	60[h]	1[i]	31[i]	28[i]
Private subsidiary agricultural sector	9,865[e]	—	5,035[e]	(4,830)[e]	914[e]	—	213[b]	(701)[e]	8,951[e]	—	4,822[b]	(4,129)[e]
Members of families of workers and employees	(4,165)[l]	—	(3,357)[l]	(808)[e]	(651)[l]	—	(213)[m]	(438)[n]	(3,514)[l]	—	(3,144)[m]	(370)[e]
Members of families of collective farmers	5,700[o]	—	(1,678)[l]	(4,022)[e]	(263)[e]	—	—	(263)[e]	(5,437)[l]	—	(1,678)[e]	(3,759)[e]
Population outside labor force	99,832[e]	(63,000)[e]	22,029[e]	(14,795)[e]	41,611[e]	(32,073)[e]	(6,380)[e]	(3,157)[e]	58,221[c]	(30,927)[e]	(15,657)[e]	(11,638)[e]
Dependents	82,122[b]	(63,000)[e]	12,860[b]	(6,255)[c]	35,007[c]	(32,073)[e]	(1,402)[b]	(431)[e]	50,415[c]	(30,927)[e]	11,465[b]	(5,824)[e]
Able-bodied students	3,300[c]	—	3,300[c]	—	—	—	(1,100)[p]	—	—	—	(2,200)[p]	—
Stipendiaries	1,717[c]	—	1,717[c]	—	943[c]	—	943[c]	—	775[c]	—	775[c]	—
Pensioners	12,423[e]	—	4,097[e]	(8,326)[e]	5,580[c]	—	(2,935)[e]	(2,645)[e]	6,843[c]	—	(1,162)[b]	(5,681)[e]
Others	269[e]	—	(55)[e]	(214)[e]	81[c]	—	—	(81)[e]	188[c]	—	(55)[e]	(133)[e]

[a] Figures are expressed in thousands; those in parentheses are estimates; dashes indicate negligible number or none. The broad age groups are: *underage*, males and females age 12–15; *able-bodied*, males age 16–59 and females age 16–54; *overage*, males age 60 and over and females age 55 and over.

[b] From the census data of Jan. 15, 1959, published in *Itogi . . . 1959 goda: SSSR*, Table 32, pp. 98–99. Discrepancy between total and sum of components is in original data.

[c] *Ibid.*, Table 30, pp. 96–97.

[d] Tsentral'noe statisticheskoe upravlenie pri Sovete ministrov SSSR, *Zhenshchiny i deti v SSSR, statisticheskii sbornik* (Moscow, 1961), p. 57.

[e] Derived either by addition or by subtraction, as appropriate.

[f] *Itogi . . . 1959 goda: SSSR*, Table 13, pp. 50–51.

[g] Closing error of 61,000. The figure of 97,793,000 shown in the table is the sum of the parts both horizontally and vertically. However, according to the 1959 census data (*ibid*, Table 32, pp. 98–99), this figure should be 97,731,139.

[h] *Ibid.*, Table 33, pp. 104–5.

[i] Computed from data in *ibid.*, Tables 33 and 39, pp. 104–5, and 117–22. The rates of employment, by sex and age given in Table 39 were applied to total employment, by sex, for corresponding branches given in Table 33. Thus employment in the socialized sector was computed by multiplying the male and female rates of employment by the appropriate age group under total employment, by sex, in the total national economy (excluding the private subsidiary economy). Figures for employment in the armed forces and in the private independent sector were then subtracted from the result in order to obtain the socialist sector employment. For determining employment by sex and age for workers and employees in the agricultural branches the same procedure was followed: computing employment in all agriculture and subtracting the computed employment of collective farmers (in agriculture) and of individual peasants.

[j] Collective farmers in nonagricultural branches are assumed to be able-bodied persons.

[k] Overage male and female independent artisans are arbitrarily estimated at 10,000 and 5,000 persons, respectively.

[l] The total number of able-bodied persons in the private subsidiary economy (5,035,000) is allocated arbitrarily as two thirds for the members of families of workers and employees and one third for the members of families of collective farmers.

[m] Able-bodied males engaged in the private subsidiary economy are all assumed to be members of families of workers and employees.

[n] Overage males employed in the private subsidiary economy are assumed to be distributed in the proportion of five eighths for members of families of workers and employees and three eighths for members of families of collective farmers.

[o] Reported to be 5.7 million, according to V. Rozdialovskaia, "Zaniatiia grazhdan SSSR po dannym perepisi naseleniia 1959 goda," *Vestnik statistiki*, No. 3 (March, 1961), 4.

[p] Able-bodied students in the nonlabor-force population are distributed arbitrarily, one third under males and two thirds under females.

[q] Males in the "Others" category are all assumed to be overage.

TABLE 30. Percentage of females in the labor-force and nonlabor-force population, by socioeconomic category and age group, 1959.[a]

Socioeconomic Category	All Ages		Underage		Able-bodied		Overage	
	Percent-age Female	Distribu-tion of Females	Percent-age Female	Distribu-tion of Females	Percent-age Female	Distribu-tion of Females	Percent-age Female	Distribu-tion of Females
Total population..........................	55.0	100.0	49.1	100.0	54.0	100.0	74.0	100.0
Total labor force..........................	51.9	49.3	48.0	0.8	50.2	75.8	67.5	38.3
Armed forces............................	–	–	–	–	–	–	–	–
Civilian labor force.......................	53.7	49.3	48.0	0.8	52.1	75.8	67.5	38.3
Socialized sector.......................	49.9	41.4	47.9	0.8	49.7	68.3	52.6	16.2
Workers and employees...............	46.7	25.6	46.3	0.2	46.7	43.9	45.5	5.0
Nonagricultural branches...........	47.3	23.2	50.8	0.1	47.4	39.9	45.8	4.3
Agricultural branches.................	41.0	2.4	42.2	0.1	40.9	3.9	43.6	0.7
Collective farmers.....................	56.1	15.8	48.4	0.6	56.2	24.4	56.5	11.3
Nonagricultural branches...........	21.5	0.1	–	–	21.5	0.2	–	–
Agricultural branches...............	56.7	15.7	48.4	0.6	56.9	24.2	56.5	11.3
Private independent sector..............	38.0	–	71.4	–	32.4	–	58.9	–
Independent artisans..................	24.1	–	–	–	23.1	–	33.3	0.2
Individual peasants...................	65.2	–	71.4	–	62.0	–	68.3	–
Private subsidiary agricultural sector.......	90.7	7.8	–	–	95.8	7.4	85.5	27.9
Members of families of workers and em-ployees..........................	84.4	3.1	–	–	93.7	4.9	45.8	2.0
Members of families of collective farmers.	95.4	4.7	–	–	100.0	2.6	93.5	19.9
Population outside labor force...............	58.3	50.7	49.1	99.2	71.1	24.2	78.7	61.7
Dependents...........................	61.4	43.9	49.1	99.2	89.2	17.7	93.1	30.9
Able-bodied students.....................		–		–	66.7	3.4	–	–
Stipendiaries...........................	45.1	0.7	–	–	45.1	1.2	–	–
Pensioners............................	55.1	6.0	–	–	28.4	1.8	68.2	30.1
Others................................	69.9	0.2	–	–	100.0	0.1	62.1	0.7

[a]See notes to Table 29.

in graphic terms (Fig. 16), showing how an optimum may properly be determined. It should be kept in mind, of course, that the optimal utilization of women as a manpower resource is but part of the general problem of the development and allocation of manpower resources.

We shall start with some simplifying assumptions, and with the caveat that we are viewing only the productive aspect of economic activity, not the welfare effects. Our first approximation to reality is concerned with the determination of an optimal utilization of male and female potential under static conditions. We assume that the talents (productive potential) of men and women are equal and are distributed in the same proportions among the members of each sex. The productive potential of males and females may be visualized in terms of two identical functions (Model A, *PM* and *PF*). The number of males and females is measured on the horizontal axes, the productive potential, on the vertical. Both males and females are arrayed by descending order of productive potential.

Full utilization of male and female potential under these assumptions would imply that the number of women in the labor force should be proportional to that in the population of working age. If the number of males and females of working age were equal, for example, equal numbers should be employed. If the proportion of women should rise, as it did in the Soviet Union as a result of events following the outbreak of World War I and culminating in World War II, the proportion of females employed should rise equally. An illustration of such an optimum is given in

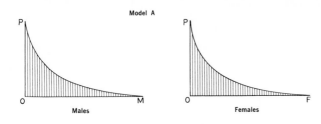

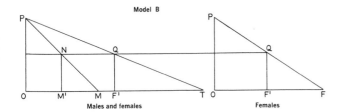

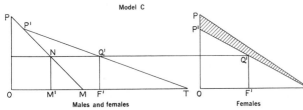

FIG. 16. Optimal proportion of male to female employment. *Model A*, productive potential; *Model B*, optimal proportion, with equal productive potential; *Model C*, optimal proportion, with lower productive potential of females.

Model B. For illustrative purposes, it is assumed that the number of women in the working ages is 50 per cent larger than that of males. It is also assumed for purposes of clarity that the productivity of males and females declines in a linear fashion. The total number of males is *OM*, that of females, *OF*. The diagram for females is combined with that for males, so that total available labor resources are *OT*, the potential contribution of females being *MT*. If full employment is represented by *OF'*, the optimal number of males employed is *OM'*, that of females, *M'F'* or *OF'*. The productivity of the marginal male, *M'N*, is equal to the productivity of the marginal female, *F'Q*, when the proportion of males and females employed is optimal. It will be observed that the number of

women employed, *M'F'* or *OF'*, is 50 per cent larger than the number of men, *OM'*. This corresponds to the relationship between the male and female populations.

In fact, of course, the productivity of females, even under the ideal circumstances of the full development of their potential, would be less than that of men because of the shorter working life of women.[13] Although individual women would bear children at different times, if at all, for simplicity the productivity curve for women is lowered by 10 to 20 per cent. Therefore, the adjusted productivity curve for women (Model C, *P'F*) lies below the potential curve. The optimal proportion of males

---

[13]Discussed in Chapter 12.

to females in the labor force can be read from Model C, if we know the full employment level. If full employment is OF', then $O'M$ males and $M'F'$ or OF' females should be employed. If males and females are employed in this proportion, the productivity of the marginal female, $F'Q'$, will be equal to that of the marginal male, $M'N$. It can be seen that the lower net productivity of females leads to an optimal proportion between males and females which is more favorable for males.

Consideration of the cost of child-care facilities introduces an additional complication into the picture. The cost of caring for children might be considered a fixed cost to society, which is borne irrespective of the methods of child care. From the standpoint of a Soviet planner, however, the women who cannot make arrangements within the family for the care of their children represent a net drain on resources which could otherwise be allocated elsewhere to the benefit of the economy. Therefore, some consideration is undoubtedly given by planners to the additional costs of the child-care facilities which would be necessary if additional women were to be drawn into the labor force. Such consideration would, of course, result in a smaller proportion of employed women at the optimum.

If we shift to more realistic assumptions by discarding the assumption that the productive potential of women is fully realized (except for the shorter working life of a woman), our method of analysis still remains valid. We simply array our available males and females as before, by descending order of productivity. If we assume that education is some indication of productivity, the smaller number of women having completed each level of education will result in the curve's falling below that of the males. Other factors will also affect the curve. With the actual productivity of women further reduced in relation to that of men, it is readily apparent that the optimal proportion of women who should be employed would be smaller than that previously indicated.

We initially assumed that labor was homo-geneous except for differences in productivity, but of course labor is not homogeneous in other respects. Particular occupations and professions require special interests, aptitudes, training, and experience, and are effectively closed to persons lacking these qualifications. Because of the high degree of specialization required in a modern complex economy, and the high costs involved in shifting one's specialization through the acquisition of new highly specialized skills, substitutability is now much more limited. As a result, the same sort of analysis we have applied to the labor force as a whole can be applied to specialized occupational groups, such as tractor drivers or chemists. Male and female tractor drivers can be arrayed in descending order of productivity, and the optimal proportion of males and females who should be employed can be determined by the same marginal principles which we have applied to the economy as a whole.

If we compare Soviet policies regarding the employment of women with those which our simple model calls for, given the relative sizes of the male and female populations of working age, educational levels, and so forth, it appears that the Soviets have, for the most part, shaped their strategy along rational economic lines. The proportion of women in the labor force has risen as the proportion of women in the population has increased. Also, as the proportion of women with specialized training has increased, the share of women employed in various specialized fields has increased. For the most part, however, the more attractive jobs requiring special training or skills have been filled largely by men; only a small share of the women fill these jobs. Most women—those who have little or no training and few skills—fill the least demanding and least desirable jobs. In jobs of this type—field work on collective farms, street cleaning, floor scrubbing—productivity is extremely low. From the standpoint of the regime, however, it is better to employ women in such occupations, since the work has to be done somehow, unpleasant or unattractive as it is.

Up to this point, our analysis has been essentially static, but the development of manpower resources, which is at the heart of economic development, is a dynamic problem. In the chapters on education and educational attainment, we shall have occasion to apply similar methods of analysis to the Soviet policies on the education and training of women.

CONCLUSIONS

The present high rate of participation of women in the Soviet Union is not without precedent. In 1926, when the country was largely agricultural, almost every woman participated in economic activity outside the home for a part of the year. As the country became industrialized and urbanized in the course of the development of the economy, there was a tendency for the participation rate of women to decline. However, the increase in the participation rate of urban women tended to offset this decline, so that there has been little change in the average participation rate. What is unique in the Soviet situation today is the very high participation rates in a country relatively advanced industrially. The continuance of a high rate of participation by women of all ages, even through the child-bearing and child-rearing ages, is another distinctive Soviet characteristic. The influence of the deficit of males on the participation of women was touched on in the preceding chapter. The resulting economic pressures, compelling women to work to make ends meet, unquestionably played a major role in keeping women in the labor force.

Although participation rates are high for women in all regions of the U.S.S.R., variations occur which appear to be related to the degree of urbanization, the influence of Moslem traditions, and the extent of the deficit of men. High rates are associated with heavily rural, non-Moslem populations afflicted with a large deficit of males. As a result, partici-pation rates tend to be high in a largely rural republic which was badly hit by the war, such as Belorussia, and low in a more urbanized republic with Moslem traditions, such as Azerbaidzhan.

The high rate of participation by women in the labor force coupled with the high proportion of women in the Soviet population has had the result that women make up approximately half of the labor force in the Soviet Union today. The importance of women in the labor force varies greatly among the different age groups, however. Up to age 35, males predominate, but the large deficit of males in the older age groups, coupled with high participation rates for women in these ages, has given women age 35 and older a majority in the labor force. This is the age group from which the leadership of an economy and a society is normally drawn. These special circumstances have made the effective utilization of women in the labor force even more vital for the Soviet Union in recent years and will continue to do so for some years to come.

As the economy has developed over recent decades, the pattern of female employment has changed considerably. In 1926, only 9.2 per cent of the women employed in the labor force were engaged in nonagricultural occupations. By 1939 this percentage had almost tripled to 26.9 per cent. The trend continued during and after the war, and the percentage reached 44.7 per cent in 1959. These changes reflect the great transformation in the employment of women as the Soviet Union was converted from a predominantly agricultural economy to one which was much more highly developed and industrialized.

The population and employment data for 1959 further emphasize the importance of women in all major employment categories. These statistics show why the party and the government must always consider their manpower policies in connection with demographic and other policies which may affect the participation of women in the labor force.

chapter

4

SOCIAL, ECONOMIC, AND LEGAL FACTORS AFFECTING EMPLOYMENT

THE HIGH participation rate of women in the Soviet labor force is the product of many factors. All these factors have the same general influence on women, whether they are in scientific, technical, or professional fields or in other occupations. Several of the most important factors—deficit of males, family size, degree of urbanization, proportion of Moslem population—have already been touched on. In this chapter, several additional factors which significantly influence the degree of participation are discussed. Some affect the general level of participation; others, such as protective legislation, affect the participation of women in certain occupations or industries.

CUSTOMS AND SOCIAL ATTITUDES

Among the factors which in the past inhibited women from working or entering certain professions were customs and social attitudes. Prior to the Revolution women had fought a vigorous battle against convention and prejudice in order to gain admission to higher educational institutions. The privileges won before 1917 came too late and in such small measure that most professions requiring special training remained traditionally male at the time of the Revolution. Only medicine and teaching were felt to be appropriate occupations for women, but science and technology

had just begun to admit a few women. It was not until the 1930's that the percentage of girls enrolled in engineering schools rose above 20 per cent,[1] and even today some parents discourage their daughters from entering the field. A young woman who had specialized in the heat treatment of metals told the author that her parents had argued for a career in teaching or medicine and, even as late as the mid-1950's, had felt that engineering was not an entirely suitable occupation for a woman. In the Central Asian republics in particular, where the Moslem customs of early marriage and confinement of women to the home have stubbornly resisted change, the Soviet regime is still fighting to alter the traditional attitudes of the indigenous population which discourage the participation of women in any but agricultural occupations. From its earliest days of power, the Communist party has considered the integration of women into the economy of these republics, especially into industry, as one of its most important tasks. The liquidation of a feudal attitude toward women through the destruction of religious custom and belief has proved a formidable task indeed.

---

[1] L. S. Souter and R. Winslade, *Women Engineers in the U.S.S.R.* (London, 1960), p. 6.

The main weapons in this struggle have been propaganda, agitation, education, and law. The propaganda efforts have been conducted largely by the Women's Affairs Sections of the party, which have stressed the importance of education and have furthered its development. Similar work has been carried on by the *Komsomol,* the trade unions, and the local governments, all of which concern themselves in varying degrees with women's affairs. During the mid-1920's, a veil-removal campaign provoked vigorous resistance. The Third Uzbek Congress of Soviets, in May, 1929, took official notice of the widespread opposition to reform and passed a decree condemning the increase of "terroristic acts" against women activists. Certain court officials were denounced because they failed to support women by not actively prosecuting social crimes.[2]

However, with the introduction of forced collectivization and the increased pace of industrialization in the 1930's, the struggle was intensified and the backbone of resistance crushed. The process was undoubtedly speeded up by the Women's Councils, which were established on collective farms and in industries in Central Asia during World War II in an attempt to provide some sort of improvement in the living and working conditions of the large numbers of female laborers in agriculture and industry. Their functions included the attraction of women into productive activities and the political education of women to fight "survivals of the past way of life."

As a result of all this, the old customs are giving way, and more and more women in Central Asia are obtaining secondary specialized and higher education and entering semiprofessional or professional employment. These young women are guided in their choice of a vocation by much the same influences and considerations as the young women in other parts of the Soviet Union. However, their aspirations may be less ambitious, because they are geared to the needs of their more backward economy. They are more likely to think in terms of becoming a secondary-school teacher rather than a research scientist or an agronomist rather than a nuclear physicist.

In the country as a whole, as today's older generation gives way to the new, a profound and far-reaching revolution in attitudes is evolving. Certain professions may be more favored by men or women, but the reasons will lie more in objective circumstances and personal preference than in custom or social attitude. Few, if any, careers are now considered taboo for women in the Soviet Union, and even further evolution in attitudes is expected.

The Soviet Union has succeeded in creating an atmosphere in which a woman feels apologetic if she does not work. The author recalls a dinner party at which he questioned each woman in turn about her work. Around the table with their husbands were a physician, a teacher, a retail executive, and a woman who confessed with embarrassment that she did not do any work at all, but stayed at home to take care of her children. This reaction was characteristic. Bearing children and caring for a home are not considered a sufficient contribution to society. Also, when most women are working, those who do not are more conspicuous in their delinquency and the moral opprobrium is increased. As a young girl from a high-income family put it, "When all your friends are working, it is no fun not to work." These responses suggest that a remolding of public opinion in support of government policies has been achieved.

The revolution in attitudes toward the place of women in the Soviet society was the product of a long and vigorous campaign by the party and the government to change and mold public opinion. All means of communication and propaganda were employed, and new organizations and publications were designed specifically to remake the image of the Russian woman. Extensive legislation was passed, but legislation alone would not have sufficed. A decree stipulating that men and women were to have equal access to higher education, for example, would have had little practical

---

[2]*Sovetskaia etnografiia,* No. 4 (1950), 84; and *Kazakhstanskaia pravda* (Dec. 20, 1950).

TABLE 31.   Percentage of respondents whose mothers had worked (Harvard Project).[a]

Occupation of Respondent's Father	Age of Respondent in 1940							
	under 26		26–35		36–45		over 45	
	%		%		%		%	
Professional........	62	(42)[b]	70	(121)	50	(69)	26	(97)
Semiprofessional.....	64	(56)	62	(161)	49	(117)	25	(183)
Worker.............	53	(49)	45	(204)	42	(137)	28	(117)
Peasant............	48	(31)	35	(251)	27	(203)	25	(266)

[a]This table is reproduced from Alex Inkeles and Raymond A. Bauer, *The Soviet Citizen* (Cambridge, Mass., 1959), p. 205.

[b]The total number of respondents on the basis of which the percentage is computed is given in parentheses.

effect if at the same time basic attitudes toward higher education for women had not been changed, and if ambitions had not been instilled into young women to enter fields where few had trod before.

In assessing the effectiveness of the regime's effort to draw women into the labor force, Inkeles and Bauer in an interview project divided the respondents into four age groups; the mothers of these respondents were thus from different generations. Overlapping periods of Russian and Soviet history, when the mothers were bearing and raising their children, could then be studied. On the basis of their data, reproduced in Table 31, Inkeles and Bauer concluded:

it . . . seems strikingly evident that there has been a marked generational trend in the likelihood that at some point in their lives women would work. Among the women who were of child bearing age in the Tsarist era only about a quarter in each social group worked outside the home at any time, whereas among the women who were bearing children in the later Soviet years the range was from about one half to almost two thirds depending on the social group.[3]

On the basis of these data we must conclude that the regime, by drawing on the younger generation rather than proportionately on all generations, has been successful in increasing the participation of women in the labor force. Also, it can be seen that the success has been greatest in attracting young women of the white-collar class and least in

drawing women of the peasant class into the labor force. These disparities provide some indication of the difficulties in reaching the older generation of women, many of whom are still of working age, and the peasant women, who traditionally have been less receptive to change.

Some comprehension of the forces which the party and the government have brought to bear in mobilizing female talent and steering it into fields of importance for industrial and military strength can be gained if one considers what would happen in the United States if the resources employed to sell soap and cigarettes on television and radio and in newspapers were used to promote the idea of women engineers and doctors. No laws would have to be changed, because attitudes would change by themselves under the influence of these media, as they have in the Soviet Union.

ECONOMIC PRESSURES AND INCENTIVES

The powerful force of economic necessity has also been on the side of the regime in encouraging women to enter the labor force. In order to maintain a standard of living which covers the basic necessities of life under Soviet conditions, it has generally been necessary for families in the urban as well as the rural areas to have two breadwinners. Although women in the rural population have traditionally worked, Soviet agricultural policies in the 1930's, which lowered farmer incomes, served to increase the economic pressures on rural women. In the urban population, dire economic need forced many

[3]Alex Inkeles and Raymond A. Bauer, *The Soviet Citizen* (Cambridge, Mass., 1959), p. 205.

women into the labor force and kept them there after marriage and even after they had children. For example, findings of the Harvard Project on the Soviet social system showed that of the women who were between ages 31 and 40 in 1940, 70 per cent of the married women, as against 80 per cent of these unmarried, reported that they had a steady occupation outside the home.[4] Among women in this age group, 84 per cent of those without children and 68 per cent of those with children reported that they were working. These figures indicate the strength of the economic pressures which kept women in the labor force even at ages when most of them would normally have desired to be in the home. Thus, the regime's emphasis on the production of producers' goods not only contributed directly to further growth, but by restricting the growth in consumption also increased the participation of women in the labor force with a resulting positive effect on output.

Political in origin but economic in impact on the participation of women in the labor force were the purges of the 1930's. The loss of a husband, in most cases the chief provider, usually forced an unemployed wife to work. In an atmosphere of sudden disappearances and secret trials, husbands and wives were concerned with the problem of the family's economic survival if the husband should be arrested. Such conditions of uncertainty induced many women to seek the security of a job of their own. One Soviet husband expressed his concern in these words:

I felt that earning everything and having my wife earn nothing made her exceptionally and completely dependent upon me for her material welfare. . . . She did not work and had no specialty. What would she have done without me? What job could she have gotten?[5]

A similar view was offered by a young woman:

You knew that you cannot count on marrying and living on the earnings of the husband. You saw how insecure a man's position was. He could be arrested at any time, and therefore every women wanted to get a profession besides getting married. Besides, when one person was working this was not enough to live on.[6]

Similarly, the modification of divorce laws after the Revolution increased the desirability of a woman's being employed or employable. While women may have gained much from the new ease in dissolving an unhappy relationship, many faced the necessity of self-support and, possibly, of furnishing whole or partial support for minor children. Even if a married women did not need or wish to work, it was good insurance for her to have a working skill in reserve or to acquire one. However, legislation in the mid-1930's made divorce more difficult and more expensive and has doubtless reduced the precautionary motive for acquiring a marketable labor skill.

The impact of World War II on the participation of women is more obvious and was, of course, much greater than that of the purges. According to the 1959 census, women in the age group 35 to 54 outnumbered men by more than 10 million. Since women do not normally become eligible for a pension until age 55, the bulk of these 10 million women were forced to find some means of support through their own efforts. The rising percentage of working women in the age group 40 to 49, which was most severely hit by the war, bears this out.

To what extent economic necessity will continue to force women into the labor force is a question to which the author attempted to find an answer during his visits to the Soviet Union in 1955 and 1962. The real income of workers and farmers has improved substantially since before the war, but interviews and conversations with Soviet men and women suggest that economic necessity continues to

---

[4] *Ibid.*, p. 206. Further mention of the effect of marriage and child rearing on the participation rate of women in the labor force is made in Ch. V.

[5] Quoted by Homer Kent Geiger, *The Urban Slavic Family and the Soviet System* (unpublished doctoral dissertation, Harvard University, 1954), p. 133.

[6] *Ibid.*

be the primary motivation for women to remain in heavy construction and farm work or in routine and monotonous occupations in industry. This does not mean, however, that with further increases in real wages for their husbands, these women would necessarily wish to withdraw entirely from the labor force. Many would prefer to shift into more attractive lower-paying occupations, particularly in the expanding service sector of the economy.

Women engaged in semiprofessional or professional work, however, indicated in many cases that they found their work intrinsically attractive and desirable; economic considerations apparently were not overriding for them. Of the two dozen professional women who were asked specifically whether they would want to continue to work if their husbands' incomes should double overnight, none expressed any desire to stop working outside the home. It is evident from the Soviet press, nevertheless, that keeping married professional women in the labor force when their husbands earn enough to support them comfortably is a chronic problem. The case of an army officer's wife illustrates this point. After finishing her specialized secondary education, Natalia Pavlovna worked as a construction mechanic in the cold processing of metals before she entered the Leningrad Institute for the Mechanization of Socialist Agriculture, from which she graduated in 1940. For four years she worked as a construction engineer, but then resigned in order to devote full time to her family. The reporter interviewing her and her husband asked whether they realized that her failure to work was socially irresponsible:

"Yes," slowly said Andrei Petrovich, "I guess that it can be said of you"—he turned to his wife—"that the Government spent a lot of money training a specialist, but the specialist left the factory for the kitchen."

Andrei Petrovich's observation was correct, and we expected that there would follow on the part of Natalia Pavlovna a sincere complaint about the unfortunate circumstances or the endlessness of the small tasks about the house. At any rate it seemed to us that a desire for creative work would be expressed—the wish to be an engineer. But nothing like that happened.

"To pass that sort of judgment with reference to me would not be correct," firmly replied Natalia Pavlovna. "A household is also an important thing. Besides, I am raising two children."

The children were standing right there, beside her. The older one, Andrei, was about 10 years old; the younger, Vladimir, 7 years old. This year he is going to go to school. When they were quite small, their mother cared for them and worked. Why did she think that such a combination was impossible now?

"The older the boys get, the more complicated it is to rear them," said Natalia Pavlovna.

It is known, however, that the working example of the parents is the strongest means of educating the children. And what does Natalia Pavlovna know about education anyhow, when she herself does not fulfill her very first obligation to society?

We wanted to hear what the head of the family thought about the matter of his wife's going to work, but no definite answer was forthcoming from him either.

"We have discussed that question more than once," he said, "and came to the following conclusion: it would be fine to find some kind of work for about two hours a day. Our material situation does not require any other decision."[7]

However, unlike Natalia Pavlovna, most professional women do choose to continue working even though their husbands have good incomes. Their motives are often complex. Some women with weak professional motivation or small sense of social obligation withdraw from the labor force when economic circumstances permit, but others with a stronger professional drive or sense of duty continue to work whether or not the added income is needed. And, of course, in the Soviet Union as elsewhere there are those women for whom the isolation and monotony of household work are a burden. In the Soviet

---

[7] *Krasnaia zvezda* (Aug. 20, 1950).

Union their number might well be swelled by the crowded and often unattractive living quarters in which days at home are spent. In the higher-income semiprofessional and professional families, even if additional earnings are not needed for food and necessities, they serve to provide some of the extras which help reduce the drabness of Soviet life. A more important motivation, however, for women in professional or semiprofessional occupations is love for their work and genuine interest in a career.

LEGISLATION AFFECTING WOMEN WORKERS

The policies of the party regarding women workers have been embodied in labor legislation, which has, from the early years of Soviet power, followed the pattern of treating women as economically equal to men, with certain exceptions and advantages dictated by their role as mothers. There has long been a body of laws and regulations which, although varying in detail of provision and effectiveness of enforcement, has been designed to give Soviet women equal job opportunities, equal pay for equal work, protection from occupations injurious to health, paid maternity leave, and security in old age. Except in Central Asia, which is a problem by itself, women's rights to education and employment are well established. Although legislation aimed at ending discrimination against women as workers has been given content and meaning in practice, protective legislation, as we shall see, has been less successful. Also, the provisions for security in old age have been until recently very limited in amount and coverage.

Early Bolshevik Legislation, 1917 to 1918. The first year of Soviet rule produced a small spate of decrees with the force of law which set the basic pattern of Soviet legislation on women. The first decree, ironically enough, contained the protective provisions which were subsequently the most revised, unenforced, and ignored of all Soviet legislation on women. This was the decree of the Council of People's Commissars of November 11,

1917, issued shortly after the Soviet seizure of power. In addition to its main purpose of ordering an eight-hour working day for everyone, it banned night work, overtime work, and underground assignments for women.[8] The enforcement of such legislation has been quite erratic. As a result, analysis of its realistic effect has been difficult.

Women's basic legal equality with men was established by the R.S.F.S.R. constitution of July 10, 1918, which discriminated heavily in favor of the honest toiler of the working class, regardless of sex, and firmly stated the obligation of every citizen to work, again, regardless of sex.[9] Decrees issued in the same year set minimum wages for specific occupations, and at least two decrees explicitly stated that women were to receive equal pay for equal work.[10] On October 31, 1918, the Council of People's Commissars set forth regulations for social insurance, including substantial provisions for the payment of maternity benefits. For women doing physical work, these benefits were to equal average earnings for a period of eight weeks before and eight weeks after confinement; for women doing mental work, for a period of six weeks before and six weeks after. Allowances were given to nursing mothers after they had resumed work, and an additional grant was stipulated, payable for seven months to manual workers and for seven and a half months to others. Anyone who employed expectant or nursing

---

[8] Margaret Dewar, *Labor Policy in the USSR, 1917–1928* (London and New York, 1956), p. 160, cites Council of People's Commissars' decree, *Sobranie uzakonenii i rasporiazhenii rabochego i krestianskogo pravitel'stva, 1917–1924,* 1917, 1–10 (hereinafter referred to as *Sobranie*).

[9] E. H. Carr, *The Bolshevik Revolution, 1917–1923* (New York, 1952), II, 199–200.

[10] The two decrees specifically mentioning equality of wages for women, according to Dewar (*op. cit.,* pp. 165, 169), were a People's Commissariat of Labor decree of Jan. 19, 1918, on wages in Petrograd engineering industries and an All-Russian Central Executive Committee (of the Soviet of Workers' and Soldiers' Deputies) decree of Sept. 22, 1918, on minima for workers in Moscow institutions.

mothers during their legal leaves was subject to fines of 1,000 to 3,000 rubles or imprisonment for one to three months,[11] and it is believed that such penalties were enforced.

The 1918 Labor Code. The bulk of the various labor decrees which appeared in 1918 were incorporated at the end of the year in a formal code, published on December 10, 1918, which was, in many respects, a statement of the ideals of the time. The Labor Code is a landmark in Soviet labor legislation, not because of its practical effect—the Civil War vitiated much of its impact—but because of its attempt to codify labor regulations. The code applied to all persons gainfully employed and was compulsory for organizations and individuals hiring labor. Thus, women working for wages and salaries were covered, but those in co-operatives and agriculture were not. The following is a brief summary of all the stipulations affecting women:[12]

(1) Women were not exempt from the requirements on obligation to work unless they were on the point of, or just recovering from, childbirth. Labor service, including the possibility of compulsory conscription, was introduced for all able-bodied citizens between ages 16 and 50, regardless of sex. Only expectant mothers during a period of eight weeks before and eight weeks after confinement were exempt.

(2) The right to work, irrespective of sex, was similarly assured. Every citizen had the right to work at his trade or profession at the accepted rate of pay, an assurance which appears to be the first blanket statement of the principle of equal pay for equal work.

(3) Protective measures for women provided the only exceptions to their right to work. The code stated that women should not be employed in night work, that they were not to work overtime under any conditions, and that they were not to hold jobs detrimental to health. A list of such jobs was to be drawn up by the People's Commissariat of Labor.

(4) Maternity was covered by the provision of extra work breaks for nursing mothers —not less than once every three hours, for a duration of not less than half an hour. The code also stipulated that social insurance benefits for maternity be paid, as established by the People's Commissariat of Labor.

Civil War. The emergency of the Civil War undoubtedly enhanced the acceptance of women in the working force in numbers and in occupations not previously the rule, or perhaps it would be more accurate to say that it reinforced the considerable position they had attained toward the end of Russia's participation in World War I. Simultaneously, however, it rendered meaningless the protective provisions for women—except those in the process of producing children—and set a precedent for all future times of stress, both military and economic.

The ban on night work was formally lifted, on October 4, 1919, by a resolution which allowed exceptions to be made. Reportedly, it had not ever been possible effectively to implement this ban because of the need for women in the communications services.[13] Overtime work for women was also "tempo-

---

[11]Council of People's Commissars' decree, cited by Dewar, *op. cit.*, pp. 172–173 (*Sobranie*, 1918, 89–906).

[12]Vserossiskii tsentral'noi Sovet professional'-nykh soiuz, *Kodeks zakonov o trude i deklaratsiia prav trudiashchegosia i eksploatiruemogo naroda* (Moscow, 1920), *passim*; and Dewar, *op. cit.*, pp. 43, 174–77.

[13]Dewar, *op. cit.*, p. 184, cites the decree of People's Commissariat of Labor, published Oct. 5, 1919 (*Sobranie*, 1919, 48–470); see also S. Kaplun, *Zhenskii trud i okhrana ego v Sovetskoi Rossii*, and V. Lebedeva, *Okhrana materinstva i mladenchestva v Sovetskoi trudovoi respublike* (published together; Moscow, 1921), p. 20.

It should be noted that this decree was stated to be temporary and, according to Dewar, could be applied only "at the request of the respective trade union organizations, with the approval of the People's Commissariat of Labor and the consent in each individual case of the local trade union committee for the protection of labour and the local labour inspector." One can only assume, in the light of Kaplun, that approval was largely a formality.

rarily" permitted in December, 1919,[14] and the conscription of women along with men for labor service in the fuel industry meant, one has to assume, that the stipulations to exempt women from heavy duties and underground work were probably being violated as well.[15]

A special appeal in April, 1919, for more men to help in the fighting on the eastern front urged that women be used as replacements in the jobs left vacant, apparently irrespective of working conditions. Some consideration based on sex difference was given, however, in an amendment in March, 1920, regarding the age groups of women subject to labor service. The upper age limit for women was lowered from age 50 to 40, and the same regulation provided that, in addition to women who were nursing or expecting a baby, those with major family responsibilities were to be relieved from labor service. Mothers in charge of children under age 8 and women looking after five or more adults were exempt.[16]

Despite the temporary suspension of general protective legislation, the rules governing maternity seem to have fared well. As food shortages grew and money from wages or benefits became meaningless, provisions were made for rations, and it was specifically stated that nursing mothers, mothers in charge of

children under age 12, and housewives responsible for three or more persons should get the same rations as nonmanual workers in Soviet institutions. These rations were substantially less advantageous than those for manual workers, but better than those for persons working in private enterprises or for the unemployed.[17]

Expectant mothers were also protected from being transferred or sent on business trips without their consent by a decree published November 24, 1920. The same decree stipulated that the exceptions made in 1919 regarding overtime and night work should not apply to expectant mothers; specifically, there was to be no overtime after the fifth month of pregnancy, none for nursing mothers, and no night work for either expectant or nursing mothers.[18] There was, it should be noted, no job protection for any mother who extended her maternity leave, and under the general rules for labor agreements, issued June 17, 1920, a maternity absence in excess of four months could be cause for dismissal.[19]

These rules, together with some other measures taken in this period, served to reinforce equal rights, as well as obligations, for working women. The 1920 rules reiterated that

---

[14]Dewar, *op. cit.*, p. 186, cites a People's Commissariat of Labor decree dated Dec. 29, 1919 (*Sobranie*, 1919, 65–587). This, too, was in theory temporary: ". . . permitted if trade union and labour inspectors confirmed that overtime by the men alone is not sufficient."

[15]Dewar, *op. cit.*, p. 46, states that men age 35 to 50 and women age 18 to 40, along with draft animals, were mobilized in some parts of the country for procurement and loading and unloading of all kinds of fuel. Other conscriptions mentioned do not distinguish between the sexes, except the one by the People's Commissariat of Labor, Oct. 30, 1920, which rounded up townswomen age 16 to 45 to sew underclothes for the Red Army (*Sobranie*, 1920, 90–468).

[16]Dewar, *op. cit.*, pp. 189–90, cites the Mar. 23, 1920 regulation by the Main Committee for General Labor Service and People's Commissariat of Labor and Social Security (*Sobranie*, 1920, 24–116).

[17]Dewar, *op. cit.*, pp. 192–93, cites the Council of People's Commissars decree of Apr. 30, 1920 (*Sobranie*, 1920, 34–165). When rationing was abolished on Sept. 6, 1921, special provision was made for people of any sex with young dependents (*ibid.*, p. 211; decree of Council of People's Commissars, *Sobranie*, 1921, 62–453).

[18]*Ibid.*, p. 200; decree of the People's Commissariat of Labor and the All-Russian Central Council of Trade Unions, Nov. 24, 1920 (*Sobranie*, 1920, 91–477). A decree in April or May, 1921, also provided that expectant mothers or those with children under age 8 should not be transferred to a different place of work without their consent (*ibid.*, p. 20; *Sobranie*, 1921, 40–42). At the time, the People's Commissariat of Labor and the Trade Unions were operating as quasi organs of the government; both were in competition with each other and the rest of the government. Occasionally, the various authorities contradicted each other, but this does not seem to have happened in their decrees on women.

[19]*Ibid.*, pp. 194–96; a Council of People's Commissars' decree (*Sobranie*, 1920, 61/62–276).

women were to receive equal pay for equal work, but they also included output quotas and explicitly stated that pay depended on work performed. The tendency for women to be less productive than men and to be in the lower, less skilled categories meant that earnings equal to those of men were probably the exception.

The Eighth Congress of Soviets, December 23 to 29, 1920, which coincided with the end of the Civil War, strongly urged that women be recruited into all economic organizations, factory administrations, and trade unions, and it noted the need for efficient use of female labor. This emphasis suggests that, in light of the conditions of the day, employment practices with regard to women were inadequate.[20]

Transition to the New Economic Policy. Ironically, no sooner was wider employment of women urged than the demobilization after the Civil War, combined with the transition from War Communism to the New Economic Policy, resulted in the dismissal of women in such numbers that the unemployment problem became particularly acute. By February, 1922, the problem had come to legislative attention; a decree was issued by the People's Commissariat of Labor to the effect that in cases of dismissal women and men were to be treated on an equal basis, but mothers with children below age 1 were to be given preference.[21] These measures to safeguard wom-

en's jobs apparently proved ineffective, and unemployment was to remain a problem until the beginning of the Five-Year Plans.[22]

Unemployment in the early 1920's seems to have had as corrosive an effect on the protective legislation for nonpregnant, non-nursing women as had the earlier emergency, and as later ones were to have. As a matter of fact, one finds that this protective legislation, which remained much the same as before, although recodified in the Labor Code of 1922, was disputed on the grounds that it contributed to a woman's inability to get a job and therefore led to prostitution. In 1924, the Commissar of Labor, V. Schmidt, viewed night work for women as a way to help them, and a woman delegate to the Russian Trade Union Convention in the same year said that it would be well to reduce the protection for women, since it was better for them to have respectable work, however arduous, than to turn to prostitution.[23] By 1925, women had reportedly been taken into the ranks of all the heavy industries, and in 1927 we find an official publication of the Central Committee arguing that to limit the enterprises in which women

---

[20]*Ibid.*, p. 202 (*Sobranie*, 1921, 1–12). The congress emphasized that local Soviets should bestir themselves to provide such facilities as laundries, crèches, and dining rooms, so that women would be sufficiently relieved of household duties to enter the labor force. These facilities are still in short supply today.

[21]*Ibid.*, p. 219; People's Commissariat of Labor decree, Feb. 20, 1922 (*Sobranie*, 1922, 18–203). This decree also provided that unmarried women and mothers of small children were not to be deprived of any housing that went with the terminated job or of any kindergarten privileges until they had found new work. The unemployment problem had, it might be noted, briefly arisen earlier, when the end of Russia's participation in World War I resulted in women's being turned out of their wartime jobs in favor of returning veterans. Susan M. Kingsbury and Mil-

dred Fairchild, *Factory, Family and Women in the Soviet Union* (New York, 1935), p. 84, note that many factory committees and trade unions in 1918 were allowing women to be dismissed, and that in April, 1918, the Petrograd Council of Trade Unions and Factory Committees insisted that dismissal should be based on need, rather than sex, with special preference given to unsupported women with babies.

[22]Judith Grunfeld, "Women's Work in Russia's Planned Economy," *Social Research*, IX, No. 1 (Feb., 1942), 22–45, cites G. N. Serebrennikov, *Zhenskii trud v SSSR* (Moscow, 1934), p. 226, who states that these measures were ineffective. She also cites the interesting fact that as late as July, 1929, 49.5 per cent of the unemployed (presumably those registered with labor exchanges) were women. The rather broad discrepancy between this figure and the share of women in the labor force suggests that unemployment was significantly higher among women. Robert W. Dunn, *Soviet Trade Unions* (New York, 1928), p. 209, states that unemployment in 1926 was "much higher" among women.

[23]Grunfeld, *op. cit.*, p. 28.

can be employed is "to swell the ranks of prostitution."[24]

The 1922 Labor Code. The Labor Code passed on October 30, 1922,[25] and effective as of November 15—probably before the unemployment problem had grown to full dimensions—was as praiseworthy as the law of 1918 on the subject of protecting women, both those with and those without dependent children. Although this code was much revised, violated, and ignored, it was the cornerstone of Soviet labor legislation for the entire period before World War II. And to this day it is the basic labor law of the Soviet Union. Like the 1918 code, it was somewhat utopian, and some of its provisions were rather broad and vague and therefore subject to varying interpretations. It was not a code once enforced in all its provisions and then later grossly violated under Stalin. It was a law which set forth an ideal never attained, and many of its original rules remained on paper until they were revised under Stalin and eventually partially restored and enforced under Khrushchev.

The 1922 Labor Code treated the subject of women in several contexts and included a special section devoted to their protection and the safeguarding of minors. The code does not concern itself with women's equal rights —to hold jobs, to acquire training, to receive equal pay for equal work—since these were already provided for by the R.S.F.S.R. constitution (July 10, 1918).

The code's provisions may be briefly summarized as follows:[26]

---

[24]Manya Gordon, *Workers before and after Lenin* (New York, 1941), p. 275, cites a pamphlet issued by the Central Committee of the Communist Party of the Soviet Union (CPSU), *Ob'edinennie opozitsii i voprosy truda* (Moscow, 1927), p. 67.

[25]According to Dewar, *op. cit.,* p. 96 (*Sobranie,* 1922, 70–903), the Labor Code was adopted Oct. 30, 1922, by the Fourth Session of the Central Executive Committee of the Soviets of Workers Deputies, then passed as a decree on Nov. 9, to become effective on Nov. 15, 1922.

[26]Dewar, *op. cit.,* pp. 96–99; and Narodnoi komissariat iustitsii SSSR, *Kodeks zakonov o*

(1) *Coverage (Art. 1).* The code covered all persons gainfully employed in all state enterprises and institutions, as well as persons hired privately. This coverage was subsequently spelled out in detail during the 1920's, with sundry supplemental regulations for persons who worked at home (cottage industry in peasant households) and for seasonal workers.[27] Article 1 apparently was not construed to cover agricultural workers, either the unpaid farmer's wife or the rural wage laborer, since its extension to kulak labor was one of the early ploys in the collectivization campaign of 1929.

(2) *Labor service (Sect. III, Art. 11–14).* The state's right to reinvoke obligatory labor service in exceptional circumstances was retained in the code. Most of the modifications of the exemption provisions in the 1918 code were also included. Specifically, obligatory labor service was to apply to all women age 18 to 40—a slight advantage over men, for whom the upper limit was age 45. Further exemptions were made for pregnant women, nursing women, and women with children under age 8 who had no one to look after them. Exemptions in consideration of family situations, health, and other factors were also stipulated, irrespective of sex.

(3) *General protection (Sect. XIII, Art. 129–37).* This special section dealing with women and minors prohibited the employment of women, irrespective of pregnancy or motherhood, in occupations involving heavy work, work detrimental to health, or underground work. A specific list of such occupations was to be drawn up by the People's Commissariat of Labor, in agreement with the trade unions, and norms for load lifting and the like were to be set. Night work was also prohibited, except when the People's Commissar of Labor, in agreement with the trade unions, permitted adult women to work in branches of production where night shifts

---

trude, s izmeneniiami na 1 iulia, 1938 (Moscow, 1938), which will hereafter be cited as *Kodeks 1938.*

[27]These regulations are taken up as they become relevant in subsequent discussions.

were necessary. Pregnant and nursing mothers were not to be engaged in either night or overtime work, and manual workers were to be entirely freed from work for eight weeks before and eight weeks after confinement, and mental workers, for six weeks before and six to eight weeks after confinement. They were not to be sent on business trips without their consent from the fifth month of pregnancy. Further, nursing mothers were to have work breaks at least once every three and a half hours for no less than half an hour, and such breaks were to be considered part of their paid working time.

(4) *Social insurance (Sect. XVII, Art. 175–80)*. Social insurance payments applied to all categories of labor covered by the code and included payments for pregnancy leave, supplementary payments during nursing, and compensation for wages lost if a mother's earnings declined as a result of time spent in breast feeding, a loss she would incur if she was being paid on a piecework basis. However, detailed rules on social insurance were not spelled out by the code.

During the period of the New Economic Policy, although considerable effort was made to implement and observe the principles laid down in the 1922 code, full enforcement was never achieved. It is nonetheless clear that the People's Commissariat of Labor, early in the New Economic Policy, did make an effort to identify and list the occupations which were detrimental to health and therefore closed to women. Its list reportedly confirmed that underground work did indeed, as the code had indicated, belong among occupations hazardous to health. On the issue of night work, regulations seem to have held the line established by the 1922 code. For example, supplemental rules on seasonal work issued by the Central Executive Committee and the Council of People's Commissars of the U.S.S.R. on June 4, 1926, permitted night work by women, except pregnant and nursing mothers. Enforcement must have been far from complete, however, because we find the Committee on a Seven-Hour Day of the People's Commissariat of Labor issuing an ordi-

nance in 1928 which again prohibited night work by pregnant women after their fifth month of pregnancy and by nursing mothers for seven months after delivery. The textile industry, for one, seems to have generally ignored these provisions, with the reported concurrence of the mothers.[28]

Maternity benefits established just prior to the 1922 code amounted to the local average monthly wage, and one fourth of this amount was paid to nursing mothers for up to nine months.[29] Social insurance at this juncture seems to have covered all hired workers and employees, regardless of how long they had held their jobs, and maternity benefits apparently were payable if either parent was insured.[30] With the introduction of the Labor Code, the situation became slightly more complicated. Working women who were themselves covered by social insurance were eligible for maternity payments equal to the full amount of wages lost—sixteen weeks being allowed for manual workers and twelve weeks for nonmanual workers. They also received additional payments, to which noninsured women whose husbands were insured were also entitled. These payments consisted of a layette allowance equal to one month's average local wage and a nursing allowance for extra baby food equal to one fourth of the average monthly wage. Eligibility for either of these payments was not dependent on the length of time the insured wife or husband had been employed.[31]

In 1927, the eligibility provisions were somewhat tightened. For receipt of all benefits, an insured woman was required to have worked for six months prior to maternity

---

[28]Kingsbury and Fairchild, *op. cit.*, p. 262; Solomon Schwarz, *Labor in the Soviet Union* (New York, 1952), p. 264; and Dewar, *op cit.*, p. 140. Dewar reports complaints in the late 1920's that protective legislation generally was not being complied with.

[29]Dewar, *op. cit.*, p. 215; Council of People's Commissars' decree, Dec. 5, 1921 (*Sobranie*, 1921, 79–688).

[30]*Ibid.*, pp. 214–15 (*Sobranie*, 1921, 76–627, 688).

[31]Schwarz, *op. cit.*, p. 318.

leave; an insured husband, for the same period prior to the birth of a child. The additional layette and nursing benefits were to be paid only to those whose income did not exceed a fixed maximum.[32]

The 1930's. After the 1922 code, no major legislation affecting women was enacted until the early 1930's. Perhaps it was believed pointless to enact legislation which could not be enforced under the conditions of female unemployment which existed at the time. Whatever the cause, there appears to have been no official stress on employing women— or, in Soviet terms, on implementing their "right" to work—until the First Five-Year Plan began to create a labor shortage. Then, abruptly, we find a whole series of measures initiated in response to the shift from a labor surplus to a labor shortage and specifically designed to draw more women into the labor force and into vocational training. Ultimately, in the 1936 constitution, there appeared a reassertion of the right of women to legal and economic equality with men.

The first of these measures, a manifesto issued on September 3, 1930, by the Central Committee of the party, called for drawing more workers' wives into production to ensure the success of the Five-Year Plan. And three days later the Council of People's Commissars authorized the R.S.F.S.R. People's Commissariat of Labor to draw up a list of trades and occupations to be reserved predominantly for women, to raise the quotas for girls in vocational schools and training classes, and to improve such services as nurseries, communal kitchens, and laundries in order to lighten domestic chores for women and enable them to join the labor force.

With the initiation of the Five-Year Plans and the resulting increased need for women in production, the earlier protective legislation began to weaken and enforcement was relaxed. While up to this time the expression of official intention had at least supported the observance of the 1922 code, in 1930 we already find the trade unions' daily newspaper advocating repeal of the nightwork restrictions for women and juveniles and a statement in *Pravda* urging that the ban on underground work for women be lifted. New scientific investigations were undertaken which reportedly proved that there were no reasons why women should not work underground, and arguments for a revision of the Labor Code appeared.[33]

On January 16, 1931, the R.S.F.S.R. People's Commissariat of Labor issued two lists of occupations which were to be reserved exclusively or predominantly for women. On May 19, 1931, however, these listings were somewhat qualified by a U.S.S.R. Council of People's Commissars decree naming occupations "in which the use of female labor should be greatly expanded." Implementation followed in the form of set quotas which obliged employers to hire a fixed percentage of women.[34] Simultaneously, similar measures were being taken to increase the number of women in vocational training. This effort was particularly important for women because lack of training had been a substantial contributing factor to their comparatively high rate of unemployment during the period of the New Economic Policy and to their remaining in comparatively low-paid jobs; their earnings averaged 60 per cent of those of men "in spite of the fact that no discrimination on the basis of sex is permitted in calculating wages."[35]

---

[32]*Ibid.* Schwarz cites Decisions of the Social Insurance Council, dated Jan. 13, 1927, and May 19, 1927, published in *Izvestiia narkomtruda* (1927), pp. 68 ff., 346 ff., and the joint decree of the Central Executive Committee and the Council of People's Commissars, Dec. 28, 1927. The fixed maximum income was 120 to 180 rubles per month (the same as that for sickness benefits). In 1931, this limitation on sick benefits was abolished, and 300 rubles was set as the maximum for eligibility for the additional maternity benefits by a decision of the Social Insurance Council dated Aug. 11, 1931, published in *Izvestiia narkomtruda* (1931), p. 508.

[33]Schwarz, *op. cit.,* p. 288; Kingsbury and Fairchild, *op. cit.,* p. 262.
[34]Schwarz, *op. cit.,* pp. 66–67.
[35]George M. Price, *Labor Protection in Soviet Russia* (New York, 1928), p. 73.

Minimum quotas for the number of girls to be accepted by factory training schools were set in December, 1929, by the U.S.S.R. People's Commissariat of Labor. They were to exceed the proportion of women already in each branch of industry and to average 35 per cent of the total number of students. These quotas were raised in September, 1930, and again, by a Central Executive Committee decree, in January, 1931.[36]

All these measures, if not carried out in every detail, were nevertheless sufficiently effective to cause the widespread use of female labor in many different occupations—including a few still ostensibly forbidden by protective legislation—to become an established fact by the mid-1930's. While it could still be remarked late in the 1920's that a "backward" attitude toward women workers continued to prevail among men in certain places, the kind of legislation which specified, and indeed compelled, the inclusion of women in the work force became quite unnecessary by the mid-1930's, and it does not seem to have been proposed at any time since then.[37] The absence of new legislation requiring equal pay for equal work also indicates that there was simply no need for it. Both Soviet and non-Soviet observers agree that nondiscriminatory pay rates were the established practice during the period of the New Economic Policy, and there is nothing to suggest any change since then.[38] It was thus rather ex post facto that the new 1936 U.S.S.R. constitution, repealing the R.S.F.S.R. constitution of 1918, made a special point of stating, in Article 122, that women had equal rights with men in all fields of economic, state, cultural, and social-political life, and that this equality was ensured by giving women equal rights to work and equal pay, time off, social insurance, and education

—plus such extras as maternity leave without loss of maintenance.[39]

Despite *de jure* and *de facto* changes in the 1922 code during the 1930's, the code was not formally revised. Perhaps Stalin thought that the 1922 code, like the 1936 constitution, was good propaganda and saw no particular reason why it should be revised or observed. In any event, illegal overtime and night work for pregnant women, as well as underground work for all women, seem to have been fairly common during the 1930's.[40] In fact, regarding underground work, the ruling influence appears to have been the discovery that it was not detrimental to women's health, and such work by women seems to have been quite frequently allowed in practice long before it was allowed by law.[41]

In the 1920's, payments compensating the working woman for wages lost in childbearing seem to have been dutifully rendered and in amounts equal to the full wages. Schwarz, however, quotes a Soviet source as saying that the actual payments for additional benefits were only half those provided by law (50 and 12.5 per cent of the local average wage for layette and nursing, respectively).[42] Then, in 1932, the benefits were simply shifted to a flat rate of 32 rubles for the layette and a total of 45 rubles in nursing benefits, or 5 rubles per month, and in 1936 they were raised to 45 and 90 rubles, or 10 rubles per month, respectively. It was in 1936, too, that the regulations for compensatory maternity benefits for working mothers were simplified by making the time period for paid maternity leave a total of sixteen weeks for all mothers,

---

[36]Schwarz, *op. cit.*, p. 68. The decree was implemented by the People's Commissariat of Labor regulations of Feb. 8, 1931.

[37]*Ibid.*, p. 67.

[38]Price, *op. cit.*, p. 73; Dewar, *op. cit.*, p. 139; Kingsbury and Fairchild, *op. cit.*, p. 264.

[39]The constitution also ensures "a wide network of maternity homes, nurseries, and kindergartens." The inadequacies of these will be discussed later.

[40]Schwarz, *op. cit.*, pp. 287–89, provides several examples.

[41]*Ibid.*, p. 74.

[42]*Ibid.*, p. 319; Schwarz cites N. A. Vigdorchik, *Social Insurance: A Popular Exposition* (Moscow, 1927), p. 183.

whether they did manual or other types of work.[43]

As a by-product of other acts tightening job mobility and enforcing job freezes for all categories of workers, eligibility rules were tightened once again in 1932. Only union members who had worked a minimum of three years, and two of these years at the same job, were now entitled to benefits in the full amount of their wages; others were to receive less than the full equivalent of their wages. In 1932 the additional benefits for layette and nursing were also contingent on consecutive employment over a specific period.[44]

In addition to the violations of regulations covering working conditions mentioned above and the limitations on eligibility, there was a general tendency for maternity leaves to be shortened and benefits reduced. The only important expansion of the privileges for mothers in the 1930's was a 1937 ruling supplemental to the Labor Code which required that pregnant women in arduous jobs be transferred to lighter work without loss in earnings.[45] This, too, was reportedly violated at times.

In 1938 the shadow of war loomed large

in the area of protective legislation, for the biggest curtailment in maternity benefits came toward the end of that year when the act of December 28 drastically cut the time period during which maternity benefits were to be paid to compensate for wages. The sixteen-week period established for all those eligible in 1936 was reduced to nine weeks—five weeks before and four weeks after the birth of a child. Eligibility for such benefits was tightened further by the requirement of seven consecutive months of employment prior to maternity leave.[46]

Prior to the 1930's, peasant women, who made up four fifths of the female population, remained a largely neglected group. There was no law relating to them apart from the customary provincial law which defined their rights and duties within the household, and contained the provision that a woman may retain control over any money she earns during the winter months.[47] The earliest Soviet legislation affecting rural women appeared in 1928, stating that a woman's rights within the household should be equal to those of the man.[48] Another legislative move made by the Soviet government which affected peasant women was the joint resolution of the Central Executive Committee and the Council of People's Commissars of February 20, 1929, which flatly extended the scope of the 1922 code, with certain emendations, to include kulak

---

[43]*Ibid.*; Decision of Social Insurance Council dated Apr. 17, 1932, published in *Izvestiia narkomtruda* (1932), pp. 265 ff.; and Decree of the Central Executive Committee and the Council of People's Commissars, June 27, 1936.

[44]Schwarz, *op. cit.*, pp. 318–20; Decisions of the Social Insurance Council of Aug. 11, 1931, and Apr. 17, 1932. The latter decision set different time periods for eligibility of working women or wives of insured men as follows: four months for women shock workers (*udarniki*), engineers, and technicians; eight months for other union members; and twelve months for everybody else.

[45]*Kodeks 1938*, p. 52, gives this information as a supplemental note (dated May 10, 1937) to the 1922 code. It seems to state that a mother must show cause to be transferred to lighter work, and Schwarz (*op. cit.*, p. 289) quotes from a letter written to a newspaper by a pregnant woman working in a mine, who had, without success, asked to be shifted to lighter work above ground.

---

[46]Schwarz, *op. cit.*, pp. 319–20; Act of Dec. 28, 1938, issued jointly by the Council of People's Commissars of the U.S.S.R., the Central Committee of the party, and the All-Union Trade Union Council. The act's title described it as "measures to increase work discipline, improve social insurance, and combat abuses in this field."

[47]Sir John Maynard, *Russia in Flux* (New York, 1951), p. 34.

[48]N. D. Kazantsev, I. V. Pavlov, and A. A. Ruskol (eds.), *Kolkhoznoe pravo* (Moscow, 1955), p. 322, cite Art. 11 of "Obshchiie nachala zemlepol'zovaniia i zemleustroistva SSSR" of 1928.

employment.[49] For the most part, however, peasant women had to wait for collectivization and for the model collective-farm statute, which superseded all legislation pertaining to kulaks, before clarification of their legal status and working conditions was made. It is interesting that at least one knowledgeable observer reported that the collective farm was fairly well received by peasant women because it allowed them to keep their own earnings.[50]

The model statute for collective farms promulgated in 1930 provided for equal membership and equal earnings per labor day (*trudoden'*) for the same work. Specifically, any person over age 16, male or female, had a right to membership, which entailed full rights to a share in the farm's net income, computed on the basis of the amount of time worked, as well as to a share in the household plot income. While the statute left the details of rules for work breaks, including those for nursing mothers, up to the individual collective farm, it did set forth other special provisions for women.

As stipulated in Article 14, maternity leave was to be provided for one month before and one month after the birth of a child, with benefits at half of the woman's average earnings according to the labor-day computation— provisions which were, however, less advantageous than those for women workers and employees, some of whom were employed in agriculture on state farms and elsewhere. Further, the farm administration was supposed to provide child-care facilities, and the state was obliged to contribute 25 per cent of the funds for maternity homes on collective farms.[51] Another more dubious "privilege" of the collective farm was that women had to share with men the obligation to do unpaid work on the roads six days each year, the peasantry being responsible for maintaining the roads, somewhat in the manner of the old *corvée*. This obligation applied to women in the age range 18 to 40, while men age 18 to 45 had to serve.[52] The statute also defined a woman's rights within the peasant household or *dvor*—the three- to four-generation peasant social unit which remains basic today, although it has begun to be undermined. Her earnings were to belong to her until she elected to turn them over to the *dvor,* and she was to have an equal voice in the distribution of income and was as eligible as a man to be head of the household.[53]

One may doubt that the male peasantry left to itself would have put all these provisions into effect, but it was not permitted to choose and decide. The collective farm system was generally implemented by loyal party members from the cities, sent out by the central government for the purpose of forcible persuasion. Also, in the early days of collectivization, most farm officials were not of peasant origin and did not share the prejudices of the peasant class. Hence, it is probable that women did have a more equal opportunity for promotion and that the traditional subordination was resisted. It should be noted also that since the middle forties, as a result of World War II and the postwar migration

---

[49]Why this was done is not clear. One would think from the 1922 code's coverage that it applied to kulaks and employees of kulaks, since it seems to say that it applies to anybody hired by or hiring anybody. Theory and practice, however, were apparently not the same.

[50]Maynard, *op. cit.,* p. 399, says that a separate wage for women was an immensely important change, which "has put the women on the side of the Soviets."

[51]Kazantsev, Pavlov, and Ruskol, *op. cit.,* pp. 85, 89–90; Decisions of the Central Executive Committee and the Council of People's Commissars of the U.S.S.R., Mar. 3, 1936.

[52]*Ibid.,* p. 255. The regulation still applied to "able-bodied" women. Excluded are pregnant women eight weeks before and after the birth of a child and women with children under age 8 in the absence of someone to look after them. Sometimes this obligation is performed by a regular road crew designated by the collective farm. See *Sbornik konsul'tatsii po voprosam kolkhoznogo prava,* ed. by P. I. Bardin (Moscow, 1955), p. 92.

[53]Kazantsev, Pavlov, and Ruskol, *op. cit.,* pp. 330–32.

of young males to the cities, the collective-farm population has become predominantly female, a fact which has inevitably given women more status and independence, although men still dominate the administrative structure and hold the better-paying jobs.[54]

The Impact of World War II. Once the threat of war became apparent, changes were made in legislation which reduced the list of occupations forbidden to women. For instance, a decree of the Council of People's Commissars of November 1, 1938, gave women "equality" to become railroad locomotive engineers and stokers, and on June 13, 1940, a decision of the All-Union Central Council of Trade Unions opened opportunities for them to work in river transport, except as stokers on steamboats and as sailors on cargo ships. Finally, on October 25, 1940, the Council of People's Commissars officially opened the mines to women, though the decree still said that they should not work in the most strenuous jobs, such as coal cutting, digging, and shoveling.[55] All restrictions on overtime were suspended, except for pregnant women from the sixth month of pregnancy and nursing mothers for the first six months of nursing. Many other provisions regarding pregnant women and mothers were for all practical purposes ignored, and military service for women was introduced by the Military Duty Law of September 3, 1939.[56]

With the outbreak of the war and the mobilization of a large portion of the able-bodied male population, women were absolutely essential to the war effort. However, by 1944, the worst of the crisis had passed, and the need to recoup population losses was felt imperative. Maternity regulations were again liberalized, although not to the extent of reverting to the original provisions. The time

period for maternity benefit payments after the birth of a child was increased from four to six weeks—the time period before confinement remaining five weeks—with two extra weeks allowed in cases of abnormal or multiple births.[57] Layette benefits increased from 45 to 120 rubles, and nursing benefits from 90 to 180 rubles, or 20 rubles per month.[58] Eligibility requirements were also soon liberalized to a minimum of three months' employment before the beginning of maternity leave in the case of a working mother applying for both regular and additional benefits, and three months' employment before the birth of a child in the case of the wife of an insured husband.[59] These maternity benefits and eligibility requirements remained in effect until after the Twentieth Party Congress.

Early Postwar Legislation. After World War II, the Soviet Union found itself heavily dependent upon its female working force. As men returned to civilian life, however, it became possible to free women from some of the heavy labor in which they had become engaged during the war. But in several branches of industry, women continued in heavy operations for a decade or more. This occurred particularly in the coal-mining and

---

[54]Family allowances, providing money benefits to mothers with many children, were introduced in the 1930's, but they are discussed in the next chapter.

[55]W. W. Kulski, *The Soviet Regime* (Syracuse, N.Y., 1956), p. 350; Schwarz, *op. cit.,* p. 74.

[56]Schwarz, *op. cit.,* p. 300; Grunfeld and Fairchild, *op. cit.,* pp. 42–43.

[57]Decree of July 8, 1944, published in *Izvestiia* (July 9, 1944), entitled: "Concerning an increase in the assistance furnished by the state to pregnant women, mothers of large families, and self-supporting mothers; extension of the protection afforded mothers and infants; introduction of the honorary title, 'Heroine Mother' and creation of the order 'Mother's Glory' and of the honorary medal, 'Medal of Motherhood.'"

[58]Schwarz, *op. cit.,* p. 320, who appears to have confused nursing and layette benefits. He says that nursing benefits increased from 45 to 120 rubles, layette benefits from 90 to 180 rubles, which conflicts with an earlier statement by him.

[59]*Ibid.,* p. 321; Schwarz cites N. G. Aleksandrov and D. M. Genkin (eds.), *Soviet Labor Law* (Moscow, 1946), p. 379. The maximum monthly income was increased again in Feb., 1947, to 500 rubles; see Schwarz, *op. cit.,* p. 321, who cites N. G. Aleksandrov, E. I. Astrakhan, S. S. Karinsky, and G. K. Moskalenko, *Labor Legislation—Commentaries to the Labor Legislation of the U.S.S.R., and to the Labor Code of the R.S.F.S.R.* (Moscow, 1947), p. 275.

construction industries.[60] Although postwar conditions were substantially changed from the prewar, little was done to change the legislative pattern established in the late 1930's until several years after Stalin's death. The only exception is a decree of the Presidium of the U.S.S.R. Supreme Soviet of May 19, 1949, which was designed to protect the working mother's right to support herself and her child and which forbade managers to refuse pregnant and nursing mothers employment on pain of punishment under Article 133 of the R.S.F.S.R. Criminal Code and corresponding provisions in the codes of other republics.[61] The decree states:

Anyone refusing to hire a pregnant woman or a mother nursing a child or lowering her pay for this reason is liable . . . to corrective labor for as long as six months or a fine up to 1,000 rubles. With repeated offense, the period of imprisonment can be raised to as long as two years.

Other income-security provisions stipulated by the decree may be summarized as follows:

(1) *Maternity leave.* For women covered by the Labor Code of 1922—in effect, all working women except collective-farm members, domestic workers, and a few others—the leave was five weeks before the birth of a child and six weeks after, with an additional two weeks in the event of an abnormal or multiple birth.[62]

(2) *Protective rules prior to leave.* Night work and overtime were as a rule forbidden to pregnant women, though exceptions could be permitted by the local union committee. Under no circumstances was overtime to be allowed after the fourth month of pregnancy. The pregnant mother's right to refuse to go on a business trip after the fourth month of pregnancy remained in force and reportedly applied, in practice, to nursing mothers as well.[63]

(3) *Transfer to lighter work.* Such transfer depended on the job a woman held and on her state of health and could be made either on doctor's orders or on her own initiative. In some jobs (unspecified) transfer was mandatory. Retainment of the same pay after transfer apparently was not a matter of course. Generally, the woman retained her previous pay only if she fulfilled the work norm that applied to the new job. In other words, whether she was shifted to a new job, or stayed in the old job with lighter duties, her pay would be computed on the basis not simply of her average earnings for the preceding six months, but also on the basis of the degree of fulfillment of the norm which applied to the new job. In effect, the preceding six months' average was taken as 100 per cent, but if she "underfulfilled" on the new job, and, for example, produced 90 per cent, then she received only 90 per cent of her previous six months' average.[64]

(4) *Time off for nursing.* As before, mothers who were nursing were given half an hour

---

[60]N. Popova, "Zhenskii trud v SSSR," *Sotsialisticheskii trud*, No. 3 (Mar., 1957), 8.

[61]A. A. Abramova, *Okhrana trudovykh prav zhenshchin v SSSR* (Moscow, 1954), pp. 27–28; see also Ministerstvo Iustitsii R.S.F.S.R., *Kodeks zakonov o brake, sem'e i opeke RSFSR* (Moscow, 1950), p. 83.

[62]Abramova, *op. cit.,* pp. 31–33, explains that if the birth was not on schedule, the total time was the same, i.e., there would have been less time before and more time after if the child was early, more before and less after if the child was late, all adding up to seventy-seven calendar days. Further, the regular vacation (usually two weeks) could be added to the maternity leave period if the woman requested it, and in this instance a woman could have her regular vacation even if she had been at the enterprise less than the eleven months required for the accrual of leave.

[63]*Ibid.,* pp. 28–29.

[64]*Ibid.,* p. 29; see also N. G. Aleksandrov (ed.), *Novoe v razvitii trudovogo prava v period mezhdu XX i XXII s"ezdami KPSS* (Moscow, 1961), p. 152. Abramova states that the provision on percentage of fulfillment applies only in certain industries and mentions the cotton textile, knitting, and tobacco industries. She also expresses her disapproval of this practice and believes it to be contrary to the resolution of the Central Executive Committee of the People's Commissars of Jan. 27, 1936, Art. 132 of the R.S.F.S.R. Labor Code of 1922, and the resolution of the Secretariat of the All-Union Central Council of Trade Unions of Jan. 19, 1938.

off every three hours; this time could be added to their lunch break or subtracted from the end of working time at the mother's own discretion.

(5) *Maternity benefits.* The regulations regarding maternity benefit payments in force for the first decade after the war remained basically those of the 1930's, and the rather complex sliding scale of eligibilities and amounts of benefits in relation to wages seems to have been carefully designed to encourage union memberships, stability on the job, productivity, and the like, with distinct advantages given to women in heavy and underground work.[65]

Specifically, all working women, except collective farmers, domestic workers, and others not covered by state insurance, were eligible for some payment during their maternity leave.[66] The minimum requirement was three months' work before the start of maternity

leave, which meant that pregnancy might antedate starting work. For young specialists who, having completed their training, had just begun working on a state assignment, even this minimum requirement was waived.

Maternity benefits for collective-farm women remained, as they do today, distinctly inferior. The leave period was still one month before and one month after the birth of the child, and the rate of benefit was still 50 per cent of earnings, computed at one twelfth of the preceding calendar year's total working days to determine the monthly rate of benefit.[67]

The regulations for the additional layette and nursing benefits, received also by some nonworking mothers, do not appear to have changed significantly in the postwar period. For these benefits, only three months of work by the mother or the insured husband were sufficient for eligibility. For students not even this was required. The income of the insured party, however, could not exceed 500 rubles (50 rubles since the 1960 currency reform) for the last month of work before the child's birth, or the last month before maternity leave in the case of the mother herself, without loss of eligibility. If both the husband and the wife were working, the lower income of the two was the determining one.[68] The al-

---

[65]Abramova, *op. cit.,* p. 39, states that at the time of writing (1953 or 1954), the maternity benefit rates described were still based on a resolution of the Central Executive Committee and the Council of People's Commissars, U.S.S.R., of June 23, 1931.

[66]Full details are given by Abramova, *op. cit.,* pp. 39–41; they are worth outlining:

Union members get the full rate of the average earnings for the full period of maternity leave: (1) if they have worked a total of three years and not less than two of them at the same enterprise; (2) if they are *stakhanovites* or shock workers who have worked a total of one year and not less than three months at the same enterprise; (3) if they are underground workers who have fulfilled their norm for two months; (4) if they are under age 18 and have worked at least one year; or (5) if they are medal holders or were partisans.

Union members get three fourths of their average earnings for the first twenty days of maternity leave and 100 per cent thereafter: (1) if they have worked at the same enterprise for two years, but less than three years in all; (2) if they have worked in mines or on steamships for one to two years; or (3) if they are under age 18 and have worked less than one year.

Union members get two thirds of their average earnings for the first twenty days and 100 per cent thereafter: (1) if they have been more than one but less than two years at the same enterprise; (2) if they have worked in mines or

on steamships less than one year; or (3) if they are construction workers who have worked less than one year, but at least ten months at the same enterprise.

Union members get two thirds of average earnings for the entire period of maternity leave if they are mothers who have worked less than one year or construction workers who have worked less than ten months.

Nonunion members get half of average earnings for the first thirty days and two thirds for the rest of the period if they have otherwise fulfilled minimum requirements.

War veterans get 100 per cent of average earnings for the entire time regardless of other considerations.

[67]*Ibid.,* p. 44.

[68]*Ibid.,* p. 45; M. Rumiantseva, A. Pergament, and G. Gromova, *Spravochnik zhenshchiny-rabotnitsy* (Moscow, 1963), pp. 115–17, confirm that these regulations have remained in force.

lowances remained a flat 120 rubles (now 12) for the layette and 180 rubles (now 18)—20 rubles (now 2) per month for nine months—for nursing; the latter allowance was paid whether the baby was nursed or bottle-fed.[69]

Legislation since the Death of Stalin, March 5, 1953. Since Stalin's death, legislation in the rights field has continued to repeat, reinforce, and slightly expand earlier provisions for pregnant and nursing mothers. A resolution of October 13, 1956, stipulated that a woman who ceased to work after having a child and returned to work within a year after the birth should retain her consecutive work status, whether she returned to the same job or not. Similarly, a decree of January 25, 1960, stated that those who, on becoming pregnant, were transferred to other work nearer their home should not lose their status of being consecutively employed.[70]

With regard to protection from arduous or dangerous work there has not been much major legislation. Underground work, which seems not only to have remained open to women, but even to have been encouraged by special incentives, such as maternity benefits, was taken up in a resolution of the Council of Ministers of the U.S.S.R. on July 13, 1957. This resolution prohibited women from doing heavy work—digging and shoveling—under ground, but it allowed them auxiliary jobs that might occasionally take them under ground. When women were removed from underground work, protection of their uninterrupted work record was provided if they took a job within six months, and their pay was continued at the average rate for up to three months during retraining if it was required.[71] Another development came on June

29, 1960, with a resolution of the U.S.S.R. Council of Ministers, which prohibited women from working in the ocean fishing fleet, except in seagoing canneries, at processing bases, and on refrigerator ships. Both these resolutions, it should be noted, provided that women holding the newly prohibited jobs be shifted to lighter work without loss of income.[72] By the fall of 1961 the shift in the fisheries industry was reported to have been completed.[73]

Considerably greater activity in these matters has been shown at the governmental level of the various republics and within individual industries. A U.S.S.R. Council of Ministers resolution of August 29, 1957, gave the various republics the right to extend, at their own discretion, the list of occupations closed to women, provided they obtained the permission of the State Committee on Labor and Wage Questions attached to the U.S.S.R. Council of Ministers and the permission of the All-Union Central Council of Trade Unions.[74]

One example of the exercise of this prerogative is a resolution of the R.S.F.S.R. Council of May 15, 1960, forbidding certain shipbuilding and ship repair jobs to women. Some industries have also been developing their own rules to protect women. For example, *Glavgaz* and the Central Committee of the Oil and Chemical Workers' Union in 1958 prohibited women from using vibrating and striking tools, such as pneumatic hammers, and stipulated that mothers should not be allowed to work with hot tar. Safety provisions established by the construction industry in 1958 forbade women to work on the construction of high smokestacks.[75]

The measure of change in frankness and honesty in discussing protective legislation is perhaps best exemplified in the attitude of a Soviet writer on women's rights, A. A.

---

[69]The food allowance was paid in two installments: 100 rubles (now 10) were paid at the time of birth and 80 (now 8) when the child was five months old. Layette was paid at the time of birth.

[70]A. A. Abramova, in N. G. Aleksandrov (ed.), *op. cit.,* p. 149.

[71]Emily Clark Brown, "A Note on Employment and Unemployment," *Soviet Studies,* No. 3 (Jan., 1961), 235.

[72]Abramova, in N. G. Aleksandrov (ed.), *op. cit.,* p. 139.

[73]E. Korshunova, "Zhenskii trud v SSSR," *Sotsialisticheskii trud,* No. 2 (Feb., 1961), p. 40.

[74]Abramova, in N. G. Aleksandrov (ed.), *op. cit.,* p. 140.

[75]*Ibid.*

Abramova. In 1954, before de-Stalinization, she claimed that the list of occupations forbidden to women was being reduced because mechanization was making many jobs much less onerous, and she cited underground mining as a case in point.[76] In 1960 she stated that the list had not been changed since 1942 and that it ought to be brought up to date, especially since technological progress had created new occupations in which women ought not to be allowed. She called for a unified, All-Union list, such as that for adolescents, and one which would pull all the scattered, decentralized rules and regulations together. She also felt that there should be legislative provisions giving women preference in lighter jobs and that the old weight-lifting rules should be revised "despite mechanization" and be made more precise.[77] Her complaints have been echoed by others in recent years who have supported her contention that women are working under conditions which are "not normal" for them and that it is necessary to re-examine and expand the list of occupations that should be closed to women.[78]

Nevertheless, some Soviet journalists continue to glorify girls who do work which is clearly undesirable. Maurice Hindus has quoted a *Pravda* article which tells the story of a team of six girls who work in the foundry of the Likhachev automobile works in Moscow.[79] Their job of filling molds with molten metal was "strenuous . . . requiring no little exertion of muscles, eyes, and nerves." But the girls walk to the factory in the morning "as though carried by the wind." One would imagine from their eagerness, the article states, that they are "hurrying to a ball, a date, a skiing party." They decide to work even harder and volunteer for Sunday construction work. But one of them, "a frail, delicate, white-faced" girl, fails to show up. Neither her fragility nor her pallor, Hindus remarks, saves her from a sharp rebuke by her teammates.

The approach to the problem of night work for women has also been one of a few, isolated regulations. Regarding this problem the textile industry, still an important employer of women, has provided a beginning, with a resolution of the U.S.S.R. Council of Ministers, adopted August 31, 1960, by which the evening and night shifts at certain plants were eliminated on Saturday in connection with the shift to a seven-hour day and a new pay scale in order to reduce the amount of night work by women. A two-day weekend was, of course, especially important for mothers on the evening or night shift. More recently, at the Twenty-Second Party Congress in 1961, the question of eliminating night work for women was raised and Khrushchev said that the Central Committee of the Party and the Government would examine the question.[80] Complete abolition of night work would, of course, be unrealistic and unsound from the point of view of the industries in which women make up a high percentage of the labor force, and it would cause considerable

---

[76] Abramova, *op. cit.,* p. 25.

[77] Abramova, in N. G. Aleksandrov (ed.), *op. cit.,* p. 138. The list of harmful occupations referred to is the one appearing in "Spisok osobo tiazhelikh i vrednykh rabot i professii, kotorym ne dopushaiutsa zhenshchiny," of the People's Commissariat of Labor of the U.S.S.R., Apr. 10, 1932, published in *Izvestiia narkomtruda SSSR,* Nos. 22–23 (1932). Among sundry specifics cited are weight-lifting norms—for men, 80 kg; for women, 20 kg; for boys age 16 to 18, 16.4 kg; and for girls the same ages, 10.25 kg—and restrictions on tractor and truck drivers, of whom it is required that they pass a medical examination once a month if they drive trucks or wheel tractors (crawler tractors being regarded as easier). Women working on wheel tractors which are not equipped with soft seats may transfer to lighter work for three days during their menstrual period on presenting a physician's certificate. If the woman is completely freed from work as a driver, she gets a social insurance benefit.

[78] V. Mel'nikov, "K dal'neishemu uluchsheniiu trudovykh uslovii," *Sotsialisticheskii trud,* No. 11 (Nov., 1959), 68–76.

[79] Maurice Hindus, *House without a Roof* (Garden City, N.Y., 1961), pp. 279–80.

[80] A. M. Rumiantseva (ed.), *Rol' zhenshchiny v sovremennom obshchestve* (Prague, 1963), p. 151.

disruption in the national economy. Instances of the resistance of managers to restrictions on the employment of women in night work have been reported in the press.[81]

While little has been accomplished in the area of protective legislation since Stalin's death, significant expansion has occurred in legislation dealing with basic benefits for working mothers, and these provisions bear quoting for purposes of comparison with those in force before Stalin's death.

(1) *Maternity leave.* A decree of the Presidium of the Supreme Soviet, U.S.S.R., of March 26, 1956, increased maternity leave from the total of 77 days previously allowed to a total of 112 days—56 days before and 56 days after confinement. The earlier provision of two extra weeks after the birth of a child in the event of multiple or abnormal delivery was retained, as was the provision that a mother may add her regular vacation to her maternity leave if she so desires. Further and rather important stipulations were contained in a resolution of the Council of Ministers, U.S.S.R., of October 13, 1956, which provided that a mother may take additional unpaid maternity leave of up to three months if she desires and then return to the same or an equivalent job without loss of pay or status, in accordance with the old 1922 Labor Code still in force. It also provided that a woman who decides to stop working entirely—in which case she gets her leave pay plus accrued vacation in a lump sum—but then returns to work within a year of the child's birth may retain her status of working consecutively. This provision is important, both in terms of the amount of maternity benefits for which she is eligible during future pregnancies and in terms of other social insurance benefits, such as sick pay and old-age and disability payments. A decree of the Presidium of the Supreme Soviet, U.S.S.R., of January 25, 1960, further provided that a

pregnant woman's transfer to work nearer her home would not result in loss of continuity status.[82]

One may infer from one Soviet source that some penalty may be attached to unpaid maternity leave if a woman insists on having children in rapid succession. Specifically, we find an argument that the unpaid time ought not to be counted in calculating a woman's average earnings over the preceding six months—on which her maternity benefits are based—even if this time did fall within the actual calendar six months.[83] Since the issue probably comes up rather seldom, the criticism may in fact be directed at the generally stingy principle which governs the computation of the average earnings on which maternity benefits are based, such as the inclusion of base vacation time or other time not worked, even when good and sufficient reasons exist for unworked time.

(2) *Maternity benefits.* The scale for maternity benefit payments to working women and the scale of eligibilities have been somewhat liberalized, notably by a resolution of the Council of Ministers, U.S.S.R., of December 6, 1956, which raised the floor under the lower benefits. There is now a flat minimum benefit, and the minimum scale is two thirds of average earnings, even for nonunion women who formerly received considerably less. The minimum eligibility requirement of three months' work has been dropped, and coverage has been expanded to include domestics working for private persons and women employed by religious organizations.[84] However, eligibility requirements for benefits at the rate of 100 per cent of average earnings do not appear to have changed significantly. The rules remain almost identical to those in force before 1956, and the system

---

[81]E.g., see the item by P. Chvertko in *Sovetskaia Kirgiziia* (Jan. 9, 1962), transl. in *The Current Digest of the Soviet Press,* XIV, No. 2, 3.

[82]Abramova, in N. G. Aleksandrov (ed.), *op. cit.,* pp. 145, 149.

[83]*Ibid.,* pp. 146–47.

[84]*Ibid.,* p. 155, from which it is possible to infer that these categories of people were not previously covered, although they should have been under the 1922 code, which is still in force, and existing social insurance regulations.

continues to favor the union member, the stable worker, "advanced" workers, and "innovators."[85]

Since the currency reform of January 1, 1961, allowances for layette and nursing have been 12 and 18 rubles, respectively, or the same as before in terms of their rather insignificant purchasing power. Recent sources also indicate that the 500-ruble (now 50) income limit means that only the lowest-paid families benefit from this provision.[86] And, although almost everybody but private farmers seem to be otherwise eligible for this benefit, it may be noted that collective farmers receive only the layette allowance.[87]

(3) *Job protection.* Mothers continue, as before, to enjoy the law's protection against being dismissed or not hired because they are pregnant. This protection applies also to single mothers and nursing mothers. One can, however, infer from one commentator's discussion of this point that enforcement is a problem and that dismissals do occur, ostensibly for other reasons.[88] The argument favoring prohibition of firing such mothers for any reason whatsoever does not seem realistic, since it would mean that a woman in danger of being dismissed for sheer incompetence could keep her job by getting pregnant. Of course, some mothers do not avail themselves of the privilege of returning to their old job at the end of their pregnancy leave. In 1959, for example, 70 of the 1,350 women employed at the Ordzhonikidze Works, Moscow's largest machine tool plant, took pregnancy leaves. Of these 70, 7 (10 per cent) did not return to the plant.[89]

(4) *Nursing provisions.* Time off for nursing has remained the same. A recent source states that even mothers whose babies are bottle-fed are allowed time off until the baby is nine months old and that this is "the firmly established policy of the All-Union Central Committee of Trade Unions and the Ministry of Health of the U.S.S.R."[90]

As is evident from the preceding pages, Soviet legislation dealing with various questions related to working women has undergone changes both as a result of varying policy and under the pressure of circumstances. Initially, a strongly idealistic policy dictated much of the legislation enacted during the period prior to the Five-Year Plans.

---

[85]Rumiantseva, Pergament, and Gromova, *op. cit.*, pp. 112–14, outline an eligibility scale noticeably similar to that summarized in n. 66; only the bottom range seems to have changed:

Union members get 100 per cent of their average earnings for the entire maternity leave period: (1) if they have worked a total of three years, of which not less than two are at the same enterprise; (2) if they are under age 18 and have worked at least one year at the same enterprise; (3) if they are former partisans or war veterans; (4) if they are medal holders; or (5) if they are innovators or advanced workers with not less than one year of total work.

Union members get three fourths of their average earnings for the first twenty days and 100 per cent for the rest of the time: (1) if they have worked two years at the same enterprise, but less than three years in all; or (2) if they are under age 18 and have worked less than one year.

Union members get two thirds of their average earnings for the first twenty days and 100 per cent for the rest of the time, if they have worked between one and two years at the same enterprise.

Union members get two thirds of their entire earnings, if they have worked less than one year.

Nonunion members get two thirds of their average earnings, no matter how long they have worked.

As before, specialists and others who have completed training and started work on a state assignment have the minimum requirements waived. They receive 100 per cent from the minute they report to work; this means that they can report to work pregnant enough to start leave immediately, with full benefits.

[86]U. S. Department of Health, Education and Welfare, Social Security Administration, *A Report on Social Security Programs in the Soviet Union* (Washington, D.C., 1960), p. 54; A. M. Rumiantseva (ed.), *op. cit.*, p. 115.

[87]Abramova, in N. G. Aleksandrov (ed.), *op. cit.*, pp. 48–49. Domestic, seasonal, and cooperative workers were included. The only exception mentioned is the private entrepreneur.

[88]*Ibid.*, pp. 148–49.

[89]"Marriage—Grounds for Firing a Woman?" *Soviet Woman*, No. 5 (1960), 12.

[90]Abramova, in N. G. Aleksandrov (ed.), *op. cit.*, p. 155.

These laws were intended not only to give women equal employment opportunities, but also to protect them from occupations and working conditions which were judged unsuitable or even harmful. However, urgent demands for manpower created by rapid industrialization led to erosion of this protective legislation, and subsequent demands created by World War II not only brought larger numbers of women into the labor force but also placed them, of necessity, in occupations generally reserved for men.

After the period of postwar economic recovery, interest in effective protective legislation has revived, and the issue of the working woman has been discussed with considerable freedom since Stalin's death. The laws pertaining to a woman's right to work and the benefits legally provided to enable working mothers to participate in the labor force are, however, only one formal aspect of the question of female employment. In another chapter we shall examine other factors which have to do with the facilitation of female employment, particularly the help in child care which the Soviet Union offers its working mothers.

CONCLUSIONS

At the time of the Revolution, Russian women were widely employed in agriculture, domestic service, and certain branches of industry. Only a small number were engaged in the professions, primarily in the fields of education and medicine. Girls had not been encouraged to obtain the higher education necessary for a professional career. Custom and social attitudes particularly discouraged women from entering fields of study, such as engineering, which were traditionally considered a male domain. Under the impact of the new regime's educational and propaganda efforts, however, these older views were modified, and many young women have entered professions in the fields of science and technology and others previously closed to women. The party and the government were, of course, the principal agents in bringing about the im-

portant changes in attitudes toward female employment which occurred. Through their monopoly of the mass media and control of the educational system, they were able to influence significantly the attitudes of large segments of the population, particularly those of the younger generation. Evidence of the success of the regime's efforts to open up new opportunities to women is the widespread employment of women in a wide variety of occupations in all sectors of the economy today. Only in some of the republics where Moslem traditions retain their influence do remnants of past beliefs continue to offer serious obstacles to the employment of women in a number of occupations.

Economic necessity has also been a powerful force contributing to the high rate of participation of women in the labor force. Two or more breadwinners have been a necessity for most families to maintain an acceptable standard of living. War widows and unmarried women typically are employed. Prior to World War II, the possibility of the loss of a husband through an easy divorce or the purges encouraged many women to seek an income of their own. At the present time, however, such uncertainties are much less significant. Also, the standard of living has risen substantially in the past decade or more, reducing the economic pressure to work simply to make ends meet. Simultaneously, however, the appetite of people for more goods has increased so that it is not evident whether the desire of women to work has been appreciably diminished by the increase in the standard of living. Rather than more women withdrawing completely from the labor force as the standard of living increases, it is probable that the number of hours worked will be reduced and part-time employment increased in response to a widespread demand by women for such arrangements.

A large body of legislation embodying Soviet policies toward women and affecting the participation of women in the labor force has been passed since the Revolution. Among the major categories are laws concerned with equal job opportunity and equal pay, the protection of women from injurious occupations, paid maternity leave and other benefits, and old-age security. Much of the basic legislation was put on the books soon after the Soviets took power. Although there have been some significant changes in the legislation since, the general outline has remained the same. There has, however, been considerable variation in the rigor with which some of the legislation, particularly protective legislation, has been enforced. At various times, protective legislation has been given only lip service, wartime being the extreme case.

In recent years, protective legislation has been more strictly enforced. Women displaced from employment by such legislation have, for the most part, been absorbed elsewhere in the economy with no loss in income. Maternity and related benefits have had the expected effect of encouraging women to enter or remain in the labor force, since they make it easier for a mother to work. On the other hand, improvements in pension payments in 1956 have encouraged more women to withdraw from the labor force when they reach the retirement age. The extension of the pension system in 1964 to cover collective farmers should have a similar effect upon women in agriculture. These developments in the various categories of legislation affecting women have had diverse effects upon the participation of women in the labor force. During most of the Soviet period the net effect, as the government intended, has been to increase the rate of female participation. During the last ten years, however, the combined impact has been less clear and may well have been neutral.

The uneven enforcement of protective legislation since the Revolution and the economic motives which have inspired in part certain of the measures should not detract from an appreciation of the pioneering role played by the Soviets in this field. The present legislation could well serve as a model for many other countries in which women make up a significant part of the labor force.

chapter

5

FAMILY VERSUS WORK

IN AN attempt to lighten the burden of mothers and free them for work outside the home, the Soviet government has developed a system of nurseries, kindergartens, camps, and other child-care institutions. It is the need for women in industry which has accounted in large part for the development of these institutions. As Kingsbury and Fairchild long ago noted, "The health of man, woman, and child is peculiarly the woman's responsibility, especially the care of the sick and the child. The crèche, the pre-school, the kindergarten, the playground, and the school must be organized and well conducted, if the mother is to be a wage earner."[1] In addition, care of the child by public institutions gives the state an opportunity to assure the welfare of the rising generation and to train the child to be a useful contributor to the goals of the state in later life.

NURSERIES

Although *yasli* or crèches are regarded as preschool educational establishments, their primary function is to serve as day nurseries for infants from two months and children up to age 3. Some nurseries operate on a permanent, year-round basis and are housed in substantial buildings, but many more function on a seasonal basis and are designed primarily

to take care of the young children of farm women during the peak agricultural season. These temporary nurseries often have little or no plant or equipment and are located in the fields where the women work, in order to make it possible for mothers to nurse their babies during the working day.

Because of the informal and *ad hoc* character of many of the temporary nurseries, the line between them and children's playgrounds, which are discussed later, is not sharply drawn. As a result, statistics on temporary nurseries must be used with caution. The purpose of the permanent and seasonal nurseries and playgrounds is identical, however, even if there is a great difference in the character and quality of the facilities.[2] To the extent that they serve to free mothers for work in the economy, they are equivalent in the result achieved.

Since only a handful of children could be cared for in nurseries prior to the Revolution, the development of nurseries has been entirely the responsibility of the Soviet government. Initially, only permanent nurseries were established, and until 1921 all were confined to the Russian republic (R.S.F.S.R.). As Table 32 indicates, the development of such facili-

---

[1]Susan M. Kingsbury and Mildred Fairchild, *Factory, Family and Women in the Soviet Union* (New York, 1935), p. 168.

[2]E. R. Ustiuzhaninova, "Detskie kolkhoznye ploshchadki," *Doshkol'noe vospitanie*, No. 5 (May, 1947), 1–5, discusses the purposes of playgrounds and suggests that parents should play a larger role in the construction and equipping of playgrounds.

TABLE 32. Number of permanent and seasonal nurseries, 1917–29.[a]

Year	U.S.S.R.		R.S.F.S.R.		Ukrainian S.S.R.		Other Republics	
	Perm.	Seas.	Perm.	Seas.	Perm.	Seas.	Perm.	Seas.
1917..........	14	–	14	–	–	–	–	–
1918..........	78	–	78	–	–	–	–	–
1919..........	126	–	126	–	–	–	–	–
1920..........	565	–	565	–	–	–	–	–
1921..........	769	46	668	–	101	46	–	–
1922..........	967	248	914	125	53	123	–	–
1923..........	535	475	447	209	88	266	–	–
1924..........	615	956	503	524	105	426	7	6
1925..........	708	2,647	536	1,853	161	749	11	45
1926..........	824	3,985	610	2,924	197	942	17	119
1927..........	944	5,622	669	4,254	193	1,123	82	245
1928..........	1,172	6,947	880	5,099	200	1,434	92	414
1929..........	1,367	9,021	1,044	6,380	200	2,021	123	620

[a]From Susan M. Kingsbury and Mildred Fairchild, *Factory, Family and Women in the Soviet Union* (New York, 1935), p. 148. Nurseries in the transport department are not included in the 1929 figures. All the figures are from a manuscript report of the R.S.F.S.R. Commissariat of Health, 1930.

ties in the Ukraine and other republics was more modest. In 1929, at the beginning of the Five-Year Plans, the R.S.F.S.R. had approximately 75 per cent of the permanent and 70 per cent of all seasonal nurseries, and the latter outnumbered the permanent nurseries almost seven to one.

The most important growth in nursery facilities occurred between 1929 and 1932, as shown in Table 33, which presents data on the number of places in urban, rural, and seasonal nurseries. Between 1929 and 1930 the number of permanent individual accommodations almost doubled for all types of nurseries and almost tripled in seasonal facilities. By 1940 the number of places in permanent nurseries had reached a peak of over 800,000 and in seasonal nurseries of more than 4 million.

Accommodations were sharply reduced during World War II, and the postwar recovery was slow.[3] In 1950 the number of permanent accommodations still fell short of the 1940 figure by about 90,000. In the same year the number of places in seasonal nurseries was less than half the prewar level. By 1955 permanent accommodations surpassed the prewar

figure by a modest margin, but seasonal nurseries showed little progress and even declined in 1957. Unfortunately, no subsequent data are available for the latter.

How adequate was the provision of these facilities? To answer this question we may compare the number of children of nursery age with the number of places available. DeWitt estimates that in 1938–1939 less than 5 per cent of the children of nursery age could be accommodated in permanent nurseries which were located primarily in urban centers.[4] Seasonal nurseries, on the other hand, which were usually in the rural areas, were equipped to handle an additional 28 per cent of the nursery group. As a result, just prior to the war about a third of the infants of nursery age could be accommodated during the summer months in some kind of nursery facility.

Recovery from wartime destruction was

---

[3]For a discussion of postwar shortages and difficulties, see N. I. Vinogradova, "Doshkol'noe vospitanie v 4-i Stalinskoi piatiletke," *Doshkol'noe vospitanie,* Nos. 9–10 (Sept.–Oct., 1946), 1–5.

[4]Nicholas DeWitt, *Education and Professional Employment in the U.S.S.R.* (Washington, D.C., 1961), p. 73. According to Frank Lorimer, *The Population of the Soviet Union: History and Prospects* (Geneva, 1946), p. 238, at the beginning of 1939 there were 14.8 million children age 0 to 38 months. This may be compared with approximately 750,000 places in permanent nurseries. If an estimated 900,000 infants up to two months of age are deducted from 14.8 million, the percentage is increased to 5.5 per cent.

TABLE 33. Number of places in Soviet nurseries, 1913–64.[a]

| Year | No. of Places in Permanent Nurseries | | | No. of Children in Seasonal Nurseries | Total No. of Children in Permanent and Seasonal Nurseries |
	Total	Urban	Rural		
1913.............	0.6	0.6	0.0	10.6	11.2
1917.............	2.2	n.a.[b]	n.a.	n.a.	n.a.
1918.............	n.a.	n.a.	n.a.	n.a.	25.2
1928.............	62.0	54.7	7.3	197.8	259.8
1929.............	64.6	56.0	8.6	179.9	257.0
1930.............	107.4	71.6	35.8	750.0	854.4
1931.............	299.9	171.5	128.4	2,271.0	2,571.7
1932.............	600.9	258.4	342.5	3,920.3	4,868.6
1933.............	n.a.	n.a.	n.a.	n.a.	4,529.3
1936.............	n.a.	n.a.	n.a.	n.a.	4,744.6
1937.............	718.2	378.1	370.1	n.a.	n.a.
1940.............	824.1	523.8	300.3	4,049.1	4,873.2
1950.............	735.5	470.1	265.0	1,813.1	2,548.6
1955.............	851.0	567.6	283.4	2,334.0	3,185.0
1956.............	904.3	604.0	300.3	2,386.8	3,291.1
1957.............	1,046.0	n.a.	n.a.	1,750.0	2,896.0
1958.............	1,135.0	n.a.	n.a.	n.a.	n.a.
1959.............	1,271.0	n.a.	n.a.	(1,500.0)	(2,771.0)
1960.............	1,402.2	n.a.	n.a.	n.a.	n.a.
1961.............	1,574.2	n.a.	n.a.	n.a.	n.a.
1962.............	1,754.0	n.a.	n.a.	n.a.	n.a.
1963.............	2,050.8	n.a.	n.a.	n.a.	n.a.
1964.............	2,253.2	n.a.	n.a.	n.a.	n.a.

[a]Figures are expressed in thousands. Figures in parentheses are estimates. The sources from which this table was compiled were as follows: cols. 1–4, for 1913, 1928, 1932, 1937, 1940, 1950, and 1955–58, Nicholas DeWitt, *Education and Professional Employment in the U.S.S.R.* (Washington, D.C., 1961), p. 74; col. 1, for 1917, *Sotsialisticheskoe stroitel'stvo SSSR* (Moscow, 1934), p. 427; col. 5, for 1918, 1933, and 1936, *Zhenshchina v SSSR* (Moscow, 1937), p. 134; cols. 1–5, for 1929–31, and col. 5, for 1932, Kingsbury and Fairchild, *op. cit.*, p. 149. Some of these figures are from special material provided Kingsbury and Fairchild by *Gosplan*, the Commissariat of Labor of the U.S.S.R., and the All-Union Council of Trade Unions. The figures in col. 4, for 1929–32, cover only seasonal nurseries in agriculture. The figure for 1959 is estimated as described in the text. The figures in col. 1, for 1959–64, are from *Narodnoe khoziaistvo SSSR v 1959 godu* (Moscow, 1960), p. 799; *Narodnoe khoziaistvo SSSR v 1960 godu* (Moscow, 1961), p. 827; *Narodnoe khoziaistvo*

SSSR v 1961 godu (Moscow, 1962), p. 609; *Narodnoe khoziaistvo SSSR v 1962 godu* (Moscow, 1963), p. 494; *Narodnoe khoziaistvo SSSR v 1963 godu* (Moscow, 1965), p. 632; and *Narodnoe khoziaistvo SSSR v 1964 godu* (Moscow, 1965), p. 742. The figures given in the tables in these sources have been adjusted upward to include nursery-aged children enrolled in combined nursery-kindergartens given in the footnotes to the tables. These were 63,000 in 1959, 142,000 in 1960, 251,000 in 1961, 382,000 in 1962, 560,000 in 1963, and 758,700 in 1964. Col. 5 (1940, 1950, 1955–57, and 1959) is the sum of cols. 1 and 4. The figures in col. 1 from 1937 to 1956 appear to omit nurseries of certain administrations, such as railroad transportation. In 1955 the difference was 56,000, and in 1956, 62,000 places; see *Narodnoe khoziaistvo SSSR v 1959 godu* (Moscow, 1960), p. 792. Such discrepancies or inconsistencies in the statistics are not sufficient, however, to distort the over-all picture.

[b]No data available.

slow, and the number of places in permanent nurseries did not reach the prewar peak until 1955. By 1962, however, some 1,750,000 places were available for nursery-aged children in permanent nurseries or in nursery-kindergartens, which could accommodate approximately 12 per cent of the children of nursery age. Evidence indicates that the number of children cared for in seasonal nurseries has never regained the prewar level. As previously noted, the number of children accommodated declined from 2,387,000 in 1956 to 1,750,000 in 1957, the last year for which data for summer nurseries alone are available.

It was reported, however, that each year between 1959 and 1962 some 3 million children were taken care of for some portion of time in seasonal nurseries and playgrounds.[5] On the basis of data on the number of children accommodated in playgrounds, approximately one half or 1.5 million of these could be expected to be accommodated in seasonal nur-

[5]*Narodnoe khoziaistvo SSSR v 1959 godu* (Moscow, 1960), p. 792; *Narodnoe khoziaistvo SSSR v 1960 godu* (Moscow, 1961), p. 827; *Narodnoe khoziaistvo SSSR v 1961 godu* (Moscow, 1962), p. 609; and *Narodnoe khoziaistvo SSSR v 1962 godu* (Moscow, 1963), p. 494.

series.[6] If a figure of slightly over 1.5 million children is assumed in 1962, an additional 10 per cent could be accommodated in seasonal nurseries, or a total of 22 per cent of the nursery-aged children could be accommodated in some sort of nursery facilities at least part of the time during the summer months.[7]

The distribution of nursery facilities differs greatly among the republics. Table 34 compares the percentage of total population in selected republics with the percentage of the total number of places in permanent nurseries in these republics.[8] The preferred position of the R.S.F.S.R. is apparent both before World War II and in more recent years. Among the major republics, the Uzbek republic seems surprisingly well supplied with

nursery facilities, but comparison with the number of nursery-aged children is not possible, since the required statistics are not available. Sharp differences between two other Central Asian republics are also revealed. The Turkmen republic is, relatively, one of the best equipped while the Kirgiz republic is one of the poorest. Very little equalization among the republics appears to have taken place since World War II.

The availability of permanent facilities differs greatly in urban and rural areas. At the time of the 1926 census the rural population outnumbered the urban by more than four to one.[9] Yet in 1928 almost eight times as many urban as rural accommodations were available in permanent nurseries (see Table 33). In 1937 the number of places in urban and rural nurseries was almost equal, but the rural population was approximately twice the urban. Three years later, the number of rural accommodations had actually declined and the number of urban increased. During the postwar period the urban and rural population reached an approximate balance, but available data for the years following World War II indicate that urban nurseries handle twice as many children as do the rural facilities.

Although during the postwar period a difference of two to one in favor of the urban

[6]*Narodnoe khoziaistvo SSSR v 1959 godu* (Moscow, 1960), pp. 738–39, reported that 1,552,700 children were accommodated in summer playgrounds in 1959. The difference of about 1.5 million between this figure and 3 million must have been accommodated in seasonal nurseries.

[7]The apparent decline in temporary nursery facilities which reduces the percentage of children accommodated in summer months below the prewar figure is probably due to stricter definitions and more reliable statistics in the postwar period.

[8]For lack of better data, the population data used are for Jan. 17, 1939, and Jan. 15, 1959, and the number of places in permanent nurseries are for the end of 1940 and the end of 1958.

[9]Lorimer, *op. cit.,* p. 67.

TABLE 34. Percentage of total population compared with percentage of total places in permanent nurseries in selected republics, 1939 and 1959.[a]

	1939			1959		
Republic	Population	Places	Ratio	Population	Places	Ratio
R.S.F.S.R.	56.8	65.5	1.2	56.3	64.8	1.2
Ukrainian S.S.R.	21.2	18.8	0.9	20.0	15.4	0.8
Belorussian S.S.R.	4.7	2.5	0.5	3.9	1.9	0.5
Uzbek S.S.R.	3.3	5.2	1.6	3.9	5.6	1.4
Kazakh S.S.R.	3.2	2.1	0.7	4.5	4.3	1.0
Georgian S.S.R.	1.9	1.3	0.7	1.9	1.3	0.7
Azerbaidzhan S.S.R.	1.7	1.8	1.1	1.8	1.2	0.7
Kirgiz S.S.R.	0.8	0.3	0.4	1.0	0.7	0.7
Turkmen S.S.R.	0.7	1.2	1.7	0.7	1.5	2.1
Other republics	5.7	1.3	0.2	6.0	3.3	0.5

[a]Calculated from data in Appendix III, Table 1, and from *Itogi . . . 1959 goda: SSSR*, p. 19. The percentages of places are calculated as of the end of 1940 and 1958. The population percentages are calculated on the basis of census data for January 17, 1939, and January 15, 1959.

areas has persisted, the situation is altered significantly when seasonal nurseries are taken into account. The data in Table 33 show that seasonal nurseries took care of from six to seven times as many children as permanent nurseries during the 1930's. But by 1957 the number of places in seasonal nurseries was less than twice that in permanent nurseries. The reason for the decline is not clear. However, seasonal nurseries still continue to help compensate for the smaller number of places available in permanent nurseries in rural areas. Further evidence of the unevenness of distribution of nursery facilities is provided by data on the distribution of facilities in the Turkmen and Kirgiz republics (see Table 35).[10] Large variations between the avail-

---

[10]See also Appendix III, Table 1, which gives the distribution of children in nurseries under all jurisdictions, by republic, for selected years from 1940 to 1962.

TABLE 35. Estimated percentage of nursery-aged children for whom accommodations were available in permanent nurseries in the Turkmen and Kirgiz republics, 1959.[a]

Locality	Children
Turkmen S.S.R.	13.2
City of Ashkhabad	16.6
Regions subordinated to the republic	11.8
Maryiskii Oblast	7.3
Tashauzskii Oblast	5.5
Chardzhouskii Oblast	38.3
Kirgiz S.S.R.	4.5
City of Frunze	20.4
Regions subordinated to the republic	3.8
Tien Shanskii Oblast	1.4
Oshsk Oblast	3.3

[a]Data on the number of permanent places in nurseries at the end of 1959 are from Tsentral'noe statisticheskoe upravlenie pri Sovete ministrov Turkmenskoi SSR, *Zhenshchina v Turkmenskoi SSR* (Ashkhabad, 1960), p. 73; and *idem*, Kirgizskoi SSR, *Zhenshchina v Kirgizskoi SSR* (Frunze, 1960), p. 86. Estimates of the population age 2 to 36 months were made as follows. On the basis of data on the population of Kazakhstan in *Narodnoe khoziaistvo Kazakhstana*, No. 3 (1961), 72, which gives the number of children under age 3, it was estimated that the children age 2 to 36 months in the Turkmen and Kirgiz republics constitute 33 per cent of the children age 0 to 9 years given in *idem*, SSSR, *Itogi Vsesoiuznoi perepisi naseleniia 1959 goda: Turkmenskaia SSR* (Moscow, 1963), p. 22, and *Itogi Vsesoiuznoi perepisi naseleniia 1959 goda: Kirgizskaia SSR* (Moscow, 1963), p. 22. It is assumed that this percentage is slightly higher in these two republics than in Kazakhstan.

ability of urban and rural nursery facilities are apparent in these republics. Such differences may be found in other parts of the Soviet Union. In many *oblasts* (the administrative units below the republican level), there is not a single collective farm with a nursery, and about half of the state farms lack a preschool institution.[11]

From the small percentages of children who can be accommodated in urban and rural nurseries, it is evident that the vast majority of Soviet children are still taken care of at home. Traditionally, the burden of caring for the young children of a working woman falls on a grandmother or some other member of the family whose earning power is low.

It would be hasty to assume from the percentage of children who can be accommodated in nurseries that the accommodations are necessarily grossly inadequate. To assess the situation properly it is necessary also to look at the demand for nursery services. It should be noted, however, that there is no free market for such services. The government not only controls the supply of nursery services but also influences the demand for these services through its control over the quality of the services offered and their cost to the parents. Unlike primary, secondary, and higher education, nurseries and kindergartens are not free. Parents must pay to send a child to a nursery according to a sliding scale which varies with family income and other circumstances, such as the number of children in the family. The scale established in 1948 and still in force today is shown in Table 36.

In computing the earnings, the pay of the father and mother is counted or, depending upon family circumstances, the income of a relative or other person who is supporting the child, alimony payments being excluded. Also included in determining the total sum of earnings are: all forms of pensions received by the persons mentioned above, as well as pen-

---

[11]I. Kuznetsev, "O chem rasskazali inspektora," *Doshkol'noe vospitanie*, No. 3 (Mar., 1964), 11.

TABLE 36. Monthly payments by parents for maintaining children in nurseries, 1948–65.[a]

	Monthly Payments			
	Time of Child's Stay			In Sanatorium, Kindergarten, or Summer Home
Parents' Total Monthly Earnings	9–10 hr.	12–14 hr.	24 hr.	
Cities or workers' villages				
up to 40...................	3.00	3.80	4.50	6.00
40–60....................	4.00	5.00	6.00	8.00
60–80....................	5.00	6.30	7.50	10.00
80–120...................	6.50	8.10	9.80	13.00
over 120..................	8.00	10.00	12.00	16.00
Rural localities				
up to 40..................	1.50	1.90	2.30	3.00
40–60....................	2.50	3.10	3.80	5.00
60–80....................	3.50	4.40	5.30	7.00
80–120...................	5.00	6.30	7.50	10.00
over 120..................	6.50	8.10	9.80	13.00

[a]Figures are given in current rubles. This table is compiled from the figures specified in Decree No. 1314, Ministry of Higher Education, U.S.S.R., Sept. 10, 1948, as quoted in

Ministervo vysshego obrazovaniia SSSR, *Vysshaia shkola, osnovnye postanovleniia, prikazy i instruktsii*, ed. by L. I. Karpov and V. A. Severtsev (Moscow, 1957), p. 487.

sions received for the child in a kindergarten or nursery, stipends, alimony support received for children who are in children's institutions, and monthly state aid received by single mothers and those with many children.

In accordance with Article 10 of the decree of the Presidium of the Supreme Soviet, July 8, 1944 (entitled, "Increasing state aid to pregnant women, single mothers, and those with many children, strengthening protection of maternity and childhood, establishing the honorary title of 'Mother-Hero,' and establishing the order of 'Maternal Glory' and the order 'Medal of Maternity'"), charges for the maintenance of children in kindergartens and nurseries are lowered for parents, relatives, or other persons supporting children: by 25 per cent, if they have two children and earnings of up to 60 rubles monthly; by 50 per cent, if they have three children and earnings of up to 40 rubles monthly; by 35 per cent, if they have three children and earnings of up to 80 rubles monthly; and by 50 per cent, if they have four or more children, regardless of their earnings. For children of the widows of servicemen and partisans killed as a result of wounds and illnesses in World War II, as well as for children of single mothers, with earnings of up to 60 rubles, payment in nurseries

and kindergartens is lowered by 50 per cent.[12]

Without actual data on household budgets, it is not possible to make a final judgment, but the present charges seem sufficiently high, particularly in relation to lower incomes, to reduce the demand for nursery services. If a grandmother is already living in a household, it is likely to be cheaper to have her care for a child. Among the alternatives of the mother's withdrawing from the labor force, hiring a nursemaid, or placing the child in a nursery, however, the latter is by far the most economical. An infant is fed and clothed at a nursery and is supplied with toys and other playthings. Some parents with whom the author spoke felt that if alternative costs were properly calculated, it would be found cheaper to care for an infant in a nursery than at home, even if a grandmother were available at home to serve as nursemaid. In any event, the demand for nurseries substantially outruns the supply—on the basis of all available evi-

[12]Decree No. 1314, Ministry of Higher Education, U.S.S.R., of Sept. 10, 1948, as amended by instructional letter No. 1-24, Main Administration of Higher Education, Ministry of Culture, U.S.S.R., Mar. 9, 1954, both quoted in *Vysshaia shkola* (Moscow, 1957), pp. 487–88.

dence.[13] There can be no doubt that the present proportion of children accommodated in permanent nurseries (about 10 per cent) falls far below the norm of 30 per cent which the Soviets would like to achieve in the short run and far below the long-range goal of caring for a majority of the children which the Soviets expressed in the program of the party presented at the Twenty-Second Party Congress.[14]

The quality of the nurseries varies greatly throughout the Soviet Union and even within such a major metropolitan area as Moscow. At one extreme, in the central part of the capital, is Nursery No. 236. Here the author found 160 children, cared for by a staff of more than twenty and housed in a substantial, if well-used, building equipped with sleeping porches, playrooms with toys, and other facilities. At the other extreme, on the outskirts of Moscow on the Tagansk road the author passed a large log hut which had been converted into a kindergarten; although it was supplied with electricity, it lacked running water. As a general rule, rural nurseries are smaller, less well equipped, and less adequately staffed. As a result, the care and training of the children suffer by comparison with urban facilities.[15] In the more remote and backward parts of the Soviet Union the facilities are even more primitive, although they may be as good as, or better than, the homes from which the children come.

Despite the physical inadequacies of nursery facilities, visitors usually have been impressed by the competence and warm devotion of the staff. The author found the administrative and other personnel of Nursery No. 236 in Moscow warm, sympathetic women who were completely dedicated to their work. The youngest children were handled in groups of fewer than twenty regularly by two women, but by three or four during "rush hours," so that a considerable amount of personal attention to each child was possible. The children follow an established regime of play, training, eating, and sleeping. After being delivered by the parents, they are undressed and reclothed for the day in the nursery, a process which is reversed before the children are picked up. The times of arrival and departure are geared to the rhythm of the parents' work day. For example, if the nursery is attached to a plant operating on three shifts, the children also attend in three shifts. As a rule, of course, they are brought early in the morning and picked up at the end of the working day. Some children are left in the nursery for the entire week, and it is claimed that they are in better health than those who are taken home every night because the nursery environment is healthier and there is less possibility of exposure to infection.

The author was repeatedly told that children in a nursery, whether there for the day or for the week, developed more rapidly than children raised at home; the regime is more regular and the meals better balanced. A program aimed at developing a child's faculties is followed—simple daily exercises to develop the motor abilities of the youngest and more elaborate exercises and tasks for the older children. Toilet training, learning to dress oneself, and other steps toward self-reliance are mastered early in the nursery, and a program to develop the proper social attitudes for a socialist society also begins in infancy. The youngest engage in group play in communal playpens holding four or five children. The older children are organized in small groups who play, paint, and model together. The attempt to foster a spirit of sharing and cooperation—and noncompetitiveness and conformity—appears to be successful at this age.

The reactions of Soviet citizens with whom the author spoke about nurseries varied considerably, but a certain consensus was apparent. A large number felt that the nurseries were run satisfactorily, but still preferred to

[13]See, for example, I. Padezhnov, "Bol'she domov dlia malen'kikh detei," *Doshkol'noe vospitanie*, No. 2 (Feb., 1963), 33–35.

[14]V. G. Davidovich, *Planirovka gorodov* (Moscow, 1947), pp. 184–88.

[15]"Vnimanie i zabotu doshkol'nomu vospitaniiu v derevne," *Doshkol'noe vospitanie*, No. 3 (Mar., 1963), 1.

raise their children in the home for the first few years; after that, sending children to kindergartens met with strong approval. On the whole, the older persons whom the author questioned tended to be less favorably inclined toward nurseries than the younger—often without a family—who stated that they would put their children in nurseries without hesitation. But even they had some reservations in the case of infants only two or three months old and favored delay until the child was six months or a year old. With the help of a grandmother or the addition of regular vacation time to the maternity leave, together with unpaid leave, such delay could be managed without a great loss of income.

From these discussions, the author gained the impression that the actual demand for nursery services might be substantially less than the number of children of nursery age would suggest, because of this general desire to keep the child at home during his first year. This circumstance, combined with the greater availability of nursery services in urban areas, helps explain the assurance by officials in a number of cities that accommodations in existing nurseries were sufficient to meet most of the demand. Nonetheless, in these same cities there are extensive plans to increase nursery facilities, which suggests that in fact demand is far from satisfied. In smaller towns and in rural areas the need for nursery facilities is, of course, even less adequately fulfilled.

KINDERGARTENS

The kindergarten is considered the first level in the Soviet educational system and admits children age 3 through 6. Its main function, like that of the nursery, is to free women for participation in the labor force. In most cases, the children are left at the kindergarten by the parents on their way to work and picked up at the end of the day. Some children, however, are left for the entire week, from Monday morning until Saturday afternoon. In the R.S.F.S.R. in 1957, 16 per cent of the children in kindergartens of de-

partments of public education were left overnight or for the week.[16] At Kindergarten No. 299 in Moscow, the author was told that almost a quarter of the children were left for the week. Some of those who were picked up each day spent almost their entire waking hours at the kindergarten—from twelve to fourteen hours. The remaining 63 per cent spent ten hours or less.

Prior to the Revolution there was only a handful of kindergartens in Russia, but shortly afterward the system was expanded rapidly. As Table 37 shows, the greatest increase in the number of children enrolled occurred between 1927 and 1932 when the number increased from 107,500 to 1,061,700, or almost ten times. The motives for expansion at this time were primarily economic. Forced industrialization required drawing as many women as possible into the industrial and other non-agricultural sectors of the economy, but during the remainder of the 1930's very little increase in numbers occurred.

Participation of increased numbers of women in the labor force during World War II caused some increase in kindergarten enrollment, but after the war it declined and did not surpass the 1945 level until 1954, the low level of births during and after the war being partially responsible. Since 1954 the expansion has been impressive and the enrollment of 3,789,700 in 1962 was more than three times the prewar level and almost two and a half times the 1954 level.

Kindergartens in urban areas at present account for four fifths of total enrollment. In rural areas, summer playgrounds are heavily relied upon for the care of children of kindergarten age. Rural kindergartens accommodated only 308,300 children in 1955 while summer playgrounds cared for 814,800.[17] Collective farmers, particularly, have to rely on summer playgrounds for the care of their

---

[16]Tsentral'noe statisticheskoe upravlenie RSFSR, *Kul'turnoe stroitel'stvo RSFSR* (Moscow, 1958), p. 335. Those listed as "boarders" numbered 5,400, and those listed as staying twenty-four hours numbered 62,000.

[17]See Appendix III, Table 2.

TABLE 37. Number, staff, and enrollment of urban and rural kindergartens and nursery-kindergartens, 1914–64.[a]

Year	Total			Urban			Rural		
	Number	Staff	Enroll-ment	Number	Staff	Enroll-ment	Number	Staff	Enroll-ment
1914	150	n.a.[b]	4.0	n.a.	n.a.	n.a.	n.a.	n.a.	n.a.
1927	2,155	6.1	107.5	1,932	5.8	99.1	223	0.4	8.4
1928	n.a.	n.a.	130.0	n.a.	n.a.	119.0	n.a.	n.a.	11.0
1932	19,611	52.1	1,061.7	10,979	37.9	710.2	8,632	14.1	351.5
1937	24,535	71.5	1,045.3	12,505	47.4	697.6	12,030	24.1	347.7
1940	23,999	75.2	1,171.5	14,427	55.0	905.4	9,572	20.2	266.1
1945	28,436	101.3	1,471.0	17,932	77.7	1,113.6	10,504	23.7	357.4
1946	27,662	97.5	1,283.2	17,539	74.9	973.5	10,123	22.6	309.7
1947	27,246	96.2	1,253.6	17,242	73.8	961.2	10,004	22.3	292.4
1948	26,143	89.3	1,054.7	17,046	69.8	838.5	9,097	19.5	216.2
1949	25,499	88.2	1,088.6	16,792	69.9	884.5	8,707	18.3	204.1
1950	25,624	92.6	1,168.8	17,055	74.3	958.1	8,569	18.3	210.7
1951	26,337	97.6	1,256.9	17,638	78.8	1,036.8	8,699	18.8	220.2
1952	27,140	104.6	1,352.6	18,325	85.2	1,121.1	8,815	19.4	231.5
1953	28,258	118.1	1,438.3	19,097	97.3	1,196.0	9,161	20.9	242.3
1954	29,896	131.0	1,577.4	20,016	107.5	1,305.3	9,880	23.5	272.1
1955	31,596	143.8	1,730.9	20,961	117.2	1,422.6	10,635	26.6	308.3
1956	33,800	155.9	1,882.0	22,100	126.5	1,541.4	11,700	29.4	340.6
1957	34,400	171.5	2,095.0	22,400	139.8	1,722.6	12,000	31.7	372.5
1958	36,800	191.9	2,354.1	24,300	157.4	1,946.4	12,500	34.5	407.7
1959	39,900	216.4	2,608.1	26,300	177.1	2,134.3	13,600	39.3	473.8
1960	43,600	243.4	3,100.9	28,600	198.5	2,408.3	15,000	44.9	564.8
1961	48,500	278.2	3,371.5	31,100	225.5	2,696.0	17,400	52.7	675.5
1962	52,700	311.8	3,789.7	33,800	251.8	3,003.2	18,900	60.0	786.5
1963	57,600	350.4	4,253.0	36,700	283.2	3,341.6	20,900	67.2	911.4
1964	62,314	399.7	4,737.3	39,600	322.9	3,688.1	22,700	76.8	1,049.2

[a]The figures for staff and enrollment are expressed in thousands. This table was compiled from data in Kul'turnoe stroitel'stvo SSSR (Moscow, 1956), pp. 190–91; Narodnoe khoziaistvo SSSR v 1956 godu (Moscow, 1957), p. 276; Narodnoe khoziaistvo SSSR v 1959 godu (Moscow, 1960), pp. 736–37; Narodnoe khoziaistvo SSSR v 1962 godu (Moscow, 1963), pp. 560–61; Narodnoe khoziaistvo SSSR v 1963 godu (Moscow, 1965), pp. 564–65; and Narodnoe khoziaistvo SSSR v 1964 godu (Moscow, 1965), pp. 676–77. In the years 1959–64 total enrollments and enroll-ments in urban areas have been adjusted downward by the number of nursery-aged children enrolled in nursery-kindergarten. The assumption is made, which is close to the truth, that all nursery-kindergartens are located in urban areas. The data for this adjustment, 63,000 in 1959, 142,000 in 1960, 251,000 in 1961, 383,000 in 1962, 560,000 in 1963, and 758,000 in 1964, are from the sources cited in Table 33 above.

[b]No data available.

children. In 1955 only 30,400 children were accommodated in collective-farm kindergartens, while 523,700 children of kindergarten age were cared for at collective-farm playgrounds.[18]

As in the case of nurseries, it is difficult to judge the adequacy of kindergarten facilities. It is clear, however, that for the Soviet Union as a whole only a relatively small percentage of the children of kindergarten age can be accommodated. In 1962 an estimated 19.3 million children were in the age group 3 to 7.[19] The reported enrollment of 3,790,000 children represents 20 per cent of the total. Because of the unequal distribution of facilities in urban and rural areas, it is estimated that 37 per cent of the urban but only 7 per cent of the rural children of kindergarten age can be accommodated in kindergartens.[20] These estimates are consistent with more recent figures for the R.S.F.S.R. alone, which

for each year from 1959 to 1989, prepared by the Bureau of the Census, U. S. Department of Commerce, in April, 1964.

[20]The estimate of the number of urban and rural children of kindergarten age was made by dividing the total for this age group into the proportions of urban (42.5 per cent) and rural (57.5 per cent) children of the age group 0 to 9 in the 1959 census (Itogi . . . 1959 goda: SSSR, pp. 60, 66).

[18]See Appendix III, Tables 3 and 4.

[19]The number of children age 3 through 6 is based on estimates of Soviet population by age

claim that 51 per cent of the urban and 11.5 per cent of the rural children can be accommodated.[21] If seasonal facilities are taken into account, the situation in rural areas is improved. The number of seasonal kindergartens and, most important, summer playgrounds was not known precisely in 1962, but it is possible that their total capacity was sufficient for a million or more children to be accommodated.[22] If so, they provided some form of supervision for an additional 10 per cent of the rural children of kindergarten age.

Kindergartens, like nurseries, are not distributed equally among the republics. Table 38 compares the percentage of the total population in selected republics with the percentage of the total number of places in kindergartens in these republics.[23] The comparison shows that the R.S.F.S.R. is relatively well equipped, while the Ukraine and Belorussia are poorly supplied. In Central Asia, too, however, there are differences; the Turkmen S.S.R. has relatively numerous facilities, while the Kirgiz S.S.R. remains backward, in spite of improvements. In twenty years, some of the widest extremes have been eliminated, but very little real equalization has occurred.

Not only are there substantial variations in the availability of kindergarten facilities among the republics, but the variations within the

---

[21]"K smotry doshkol'nykh uchrezhdenii sela," *Doshkol'noe vospitanie,* No. 8 (Aug., 1964), 26.

[22]In 1955 a total of 971,000 children were cared for in summer playgrounds (Appendix III, Table 4). Of these, 815,000 were in rural areas (Appendix III, Table 2), of which number 771,-000 were in playgrounds of collective farms. Of these, 524,000, or 68 per cent, were age 3 to 7. Accordingly, we may assume that some 550,000 of the 815,000 children in rural areas were of kindergarten age. By 1959 the total number of children accommodated had increased by more than 50 per cent to 1,554,000 (*Narodnoe khoziaistvo SSSR v 1959 godu,* pp. 738–39). It is not unreasonable to assume that further expansion has occurred since then, in line with the expansion of other child-care facilities.

[23]See the comment on Table 34 for the years employed in the comparison. Unfortunately, data on the population of kindergarten age are not available for the republics.

TABLE 38. Percentage of total population compared with percentage of total places in permanent kindergartens in selected republics, 1939 and 1959.[a]

Republic	1939			1959		
	Population	Places	Ratio	Population	Places	Ratio
R.S.F.S.R..........	56.8	64.2	1.1	56.3	70.3	1.2
Ukrainian S.S.R.....	21.2	14.7	0.7	20.0	12.4	0.6
Belorussian S.S.R....	4.7	3.9	0.8	3.9	2.0	0.5
Uzbek S.S.R........	3.3	2.9	0.9	3.9	3.4	0.9
Kazakh S.S.R.......	3.2	1.8	0.6	4.5	3.1	0.7
Georgian S.S.R......	1.9	3.3	1.7	1.9	1.6	0.8
Azerbaidzhan S.S.R..	1.7	3.7	2.2	1.8	1.4	0.8
Kirgiz S.S.R........	0.8	0.3	0.4	1.0	0.8	0.8
Turkmen S.S.R......	0.7	1.4	2.0	0.7	1.2	1.7
Other republics.....	5.7	3.8	0.7	6.0	3.8	0.6

[a]Calculated from data in Appendix III, Table 1, and *Itogi . . . 1959 goda: SSSR,* p. 19. The percentages of places are calculated as of the end of 1940 and 1958. The population percentages are calculated on the basis of census data for Jan. 17, 1939, and Jan. 15, 1959.

republics are also large. For example, Table 39, showing the estimated percentage of children of kindergarten age who could be accommodated in various cities and geographical regions of the Turkmen and Kirgiz republics in 1959, reveals a marked difference between urban and rural areas. The kindergarten facilities in the major urban centers of these two republics are sufficient to accommodate nearly 40 per cent of the estimated number of children of kindergarten age. Rural facilities, by contrast, are able to accommodate

TABLE 39. Estimated percentage of kindergarten-aged children for whom accommodations were available in permanent kindergartens in the Turkmen and Kirgiz republics, 1959.[a]

Locality	Children
Turkmen S.S.R..........................	13.3
City of Ashkhabad....................	37.9
Regions subordinated to the republics....	18.7
Maryiskii Oblast......................	8.0
Tashauzkii Oblast.....................	10.9
Chardzhouskii Oblast.................	45.1
Kirgiz S.S.R............................	8.6
City of Frunze........................	39.8
Regions subordinated to the republic.....	10.3
Tien Shanskii Oblast..................	4.5
Oshsk Oblast.........................	6.4

[a]For the sources of these data, see Table 35, n. On the basis of the data for the Kazakh republic, it is estimated that 41 per cent of the age group 0 to 9 in the two republics is between age 3 and 7. This may do some violence to reality, but should not alter the picture appreciably.

only 5 to 10 per cent of the relevant age group. These figures suggest that in the large cities, where the government is particularly eager to attract women into the productive labor force, the percentage of children who can be accommodated is substantially larger than the average figures for the U.S.S.R. as a whole, or for urban areas as a whole, would suggest. Moscow is a prime illustration of the concentration of child-care facilities. Taking nursery- and kindergarten-aged children together, 48 per cent of them are cared for in preschool institutions, 30 per cent in nurseries, and 60 per cent in kindergartens.[24] Plans call for increasing the percentage accommodated to 66 per cent by 1966.[25]

Largely inspired by dwindling additions to the labor force in the late 1950's and early 1960's as a result of wartime conditions and

postwar birth deficit, the government, in a decree of May, 1959, called for the reorganization and expansion of preschool child-care facilities.[26] Economic and other organizations administering kindergarten facilities were asked to expand their program and to give this effort high priority in the allocation of construction materials and equipment. At the same time, the decree called for intensified "advertising" of preschool educational institutions, which seems to indicate that, although kindergartens appear to be more acceptable to Soviet parents than nurseries, some resistance to the former remains. As in the case of nurseries, the cost and the quality of the service largely account for this reluctance.

For kindergarten care, fees are determined according to a sliding scale similar to that which applies to nurseries. However, the scale is from 50 kopeks to 4 rubles higher than the nursery scale, depending upon family income and the location and type of kindergarten. As Table 40 indicates, for a family with earnings of 120 or more rubles per month—which is typical of urban families where both the husband and wife work—the cost per month for day care would be 10 rubles per month per child if there were fewer than four children

[24]A. Kalashaikov and A. Pegov, "O rasshirenii seti detskikh doshkol'nykh uchrezhdeniakh v gor. Moskve na 1963–1965 gody, reshenie ispolnitel'nogo komiteta Moskovskogo gorodskogo Soveta deputatov trudiashchiksia ot 21 Fevralia, 1963 g., No. 915," *Biulleten' ispolnitel'nogo komiteta Moskovskogo gorodskogo Soveta deputatov trudiashchikhsia,* No. 7 (Apr., 1963), 7. Where the remaining 10 per cent of the children in child-care institutions are cared for is not indicated, possibly in children's homes.

[25]*Ibid.,* p. 8.

[26]*Pravda,* May 28, 1959.

TABLE 40. Monthly payments by parents for maintaining children in kindergartens, 1948–65.[a]

	Monthly Payments			
	Time of Child's Stay			In Sanatorium, Kindergarten, or Summer Home
Parents' Total Monthly Earnings	9–10 hr.	12–14 hr.	24 hr.	
Cities and workers' villages				
Up to 40	4.00	5.00	6.00	8.00
40–60	5.50	6.90	8.30	11.00
60–80	7.00	8.80	10.50	14.00
80–120	8.50	10.60	12.80	17.00
Over 120	10.00	12.55	15.00	20.00
Rural localities				
Up to 40	3.00	3.80	4.50	6.00
40–60	4.50	5.60	6.80	9.00
60–80	6.00	7.50	9.00	12.00
80–120	7.50	9.40	11.30	15.00
Over 120	9.00	11.30	13.50	18.00

[a]Figures are given in current rubles. For the source of this table, see Table 36, n.

in the family.[27] If the child stays for an "extended day," that is, from twelve to fourteen hours, the charge is 12.50 rubles per month, a significant expense for a family making 120 rubles per month. Here, however, as in the case of nurseries, the burden is offset to some extent by such benefits as food, clothing, and toys which are provided for the permanent use of the children.

The quality and attractiveness of the service provided by the kindergartens vary widely. In major urban centers, such as Moscow, Leningrad, Kiev, Kharkov, and other cities which the author visited, the facilities are good by Soviet standards. In Kharkov, for example, Kindergarten No. 36, located in the center of the city, was set back from the street in a courtyard among trees and shrubs. The setting was pleasant, although the building was in a state of repair typical of older Soviet buildings. The children were playing outside with an ample supply of toys, modeling clay, crayons, books, and the like. The kindergarten on a state farm, which the author also visited, was much less well equipped.

The director of the kindergarten in Kharkov stated that her experience had been that parents prefer to send their children to kindergartens not only to free the mother for participation in the labor force but also to further the child's own development. She felt that children are better fed and cared for than at home, a view which was supported in conversations with a number of young mothers, who expressed no hesitation about sending their children to a kindergarten.[28] Thus, it would appear that the government's efforts to win acceptance of kindergartens are succeeding, particularly among younger parents, and that demand for kindergarten services continues to outrun the supply.

----

[27]If there were four or more children in the family, the charges would be reduced 50 per cent, regardless of income. This and other modifications in the basic charges apply to both nurseries and kindergartens.

[28]Claims of better health and faster development may be found in E. I. Volkova, "30 let doshkol'nogo vospitaniia," *Doshkol'noe vospitanie*, No. 10 (Oct., 1947), 13.

BOARDING SCHOOLS

For several decades, dormitory and boarding facilities have been provided for school children in grades five to ten primarily in rural areas, where schools with grades above the primary level are not established unless there is a minimum enrollment of 50 to 100 pupils. In sparsely populated districts many pupils may live too far away to make a daily trip on foot.[29] Some of these children may board with relatives or friends who live nearer the school, but others will be furnished board and room during the week in some sort of communal facilities. Usually these facilities are quite primitive in rural areas and lack running water and indoor toilets. Regular boarding schools are a more recent innovation and stem from a proposal by Khrushchev which was implemented by the 1956 Party Congress. Contrary to the initial impression, the new boarding schools did not represent a radical departure from Soviet educational policy. Rather than serving the elite, as was initially understood, the boarding schools have given priority to children with an unsatisfactory home life, to underprivileged children, such as children from broken homes or children whose parents cannot provide adequate educational opportunities, and to problem children. In addition, children of parents who are both professionally employed are given preference. A boarding school visited by the author on the outskirts of Alma-Ata in the Kazakh republic may serve as an illustration of admission policy. The director reported that the parents of most of his pupils were shepherds; it was difficult for these migratory parents to provide for their children's education. A smaller number of pupils were from professional families in which both parents worked and grandparents or relatives were not available to help care for the children. To

----

[29]A 1948 regulation states that such facilities are designed for children living 3 or more kilometers from school; see M. M. Deineko (ed.), *Spravochnik direktora shkoly* (2d ed.; Moscow, 1955), pp. 172–78, cited in DeWitt, *op. cit.*, p. 100.

free parents for productive work was unquestionably a strong motive in assuring boarding care.

Fees for children in boarding schools vary, depending upon family income, as indicated in Table 41. For this fee, the children are fed, clothed, housed, and educated. At the school visited by the author the charges were quite low because of size of family and other exemptions. The parents of 18 per cent of the pupils made no contribution, and 52 per cent paid only 3 to 5 rubles per month. Another 27 per cent paid 5 to 10 rubles, and only 3 per cent paid 10 or more rubles per month. The family income figures to which these payments correspond indicate that the parents of these children do not form an elite group.[30] For those in higher income brackets the monthly charges can become a rather significant part of the family budget. For example,

[30]Members of the Comparative Education Society Field Study in 1958 found that at Boarding School No. 1 in Tashkent 40 per cent of the parents paid nothing. At School No. 13 in Moscow, 21 per cent paid nothing; see George F. Bereday *et al.* (eds.), *The Changing Soviet School* (Cambridge, Mass., 1960), p. 210. The present writer was told that 25 per cent of the pupils in Leningrad boarding schools were admitted free.

TABLE 41. Cost of attending a boarding school.[a]

Parents' Monthly Income	Monthly Charge (per student)	Percentage Reduction for Families with	
		3 Children	4 or More
To 35.........	6.00	35	50
35–40.........	8.00	35	50
40–50.........	10.00	35	50
50–60.........	12.00	35	50
60–70.........	15.00	35	50
70–80.........	18.50	35	50
80–90.........	22.50	35	50
90–100.........	27.00	30	40
100–120........	32.00	25	40
120–140........	37.00	25	40
140–160........	42.00	20	30
180–200........	53.00	10	20
200 or more....	56.00	10	20

[a]Figures in cols. 1 and 2 are expressed in current rubles. This table is based on Annex No. 1 to a decree of the Ministry of Education of the R.S.F.S.R., No. 387, Sept. 28, 1956, presented in *V pomoshch rabotnikam shkol-internatov* (Moscow, 1956), p. 10. Details on how the family income is computed are also given. Data on the 160–180 income category were not given.

a family with a combined income of 120 to 140 rubles per month, which is not unusual, would find that maintaining an only child in a boarding school would take close to 30 per cent of its monthly income. A family such as this might well hesitate before sending the child to a boarding school.

In 1954, 500,000 out of 9.2 million pupils in grades five to ten in the R.S.F.S.R. were using boarding facilities.[31] The new boarding schools are located primarily in urban areas or on the outskirts of major cities. Variations in availability exist not only between urban and rural areas, but also among the republics. In the Latvian republic, 40,000, or 14.8 per cent, of the 270,000 pupils of primary and secondary school age in 1959 were in boarding schools, while in the Kirgiz republic only about 2 per cent of the total were so enrolled.[32]

The expansion of boarding-school facilities has been achieved partly through the conversion of children's homes and orphanages into boarding schools, as well as through the conversion of regular schools in which classrooms have been replaced with dormitory facilities. New buildings specifically designed for boarding schools, such as *Internat* No. 2 in Alma-Ata, have been constructed, and extensive building programs in the environs of Moscow, Leningrad, and other cities have been reported. The actual rate of expansion in boarding-school enrollment is likely to continue to depend mainly on the progress of the construction program, for there are still waiting lines for every available space. The excess demand is being met in some areas, however. In Leningrad, for example, the author was told that in 1956, when seven boarding schools were established, there were 1,500 places and ten applicants for every available

[31]DeWitt, *op cit.,* p. 100; and Central Statistical Board of the U.S.S.R., Council of Ministers, *Cultural Progress in the U.S.S.R.* (Moscow, 1958), p. 130.

[32]DeWitt, *op. cit.,* p. 101, who cites the *Bol'shaia Sovetskaia entsiklopediia* (2d ed.), VI, 120, and *SSSR v tsifrakh v 1958 godu* (Moscow, 1959), p. 400.

space. By 1961, sixty-six boarding schools were in operation with 27,330 places. Construction had largely caught up with demand, it was said, but the plan for an additional 30,000 places by 1965 remained in force.

As yet it is too early to know how important a part boarding schools will play in freeing women for participation in the labor force. Unfortunately, very little has been published about actual progress in the boarding-school program. In recent years the enrollment figures published in Soviet sources give only the combined totals for pupils in both boarding schools and schools with a prolonged day. In 1961, 600,000 children were reported enrolled in boarding schools.[33] A year later, 9,200,000 children were expected to be enrolled in boarding schools and 1,160,000 in schools with a prolonged day.[34] By 1965 enrollment in boarding schools apparently was originally expected to approach 1.5 million children.[35] The target date since then, however, has been moved back to 1967. With regard to the ultimate aim of the government, both Khrushchev and the Minister of Higher Education, V. Yeliutin, expressed the belief that boarding-school education is desirable for all Soviet children.[36] There is no indication that this aim has been changed.

Whether the belief that boarding-school education is desirable for all children is shared by Soviet mothers is doubtful. Maurice Hindus reports:

Except for mothers of large families who are poor and live in crowded quarters, women,

whether shop workers or college graduates, do not speak well of the plan. Overwhelmingly they do not want to be separated from their sons and daughters at the age of seven, even if they come home for the weekends and holidays. "Boys and girls," a woman biologist told me, "are so young at that age. They need a mother's affection and a father's guidance all the time. No teachers, however good they may be, can take the place of fathers and mothers for them."[37]

These views were echoed in conversations the present writer had with Soviet parents in 1962 and 1965, although the younger fathers and mothers showed a more favorable attitude.

OTHER CHILD-CARE FACILITIES

Apart from their educational functions, ordinary, nonboarding schools serve admirably to care for older children during most of the working day. However, school children too young to fend for themselves after school hours, or before school if the child attends a second shift, must be supervised and cared for while the mother and father are away at work. The help of grandparents, older relatives living at home, neighbors, or some other arrangement is required in such instances. Activities organized by various youth organizations, such as the Young Pioneers, provide important help.

An indication of the kinds and numbers of extracurricular facilities available to Soviet youths in recent years is provided by Table 42. Typically, at age 10 or 11 Soviet children join afterschool clubs, or circles, as they are called, where they may develop and pursue hobbies and other interests. The circles are organized by the school or by the Pioneer organization and may be academic, technical, or artistic. Young scientists may make apparatus and carry out experiments in physics, chemistry, or biology laboratories. Other circles include map making, literature, drama, foreign languages, painting, sculpting, dancing, chess, gymnastics, athletics, and games.

---

[33]Richard McFeely, quoted by Vera and David Mace, *The Soviet Family* (New York, 1963), p. 290.

[34]A. M. Rumiantsev (ed.), *Rol' zhenshchiny v sovremennom obshchestva* (Prague, 1963), p. 152.

[35]DeWitt, *op. cit.,* p. 101. A goal of 2.5 million places in 1965 included enrollment in schools with an extended school day. In the fall of 1960 enrollment in this type of school numbered 525,000 pupils (*Pravda*, Dec. 21, 1960). Taking into account expansion in this enrollment, one must question whether planned enrollment in boarding schools could have exceeded 1.5 million.

[36]Bereday *et al., op. cit.,* p. 212.

---

[37]Maurice Hindus, *House without a Roof* (New York, 1961), p. 291.

TABLE 42. Number of extracurricular children's institutions of the Ministries of Education in the Union republics and of the Ministry of Railways.[a]

Institution	1956	1959	1960	1961	1962
Young Pioneer palaces and houses..............	2,381	2,908	3,014	3,148	3,229
Young technicians' centers..	258	320	338	348	361
Young naturalists' centers..	214	254	269	272	275
Excursion and tourist centers...................	135	146	149	147	167
Children's parks..........	135	158	170	170	174
Children's railways.......	30	33	32	33	33

[a]Figures are for the beginning of each year. This table is based on *Zhenshchiny i deti v SSSR* (Moscow, 1963), p. 149.

Circles meet after school hours and are voluntary. In theory a child may belong to no more than two. Through participation a child can discover his interests and talents and is helped in deciding his future career. The availability and quality of these facilities vary greatly, of course, the best facilities being in the major urban centers, such as Moscow, Leningrad, Kiev, etc.[38] As an example of the best type, we have this description by Deana Levin:

. . . In school 157 in Leningrad there are forty-five circles attended by about 650 children—that is just over half the total number of pupils. There is a choir of 130 voices, eight history circles, eight chemistry circles, six metal and woodwork circles and many others in physics, photography, radio, cinema, biology and artistic pursuits.[39]

Pioneer palaces and houses, young naturalists' centers, excursion and tourist stations, and children's parks have increased about 30 per cent in number since 1956, but these facilities are still unable to accommodate all the children who would like to participate and frequently have been forced to limit children to one or two afternoons a week.[40] The growth in the number of young technicians' centers has been somewhat more rapid, but

the rate of increase in extracurricular facilities does not reflect a policy of giving them top priority.

The extended school day appears to be a cheaper alternative and serious rival to boarding schools as a device for freeing women for participation in the labor force. Unlike the boarding school, which has aims and purposes beyond simply sharing women's family responsibilities, the longer school day serves to keep the children constructively occupied and supervised after regular school hours until their parents have returned from work. Two types of provisions are made: pupils may stay at school nine to twelve hours daily under the supervision of a teacher, and have their meals there; or they may participate in day groups, operating in union clubs or in apartment buildings and supervised by a teacher from a nearby school after regular school hours. In the latter case, meals are not provided. Both types of activities are financed in part by the trade unions of the enterprises where the parents are employed.[41]

In 1960 enrollment in longer school-day programs already numbered 525,000 and within two years had doubled.[42] Conversations with school administrators and parents in 1962 and 1965 indicated that this form of child care was very popular and would be expanded substantially in future years. Such further expansion can be achieved easily and economically with existing buildings and facilities and should not evoke the negative reactions from some parents which the full-scale boarding school does.

Summer vacations present another problem and require special seasonal facilities. Playgrounds, which have already been discussed, and Pioneer camps are provided in most parts of the country. The former serve mainly rural children while the latter take care of urban children either in city camps or in the country. Although the number and capacity of these camps have increased by 60 per cent

[38]See Deana Levin, *Soviet Education Today* (New York, 1959), pp. 48–58; and V. Petrova, "After-school Centre for Children," *Soviet Woman*, No. 12 (Dec., 1958), 17–19.

[39]Levin, *op. cit.*, p. 49.

[40]See Appendix III, Table 5, for data on these facilities.

[41]DeWitt, *op. cit.*, p. 102.

[42]*Pravda*, Dec. 21, 1960; Rumiantsev, *op. cit.*, p. 152.

since 1950,[43] some areas of the Soviet Union are very inadequately supplied, and altogether only about 15 per cent of the children in the age group 7 to 17 are accommodated for a month or more in the course of the summer.[44]

The inadequacy of summer child-care facilities is indicated by the higher turnover of women workers in the summer when they leave to look after their children during the holidays. The authors of a Soviet sociological study which discusses this problem urge the construction of more facilities:

Economic calculations show that we would stand to gain a lot from extra investment in building children's establishments at factories where female labor is preponderant. We would get more stable cadres at these enterprises, more skilled cadres, and consequently save on production.[45]

Similar concern for the economic impact of inadequate child-care facilities is expressed by N. Popova:

The number of kindergartens and nurseries in our country constantly increases, but the demand for them is still not fully covered. . . . Many thousands of women who have children would seek work but cannot because the administrators of enterprises suffering from a shortage of labor cannot attract them into employment because of a lack of places in kindergartens and nurseries.[46]

Popova urges that child-care institutions be increased to meet the demand so that "the mind of any mother working at a plant or organization will be at rest about her children, ensuring a high productivity of labor."[47]

LIGHTENING THE BURDEN OF HOUSEWORK

The burden of domestic duties affects a woman's contribution to the economy in two ways. First, it may deter her from entering or remaining in the labor force while her children are young. Although a childless couple is not likely to find the task of shopping, preparing food, and taking care of other necessary chores a hindrance to the wife's participating in the labor force, a woman who must care for an entire family may find housework a serious deterrent to her participation in the labor force. According to figures cited by Shishkin, a woman with a family who also has a job will be busy for three more hours a day than the full-time housewife. The woman worker-housewife typically has two hours less time for self-education, reading, entertainment, and rest and one and a half hours less sleep.[48] Second, the productivity of a woman overburdened with housework is likely to be reduced.[49]

The number of persons doing housework who conceivably might be drawn into the labor force is substantial. According to census data, some 12.8 million persons in the able-bodied age group were engaged in household work in January of 1959. Of these, 11.5 million were women, many of whom had children young enough to require considerable care. However, 4.7 million did not have children under age 14. If the household tasks were made easier, some of the 11.5 million women, particularly those without young children, could enter the labor force.[50] The extent of the housework burden and of its ad-

---

[43]See Appendix III, Tables 6 and 7.

[44]In 1962, 4.1 million children were accommodated in Pioneer camps out of an estimated 27 million children between age 7 and 17. This estimate is based on unpublished projections made by the Bureau of the Census, U. S. Department of Commerce, June, 1962, and on data in Appendix III, Table 7.

[45]Foreign Broadcast Information Service, "Sociologists Reveal Labor Turnover Factors," *Daily Report: U.S.S.R. and East Europe* (July 28, 1964), p. 10.

[46]N. Popova, "Zhenskii trud v SSSR," *Sotsialisticheskii trud,* No. 3 (Mar., 1957), 6.

[47]*Ibid.,* p. 7.

[48]*Trudovye resursy SSSR* ed. by N. I. Shishkin (Moscow, 1961), p. 146.

[49]V. D. Patrushev, *Intensivnost' truda pri sotsializme* (Moscow, 1963), pp. 198–99, cites data showing a loss of productivity due to less free time or fewer hours of sleep than normal.

[50]*Ibid.,* p. 149; and *Itogi . . . 1959 goda: SSSR,* p. 99.

verse effects will be examined here, drawing on time-use studies made in the Soviet Union in recent years.

Soviet interest in the distribution of time among various activities has been stimulated by the program of reducing the work week, initiated several years ago. This policy is aimed, in part, at increasing the participation rate of women in the labor force, particularly women with families. Its successful implementation depends not only upon the provision of adequate child-care facilities, but also upon reducing the time required for household chores. Time-use studies provide the information necessary to assess the problem, and they also help uncover untapped reserves of "free" time.[51] For example, improved pen-

---

[51] A partial list of Soviet writings on this subject includes: V. D. Patrushev, *Intensivnost' truda pri sotsializme* (Moscow, 1963), Pt. III; Nauchno-issledovatel'skii institut truda, *Voprosy truda,* No. 4 (Moscow, 1959); G. Chufarova, "O rezhimakh truda i otdykha pri dalneishem sokrashchenii rabochego vremeni," *Biulleten' nauchnoi informatsii, Trud i zarabotnaia plata,* No. 9 (1961); P. Maslov, "Vremia v bytu," *Novy Mir,* No. 10 (1960), 157–65, and "Vnerabochee vremia v usloviakh perekhoda ot sotsializma k kommunizmu, *Voprosy ekonomiki,* No. 12 (1961), 59–70; N. Klimov, *Rabochii den' v obshchestve stroiashchem kommunizm* (Moscow, 1961); S. G. Strumilin, *Problemy ekonomiki truda* (Moscow, 1957), pp. 169–359; G. A. Prudenskii, "Voprosy ucheta vnerabochego vremeni," *Voprosy ekonomiki,* No. 4 (1959), 84–90; G. A. Prudenskii (ed.), *Vnerabochee vremia trudiashchikhsia* (Novosibirsk, 1961), and *Vremia i trud* (Moscow, 1964); E. Beliaev *et al.,* "Izuchenie biudzheta vremeni trudiashchikhsia kak odin iz metodov konkretno-sotsiologicheskogo issledovaniia," *Vestnik Leningradskogo universiteta, Seriia ekonomiki, filosofii i prava,* vypusk 4, No. 23 (1961), 96–110; and G. S. Petrosian, *Vnerabochee vremia trudiashchikhsia v SSSR* (Moscow, 1965), and "O ratsional'nom ispol'zovanii vnerabochego vremeni trudiashchikhsia," *Voprosy ekonomiki,* No. 4 (1963), 32–41; V. G. Baikova *et al., Svobodnoe vremia i vsestoronnee razvitie lichnosti* (Moscow, 1965); and V. I. Boltov, *Vnerabochee vremia i uroven' zhizni trudiashchikhsia* (Novosibirsk, 1964). An excellent English source which presents and interprets much of this material is M. Yanowitch, "Soviet Patterns of Time Use and Concepts of Leisure," *Soviet Studies,* No. 1 (July, 1963), 17–37.

---

sion provisions have led to an increased number of pensioners, many of whom are physically able to work. Drawing some of these pensioners back into the labor force to perform on a part-time basis some of the functions of mothers or housewives would not only free younger women for regular work, but might also be helpful to the well-being of the pensioners themselves.

In most Soviet time-use studies the following categories have been employed:

(1) *Socially useful labor time.* This includes regular and overtime work and time spent in private household production, such as working on private garden plots.

(2) *Nonworking time connected with the job.* This includes chiefly travel time to and from work, as well as time spent in preparing and cleaning up the work place.

(3) *Time spent on household chores.* This includes shopping, the preparation of food, cleaning, sewing, laundering, and care of children. In some studies personal care is included in this category.

(4) *Time spent on physiological needs.* This includes eating and sleeping. In some studies personal care is included in this category.

(5) *Free time.* This includes time spent studying, reading, watching television, attending motion pictures or the theater, sports, hobbies, entertaining and being entertained, civic activities, educating children, and "inactive rest." Any miscellaneous activities not included in the previous categories are also included here.[52]

Our interest is focused on the third category—time spent on household chores. Of particular interest are the changes which have occurred over the years in the number of hours allocated to this activity. Equally interesting are the factors that account for changes or differences in the amount of time spent on household duties. Although our attention will

---

[52] Where there is an overlap or duplication of functions, such as taking a child to a soccer match, the time expended is assigned only to the "primary" activity.

be focused on time spent on household chores, the allocation of time to one category is inter-related with time spent in other functions. Since the time spent on household chores alone in one day is influenced by the amount of time spent in other ways, it will be necessary to examine time budgets for the entire twenty-four-hour period.

Unfortunately, lack of systematic data on time budgets and of a single generally accepted method for studying them makes precise comparison of changes over a period of time impossible. Some idea, however, of the reduction in the time spent on housework in the Soviet Union can be obtained from data presented by Petrosian.[53] He reports that working women in Moscow in 1923 spent 6 hours and 2 minutes on housework on week-days; in 1958 the figure came to 3 hours and 20 minutes. In Novosibirsk in 1959 the expenditure of time was 4 hours and 3 minutes and in Novokuznetsk 3 hours and 43 minutes. In Moscow in 1923, women spent 2 hours and 54 minutes in preparing food, while in Novosibirsk in 1959 they spent 49 minutes, in Novokuznetsk 58 minutes, and in Krasnoiarsk 1 hour and 12 minutes.

[53] Petrosian, in *Voprosy ekonomiki, op. cit.,* pp. 36–37.

A more detailed view may be obtained by comparing a recent study with Strumilin's 1922 study of 145 households in Moscow, Petrograd, and Ivanovo-Voznesensk. One of the largest, made at the beginning of 1960, covered over 5,000 men and women workers in Krasnoiarsk Krai. The findings of these two studies, presented in Tables 43 and 44, show that if the time spent on the job is kept constant by comparing the Strumilin data with the Krasnoiarsk data for an 8-hour work day, a significant though hardly dramatic reduction in time spent on household chores by working women can be observed. In 1922 the women in the sample spent 4.4 hours a day, or 18.3 per cent of their time, on household chores, while in 1960 the number of hours was reduced to 3.6 a day, or 15.2 per cent of their time. However, when the work day is reduced to 6 or 7 hours, women tend to increase the time spent on housework. For example, at the beginning of 1960 women in Krasnoiarsk Krai who worked a 7-hour day spent 4.7 hours a day on housework, and those who worked 6 hours a day spent 4.9 hours.

Women's liberation from housework is taking place partly because of a redistribution of work among other members of the family. A radical break with the old notion that men

TABLE 43. Time budgets of male and female workers in 1922 and at the beginning of 1960.[a]

	1922		At the Beginning of 1960											
	Moscow, Petrograd, Ivanovo-Voznesensk		Krasnoiarsk Krai						City of Krasnoiarsk					
			8-hr. work day		7-hr. work day		6-hr. work day		8-hr. work day		7-hr. work day		6-hr. work day	
Time Use	M	F	M	F	M	F	M	F	M	F	M	F	M	F
Socially useful labor time.............	9.4	9.1	10.6	9.9	9.5	8.9	9.1	8.3	9.8	9.3	8.5	8.4	7.7	7.7
Socialized production................	8.5	8.2	8.1	8.1	7.1	7.0	6.5	6.2	7.8	7.6	7.0	6.9	5.9	6.0
Private household production.........	0.1	0.3	1.0	0.7	0.5	0.5	0.5	0.7	0.5	0.4	–	0.3	–	0.2
Time spent on household chores........	1.4	4.4	1.4	3.6	1.9	4.7	2.0	4.9	1.6	3.8	1.9	4.8	2.5	3.6
Shopping.........................	0.2	0.6	0.3	0.7	0.4	0.7	0.5	0.8	0.4	0.7	0.6	0.7	0.4	0.7
Preparation of food.................	0.7	1.9	0.2	1.4	0.3	1.5	0.3	1.6	0.3	1.4	0.3	1.7	0.6	1.1
Cleaning.........................	0.3	0.6	0.3	0.6	0.4	0.7	0.3	0.6	0.4	0.6	0.4	0.8	0.1	0.5
Sewing, laundering, and care of shoes..	0.1	0.7	0.1	0.5	0.1	0.8	0.1	0.7	0.1	0.6	0.1	0.8	0.3	0.4
Care of children....................	0.1	0.6	0.3	0.4	0.5	0.8	0.6	1.1	0.4	0.4	0.4	0.7	0.9	0.7
Other............................	–	–	0.2	0.1	0.2	0.1	0.2	0.2	0.2	0.1	0.1	0.1	0.2	0.3
Time spent on physiological needs......	10.2	8.5	9.4	8.5	9.1	8.5	9.1	8.3	9.3	8.2	9.6	8.8	10.1	8.7
Sleep............................	8.0	6.7	7.5	6.9	7.4	6.9	7.5	7.0	7.4	6.7	7.6	7.1	8.0	7.3
Free time.........................	3.0	2.0	2.6	2.0	3.5	2.0	3.8	2.5	3.3	2.8	4.1	2.0	3.8	4.0
Total........................	24.0	24.0	24.0	24.0	24.0	24.0	24.0	24.0	24.0	24.0	24.0	24.0	24.0	24.0

[a] Figures express hours per day. This table is based on figures from Appendix III, Table 12.

TABLE 44. Percentage allocation of time of male and female workers in 1922 and at the beginning of 1960.[a]

	1922		At the Beginning of 1960											
	Moscow, Petrograd, Ivanovo-Voznesensk		Krasnoiarsk Krai						City of Krasnoiarsk					
			8-hr. work day		7-hr. work day		6-hr. work day		8-hr. work day		7-hr. work day		6-hr. work day	
Time Use	M	F	M	F	M	F	M	F	M	F	M	F	M	F
Socially useful labor time..............	39.3	37.8	44.3	41.3	39.6	37.0	37.9	34.5	40.7	38.7	35.3	35.0	32.0	31.9
Productive labor time..............	35.9	35.4	37.9	36.5	31.7	31.3	29.1	28.5	34.3	33.1	29.3	29.8	24.8	25.8
Socialized production..............	35.6	34.0	33.6	33.8	29.5	29.0	26.9	25.8	32.3	31.5	29.3	28.5	24.7	24.8
Private household production.......	0.3	1.4	4.3	2.7	2.2	2.3	2.2	2.7	2.0	1.6	–	1.3	0.1	1.0
Nonwork time connected with the job	3.4	2.4	6.4	4.8	7.9	5.7	8.8	6.0	6.4	5.6	6.0	5.2	7.2	6.1
Time spent on household chores........	5.9	18.3	5.7	15.2	8.0	19.4	8.1	20.3	6.8	15.8	7.8	19.9	10.2	15.1
Time spent on physiological needs.......	42.5	35.4	39.0	35.4	37.9	35.3	38.1	34.6	38.8	34.0	39.9	36.8	42.0	36.2
Sleep............................	33.3	27.9	31.3	28.8	30.8	28.8	31.3	29.2	30.8	27.9	32.7	29.6	33.3	30.4
Free time..........................	12.3	8.5	11.0	8.1	14.5	8.3	15.9	10.6	13.7	11.5	17.0	8.3	15.8	16.8
Total......................	100.0	100.0	100.0	100.0	100.0	100.0	100.0	100.0	100.0	100.0	100.0	100.0	100.0	100.0

[a]Based on V. D. Patrushev, *Intensivnost' truda pri sotsializme* (Moscow, 1963), pp. 218–19.

should not help in the home has occurred. In 1922 men spent only about a third as much time on household chores as women. A recent study in the town of Gorky has shown that men now spend two thirds as much time as women on housework and personal care. However, if only women with families are considered, their husbands spend only one third as much time.[54] Changes in this regard since the 1920's are also indicated by Petrosian, who states that in 1923 men spent two fifths as much time as working women on housework, while in 1959 they spent two thirds as much time. Put in different terms, this means that in 1923 a man had 120 per cent more free time than the working woman, but in 1959 he had only 30 to 40 per cent more. By 1960 the time spent by men in preparing food had been sharply reduced, but men spent more time in shopping and child care. The preparation of food is the only aspect of housework which shows a substantial increase in efficiency; shopping takes just as much time today as in 1922. Care of children is the household activity which now consumes most of the time saved in other ways. If the modern Soviet mother works an 8-hour day, she spends less time on the "care" of her children (24 minutes a day) than in 1922

(36 minutes), but if she works a 7-hour day she will spend more time (48 minutes). Thus, certain types of household activities may gain when others lose, instead of the time gained being allocated to amusement, sleep, or other activities. Only women working a 6-hour day are able to add as much as a half hour to their free time. Men working a 6-hour rather than an 8-hour day, on the other hand, have added 1 hour and 12 minutes a day to their free time.

The heavy burden which falls on working women is also dramatically reflected in the difference in the time spent for sleep. In 1922 the men in the sample averaged 1.3 hours more sleep than women. In 1960 women slept little more than in 1922, regardless of how short the work day, while men averaged a half hour less a night regardless of the length of the work day. We find, therefore, that a working woman will spend substantially more time on housework, sleep fewer hours, and have less free time than her husband.[55]

The average figures we have been examining conceal considerable differences in time-use patterns among households. A study presenting data on families in Leningrad, Tbilisi, and Pavlovo-Posad, a small town near Mos-

---

[54]V. Olshanskii, "Operatsia na konkretno-sotsiologicheskie issledovaniia (zametki sotsialoga)," *Partinaia zhizn'*, No. 15 (1963), 59–60.

[55]The pattern of time allocation revealed above is borne out by a study in Leningrad in 1961 of sixty-two workers and thirty-eight engineering-

TABLE 45. Distribution of families by hours spent on housework and in the preparation of meals and washing dishes in Leningrad, Tbilisi, and Pavlovo-Posad.[a]

Time Spent	Tbilisi	Leningrad	Pavlovo-Posad
Housework	%	%	%
To 1 hr............	15	9	–
1–3 hr............	24	15	7
3–5 hr............	36	26	18
Over 5 hr.........	25	50	75
Total........	100	100	100
Preparation of meals and washing dishes			
To 1 hr............	40	34	10
1–2 hr............	40	32	45
Over 2 hr.........	20	34	45
Total........	100	100	100

[a]Based on Nauchno-issledovatel'skii institut truda, *Voprosy truda*, No. 4 (Moscow, 1959), 226.

cow, provides some insights into these differences. Table 45 shows not only wide variations in the amount of time spent on housework and food preparation among families in a single locality, but also considerable variation among different localities. Less time is spent on housework and the perparation of food in Tbilisi than in Leningrad and Pavlovo-Posad. These differences, of course, are explained by the greater ease in shopping in a city such as Tbilisi, where locally grown foodstuffs are available in greater abundance during much of the year. The exceptionally large amount of time spent on household chores in

technical personnel and office employees. Their weekly time-expenditure patterns were as follows:

	Males hr.	%	Females hr.	%
Actual working time .	44.2	26.3	40.3	24.0
Nonworking time connected with job ...	10.6	6.3	10.2	6.1
Household chores and personal care	9.2	5.5	22.0	13.1
Eating and sleeping ..	61.3	36.5	58.6	34.9
Free time	42.7	25.4	36.8	21.9
	168.0	100.0	168.0	100.0

These figures are based on data in Yanowitch, *op. cit.,* p. 22. Because of rounding, the right column does not add up to 168 hours.

Pavlovo-Posad reflects the lack of amenities in a small town. It is not likely that many of the families have running water; therefore, the simple act of washing dishes would require hauling water and heating it. The availability of consumer durables in Pavlovo-Posad is also probably quite limited. As a result, the women of Pavlovo-Posad devoted an average of 90 hours per week to housework, compared with some 80 hours for women in other localities. The comparison shows more clearly than do Tables 43 and 44 the effects which improvements in the availability of consumers' goods and basic household equipment can have in reducing the amount of time required for household chores. It appears that in order to attract more women to or retain them in the labor force marked improvements are required in these two areas.[56]

Any significant reduction in the burden of housework for Soviet women will depend primarily upon two developments—a marked improvement in housing conditions and a more widespread provision of labor-saving consumers' goods on a private and communal basis. Up to the present time progress in both of these directions has been slow. Per capita living space in the urban areas of the Soviet Union has yet to return to the levels of 1923. In 1926, when the space per capita was approximately the same as it is today, 53.6 per cent of the urban families lived in a single room and 11.7 per cent of the urban families lived in only part of a room. The proportion of families having a separate kitchen was 23.5 per cent; 36.5 per cent used kitchens in common; 22.3 per cent had no kitchen at all; and 11.1 per cent of the families used the kitchen for living space. In Sosnovy's opinion, "It may be assumed today, with only a very slight increase over 1926 in the per capita living

[56]We can also see the effect of family size on time spent for housework, child care, and rest and sleep. As Table 46 indicates, and as is to be expected, a family with one or more dependents spends substantially more time each day on housework and child care than a married couple with grown children.

TABLE 46. Time spent by working women on housework and child care and on rest and sleep.[a]

Family Size	Leningrad				Tbilisi				Pavlovo-Posad			
	Number of Budgets	Housework & Child Care	Rest & Sleep	Sleep Alone	Number of Budgets	Housework & Child Care	Rest & Sleep	Sleep Alone	Number of Budgets	Housework & Child Care	Rest & Sleep	Sleep Alone
		hr. min.	*hr. min.*	*hr. min.*		*hr. min.*	*hr. min.*	*hr. min.*		*hr. min.*	*hr. min.*	*hr. min.*
One person or no child...	62	2 10	9 40	7 10	18	1 50	10 10	7 30	12	2 05	10 30	8 0
Family with only grown children.............	7	3 35	9 20	7 0	7	3 30	9 10	7 30	14	3 50	9 40	8 0
Family with one or more children or dependent...	58	5 10	9 30	6 35	28	4 0	8 50	7 20	22	5 45	8 10	7 20

[a]Based on Nauchno-issledovatel'skii institut truda, *Voprosy truda*, No. 4 (Moscow, 1959), p. 226.

space, many of the conditions described above still exist."[57]

Under such crowded conditions the preparation of meals is particularly difficult, a difficulty further compounded by the absence of running water for approximately two thirds of the city population. The bulk of urban families must carry their water for cooking and washing in buckets from a communal tap or pump. In rural areas, where conditions are even more primitive, a household with running water is a rare exception. Hot water is practically unavailable even in the cities, where it is estimated that less than 3 per cent of the urban population is supplied with hot water; even in Moscow only 10 per cent of all apartments have hot water.[58] This means that almost every drop of hot water in the Soviet Union must be heated in a pot on the stove, and the family laundry alone can take the equivalent of two strenuous days a week.[59] The washing of laundry has to be fitted somehow into the evenings and days off, and generally has to be done at home. Public facilities for laundry and dry-cleaning exist only in the largest cities and even there most inadequately. Although some progress has been

[57]Timothy Sosnovy, "The Soviet City," in U. S. Congress, Joint Economic Committee, *Dimensions of Soviet Economic Power* (Washington, D.C., 1962), pp. 331–32.

[58]See Table 47 and *Ekonomicheskaia gazeta* (Oct. 6, 1960), p. 3.

[59]Elena Whiteside, "For Soviet Women: A 13-Hour Day," *The New York Times Magazine* (Nov. 17, 1963), 28.

TABLE 47. Percentage of urban population provided with municipal utilities, 1927, 1939, and 1956.[a]

Type of Municipal Utility	1927	1939	1956
Electric lighting............	40.7	84.8	89.3
Running water..............	25.9	38.7	34.0
Plumbing.................	17.5	28.1	31.4
Central heating.............	n.a.[b]	11.1	22.4
Gas......................	–	n.a.	15.6
Bath.....................	n.a.	7.5	8.9
Hot water.................	–	0.7	2.2

[a]Adapted from Sosnovy, *op. cit.*, p. 337.
[b]No data available.

made in providing these services, it will be many years before they are available to the average Soviet citizen.

Because of the lack of such equipment as washing machines, vacuum cleaners, and other household appliances, almost any household chore takes a Soviet woman much longer than it does an American woman. The only major consumer durable which has been produced in quantity is sewing machines. Household refrigerators and washing machines have come into production in large numbers only in the last decade (see Table 48). Substantial further increases in the production of these consumer items have been scheduled, but many other appliances which are common in the United States—dishwashers, clothes dryers, food freezers, and smaller electrical appliances—are virtually unknown to the Soviet public.

The statistics on living space, utilities, and household durable goods paint a bleak picture for the average Soviet housewife. Her burdens do not end with work in the home itself.

TABLE 48. Production of consumer durables, selected years, 1940–64.[a]

Commodity	1940	1950	1952	1953	1955	1956	1957	1958	1959	1960	1961	1962	1963	1964
Sewing machines...........	175	502	804	993	1611	1914	2267	2686	2941	3096	3292	3341	2604	1564
Refrigerators..............	3.5	1.2	31.1	49	151	224	309	360	426	530	687	838	911	1134
Washing machines.........	–	0.3	4.3	3.5	87	195	377	464	648	896	1286	1797	2282	2861
Vacuum cleaners...........	–	6.1	22.5	46	131	175	262	245	368	501	497	626	728	765
Electric irons..............	420	508	1167	1713	5291	1759	1655	2144	3408	5006	7124	8445	8654	6905
Electric hot plates..........	726	1689	2238	3001	4584	4192	3473	4309	5358	6875	7834	8899	9126	6727
Electric tea and coffee makers	76	154	206	242	485	363	91	81	105	103	158	196	249	284

[a]Figures are expressed in thousands. This table is based on data from *Narodnoe khoziaistvo SSSR v 1958 godu* (Moscow, 1959), pp. 298–99; *Narodnoe khoziaistvo SSSR v 1961 godu* (Moscow, 1962), p. 262; *Narodnoe khoziaistvo SSSR v 1962 godu* (Moscow, 1963), p. 202; and *Narodnoe khoziaistvo SSSR v 1964 godu* (Moscow, 1965), p. 224. In the years for which data are available, actual sales of these products differ somewhat from the above figures because of exports and imports and the time lag between production and distribution. Any deviations are not large, however, so that the more complete production data give a good picture of progress over the years.

Shopping is an extremely time-consuming task, whether for clothing or for food, and the latter must be bought each day during the warm months because of the lack of refrigeration. Much time is often lost in a search among state stores or through a collective-farm market for the desired product. Although food distribution is improving, it remains one of the most backward sectors of the Soviet economy.

One method of reducing the burden of purchasing and preparing food has been to provide restaurants and other public eating facilities. The first factory kitchens were opened in the big industrial centers in 1925, and later in all the towns of the U.S.S.R. By the end of 1932 these kitchens served more than 70 per cent of the workers in the main branches of industry.[60] For families with small children, however, public eating facilities seldom offer a satisfactory alternative to preparing one's own meals. Furthermore, it is the working woman with children who is in the greatest need of relief from household responsibilities, but restaurants can offer little relief because the number of restaurants and other public facilities is small and has experienced a relatively modest growth over the past twenty-five years (see Table 49). Furthermore, the cost would be prohibitive if families used them frequently.

A new type of public catering establishment which has developed recently is the take-home service, through which prepared

dishes can be purchased and taken home for serving, and shops which sell ready-to-cook food are also increasing in popularity. At the beginning of 1962, however, there were only 1,067 of the former and 2,736 of the latter.

Sufficient commitment of resources to lighten household duties has not yet been made by the government, despite statements of sincere intent, and the result is that the Soviet worker-housewife continues to bear a heavy and disproportionate burden compared with men. Conversations with women of different ages in a variety of walks of life indicate, however, that Soviet women today feel more optimistic about their future lot. Improvements in their life, although small, are visible and are felt. Young women in particular seem to take new pride in their femininity and are finding time, at least in the major cities, to make themselves attractive in addition to coping with their other daily responsibilities.

CONCLUSIONS

The varied and extensive child-care facilities provided in the Soviet Union at the present time play an important role in freeing women with young children for participation in the labor force. As we have seen, however, the demand for the services these institutions provide continues to outrun the supply. Although the government has allocated substantial investment funds over the years to the expansion of these facilities, it has been unwilling to give this task sufficiently high priority to satisfy the demand.

According to our estimates, approximately 12 per cent of the children of nursery age and 20 per cent of the children of kindergarten age can be accommodated in permanent child-care facilities. Most of these facilities are in urban centers. Only 10 per cent of the child-care institutions in 1961—nurseries and kindergartens—were located on collective farms.[61] There, most nurseries and kinder-

---

[60]Vera Bilshai, *The Status of Women in the Soviet Union* (Moscow, 1957), p. 49.

TABLE 49. Number of public catering establishments.[a]

Facilities	1935	1940	1950	1955	1960	1961
Dining rooms and restaurants......	40.2	44.5	31.0	43.1	59.9	67.2
Tea rooms........	n.a.[b]	2.4	8.9	9.7	6.5	6.0
Lunch bars and canteens........	n.a.	40.6	55.4	65.2	80.7	82.2

[a]Figures are expressed in thousands, as of the end of each year. This table is based on data from *Socialist Construction in the U.S.S.R.* (Moscow, 1936), p. 418; and *Zhenshchiny i deti v SSSR* (Moscow, 1963), p. 75.
[b]No data available.

---

[61]I. D. Laptev, *Material'noe stimulirovanie razvitiia kolkhoznogo proizvodstva* (Moscow, 1963), p. 237.

gartens operate only during the summer months and fail to free women from much of their housework or to provide adequate training for the children. If these seasonal facilities are taken into account, however, about a quarter of all nursery- and kindergarten-aged children can be accommodated in some sort of nursery or kindergarten facility in the summer.[62]

Since only a fraction of preschool-aged children can be accommodated in child-care institutions, most working women are compelled to make their own arrangements for the care of their young children by members of the family or in other ways. From the standpoint of the working mothers' welfare, this policy has not been beneficial. However, from the standpoint of the regime's overriding goal of economic growth, reduced welfare for the working mother and a slightly lower participation of women in the labor force have apparently been deemed more desirable than the diversion of more investment funds and other resources to child-care facilities.

As a result, one must accept with reservation the assertion of the Twenty-Year Program of the party that "In the nearest future, state and public homes for children will be able to take the great majority of children of preschool age. In both town and country there will be full satisfaction of the demand for crèches and kindergartens."[63] Past experience suggests that these goals may be sacrificed to others with a higher priority and that their realization will occur in the distant rather than in the near future.

It is difficult to pass judgment on the government's strategy regarding housing, consumers' goods, and the provision of services affecting the burden of housework. To do so would require that answers be found to such questions as whether more investment in labor-saving devices for the household would have encouraged a sufficiently larger number of women to enter the labor force or increased the productivity of those already in the labor force sufficiently to more than offset the negative effect on the rate of growth which a diversion of resources to the consumer sector would have entailed. Unfortunately, the data necessary to provide the basis for an answer to this question are not available. In the final analysis, of course, the answer depends not only upon adequate data but also upon the criteria used in evaluating the planners' strategy. What may appear correct in the light of planners' preferences may not be so from the standpoint of the women involved or from the standpoint of the general welfare of society.

---

[62]*Ibid.*, p. 237. Laptev states that in the busiest period seasonal facilities can handle 25 per cent of preschool collective-farm children. This suggests a higher over-all figure than that mentioned above.

[63]*Pravda* (Oct. 18, 1961).

chapter

6

EDUCATION AND TRAINING

IN THE Soviet Union, as elsewhere, economic progress is dependent upon the development of an appropriately trained labor pool at all levels, from the unskilled farm or industrial laborers to the semiprofessional and professional workers. For women as well as for men, the level and importance of their participation in the Soviet economy will be determined in large part by the level of their educational attainments. For this reason the policies of the Soviet government toward the education of women will indicate broadly its attitude toward their place in the economy. In this chapter an attempt will be made to determine, both from official statements and from actual educational practices, the policies of the Soviet government toward the education of women. To this end, regional differences and major trends in the participation of women in primary, secondary, and higher education will be examined and interpreted.

THE TSARIST LEGACY

The Russian Tsars viewed education with mixed feelings. On the one hand, they realized that without a modern system of widespread education their country would lag behind the countries of the West in economic and military power. On the other hand, they feared education as a threat to their system. Schools, particularly universities, were regarded as incubators of heresy and revolution. Consequently, Tsarist educational policy was characterized by ambivalence and contradiction. In such an atmosphere it was not surprising that the education of women was looked upon with disfavor during the frequent periods of reaction.

The beginnings of state education for girls came under Catherine II, who, with Ivan Betskoy, wrote "A general statute for the education of the youth of both sexes," which was issued in 1764. The only concrete result of this project, however, was the establishment of two boarding schools for girls, the Smolny Institute in St. Petersburg and the Novodevichy Convent Institute in Moscow. The former was to train girls of noble origin, and the latter, girls of the lower class. By 1794, 440 girls had graduated from the former, and 410 from the latter. These were the first state institutions for the training of girls in Russia and, indeed, in Europe.[1]

Girls also began to be accepted into gymnasiums. However, after 1808 data show only "pupils" without indicating their sex. It is not certain, therefore, how many of the students were girls after that date. District schools accepted girls up to 1829, and only later did the statutes of Nicholas I forbid girls to enter district and provincial schools. Thus, under Nicholas I many of the advances initiated by Catherine II were rescinded.[2]

---

[1]Nicholas Hans, *History of Russian Educational Policy (1701–1917)* (New York, 1964), pp. 18–19.

[2]*Ibid.*, pp. 56–57.

Important developments in the education of girls and women occurred during the reign of Alexander II. Already, he felt, the "institutes" which provided for the daughters of the nobility and the official class and the schools for the daughters of priests constituted together a public provision for girls' education "which might challenge comparison with that made by any other country in Europe in the middle of the last century."[3] Nevertheless, the daughters of the growing urban middle class remained unprovided for. The Minister of Public Instruction, A. S. Nerov, recognizing the need, stated, "Russia has up to the present only had in view one half the population—namely, the males. It would be of the greatest benefit to our country to establish day girls' schools in provincial and district towns and even in large villages."[4] Accordingly, in 1858 two types of schools for girls were created: a three-year school and a six-year school. During the decade of the 1860's, 94 of the former and 37 of the latter were established in various parts of Russia by private individuals and public bodies.[5] In 1870 these schools acquired the form which continued until the Revolution. The six-year school gained a year and became a gymnasium and the three-year school became a progymnasium with a course of three years or more. Provisions were also made for state aid to supplement private support. A supplementary one-year course in pedagogy was also added to the gymnasiums for those girls who desired to become teachers.[6] At the same time, the girls' institutions were modernized and the class character modified.[7]

The enrollment of girls in all types of institutions increased in the next decades. At the primary level the enrollment of girls increased from 121,000 in 1871 to 2,700,000 in 1914.[8] Around the turn of the century one out of every four children receiving primary education was a girl.[9] In 1914, 55 per cent of the 685,611 pupils enrolled in public secondary education were girls.[10] These relatively high percentages reflected a remarkable advance over the prevailing view held so short a time before that anything beyond the rudiments of reading and writing was superfluous for the daughters of the most aristocratic families and that even these rudiments were unnecessary for peasant girls.

The development of secondary education for girls naturally gave rise to a demand for higher education for women. When the restrictions of Nicholas I on higher education for women were rescinded, the authorities of Russian universities interpreted the new policy very liberally and opened the doors of their lecture rooms to women as "auditors." This practice was brought to a halt in 1863, however, when a new university statute excluding women was adopted.[11] The goal of higher education for women continued to be pursued, however, by feminists and others recognizing the need for women belonging to the poorer gentry to acquire the means of self-support. Failing to be admitted in their own universities, many Russian women went abroad to obtain their higher education, especially to Switzerland, where the universities had recently been opened to women.[12]

In 1868 the University of St. Petersburg was petitioned by several groups to offer systematic university instruction to women. On the basis of a report by a commission of professors, the university council approved the

---

[3] Great Britain, Board of Education, *Education in Russia* (Special Reports on Educational Subjects, XXIII; London, 1909), p. 124.

[4] Quoted by Hans, *op. cit.*, p. 96.

[5] Great Britain, Board of Education, *op. cit.*, p. 124.

[6] William H. E. Johnson, *Russia's Educational Heritage* (Pittsburgh, 1950), p. 146.

[7] Hans, *op. cit.*, pp. 96–97.

[8] L. D. Filippova, "Iz istorii zhenskogo obrazovaniia v Rossii," *Voprosy istorii*, No. 2 (Feb., 1963), 211.

[9] Great Britain, Board of Education, *op. cit.*, p. 320. The percentage of girls in the villages was much lower than in the towns.

[10] Johnson, *op. cit.*, p. 196. Secondary education was available only in towns; hence the higher percentage of girls.

[11] Hans, *op. cit.*, p. 128.

[12] Great Britain, Board of Education, *op. cit.*, p. 125.

establishment of women's higher courses, although not within the university itself. Meanwhile, since existing secondary schools for girls did not provide adequate preparation for university studies, special preparatory courses were organized. The courses opened with government approval in 1870 and admitted 767 women. The lectures took place in the evening, and laboratory work was done at the university on Sundays and holy days, when the male students were absent. The subjects included Russian history and literature, general history, law, botany, zoology, geology, human anatomy and physiology, and inorganic and organic chemistry.[13]

The example of St. Petersburg was followed by other university towns. In 1872 a second institution for the higher education of women was established in Moscow. Higher medical education for women also began in this year, at the Military Medical Academy in St. Petersburg. The training of midwives had begun in 1785 under Catherine II.[14]

In 1876, in an attempt to strengthen the higher education of women, Alexander II confirmed a plan drawn up by Count Dmitry Tolstoy for the establishment in university towns of women's higher courses approximating the university courses for men. The government had special motives in issuing the decree. First, it would no longer be necessary for women desiring a higher education to study abroad, where they were exposed to radical ideas, and, second, the supply of qualified schoolteachers, who were desperately needed, could be expanded. In addition to the courses already established in St. Petersburg and Moscow, courses were established in Kazan

(1876), Kiev (1878), and Odessa (1879). By 1881 a total of 2,000 women were enrolled.[15]

During the reign of Alexander III, the education of women encountered difficulties. In 1886, apparently as a result of political activity, the admission of new students to the women's courses was prohibited, pending the drawing up of new statutes. As a result, the last group graduated in 1889, except in St. Petersburg where the courses had just acquired a new statute. This statute limited enrollment and effectively placed the courses under the control of the Ministry of Public Instruction.[16] Higher medical education also suffered. Admission to the medical courses which had been transferred after the first four years to the Nicholas Military Hospital was closed in 1882, and lectures ceased in 1886 when the last of the students graduated. Higher medical education for women was not resumed until 1897, when the Medical Institute for Women was opened in St. Petersburg as a separate institution under the Ministry of Public Instruction.[17]

In 1900 higher courses for women were founded in Moscow. This was followed by courses in Odessa (1903) and private courses in St. Petersburg (1903) in addition to the courses already established. By 1904, some 5,000 women were enrolled in the major university centers. After the political turmoil of 1905, additional courses were opened in Kiev and Kazan (1906), Kharkov (1907), Dorpat and Tiflis (1908), and Tomsk and Novocherkask (1909). By 1910 the number of women students had increased to 20,000 at twenty institutions and constituted more than a fifth of the total enrollment in higher education. Repressive measures again followed student political activity, but in 1915 women were again permitted to enter state universities.[18] By 1916 rapid gains were made and

---

[13]*Ibid.*, p. 126; Hans, *op. cit.*, p. 129; and Helen Stasova, "How Russian Women Won the Right to Higher Education," *Soviet Woman*, No. 4 (July–Aug., 1946), 49–50. It should be remembered that the first college for women in England—Girton College at Cambridge—was founded only in 1869.

[14]Hans, *op. cit.*, p. 130; E. D. Zabludovskaia, "Pervye zhenshchiny-vrachi v Rossii," *Istoriia meditsiny*, No. 10 (1964), 25–30; and I. G. Lavrova, "Russkie zhenshchiny-khirugi," *Istoriia meditsiny*, No. 12 (1956), 27–28.

[15]Hans, *op. cit.*, p. 131.

[16]*Ibid.*, p. 147; Great Britain, Board of Education, *op. cit.*, pp. 148–49.

[17]Great Britain, Board of Education, *op. cit.*, p. 149; Hans, *op. cit.*, p. 175.

[18]Hans, *op. cit.*, p. 200.

women constituted 30,000, or almost a quarter, of the 125,000 students in higher education.[19] It may be fairly said that despite the difficulties encountered, the education of women was making good progress on the eve of the Revolution and that women constituted a substantial share of total enrollments in higher education.

EARLY SOVIET EDUCATIONAL POLICIES TOWARD WOMEN

The Bolshevik leaders were passionate believers in education—in education not only as a major instrument for improving the lot of the masses, but also as an essential tool in retaining and expanding their own power. At the First Congress of Teachers in 1918, Lenin stated: "The victory of the revolution can only be consolidated by the school—the training of future generations will anchor everything won by the revolution."[20] To effect this consolidation, vast changes in educational policy and practice were introduced in the early years of the Soviet regime. Basic to the new thought was the principle of access to education regardless of sex. These views can be traced back to Engels, whose book *The Origin of the Family, Private Property and the State* is a Marxist classic which permeated the thinking of the Bolshevik leaders. Engels protested that the modern family was founded on "the open or concealed domestic slavery of the wife."[21] In his opinion, the only solution to the exploitation of wives was to take women out of the home and give them a role in the country's productive industrial life. This solution presupposed, of course, that women receive the training and education necessary to fit them for their new status. From the start, therefore, the new regime took measures to secure for Soviet women equality of opportunity in the educational institutions of the U.S.S.R.

In the first annual report of the People's Commissar of Education, Anatol V. Lunacharsky stated:

In place of school of all varieties and kinds—which formerly were sharply divided into a lower school for the plain people, and the middle school for the privileged classes and the well-to-do people, and divided further into schools for boys and those for girls, into technical and classical secondary schools, general and special school institutions—the Commissariat has introduced the Unified Workers' School, covering the entire length of the course of instruction.

. . . In principle, every child of the Russian Republic enters a school of an identical type and has the same chances as every other to complete the higher education.

. . . Our school will be in fact accessible to all.[22]

Guarantees of equal access to higher education were also provided in an act signed in 1918 by Lenin, as Chairman of the Soviet Peoples' Commissars of the R.S.F.S.R. The relevant sections read:

Every person reaching the age of 16, regardless of citizenship and sex, can be admitted as a member of the student body of any of the higher institutions of learning without submitting a diploma or testimonial papers attesting graduation from a secondary or other school.

All school institutions of the Republic, in conformity with the decree on joint instruction, dated May 27, 1918, are thrown open to all, regardless of sex. All persons responsible for violating this decree shall be tried by the Revolutionary Tribunal.[23]

---

[19]*Ibid.*, pp. 203–4.

[20]Quoted by Manya Gordon, *Workers before and after Lenin* (New York, 1941), p. 433.

[21]Frederick Engels, *The Origin of the Family, Private Property and the State, in the Light of the Researches of Lewis H. Morgan* (New York, 1942), p. 65.

[22]Quoted by Daniel B. Leary, *Education and Autocracy in Russia from the Origins to the Bolsheviki* (Buffalo, N.Y., 1919), pp. 113–14. It should be noted that "class enemies" or their sons and daughters were excluded or discriminated against in practice.

[23]Quoted by George Z. F. Bereday *et al.* (eds.), *The Changing Soviet School* (Cambridge, Mass., 1960), p. 53.

These principles were reiterated in the comprehensive statement of the aims and organization of Soviet education set forth at the Eighth Congress of the Communist Party in 1919. Since the principles expressed in the statement represented so complete a departure from those prevailing before the Revolution, they are worth quoting in full:

1. The introduction of free and compulsory general and technical education (instruction in the theory and practice of the principal branches of production) for all children of both sexes up to the ages of 17.

2. The establishment of a system of pre-school instruction: nurseries, kindergartens, homes, etc., to improve the social development of women and assist in their emancipation.

3. Full realization of the principle of a uniform industrial labor school with instruction in the native language, with co-education for children of both sexes, free from religious influences; a school where teaching is closely connected with socially useful labor and which prepares members of a communist society.

4. The supply of all pupils with food, clothes, boots, and school appliances at the cost of the state.

5. The preparation of a new staff of teachers who are imbued with the ideas of Communism.

6. Bringing the toiling masses to take an active part in educational work (the development of councils of public education, mobilization of educated people, etc.).

7. General state assistance to self-education and the intellectual development of workers and peasants (creation of a system of institutions for education outside of the schools, such as libraries, schools for adults, people's palaces and universities, courses of lectures, cinemas, studios, etc.).

8. Spreading of professional education on a large scale for persons from the age of 17, in connection with technical knowledge.

9. Making all universities accessible to all desiring to study, particularly to workmen; attracting all people able to lecture to become instructors in these universities; abolishing all artificial barriers standing in the way of young scientists reaching professorial chairs; financial support of students in order to offer the proletarians and the peasants the fullest opportunity to take advantage of the universities.

10. Opening and making accessible to the toiling masses all the art treasures which were created by the exploitation of their labor, and which were formerly at the exclusive disposal of the exploiters.

11. The development of the propaganda of communist ideas on a wide scale and for that purpose the utilization of state resources and apparatus.[24]

Nearly five decades later, many of these aims have yet to be realized. In the area of women's rights, however, the gains were immediate and tangible. Education at all levels was thrown open to women, and they responded enthusiastically by entering many institutions and fields previously closed to them. An adequate system of nurseries and kindergartens has yet to be fully provided, but at least the government went on record as recognizing the importance of these institutions for releasing women from their traditional restriction to the home and took concrete steps to expand the availability of child-care institutions.

The implementation of the Soviet educational program in the 1920's was severely hampered by the ravages of World War I and the ensuing Civil War. The loss of teaching personnel by exile and untimely death, the prostration of the economy, particularly the industrial sector, and the many uncertainties, both physical and psychological, of the postwar chaos blunted the idealism of the new leadership.

But inadequate means to implement the new educational program was only one of several causes of the difficulties which plagued Soviet education during this decade. It was a period of widespread experimentation, and many of the ideas of liberal Western educators—Dewey, Montessori, Kerchensteiner—were tried and often misapplied with damaging results. Homework and examinations were abolished, and corporal punishment was prohibited. The management of the school was

---

[24]*Ibid.*, pp. 53–55.

turned over to the "school collective," which embraced, in addition to the teachers, the school children themselves, the nonacademic employees, and representatives of the working population of the area. The authority of the teachers was nil, and formal instruction was abandoned. Schoolwork became a series of "projects" involving the observation of life and work in factory and field. Imparting the basic skills of reading, writing, and arithmetic in the first four grades was abandoned, as was the teaching of the so-called "routine" subjects—Russian, literature, history, geography, and mathematics—in the intermediate schools.[25] Thus, at the very time the schools opened their doors to women, the quality of education was in decline. As a result, women who obtained their basic or even specialized training during the 1920's often had gaps in their education which seriously limited their contribution in later years.

EDUCATIONAL POLICIES IN THE STALIN ERA

The imperatives of rapid industrialization led to a number of adjustments in Soviet economic and social policy and practice. In the realm of economic policy, for example, money incentives were strengthened and inequality in earnings blessed. In the area of social policy, the family, once considered a threat to the indoctrination of the young by the regime, was now recognized as playing an essential role in conditioning the child to accept the discipline demanded by the new industrial order. As a result, various measures designed to strengthen and stabilize the family were passed. Similarly, the educational system acquired new importance because of its vital role in the process of industrialization. Millions of young people had to be trained to take their place in industry. They needed not only basic skills but also habits of systematic learning and self-discipline necessary for participation in the industrial order. They also needed to learn the fundamentals of natural science, both for direct and immediate application in the factory and as a basis for further scientific and technical training in higher educational institutions. This new educational emphasis, based upon the needs of an industrial society, was not, however, introduced at the expense of inculcating communist attitudes in the young. Communist indoctrination continued as a conspicuous cornerstone of educational policy.

In the early 1930's a series of decrees put the new educational policy into practice. Formal class instruction was restored, together with homework, examinations, and grades. Teachers were again given full authority over their students, and discipline was tightened. The curriculum was strengthened by a renewed emphasis on fundamentals. In 1934 an entrance examination covering a student's work in secondary school was required for admission to certain higher educational institutions; two years later these requirements were made uniform for admission to all higher educational institutions.[26]

Prior to the Revolution, separation of the sexes was the general rule in secondary and higher educational institutions. Since the Revolution, Soviet schools have in principle been coeducational. The exceptions have been certain of the military service schools and a number of secondary schools in the 1940's and early 1950's. Early in World War II, experiments in separating the sexes were begun in a number of secondary schools in Moscow. After experiments in other major cities, separate education was introduced in 76 cities in the 1944–45 school year, and the following year the principle was extended to 146 cities. This separation was encouraged by the wartime need to provide boys with intensive military training. The curriculum, course content, texts, and instruction methods all remained the same for both sexes. In some schools all ten grades were segregated, in others only the intermediate and upper grades.

---

[25] Gordon, *op. cit.*, pp. 434–39.

[26] Nicholas DeWitt, *Education and Professional Employment in the U.S.S.R.* (Washington, D.C., 1961), pp. 32–33.

The proportion of students participating in separate education was never large. In 1943–44 only 7.2 per cent of the total enrollment in the R.S.F.S.R. was involved. Data are not available for intervening years, but when the experiment was abandoned some ten years later, in 1954, only about 13 per cent of the pupils were involved.[27] One might well ask why separation of the sexes on even this limited scale was not abandoned at the end of the war. There seems to be no ready explanation for the delay. DeWitt ties the timing to the wartime deficit in births; in 1954 the children born in the early 1940's were entering their teens. He explains:

The declining enrollment in the upper grades created obvious complications in regard to the utilization of both school facilities and teachers. Separate facilities for boys and girls in view of the declining enrollment led to smaller size classes, which had to be consolidated, thus leaving some schoolrooms idle as well as reducing the load upon the individual teachers. The merging of even the limited number of schools conducting separate education undoubtedly helped to eliminate some of these complications.[28]

DeWitt also observes that the higher proportion of girls attending the upper grades of Soviet secondary schools during the mid-1950's was a further obstacle to the full use

[27]*Ibid.*, p. 57.
[28]*Ibid.*, pp. 57–58.

of facilities and teachers and may have contributed to the decision to abandon separate education completely.[29]

GIRLS IN PRIMARY AND GENERAL SECONDARY EDUCATION

Before the Revolution girls made up about a third of the enrollment in primary and secondary schools. After it, the percentage edged upward, reaching about 40 per cent during the 1920's. During the 1930's female enrollment rose to 48 per cent of the total and has remained close to this level ever since. Table 50 shows that in the 1920's girls made up only a little over a third of the enrollment in rural schools, but almost half of the enrollment in urban schools. By the end of the 1930's, however, girls were almost as well represented in rural as in urban schools, reflecting a change in the attitudes of the rural population toward education for girls brought about by the modernization of the economy and the proselytizing efforts of the government and party.

[29]*Ibid.*, p. 58. Apart from military schools, such as the Suvorov and Nakhimov Academies, the only separate schools at present are some boarding schools and certain normal schools and pedagogical institutes training teachers in the Central Asian republics and the Caucasus area, where separation conforms with the traditional social custom of the native Moslem population.

TABLE 50. Percentage of girls in Soviet primary and secondary schools, 1927–61.[a]

Beginning of School Year	Total				Urban				Rural			
		Grades				Grades				Grades		
	Total	1–4	5–7	8–10	Total	1–4	5–7	8–10	Total	1–4	5–7	8–10
1927	40	39	44	–	48	47	49	–	36	37	32	–
1938	48	48	47	–	49	48	51	–	47	47	45	–
1940	48	47	49	53	50	48	52	56	47	47	47	50
1950	–	–	–	55	–	–	–	57	–	–	–	51
1955	50	48	49	55	51	48	50	58	48	48	48	52
1959	49	48	49	54	50	48	50	58	48	48	49	48
1960	49	48	49	54	50	48	50	58	48	48	48	49
1961	49	48	48	55	50	49	49	58	48	48	48	50

[a]After 1958, an eighth year was added to elementary school and an eleventh year to the secondary school curriculum. In 1964, the system reverted to the pre-1958 sequence. This table is based on data from *Kul'turnoe stroitel'stvo* (Moscow, 1940), p. 65; *Kul'turnoe stroitel'stvo* (Moscow, 1956), pp. 176–77; *Vestnik statistiki*, No. 6 (1956), 96, and No. 3 (1962), 94.

TABLE 51. Percentage of girls in Soviet secondary schools in representative republics, 1955.[a]

Republic	Total	Urban	Rural
Latvian S.S.R.	62.5	62.4	62.7
Estonian S.S.R.	61.8	61.7	62.7
Lithuanian S.S.R.	61.4	61.2	61.7
R.S.F.S.R.	59.2	60.3	57.6
U.S.S.R.	55.4	58.2	51.9
Kirgiz S.S.R.	42.8	53.0	36.1
Turkmen S.S.R.	37.7	42.0	33.7
Uzbek S.S.R.	32.6	48.0	25.7
Tadzhik S.S.R.	30.4	42.2	21.8

[a]Republics are ranked in decreasing percentages of total enrollment. For the source of this table, see Appendix IV, Table 1.

Soviet primary and general secondary education is divided into three levels: grades 1–4, constituting four-year or primary education; grades 5–7, constituting seven-year or junior secondary education, and grades 8–10 (between 1958 and 1964 grades 8–11), constituting ten-year or senior secondary education. Of particular interest is the high percentage of girls enrolled in grades eight to ten, or, since the reform of 1958, in grades eight to eleven. This anomaly is particularly marked in the urban areas, where almost three fifths of the enrollment in the upper grades has been female. In the rural areas, however, the number of boys and girls enrolled was nearly equal. The substantially higher percentage of girls in the higher grades of city schools reflects the tendency among boys to enter the labor force at an earlier age than girls.[30] In the rural areas girls as well as boys tend to leave school early.

The proportions of girls enrolled in the upper grades vary considerably from region to region in the Soviet Union. Table 51 shows the extremes. In the Baltic republics girls predominate in the upper grades, while in the Central Asian republics they make up a relatively small proportion of the enrollment. The high drop-out rate of the latter reflects the failure of the Soviet regime to liquidate "survivals of the past" in these regions. There is still a basic hostility on the part of the native Moslem population toward the education of women. Teenage girls' remaining in school interferes with the customary early marriages, and for Moslems marriage has an important economic aspect. The parents of a girl expect and receive from the bridegroom a sizable *kalym*—money, goods, or services—which is considered compensation for the expense incurred in rearing her. Women are, therefore, an economic asset to a Moslem family. Their integration into the Soviet system of education delays, if it does not prevent, the acquisition of tangible wealth by the family. As a result, few Moslem girls are permitted to remain in the upper grades, in spite of the Soviet government's efforts to eradicate reactionary traditions. Recurring references in the press to the purchase of brides in their early teens attest how deeply rooted is this custom. A recent example describes the sale of a daughter at age 5 and then again, in violation of the original agreement, at age seventeen.[31] In the Tadzhik republic in 1950, for example, Tadzhik and Uzbek girls were reported to comprise only 1 per cent of all pupils in the tenth grade although they comprised almost a third of the boys and girls of that age group.[32]

Revolutionizing the status of women in the predominantly Moslem republics can be accomplished only through the destruction of many religious beliefs and social customs. Although much progress has been made among the younger generations in the urban centers, custom and tradition still exert a powerful influence in the rural areas. Despite their great influence, the party and central government have had to move warily in their attempts to reverse the course of many centuries. In the Turkmen S.S.R., the percentage

[30]The draft should not affect the proportion of male enrollment, since most secondary schoolboys are under the induction age.

[31]*Sovetskaia Kirgiziia* (Apr. 11, 1961). For other examples, see *Sovetskaia Kirgiziia* (Oct. 11, 1960).

[32]*Kommunist Tadzhikistana* (Sept. 15, 1950). The Tadzhik republic's population includes a large number of Uzbeks, who make up the second largest nationality group in the republic.

of girls in grades one to seven increased from 32.6 per cent in 1925 to 43.8 per cent in 1938. In rural schools the increase was from 14.4 to 42.9 per cent.[33] By 1950 the over-all percentage had increased only slightly, to 47 per cent, where it still remained in 1959.[34] In these grades there was no longer a significant urban-rural difference. In the Uzbek S.S.R., another illustration, the percentage of girls rose sharply from 26.1 per cent in 1927 to 42.7 per cent in 1938, while in the rural areas the increase was from 11.5 to 41.7 per cent.[35] By 1955 the over-all percentage was approximately 46 per cent, and the urban-rural difference had largely disappeared.[36] In the higher grades the situation remains less favorable to girls, particularly in rural areas. As Table 52 shows, the percentage of Moslem and non-Moslem girls in the upper three grades has been increasing at a slow rate in the Kirgiz and Turkmen republics but not at all in the Tadzhik republic. Soviet authorities explain the decline in the latter case by an increase in the number of rural schools, where the percentage of girls is always smaller. Since Table 52 includes both non-Moslem and Moslem girls, the actual situation of native girls is not clearly shown. More indicative of the real situation are data showing that

[33]S. Gurevich and I. Gurevich, "O statisticheskikh sbornik mestnikh organov narodnokhoziaistvennogo ucheta," *Planovoe khoziaistvo,* No. 3 (1940), 118.

[34]*Zhenshchina v Turkmenskoi SSR* (Ashkhabad, 1960), p. 66.

[35]Gurevich and Gurevich, *op. cit.,* p. 118.

[36]Central Statistical Board of the U.S.S.R., Council of Ministers, *Cultural Progress in the U.S.S.R.* (Moscow, 1958), pp. 182–83, trans. of *Kul'turnoe stroitel'stvo SSSR* (Moscow, 1956).

out of every 100 Turkmen girls entering the first grade, only 15 to 20 finish the seventh grade, and of the original 100 girls only 5 to 7 complete a secondary education.[37]

From a review of the educational statistics which are available, it is evident that boys and girls in all parts of the Soviet Union have approximately equal chances of completing seven years of schooling. However, girls have a greater chance than boys of completing a secondary education—with the exception of girls in Central Asia and Transcaucasia. Boys are more likely to drop out because of economic necessity, entrance into vocational or technical schools, or, in the case of over-aged boys, military service. The high enrollment rate for girls is of great significance in view of the uniform academic curriculum, heavily weighted with science, which is required throughout the entire primary and general secondary school system. This uniform curriculum for both sexes unquestionably has a strong favorable influence upon the attitude of girls toward mathematics and science. Also, the polytechnical orientation which characterized Soviet education in the 1920's and which has been re-emphasized since the reform of 1958 serves to familiarize girls as well as boys with the practical applications of science. When girls are given no opportunity to study cooking or dress design but must take the same scientific and technical courses as boys, it is natural that many develop an interest in these subjects. Talents are nourished which might have lain perpetually dormant in another cultural and educational environment.

Upon graduation, boys and girls have es-

[37]*Turkmenskaia iskra* (Aug. 18, 1960).

TABLE 52. Percentage of girls in Soviet secondary schools in certain Central Asian republics, 1950, 1955, and 1959.[a]

Republic	Total			Urban			Rural		
	1950	1955	1959	1950	1955	1959	1950	1955	1959
Kirgiz S.S.R.	37	43	44	50	53	55	30	36	39
Turkmen S.S.R.	32	38	41	38	42	45	23	34	38
Tadzhik S.S.R.	31	30	29	37	42	40	23	22	24

[a]Based on *Zhenshchina v Kirgizskoi SSR* (Frunze, 1960), p. 70; *Zhenshchina v Turkmenskoi SSR* (Ashkhabad, 1960), p. 66; *Zhenshchina v Tadzhikskoi SSR* (Stalinabad, 1960), pp. 78–79; and *Kul'turnoe stroitel'stvo SSSR* (Moscow, 1956), pp. 176–77.

sentially the same options open to them. Science careers are not frustrated because of an earlier failure to take essential courses or the selection of a noncollege-preparatory curriculum. On the contrary, the Soviet school environment as well as the over-all social environment encourages both sexes to develop and pursue their interests in science and technology.

WOMEN STUDENTS IN SPECIALIZED SECONDARY EDUCATION

Every industrialized economy requires a large supply of specialized workers with a secondary education. In the United States many in this category receive their training on the job or through public vocational high schools or private vocational and trade schools. Since industrialization proceeded gradually in the United States, these sources of supply, supplemented by skilled immigrants, were sufficient to provide for the needs of our developing economy. In the Soviet Union, on the other hand, the decision to industrialize at a forced pace required that the state make special provisions for the training of semiprofessional workers. The system of specialized secondary educational institutions developed during the 1930's was designed to fill this need.

Since there are no real counterparts of the Soviet specialized secondary schools in the United States, concrete illustrations are necessary of the type of training offered in these schools and the kind of work for which the specialist is prepared. In the field of medicine, for example, a Soviet midwife, medical aide, or nurse receives specialized training at a secondary medical school. Soviet dentists and veterinarians are also largely trained in specialized secondary schools, while their American counterparts are trained at the college level.

In the Soviet Union women predominate in such semiprofessional occupations as laboratory technicians, accountants, and bookkeepers. Table 53 indicates the increasing importance of women in these and other fields.

In 1927, women comprised a little under two fifths of the enrollment in the specialized secondary educational institutions, and during the 1930's the proportion of women increased. A decree issued in February, 1929, required that by the fall of 1930 at least 30 per cent of the enrollees at every institution be girls. In most schools the percentage of girls was above the required level, but at some individual institutions there was a forced expansion of female enrollment, and by the outbreak of the war in 1941 women made up more than half the total. During the war the share of women in the total enrollment rose to almost 70 per cent. For a few years after the war both their number and their share of the total declined, and, while the absolute number of women is now almost twice the 1950 figure, the proportion of women in the total enrollment is now slightly less than half.

The distribution of women among broad fields of specialization has remained essentially the same since the 1920's. Women have strongly predominated in health and medicine, education, economics, including accounting, and law. The preponderance of women enrolled in medicine and health has been particularly striking—83 to 90 per cent of the total. The percentage of women enrolled in education, art, cinematography, economics, and law is also extremely high at the present time, more than three fourths of the total in these fields. In the combined field of industry, construction, transportation, and communications the proportion of women students, which was initially less than one tenth, has remained relatively low, averaging about a third of the enrollment; in agriculture the experience has been similar. However, during the war period there were as many women as men enrolled in the former field and twice as many in the latter.

Regional differences similar to those in the upper grades of the general secondary schools exist in the proportion of girls enrolled in specialized secondary schools. Table 54 shows that the proportion of women students in specialized secondary education in the Tadzhik republic (36 per cent) is lower than that in

TABLE 53. Women among day and evening students enrolled in specialized secondary educational institutions, by field, 1927–64.[a]

	Enrollment (in thousands)		Percentage of Women Enrolled					
Year[b]	Total	Women	All Fields	Indus- trial[c]	Agricul- tural	Socio- economic	Health[c]	Educa- tion[c]
1927.............	189.4	72.0	37.6	9.5	15.4	36.3	89.3	53.5
1930.............	586.8	(323.5)[d]	38.8	25.8	31.0	48.2	87.3	51.9
1932.............	723.7	(227.7)	44.7	28.5	33.5	51.9	85.6	54.1
1933.............	588.9	(258.5)	43.9	30.1	30.1	54.5	80.7	54.6
1934.............	671.5	(296.1)	44.1	29.6	31.6	54.6	79.7	55.2
1935.............	712.9	(306.5)	43.0	26.0	30.2	52.3	76.3	54.3
1936.............	768.9	(359.1)	46.7	26.8	29.3	51.1	79.9	55.9
1937.............	862.5	(445.1)	51.6	25.9	28.7	50.2	83.3	57.0
1940.............	819.5	447.8	54.6	32.0	37.0	60.0	83.0	60.0
1945.............	907.0	627.2	69.1	50.0	66.0	79.0	93.0	83.0
1950.............	1,116.9	598.2	53.6	35.0	41.0	73.0	85.0	77.0
1955.............	1,673.9	916.9	54.8	42.0	43.0	82.0	89.0	80.0
1956.............	1,660.7	(863.7)	52.0	39.0	44.0	n.a.[e]	89.0	78.0
1957.............	1,540.2	(739.1)	48.0	37.0	38.0	n.a.	86.0	79.0
1958.............	1,427.9	(672.1)	47.0	34.0	38.0	n.a.	84.0	76.0
1959.............	1,384.7	(637.0)	46.0	33.0	36.0	n.a.	83.0	77.0
1960.............	1,461.1	(686.7)	47.0	33.0	38.0	75.0	84.0	76.0
1961.............	1,634.0	784.3	48.0	33.0	38.0	74.0	85.0	77.0
1962.............	1,799.1	(883.3)	49.0	34.0	38.0	n.a.	86.0	79.0
1963.............	2,010.0	(984.9)	49.0	34.0	38.0	n.a.	87.0	80.0
1964.............	2,220.0	(1,087.8)	49.0	34.0	37.0	n.a.	87.0	80.0

[a]Excluding correspondence students. Sources for this table were as follows: for 1927, 1940, 1945, 1950, 1955, 1958–61, *Srednee spetsial'noe obrazovanie v SSSR* (Moscow, 1962), p. 92; for 1930, 1932–37, 1956–57, DeWitt, *op. cit.*, p. 613; the totals are from *Kul'turnoe stroitel'stvo* (Moscow, 1956), p. 201, and *Srednee spetsial'noe obrazovanie v SSSR* (Moscow, 1962), p. 69; all 1962 data are from *Narodnoe khoziaistvo SSSR v 1962 godu* (Moscow, 1963), p. 573; all data for 1963 are derived from *Narodnoe khoziaistvo SSSR v 1963 godu* (Moscow, 1965), pp. 566, 578; 1964 data are from *Narodnoe khoziaistvo SSSR v 1964*

godu (Moscow, 1965), pp. 678, 690.
[b]At the beginning of the academic year.
[c]The industrial field is used here to signify the related fields of industry, construction, transport, and communications. Similarly, the health field includes physical culture and sport; and education, the fields of art and cinematography.
[d]Figures in parentheses are derived from total enrollment and the percentage given for women.
[e]No data available.

TABLE 54. Specialized secondary education enrollment and the proportion of women of local nationality enrolled, Tadzhik S.S.R., 1959.[a]

		Women of All Nationalities		Women of Local Nationality		
Field	Total Enrollment[b]	Number Enrolled	Percentage of Total Enrollment	Number Enrolled[c]	Percentage of Total Enrollment	Percentage of All Women
Industrial.................	1,778	569	32	25	1	4
Agricultural.............	3,663	586	16	69	2	12
Socioeconomic[d].............	1,716	563	33	141	8	25
Health....................	2,326	1,675	72	558	24	33
Educational-cultural.........	2,089	773	37	410	20	53
Total....................	11,572	4,166	36	1,193	10	29

[a]Calculated from *Zhenshchina v Tadzhikskoi SSR* (Stalinabad, 1960), pp. 75–77.
[b]Calculated from the figures on the number and percentage of women.
[c]Tadzhiks and Uzbeks.
[d]Calculated as a residual.

TABLE 55. Total specialized secondary education enrollment and the proportion of women of local nationality in total enrollment, Turkmen S.S.R., 1959.[a]

Field	Total Enrollment[b]	Women of All Nationalities			Women of Local Nationality		
		Number Enrolled	Percentage of Total Enrollment		Number Enrolled[c]	Percentage of Total Enrollment	Percentage of All Women
Industrial..................	3,293	922	28		44	1	5
Agricultural...............	4,815	626	13		139	3	22
Socioeconomic[d]............	642	468	73		64	10	14
Health....................	2,329	1,607	69		371	16	23
Educational-cultural........	1,600	688	43		245	15	36
Total..................	12,679	4,311	34		863	7	20

[a]Calculated from *Zhenshchina v Turkmenskoi SSR* (Ashkhabad, 1960), pp. 64–65.
[b]Calculated from the figures on the number and percentage of women.
[c]Turkmen.
[d]Calculated as a residual.

the U.S.S.R. as a whole (46 per cent) and that the percentage of women students of local nationality, Tadzhiks and Uzbeks in this case, is disproportionately low. These two ethnic groups made up 76 per cent of the population of the republic in 1959, but provided only 29 per cent of the women students. A similar but even more extreme pattern is shown in Table 55 for the Turkmen S.S.R. Although Turkmen made up 61 per cent of the population, only 20 per cent of the women enrolled in specialized secondary education were of Turkmen nationality. Less complete data are available on enrollment in the Kirgiz republic, but the situation there is comparable. In the industrial, agricultural, health, and educational fields women accounted for 26, 15,

83, and 64 per cent, respectively, of the enrollment, and 40 per cent of the total enrollment (see Table 56). However, women of Kirgiz origin comprised only 9, 18, 27, and 30 per cent, respectively, of the enrollment in these fields, and 20 per cent of total enrollment, although native Kirgiz comprised 41 per cent of the total population of the republic.[38]

WOMEN STUDENTS IN HIGHER EDUCATIONAL INSTITUTIONS

As we have previously indicated, the percentage of women enrolled in higher educational institutions before the Revolution, although increasing, was limited. Since then, however, Soviet higher educational institutions have been completely coeducational, and the admission rules have affirmed the equality of the sexes and have applied in principle the same standards to women as to men (see Table 57). By 1926, the proportion of women had grown to 31 per cent.[39] This figure remained fairly stable until 1932. However, with the intensification of the industrialization drive in the late 1920's, special efforts were made to expand the enrollment of women in higher educational institutions. In February,

TABLE 56. Proportion of women enrolled in specialized secondary educational institutions, Tadzhik, Turkmen, and Kirgiz republics, 1950 and 1959.[a]

Field	Tadzhik S.S.R.		Turkmen S.S.R.		Kirgiz S.S.R.	
	1950	1959	1950	1959	1950	1959
Industrial........	28	32	26	28	18	26
Agricultural......	10	16	14	13	15	15
Health...........	60	72	42	69	87	83
Educational-cultural........	26	37	42	43	50	64
Total.........	28	36	33	34	41	40

[a]Calculated from *Zhenshchina v Tadzhikskoi SSR* (Stalinabad, 1960), pp. 75, 77; *Zhenshchina v Turkmenskoi SSR* (Ashkhabad, 1960), pp. 64–65; and *Zhenshchina v Kirgizkoi SSR* (Frunze, 1960), pp. 77–78.

[38]*Zhenshchina v Kirgizkoi SSR* (Frunze, 1960), pp. 77–78; *Itogi . . . 1959 goda: SSSR*, p. 208.
[39]DeWitt, *op. cit.*, p. 346.

TABLE 57. Women among day and evening students enrolled in higher educational institutions, by field, 1926–64.[a]

	Enrollment (in thousands)		Percentage of Women Enrolled					
Year[b]	Total	Women	All Fields	Engineering-industrial	Agricultural	Socio-economic	Medicine	Educational-cultural
1926	168.0	(51.9)[c]	30.9	7.2	16.3	16.5	52.0	48.0
1927	168.5	(48.0)	28.5	13.4	17.4	21.1	52.0	48.7
1928	176.6	(51.4)	29.1	14.3	18.4	22.4	54.0	49.0
1929	204.2	(59.6)	29.2	15.6	20.4	19.4	56.0	46.7
1930	287.9	(81.5)	28.3	15.5	25.4	24.8	58.0	44.4
1931	405.9	(125.0)	30.8	17.7	28.1	29.8	64.7	46.9
1932	504.4	(168.0)	33.3	19.8	30.6	34.9	71.4	49.3
1933	458.3	(167.3)	36.5	22.4	32.1	36.0	75.1	50.2
1934	527.3	(200.4)	38.0	23.3	31.8	39.0	71.2	48.4
1935	563.5	(222.6)	39.5	25.6	30.2	40.1	69.0	46.8
1936	542.0	(222.2)	41.0	26.6	29.3	39.7	68.8	47.4
1937	547.0	(235.8)	43.1	28.0	30.2	41.3	67.5	48.2
1940	585.0	(330.3)	58.0	40.3	46.1	63.6	74.1	66.5
1945[d]	539.2	(323.5)	77.0	60.0	79.0	77.0	90.0	84.0
1950	845.1	(448.7)	53.1	30.3	39.3	57.0	64.9	71.9
1955	1,227.9	(642.2)	52.3	35.4	39.3	67.0	69.1	72.1
1956	1,277.9	(651.7)	51.0	36.0	39.0	n.a.[e]	69.0	70.0
1957	1,320.3	(646.9)	49.0	33.0	34.0	n.a.	65.0	66.0
1958	1,332.9	(626.5)	47.0	32.0	31.0	n.a.	62.0	65.0
1959	1,341.6	(603.7)	45.0	31.0	28.0	n.a.	59.0	63.0
1960	1,400.4	(602.2)	43.0	30.0	27.0	49.0[d]	56.0	63.0
1961	1,511.0	(634.6)	42.0	28.0	26.0	n.a.	55.0	62.0
1962	1,661.0	(697.6)	42.0	28.0	25.0	n.a.	54.0	62.0
1963	1,822.0	(783.5)	43.0	29.0	25.0	n.a.	53.0	64.0
1964	2,020.0	(868.6)	43.0	29.0	25.0	n.a.	53.0	64.0

[a]The sources of this table were as follows: through 1956, except 1945, DeWitt, op. cit., p. 654; for 1956–58, Narodnoe khoziaistvo SSSR v 1959 godu (Moscow, 1960), p. 751; for 1959–61, Narodnoe khoziaistvo SSSR v 1961 godu (Moscow, 1962), p. 699; for 1945 and the socioeconomic field in 1960, Vysshee obrazovanie v SSSR (Moscow, 1961), p. 86; totals for men and women or for women alone are based on Zhenshchina v SSSR (Moscow, 1937), p. 121; Kul'turnoe stroitel'stvo (Moscow, 1956), pp. 201–2; Vysshee obrazovanie v SSSR (Moscow, 1961), p. 80; and Narodnoe khoziaistvo SSSR v 1961 godu (Moscow, 1962), p. 688. All 1962 data are from Narodnoe khoziaistvo SSSR v 1962 godu (Moscow, 1963), pp. 572–73. All 1963 data are from Narodnoe khoziaistvo SSSR v 1963 godu (Moscow, 1965), pp. 566, 578. 1964 data are from Narodnoe khoziaistvo SSSR v 1964 godu (Moscow, 1965), pp. 678, 690.

[b]At the beginning of the academic year.

[c]Figures in parentheses are derived from total enrollment and the percentage given for women.

[d]Percentages for all fields in 1945 and for the socioeconomic field in 1960 refer to the total enrollment in higher educational institutions, including correspondence students. The percentage of women by field in 1960 is identical for regular and total enrollment. In 1940, 1950, and 1955, years in which both sets of data are available, they differ (when rounded) only in the educational-cultural field. The percentage of women in total enrollment in these years is given as 66, 71, and 71 per cent, respectively, in Vysshee obrazovanie v SSSR (Moscow, 1961), p. 86. It is not likely, therefore, that the 1945 percentages and the socioeconomic percentage for 1960 are seriously inconsistent with the rest for the table.

[e]No data available.

1929, the government issued a decree reserving for women 20 per cent of admissions to higher educational institutions as of September, 1929, and 25 per cent of admissions as of September, 1930.[40] Since women already made up almost 30 per cent of the total enrollment in higher educational institutions, it was primarily in institutions in the indus-

[40]Ibid.; and E. Lishchina, "Podgotovka spetsialistov," V edinom stroiu (Moscow, 1960), p. 317.

trial field and in the agricultural and socioeconomic fields, in which enrollments were 15 and 20 per cent, respectively, that the regulation made itself felt. It took until 1935 for the enrollment of women in the engineering and industrial fields to pass the 25 per cent mark. By this time the percentage in agriculture had risen to 30 per cent, and in the socioeconomic fields to 40 per cent. The over-all percentage of women in higher education in 1935, however, was almost 40 per cent, owing to the large numbers of women in health and education. The over-all percentage of women continued to increase in the late 1930's and had reached 43 per cent by 1937. Between 1937 and 1940 there was a very sharp increase, and the proportion of women students rose to 58 per cent of the total. Even in engineering the proportion reached 40 per cent.[41] Two explanations for this phenomenon are offered by DeWitt:

First, enrollments in education and medical programs expanded greatly during this period, and women had always accounted for a major proportion of enrollment in these fields. Secondly, the military draft just prior to World War II drained off many young men eligible for higher education.[42]

By the beginning of the school year in 1945 women constituted 77 per cent of total university enrollment. DeWitt notes that Western observers reported the 1946–49 graduating classes to be composed largely of women.[43] However, by 1950 the proportion of women was well below the 1940 level, and by 1955 had declined sharply to 52 per cent, which reflected accurately the proportion of men and women in the college-age population. The decline continued, however, after this "normal" level was reached. Each year the proportion declined one or two percentage points

until the proportion reached 42 per cent in 1962.

It seems that this further decline did not simply represent the return of the ratio of male and female students applying for admission to a more normal relationship. The data presented in Table 58 indicate that at Moscow State University, the largest in the Soviet Union, the proportion of women admitted to the science faculties in 1964 was considerably smaller than the proportion who applied. Somewhere between the application stage and final admission a larger proportion of women than of men was eliminated. In view of the excellent performance of girls in secondary school in all subjects, including mathematics and the sciences, it is unlikely that their scores on entrance examinations were lower than those of boys. The causes for the high attrition rate would seem to lie elsewhere.

Several explanations for the reduction in the proportion of women admitted may be suggested, though they are difficult to substantiate. There is the possibility that a quota system or other preferential treatment for men has been instituted in order to reduce the percentage of women in some fields. For example, the writer was told by a medical official that once the cut-off score on the entrance examination had been determined, all men with this score were accepted before the remaining vacancies were filled by women. In addition, students of two medical institutes stated that men were admitted who had re-

---

[41]DeWitt, op. cit., p. 346.
[42]Ibid.
[43]Ibid., pp. 346–47.

TABLE 58. Number and percentage of women applying for admission and the ratios of male and female applicants admitted to the science faculties of Moscow State University, fall of 1964.[a]

Science Faculties	Applicants			Acceptances			Applicants per Acceptance	
	Total	Women	Women %	Total	Women	Women %	Men	Women
Mechanics-mathematics...	3,045	1,302	43	480	122	25	4.9	10.7
Physics	3,469	1,013	29	480	116	24	6.7	8.7
Chemistry	1,917	1,335	70	301	160	53	4.1	8.3
Biology	1,902	1,293	68	282	149	53	4.6	8.7
Geography	865	394	45	173	60	35	4.2	6.6
Geology	877	310	35	166	44	27	4.6	7.0
Total	12,075	5,647	47	1,882	651	35	5.2	8.7

[a]Based on data supplied by the university.

ceived entrance examination scores one point —out of twenty—below the cut-off point applied to women applicants. Undoubtedly the changes in the admission regulations for higher education which followed the school reforms in 1958 had an effect on the proportion of women enrolled in higher educational institutions.[44] Prior to the fall of 1955, graduates of secondary schools who received gold or silver medals and the top 5 per cent of the graduates of specialized secondary schools were admitted without entrance examinations. This group of preferred applicants was limited, however, to 40 per cent of the planned admissions, the remaining places being filled on the basis of examination scores. A new element was introduced in the fall of 1955. Veterans and persons with two or more years of employment experience were given priority, "all other competitive conditions being equal."

In 1956 and 1957 silver medalists and honors graduates of specialized secondary schools were required at a number of institutions to take an examination in their most important subject. In 1958 persons with gold and silver medals and honors graduates of specialized secondary schools were admitted "on the same basis as everybody else," first priority in admission being given to veterans of World War II and second priority to ordinary veterans and persons with two or more years of employment experience. The proportion of applicants in these two categories was not to exceed 80 per cent of planned admissions. The remaining 20 per cent were to be admitted on the basis of the general entrance competition; however, persons with gold or silver medals and honors graduates were to be given preference, "all other competitive conditions being equal."

In 1959 preference was given, first, to veterans of World War II who received gold or silver medals or were honors graduates. After these admissions, preference was given: (1) to persons who had shown themselves to be outstanding workers during two or more years of employment, and (2) to veterans of World War II and persons discharged from service in the army and navy who had the highest scores on the entrance examinations. As in 1958, at least 20 per cent of planned admissions were to be reserved for general competition. In this category gold and silver medalists and honors graduates of specialized secondary schools were to be given preference, "all other competitive conditions being equal."

The most distinctive new element introduced in 1959 was the restriction of applicants for the fields of journalism, law, literature, philosophy, and economics to persons with two or more years of employment experience. Also, the fields of international relations, pedagogy, medicine, stomatology, and pharmacy were to be filled primarily by persons who had had two or more years of work experience. Graduates of specialized secondary schools were accepted only if they had completed three years of practical work or had two years of military service (except for the top 5 per cent of the graduating class, provided they planned to continue their training in the field of their specialization). Thus, in line with the educational reforms of 1958, work experience began to become an essential precondition for admission to higher education.

In 1960 a new element was added to the admission regulations. First priority was given to persons with two or more years of employment experience who were assigned to study in higher educational institutions by industrial and construction enterprises and state and collective farms, provided the applicant passed the entrance examination. It is reported that such students made up almost 20 per cent of all those admitted to higher educational institutions in the Ukraine in 1960.[45] Next in the sequence of admission were applicants who had outstanding work records and two or

[44]The following discussion is based on the yearly handbooks for students entering higher educational institutions which give the rules for admission; it is also based on DeWitt, *op. cit.*, pp. 248–58.

[45]"Gotovit'sia k priemu uzhe sevodnia," *Vestnik vysshei shkoly*, No. 1 (Jan., 1961), 3.

more years of employment experience and persons discharged from service in the military. The same fields as in 1959 gave preference to or were open only to persons with two or more years of employment experience. Furthermore, in certain unspecified fields of work where the employment of women was considered hazardous, women were not permitted to apply.[46] Mining, metallurgy, and certain branches of the chemical industry were mentioned specifically in the 1961 rules.

In 1961 priority in admission was given to persons with two or more years of employment experience and also to persons discharged from military service after serving not less than two years, including time spent studying in military schools (other than the Nachimov and Suvorov schools for cadets). The other provisions remained essentially the same as in 1960 except that special preference was no longer given to persons sent by enterprises or farms, and no mention of World War II veterans was made. No important changes were made in the 1962 or 1963 regulations.

In 1964, however, there was a reversion to the more detailed elaboration of priorities and preferences characteristic of some earlier years. The requirement for admission as a regular, full-time student with two years of work experience or equivalent military service has been reiterated. Graduates of specialized secondary educational institutions are required to have worked at least three years or to have been in the top 5 per cent of their class. Similarly, graduates of technical schools must have three years of work experience. Four years of experience are required of persons having a secondary education and trained in industrial reserve or factory schools. Women continue to be excluded from certain fields considered unhealthful.

No entrance examinations are required for veterans of World War II who are gold and silver medal winners or honors graduates from general secondary schools or specialized secondary schools. Also, persons discharged

from military service who have completed higher military training or who have begun higher civilian or military training are not required to take an entrance examination for admission as regular day students within a three-year period of their discharge.

Priority for admission is given to the following categories of applicants, who need only pass the entrance examination with a satisfactory grade for admission as regular day students: (1) veterans of World War II; (2) outstanding workers sponsored by industrial, agricultural, and other organizations; and (3) officers and persons of other ranks who have served extra tours of duty in the military services or the K.G.B. (secret police) who were discharged for reasons of health, age, or reduction in force, and who have a secondary education.

After the above preferences are taken into account in the admission of students, those applicants successfully passing the entrance examination are to be admitted in the following order: (1) persons with outstanding work records who have worked not less than two years and persons discharged from military service who have served not less than two years; and (2) persons who have worked not less than two years in agriculture who are applying for enrollment in agricultural institutes or in agricultural and biological specialties in other higher educational institutions. For applicants with less than two years of practical work experience, 20 per cent of the planned number of admissions is to be reserved. The selection of these applicants is made on a competitive basis.

These changes in admissions regulations reflect a downgrading in the past decade of the importance of purely intellectual achievement as a criterion for admission to higher education and an increase in the importance of employment experience or military service. The effect of these changes has not, of course, been neutral with respect to men and women. The preference given veterans and persons discharged from military service has clearly worked to the advantage of males. Also, the insistence upon employment experience would

---

[46]*Izvestiia* (Apr. 6, 1960).

appear to have had a more restrictive effect upon the admission of women. During the two-year work period, women would seem more likely than men to be deflected from continuing their further education by marriage and family commitments.

The author found a number of university and institute administrators unhappy about the change in emphasis. Competition among students lacking work experience who were seeking to be included among the 20 per cent admitted directly from secondary school was very intense, and many excellent students had to be turned down. Conversely, there was much less competition among students who had two or more years of work experience, and many of these were admitted who were not as well qualified academically as those admitted among the restricted group. It is not surprising, therefore, that a major reversal in policy occurred in 1965 following the replacement of Khrushchev. Although the 1965 admissions regulations superficially appear to continue to favor applicants who have had work experience or military service, the 20 per cent limitation on the proportion of students who may be admitted directly from secondary school or before completing the work requirement has been lifted.[47] At present, the proportion of students admitted without adequate work experience may correspond to the proportion of all applicants who lack work experience. In other words, if half the applicants for admission to an institution apply directly from secondary school, half the students admitted may come from among this group. It will be interesting to see whether the percentage of women enrolled in higher education, which appears to have been stabilized at about 43 per cent in recent years, will now increase.

An economic rationale can be found in the recent reduction in the percentage of women enrolled in higher education. The theoretical framework employed is the same as that discussed in Chapter 3 in connection with the optimal proportion of women in the labor force. The analysis presented there was essentially static, but with modifications this method can contribute to an understanding of Soviet policies concerning upgrading the quality of the female labor force in recent decades. As we have indicated earlier, at the time of the Revolution women were one of Russia's least developed resources. Although the potential of older, rural women still remains largely unrealized, the younger generation of women has received substantially more education and training than their predecessors, and their productivity has accordingly been sharply increased. The result can be visualized as a raising of the left end of the productivity curve for women,[48] with the result that women become increasingly more competitive with men and able to replace them in the more productive occupations as their educational level rises.

In planning the supply of specialists, such as chemists, the task of planners is complicated by the long lead time required and the high costs of training either an oversupply or an undersupply of chemists. The former would represent a wasteful investment in human capital, and the latter would constitute a bottleneck to economic development, as indeed it recently has. In addition to the question of the quantity of specialists who should be trained, there is the question which interests us most—what is the optimal proportion of males and females who should receive a particular type of training? Taking higher education as an illustration and sidestepping the important question of the total number of persons who should receive a higher education, the proportion of males and females should be determined on the basis of expected productivity. If the scholarly potential of men and women is assumed to be equal, the expected productivity of females will nevertheless be lower on the average than that of males for a variety of reasons, including lost

---

[47]Ministerstvo vysshego i srednogo spetsial'no obrazovaniia SSSR, *Spravochnik dlia postupaiushchikh v vysshie uchebnye zavedeniia SSSR v 1965 g.* (Moscow, 1965), pp. 3–10, and *Pravda*, March 20, translated in *The Current Digest of the Soviet Press*, XVII, No. 10, (Mar. 31, 1965), 9–13.

[48]See pp. 48–50.

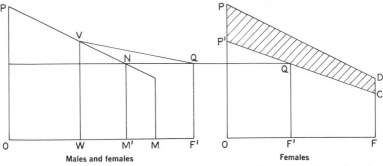

Fig. 17. Optimal proportion of male and female enrollment in higher education.

work time, a shorter working life, family distractions, and so forth. Therefore, expected productivity is lower by the amount of the shaded area $PP'CD$ in Figure 17. According to this figure, males should be admitted to higher educational institutions up to the number OW before any women are admitted. From this point, men and women should be admitted on the basis of their net productivity until all the places are filled. At the cut-off point, OF', the expected productivity of the last male $(M'N)$ and the last female $(F'Q)$ admitted should be equal. Although the intellectual capacity of the last female will be higher than that of the last male, expected returns should be equal. The proportion of males and females admitted can be read from the diagram, males being represented by the quantity OM' and females by the quantity $M'F$ or OF'. It can be seen that the greater the productivity loss of females—whatever the cause may be—the higher the proportion of males who should be admitted. In order to enroll the optimal proportion of males and females, admission standards for females should be set higher than those for males. What may appear to be discrimination, therefore, is good economics. Nor is it difficult to see that the larger the number of females in relation to males capable of acquiring a higher education, the larger the proportion of females who should be admitted. The high proportion of females enrolled in higher education in the decade following the war put this logic into effect. Also, as should be expected from our analysis, with the restoration of a balance of the sexes in the college age group, the proportion of females in higher education has declined. Although Soviet educational

planners may not think along precisely the lines just presented, their actions suggest that they are motivated by the same basic considerations and have arrived at similar conclusions, which have not, however, been publicly expressed.

Considerable changes in the proportion of women have occurred in the broad areas of study for which enrollment data have been published. Examination of Table 57 shows that since the 1920's health and education have been the fields of study in which women have been most numerous. As early as 1926, women comprised more than half the enrollment in these areas. In the agricultural and the socioeconomic disciplines, however, women made up only 16 per cent of the enrollment, and in engineering, a meager 7 per cent. Apart from a doubling of the percentage of women in engineering and smaller increases in the agricultural and socioeconomic fields, the situation changed little during the 1920's. However, as the industrialization drive gained momentum in the early 1930's, some very significant shifts occurred. We have already noted that the over-all percentage of women in higher education increased substantially during the 1930's. Although this increase came in all areas, the most spectacular increases occurred in the engineering and socioeconomic fields. In the latter, the proportion of women rose from 25 per cent in 1930 to 41 per cent in 1937. In engineering, the increase was from 15 to 28 per cent. During the war the enrollment of women in all fields increased still further and reached the highest level achieved so far.

In the postwar period, as we noted above, the proportion of women in total enrollment has gradually subsided toward the prewar level, and in connection with this decline the pattern of enrollment by fields exhibits some change. Women still predominate strongly in health and education, but in the health field their relative importance has declined noticeably, dropping from 69 per cent in 1955 to 54 per cent in 1962. The decline over the same period in the educational-cultural field has been from 72 to 62 per cent, in the agricultural field from 39 to 25 per cent, and in engineering from 35 to 28 per cent. Whether these downward trends will continue cannot be determined, since the reason for the change in pattern is not yet fully understood. In view of the recent changes in admissions requirements, however, it would seem likely that the percentage of women in total enrollment will stabilize or even increase slightly.

REGIONAL DIFFERENCES

To what extent is higher education equally available to all intellectually qualified young women in all parts of the Soviet Union? An examination of the statistics showing the proportion of women enrolled in higher education by republic and by nationality group reveals some wide discrepancies. In most of the non-Russian republics and autonomous national republics, with the exception of the Baltic area, the proportion of women enrolled in higher educational institutions is lower than the national average. For example, in 1960 women made up only 30 and 34 per cent, respectively, of the enrollment in the Tadzhik

and the Azerbaidzhan republics, while the national average was 43 per cent.[49]

A closer look at the situation is afforded by detailed statistics of 1959 for the Tadzhik republic, the most backward in regard to the enrollment of women. Table 59 reveals that the proportion of women students in higher education in this republic was 30 per cent, or well below the average for the U.S.S.R. in that year (45 per cent). Of the 5,667 women enrolled, those of local nationality comprised only 1,630, a third, although Tadzhiks and Uzbeks comprised three fourths of the total population. Table 60 gives similar data for the Turkmen republic, where the proportion of women enrolled is substantially below the national average, and the share of women of local nationality is disproportionately small. Instead of the three fifths of enrollments which would correspond to their proportion of the population, they account for less than a third. Again, agriculture was the least popular field for all women and particularly for women of local nationality. Both tables show that the educational-cultural field, usually very popular among women, who make up 63 per cent of the enrollment on the All-Union level, apparently has no such appeal in the Tadzhik and Turkmen republics. Here men are still a majority in the teacher-training programs, where most of the enrollment in the educational-cultural field is to be found.

Further insights are provided when we shift our focus from the differences among repub-

---

[49]See Appendix IV, Table 3.

Table 59. Higher educational enrollment and the proportion of women of local nationality enrolled, Tadzhik S.S.R., 1959.[a]

Field	Total Enrollment	Women of All Nationalities		Women of Local Nationality		
		Number Enrolled	Percentage of Total Enrollment	Number Enrolled[b]	Percentage of Total Enrollment	Percentage of All Women
Engineering..................	820	181	22	81	10	45
Agricultural.................	2,620	366	14	44	2	12
Medicine....................	1,640	950	58	219	13	23
Educational-cultural..........	13,800	4,171	30	1,286	9	31
Total....................	18,900	5,667	30	1,630	9	29

[a]Calculated from *Zhenshchina v Tadzhikskoi SSR* (Stalinabad, 1960), pp. 74–77.
[b]Tadzhiks and Uzbeks. These nationality groups make up 76 per cent of the population.

lics to differences among nationality groups. As the previous two tables have shown, the combination of native and non-native nationalities in the statistics of the Central Asian republics tends to obscure the much more limited participation of women of local nationalities in higher education in these areas. The highest percentage of women enrolled in higher education is among the Baltic nationalities.[50] Women made up 48 per cent of the enrollment of Latvians and Estonians and 47 per cent of the Lithuanians in higher educational institutions in 1960. These high percentages reflect the more advanced social and cultural conditions in the Baltic area. The Russians followed with 46 per cent, and the Georgians were close behind with 45 per cent. The high percentage among the latter is in accord with their long cultural traditions, the strong desire for higher education which these traditions have reinforced, and the relatively important and independent position of women in their culture. These are the only nationality groups which have a percentage of women in higher education above the national average of 43 per cent. In striking contrast are the Moslem nationality groups in Central Asia. Of all the Uzbeks enrolled in higher education only 25 per cent were women; of the Turkmen, 21 per cent; and of the Tadzhiks, 16 per cent.

Table 61 combines our two approaches and shows the percentage of women enrolled in

[50]See Appendix IV, Tables 2 and 3.

higher educational institutions in 1960 by republic and by nationality for a selected group of republics and nationalities. A number of interesting points emerge from this table. The higher percentage of Slavic women—Russians, Ukrainians, and Belorussians—enrolled in higher education persists regardless of the republic considered. In fact, the percentage of Russian and Ukrainian women rises to well over 50 per cent in the more backward republics, suggesting that a considerable number of male students of these nationalities seek their education at institutions in European Russia where they feel the instruction and facilities are superior. However, the effect of this migration is probably in part canceled by male students from European Russia who may fear the more intense competition for admission there and apply to higher educational institutions in the hinterland.

Another pattern is observable in Table 61. With the exception of the Slavic nationalities, the percentage of girls is usually higher for a nationality group in its own republic than elsewhere. Starting with the Georgian and Georgian S.S.R. cell (47.3 per cent), the figures along the diagonal tend to be higher than the numbers in the other cells. It is particularly interesting to compare the figures along the diagonal with the corresponding figure for the R.S.F.S.R. In every republic except the Tadzhik the percentage of women of a given nationality enrolled in higher education is significantly above the percentage for that group in the R.S.F.S.R. Outside their own republics these nationality groups are

TABLE 60. Higher educational enrollment and the proportion of women of local nationality enrolled, Turkmen S.S.R., 1959.[a]

Field	Total Enrollment	Women of All Nationalities			Women of Local Nationality		
		Number Enrolled	Percentage of Total Enrollment		Number Enrolled[b]	Percentage of Total Enrollment	Percentage of All Women
Engineering.................	–	–	–		–	–	–
Agricultural.................	2,916	554	19		89	3	16
Medicine...................	1,997	1,238	62		457	23	37
Educational-cultural	7,908	3,005	38		1,039	13	35
Total...................	12,624	4,797	38		1,585	13	33

[a]Calculated from *Zhenshchina v Turkmenskoi SSR* (Ashkhabad, 1960), pp. 64–65.

[b]Turkmen. This nationality group makes up 61 per cent of the population.

TABLE 61. Percentage of women of total enrollment in higher educational institutions, by republic and nationality, 1960.[a]

Nationality	Republic							
	R.S.F.S.R.	Georgian	Azer-baidzhan	Uzbek	Kazakh	Kirgiz	Tadzhik	Turkmen
All nationalities.........	44.7	46.8	33.7	35.8	45.8	42.0	29.5	36.7
Russian.................	46.3	43.8	50.1	54.2	56.0	54.7	63.4	58.4
Ukrainian...............	36.2	46.4	44.4	45.7	48.0	51.9	54.6	49.3
Belorussian.............	33.5	20.4[b]	40.9[b]	43.8	33.9	56.8[b]	37.2	48.1[b]
Georgian...............	28.1	47.3	42.2	53.1	25.0[b]	41.7	50.0[b]	28.4[b]
Azerbaidzhan...........	19.9	22.8	28.1	28.7	13.2[b]	14.3	20.0[b]	50.0
Uzbek..................	21.0	–	–	25.5	27.1	32.6	14.2	24.9
Kazakh.................	18.7	–	–	17.2	35.7	33.5	14.1	20.0
Kirgiz.................	19.4	–	–	26.1	5.1[b]	30.7	22.5[b]	–
Tadzhik.................	19.2	–	35.0[b]	23.0	–	27.3[b]	14.3	–
Turkmen...............	15.0	–	16.5	11.7	–	–	10.0[b]	22.6

[a]From *Vysshee obrazovanie v SSSR* (Moscow, 1961), pp. 128–57.

[b]Fewer than 100 women enrolled. A dash indicates 10 or fewer women enrolled.

TABLE 62. Nationality groups as percentage of total population of selected republics in 1959 compared with the share of women of a given nationality in the total enrollment of women in higher education in 1960.[a]

Nationality	Uzbek S.S.R.		Kirgiz S.S.R.		Tadzhik S.S.R.		Turkmen S.S.R.		Kazakh S.S.R.	
	a	b	a	b	a	b	a	b	a	b
Russian.................	13.5	39.3	30.2	47.5	13.3	50.4	17.3	47.3	42.7	53.9
Ukrainian...............	1.1	3.2	6.6	6.4	1.4	4.7	1.4	2.8	8.2	5.3
Belorussian.............	0.1	0.5	0.2	0.3	*	0.3	*	0.3	1.2	0.4
Slavs..................	14.7	43.0	37.0	54.2	14.7	55.2	18.7	50.2	52.1	59.6
Uzbek..................	62.2	33.6	10.6	1.4	23.0	8.3	8.3	1.8	1.5	0.2
Kirgiz.................	1.1	0.5	40.5	34.4	1.3	–	–	–	–	–
Tadzhik.................	3.8	1.2	0.7	–	53.1	23.1	–	–	–	–
Turkmen...............	0.7	0.3	–	–	0.4	–	60.9	34.2	–	–
Kazakh.................	4.1	2.4	1.0	1.1	0.6	–	4.6	0.8	30.0	31.7
Moslems..............	71.9	38.0	52.8	36.9	78.4	31.4	73.8	36.8	31.5	31.9

[a]a, percentage of total population; b, percentage of women students; asterisk indicates negligible percentage. This table is based on *Vysshee obrazovanie v SSSR* (Moscow, 1961), Table 29, pp. 128–57, and *Itogi . . . 1959 goda: SSSR*, pp. 206–8.

less likely to be incorporated in the processes of modernization which have brought more women to higher educational institutions.

The more advantageous position of women of Slavic nationality—Russian, Ukrainian, and Belorussian—in the more backward Central Asian republics and Kazakhstan is reflected in Table 62, which compares the percentages of the Slavic and various local nationality groups in the total population of a republic with the percentages of women of these nationality groups in the total enrollment of women in higher education in the

republic in 1960. For example, in the Uzbek S.S.R., Russians comprised 13.5 per cent of the population in 1959, but Russian women made up 39.3 per cent of the enrollment of women in higher education in 1960. Uzbeks, on the other hand, made up 62.2 per cent of the population, but Uzbek women, only 33.6 per cent of the women enrolled in higher education. The most extreme case is that of the Tadzhik S.S.R., where the Slavic nationalities comprised only 14.7 per cent of the population, but 55.2 per cent of the women enrolled in higher education, and Uzbek and

Tadzhik women only 31.4 per cent of the women enrolled in higher education, although Uzbeks and Tadzhiks made up 76.1 per cent of the population. The Kazakh republic, which is not a part of Central Asia and which has been much more thoroughly Russianized than the Central Asian republics, presents quite a different picture. The representation of Kazakh women in higher educational enrollment is almost exactly proportional to the share of Kazakhs in the population of the republic.

It is clear from our previous discussion that equality of the sexes in higher education is far from being a reality in Central Asia. But how much progress has been made? Although the gains since the 1920's have unquestionably been great, progress in the past decade has been rather halting, as Table 63

TABLE 63. Percentage of women enrolled in higher educational institutions, by field, 1950 and 1959, in the Tadzhik, Kirgiz, and Turkmen republics.[a]

Field	Tadzhik S.S.R.		Kirgiz S.S.R.		Turkmen S.S.R.	
	1950	1959	1950	1959	1950	1959
Engineering......	–	22	–	19	–	–
Agricultural......	19	14	22	16	23	19
Health..........	58	58	50	45	49	62
Educational-cultural........	33	30	39	53	25	38
Total..........	36	30	38	42	29	38

[a]Based on *Zhenshchina v Tadzhikskoi SSR* (Stalinabad, 1960), pp. 74–77; *Zhenshchina v Kirgizkoi SSR* (Frunze, 1960), pp. 77–78; and *Zhenshchina v Turkmenskoi SSR* (Ashkabad, 1960), pp. 64–65.

indicates. In fact, in the Tadzhik S.S.R. the proportion of women enrolled in higher education has declined, and in the Kirgiz S.S.R. the improvement has been only nominal. Only in the Turkmen S.S.R. has improvement been significant.[51]

The lag in higher education for women in the Central Asian and some of the other non-Russian republics is not due to any "imperialist" policies on the part of the Soviet govern-

---

[51]Comparable data are not available for the Uzbek S.S.R.

ment. Quite the contrary. Sincere efforts are being made to alter or stamp out obstructive traditions, the so-called "survivals of a feudal-bey attitude" toward women. Conversations with Uzbek school officials and teachers in Tashkent, Samarkand, and Bukhara convinced the author that they are now as anxious as the central government to give Uzbek women an equal opportunity for education at all levels. This progressive spirit was much in evidence at the Bukhara Pedagogical Institute, where women make up over half of both the faculty and the student body. About 40 per cent of the students were reported to be Uzbeks, and of these, 40 per cent were women. Uzbek girls were in evidence in every classroom and laboratory, including the physics and other natural science laboratories. There seems little doubt that the goal of equality for women in education will be achieved eventually, but how long this will take is difficult to predict. The rather slow progress in recent years suggests that it will be many decades.

CONCLUSIONS

In the last decades prior to the Revolution, considerable progress was being made in the education of young women at all levels. Even at universities, where women had only recently been admitted, women made up almost 25 per cent of the enrollment. Since the Revolution, education became available to a much larger proportion of the population, and women were among the major beneficiaries of this expansion. At the lower levels of the educational system—grades one through ten—the proportion of girls has been almost equal to that of boys except in the higher grades of the more backward republics, where girls typically withdraw from school earlier than boys. In specialized secondary education the proportion of young women exceeded that of men by the late 1930's, while in higher education, where the share of women grew more slowly, it exceeded that of men substantially by 1940.

After reaching a peak during World War

II, the proportion of women enrolled in specialized secondary and higher education declined sharply by the first half of the 1950's to a level consistent with the proportion of women in the student-aged population. With a return to normal of the male-female ratio in the student age groups, the proportion of women has declined further—slightly in specialized secondary education and sharply in higher education—reflecting, in large part, changes in the admissions regulations of higher educational institutions, which have tended to favor men. Although equality between the sexes in access to education remains the stated public policy of the Soviet regime, recent practice apparently has departed from this principle. The reason for this appears to be economic. It was pointed out that if educational resources are limited, they can be utilized most efficiently only if devoted to those persons whose expected productivity is greatest. Since the productivity of women in the course of their professional careers is likely, on the average, to be less than that of men for a number of reasons (see Chapter 12), higher admission standards for women are economically justifiable. Current Soviet admission policies favoring men probably do not, therefore, reflect a discriminatory attitude against women in the usual sense, but simply the desire of the educational planners to utilize limited resources to the best effect. Thus, practical considerations of efficiency appear to be overriding the principle of equality even though support of the principle continues to be stoutly maintained.

Substantial regional differences in the proportion of women enrolled in the higher levels of education continue to exist in the Soviet Union. Particularly backward are the Central Asian and some of the other non-Slavic republics. These republics continue to lag despite the impressive progress made in earlier decades and despite the continued efforts of the government to eradicate the customs and attitudes which have tended to inhibit the education of young women in the past. Judging from the slow progress in recent years, future gains will not be achieved without great effort.

chapter
7

SPECIALIZED TRAINING

IN A PLANNED economy which emphasizes growth, it is important that the output of specialists by the educational system be closely geared to the manpower needs of the economy. This is not achieved easily for a number of reasons. It is difficult, or even impossible, to foresee specific manpower needs far enough in advance to assure the required supply because of the long lead time necessary to train a productive professional in such fields as science and technology. Furthermore, when education is as narrowly specialized as most Soviet training, readjustments in supply at midstream are particularly difficult. There is also a problem of attracting the appropriate number of young people with the requisite qualifications and capacities to the fields in which needs are anticipated.

It is a misconception that Soviet youngsters are told by the government what they should study and what career they should follow. On the contrary, from its inception the government has adhered, broadly speaking, to the principle of freedom of choice in employment. There are exceptions, the most obvious being the employment of forced labor on major construction projects and in mining and forestry. Young men face a period of military service, but specialists—scientists or engineers—can usually win exemption from conventional military service or even from any military service. Also, some youths have been drafted into the labor reserve schools. Another notable exception to the policy of a free labor market is the assignment by the government of graduates from vocational specialized secondary and higher educational institutions to specified positions for a period of two to four years—a measure taken to supply workers and specialists where they are most needed. In addition to these exceptions, there may be pressure from political organizations, such as the Komsomol, on individuals or groups of individuals to undertake certain assignments, such as migration to the Virgin Lands; or the party may bring pressure to bear on an individual engineer or scientist to undertake a high-priority assignment.

In general, however, the Soviet system relies upon incentives to attract manpower and woman power where it is needed, and the most important incentive has been monetary. After the Revolution, Lenin and other theorists expected pecuniary motivation to become less important, but after the inauguration of the industrialization drive, a formal about-face regarding wage equalization was made by Stalin in his famous 1931 speech to industrial managers.[1] At this time, he proclaimed the doctrinal orthodoxy of money incentives, and increases in wage and salary differentials soon followed. These were reinforced by other incentives: honors, awards, perquisites, and prestige.

---

[1] J. Stalin, *Problems of Leninism* (Moscow, 1940), pp. 371–73.

The attractiveness of professions such as engineering and science was heightened by the full force of the Soviet propaganda machine, operating through party agitators, the press, and radio. Even the arts were enlisted in the task. Films, novels, plays, poetry, and paintings all contributed to enhancing the image of the scientist, engineer, and technician in the eyes of the public, particularly the young. The publicity reserved for movie and sports stars in the West was given to the achievements of these technical men and women. Thus, the regime enhanced the attractiveness of certain key professions and specialties to assure the educational system a sufficient supply of applicants in specific fields.

Little real planning of manpower was attempted until the industrialization drive began at the end of the 1920's, when the training of specialists to meet planned needs became vitally important to the rapid development of the economy. During the 1930's a shortage of qualified secondary-school graduates necessitated the admission of inadequately prepared candidates into technical institutes and universities. During this period the major problem of the planners was to attract and prepare a sufficient number of specialists in fields, such as engineering, which were essential to economic development.

After World War II the annual supply of secondary-school graduates increased substantially and by 1950 equaled the number of acceptances into the full-time day programs of higher educational institutions. In the years following, graduations from secondary schools expanded even more rapidly, while admissions to the full-time day programs of higher educational institutions decreased slightly. By 1957 almost six times as many students completed their secondary education as could be admitted as full-time students to institutions of higher learning. Under these circumstances the task of the manpower planners was easier. Given an excess of eager applicants for the key specialties and professions, the flow of newly trained specialists could be regulated by enlarging or reducing the numbers per-

mitted to enter the educational pipelines. By opening the gates where more specialists were needed and closing others, the flow could be deflected into those channels, or specialties, for which the demand was greatest.

The excess of secondary-school graduates relative to space in higher educational institutions has dropped sharply in recent years—a reflection of the low birth rates and high infant mortality during the war years. However, the number of those desiring admission to higher education has continued to grow, and a further increase in secondary school graduates can be expected in the future, since the sharply reduced crop of war babies will have passed through the secondary-school age by 1962–63. The next decade should witness, therefore, mounting pressure by qualified students for advanced training. Manpower planners will continue to work with an excess demand for education in most specialties, which will ease their task of meeting specific needs.

The eagerness for higher education in the Soviet Union may be explained primarily by the circumstance that the chance of achieving a position with high status and income is largely determined by one's education. Talent, industry, and perseverance are also required, but without the necessary higher educational training, ability and effort provide no assurance of success. As a result, any advanced degree is preferable to no degree at all, but certain fields of study and certain institutions are particularly popular because of their special attractions. Stipends vary by field, and institutions vary greatly in quality. Awareness of the intense competition for admission to desirable specialties in the better institutions may discourage all but the most able applicants. This circumstance accounts for some of the unexpected differences in the ratios of applicants to vacancies at a number of Soviet higher educational establishments. For example, DeWitt reports seven applicants for every vacancy at the Azerbaidzhan Medical Institute in 1957, but only four applicants for every vacancy at the Moscow State University in the same year.[2] In all probability, many more students than the four-to-one ratio indicates would have liked to enter the Moscow State University but did not consider it worth trying because of the strong likelihood of failure.

There are also substantial variations in the ratio of applicants to acceptances among the various disciplines offered by any one institution. For example, when the author visited the Bauman Higher Technical School in Moscow in 1955, one of the Soviet Union's elite engineering institutions, there were ten to twelve applicants for every acceptance in the specialties of machine tool and electromechanical apparatus design, while there were only two to three applicants for every acceptance in hydraulic turbine and hydraulic machine design and in the design of hoisting and materials handling equipment.

The proportion of girls applying for admission to various higher educational institutions and specialties is not determined by the government. A girl's decision in this regard, like a boy's, is her own. Of course, a variety of factors may influence her decision: her family, her teachers, her friends, her earlier education, her talents and interests, the attractiveness for her of possible alternative careers, and so forth. If the effect of these influences is to encourage a substantially larger number of girls than boys to apply for a particular field, like medicine, the result, given equal test results and political reliability between the sexes, is that the percentage of girls among the applicants selected for admission is also high. With its stated commitment against discrimination between the sexes, the government cannot openly influence the ratio of male to female students except through legislation designed to protect women from unhealthful occupations or through efforts to alter the public image of the suitability of an occupation, such as engineering, for women. In practice, however, we have observed that the

double standard is not dead. Indirectly discriminatory admissions policies, some covert prejudice in favor of men, and informal quotas may handicap a woman in the Soviet Union, as elsewhere. The high percentage of women enrolled in higher education and the high percentage enrolled in many traditionally "male" specialties in the areas of science and technology demonstrate, however, that prejudice per se has been largely if not completely overcome in the interests of equality and the efficient utilization of the talents of women.

In this chapter we investigate how well the Soviets have succeeded in attracting women to the fields of science and technology. The training of women in science and technology at both the undergraduate and the postgraduate levels in universities and institutes is surveyed. The treatment is largely statistical, since this is not the place to evaluate the quality of the training, which is identical for men and women.[3]

WOMEN STUDENTS IN SCIENCE, SCIENCE TEACHING, AND TECHNOLOGY

Before discussing in detail the higher education of women in the fields of science, engineering, and medicine, it is necessary to have clearly in mind the different types of institutions offering higher educational training in these fields.

Engineering Institutes. Students of technology trained in the 191 engineering institutes provided the largest flow of male and female graduates, or 32.2 per cent of the total number of graduates of higher education in 1959.

Agricultural and Medical Institutes and the Universities. Pure and applied scientists comprised the second largest group, or 21.3 per cent, of the total number of graduates from higher educational institutions. The applied

[2]Nicholas DeWitt, *Education and Professional Employment in the U.S.S.R.* (Washington, D.C., 1961), p. 264.

[3]For qualitative evaluations, see DeWitt, *op. cit.,* and Alexander G. Korol, *Soviet Education for Science and Technology* (Cambridge, Mass., 1957).

scientists are divided into two major sub-groups: the agricultural scientists, including agronomists and veterinarians (10.2 per cent), and the physicians (8.0 per cent). These two subgroups received their training in 109 agricultural institutes and 95 medical institutes. Although some of these graduates—for example, botanists trained at agricultural institutes—might more accurately be classified as pure rather than applied scientists, we reserve the category of pure scientists (an estimated 3.1 per cent) for those graduates of the forty universities who have been trained in the mathematical, physical, and biological sciences for employment as scientific research workers and not as secondary-school science teachers.

Pedagogical Institutes and University Teacher Training Programs. Teachers of science for the secondary schools make up the third group of graduates, or an estimated 14.9 per cent of the total. About four fifths (11.8 per cent) of these teachers are estimated to have been trained at those institutes having science departments among the 256 pedagogical and related cultural institutes. The remainder (3.1 per cent) were graduated from the forty universities.[4]

Graduates in science, science teaching, and technology together made up 68.4 per cent of

the total of graduates from higher educational institutions in 1959.[5] The following discussion of the proportion of women enrolled in each of these fields deals, therefore, with the areas in which a substantial majority of the students in higher education are enrolled.

WOMEN ENROLLED IN ENGINEERING

We have mentioned that the proportion of women enrolled in engineering courses quadrupled between 1926 and 1939; with the exception of the war and immediate postwar period, this proportion has fluctuated between 26 and 36 per cent for the last twenty-five years and stood at 29 per cent in 1963. Engineering covers a multitude of occupations; Table 64 shows the percentage of women en-

TABLE 64. Percentage of women enrolled in engineering-industrial institutes, 1956–57.[a]

Specialty Groups	Women
	%
Technology of the food products industry.....	74.5
Technology of the consumers' goods industry .	74.0
Hydrology and meteorology..............	63.0
Chemical engineering....................	60.0
Geodesy and cartography................	58.0
Radio engineering and communications.....	35.3
Timber engineering and technology of wood processing, cellulose, and paper manufacturing................................	34.5
Metallurgy............................	31.5
Geology and exploration of mineral deposits..	31.0
Power engineering......................	27.4
Machine building and instrument construction	23.8
Transportation.........................	22.6
Mining engineering.....................	16.6
All engineering fields...................	36.0

[a]Based on V. E. Komarov, *Ekonomicheskie osnovy podgotovki spetsialistov dlia norodnogo khoziaistva* (Moscow, 1959), p. 192.

rolled in thirteen of the most important specialty groups in the 1956–57 academic year, when women made up 36.0 per cent of the enrollment. The percentages range from 16.6 per cent for mining engineering to 74.5 per cent for food products technology. Other specialty groups in which women predominated

---

[4]The numbers of educational institutions apply to the 1959 academic year and are from DeWitt, *op. cit.,* pp. 748–49. The percentages of graduates in 1959 are adapted from DeWitt (Table IV-51, p. 341). It is assumed here that one half of the university graduates in the fields of the mathematical, physical, and biological sciences entered teaching. This is a smaller proportion than that required by law as of the 1955–56 academic year. Supposedly, from that time on "Not fewer than 80 per cent of those graduating from the faculties of Philology, History, Geography, and Biology; and not fewer than 60 per cent of the graduates of the Physics, Mathematics, and Chemistry faculties shall be directed to teach in the secondary schools" (quoted in Korol, *op. cit.,* p. 272). These regulations were not put into effect fully. See Norton T. Dodge, "Recent Changes in the Training of Soviet Secondary School Teachers," in *The Politics of Soviet Education,* ed. by George Z. F. Bereday and Jaan Pennar (New York, 1960), pp. 146–47.

[5]DeWitt, *op. cit.,* p. 328.

were consumers' goods industry technology (74.0 per cent), hydrology and meteorology (63.0 per cent), and chemical engineering (60.0 per cent). These groups, in contrast to mining engineering, transportation, and machine building, are those in which working conditions favor the employment of women.

The considerable differences in the proportions of women enrolled in the various fields of engineering presented in Table 64 are substantiated by data reported by the author and other visitors to the Soviet Union on the percentages of women enrolled in a number of different engineering institutes. In Table 65 data on a number of institutes and some of their specialties are presented. The proportion of women at the polytechnical institutes, all of which provide a broad curriculum in a number of fields, has remained close to the over-all average for engineering. The author

TABLE 65. Percentage of women enrolled in selected engineering institutes.[a]

Institution and Specialty	Women	Institution and Specialty	Women
	%		%
Ashkabad Polytechnical Institute, Ashkabad		Institute of City Planning and Construction, Stalingrad	
Total, 1965	20	Total, 1955	50
Construction	33	Heat treatment	60
Mechanical-technical	25–30	Moscow Institute of Power Engineering, Moscow	
Petroleum engineering	15		
Baku Polytechnical Institute, Baku		Total, *1960*	35
Total, *1960*	22	Total, 1960	45
Total, 1965	27–30	Total, 1965	30
Textile and light industry	50	Institute of Railway Transport,[b] Moscow	
Construction	30	Total, 1960	–
Electro-technical	25	Bridges and tunnels	35
Mechanical	12–15	Airport construction	35
Bauman Higher Technical School, Moscow		Road vehicle maintenance	10
Total, 1955	25	Institute of Railway Transport, Rostov	
Metallurgy	50–60	Total, *1960*	41
Total, *1960*	27	Institute of Railway Transport, Tashkent	
Erevan Polytechnical Institute, Erevan		Total, *1960*	25
Total, 1965	24	Moscow Engineering-Economic Institute, Moscow	
Kharkov Polytechnical Institute, Kharkov			
Total, 1955	35	Total, *1960*	40
Total, *1960*	30	Total, 1962	50
Total, 1960	30–35	Leningrad Mining Institute, Leningrad	
Total, 1962	30	Total, *1960*	30
Leningrad Polytechnical Institute, Leningrad		Institute of Building Construction, Kharkov	
Total, *1960*	27	Total, *1960*	35
Total, 1960	30–35	Heating and ventilation	50+
Engineering economics	95	Water supply and sewage systems	40
Total, 1965	32	Industrial construction	25
Engineering economics	50	Civil engineering	25
Novocherkassk Polytechnical Institute, Rostov		Rostov Institute of Agricultural Machinery Building, Rostov	
Total, *1960*	30	Total, *1960*	30–33
Kiev Construction Engineering Institute, Kiev		Tashkent Textile Institute, Tashkent	
Total, 1965	20	Total, *1960*	49

[a]The following sources were used for the compilation of this table: for 1955, Homer L. and Norton T. Dodge, *Notes on Visits to Educational Institutions in the U.S.S.R., April 20 to May 21, 1955* (Cambridge, Mass., 1955), pp. 34, 80, 141; for 1960, Engineers Joint Council, *The Training, Placement and Utilization of Engineers and Technicians in the Soviet Union* (New York, 1961), pp. 94–95; for 1960, L. S. Souter and R. Winslade, *Women Engineers in the U.S.S.R.* (London, 1960), pp. 9–10; for 1962, Norton T. Dodge, *The Utilization of Women in Soviet Science and Technology, Report A* (College Park, Md., 1963), pp. 19, 36, 47; and for 1965, data collected by the author at the respective institutes, with the exception of the Moscow Institute of Power Engineering and the Kiev Construction Engineering Institute, which were reported by Henry Chauncey, *Interviews with Soviet Educators on Recent Developments and the Current Status of Education in the U.S.S.R.* (Princeton, 1965), pp. 65, 191.

[b]The title "Institute of Ways of Communications" given by Souter and Winslade does not correspond to any of the institutes listed in Soviet handbooks on higher educational institutions (see DeWitt, *op. cit*., pp. 681–700). It would appear, however, that this institute must be the Institute of Railway Transport, although the specialties mentioned do not fit precisely those given by DeWitt (p. 694).

was told that the proportion of women enrolled in chemical engineering, metallurgy, and heat treatment of metals in these general engineering institutions was particularly large, varying between 50 and 60 per cent. Engineering economics, which is concerned with production planning, is a field which also attracted a high percentage of women. There was considerable variation in the enrollment among the various branches of construction engineering, the maintenance of road vehicles being especially unpopular.

In recent years the number of women graduates in several engineering fields has exceeded employment opportunities. Jobs have been particularly scarce in such areas as mining and certain types of chemical manufacture and machine building—fields from which the government has attempted to exclude women.[6] A professor of fuel technology, for example, told the author that he could not recommend that a girl enter his field. He felt that the work was unsuited for women for health reasons and was convinced that it would be difficult to utilize a woman effectively because of limited employment possibilities. He cited as an illustration the coke and coal-tar industry's opposition to having more than 5 per cent women among its workers and engineers.

What attracts Soviet women to engineering? What are the factors which influence their choice of career? The author asked these questions of a number of the women teaching at the Kharkov Polytechnic Institute. A middle-aged associate professor (*dotsent*) who taught in the heat-treating department had found science interesting when she was quite young but could not refer to any particularly decisive influence. Her choice developed out of her school experience in which she had become interested in physics and mathematics. She pointed out that young girls today are much more exposed to technology than she had been twenty-five years ago, through the practical work now required in grades nine to

eleven and through on-the-job experience in factories, where many girls are employed upon completion of their secondary schooling. It seemed to her natural for a girl to obtain advanced training in her field after two or more years of actual work experience. Another woman, an associate professor in the electrochemical field, said that her interest in science was inspired by her chemistry teacher in the ten-year school. After three years of work in a factory, she entered the chemistry faculty of the University of Kharkov. She then worked for ten years in a chemical plant, ending as a shop supervisor, before entering the Kharkov Polytechnic Institute for graduate training. A woman mechanical engineer said that her interest developed at a specialized secondary school, or *tekhnikum*, which trained machinists. She found she liked to operate machine tools, and from this her interest in mechanical engineering evolved. Upon graduation she entered the Kharkov Polytechnic Institute and specialized in metal-cutting machines.

While visiting the heat-treating laboratory, the author asked a number of students—all girls—how they had chosen this field. Contact with an inspiring teacher and good grades in mathematics and science seemed to have provided the stimulus for their careers. Salary considerations did not appear to have had any direct influence upon their decisions. However, the heat treatment of metals particularly appealed to them because it did not involve heavy work. From these and other discussions it appears that students and teachers lack concrete and specific reasons for choosing the fields in which they are working. Interest seems to have been stimulated by good teachers, success in school, and the home environment. Also, engineering has always been depicted in the Soviet Union as a field in which a girl or boy can make a vital contribution to the industrial growth of the nation. The relatively high pay of engineers might be expected to offer a special attraction, but in none of the explanations did the author find financial rewards playing a conscious role in the choice

[6]*Ibid.*, p. 348.

of field. Although monetary incentives and attendant prestige undoubtedly color the public image of engineering, other factors were apparently felt to be of greater importance.

WOMEN ENROLLED IN THE APPLIED SCIENCES

Women enrolled in the applied sciences may be divided into those in the agricultural sciences and those in medicine.

Agricultural Sciences. The enrollment of women in agricultural courses since 1926 has followed the same course already noted in disciplines other than health and education. The percentage rose substantially during the 1930's, reached a peak during World War II, and declined steadily, to a level of 25 per cent in 1962, where it has remained for the past two years.

The choice of specialties by women at the Institute of Agriculture in Alma Ata, which the author visited in 1962, although not necessarily a faithful reflection of attitudes in the more heavily industrialized European U.S.S.R., illustrates some of the differences in the popularity of various fields of specialization for women. Approximately 40 per cent of the students at the Institute are girls, but most of them shy away from fields requiring mechanical work. The dean explained that the largest faculty was that devoted to mechanization of agriculture, but few women are enrolled in it. However, the second largest faculty, that of agronomy, is very popular with girls, and particularly the botany department. Indeed, no male students at all were observed working in the botany laboratories. Of the sixteen staff members, only one is a man. Professor Olga Troitskaia, the enthusiastic septuagenarian who heads the department, pointed out by way of explanation that women have been interested in plants from the beginning of history. When the first nomads settled down long enough to raise a crop, men were the hunters and women the cultivators.

Medicine. A number of factors explain the high percentage of girls studying medicine. Care of the sick is a traditional activity for women. As Madame Kovrigina, former Minister of Health, commented to the writer, "Medicine is close to the nature of women. It tends to satisfy their maternal instincts." Also, the six-hour day required of medical workers is an hour shorter than the present factory day. Physicians may put in extra time for extra pay, but a woman physician with children can limit herself, if she desires, to six hours and also can arrange her working hours so that they do not interfere unduly with her home life. The author was told, for example, that in hospitals men are asked to take more night duty than women. If women are compelled by economic and other pressures to be gainfully employed, medicine is clearly one of the most attractive fields of work. The government has taken advantage of this fact by paying physicians no more than necessary to attract a "sufficient" number into the profession. The relatively low salaries, corresponding to those of industrial workers, have also contributed to the domination of the field by women.

Precisely what factors have caused the decline in female enrollment in university-level medical courses between 1956 (69 per cent) and 1964 (53 per cent) is not clear. Conversations with education officials suggest that they would like to have about the same number of men as women in the field. When pressed as to why it was necessary to restore the balance of the sexes, one professor, the deputy head of an institute, said that men seemed to be better suited than women for some fields, such as surgery. This opinion was shared by others who felt that male surgeons were more detached from their work emotionally and prepared to take bolder action when necessary. However, even prior to the cutback in the percentage of girls enrolled in medical institutes, surgery tended to be dominated by men. Other reasons must, therefore, be found for the increase in male students. One might be defense considerations, which would dictate that the number of male physicians ready for mobilization in time of war should not be permitted to sink below a certain minimum. In 1959 civilian male physicians age 20 to 29 numbered only 15,355, while those age 30 to 39 numbered 23,615.[7] The shortage of male physicians of military age would have become even more acute during the present decade if girls had continued to make up two thirds or more of the enrollment in the medical institutes. Another reason is the difficulty of assigning young women to posts in remote rural areas. If a girl marries before completing her studies, she may not upon graduation be assigned apart from her husband. Indeed, the author was told that in major cities girls often schedule their marriages to local men prior to graduation in order to avoid being consigned to the dreary and limited life of some remote village. Life in such a place, including marriage op-

portunities, presents an appalling prospect to many educated girls accustomed to city living.

THE MAJOR SCIENTIFIC FIELDS

Unfortunately, Soviet statistics on the enrollment of women in the natural sciences have not been published, and the scattered data available from Soviet sources and from visitors' reports are very limited. However, on the basis of the author's visit to a number of institutions and reports received from others, some fairly reliable judgments can be made. The evidence is briefly summarized before the resulting estimates of the percentage of female enrollment in the various scientific fields are presented. Detailed information is available for only six universities: Uzhgorod State University, founded in 1945; Voronezh State University, established in 1918; Odessa State University, founded in 1865; Tartu State University, founded in 1637 and taken over by the Soviets in 1940; Tbilisi State University, founded in 1918; and Erevan State Uni-

---

[7]Calculated from *Itogi 1959 . . . goda: SSSR,* pp. 139, 144, 164, 168.

TABLE 66. Total enrollment and percentage of women enrolled in day division, by faculty, Voronezh State University, 1950, 1960, and 1963.[a]

	1950		1960		1963	
Faculties	Total	Women	Total	Women	Total	Women
Science		%		%		%
Mechanics-mathematics.....	108	43	480	55	659	61
Physics..................	212	49	589	31	936	34
Chemistry................	227	68	299	75	403	82
Biology-soil science........	301	90	402	80	472	74
Geology.................	173	41	216	17	202	24
Total..................	1,021	64	1,986	54	2,672	54
Other						
Geography...............	216	82	304	69	304	70
Economics...............	–	–	116	80	301	78
Law....................	–	–	102	33	134	26
History.................	153	54	200	41	231	30
Literature...............	196	74	243	72	291	81
Romance and Germanic literature...............	–	–	–	–	273	80
Total..................	565	72	965	62	1,534	66
Total.....................	1,586	66	2,951	55	4,206	58

[a]Based on a communication to the author from the university.

versity, founded in 1921.[8] The proportion of women enrolled in various fields at the six universities for which detailed data are available is shown in Tables 66 through 71.

It will be noted that women make up a higher percentage of university enrollment than of enrollment in the educational-cultural category as a whole. In the scientific fields at the universities, the proportion of women is particularly high in the chemical and biological sciences; in the nonscientific fields the proportion is particularly high in literature and languages. Even in mathematics and physics the proportion of women is quite high. It is equally evident that there is considerable variation from institution to institution and even from year to year. If these figures are representative of the proportion of women enrolled in universities, the conclusion is un-

avoidable that the decline in the over-all proportion of women enrolled in higher education has occurred primarily in other types of higher

TABLE 67. Percentage of women enrolled, by faculty, Uzhgorod State University, 1950, 1955, and 1963.[a]

	1950	1955	1963	
Faculties	Day	Day	Day	Eve-ning
Science				
Physics-mathematics...	33	47	56	33
Chemistry............	43	59	41	66
Biology..............	25	64	55	69
Medicine............	41	55	71	55
Other				
History..............	38	40	28	–
Literature...........	62	49	81	79
Total.................	47	59	58	55

[a]Based on a communication to the author from the university.

[8]Based on data in Tsentral'noe statisticheskoe upravlenie pri Sovete ministrov SSSR, *Kul'turnoe stroitel'stvo SSSR* (Moscow, 1956), pp. 218–29, and *Vysshee obrazovanie v SSSR* (Moscow, 1961), pp. 178–200. Uzhgorod had an enrollment of only 1,629 evening and daytime students in 1955 and 1,858 in 1960. Among state universities it ranked thirty-first out of thirty-three in enrollment in 1955 and thirty-fifth out of forty in 1960. If correspondence students are included in 1960, the rank is raised to thirteenth. Voronezh had 2,313 evening and daytime students in 1955 and ranked twenty-fourth, and 3,820 in 1960, when it ranked eighteenth. For the latter year, correspondence students raised the rank to ninth. Odessa had 2,118 evening and daytime students in 1955 and ranked twenty-third in 1955, and 3,224 students in 1960, when it ranked nineteenth. The inclusion of correspondence students in 1960 raised the rank to seventh. Tartu had 2,870 evening and daytime students in 1955 and ranked eighteenth in size. In 1960 the enrollment was 2,934 and the rank, twenty-fourth. The inclusion of correspondence students dropped it to twenty-ninth place. Tbilisi had 4,865 evening and daytime students in 1955 and ranked fourth. In 1960 the enrollment was 6,472 and the rank, third. For the latter year, the inclusion of correspondence students reduced the rank to fifth. Erevan had 3,141 evening and day students in 1955 and ranked fifteenth, and 4,079 in 1960, when the rank increased to ninth. The inclusion of correspondence students in 1960 dropped its rank to twentieth. Voronezh, Odessa, and Tartu, therefore, had close to the median evening and day-

time enrollment, while Uzhgorod State University was one of the smaller institutions of its kind. Erevan is now one of the larger universities in terms of evening and daytime enrollment, while Tbilisi is one of the largest universities. All but Uzhgorod carry on graduate work. In terms of size and character, therefore, the six universities are fairly representative. It is impossible to know, however, whether the pattern of enrollment of women which they reveal is representative of the entire university enrollment.

In addition to these six schools, some information was obtained on others. The Uzbek State University in Samarkand, founded in 1933, is very near the median size. In 1955, with an evening and daytime enrollment of 1,694 students, it ranked twentieth, but by 1960, with an increase in enrollment to 3,337, it tied for twenty-second place. At the time of my visit, at the end of the 1961–62 academic year, the enrollment was 3,200 daytime and 1,200 evening students. The pattern of female enrollment in the various fields was close to that displayed by the other universities, but the proportion of women tended to be slightly lower. For example, 63 per cent of the students enrolled in the chemistry faculty, 26 per cent in the combined physics and mathematics-mechanics faculty, and 49 per cent in the literature faculty were women. These lower percentages reflect the continuing influence of Moslem cultural patterns in the Uzbek republic. At the University of Kharkov, on the other hand, women were reported to make up approximately half the enrollment in the physics faculty.

TABLE 68. Total enrollment and percentage of women enrolled in day division, by faculty, Tartu State University, 1950, 1960, and 1963.[a]

Faculties	1950 Total	1950 Women	1960 Total	1960 Women	1963 Total	1963 Women
		%		%		%
Science						
Physics-mathematics........	219	46	516	47	632	53
Biology-geography.........	209	67	214	62	306	68
Medicine................	950	59	1,275	78	1,202	80
Total.................	1,378	58	2,005	68	2,140	70
Other						
History-literature..........	502	73	555	77	720	79
Law-economics...........	249	34	275	43	263	59
Physical culture...........	96	46	99	32	136	49
Total.................	847	59	929	62	1,119	70
Total.....................	2,225	58	2,934	66	3,259	70

[a]Based on a communication to the author from the university. The faculties of veterinary, agricultural, and forestry science, which were transferred to the Estonian Academy of Agriculture in 1951, are omitted from the 1950 as well as later figures. The percentages of women were 28, 46, and 13, respectively, in 1950.

educational institutions, such as technical and medical institutes.

On the basis of the data available on individual universities, we estimate that more than three fourths and possibly as many as four fifths of the students enrolled in biology and its various subfields, such as zoology and botany, are women. Almost as high a proportion of women, possibly two thirds or more of the students, is to be found in chemistry. Perhaps two fifths to one half of students in mathematics are women. The percentages enrolled in the other sciences—physics, geology, and the agricultural sciences—probably range from one fourth to two fifths.

Many of the women enrolled in university science courses enter research institutes or continue for advanced degrees. Those who are less capable are likely to become secondary-school teachers. About half of the university graduates in the sciences go into teaching.

SCIENCE TEACHING

Teaching in primary and secondary schools is a popular field for women—for many of the same reasons that medicine is popular. For a woman with a family, the possibility of shorter hours and the personal attraction of

the work offer a real incentive. As in medicine, the basic schedule is six hours a day. Because of the low salary schedule, however, many teachers do extra work for additional income. Science teachers, for example, receive extra pay for setting up laboratory experi-

TABLE 69. Percentage of women enrolled in day division, by faculty, Odessa State University, 1950, 1960, and 1963.[a]

Faculties	1950	1960	1963
Science			
Physics-mathematics.........	55	–	–
Mathematics.............	–	71	65
Physics..................	–	52	49
Chemistry................	91	85	85
Biology..................	93	86	80
Geology.................	55	–	–
Other			
History..................	55	48	32
Literature			
Russian................	85	80	74
Ukrainian..............	81	86	86
Economics................	61	–	–
Geography................	87	78	70
Law....................	40	–	–
Foreign languages			
English................	–	86	80
German................	–	86	82
French................	–	92	90
Spanish................	–	–	78
Total.......................	67	75	70

[a]Based on a communication to the author from the university.

TABLE 70. Enrollment and percentage of women enrolled in day, evening, and correspondence divisions, by faculty, Erevan State University, 1964.[a]

Faculties	Day Students		Evening Students		Correspondence Students	
	Total	Women	Total	Women	Total	Women
		%		%		%
Science						
Mathematics..................	385	32	113	39	35	13
Physics......................	542	31	205	30	–	–
Chemistry....................	378	66	60	40	–	–
Biology......................	507	81	336	82	–	–
Geology.....................	122	7	–	–	–	–
Total.....................	1,934	50	714	57	35	13
Other						
Economics...................	412	41	381	44	560	34
Economics of trade............	110	25	180	31	286	27
Law.........................	140	11	241	11	463	12
History......................	222	26	–	–	47	47
Geography...................	110	53	–	–	–	–
Philology....................	963	70	276	78	658	58
Total.....................	1,957	51	1,078	43	2,014	36
Total.........................	3,891	51	1,792	49	2,049	36

[a]Based on a communication to the author from the university.

ments. Others teach additional hours. In primary and secondary teaching, as in medicine, the attraction the profession holds for women

TABLE 71. Enrollment and percentage of women enrolled in day division, by faculty, Tbilisi State University, 1964.[a]

Faculties	Total	Women
Science		%
Mechanics-mathematics......	500	48
Physics....................	861	42
Chemistry.................	389	78
Biology...................	349	88
Geology..................	282	29
Cybernetics...............	325	52
Total.................	2,706	54
Other		
Economics................	783	34
Law......................	151	19
Philosophy................	122	47
History...................	235	38
Philology.................	725	68
Western European languages and literature.............	498	94
Oriental studies............	254	60
Total.................	2,768	56
Total.........................	5,554	54

[a]Based on a communication to the author from the university.

has made possible the recruitment of sufficient personnel, even at low salaries, which, in turn, cause men to avoid teaching on the primary and secondary level and to seek better-compensated work in teaching at higher levels, research, and administration.

Although no official data have been published on the percentage of women enrolled in the teacher training programs of the universities or the pedagogical and related institutes, there can be little doubt that the total percentage of women in programs devoted to training secondary-school teachers is somewhat higher than that of women enrolled in the entire educational-cultural field, which includes students destined for careers in which the percentage of women employed is smaller. Therefore, the percentage of women being trained for teaching in 1964 was very likely larger than the 64 per cent enrolled in the educational-cultural fields.[9] Since the percentage of women enrolled in scientific fields appears to be somewhat below the average for all fields, it is probable that the proportion of

[9]See Table 57.

women being trained for teaching science was in the neighborhood of 60 per cent.

Support for this view was provided by conversations with teachers and officials concerned with the training of secondary-school teachers. They said that women made up the bulk of the enrollment in the scientific and mathematical as well as other fields. There are indications that in the pedagogical institutes the percentage of women enrolled in science is larger than in the universities. At the Pedagogical Institute in Rostov-on-Don, for example, the author found that 70 to 75 per cent of the total enrollment in 1955 was women. In the physics faculty they comprised an unexpectedly high 80 per cent. Usually, however, biology and chemistry were reported to be the most popular science fields for young women.

WOMEN IN GRADUATE TRAINING

Graduates of Soviet higher educational institutions who plan to pursue a career in research or teaching in higher education must continue their training at the graduate level and acquire one or both of the two Soviet academic degrees. The first of these, which corresponds roughly to our Ph.D. degree, is called the candidate degree (*Kandidat nauk*). The second, the doctor's degree (*Doktor nauk*), has no real equivalent in the United States. It is usually acquired by seasoned scholars, often in their forties, on the basis of some significant contribution to research. It might best be compared to the doctorate awarded in the Scandinavian countries.[10] The candidate degree may be earned either through completion of formal training, with examinations and defense of a dissertation, or on a

merit basis as recognition for outstanding work, without examinations or thesis defense. Except for the twenty-year period 1937 to 1956, there has been no formal training for the doctorate. The degree is awarded either after public defense of a dissertation or on the basis of other outstanding work.[11]

Formal work toward an advanced degree may be done at a regular higher educational institution offering graduate training, such as the University of Moscow or the Kharkov Polytechnical Institute, at research institutes and laboratories of the Academies of Sciences, such as the Vavilov Institute of Physical Problems, and at certain industrial research institutes. In 1960 universities and technical institutes accommodated 56 per cent of the graduate students, and research institutes, the remaining 44 per cent (see Table 72). The proportion of women being trained at each type of institution was almost identical to that of men.[12]

With increasing demands for highly trained manpower, the proportion of women among graduate students rose steadily from the beginning of the first Five-Year Plan until World War II. At the end of 1931, 23 per cent of the graduate students enrolled in

---

[10]According to A. Ia. Sinetskii, *Professorsko-prepodavatel'skie kadry vysshei shkoly SSSR* (Moscow, 1950), pp. 178–79, 43.7 per cent of the persons receiving doctorates did so fifteen or more years after completing their undergraduate training. Only 13.8 per cent received the degree in less than ten years. The gap between the candidate and doctorate was usually four to eight years.

[11]For a full discussion of Soviet advanced degrees, see DeWitt, *op. cit.*, pp. 373–496.

[12]Just before the war the proportion of women graduate students in research institutes was greater than that in higher educational institutions. K. Galkin, *The Training of Scientists in the Soviet Union* (Moscow, 1959), p. 123, reports that on January 1, 1939, 30.6 per cent of the graduate students at higher educational institutions were women, but that the proportion of women at research institutes was 36.2 per cent.

TABLE 72. Enrollment of graduate students, by type of institution, 1960.[a]

	Total	Higher Educational Institutions	Scientific Research Establishments
		%	%
Total..........	36,754	20,406	56	16,348	44
Men...........	28,349	15,626	55	12,723	45
Women.......	8,405	4,780	57	3,625	43

[a]Based on Tsentral'noe statisticheskoe upravlenie pri Sovete ministrov SSSR, *Vysshee obrazovanie v SSSR* (Moscow, 1961), p. 224.

higher educational institutions and research establishments were women; just prior to the war the proportion had increased to 32 per cent (see Table 73). The proportion increased further in the immediate postwar period, but declined from 41 per cent in 1947 to 29 per cent in 1956, and to 23 per cent in 1960.

Wide variations from year to year may occur at an individual institution. At Voronezh State University, for which some recent data are available, 26 of the 41 graduate students (63 per cent) were women in 1959, 32 of 100 in 1961, 30 of 146 (21 per cent) in 1962, and 35 of 185 (19 per cent) in 1963.[13] In this

---

[13]From a communication to the author from the university. At the time of the author's visit to the University of Samarkand in 1962, 15 of the 66 *aspirants* (23 per cent) were women. In 1965, the author was told, 32 of 97 *aspirants* (33 per cent) at Ashkhabad State University and 74 of 200 *aspirants* (37 per cent) at Erevan State University were women.

instance, the sharp decline in the percentage of women graduate students was due to a sharp increase in the male enrollment, while the female enrollment remained relatively stable. This mirrors the pattern for the entire U.S.S.R., at least until recent years. The enrollment data for 1961 suggest that the decline in the proportion of women shown in Table 70 may have been reversed.

The distribution of women graduate students among the various fields of study was quite uneven. As shown in Table 74, the fields of public health and education account for between 60 and 70 per cent of the female enrollment in graduate programs, while only a very small proportion of women graduate students are in the fields of transportation and communication, the socioeconomic fields, and art. Public health and education are also the fields in which women make up the largest percentage of the enrollment in both types of graduate training. Women comprise approxi-

TABLE 73. Graduate students, by type of institution, 1929–61.[a]

	Males and Females			Males			Females					
Year	Total	Higher Educ. Inst.	Res. Estab.	Total	Higher Educ. Inst.	Res. Estab.	Total	Higher Educ. Inst.	Res. Estab.	Total	Higher Educ. Inst.	Res. Estab.
										%	%	%
1929	3,000	2,000	1,000	–	–	867	–	–	233	–	–	23.3
1931	–	7,400	–	–	(5,984)	–	–	(1,416)	–	23.0	19.0	19.9
1932	14,800	8,400	6,400	–	–	4,920	–	–	1,480	–	–	23.2
1934	10,600	6,300	4,300	–	–	3,143	–	–	1,157	–	–	36.9
1935	9,800	6,300	3,500	–	–	2,410	–	–	990	–	–	28.3
1938	12,186	9,175	3,011	8,288	6,367	1,921	3,898	2,808	1,090	32.0	30.6	36.2
1940	16,900	13,200	6,700	–	(7,458)	–	–	(5,742)	–	–	43.5	–
1946	–	9,536	–	–	5,439	–	–	4,097	–	–	43.2	–
1947	15,800	–	–	9,300	–	–	6,500	–	–	41.0	–	–
1950	21,900	–	–	13,312	–	–	8,588	–	–	39.0	–	–
1955	29,400	21,400	8,000	20,200	–	–	9,200	–	–	31.0	–	–
1956	25,500	17,800	7,800	18,100	–	–	7,400	–	–	29.0	–	–
1960	36,754	20,406	16,348	28,349	15,626	12,723	8,405	4,780	3,625	22.9	23.4	22.2
1961	47,560	27,066	20,494	35,812	20,020	15,792	11,748	7,046	4,702	24.7	–	–

[a]At the end of each calendar year. Total figures for 1929, 1932, 1934, 1935, 1938, and 1940 are from K. T. Galkin, *Vysshee obrazovanie i podgotovka nauchnykh kadrov v SSSR* (Moscow, 1958), p. 110; for 1947, 1950, 1955, and 1956, from *Kul'turnoe stroitel'stvo SSSR* (Moscow, 1956), p. 255; and for 1960, from *Vysshee obrazovanie i SSSR* (Moscow, 1961), pp. 223–24; for 1929, 1932, 1934, and 1935, from *Zhenshchina v SSSR* (Moscow, 1937), p. 110. The 1929 figure is for April 1, 1929; the 1931 total percentage (23 per cent) is from Galkin, *The Training of Scientists in the Soviet Union* (Moscow, 1959), p. 122, which conflicts with the other 1931 figures (19.0 and 19.9 per cent) from Galkin, *Vysshee obrazovanie*, p. 115. The 1938 figures for males and females are from *Kul'turnoe stroitel'stvo SSSR* (Moscow, Leningrad, 1940), p. 242; the 1940 percentage for females, from Galkin, *Vysshee obrazovanie*, p. 115; for 1946, November 5, 1947, from A. Ia. Sinetskii, *Professorsko-prepodo-vatel'skie kadry vysshei shkoly SSSR* (Moscow, 1950), p. 183; for 1950, 1955, and 1956, female enrollment and percentages are from *Narodnoe khoziaistvo SSSR v 1956 godu*, p. 261; for 1960, female enrollment and percentages, from *Vysshee obrazovanie v SSSR*, pp. 223–24; 1961 female enrollment and percentages are calculated from data in *Izvestiia*, September 17, 1963, and *Narodnoe khoziaistvo SSSR v 1962 godu* (Moscow, 1963), p. 587. The author is indebted to Mr. Nicholas Rokitiansky for pointing out the *Izvestiia* figures on female enrollment, which were published in response to a letter he wrote the editor.

mately 70 per cent of the students in the former field. More recent data for the Tartu State University illustrate the heavy concentration of women in history and philology in the universities. At Tartu in 1964, 40 per cent of the women graduate students were enrolled in these fields.[14]

Official data on the granting of candidate degrees to women are available only for the period from 1946 to 1953 (see Table 75).

[14]From a communication to the author from the university.

TABLE 74. Number and distribution of women graduate students, by type of institution and by field, 1938.[a]

		Women		
Type of Institution and Field	Total Enroll-ment	Enroll-ment	Per Cent	Distri-bution by Field
Higher educational institutions				
Industry and construction...	2,748	393	14.3	14.0
Transportation and com-munication.............	662	62	9.4	2.2
Agriculture..............	849	169	19.9	6.0
Socioeconomic..........	661	132	20.0	4.7
Education...............	2,296	792	34.5	28.2
Art.....................	270	97	35.9	3.5
Public health.............	1,689	1,163	68.9	41.4
Total.................	9,175	2,808	30.6	100.0
Research establishments				
Industry and construction...	519	140	27.0	12.8
Transportation and com-munication.............	55	4	7.3	0.4
Agriculture..............	462	123	26.6	11.3
Socioeconomic..........	57	14	24.6	1.3
Education...............	746	204	27.3	18.7
Art.....................	75	4	5.3	0.4
Public health.............	679	489	72.0	44.8
Academies of sciences.......	418	112	26.6	10.3
Total.................	3,011	1,070	36.2	100.0
Total of above				
Industry and construction...	3,267	533	16.3	13.7
Transportation and com-munication.............	717	66	9.2	1.7
Agriculture..............	1,311	292	22.3	7.5
Socioeconomic..........	718	146	20.3	3.7
Education...............	3,042	996	32.7	25.6
Art.....................	345	101	29.3	2.6
Public health.............	2,368	1,652	69.8	42.4
Academies of sciences.......	418	112	26.6	2.9
Total.....................	12,186	3,898	30.0	100.0

[a]At the end of the year. This table is based on *Kul'turnoe stroitel'stvo SSSR* (Moscow, Leningrad, 1940), p. 242.

Nevertheless, at least two thirds of the holders of candidate degrees in 1953 received their degree during these eight years. All together, women received 31 per cent of the degrees awarded. In each year the proportion of women graduates was slightly below the proportion enrolled in the several preceding years, which suggests that the attrition rate among women graduate students is higher than among men.

TABLE 75. Number and percentage of women granted candidate degrees, 1946–53.[a]

Year	Total Number of Candidates Certified	Number of Women Candidates	Percentage of Women
1946......	3,188	940	29
1947......	4,750	1,422	30
1948......	5,642	1,655	29
1949......	4,264	1,193	28
1950......	4,910	1,516	30
1951......	5,564	1,811	32
1952......	6,702	2,275	34
1953......	8,534	2,946	34
Total....	43,554	13,756	31

[a]Based on K. Galkin, *The Training of Scientists in the Soviet Union* (Moscow, 1959), p. 125. In the two-year period 1955–56 "over 5.5 thousand women received the candidate degree," according to K. T. Galkin, "Iz istorii attestatsii nauchno-pedogogicheskikh kadrov," *Vestnik vysshei shkoly*, No. 9 (Sept., 1957), 48.

Further insights into the proportion and distribution of women degree recipients among fields of study can be obtained from the published lists of dissertations received by the Lenin and Central Medical libraries. Although the data have been sparse and intermittent until recent years and only the names of the authors which are unequivocally male or female on the basis of the ending of the family name can be used, it is felt that a fairly accurate picture of the pattern which has evolved since the prewar period can be obtained. In Table 76 the estimated percentage of women receiving candidate degrees by major scientific fields is shown.[15] Nonscientific

[15]Appendix V, Table 1, gives the total number of dissertations received in each field of study, including the principal nonscientific fields, the percentage distribution of these among all

TABLE 76. Estimated percentage of women receiving candidate degrees, by field, selected years.[a]

Field	1936–37	1956–58	1959–61	1962–64
Pure science.............	23.8	38.3	33.6	25.5
Physics, mathematics...	6.1	23.1	15.3	16.8
Chemistry.............	25.9	52.6	50.7	38.2
Biology...............	36.8	66.5	52.2	53.2
Geology...............	22.7	27.0	26.8	26.9
Applied science..........	19.0	31.4	30.1	30.1
Technology............	4.4	18.5	15.8	12.4
Agriculture, veterinary medicine............	19.5	36.3	33.1	28.6
Medicine..............	28.6	54.4	52.7	47.0
Total...................	20.4	33.4	30.9	28.7
Nonscientific fields.......	21.0	31.5	27.2	25.3
Total, all fields..........	20.5	32.8	30.0	27.9

[a]This table was compiled from figures presented in Appendix V, Table 1.

fields, which account for less than a quarter of the total in recent years, are lumped together into one category.

The percentage of women among all recipients of the candidate degree increased from 20.5 to 32.8 per cent between 1936–37 and 1956–58 and then declined slightly in recent years. Looking at the broad breakdown between scientific and nonscientific fields, we find that the percentage of women receiving degrees has been very similar in each of the four periods covered. Within science, however, there has been considerable variation among the fields. In recent years the percentage of women has been very high in the fields of chemistry, biology, and medicine. The smallest proportion of female degree recipients has consistently been in the field of technology. Physics and mathematics also have a relatively low proportion of female de-

gree recipients. Nonetheless, women have made up approximately one sixth of those receiving candidate degrees in physics and mathematics in recent years.[16]

The proportion of women receiving doctoral degrees in various fields of study follows closely the pattern already observed for recipients of candidate degrees, but with some variations. Women make up a relatively high proportion of those receiving degrees in the fields of medicine, chemistry, and biology. The percentage of women in the nonscientific fields is now relatively low after a substantial decline since 1956. The proportion of women in all fields decreases as the degree ladder is climbed. The reduction in the proportion of women is particularly marked at the doctoral level. According to estimates of the percentage of women among doctoral degree recipients (see Table 77), approximately 10 per cent were women in 1936–37, 15 per cent in 1956–58, 18 per cent in 1959–61, and 21 per cent in 1962–64. Although the percentage of women receiving doctoral degrees still remains well below that of women receiving candidate degrees, it has risen significantly during the past two and a half decades.[17]

In an examination of the productivity of women scientists and other professional women in Chapter 12, a tendency toward an inverse relationship between the level of

---

fields, the proportion of the dissertations authored by persons with unequivocally male or female family names, and the percentage of women among this group. Where the initial number of dissertations is small and the "sample" of names small as well, the percentage of women among the sample might differ widely from that of the total if it were known. As the number of dissertations increases, as it does in recent years, we can assume that the percentages, at least for the larger fields or groupings, reflect fairly accurately the actual percentages of women receiving degrees.

[16]A tabulation of candidate dissertations in the field of science and technology made by Professor John B. Parrish, "Professional Womanpower as a Soviet Resource," *Quarterly Review of Economics and Business* (Autumn, 1964), 55–61, indicated that women earned about 25 per cent of the candidate degrees awarded in the 1955–58 period. In the biological sciences, the percentage was 53.4; in the physical sciences, 28.6; in mathematics, 16.2; and in engineering, 14.8.

[17]These estimated percentages agree closely with more direct evidence from DeWitt, *op. cit.*, pp. 756–57, who estimated that 978 doctor degrees were awarded in 1940 from a five-year total presented in Galkin, *Vysshee obrazovanie*, p. 155. Galkin also gives a figure of 42 female degree recipients in 1940, or approximately 4 per cent. During the five-year period ending in 1955, 2,886 doctoral degrees were awarded, of which 376, or 13 per cent, were awarded to women (*ibid.*, p. 125, and DeWitt, *op. cit.*, p. 756).

TABLE 77. Estimated percentage of women receiving doctoral degrees, by field, selected years.[a]

Field	1936–37	1941–45	1956–58	1959–61	1962–64
Pure science....................	15.1	10.5	8.3	15.4	16.8
Physics, mathematics...........	7.7	2.8	0.0	4.3	7.7
Chemistry....................	8.3	8.5	17.6	17.8	40.0
Biology......................	23.8	14.5	28.6	36.0	30.8
Geology.....................	9.1	12.5	10.5	10.4	23.1
Applied science................	8.4	0.9	15.5	18.9	26.3
Technology..................	0.0	0.5	3.6	4.2	2.9
Agriculture, veterinary medicine...	0.0	2.7	12.5	11.1	13.0
Medicine.....................	10.7	–	51.2	41.0	42.3
Total........................	9.6	5.3	13.1	18.0	23.7
Nonscientific fields..............	8.3	6.5	19.8	16.3	11.3
Total, all fields.................	9.6	5.5	14.8	17.7	21.2

[a]See Appendix V, Table 2.

scientific research and scholarship and the ratio of women contributors is evident. The higher the research or academic rank, the lower the proportion of women. Similarly, there are fewer women among those receiving candidate degrees than among those completing an undergraduate education, and there are still fewer women among those receiving doctorates. Apparently the distractions of family and other responsibilities have their greatest impact at the higher levels of creative work. Employing the same graphic analysis used in examining the situation at the undergraduate level (Fig. 17), we must assume in Figure 18 a more substantial difference between the expected and potential productivity of women having a capacity of graduate work than among those capable of undergraduate work. It will be seen from Figure 18 that the optimal proportion of females who should be admitted to graduate training, if efficiency is the criterion, is relatively small.[18] Hence, the small proportion of female graduate students re-

[18]The diagram and its interpretation follow Fig. 17, p. 117. Males should be admitted to graduate training up to the number *OW* before any women are admitted. From this point, men and women should be admitted on the basis of their net productivity until all places are filled. At the cutoff point, *OF'*, the expected productivity of the last male (*M'N*) and the last female (*F'Q*) admitted should be equal.

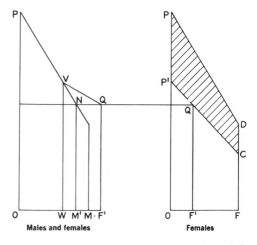

FIG. 18. Optimal proportion of male and female enrollment in graduate education.

ceiving the candidate degree and the still smaller proportion receiving the doctorate are to be expected and represent a rational use of limited resources. Indeed, it probably would be a mistake from the standpoint of the efficient use of resources for the government to press for a more equal ratio of women to men.

CONCLUSIONS

A uniform curriculum through the tenth grade, with some regional variations incorporating native languages and literature, ensures that girls in the Soviet Union receive as much training in the sciences and mathematics as boys. As a result, young women are as well prepared formally as are young men to enter scientific or technical fields at the specialized secondary or higher educational level. The success of the Soviet Union in attracting women to the fields of science and technology at these higher educational levels is clearly apparent from the statistics on enrollment by field of study. In 1964 women made up 29 per cent of the students enrolled in engineering, 25 per cent of those in agriculture, 52 per cent of those in medicine, and 64 per cent of those in the cultural-educational fields. On the basis of available data on university enrollments, it is estimated that three fourths to four fifths of the students enrolled in biology, more than two thirds of those in chemistry, two fifths to a half in mathematics, and a quarter to two fifths in physics, geology, and the agricultural sciences are women. These are impressive percentages and have been achieved, in part, through the efforts of the regime to alter the public image of various professions for women. Forty years ago, parents would steer their daughters away from a field such as engineering. Now such fields have become quite acceptable for women. The development of talents of women which would otherwise have been wasted has been of great benefit to the Soviet economy and is a distinct accomplishment.

The pattern of enrollment of women among fields in graduate study is similar to that at the undergraduate level, but the proportion of women in each field is generally lower. In recent years, women have received about 30 per cent of the candidate degrees and 20 per cent of the doctoral degrees. The smaller proportion of women among scholars obtaining the candidate and doctoral degrees seems to reflect the same considerations of efficiency which help explain the reduction in the percentage of women enrolled in higher education in the past decade. Because of the lower average productivity of women professionals, the rational use of scarce educational resources at these highest levels would call for a reduction in the proportion of women from the proportion trained at the undergraduate level. It seems probable, however, that a process of self-selection has been at work in this instance rather than any overt or covert form of restriction. Because of greater conflicts with one's career which usually come with being a woman, fewer women than men appear to want to undertake the rigors of advanced training. Hence, women can be expected to make up a smaller proportion of graduate students regardless of government policy.

Changes in the proportion of women enrolled in the various levels of the educational system suggest that Soviet manpower planners and educational administrators have been consciously or unconsciously following economic principles aimed at the rational utilization of their limited educational resources. Such a policy called for substantial increases in the proportion of women receiving various forms of specialized or graduate training until after World War II. With a return to more normal conditions in the postwar period, the proportion of women enrolled in secondary specialized or higher educational institutions declined. We have seen that this decline can be fully justified on purely economic grounds. Stabilization in the past few years of the proportion of women enrolled suggests that a new equilibrium at a relatively high level, but below the proportion of women in the population of college age, may have been found which will continue so long as underlying conditions remain unchanged.

We may conclude that the Soviets have been markedly successful in their efforts to educate women, and, in particular, to interest them in fields such as science, technology, and medicine, in which relatively few women have been interested in other parts of the world. As a result, they have been able to develop and to employ rare talents which otherwise would have been lost to their society and to its development.

chapter
8

EDUCATIONAL ATTAINMENT

In Chapters 6 and 7 an attempt was made, by analyzing the pattern of participation of women in the various educational programs provided by the government, to gain some insight into Soviet policies on manpower utilization. In this chapter the success of the educational programs over the years in developing the cadres of trained personnel needed in the Soviet economy will be examined. We shall look at the educational attainments of Soviet women, comparing them with those of men and with the attainments of women at earlier dates. We shall first discuss the degree of literacy among Soviet women—an indication of the extent to which primary education has been made available—and then turn to their higher educational attainment.

THE ATTACK ON ILLITERACY
AMONG WOMEN

With the inauguration of the Five-Year Plans, the equalitarian aims of the early Soviet educational policy received strong reinforcement from the imperatives of economic development. In order to utilize more fully the vast human resources of Russia in building a modern industrial society, it was necessary to provide as rapidly as possible both the rudimentary knowledge and skills needed by industrial workers and the more sophisticated knowledge and skills needed by the technicians, engineers, scientists, and managers. However, it was not until the First Five-Year

Plan (1928–32) that the attack on illiteracy, so prevalent among Russian women at the time, began to open all levels of education and all types of careers to them.

The two great segments of the population whose basic education had been neglected were the rural population as a whole and women. Among rural women, where these two categories overlapped, illiteracy was particularly high. In 1926, for example, it was almost five times as high as among urban males. With this initial disparity and the total population now moving toward 100 per cent literacy, the reported improvement in the literacy rate of women, and of rural women in particular, is very impressive.

In order to serve as an accurate measure of the rate of improvement, however, the literacy rate must be based upon a consistent definition of literacy. This has not, unfortunately, been the case in the Soviet censuses. In prerevolutionary Russia, literacy was defined as "the ability to read and write proficiently" and was determined by a standard test. In the 1926 population census, this definition was changed to "ability to read" and no standard test was required. In the 1939 and 1959 censuses, a slightly altered definition, "ability to read or write,"[1] was applied,

---

[1] Frank Lorimer, *The Population of the Soviet Union: History and Prospects* (Geneva, 1946), pp. 198–99, and Nicholas DeWitt, *Education and Professional Employment in the U.S.S.R.* (Washington, D.C., 1961), pp. 71–72.

but, again, no standard test of proficiency was required. Thus, in the absence of such a test, the ability to read some of the common political slogans on banners or to sign one's name was often judged evidence of literacy. Hence, many persons reported literate would properly have to be considered functionally illiterate. As a result, it is difficult to make adequate comparisons among the literacy rates given in the various census returns.

The change in definition and the relaxation of testing methods in the 1926 census probably caused the greatest upward bias in the reported figures; the further relaxation in definition in 1939, coupled with the atmosphere in which that census was taken, undoubtedly resulted in additional exaggeration. Nevertheless, it cannot be denied that the general educational level has risen impressively under the Soviet regime and is strikingly higher than it was half a century ago. Data on literacy rates from the censuses of 1897, 1926, 1939, and 1959 are summarized in Table 78.

At the end of the century the great bulk of the Russian population was illiterate. According to the 1897 census figures for the age group 9 to 49, only 40.3 per cent of the men and 16.6 per cent of the women were literate. The disparity between the literacy of males and females was matched by the disparity between urban and rural literacy rates: 57.0 per cent of the urban population was literate, but only 23.8 per cent of the rural population was literate. Two thirds of the urban males, but only slightly more than a third of the rural males, were literate. Nearly half the urban women could read and write, but only one eighth of the rural women were literate; among women in rural areas over age 50, the literacy rate was only 4.1 per cent.[2]

Before the Revolution, social class was the principal determinant of educational opportunities. And the poorer the class, the lower the relative attainment of women. Among the noble and official class, 73.2 per cent of the males and 69.2 per cent of the females were literate. The percentages for the Christian clergy and their families were similar. Among the urban population of all ages, 50.1 per cent of the males and 31.1 per cent of the females were literate. In the rural areas, the rates dropped to 27.4 and 9.7 per cent, respectively.[3]

The inequities of education under the tsars are further illustrated by comparing the literacy rates in the areas on the southern periphery of the country with the average for the empire as a whole. As against an average for the empire in 1897 of 28.4 per cent for both sexes in the age group 9 to 49, the literacy rate in the area of what became the Tadzhik republic was 2.3 per cent; in the Kirgiz area, 3.1 per cent; and in the Uzbek area, 3.6 per cent. The Moslem cultural traditions relegating women to the status of chattels were responsible for the especially low literacy rates of women in the regions which now constitute these three republics, particu-

TABLE 78. Percentage of literacy of the urban and rural population, age 9–49, by sex, 1897, 1926, 1939, and 1959.[a]

Census Year	Total	Males	Females
Urban and rural			
1897............	28.4	40.3	16.6
1926............	56.6	71.5	42.7
1939............	87.4	93.5	81.6
1959............	98.5	99.3	97.8
Urban			
1897............	57.0	66.1	45.7
1926............	80.9	88.0	73.9
1939............	93.8	97.1	90.7
1959............	98.7	99.5	98.1
Rural			
1897............	23.8	35.5	12.5
1926............	50.6	67.3	35.4
1939............	84.0	91.6	76.8
1959............	98.2	99.1	97.5

[a]Based on *Itogi . . . 1959 goda: SSSR*, p. 88. The data refer to different territories. The 1939 and 1959 figures refer to the territory with present boundaries. The 1897 figures refer to the same territory except for Galicia and northern Bukovina. The 1926 figures exclude the Baltic States and the western *oblasts* of the Ukraine and Belorussia.

[2]For the literacy rates of the urban and rural population of each republic, see Appendix VI, Table 1.

[3]William H. E. Johnson, *Russia's Educational Heritage* (Pittsburgh, 1950), p. 284. These figures refer to persons of all ages.

larly in the rural areas. The rates for the other southern areas were only slightly higher.[4]

Progress in increasing the literacy rate during the last years of the tsarist regime came to a halt with the outbreak of World War I, which initiated a difficult period for Russian education. And the decline in the literacy rate among persons of schol age was sharply accelerated after the Revolution because of the disruptions in school caused by the Civil War.[5]

The fight against illiteracy was, nevertheless, considered one of the government's most important tasks, and a major effort to reduce illiteracy was made on the local level at the end of the Civil War. Almost a fifth of the local educational budgets was reserved by a decree of the Commissariat of Public Education for adult education.[6] By 1926 the efforts of the new regime to increase literacy began to bear fruit. Even if allowance for an upward bias in the statistics is made, the results are impressive. The over-all literacy rate for both sexes, age 9 to 49, was reported to have doubled. Among all women the rate increased almost two and a half times, while among rural women it almost tripled. Almost two thirds of the remaining illiterates, however, were women. The worst concentrations were in the Central Asian republics, where over 90 per cent of the women remained illiterate.

As previously mentioned, a special campaign to eradicate illiteracy was launched in the interests of rapid industrialization during the First Five-Year Plan.[7] It was officially claimed that 45 million persons were taught to read and write during the drive, bringing the rate for all persons age 9 to 49 to almost 90 per cent.[8] A special effort was made with women. For example, women workers with children and older women who found study particularly difficult were tutored at home. Also, child-care facilities were provided to enable mothers to attend classes.[9] As a result, the census of 1939 reported the literacy rate for women age 9 to 49 to be over 80 per cent, only 12 percentage points below that for men. It will be seen, however, that the illiteracy rate among women remained nearly three times as high as among men. The urban-rural difference was also narrowed, but the literacy rate of 76.8 per cent among rural women still lagged 14 percentage points behind that of urban women, while rural men lagged only 5.5 percentage points behind urban men. Even in Central Asia, the reported 1939 rates were not far behind the national average. In none of these republics was a literacy rate of less than 66.5 per cent reported for rural women. Moldavia alone, with a literacy rate of only 28.4 per cent, stood out as a pocket of female illiteracy.

Among older women throughout the U.S.S.R., illiteracy remained high despite the special efforts to combat it. The literacy rate for women over 50 years of age was only 24.8 per cent: 46.4 per cent in the cities, 15.8 per cent in rural areas. Also, among rural men in this age group the rate was less than a third the rate among urban men.

By the 1959 census, illiteracy as then defined was virtually wiped out in all segments of the population except among the aged. In the age group 9 to 49, the reported literacy rate was 98.5 per cent. The lowest rate reported in the entire Soviet Union—for rural women in the Turkmen republic—was 93.2 per cent.

The 1959 figures on literacy by republic provide evidence of the transformation in the status of women, particularly in Central Asia and in republics on the southern perimeter of

---

[4]See Appendix VI, Table 1.
[5]Manya Gordon, *Workers before and after Lenin* (New York, 1941), p. 436.
[6]Nicholas Hans and Sergius Hessen, *Educational Policy in Soviet Russia* (London, 1930), p. 80.
[7]Susan M. Kingsbury and Mildred Fairchild, *Factory, Family and Women in the Soviet Union* (New York, 1935), pp. 169–72.

[8]Gosplan SSSR, *Itogi vypolneniia pervogo piatiletnego plana razvitiia narodnogo khoziaistva SSSR* (Moscow, 1935), p. 222.
[9]Kingsbury and Fairchild, *op. cit.*, p. 169.

the Soviet Union. To cite the most extreme case, less than 1 per cent of all women in the Tadzhik republic were reported literate in 1926, but by 1939 the percentage had increased to 77.5 and by 1959 to 94.6.[10] In the Kirgiz, Turkmen, and Uzbek republics, where the literacy rate ranged from 7.3 to 8.8 per cent in 1926, literacy among women was reported to have increased to between 93.4 and 97.3 per cent in 1959. Similar, though slightly less dramatic, transformations occurred in the Kazakh, Azerbaidzhan, and Armenian republics.

LEVELS OF EDUCATIONAL ATTAINMENT

The larger number of women in the able-bodied age groups of the Soviet population make it possible for women with a given level of education to outnumber men at the same level, even though the proportion of women who have attained this educational level is smaller than the proportion of men. In assessing the extent to which the Soviets have de-

[10]See Appendix VI, Table 1.

veloped their female potential, it is necessary to examine educational attainment in the light of this fact. Table 79, showing the 1939 and 1959 census data on the number of men and women in the entire population and in the able-bodied age groups with secondary and higher education, enables us to draw some conclusions regarding the relative size of the pools of educated men and women from which the educated labor force may be drawn in the Soviet Union. Looking at the population in the able-bodied groups, we find that in 1939 women accounted for 44.5 per cent of the persons with some secondary education and in 1959 for 52.8 per cent, but the increase in the relative importance of women among those who completed a higher education has been even more striking. In 1939 women accounted for only 32.3 per cent of those in the able-bodied age group with a higher education. By 1959 this figure had grown to 48.6 per cent. This development reflects, of course, both the increasing number of women completing higher education in recent decades and the loss of male lives in this age group during World War II.

At each level of educational attainment, ur-

TABLE 79. Men and women with secondary and higher education, 1939 and 1959.[a]

| | Total Population | | | | Able-bodied Age Groups[b] | | | |
| | Higher Education | | Secondary Education[c] | | Higher Education | | Secondary Education[c] | |
Population	1939	1959	1939	1959	1939	1959	1939	1959
Total	1,177,081	3,777,535	14,689,330	54,929,658	1,051,594	3,487,454	12,298,413	51,596,323
Males	799,207	1,933,226	8,053,185	25,711,231	711,980	1,791,596	6,830,353	24,346,348
Females	377,874	1,844,309	6,636,145	29,218,427	339,614	1,695,858	5,468,060	27,249,975
Females	32.1%	48.8%	45.2%	53.2%	32.3%	48.6%	44.5%	52.8%
Urban	956,179	3,169,391	9,805,745	34,457,715	855,994	2,902,885	8,291,005	32,362,280
Males	628,494	1,594,870	4,954,040	15,530,976	560,595	1,467,268	4,236,533	14,758,428
Females	327,685	1,574,521	4,851,705	18,926,739	295,399	1,435,617	4,054,472	17,603,852
Females	34.3%	49.7%	49.5%	54.9%	34.5%	49.5%	48.9%	54.4%
Rural	220,902	608,144	4,883,585	20,471,943	195,600	584,569	4,007,408	19,234,043
Male	170,713	338,356	3,099,145	10,180,255	151,385	324,328	2,593,820	9,587,920
Females	50,189	269,788	1,784,440	10,291,688	44,215	260,241	1,413,588	9,646,123
Females	22.7%	44.4%	36.5%	50.3%	22.6%	44.5%	35.3%	50.2%

[a]Figures represent absolute numbers. The 1939 figures in every instance are for boundaries prior to Sept. 17, 1939. This table is based on figures from *Itogi ... 1959 goda: SSSR*, p. 81.

[b]Men, age 16–59; women, age 16–54.
[c]Including those with incomplete secondary or incomplete higher education.

ban women make up a higher percentage than rural women. This urban-rural disparity was particularly marked in 1939, but since then the gap has been significantly narrowed. In 1959, for example, women accounted for 44.5 per cent of the able-bodied rural and 49.5 per cent of the able-bodied urban population with a higher education. This gap has narrowed considerably from the 11.9 percentage point difference which existed in 1939. There also has been a comparable narrowing of the urban-rural difference for women at the secondary educational level.

By combining data in Table 79 with population data, we derive Table 80, showing the number of persons per thousand who have reached various levels of education. An initial examination of the combined figures for urban and rural population reveals that in both 1939 and 1959 the proportion of men with a secondary or a higher education was greater than the proportion of women, and considerably so in the case of the latter. In 1939 more than twice as many men as women per thousand in the able-bodied age group had a higher education, but by 1959 the gap had been narrowed, and the proportion of men was only 30 per cent greater than women.

For both men and women, the level of educational achievement still remains much higher in urban than in rural areas. In 1959 the proportion of persons with a higher edu-cation was more than five times as high in the city as in the country, and the low educational level in the rural areas was even lower for women than for men. In 1959, 35 males per thousand in the urban population had a higher education, while in the rural population only 7 had this distinction, yielding a ratio of 5 to 1 in favor of the urban population. The rates for women, however, were 29 and 4, a ratio of over 7 to 1. And although the disparities are smaller at the lower educational levels, the general pattern remains much the same.

We have noted before that generally lower motivation and restricted educational opportunities in rural areas result in the enrollment in higher educational institutions of a much smaller proportion of the rural than urban population, particularly of women. The problem of low enrollment is further compounded by the smaller number of rural jobs requiring advanced educational training, which in many cases causes persons who have acquired a higher education to migrate to the cities. Lower job availability alone would result in a lower level of educational achievement among the rural population.

In rural areas more than two thirds of the able-bodied age group have fewer than four years of schooling. Nevertheless, the improvement over the years has been considerable. As Table 80 shows, the gains of the rural

TABLE 80. Proportion of men and women with secondary and higher education, 1939 and 1959.[a]

| | Total Population | | | | | | Able-bodied Age Groups[b] | | | | | |
| | Higher Education | | Secondary Education[c] | | Less than 7-yr. Education | | Higher Education | | Secondary Education[c] | | Less than 7-yr. Education | |
Population	1939	1959	1939	1959	1939	1959	1939	1959	1939	1959	1939	1959
Total............	6	18	77	263	917	719	12	29	135	431	853	540
Males..........	9	21	88	273	903	706	16	33	153	442	831	525
Females........	4	16	67	255	929	729	7	26	118	421	875	553
Urban............	16	32	162	344	822	624	25	47	239	520	736	433
Males..........	22	35	171	344	807	621	33	51	249	514	718	435
Females........	10	29	154	346	836	625	17	43	230	526	753	431
Rural............	2	6	37	188	961	806	3	10	71	334	926	656
Males..........	3	7	50	208	947	785	5	12	94	364	901	624
Females........	1	4	26	172	973	824	2	8	49	308	949	684

[a]Figures represent the number of persons per thousand. The 1939 figures in every instance are for boundaries prior to Sept. 17, 1939. For the source of these data, see Table 79, n.

[b]Men, age 16–59; women, age 16–54.
[c]Including those with incomplete secondary or incomplete higher education.

population have been much higher in relative numbers than those of the urban population at both the higher and the secondary educational levels. While the attainment rate for men with a higher education more than doubled between 1939 and 1959, the rate for women quadrupled, and at the lower educational levels there was a sixfold increase for women, but only a fourfold increase for men.

Table 81 shows the educational levels of urban and rural workers, employees, and collective farmers in 1939 and 1959. Examination of this table shows an over-all increase of 350 per cent in the proportion of persons with a higher or secondary education, including those with incomplete secondary education. For males the increase was 320 per cent and for females 410 per cent. Among employees the increase was only 170 per cent, while among collective farm workers it was 1,260 per cent. Also we see reflected the relatively greater educational advances made by rural women as compared with their urban counterparts.

As indicated in Table 81, the differences among the educational levels of workers, employees, and collective farmers have narrowed significantly, but they still remain large. Since the educational needs of these three social groups differ considerably, it can be anticipated that future narrowing will be less than in the past. It is not likely that collective farmers will ever achieve the educational levels of workers and employees, because the educational demands of their work will remain less rigorous.

THE EDUCATIONALLY DEPRIVED

A four-year elementary education did not become compulsory until the fall of 1930. Compulsory seven-year education was introduced in major urban and industrial centers only in 1943 and was supposed to become universally compulsory in 1949. In the statistics of educational attainment the proportions of the population who have not completed a four- or seven-year education are of special interest since these indicate the scope of the problem of the educationally deprived which still confronts the Soviet Union.

Although impressive gains have been made in the number of women who have acquired higher or secondary education, nevertheless, over half the women in the Soviet Union have received less than a seven-year education. Indeed, a surprisingly large number have received less than a four-year education. Table 82 shows the number of men and women age 15 and over and in the able-bodied age group who in 1959 had had less than a seven-year education. There were 53.9 million women and 35.6 million men age 15 and over with less than a seven-year education. Women accounted for 57.3 per cent of the population age 15 and over, but for 60.2 per cent of

TABLE 81. Male and female workers, employees, and collective farmers in the urban and rural population with higher or secondary education, 1939 and 1959.[a]

Population	Total			Workers			Employees			Collective Farmers		
	1939	1959	Ratio	1939	1959	Ratio	1939	1959	Ratio	1939	1959	Ratio
Total..........	123	433	3.5	82	386	4.7	519	893	1.7	18	226	12.6
Males........	136	434	3.2	100	393	3.9	455	859	1.9	26	261	10.0
Females.....	104	431	4.1	44	377	8.6	639	921	1.4	11	198	18.0
Urban..........	242	564	2.3	96	424	4.4	555	898	1.6	50	241	4.8
Males........	235	537	2.3	122	430	3.5	496	872	1.8	63	287	4.6
Females.....	255	597	2.3	54	413	7.6	641	918	1.4	26	193	7.4
Rural..........	63	316	5.0	60	311	5.2	454	879	1.9	17	226	13.3
Males........	81	337	4.2	73	320	4.4	394	828	2.1	24	260	10.8
Females.......	42	294	7.0	27	296	11.0	632	927	1.5	10	198	19.8

[a]Including those with incomplete secondary or incomplete higher education. Figures represent the number of persons per thousand. This table is based on *Itogi . . . 1959 goda: SSSR*, p. 116.

TABLE 82. Number and percentage of persons with less than a seven-year education in the population age 15 and over and in the able-bodied age group, 1959.[a]

Education of Population	Total	Males	Females	Females
				%
Age 15 and over.......	148,186	63,232	84,954	57.3
7-year or more.......	58,708	27,645	31,063	52.9
Less than 7-year.....	89,478	35,587	53,891	60.2
Less than 7-year.....	60.4%	56.3%	63.4%	
Able-bodied age group[b].	119,822	55,072	64,750	54.0
7-year or more.......	55,084	26,138	28,946	52.5
Less than 7-year.....	64,738	28,934	35,804	55.3
Less than 7-year.....	54.0%	52.5%	55.3%	

[a]Figures are expressed in thousands. This table is based on data derived from *Itogi . . . 1959 goda: SSSR*, pp. 54, 56, 58, 81, and 98, and *Zhenshchiny i deti v SSSR* (Moscow, 1961), p. 57.
[b]Males, age 16–59; females, age 16–54.

those age 15 and over with less than a seven-year education. Furthermore, 56.3 per cent of the males and 63.4 per cent of the women in this age group had had less than a seven-year education; in the able-bodied group, these figures were 52.5 and 55.3, respectively.

The very large number of uneducated women and the contrast between the educational achievement of men and women are shown even more dramatically in Table 83, which focuses on persons with less than a four-year education. It can be seen that over a third of the population age 20 and over had not completed a four-year education. There were 12.5 million men, constituting 22.9 per cent of the male population in this age group, and almost three times as many women, constituting 44.2 per cent of the women age 20 and over. Expressed in slightly different terms, women age 20 and over made up 58.4 per cent of the population in this age group and yet accounted for 73.0 per cent of those in

TABLE 83. Number and percentage of persons with less than a four-year education in the population age 20 and over, 1959.[a]

Education of Population	Total	Males	Females	Females
				%
Age 20 and over.......	130,656	54,376	76,280	58.4
Less than 4-year.....	46,144	12,455	33,688	73.0
Less than 4-year.....	35.3%	22.9%	44.2%	

[a]Figures are expressed in thousands. This table is derived from data in *Itogi . . . 1959 goda: SSSR*, pp. 74–75.

this group who had had less than a four-year education.

In order to gauge the economic significance of the low level of educational attainment by so large a segment of the Soviet population, an additional table has been compiled (Table 84), eliminating men age 60 and over and women age 55 and over. The age grouping is that of the able-bodied, except for the omission of the age group 16 to 19.[11] Since the oldest age groups have the lowest levels of educational attainment, the confinement of our data to the working-age group somewhat improves the picture of the educational level. Nevertheless, a quarter of the population in this group had less than a four-year education. Again the urban-rural and male-female differences are substantial: only a sixth of the urban population, but a third of the rural population, in this age group had less than a four-year education. Among both the urban and rural populations the proportion of women with fewer than four years of schooling was approximately double that of men, but, surprisingly, the discrepancy was slightly greater in urban areas. Women accounted for more than two thirds of the persons with less than a four-year education among both the urban and the rural populations.

Previous educational policies left the Soviets with a difficult heritage. Improvement was obstructed by the Civil War, collectivization, and World War II, all of which increased the immense problems involved in raising the educational level of the population. At least another generation will be required before the percentage of educationally deprived, particularly among women, is reduced to insignificant levels.

AGE AND URBAN-RURAL DISPARITIES IN EDUCATIONAL ATTAINMENT

As would be expected in a rapidly developing country, the distribution of educational attainment in the Soviet Union varies widely

[11]An absence of data necessitates beginning the figures at age 20 rather than 16.

TABLE 84. Number and percentage of persons with less than a four-year education in the able-bodied age group, 1959.[a]

Education of Population	Total	Males	Females	Females
				%
Total				
Women age 20–54 and men age 20–59.....	105,146,374	47,731,901	57,414,473	54.6
Less than 4-year....................	26,833,950	8,038,514	17,795,436	66.3
Less than 4-year....................	25.5%	16.8%	31.9%	
Urban				
Women age 20–54 and men age 20–59.....	54,893,897	25,143,287	29,750,610	54.2
Less than 4-year....................	8,751,698	2,616,043	6,135,655	70.1
Less than 4-year....................	15.9%	10.4%	20.6%	
Rural				
Women age 20–54 and men age 20–59.....	50,251,477	22,588,614	27,663,863	55.1
Less than 4-year....................	16,768,418	5,373,268	11,395,150	68.0
Less than 4-year....................	33.4%	23.8%	41.2%	

[a]Except for the omission of the age group 16–19. This table is derived from *Itogi . . . 1959 goda: SSSR*, pp. 74–79.

with age. The educational achievement of the younger age groups is dramatically higher than that of the older, reflecting the much larger numbers educated at all levels since the Revolution. The improvement is particularly marked for women.[12] In the younger age groups the educational attainment of women is as high or higher than that of men. In the age groups 40 and above, however, the percentage of women with secondary or higher education declines sharply with advancing age, both absolutely and in relation to that of men.

The devastating impact of World War II is illustrated by Figure 19. Instead of a steady improvement in educational attainment from the oldest to the youngest age groups, one finds an abnormally low percentage with higher education in the age group 30 to 34 and with secondary education in the age group 25 to 29. In the latter age group the percentage of persons with an elementary and incomplete seven-year education is abnormally high. The pattern revealed in Figure 19 indicates that many in the age group which passed from ages 7 to 12 to ages 12 to 17 during the period 1941 to 1946, when the

devastation and disruption of war were greatest, were kept from completing the usual seven-year education.

Figures 20 and 21 indicate considerable urban-rural differences in educational attainment. In the earlier age groups, considerably more rural than urban women had only an elementary or incomplete seven-year education. Indeed, the number of rural men who continued their education is smaller than the number of urban women. Among rural women age 20 to 24, only 549 per 1,000 obtained some form of secondary education, but among urban women the rate was 783 per 1,000. Rural women over age 45 were practically uneducated. In the age group 45 to 49, for example, only 132 per 1,000 had an elementary, 34 a secondary, and 2 a higher education. For the age group 55 to 59, these rates fell to 89, 18, and 2, respectively. In contrast, the figures for urban women in the latter group were 189, 149, and 25. We may conclude that among women secondary education and, to an even greater extent, higher education are largely for the young, especially young urban women, and that rural women even in the younger age groups are likely to have substantially less education than their city cousins.

[12]See Appendix VI, Tables 2–4.

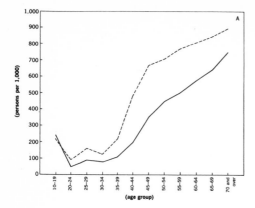

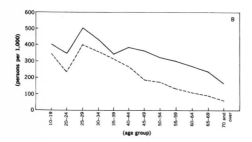

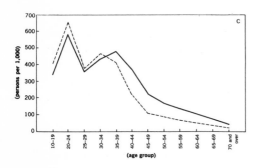

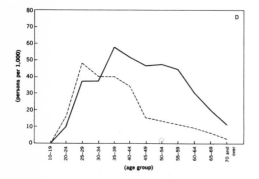

REGIONAL DIFFERENCES IN EDUCATIONAL ATTAINMENT

Differences in educational attainment among the republics are also substantial, reflecting their differing stages of economic and cultural development. Table 85 shows the number of persons per thousand in 1959 with a higher or secondary education in the able-bodied age groups of each republic. The urban and rural rates are also shown. The highest proportions of women with a higher education were found in Georgia (55 per 1,000) and Armenia (44 per 1,000), where past cultural traditions have been favorable to the education of both men and women. Although women have fewer advantages in these republics in other respects, their level of educational achievement is high. The urban-rural differential remained large, however. In Armenia, more than six times as many urban as rural women per thousand had a higher education; in Georgia, the differential was very near the over-all average of 5.4 to 1.

Next in rank in higher education were the Baltic republics of Latvia (33 per 1,000) and Estonia (32 per 1,000). However, Lithuania (20 per 1,000) lagged behind the national average. Despite the relatively high over-all level of education in the Latvian and Estonian republics, the urban-rural differences there were great, and the level of education in the rural areas of both fell below the national average. In Lithuania, the difference was particularly great and was the prime cause of the low average achievement. The only other republics which exceeded the national average of 26 per 1,000 were Azerbaidzhan (30 per 1,000) and the R.S.F.S.R. (28 per 1,000). Urban-rural differences in Azerbaidzhan were

FIG. 19. Educational level of the urban and rural population, by age and sex, January 15, 1959. *Solid lines,* males; *broken lines,* females. *A,* less than a four-year education; *B,* elementary and incomplete seven-year education; *C,* seven-year, incomplete secondary, secondary, and incomplete higher education; *D,* higher education. See Appendix VI, Table 2.

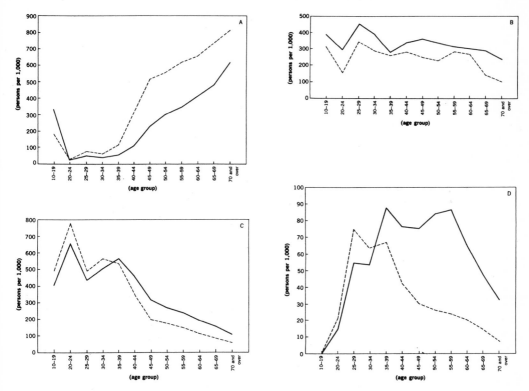

Fig. 20. Educational level of the urban population, by age and sex, January 15, 1959. *Solid lines,* males; *broken lines,* females. *A,* less than a four-year education; *B,* elementary and incomplete seven-year education; *C,* seven-year, incomplete secondary, secondary, and incomplete higher education; *D,* higher education. See Appendix VI, Table 2.

TABLE 85. Persons of able-bodied age with higher and secondary education, by republic, 1959.[a]

Republic	Higher Education						Secondary Education[b]						Less than 7-yr. Education					
	Total		Urban		Rural		Total		Urban		Rural		Total		Urban		Rural	
	M	F	M	F	M	F	M	F	M	F	M	F	M	F	M	F	M	F
U.S.S.R.	33	26	51	43	12	8	442	421	514	526	364	308	525	553	435	431	624	684
R.S.F.S.R.	33	28	49	42	12	9	426	427	493	520	338	308	541	545	458	438	650	683
Ukrainian S.S.R.	30	23	50	41	10	7	473	420	558	548	386	301	497	557	392	411	604	692
Belorussian S.S.R.	23	19	50	42	9	6	392	363	558	572	306	252	585	618	392	386	685	742
Uzbek S.S.R.	31	20	57	43	15	4	501	405	539	491	477	350	468	575	404	466	508	646
Kazakh S.S.R.	26	18	37	30	16	8	457	399	495	478	424	325	517	583	468	492	560	667
Georgian S.S.R.	72	55	116	92	34	22	522	526	584	611	468	449	406	419	300	297	498	529
Azerbaidzhan S.S.R.	48	30	72	52	21	5	543	431	560	502	525	350	409	539	368	446	454	645
Lithuanian S.S.R.	24	20	49	40	6	5	270	287	431	454	155	159	706	693	520	506	839	836
Moldavian S.S.R.	19	16	56	48	7	5	334	278	497	492	282	207	647	706	447	460	711	788
Latvian S.S.R.	33	33	49	49	10	9	511	538	599	630	386	400	456	429	352	321	604	591
Kirgiz S.S.R.	30	22	50	41	17	9	482	397	531	497	452	332	488	581	419	462	531	659
Tadzhik S.S.R.	25	16	48	36	12	3	461	358	500	442	439	307	514	626	452	522	549	690
Armenian S.S.R.	58	44	86	71	26	11	542	509	579	589	498	418	400	447	335	340	476	571
Turkmen S.S.R.	31	19	43	34	19	4	518	455	525	476	511	431	451	526	432	490	470	565
Estonian S.S.R.	35	32	50	45	13	11	446	509	538	601	306	361	519	459	412	354	681	628

[a]Figures represent the number of persons per thousand. Males, age 16–59; females, age 16–54. This table was compiled from census data for Jan. 15, 1959, in *Itogi . . . 1959 goda: SSSR,* p. 87.

[b]Including those with incomplete secondary or incomplete higher education.

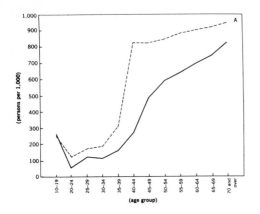

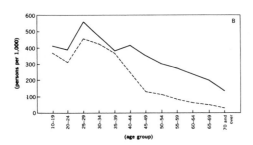

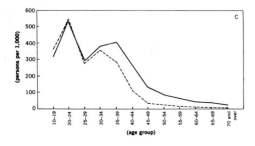

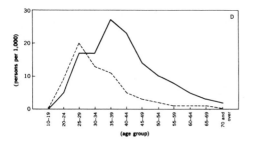

also unusually large—ten times as many women in the urban as in the rural areas had a higher education.

As in other respects, educationally, the Central Asian republics are among the most backward—only Moldavia lags still farther behind. In the Central Asian republics the number of women with a higher education varied from 16 to 20 per 1,000, and the urban-rural differences in these areas were the sharpest in the Soviet Union. In the Uzbek republic, the largest of the four, the number of women with a higher education was 43 per 1,000 in the urban areas, but only 4 per 1,000 in the rural areas.

A similar but less extreme pattern of uneven achievement is seen for secondary education. In Latvia, Georgia, Armenia, and Estonia over half the able-bodied women had had a secondary education. Again, Lithuania made a much poorer showing than her Baltic neighbors and almost matched Moldavia for the distinction of having the lowest proportion of women with a secondary education. The proportion in the Central Asian republics varied from a low of 358 per 1,000 in the Tadzhik republic to a high of 455 per 1,000 in the Turkmen republic, and although higher education for women in the Central Asian republics is relatively rare, the proportion of women with a secondary education in these areas was not far from the over-all average of 421 per 1,000, which represents a substantial accomplishment.

Among the most revealing statistics on educational achievement are those showing the proportion of men and women in the able-bodied age group who have had fewer than seven years of schooling. Despite the considerable advances made in Soviet education

Fig. 21. Educational level of the rural population, by age and sex, January 15, 1959. *Solid lines,* males; *broken lines,* females. *A,* less than a four-year education; *B,* elementary and incomplete seven-year education; *C,* Seven-year, incomplete secondary, secondary, and incomplete higher education; *D,* higher education. See Appendix VI, Table 2.

and the vastly improved educational opportunities for women, in only three republics—Lithuania, Latvia, and Estonia—was the proportion of women with fewer than seven years of education less than that of men; and only in Georgia, Latvia, Armenia, and Estonia were there fewer able-bodied women with less than a seven-year education than with more than seven years. In the other republics a majority of the female working-age population had had less than a seven-year education. In both Lithuania and Moldavia the proportion was close to 70 per cent. However, both these republics came under firm Soviet rule only after World War II, and the full effect of Soviet educational policy is not yet evident.

The educational backwardness of rural women is also strikingly illustrated by the figures in Table 85. A glance at the right-hand columns shows that, typically, two thirds of the rural women in the working-age group had had fewer than seven years of education. In the most backward republics in this respect—Lithuania, Moldavia, and Belorussia—three quarters or more of the rural women in the working ages had had fewer than seven years of schooling.

GAINS IN EDUCATIONAL LEVELS IN THE U.S.S.R. AND IN THE UNION REPUBLICS

Table 86 shows the substantial rise in the number of persons with higher and secondary education in the republics between 1939 and 1959. For the Soviet Union as a whole, the number of males with a higher education increased 240 per cent, and the number of women increased 490 per cent. At the secondary level, the gain over the same period was 320 per cent for men and 440 per cent for women.

If one examines the improvement in educational achievement reflected in the figures for nationality groups, one finds disparities similar to those revealed by the statistics for the republics, but greatly accentuated by the exclusion from the picture of persons of Russian nationality, who make up a large component of the population in most areas of the Soviet Union and whose educational tradition has been generally more advanced than that of most other nationality groups. For example, the number of women per thousand of all nationalities who had a higher or secondary education in the Uzbek and Turkmen re-

TABLE 86. Men and women with higher and secondary education, by republic, 1939 and 1959.[a]

| | Higher Education | | | | | | | | | |
| | 1939 | | 1959 | | Increase | | 1939 | | 1959 | |
Republic	Males	Females	Males	Females	M	F	M	F	M	F
					times		*per 1,000*			
U.S.S.R.	799,207	377,874	1,933,226	1,844,309	2.4	4.9	9	4	21	16
R.S.F.S.R.	472,192	237,301	1,128,529	1,137,411	2.4	4.8	9	4	22	17
Ukrainian S.S.R.	184,695	87,257	368,514	346,924	2.0	4.0	10	4	20	15
Belorussian S.S.R.	22,704	10,299	48,062	47,596	2.1	4.6	5	2	13	11
Uzbek S.S.R.	14,067	5,669	62,336	42,577	4.4	7.5	4	2	16	10
Kazakh S.S.R.	20,850	6,604	64,689	49,269	3.1	7.5	7	2	15	10
Georgian S.S.R.	27,522	12,192	81,731	71,687	3.0	5.9	16	7	44	33
Azerbaidzhan S.S.R.	16,172	5,437	45,697	31,547	2.8	5.8	10	3	26	16
Lithuanian S.S.R.	4,900	1,500	18,597	16,792	3.8	11.2	4	1	15	11
Moldavian S.S.R.	4,959	2,383	15,299	14,232	3.1	6.0	4	2	11	9
Latvian S.S.R.	11,500	2,400	20,693	23,711	1.8	9.9	13	2	23	20
Kirgiz S.S.R.	2,403	847	15,152	12,042	6.3	14.2	3	1	16	11
Tadzhik S.S.R.	2,245	737	12,467	8,215	5.6	11.2	3	1	13	8
Armenian S.S.R.	5,122	2,401	26,969	21,803	5.3	9.1	8	4	32	24
Turkmen S.S.R.	2,969	1,063	12,029	7,782	4.1	7.3	5	2	16	10
Estonian S.S.R.	6,907	1,784	12,462	12,721	1.8	7.1	14	3	24	19

TABLE 86. Men and women with higher and secondary education, by republic, 1939 and 1959.[a]—*continued*

	Secondary Education[b]									
	1939		1959		Increase		1939		1959	
Republic	Males	Females	Males	Females	M	F	M	F	M	F
					times		*per 1,000*			
U.S.S.R.	8,053,185	6,636,145	25,711,231	29,218,427	3.2	4.4	88	67	273	255
R.S.F.S.R.	4,363,515	3,927,442	13,966,825	16,936,916	3.2	4.3	85	69	267	260
Ukrainian S.S.R.	2,011,733	1,613,397	5,730,073	6,242,619	2.9	3.9	104	76	308	268
Belorussian S.S.R.	348,665	246,538	844,988	969,028	2.4	3.9	81	54	236	216
Uzbek S.S.R.	156,905	88,652	1,026,296	870,404	6.5	9.8	48	29	264	206
Kazakh S.S.R.	254,234	110,701	1,142,980	1,072,195	4.5	9.7	80	38	258	219
Georgian S.S.R.	216,813	184,607	584,212	686,497	2.7	3.7	123	104	314	315
Azerbaidzhan S.S.R.	151,772	82,740	518,659	448,630	3.4	5.4	92	53	295	231
Lithuanian S.S.R.	115,200	69,100	215,644	260,408	1.9	3.8	83	46	173	178
Moldavian S.S.R.	56,129	41,161	271,236	263,347	4.8	6.4	46	33	203	169
Latvian S.S.R.	148,300	116,200	318,269	403,953	2.2	3.5	167	116	346	344
Kirgiz S.S.R.	30,114	17,234	247,745	222,612	8.2	12.9	41	24	254	205
Tadzhik S.S.R.	27,981	12,287	236,928	188,633	8.5	15.4	36	17	246	186
Armenian S.S.R.	67,090	37,391	250,749	257,369	3.7	6.9	103	59	298	280
Turkmen S.S.R.	37,220	20,636	201,815	186,609	5.4	9.0	58	34	276	237
Estonian S.S.R.	67,514	68,059	154,812	209,207	2.3	3.1	138	121	294	312

[a]Based on *Itogi . . . 1959 goda: SSSR*, p. 86. Rates per 1,000 are based on total male or female population.

[b]Including those with incomplete secondary or incomplete higher education.

publics increased seven times between 1939 and 1959, but the number of Uzbek women rose from 6 to 165 per 1,000, or twenty-seven times, and the number of Turkmen women from 3 to 205 per 1,000, or sixty-eight times.[13]

EDUCATIONAL ATTAINMENT BY SOCIOECONOMIC GROUP

When the educational attainment of the population as a whole is considered from the standpoint of socioeconomic group—employees, workers, collective farmers, and their families—rather than from the standpoint of urban-rural grouping, even greater differences based upon sex and age are evident. Examination of Figure 22 shows the almost complete concentration among the employee groups and their families of persons with higher, incomplete higher, and specialized secondary education.[14] Few workers and even fewer collective farmers and their families have achieved these levels of education, and

[13]See Table 86 and Appendix VI, Tables 5 and 6.

[14]See also Appendix VI, Table 7.

the number of women in these two categories with higher and specialized secondary education is negligible.

The situation does not differ radically for general secondary education. Again, the concentration of persons who have completed this level of training is among employees and their families. Few workers and very few collective farmers and their families have a general secondary education.

The proportion of women with general secondary education in 1959 was higher than that of men in the case of employees—151 women as compared with 130 men per 1,000 age 10 and over—but was significantly lower in the case of workers and collective farmers. Among the former, there were 55 men and 46 women per 1,000 age 10 and over with a secondary education; among the latter, 33 men and only 18 women per 1,000. Persons with a four-year education or less represent the reverse side of the coin. Here, the incidence is highest among the older female collective farmers, where the proportion approaches 100 per cent, but it remains very high (about 70 per cent) among the older women workers and employees as well.

EDUCATIONAL ATTAINMENT BY OCCUPATIONAL GROUP AND ECONOMIC BRANCH

At this point it is relevant to examine the educational levels of those gainfully employed, both in terms of the three main occupational groups—workers, employees, and collective farmers—and in terms of branches within the Soviet national economy. Here again, the basic pattern is one of great disparities, which, however, are not to be interpreted in the same manner as the disparities in enrollment in secondary or higher educational institutions; for here the interpretation must take into account not only differences in cultural and social traditions and in the quality and availability of educational facilities in urban and rural areas, but also differences in the educational requirements for the various occupational groups and branches of the economy. The latter factor is, of course, the most important cause of variations in educational achievement. Even with complete equality of educational opportunity, the educational level of a lathe operator or a field worker is not the same as that of an engineer or a scientist.

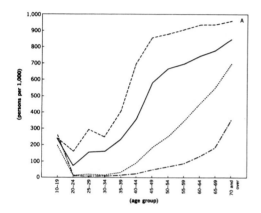

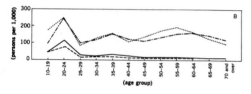

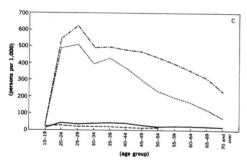

FIG. 22. Educational level of employees and collective farmers and their families, by age and sex, January 15, 1959. *Solid lines,* male members of collective-farm families; *broken lines,* female members of collective-farm families; *dotted and broken lines,* male members of families of employees; *dotted lines,* female members of families of employees. *A,* less than a four-year education; *B,* general secondary education; *C,* higher, incomplete higher, or specialized secondary education. See Appendix VI, Table 7.

Some discrepancies between urban-rural and occupational status should be noted, however. For example, over 10 per cent of the workers and employees are engaged, not in industry or other urban occupations, but in agriculture, primarily in the state farm system. Conversely, almost 2 per cent of the collective farmers are engaged in nonagricultural branches of the economy. A man may remain a member of a collective farm but work in a factory in the city, a type of overlapping in categorization which explains the figures on the educational level of collective farmers included in the urban population.

The data presented in Table 87 do not hold any surprises. The relatively high level of education among employees and the relatively low level among collective farmers are to be expected. The tendency for women employees to have an education comparable to that of men is also predictable, as is the tendency for women collective farmers to have a much lower level of education than men. These relationships among the employed population mirror very closely those among the population as a whole.

The National Economy. If we consider

TABLE 87. Educational level of the employed population, by socioeconomic group and sex, 1959.[a]

Socioeconomic Group	Higher, Incomplete Higher, or Specialized Secondary Education		General Secondary Education		Incomplete Secondary Education		Primary and Incomplete 7-year Education		Less than 4-yr. Education	
	M	F	M	F	M	F	M	F	M	F
Urban and Rural										
Total.....................	103	116	60	68	271	247	386	272	180	297
Workers..................	23	16	56	63	314	298	459	353	148	270
Employees................	508	476	124	161	227	284	121	69	20	10
Collective farmers..........	14	6	29	18	218	174	413	308	326	494
Urban										
Total.....................	153	184	82	109	302	304	362	243	101	160
Workers..................	27	19	67	76	336	318	449	350	121	237
Employees................	533	459	129	169	210	290	110	71	18	11
Collective farmers..........	28	10	38	23	221	160	420	292	293	515
Rural										
Total.....................	56	60	40	34	241	200	408	295	255	411
Workers..................	14	9	36	34	270	253	480	361	200	343
Employees................	450	523	113	139	265	265	146	64	26	9
Collective farmers..........	13	6	29	18	218	174	412	309	328	493

[a]Figures represent the number of persons per thousand. This table is based on data from *Itogi . . . 1959 goda: SSSR*, p. 115.

the economy as a whole in 1959,[15] except private subsidiary agriculture, only a few more males (34) than females (32) per thousand employed had had a higher education. However, a significantly larger proportion of females (84) than males (69) per thousand employed had had a specialized secondary education. The proportion of males (331) and females (315) per thousand employed with a general secondary and incomplete secondary education was almost the same, while among those with an incomplete seven-year and elementary education the proportion of males (386) per thousand employed was substantially above that of women (272). The remaining part of the employed population, with less than a four-year education, contained a substantially larger proportion of women (297) than of men (180) per thousand employed.

Industry. The pattern of education for those in the industrial sector differed somewhat from the over-all pattern. Fewer women

showed either very high or very low levels of educational achievement. Again the proportion of men with a higher education (22) was larger than that of women (17), and this relationship extended substantially to men (65) and women (61) with specialized secondary and incomplete higher education. However, the proportion of women (470) with a general secondary education and incomplete secondary education substantially exceeded that of men (395). The proportion of men (409) again exceeded that of women (301) with incomplete seven-year and elementary education, but the situation was reversed with regard to men (109) and women (151) with fewer than four years of schooling.

From these figures we may conclude that industry utilizes primarily persons who have reached the intermediate levels of education. Few have less than a primary education or more than a general secondary education. Almost half the women employed in industry have a general secondary or incomplete secondary education. The concentration of

[15]See Appendix VI, Table 8.

women at these intermediate educational levels may be explained by the many women in production work and by the women who make up the vast majority of white-collar employees in industry.

Some interesting differences emerge among the constituent industries. In 1959, the proportion of women with higher education significantly exceeded that of men in a number of chemical, petroleum, and petroleum- and fuel-refining industries. In the case of petroleum refining, 59 women as opposed to 39 men per thousand employed had had a higher education. The proportion of women in petroleum production and refining with an incomplete higher or specialized secondary education was also substantially higher than that of men.

Construction. The educational attainment of the bulk of the women in the construction sector of the economy ranges from the elementary to the general secondary level. Only the planning phase of construction requires and attracts women with higher education. The bulk of the women are painters, plasterers, and white-collar workers who do not need advanced training.

Agriculture. The educational attainments of women in rural areas and of women collective farmers in particular have been very low. The data for 1959 confirm this. Almost three quarters of the women engaged in private farming and almost half the women working on collective farms had had fewer than four years of schooling. The educational level of women working on state farms was little better. The small number of women employed in repair technical stations had had a substantially higher level of education. However, it is only at the administrative level that a relatively high proportion of women had achieved a higher (177) or specialized secondary education (216). Also, the proportion of women with a higher (145) or specialized secondary education (240) employed in veterinary and other establishments serving agriculture exceeded that of men.

Transportation and Communications. The pattern in transportation is similar to that in

the industrial sector; however, almost 70 per cent of the women in communications in 1959 had had a general secondary or incomplete secondary education.

Trade and Public Dining, Procurement, and Supply. The pattern of educational achievement in these sectors is similar to that in the industrial sector. There was a relatively small percentage of women with a higher or specialized secondary education, but the proportion with a general or incomplete secondary education was quite high and exceeded that of men.

Housing and Communal Service. The general educational level in these activities is low: approximately two thirds of the women had had less than a seven-year education. The proportion of men with higher or specialized secondary education was considerably higher.

Health. The general level of education in the health field is high. More than two fifths of the women employed in medical institutions in 1959 had completed a higher or specialized secondary education. However, the educational level of men in this field is still higher. The proportion of men with a higher education (190) exceeded by a substantial margin that of women (99), but the relationship was reversed for incomplete higher and specialized secondary education, where men numbered 212 per 1,000 and women 336.

Education. The highest levels of educational attainment are to be found among persons working in education. As might be expected, the levels of attainment increase as one moves from those employed in primary and secondary education through those in specialized secondary education to those in higher education. But as one goes up the academic ladder, the proportion of women with a higher education tends to decline. In higher educational institutions in 1959, the proportion of women with a higher education was approximately 70 per cent that of men. In general education the number of women per thousand was 79 per cent that of men, while in specialized secondary educational institutions the figure rose to 88 per cent. In other types of educational institutions, the proportion of women with a higher education exceeded the proportion of men.

Science and Science Service. In this field as a whole the educational level of both men and women is high but, surprisingly, the proportion of women with a higher education exceeds that of men. Out of every 1,000 women employed in this field in 1959, 219 had had a higher education, as compared with 209 men. The differential in favor of women was even greater for incomplete higher and specialized secondary education, women numbering 194 and men 143 per 1,000. The proportions were more nearly equal for general secondary and incomplete secondary education, 366 women and 306 men per 1,000.

Two further breakdowns within the science field can be made. The first covers persons employed in scientific research institutions and auxiliary organizations. Here the proportion of men (293) exceeded that of women (255) with a higher education. However, the proportion of women (231) exceeded that of men (150) with an incomplete higher or specialized secondary education, and the proportion of women (336) slightly exceeded that of men (306) with a general or incomplete secondary education. The second breakdown covers persons employed in design and planning organizations, excluding construction, geological prospecting, and hydrometeorological work. The general level of education in these fields was lower than in scientific research institutes, but the proportions of women with a higher education (162), an incomplete higher and specialized secondary education (231), and a general and incomplete secondary education (413) are larger than those of men (139, 150, and 355, respectively).

In almost all branches of the economy, as we have seen, the proportion of men with a higher education is greater than that of women, but in most instances the position is reversed with regard to incomplete higher and specialized secondary education. For example, in the field of education a smaller proportion of women than men have a higher education; a substantially larger proportion of women have an incomplete higher or specialized secondary education. In medical institutions in 1959, the proportion of men with a higher education was almost twice that of women, but 34 per cent of the women and only 21 per cent of the men had had an incomplete higher or specialized secondary education. In scientific research institutions, 26 per cent of the women and 29 per cent of the men had completed a higher education, but 17 per cent of the women and only 14 per cent of the men had had an incomplete higher or specialized secondary education. In these three important fields—education, medicine, and science—Soviet women have a relatively high level of educational training.

TRENDS IN THE EDUCATIONAL ATTAINMENT OF THE EMPLOYED POPULATION

The improvement in the educational level of the working population which resulted from the extensive program to expand education during the industrialization drive is reflected in Table 88. The change in the proportion of both urban and rural women engaged in physical and mental work—roughly equivalent to blue-collar and white-collar work—who had completed higher or secondary education was striking. The over-all rate increased from 104 per 1,000 in 1939 to 431 in 1959, and the gain was particularly dramatic in the case of women doing physical work, who showed an increase from 21 to 284 per 1,000.

The urban-rural differences were considerably narrowed by 1959. In 1939 almost three times as many males per thousand in the urban as in the rural population had had a higher or secondary education. By 1959 the urban rate was only a little over one and a half times the rural. For women the narrowing was even more impressive. An urban rate six times the rural in 1939 was reduced to two times the rural in 1959. A similar change occurred in the differences between the educational levels of persons employed in physi-

TABLE 88. Educational level of the urban and rural population employed in physical and mental work, 1959.[a]

Population	Higher and Secondary Education, Including Incomplete Secondary Education				Higher, Incomplete Higher, and Specialized Secondary Education		General Secondary and Incomplete Secondary Education	
	1939		1959		1959		1959	
	M	F	M	F	M	F	M	F
Urban and Rural								
Total employed	136	104	434	431	103	116	331	315
Employed primarily in physical work	61	21	343	284	18	9	325	275
Employed primarily in mental work	429	635	844	918	485	468	359	450
Urban								
Total employed	235	255	537	597	153	184	384	413
Employed primarily in physical work	114	54	426	404	27	19	399	385
Employed primarily in mental work	510	654	868	917	528	458	340	459
Rural								
Total employed	81	42	337	294	56	60	281	234
Employed primarily in physical work	36	11	275	214	10	4	265	210
Employed primarily in mental work	335	586	799	920	404	498	395	422

[a]Figures represent the number of persons per thousand. This table is based on data from *Itogi ... 1959 goda: SSSR*, pp. 174, 176.

cal work and those of persons employed in mental work. In 1939 the number of men per thousand employed in mental work who had had a higher or secondary education was seven times the number of those engaged in physical labor, while the female increased thirtyfold. By 1959 the differentials had been reduced to two and a half and to slightly over three. These figures show very clearly the profound improvement in the basic educational level of the working population. While extensive differentials among the various components of the population remain, the extreme differences have been sharply reduced. In this leveling process women have been the principal beneficiaries.

Additional light on the improvement in the educational attainments of employed women between 1939 and 1959 is shed in Table 89, which shows the educational level of women in various occupations. Among those involving physical work, the greatest improvement was made in occupations for which the 1939 educational level was particularly low. Thus, the number of milkmaids and animal tenders with a secondary or higher education in-

creased from 4 to 241 per 1,000. In agricultural occupations as a whole, the increase was from 9 to 192 women per 1,000. Among women construction workers an increase from 24 to 434 per 1,000 was achieved. The largest absolute increases occurred in skilled labor. Among female metal and chemical workers the absolute gains were 447 and 434 per 1,000, respectively; women in construction and transportation showed gains of 410 and 477 per 1,000.

The gains among women engaged primarily in mental work were less dramatic, since the level in 1939 was already fairly high. The highest initial level, and consequently the smallest increase, applied to scientific workers and teachers. In 1939, 901 women per 1,000 in these fields had had a higher or secondary education. By 1959, all but 5 out of every 1,000 employed in science or education had achieved this level. Although the breakdown of the educational levels achieved by women in these scientific and technical fields is not so detailed as would be desirable, it is clear that substantial progress was made in raising the qualifications of women workers in these

TABLE 89. Educational level of women in various occupations, 1939 and 1959.[a]

Occupation	Secondary or Higher Education[b]		Increase	Occupation	Secondary or Higher Education[b]		Increase
	1939	1959			1939	1959	
			times				*times*
Primarily physical...............	21	284	13.5	Auto transport and urban electric transport workers............	111	588	5.3
Metallurgy and metal workers....	122	569	4.7	Drivers of streetcars, subway trains, and trolley buses.....	99	668	6.7
Lathe operators..............	228	707	3.1				
Milling machine operators.....	173	669	3.9	Conductors of autobuses, street-cars, and trolley buses.......	70	642	9.2
Operators of planers, mortizing, drilling, grinding, automatic, and other machines.........	55	534	9.7	Workers in public dining........	31	409	13.2
Electrical and gas welders......	129	509	4.9	Primarily mental.................	635	918	1.4
Press and stamping machine op-erators...................	45	504	11.2	Heads of organs of government administration, the party, Kom-somol, trade unions, co-opera-tives, and other social organiza-tions and their structural subdi-visions......................	509	946	1.9
Watchmakers and jewelers.....	279	783	2.8				
Electricians..................	379	763	2.0				
Chemical workers..............	101	535	5.3				
Woodworkers.................	32	389	12.2				
Paper industry workers.........	63	404	6.4	Heads of enterprises (in industry, construction, agriculture, fores-try, transportation, and com-munications) and their struc-tural subdivisions............	386	895	2.3
Printers......................	178	651	3.7				
Textile workers...............	55	483	8.8				
Garment workers..............	78	582	7.4				
Leather workers...............	66	430	6.5	Engineering technical workers....	753	952	1.3
Footwear workers..............	88	547	6.2	Agronomists, zootechnicians, vet-erinarian workers, and foresters.	840	981	1.2
Food industry workers..........	42	442	10.5	Medical workers...............	654	969	1.5
Construction workers..........	24	434	18.1	Scientific workers and teachers....	901	995	1.1
Agricultural workers..........	9	192	21.3	Cultural-educational workers.....	694	978	1.4
Heads of farms and brigadiers of livestock brigades.........	20	452	22.6	Workers in the arts..............	743	912	1.2
Brigadiers of tractor, field, com-plex, and other brigades.....	32	423	13.2	Communications workers........	375	805	1.2
Field-team leader..............	26	310	11.9	Trade, public dining, procurement, and supply workers...........	204	776	3.8
Milkmaids and women caring for cattle, sheep, horses, pigs, and poultry................	4	241	60.3	Planners and bookkeepers........	669	931	1.4
Railway workers...............	29	377	13.0	Workers in communal enterprises, repairs, and other services......	203	556	2.7

[a]Based on Tsentral'noe statisticheskoe upravlenie pri Sovete ministrov SSSR, *Zhenshchiny i deti v SSSR* (2d ed.; Moscow,

1963), pp. 62–63.
[b]Number of persons per thousand.

fields in the decades between 1939 and 1959.[16]

CONCLUSIONS

It is clear that the Soviet Union has made great progress in raising the educational levels of the population and the labor force, and women have been among the principal bene-ficiaries of this process. For all practical pur-poses illiteracy among women has been wiped out except in the older generation and in some of the more backward areas of the country. The most striking improvement has been achieved by women in rural areas and in some of the less developed republics where Moslem traditions kept women from acquir-ing an education. It should not be overlooked, however, that a third of the persons in prime working ages still have less than a four-year education and that two thirds of this group are women. Although most of these educa-tionally deprived women are considered lit-erate, they lack all but the most rudimentary education. As a result, they are fit only for the least skilled jobs—agricultural field work, cleaning, street sweeping, and the like. They appear to have been deliberately neglected,

[16]The data in Appendix VI, Table 8, although not directly comparable to those presented in Table 89, suggest that many women in science and technology had had a higher or specialized secondary education, and the age distribution in-dicates that within another decade the educational levels of women in this area will be very high indeed.

while the regime concentrated its attention and scarce educational resources on the younger generations, particularly those growing up in urban areas. Only time will eradicate this large group of poorly educated women, and at least another generation will be required. Where the educational priorities were higher, the results have been much better. The Soviet government has succeeded in substantially raising the level of educational attainment of men and women in those occupational fields which are critical for economic growth and development. For women, this improvement has been particularly important, since it has enabled them to enter many of the more interesting and attractive occupations, which had previously been closed to them.

Substantial regional, age, and occupational differentials, along with sex differences, result in very wide differentials among the extreme groups. Over the years these differences have been dramatically narrowed as the most backward areas and occupations have advanced more rapidly than those which have been in the lead. It is certainly not the aim of Soviet policy makers to eliminate these differences, but there can be no doubt that they will continue to strive to raise both the minimum and the average level of education. As in the past, women will be major beneficiaries of this effort, but in many respects the battle for women's education has already been won. As we have seen earlier, the economic justification for women's lagging behind men in educational achievement is found in their lower productivity during their working life. The war and resulting shortages of males apparently led Soviet planners to train more women at higher levels than would normally be justified. With the passing of the present older generation, the educational levels achieved by women will not, therefore, differ greatly from those achieved by men. In general, the level of educational attainment of women lags behind that of men, but because there are more women in the population, particularly in the older age groups, the number of women with a given level of education is sometimes greater.

chapter
9

NONPROFESSIONAL OCCUPATIONS

IN ALL MAJOR sectors of the Soviet economy the proportion of women employed is large, and to a visitor at a collective farm, factory, or construction site it is immediately evident that women perform a large share of the physical labor. The employment of women in unskilled and skilled physical labor is not, however, a recent phenomenon. Before the Revolution women were widely employed in agriculture; today, with the new attitude toward women and the more highly developed economy, they are distributed in a much more diversified pattern. The characteristic figure remains, however—the woman with the hoe —but many other agricultural occupations have been opened to women possessing sufficient talent and ambition; and in the sectors of the economy which have grown most rapidly, women have been utilized in large numbers to make up for manpower deficiencies. Women may be found in the foundry, forge, and machine shop. They man the assembly lines of industries, ranging from the automotive to the electronic. In transportation they operate the signal systems and drive buses. In construction they plaster, paint, and lay the bricks. In communications they man the switchboards and teletypes. In the stores they are sales clerks. In hotels and restaurants, they clean and they serve food. Throughout all sectors of the economy they form the bulk of the nonprofessional workers.

We view as nonprofessional that category of workers who are classified in the Soviet census as employed in predominantly "physical labor." For convenience these may be thought of as "blue-collar" workers. However, some of the workers and employees listed in the census as occupied in "mental labor," such as sales clerks and secretaries, should be classified as nonprofessional workers even though they are in "white-collar" occupations. Without completely reworking the employment data of the census, it is impossible to eliminate these inconsistencies in classification. There are, however, very few workers employed in "physical labor" who could be considered semiprofessional or professional workers. "Physical labor" also includes the great bulk of the nonprofessional workers. Therefore, it is a useful category for our analysis. On January 15, 1959, according to census data, women accounted for 46.5 per cent of those employed in physical labor. The imbalance of the sex ratio in the age groups most seriously affected by the war is sufficiently great so that women outnumber men in the less skilled and heavier occupations, especially in agriculture (see Figs. 23, 24, and 25).

The following discussion describes the structure of nonprofessional agricultural employment, which accounts for over 40 per cent of total civilian employment, and then proceeds to a consideration of the employment of women in nonprofessional occupa-

160

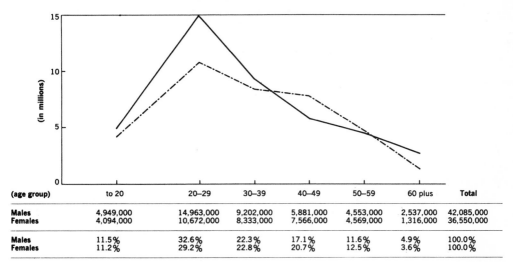

(age group)	to 20	20–29	30–39	40–49	50–59	60 plus	Total
Males	4,949,000	14,963,000	9,202,000	5,881,000	4,553,000	2,537,000	42,085,000
Females	4,094,000	10,672,000	8,333,000	7,566,000	4,569,000	1,316,000	36,550,000
Males	11.5%	32.6%	22.3%	17.1%	11.6%	4.9%	100.0%
Females	11.2%	29.2%	22.8%	20.7%	12.5%	3.6%	100.0%

FIG. 23. Age distribution of males and females employed in predominantly physical occupations, 1959. *Solid line,* males; *broken line,* females. Calculated from *Itogi . . . 1959 goda: SSSR,* pp. 132, 142, 161, 167.

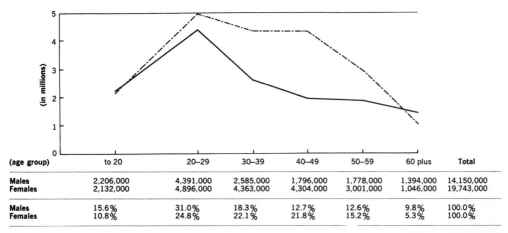

(age group)	to 20	20–29	30–39	40–49	50–59	60 plus	Total
Males	2,206,000	4,391,000	2,585,000	1,796,000	1,778,000	1,394,000	14,150,000
Females	2,132,000	4,896,000	4,363,000	4,304,000	3,001,000	1,046,000	19,743,000
Males	15.6%	31.0%	18.3%	12.7%	12.6%	9.8%	100.0%
Females	10.8%	24.8%	22.1%	21.8%	15.2%	5.3%	100.0%

FIG. 24. Age distribution of males and females employed in predominantly physical occupations in agriculture, except private subsidiary agriculture, 1959. *Solid line,* males; *broken line,* females. Calculated from *Itogi . . . 1959 goda: SSSR,* pp. 136, 143, 162–63, 168.

tions in industry and other sectors of the economy.[1] Data from the 1959 census are used because they provide detailed socio-economic characteristics not readily obtainable from the regular employment statistics,

which are based on establishment reports. The census divides the civilian economy into two sectors: the socialized and private independent sector and the private subsidiary sector (see Table 90). Since the latter is comprised chiefly of persons cultivating private agricultural plots, it has been necessary to recombine the census data into appropriate agricultural and nonagricultural groupings.

---

[1] Census data on women employed in semi-professional and professional occupations are dealt with in detail in the next chapter.

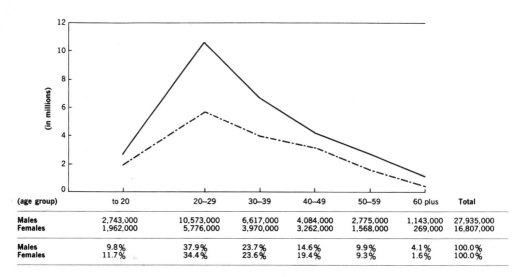

(age group)	to 20	20–29	30–39	40–49	50–59	60 plus	Total
Males	2,743,000	10,573,000	6,617,000	4,084,000	2,775,000	1,143,000	27,935,000
Females	1,962,000	5,776,000	3,970,000	3,262,000	1,568,000	269,000	16,807,000
Males	9.8%	37.9%	23.7%	14.6%	9.9%	4.1%	100.0%
Females	11.7%	34.4%	23.6%	19.4%	9.3%	1.6%	100.0%

FIG. 25. Age distribution of males and females employed in predominantly physical occupations other than in agriculture, 1959. *Solid line,* males; *broken line,* females. Calculated from *Itogi . . . 1959 goda: SSSR,* pp. 132, 142, 161, 167, and from data in Fig. 24.

TABLE 90. Civilian labor force, by socioeconomic category, branch, and sex, 1959.[a]

Labor Force Category	Total	Men	Percentage Distribution	Women	Percentage Distribution	Percentage of Women
Total civilian labor force....................	105,372	48,817	100.0	56,555	100.0	53.7
Socialized and private independent sector......	95,507	47,904	98.1	47,604	84.2	49.8
Branches of material production............	80,863	42,520	87.1	38,342	67.8	47.4
Industry, construction, transport, and communications........................	36,575	22,423	45.9	14,152	25.0	38.7
Agriculture............................	38,426	17,662	36.2	20,764	36.7	54.0
Collective farmers....................	31,723	13,731	28.1	17,992	31.8	56.7
Workers and employees................	6,611	3,898	8.0	2,713	4.8	41.0
Individual peasants...................	92	32	0.1	60	0.1	65.2
Trade, public dining, etc................	5,171	1,993	4.1	3,178	5.6	61.5
Other branches........................	691	442	0.9	248	0.4	35.9
Branches of nonmaterial production.........	14,453	5,249	10.8	9,204	16.3	63.7
Education, science, and public health......	9,793	2,865	5.9	6,928	12.3	70.7
Housing, communal economy administration, finance-credit system..............	4,660	2,384	4.9	2,276	4.0	48.8
Unknown..............................	191	133	0.3	58	0.1	30.4
Private subsidiary agricultural sector..........	9,865	914	1.9	8,951	15.8	90.7

[a]Figures are expressed in thousands. Since they are independently rounded, sums may not equal totals. This table is based on data in *Itogi . . . 1959 goda: SSSR,* Tables 30 and 33, pp. 96–97, 104–5.

WOMEN WORKERS IN AGRICULTURE

The large number of agricultural workers in the civilian labor force (46 per cent) and the high proportion of women in the agri- cultural labor force (54 per cent in the socialized and private independent sector and 91 per cent in the private subsidiary sector) and the high proportion of working women who are occupied in agriculture (53 per cent) are some of the most striking characteristics of the Russian economy revealed by the 1959 census.[2]

Four categories of workers were employed in agriculture. The bulk (31.7 million) were members of and contributed most of their labor to collective farms. At the same time more than 9.8 million persons were engaged primarily in private subsidiary farming; these were mostly members of collective farm families and members of families of workers and employees in the state farm sector and those in other sectors of the economy who worked on private garden plots raising vegetables, livestock, and other agricultural products for their own use and the market. Some 6.6 million workers and employees were engaged in agriculture, primarily on state farms. The employment status of these state farm workers and employees is comparable to that of workers and employees in industry or other sectors of the state economy, but their function is agricultural.[3] The fourth category of agricultural worker—individual peasants— has almost passed out of existence. In 1959 only 92,000 individual peasant families were left in the Soviet economy. Of the three significant categories of agricultural workers, women made up 57 per cent of the collective farmers, 91 per cent of the workers in private subsidiary agriculture, and 41 per cent of the workers and employees in the agricultural sector.

Women still perform much of the "physical" agricultural work. A comparison of the proportion of women and men among those engaged in primarily physical agricultural occupations (excluding those in the private subsidiary economy) for the years 1926, 1939, and 1959 reveals little or no improvement in the position of women in this respect over the years.[4] The proportion in 1926 was 50 per cent, and in both 1939 and 1959 it stood at 58 per cent. However, the absolute number of women has declined to slightly over 55 per cent of the 1926 level, corresponding, of course, to the over-all decline in the number of persons employed in agriculture.

Many young women in rural areas enter industry, construction, trade, and the professions, while the older women, who lack mobility, remain behind. This tendency for older persons to stay in agriculture while the younger people shift into industry or other expanding sectors of the economy is a phenomenon which has been observed in the development of other countries. The Soviet case is illustrated by Figure 24, showing the age distribution of males and females employed in physical occupations in agriculture, with the exception of the private subsidiary sector. Here we see a higher percentage of the employed males and females in the older age groups than is true for other sectors. Women in this sector tend to be older than men; approximately 42 per cent of the women were age 40 or older as against 35 per cent of the men. Only in the age group 60 and above do we find a substantial proportion of men. Women of this age are likely to shift to work in the private subsidiary sector, while men tend to continue working in the socialized sector. Women in unskilled and unspecified agricultural work, which includes the vast majority, tend to be a bit older than women in the skilled or semiskilled agricultural occu-

---

[2]Although the proportion of persons engaged in agriculture is large, it is slightly understated because of the census-processing methodology. Farm chairmen and their deputies, agronomists, and other specialists employed in agricultural occupations are classified under "Administration" and other headings and consequently are not listed under the main heading of "Agricultural Occupations" (*Itogi . . . 1959 goda: SSSR,* Table 46, pp. 162–64).

[3]The combined term "worker and employee"

---

has a very specific meaning in Soviet terminology. Persons so designated are paid wages or a salary by the state and possess a specified set of fringe benefits, including pension rights and rights to vacation.

[4]See Appendix VII, Table 1.

pations. Approximately 46 per cent of these women were in the age group 40 and over.[5]

Women on Collective Farms. Prior to World War II the trend in the proportion of female able-bodied collective farmers was

[5]*Itogi . . . 1959 goda: SSSR*, p. 143. For further data on the age-sex distribution in certain agricultural occupations, see Appendix VII, Fig. 1.

upward. As shown in Table 91, women made up 46 per cent of the total number of able-bodied collective farmers in 1936 and 53 per cent in 1938. During the war, owing to the draft and the transfer of men into industry and of youngsters into labor reserve schools, the proportion of able-bodied women collective farmers climbed to a record high of 78 to 80 per cent. The postwar high of 63 to 64

TABLE 91. Contribution of able-bodied women to collective farm labor, selected years, 1936–62.[a]

Year	Number of Able-bodied Women	Percentage of Women (of total able-bodied farmers who work)	Percentage of Total Labor Days (*trudodni*) (earned by able-bodied farmers) Earned by Women	Index of Average Number of Labor Days Earned by Women (1940 = 100)
1936	17,896.2[b]	46.2[b]	n.a.	n.a.
1938	18,705.8[b]	52.7[b]	n.a.	n.a.
1940	17,275.0[c]	54[d]	42[d]	100[d]
1941	8,485.1[e]	52[e]	40[e]	n.a.
1942	8,913.7[e]	60[e]	n.a.	n.a.
1943	9,191.6[e]	72[e]	n.a.	n.a.
1944	8,575.9[e]	76[e]	70[e]	n.a.
1945	8,216.0[e]	76[e]	n.a.	n.a.
1950	(18,306)[f]	64[g]	n.a.	n.a.
1953	(16,859)[f]	63[d]	52[d]	122[d]
1955	(17,336)[f]	61[d]	50[d]	139[d]
1957	(16,342)[f]	59[d]	48[d]	138[d]
1958	(15,950)[f]	58[d]	47[d]	140[d]
1959	(14,916)[f]	57[g]	49[d]	n.a.
1961	(12,264)[f]	56[h]	48[i]	n.a.
1962	(11,872)[f]	56[j]	48[i]	n.a.

[a]By census definition, able-bodied women are age 16 to 54, and able-bodied men are age 16 to 59; n.a., no data available and no estimate made; figures in parentheses are estimates.

[b]From E. Orlikova, "Sovetskaia zhenshchina v obshchestvennom proizvodstve," *Problemy ekonomiki*, No. 7 (July, 1940), 119.

[c]From Iu. V. Arutiunian and V. P. Danilov, "Svod otchetov kolkhozov strany v period Otechestvennoi Voiny," *Istoricheskii arkhiv*, No. 6 (Nov.-Dec., 1962), 30.

[d]From Tsentral'noe statisticheskoe upravlenie pri Sovete ministrov SSSR, *Zhenshchiny i deti v SSSR* (Moscow, 1961), p. 129. Datum for 1959 in col. 4 is in terms of man-days.

[e]From Iu. V. Arutiunian, *Sovetskoe krest'ianstvo v gody velikoi otechestvennoi voiny* (Moscow, 1963), pp. 66–67.

[f]Estimated by multiplying the percentage of women able-bodied participants in col. 3 times the total number of able-bodied participants in corresponding years. For 1950 (28,603,-000), 1953 (26,761,000), and 1957 (27,699,000), from Iu. V. Arutiunian, *Mekhanizatory sel'skogo khoziaistva v 1929–1957 gg.* (*Formirovanie kadrov massovykh kvalifikatsii*) (Moscow, 1960), p. 271. Excluding able-bodied farmers working in state industry, transport, etc., 1955 (28,419,000) and 1956 (29,382,-000) were estimated by multiplying the average number of able-bodied collective farmers (from V. G. Venzher, *Voprosy ispol'zovaniia zakona stoimosti v kolkhoznom proizvodstve* [Moscow, 1960], p. 79) by the number of agricultural collective farms (Tsentral'noe statisticheskoe upravlenie pri Sovete ministrov SSSR, *Narodnoe khoziaistvo SSSR v 1956 godu* [Moscow, 1957], p. 140, and *Narodnoe khoziaistvo SSSR v 1959 godu* [Moscow, 1960], p. 423). For 1958 a total of 27,500,000 was reported in Akademiia nauk SSSR, Institut ekonomiki, *Osobennosti i faktory razmeshcheniia otraslei narodnogo khoziaistva SSSR*,

ed. by Iu. G. Feigin *et al.* (Moscow, 1960), p. 404. Excluding members working in state establishments and institutions and full-time students, for 1959 (26,168,800) the total number was estimated by multiplying the total number of collective farmer participants by the percentage of able-bodied collective farmers (35,411,100 × 0.739), Nauchno-issledovatel'skii institut truda gosudarstvennogo komiteta Soveta ministrov SSSR po voprosam truda i zarabotnoi platy, *Trudovye resursy SSSR* (*Problemy raspredeleniia i ispol'zovaniia*), ed. by N. I. Shishkin (Moscow 1961), pp. 98–99; and for 1961 and 1962, total number of able-bodied participants of 30,400,000 and 29,559,000, respectively, are given in E. S. Karnaukhova, "Utilization of Labor Resources in Collective Farms," in *Puti povysheniia proizvoditel'nosti truda v sel'skom khoziaistve SSSR*, ed. by E. S. Karnaukhova and M. I. Kozlov (Moscow, 1964), p. 56.

[g]From *Zhenshchina v SSSR* (Moscow, 1960), p. 42.

[h]From *Zhenshchiny i deti v SSSR* (Moscow, 1963), p. 109.

[i]Estimated as follows: *ibid.* gives 171 and 173 man-days worked by able-bodied women in 1961 and 1962, which when multiplied by the number of able-bodied women (column 2) yields 2,097 and 2,054 million man-days worked by able-bodied women. Total number of man-days worked by all able-bodied collective farmers was obtained by multiplying the average number of able-bodied participants (21,900,000 and 21,200,000 in 1961 and 1962, ibid., p. 63) by the average number of man-days worked by each (198 and 199, *ibid.*, p. 63). Thus, in 1961, 2,097 million man-days ÷ 4,336 million man-days equals 48 per cent and in 1962, 2,054 million man-days ÷ 4,219 million man-days equals 49 per cent.

[j]From G. I. Shmelev, *Raspredelenie ispol'zovanie truda v kolkhozakh* (Moscow, 1964), p. 113.

per cent was reached in 1950–53, when, as a consequence of the Korean conflict, the government was drafting men away from the fields into the army or shifting them to industry. In 1961, the date of the last available information, the ratio had declined to 56 per cent.

In those years for which data for the various republics are available (1958, 1959, and 1961; see Table 92), the highest female participation in collective farming was in the Ukraine; the lowest was in the Tadzhik S.S.R., the only republic in which the proportion of women fell below 50 per cent. In the Ukraine and other European republics, the opportunities for men to find employment in other well-developed and diversified branches of the national economy, such as industry and construction, have been an important reason for the high proportion of women in agriculture. Conversely, the Tadzhik S.S.R. is among the least developed of the republics and consequently offers to the male population little alternative to agricultural employment. In the Central Asian republics, the traditional local

pattern of high male and low female participation in agriculture, as in most other branches of the economy, has not been overcome.

The contribution of women to collective farm labor can be measured in several ways: in terms of the absolute numbers, the proportion of women compared to men, the proportion of labor days (*trudodni*) earned by women, and the proportion of man-days worked by women. In Table 91 (col. 2), we find that the female contribution measured in absolute numbers shows a substantial decline from 1950, when the number of women collective farmers was almost 3.5 million larger than in 1959, and almost 6.5 million larger than in 1962. The proportion of women among able-bodied farmers who are working on collective farms still remains several percentage points higher than in the late 1930's in spite of the steady decline since the peak of 76 per cent during the war years. The decline since 1950 in both the number of collective farm women working and their proportion of the total since 1950 reflects, of

TABLE 92. Percentage of women among able-bodied collective farmers, by republic, selected years, 1940–61.

	1940	1950	1951	1952	1953	1954	1955	1956	1957	1958[a]	1959[b]	1961[c]
U.S.S.R.	54[b]	64[a]	–	–	63[b]	–	61[b]	–	59[b]	58	57	56
R.S.F.S.R.	–	–	–	–	–	–	–	–	–	59	58	57
Ukrainian S.S.R.	–	–	–	–	–	–	–	–	–	60	59	58
Belorussian S.S.R.	–	–	–	–	–	–	–	–	–	59	59	58
Uzbek S.S.R.	–	–	–	–	–	–	–	–	–	52	51	52
Kazakh S.S.R.	–	–	–	–	–	–	–	–	–	52	51	51
Georgian S.S.R.	–	–	–	–	–	–	–	–	–	52	51	51
Azerbaidzhan S.S.R.	–	–	–	–	–	–	–	–	–	54	55	53
Lithuanian S.S.R.	–	–	–	–	–	–	–	–	–	53	53	52
Moldavian S.S.R.	–	58[d]	–	–	59[d]	–	58[d]	–	55[d]	55	54	54
Latvian S.S.R.	–	–	–	–	–	–	–	–	–	57	56	56
Kirgiz S.S.R.	46[e]	56[e]	–	–	–	–	54[e]	53[e]	52[e]	52	52	51
Tadzhik S.S.R.	43[f]	51[f]	–	–	–	–	50[f]	50[f]	49[f]	49	49	48
Armenian S.S.R.	46[g]	56[g]	57[g]	58[g]	57[g]	56[g]	56[g]	54[g]	53[g]	52	52	51
Turkmen S.S.R.	47[h]	54[h]	–	–	–	–	54[h]	53[h]	53[h]	53	52	52
Estonian S.S.R.	–	–	–	–	–	–	–	–	–	59	58	56

[a]From Tsentral'noe statisticheskoe upravlenie pri Sovete ministrov SSSR, *Zhenshchina v SSSR* (Moscow, 1960), p. 42.
[b]From *Zhenshchiny i deti v SSSR* (Moscow, 1961), p. 129.
[c]From *Zhenshchiny i deti v SSSR* (Moscow, 1963), p. 109.
[d]From Tsentral'noe statisticheskoe upravlenie pri Sovete ministrov Moldavskoi SSR, *Zhenshchina Moldavii* (Kishinev, 1961), p. 27.
[e]From Tsentral'noe statisticheskoe upravlenie pri Sovete ministrov Kirgizskoi SSR, *Zhenshchina v Kirgizskoi SSR* (Frunze, 1960), p. 34.

[f]From Tsentral'noe statisticheskoe upravlenie pri Sovete ministrov Tadzhikskoi SSR, *Zhenshchina v Tadzhikskoi SSR* (Stalinabad, 1960), p. 32.
[g]From Tsentral'noe statisticheskoe upravlenie pri Sovete ministrov Armianskoi SSR, *Sel'skoe khoziaistvo Armianskoi SSR* (Erevan, 1961), pp. 458–59. Computed from data on actual number of female and total able-bodied participants.
[h]From Tsentral'noe statisticheskoe upravlenie pri Sovete ministrov Turkmenskoi SSR, *Zhenshchina v Turkmenskoi SSR* (Ashkhabad, 1960), p. 35.

course, the increase in the efficiency of labor on the collective farms in the decade of the 1950's.

In applying the third measure, we must remember that the labor day is not a measure of time worked but is determined by the type and quality of work performed. A brigadier or tractor driver earns more labor days per shift than an ordinary worker in a field brigade. Local rates are based on national minimums for certain occupations but still vary from region to region. The coefficient for men is higher, as a rule, because they do more complicated and harder work.[6] The situation in the Ukraine in 1957 can be considered fairly typical. Able-bodied males received 1.91 labor days for every man-day on the average while women received only 1.68. Typically, women contribute less work measured in labor days during the year than men because of the smaller final coefficient and the fewer man-days worked.

The different expectations for the two sexes are reflected in the minimum number of labor days required of men and women. The number which must be earned by women is smaller than the number required of men. At the "New Life" collective farm in Tambov Oblast, for example, the minimum for men was 350 labor days and for women, 250. At the "Khrushchev" collective near Moscow the minimum for men was 250 labor days and for women, 200.[7] In 1957 at the "Kirov" collective farm in Kharkov Oblast the minimum for males age 18 to 50 was 300 labor days and for males age 50 to 60, 250 labor days. For women age 18 to 40 the minimum was 200 days and for women age 40 to 50 and for nursing mothers the minimum was 150.[8] As a result of the smaller number of labor days worked by women, the series showing the percentage of labor days earned by women collective farmers (Table 91) averages some

10 percentage points, or approximately a fifth, below the percentage of women collective farmers.[9] The importance of female participation in the agricultural labor force is, therefore, obviously exaggerated unless allowance is made for the difference between the number of available women laborers and the work they actually perform.

For an examination of the distribution of man-days of input by women in relation to men, the only national data available are for 1959, when those able-bodied females required to earn the minimum number of labor days averaged 67 man-days less work than males,[10] but 1956–58 data for Krasnodar Krai, a fairly typical agricultural region, are sufficiently similar in their internal distribution to the 1959 national data to permit us to juxtapose them, as shown in Tables 93 and 94.

It is evident that although women constituted 57 per cent of the able-bodied collective farmers in 1959 (see Table 91), they contributed only 46.4 per cent of the total man-hours expended on all types of activity—on the collective farms, in the state sector, for private citizens, and on their own garden plots (see Table 93). By far the largest share of their time was contributed to the collective farms. For the four-year period 1956 to 1959, women devoted approximately 58 per cent of their work time to the collective farm (see Table 94). The next largest claim on their time was work in the private subsidiary economy—on private plots, in woodcutting, fishing, hunting, and as independent artisans. In no year for which data are given did women work less than a third of their time in private activity.[11]

---

[9]The 1959 figure of 49 per cent is for mandays worked, however. A shift is being made to this form of reporting collective-farm labor inputs.

[10]M. P. Vasilenko, *Puti preodoleniia sezonnosti truda v kolkhozakh* (Moscow, 1962), p. 53.

[11]It is interesting to note that the closer a collective farm is to an urban center, the fewer labor days worked, particularly by female labor, because of the higher returns from work on private

---

[6]I. Paskhaver, *Balans trudovykh resursov kolkhozov* (Kiev, 1961), p. 74.

[7]Ol'ga Danilovna Dubinskaia, *Prava i obiazanosti chlenov kolkhoza* (Moscow, 1957), p. 34.

[8]Paskhaver, *op. cit.*, p. 264.

TABLE 93. Labor inputs of all collective farmers, in percentages of man-hours worked by each group, 1959.[a]

Place of Work	Adults			Youths			Averages by All Groups
	Males 16–59	Females 16–54	Overaged and Invalids	Males 14–15	Females 14–15	Both Sexes 12–13	
Collective farms..........................	75.0	56.35	38.0	65.4	61.8	33.7	60.7
State and co-operative organizations........	12.8	9.05	3.1	2.2	4.4	0.8	9.5
For individual citizens....................	1.9	0.20	1.0	7.9	1.2	6.0	1.1
Private plots, in procurement and gathering of timber products, in fishing and hunting, in independent artisan-trade work........	10.3	34.4	57.9	24.5	32.6	59.5	28.7
Total.................................	100.0	100.0	100.0	100.0	100.0	100.0	100.0
Total in all activities....................	37.2	46.4	14.0		2.4		100.0

[a]Based on data from M. P. Vasilenko, *Puti preodoleniia sezonnosti truda v kolkhozakh* (Moscow, 1963), pp. 23–24.

TABLE 94. Labor inputs of able-bodied male and female collective farmers in Krasnodar Krai, in percentages of man-hours worked by each group, 1956–58.[a]

Place of Work	Males, 16–59			Females, 16–54		
	1956	1957	1958	1956	1957	1958
Collective farms.....................	78.1	80.0	78.6	57.6	56.5	55.7
State and co-operative organizations.....	10.6	10.4	12.5	6.3	7.9	10.0
For individuals......................	1.1	1.2	0.5	0.1	0.3	0.1
Private subsidiary sector..............	10.2	8.4	8.4	36.0	35.3	34.2
Total.............................	100.0	100.0	100.0	100.0	100.0	100.0

[a]Based on data from B. I. Braginskii, *Proizvoditel'nost' truda v sel'skom khoziaistve, metodika ucheta i planirovaniia* (Moscow, 1962), p. 194.

Because female collective farmers devote substantially more of their time to private plots than do men, women accounted for 80.6 per cent of the labor time spent in the private subsidiary agricultural economy. Men, on the other hand, devoted over a third again as much of their time as women to work on collective farms, while, largely as a result of their private work, women contributed only 48.6 per cent of the labor time spent on collective farms. Their share in the work of

plots. See V. Komarevskaia, V. Luzgina, and V. Shatskii, "Ispol'zovanie i material'oe stimulirovnaie sel'skokhoziaistvennogo truda v raionakh Bratsko-Taishetskogo promyshlennogo uzla," in *Ispol'zovanie trudovykh resursov v sel'skom khoziaistvo SSSR,* ed. by I. A. Borodin (Moscow, 1964), p. 211.

state and co-operative organizations was slightly smaller. However, when all agricultural activities are taken together, including work on private plots, women accounted for 55.5 per cent of the total labor inputs, measured in man-hours, of able-bodied men and women in 1959.[12] This total is close to the share of able-bodied women on collective farms (57 per cent).

In 1959, despite the high participation rate of women in collective agriculture, 4.1 per cent of the women collective farmers who were required to earn the minimum number of days did not work even one day, while 14.1 per cent of the females who occasionally put in some work on the collective did not earn the obligatory minimum number of labor

[12]Derived from data in Table 93.

days.[13] This discrepancy from the state norm was due principally to women's devoting their energies to private plots and the home. It is interesting that the percentage of completely nonparticipating women in 1959 (4.1 per cent) was higher than the corresponding rate in 1953 at the time of the Korean War (3.3 per cent, as shown in Table 95), when the mobilization of men would have placed greater responsibility for farm production upon women. Table 95 shows the tendency of women to work little more than the required number of days while a substantial number of men earned more than 400 labor days.

TABLE 95. Utilization of collective-farm labor resources, by sex, 1953.[a]

Number of Labor Days Earned	Percentage		
	Total	Men	Women
None	2.6	1.4	3.3
1–50	5.8	2.5	7.6
51–100	7.0	3.0	9.3
101–200	26.4	15.9	32.3
201–300	21.8	20.7	22.3
301–400	15.7	20.9	12.8
More than 400	20.7	35.6	12.4
Total	100.0	100.0	100.0
100 or less	15.4	6.9	20.2

[a]*Trudovye resursy SSSR*, ed. by N. I. Shishkin (Moscow, 1961), p. 109.

That some collective farmers do not perform their share of work or do not participate at all contributes to the acute labor shortage existing during the harvest period. This shortage and probably also poor planning and insufficient working equipment often require the importation of extra hands from the cities to aid in the harvest. For example, in Kazakhstan in September, 1958, 115,300 workers, employees, and students were used on collective farms to bring in the crop. They amounted to a sixth of the collective farmers

and repair-technical station workers who worked in Kazakhstan that month. At the same time in that republic there were 18,400 able-bodied farmers, reported to be mostly women, who did not work at all, and another 34,500 who did not earn the minimum number of labor days during the year. These figures may be compared with the annual average number of 3,500 hired wage workers employed on the collective farms in Kazakhstan during 1958 and about 40,000 harvest hands (converted to an average annual basis) who were brought in temporarily during periods of peak labor demand, as in September.[14]

In appraising the participation of women on collective farms, we must consider the structure of female employment not only in terms of aggregate numbers and percentages, but also in terms of the specific type of agricultural activity in which they are engaged. Among women collective farmers 97 per cent are engaged in physical labor. For men the proportion is 82 per cent.[15] It is no wonder then that as recently as December 26, 1961, Khrushchev is reported to have stated at a regional farm conference in Kiev:

We all know what an enormous role women play in all the sectors in the building of communism. But for some reason there are few women in this hall. Just take a pair of binoculars and have a look around. What is the reason for this? It will be said that it is mainly administrative workers who are present here. It turns out that it is the men who do the administrating and the women who do the work.[16]

Further evidence of the type of work performed by women engaged in agriculture is provided by Table 96, according to which 83 per cent or 14.5 of 17.4 million women collective farmers employed in physical labor are

[13]*Trudovye resursy SSSR*, ed. by N. I. Shishkin (Moscow, 1961), p. 109. For failure to work the required minimum number of labor days, pay is typically reduced 10 per cent. See Dubinskaia, *op. cit.*, p. 34.

[14]B. I. Braginskii, *Proizvoditel'nost' truda v sel'skom khoziaistve (metodika ucheta i planirovaniia)* (Moscow, 1962), pp. 97–98.
[15]*Itogi . . . 1959 goda: SSSR*, Tables 33, 46, pp. 104–5, 160.
[16]*Izvestiia* (Dec. 26, 1961).

TABLE 96. Number and percentage of women among collective farmers employed in predominantly physical labor in agriculture, by occupation, January 15, 1959.[a]

Occupation	Number		Percentage Female
	Total	Female	
Total employed in physical labor...................	28,728,425	17,420,143	60.6
Administrative and supervisory personnel			
Heads of livestock and poultry subfarms...........	134,983	20,227	15.0
Brigadiers of field brigades......................	232,772	19,295	8.3
Brigadiers of livestock brigades..................	31,697	4,043	12.8
Other brigadiers...............................	195,940	10,256	5.2
Skilled workers and junior supervisory personnel			
Bookkeepers..................................	23,443	4,363	18.6
Tractor and combine drivers.....................	1,259,261	9,571	0.8
Implement handlers and workers on agricultural machinery...................................	124,751	1,774	1.4
Field-team leaders.............................	149,666	130,664	87.3
Specialized agricultural workers			
Workers in plant breeding and feed production.....	524,606	374,167	71.3
Cattle farm workers............................	701,449	423,786	60.4
Milking personnel..............................	1,150,363	1,136,923	98.8
Stablemen and grooms..........................	716,017	50,708	7.1
Swineherds....................................	420,541	381,145	90.6
Herdsmen, drovers, shepherds...................	550,657	96,356	17.5
Other livestock workers.........................	113,874	23,920	21.0
Poultry workers................................	116,557	108,886	93.4
Beekeepers....................................	62,603	9,497	15.2
Orchard and vineyard workers...................	50,854	20,887	41.1
Vegetable and melon growers....................	56,539	45,546	80.6
Irrigators.....................................	7,975	861	10.8
Nonspecialized agricultural workers...............	21,991,868	14,523,178	66.0

[a]Based on data from *Itogi . . . 1959 goda: SSSR*, pp. 159–60.

nonspecialized and unskilled, as against 66 per cent of male collective farmers. In addition, although they comprise 60 per cent of the collective farmers engaged in physical labor, they make up 66 per cent of the unskilled collective farmers of both sexes. Of those engaged in managerial work of the limited type (heads of subfarms and brigadiers), women number only about 12 per cent of the total. Among bookkeepers the percentage of women is only slightly higher (19 per cent). Only among field-team leaders do they play a preponderant role (87 per cent), and this is basically a foreman type of position. In three of the occupations, those of swineherd, milking worker, and poultry worker, women number more than 90 per cent.

Of the two major branches of collective farm activity—crop growing and animal husbandry—the former is of course highly seasonal, while the latter requires constant attendance and therefore provides employment throughout the year. According to the 1959 census, women comprised 57 per cent (2,-244,342) of the 4.4 million workers in animal husbandry, including poultry raising. Most of the women working in animal husbandry are girls and young women with children of preschool age.[17] This seems to be particularly true of the milkmaids and poultry workers.[18] However, the proportion of collective farm women employed in animal husbandry is small (12.8 per cent) compared with all women collective farmers employed primarily

[17]The category of animal husbandry workers includes cattle farm workers, milkmaids, stablemen, grooms, swineherds, herdsmen, drovers, shepherds, and other livestock workers (see Table 96).

[18]G. Shmelev and V. Ladenkov, "Ispol'zovanie zhenskogo truda v kolkhozakh," *Ekonomika sel'skogo khoziaistva* (Oct., 1962), p. 30.

in physical labor.[19] The overwhelming proportion of women (86.8 per cent) are employed in field work—the planting, cultivating, and harvesting of crops—which is highly seasonal.[20] This being the case, many women are able to devote substantial amounts of time during the rest of the year to their private plots, to the care of children, and to other household duties. Data from Rostov Oblast indicate the monthly variations in the rates of female participation. In 1960, fewer than 57 per cent of the women employed in July worked in the months of November, December, January, and February; for men the lowest rate, 67.1 per cent, was reached in December.[21]

The prospects are slim for a substantial increase in the labor inputs of women to socialized agriculture. A total of 45 per cent of the able-bodied women dependents outside the Soviet labor force have children under age 7, and 59 per cent have children under age 14.[22] The percentage among women collective farmers probably would not differ greatly, since rural families generally are larger than urban families. Until more adequate childcare facilities are available in rural areas, the majority of housewives who have young children are not likely to want to leave the home for work on other than a seasonal basis. The preference of women for seasonal work has tended to discourage them from developing the knowledge and skills required for the more attractive kinds of work in agriculture.

It is young men rather than girls who are encouraged or actually sent by collective farms to obtain specialized training in some agricultural field. As a result, most women in agriculture spend their lives doing the least interesting and least challenging work.

After the abolition of the machine tractor stations (MTS) in 1958 and the sale of most of their machinery to the collectives, the bulk of the MTS workers were also transferred to the collective farms, and by the time of the 1959 census were classified as collective farmers.[23] For this reason, MTS workers are discussed in this section. The jobs performed by the MTS workers—who numbered 3.1 million in 1954—both before and after the 1958 shift were usually among the more highly skilled and better-paying jobs in agriculture. As Table 97 indicates, the proportion of women in

TABLE 97. Percentage of women among MTS personnel, by occupation, 1948, 1950, and 1954.[a]

	Percentage of Women		
Categories of Workers	May 1, 1948	May 5, 1950	May 5, 1954
Total of all MTS personnel.......	7.6	5.6	9.3
Personnel servicing tractors and agricultural machinery...........	7.5	5.5	3.9
Drivers........................	1.1	1.3	0.7
Repair workers...................	4.4	4.0	3.3
Workers employed on construction..	n.a.	22.0	35.7
Wage workers of subsidiary units, dining halls, kindergartens, and others......................	44.6	37.3	53.6

[a]Based on Appendix VII, Tables 3, 4, and 5.

these occupations was very small. Despite the omnipresence of the sturdy girl tractor driver in Soviet fiction, she remains largely a creature of the propaganda mill.[24] Only during World War II did women make up a significant percentage of those employed in the machine tractor stations as drivers or mechanics. The author of an important study

---

[19]*Ibid.* According to Shishkin, *op. cit.,* p. 99, the corresponding percentages for both sexes from collective farm annual reports for 1956, 1958, and 1959 are 11.7, 12.1, and 12.6 per cent, respectively.

[20]For both sexes, Shishkin (*ibid.*) gives 79.8, 78.8, and 78.2 per cent in 1956, 1958, and 1959, respectively.

[21]Shmelev and Ladenkov, *op. cit.,* p. 29. For earlier but similar figures, see B. Babynin, "Trudovye resursy kolkhozov i ikh ispol'zovanie," *Problemy ekonomiki,* No. 2 (1940), 71.

[22]F. I. Kotov, *Problemy truda i zarabotnoi platy v period perekhoda k kommunizmu* (Moscow, 1963), p. 192; *Itogi . . . 1959 goda: SSSR,* p. 99; cf. Shishkin, *op. cit.,* p. 154.

[23]Only a small number remained to staff the repair-technical stations, which continued to supply the collective farms with fuel and parts and to service equipment.

[24]Almost all female tractor or combine drivers are in the age group 20–35. See Appendix VII, Table 2.

on agriculture during the war has described the importance of women in mechanized work during this period: "Women could be seen even behind the wheel of a tractor or combine or in the shop behind a lathe. They plowed the fields, herded cattle, carried heavy sacks, and often slept in the fields. After a day's work, sitting next to a kerosene lamp or in the flickering light of a chip, they knitted warm clothes for the fighting men."[25] The district of Rostov in 1943 is illustrative. There, 41 per cent of the tractor drivers and 50 per cent of the combine operators were women.[26]

The important role women played in the machine tractor stations during the war did not persist, as the following long, frank quotation indicates:

As is known, the war made women a basic part of production not only in collective farms but also in MTS's. If women had continued to maintain their role in the MTS in the postwar period, then the reduction in total labor resources in the villages would not have placed the machine tractor stations in a less favorable position than existed in the prewar period. In comparison with the prewar period, the MTS's would have had the advantage of having their basic cadres composed not only of men (before the war men were 90–95 per cent of the mechanized personnel), but also of women. In practice it turned out, however, that the changes in MTS cadres which took place during the war disappeared with the end of the war. As soon as the war ended a mass exodus of women from the machine tractor stations began. . . .

On January 1, 1947, women comprised 17.4 per cent of the tractor drivers, on January 1, 1948, 9 per cent, and on January 1, 1949, 5 per cent. In other words during these two postwar years, women reverted to their prewar norm. In 1945–49, mechanized cadres were composed mainly of men, as in the prewar period. . . .

During the war women went to work in

MTS's because of extreme necessity. When this need no longer existed, conditions in MTS did not attract women. It is sufficient to state that there were no kindergartens or nurseries.

Finally, not only the MTS's needed labor; the collective farms had a large demand for workers; they needed milkmaids, swineherds, field workers. Women entered this kind of employment more willingly than employment as mechanized personnel. For the latter jobs, almost without exception, they would have to live for a long time away from their families and homes, at a field station or at repair workshops. This was the main reason for the exodus of women from machine tractor stations. . . .[27]

The percentage of women engaged in occupations involving mechanical work connected with agriculture continued to decline during the 1950's, as indicated by a comparison of Tables 96 and 97. By January 15, 1959, about 400,000 tractor and combine drivers remained to be shifted to the collective farms from repair-technical stations.[28] Of the nearly 1.3 million drivers already on the collective farm rolls, fewer than 10,000, or about 0.8 per cent, were women. Thus, the dominance of men in this type of work was almost complete by 1959, and the driving, repair, and maintenance of tractors, combines, and trucks remain today almost exclusively in the male domain.

Women in the Private Subsidiary Economy. Work in the private subsidiary economy consists almost entirely of work on private garden plots. Only a negligible amount of handicraft work is included. These garden plots are among the last remnants of private enterprise in the Soviet Union and have been tolerated for very practical reasons. Through intensive cultivation, in 1959, these plots, which occupied only 3.7 per cent of the sown area, accounted for a substantial share

[25]Iu. V. Arutiunian, *Sovetskoe krest'ianstvo v gody Velikoi otechestvennoi voiny* (Moscow, 1963), pp. 113–14.

[26]*Izvestiia* (Aug. 18, 1943).

[27]Iu. V. Arutiunian, *Mekhanizatory sel'skogo khoziaistva SSSR v 1929–1957 gg. (formirovanie kadrov massovykh kvalifikatsii)* (Moscow, 1960), pp. 114–16.

[28]See Table 96 and *Narodnoe khoziaistvo SSSR v 1960 godu* (Moscow, 1961), p. 527.

of total farm output, particularly of certain key products, such as potatoes (64 per cent), vegetables (46 per cent), fruit and berries (67 per cent), meat (41 per cent), milk (47 per cent), and eggs (81 per cent).[29] By 1961 the sown area of the plots had shrunk to 3.3 per cent and the share in the production of potatoes had declined slightly to 63 per cent, vegetables to 44 per cent, fruits and berries to 64 per cent, milk to 46 per cent, and eggs to 79 per cent. The share of meat production actually increased slightly to 45 per cent. Hence, the production of the private plots continues to remain important despite the decline.[30]

For many Soviet citizens the plots provide important food products which would not otherwise be available. They are cultivated by three major groups: members of families of collective farmers, of state farm workers, and of other workers and employees. The first is the largest group, accounting for 58 per cent of the total number reported employed in this sector by the 1959 census. The allocation of the remaining 42 per cent between families of state farm workers and of other workers and employees cannot be made with precision. It is estimated that the former account for approximately 30 per cent, and the latter, for 12 per cent.[31] When employment is converted

to man-year equivalents, so that labor inputs from all sources are taken into account, the share of families of collective farmers, including the labor of persons classified as collective farmers but who work on the plots in their spare time, is estimated to have been 71 per cent in 1959.[32] No further breakdown of the remainder has been attempted.

Women account for the great majority of the workers in the private subsidiary economy. According to the 1959 census figures, almost 9 million women made up 91 per cent of the workers of both sexes (Table 98). Among the able-bodied age groups their share was even larger (96 per cent), since men in this age group are usually engaged in full-time socialized occupations. Their share among over- and under-aged workers was slightly smaller (86 per cent). A very high percentage of the persons employed in the private subsidiary sector are in the over-aged group—age 60 and over in the case of men and age 55 and over in the case of women. Among women of all ages employed in this sector, 46 per cent are in the over-aged group.[33] Some of these women continue to work for many years beyond the normal retirement age. Readers of Abramov's novel *The New Life* will recall the elderly woman who supported herself by the produce of her

---

[29]These figures are for 1959 and are calculated from *Sel'skoe khoziaistvo SSSR* (Moscow, 1960), pp. 235–38, 240–43, 348, 350–51, 354–56, 359.

[30]Calculated from *Narodnoe khoziaistvo SSSR v 1961 godu* (Moscow, 1962), pp. 300, 319, 321, 376, 391.

[31]In making this estimate the author assumes that the urban element in employment in the private subsidiary sector reflects fairly accurately the proportion of nonstate farm workers and employees. The presumption is that members of families of collective or state farm workers who live in urban areas are balanced by members of families of other workers and employees who live in rural areas and who are engaged in private subsidiary agriculture. Even if the census provided this breakdown, reservations about the validity of the data would be necessary. It may be presumed that many collective farmers who devoted much of their time to their plots were listed by census takers as working on the collec-

tive farms even though the number of labor days earned was small. As an example of the cultivation of urban or suburban garden plots by families of workers and employees, the city of Saratov was reported to have more than 2,000 acres under cultivation by 13,339 families. See S. A. Osipov, "Flowering Gardens," *Soviet Woman*, No. 4 (1960), 11.

[32]Weitzman, Feshbach, and Kulchycka, *op. cit.*, p. 602.

[33]The number of under-aged workers in the private subsidiary sector is small, and is ignored in our discussion (see Appendix VII, Table 6). It should be remembered that the census classifications would not classify a pupil who worked on the family plot during the summer months as employed in private subsidiary agriculture. This is a major reason that the census data are not helpful in analyzing actual labor inputs into the subsidiary sector.

TABLE 98. Percentage of women employed in the private subsidiary sector, by age, urban and rural residence, and republic, 1959.[a]

Republic	Age Distribution of Women		Percentage of Women among			Percentage of Women among		Percentage of Women Employed Who Are Rural
	Able-bodied Age Group	Over- or Under-aged	All Ages	Able-bodied Age Group	Over- or Under-aged	Urban Workers	Rural Workers	
U.S.S.R.	53.9	46.1	90.7	95.8	85.5	83.5	90.3	88.7
R.S.F.S.R.	57.4	42.6	93.4	97.4	88.6	96.2	93.1	89.8
Ukrainian S.S.R.	43.6	56.4	89.0	94.1	85.5	94.9	88.1	85.6
Belorussian S.S.R.	44.9	55.1	89.2	94.5	85.3	93.7	88.7	89.9
Uzbek S.S.R.	53.2	46.8	78.0	88.4	68.7	84.4	77.6	94.6
Kazakh S.S.R.	76.1	23.9	93.1	97.8	80.9	92.7	93.2	87.5
Georgian S.S.R.	58.8	41.2	84.6	90.2	77.8	87.4	84.3	88.5
Azerbaidzhan S.S.R.	60.8	39.2	88.5	92.2	83.3	89.8	88.3	84.1
Lithuanian S.S.R.	51.5	48.5	87.0	92.7	81.6	87.6	87.0	92.7
Moldavian S.S.R.	48.9	51.1	90.7	94.9	86.9	94.4	90.3	91.8
Latvian S.S.R.	44.9	55.1	87.8	94.5	82.8	89.0	85.9	87.2
Kirgiz S.S.R.	53.5	46.5	83.2	93.9	73.5	89.5	82.5	89.4
Tadzhik S.S.R.	66.5	33.5	86.5	94.0	74.4	92.1	85.7	86.8
Armenian S.S.R.	62.0	38.0	88.3	94.0	80.4	88.1	88.4	91.8
Turkmen S.S.R.	60.1	39.9	78.3	86.2	68.7	91.1	76.2	84.3
Estonian S.S.R.	23.7	76.3	82.9	89.1	67.6	75.4	83.3	95.2

[a]Calculated from *Itogi . . . 1959 goda: SSSR*, pp. 99 and 101.

garden plot.[34] More typical would be the grandmother who leaves the socialized labor force to take care of the grandchildren and the garden plot, often before retirement age is reached, since the daughter or daughter-in-law is likely to be a better earner in the socialized sector. Garden work does not, of course, require much training, and even the urban grandmother is likely to have acquired all the knowledge necessary.

Women on State Farms and in Other State Agricultural Enterprises. The third group of agricultural workers are those employed on state farms and other state agricultural enterprises, such as repair-technical stations. This sizable group of workers and employees, numbering 6.6 million in 1959, have the same employment status as workers and employees in industry, construction, and other nonagricultural branches of the economy.[35] They earn regular wages, are covered by social insurance, receive regular vacations, and so

forth. Thus they occupy a privileged position as compared to collective farmers. Most of them, like collective farmers, are also provided with private garden plots. The proportion of women among this group is smaller than among collective farmers, amounting to only 41 per cent.[36] However, women employed in state agriculture, like women collective farmers, are primarily assigned to the less skilled jobs. Of the 2.7 million women employed in this sector, almost 2.3 million, or 84 per cent, were reported by the 1959 census as engaged in predominantly physical labor. Approximately half of all the women working on state farms or other state enterprises were employed as nonspecialized workers and made up 63.4 per cent of all those employed in this category.

The percentage of women varies widely among the different occupations, and the pattern shown for workers and employees in Table 99 is similar to that for collective farmers. More than 99 per cent of the milking personnel on state farms are women. Other occupations in which women make up more

[34]Feodor Abramov, *The New Life* (New York, 1964).
[35]See Table 90, entry for "Agriculture, Workers and Employees."

[36]*Ibid.*

TABLE 99. Number and percentage of women among state farm and other workers of state agricultural enterprises employed in predominantly physical labor, January 15, 1959.[a]

Occupation	Number		Percentage of Females
	Total	Females	
Total employed in physical labor....................	5,071,233	2,261,473	44.6
Administrative and supervisory personnel			
Heads of livestock and poultry farms...............	8,114	2,046	25.2
Brigadiers of field brigades.........................	26,364	3,396	12.9
Brigadiers of livestock brigades....................	42,790	7,718	18.0
Other brigadiers.................................	66,948	6,243	9.3
Skilled workers and junior supervisory personnel			
Bookkeepers....................................	6,671	1,835	27.5
Tractor and combine drivers......................	1,130,031	7,669	0.7
Implement handlers and workers on agricultural machinery...................................	25,481	1,296	5.1
Field-team leaders...............................	6,839	5,845	85.5
Specialized agricultural workers			
Workers in plant breeding and feed production.......	86,661	58,297	67.3
Cattle farm workers.............................	260,014	122,178	47.0
Milking personnel...............................	281,126	278,686	99.1
Stablemen and grooms...........................	299,274	34,852	11.6
Swineherds.....................................	142,601	132,682	93.0
Herdsmen, drovers, shepherds....................	202,958	44,655	22.0
Other livestock workers..........................	74,681	38,812	52.0
Poultry workers.................................	45,596	42,996	94.3
Beekeepers.....................................	17,383	4,085	23.5
Orchard and vineyard workers....................	55,541	34,441	62.0
Vegetable and melon growers.....................	28,290	22,118	78.2
Irrigators......................................	11,635	2,154	18.5
Nonspecialized agricultural workers..................	2,130,267	1,350,240	63.4

[a]*Itogi . . . 1959 goda: SSSR*, pp. 159–60.

than 90 per cent of the total are swine herding and poultry raising. More than 60 per cent of those employed as field-team leaders, vegetable and melon growers, orchard and vineyard workers, workers in plant breeding and feed production are women. However, by far the largest number of workers are employed in the unskilled, nonspecialized category, in which women make up 63.4 per cent of the total. The smallest percentage of women is in occupations requiring administrative responsibility (heads of subfarms and brigadiers), mechanical ability (tractor drivers), a nomadic existence (herdsmen and shepherds), or in those by long custom dominated by males (stablemen and grooms). In none of these occupations does the percentage of women exceed 27 per cent.

If we consider the collective farm and state farm sector together, we find that 80.7 per cent or 15.9 million of the 19.7 million women wage workers and collective farmers

are unskilled.[37] These women represent 66 per cent of the total of unskilled farmers of both sexes. Of those engaged in administrative work of the limited type, women number only about 20 per cent. Only among field-team leaders are they preponderant (87.2 per cent); this is basically a foreman type of position, and the workers supervised are predominantly women.

Since the three categories of agriculture discussed above include over half the women in the Soviet labor force, the majority of Soviet women are still engaged in heavy, backbreaking physical labor. Anyone who has traveled in rural Russia or visited a collective farm market will recognize these women. They have the deeply tanned, heavily lined faces of people who have spent their lives outdoors. Their hands are rough; their bodies are thick; they have become old before their

[37]See Appendix VII, Table 5.

time. Later in this study, when we examine the role of women in industry and in the professions, we should not forget that for every woman pursuing a challenging or stimulating career, there is a brigade of farm women bent to their tasks in the fields. Up to the present, the rhythm and pattern of these women's lives have been little touched by the twentieth century.

Women Workers and Employees in Non-agricultural Branches of the Economy. Visitors to the Soviet Union in recent years have found women doing all kinds of work in the nonagricultural fields. Justice Douglas, for example, has remarked:

I saw women digging ditches, loading freight cars with rocks, shoveling dirt at the hydroelectric dam on the Ob River, laying concrete, using welding torches, pouring molten metal, operating overhead cranes in Siberian factories, cleaning streets, driving trucks, operating streetcars, unloading baggage and express, serving as switchmen, flagmen, and porters on trains, and doing every conceivable kind of work in meatpacking plants.[38]

This widespread employment of women represented the end result of a variety of pressures building up since the Revolution which have led to the employment of Soviet women in nearly every walk of life. At different times the pressures which have been of the greatest importance have changed. During the 1920's agitation for an increase in the employment of women was motivated by a desire to relieve unemployment and to secure the economic independence of women rather than to mobilize unused manpower reserves because of a labor shortage. The authors of the First Five-Year Plan were not moved by the pressure of labor shortages to plan a substantial increase in the proportion of employed women, but they were concerned that in the absence of countermeasures the rapid expansion of heavy industry, in which the proportion of women was relatively low, would lower the proportion of women employed in the economy as a whole.[39] Vigorous efforts promoting the employment of female labor were expected, not just to maintain, but to increase the proportion of women workers and employees from 27.0 per cent in 1927–28 to 32.5 per cent in 1932–33.[40]

When a shortage of labor began to be felt in 1930, the employment of women acquired a new urgency. In order to fulfill the plan, it had become necessary to draw more women into production. A detailed plan was worked out in the spring of 1930 which raised the target of the First Five-Year Plan, to 34 to 35 per cent women in all occupations.[41] The increase was to be largest in the production of capital goods, where the percentage was scheduled to rise from 10.3 per cent in 1928–29 to 20.2 per cent in 1932–33. A sharp increase in the number of women was also planned for the construction industry, trade, and education. In the consumers' goods industries, where the percentage of women was already high, the percentage was to increase from 51.6 to 58.8 per cent.

The bulk of the new women workers were to be recruited from among housewives. As Solomon Schwarz points out, the utilization of urban manpower was an "alluring prospect." It permitted an increase in the labor supply without aggravating the housing and food shortages in the cities and hopefully reduced the high rate of labor turnover.[42]

Schwarz also quotes a leading economic journal as stating as early as the spring of 1931:

Economic, Soviet, and Party organs will have to consider that even in peacetime the problem of women workers is of greatest importance to national defense, for the training of manpower takes time and vocational skill

---

[38]William O. Douglas, *Russian Journey* (Garden City, N.Y., 1956), p. 129.

[39]*Five-Year Plan of Economic Construction of the U.S.S.R.* (Moscow, 1929), Vol. II, p. 180.
[40]*Ibid.*
[41]E. Bronshtein, "Blizhaishie perspektivy zhenskogo truda," *Na planovom fronte,* No. 11 (1930), 52.
[42]Schwarz, *op. cit.,* p. 66.

is determined not only by an apprenticeship but by practical experience on the job.[43]

To encourage the employment of women, lists of trades and professions to be reserved exclusively or predominantly for women were drawn up and issued by the People's Commissariat of Labor of the R.S.F.S.R. on January 16, 1931, and minimum quotas for girls in vocational schools and training classes were increased. These lists were superseded by a less specific and restrictive All-Union list of occupations "in which the use of females shall be greatly expanded."[44] As a result, planning agencies set quotas for the various industries requiring plant managers to employ a given percentage of women.[45] Schwarz points out that by the mid-1930's the job was believed accomplished and that the quotas fell out of use.

By the end of the 1930's the measures taken to encourage the employment of women in industry had largely served their purposes. The numbers of women workers and employees had risen sharply. As Schwarz emphasizes, "Women made up the overwhelming majority of the newly employed workers. Between 1932 and 1937 total employment increased by 4,047,000, of which 3,350,000, or 82 per cent, comprised women."[46] The largest gains were made in industries in which few women workers had been employed. Nevertheless, although the number of female workers and employees increased threefold between 1927 and 1937, the over-all increase in workers and employees was so great that the percentage of women increased only from 27.0 to 39.3 per cent.

During World War II, the share of women workers and employees increased greatly. By 1942 the share of women among workers and employees, including those women employed on state farms, had risen to 53 per cent, from 38 per cent in 1940. In industry the increase was from 41 to 52 per cent; on the railways, from 25 to 36 per cent; in communications, from 48 to 67 per cent; in public utilities, from 42 to 64 per cent; in trade, from 37 to 55 per cent; and in public catering, from 67 to 83 per cent. The proportion of women in educational institutions increased from 58 to 73 per cent; in health services, from 76 to 83 per cent; and in government administration, from 35 to 55 per cent.[47]

The increased role of women was also reflected in various skilled occupations in industry, where few women had been employed previously. The proportion of women operating steam engines increased from 6 per cent in the beginning of 1941 to 33 per cent at the end of 1942; women compressor operators, from 27 to 44 per cent; and stokers, from 6 to 27 per cent. During the same period the proportion of women lathe operators increased from 16 to 33 per cent; welders, from 17 to 31 per cent; hand molders, from 17 to 32 per cent; machine molders, from 29 to 39 per cent; fitters, from 3.9 to 12 per cent; forge, hammer, and die press operators, from 11 to 50 per cent; electricians working at electric substations, from 32 to 50 per cent. The proportion of women automobile drivers also increased, from 3.5 to 19 per cent; and women loaders, from 17 to 40 per cent.[48] After 1942 the employment of women appears to have continued to expand. In the iron and steel industry women accounted for 40 per cent of the employment by the spring of 1944, an increase of 15 percentage points since 1939.[49] In the oil fields and coal mines the percentage of women continued to grow. In the Baku oil fields, where few women had been employed before the war, women made up 30 to 40 per cent of the labor force.[50]

[43]S. Gimmelfarb, "Likvidatsiia bezrabotitsy v SSSR i problema kadrov," *Problemy ekonomiki* (April-May, 1931), p. 31; quoted by Schwarz, *op. cit.*, p. 66.

[44]*Izvestiia Narkomtruda* (1931), p. 268; cited in Schwarz, *op. cit.*, p. 67.

[45]Schwarz, *op. cit.*, p. 67.

[46]*Ibid.*, p. 72.

[47]N. A. Voznesensky, *Soviet Economy during the Second World War* (New York, 1949), p. 92.

[48]*Ibid.*

[49]*Pravda* (Mar. 8, 1944); quoted by Schwarz, *op. cit.*, p. 74.

[50]*Trud* (Dec. 11, 1943); quoted by Schwarz, *op. cit.*, p. 74.

In some of the mine pits women became a majority of the miners.[51]

With the basic strategy of Soviet economic development directed toward the expansion of industry, the participation of women in this branch of the economy has increased at a rapid pace. The number of women in industry grew over tenfold during the years 1929 to 1964 (see Table 100), thus almost exactly paralleling the rate of increase of women workers and employees in all nonagricultural branches of the economy. Table 101 reveals that, in terms of their distribution among the various branches of industry, not only have women wage workers continued their predominance in such traditional activities as the textile and clothing industries, but their contribution as wage workers has risen to significant proportions in many other branches of industry. For example, on January 1, 1962, they comprised over 38 per cent of the workers in the oil-refining industry, almost 39 per cent in machine building and metalworking, about 44 per cent in the paper industry, and over 54 per cent in the food industry.

Census data showing a breakdown of occupations involving primarily physical labor reveal a similar pattern. Women made up 70 per cent of the printing workers engaged in physical labor, 62 per cent of those in the paper industry, and 57 per cent of the chemical workers. These high percentages, particularly in the chemical industry, do not seem to be compatible with the legal prohibition against the employment of women in many of the so-called "hot, heavy, and hazardous occupations."

In some of the more narrowly defined industrial occupations the percentage of women is also surprisingly high. For example, women make up 64 per cent of the forge and press operators and 48 per cent of other machine tool operators.[52] In any Soviet factory one will find women doing unexpected tasks. The author recalls seeing women doing most of the actual production work in a number of machine and assembly shops at the Kharkov Tractor Plant. In the shop producing fuel injection apparatus, which calls for very high tolerances, the work force was almost exclusively made up of women. The foreman—a man—said that for such delicate and exacting work women were much preferred to men. One expected that the balance would be redressed in the steel foundry and that the bulk of the production personnel there would be men. This was not the case, however. A substantial share of the workers handling the molds and manning the casting carousels were women.

One also finds surprisingly high percentages of women in construction work, where women workers and employees increased between 1929 and 1962 from less than 7 to 29 per cent of the total. The woman plasterer or painter has become a familiar sight at any construction site. The number of women engaged in both these occupations has increased manyfold since the war, and women comprised more than half of the total employment in each occupation at the time of the 1959 census.

Another occupational area in which women play an unexpectedly important role is public transportation. Although women make up less than 1 per cent of the automobile and truck drivers, they comprise 57 per cent of the subway, trolley, and trolley-bus drivers and 94 per cent of the conductors on these vehicles.

The role of women has also grown considerably in sectors of the economy in which their presence might be expected. For example, two thirds of the persons providing communal and household services are women, as are almost three fourths of the postal workers and letter carriers, nine tenths of the public dining workers, and nearly all nurses, nursemaids, and orderlies.

The regional distribution of women workers and employees (Table 102) shows a persistently higher percentage in the R.S.F.S.R., Belorussia, and the Ukraine than in the non-Slavic republics, particularly the Central Asian republics. Women also make up a rela-

---

[51]*Pravda* (Sept. 7 and Dec. 6, 1944); quoted by Schwarz, *op. cit.,* pp. 74–75.

[52]See Appendix VII, Table 1.

TABLE 100. Number and percentage of women workers and employees, by branch of the economy, selected years, 1929–64.*

Branch of the Economy	1929[a, b]		1930[c]		1931[c]		1932[c]	
		%		%		%		%
Total national economy	3,118	27	3,877	26.7	4,197	26.9	6,007	27.4
Industry	1,109	28	–	–	–	–	–	–
Large-scale industry	–	–	1,236	29.0	1,440	29.3	2,043	32.2
Construction	64	7	156	9.6	189	10.1	380	12.8
State farms and subsidiary agricultural enterprises	416	28	425	27.4	421	23.1	394	21.3
MTS and RTS	–	–	–	–	–	–	–	–
Transport and communications	155	11[i]	–	–	–	–	–	–
Transport	122	9	146	9.7	173	10.2	243	11.6
Communications	33	28	–	–	–	–	–	–
Trade, public dining, procurement, material-technical supply	133	19	279	28.0	405	34.6	675	38.9
Trade	–	16[e]	179[i]	22.0[i]	–	–	–	–
Public dining	–	46[e]	100[i]	55.5[i]	–	–	–	–
Public health	283	65	320[i]	67.1[i]	358[i]	69.0[i]	426[i]	70.2[i]
Education, science, and scientific services	449	54	482[i]	52.3[i]	514[i]	50.4[i]	692[i]	53.6[i]
Education	–	–	–	–	–	–	–	–
Science and scientific services	–	–	–	–	–	–	–	–
Government and social institutions; credit and insurance	255	19	332[i]	22.6[i]	373[i]	24.1[i]	475[i]	25.8[i]
Government and social	–	–	–	–	–	–	–	–
Credit and insurance	–	–	–	–	–	–	–	–
Other branches[k]	(284)	(31)	(501)	(30)	(324)	(31)	(679)	(21)

TABLE 100. Number and percentage of women workers and employees, by branch of the economy, selected years, 1929–64.*—*continued*

Branch of the Economy	1950[a, b]		1952[d]		1955[e]		1956[e]	
Total national economy	18,397	47	20,300[a]	48	21,674[a]	45	22,691[a]	45
Industry	6,421	45	(7,156)	46	(7,815)	45	(8,306)	45
Large-scale industry	–	–	–	–	–	–	–	–
Construction	845	33	(948)	34	(989)	31	(1,064)	31
State farms and subsidiary agricultural enterprises	1,193	49	(1,089)	43	(1,303)	46	(1,268)	43
MTS and RTS	108[b]	16	–	–	(276)	9	(202)	7
Transport and communications	1,530	34[e]	(1,717)	(33)	(1,864)	33	(1,940)	33
Transport	1,212	30	(1,378)	30	–	–	–	–
Communications	318	59	(339)	60	–	–	–	–
Trade, public dining, procurement, material-technical supply	1,922	58	(2,097)	60	(2,409)	(64)	(2,515)	(64)
Trade	–	52[e]	–	–	(1,699)	58	(1,775)	59
Public dining	–	80[e]	–	–	(710)	83	(740)	83
Public health	1,729	84	(1,892)	85	(2,233)	85	(2,363)	85
Education, science, and scientific services	2,579	64	(2,809)	(64)	–	–	–	–
Education	–	–	(2,453)	69	(3,116)	68	(3,183)	67
Science and scientific services	–	–	(326)	43	–	–	–	–
Government and social institutions; credit and insurance	945	45	(959)	(47)	(797)	49	(804)	50
Government and social	–	–	(804)	45	–	–	–	–
Credit and insurance	–	–	(155)	59	–	–	–	–
Other branches[k]	(1,125)	(35)	(1,643)	(41)	(872)	(24)	(1,046)	(27)

*Absolute numbers are expressed in thousands; –, data not available and no estimate made; parentheses indicate estimates.

[a]From *Zhenshchiny i deti v SSSR* (Moscow, 1963), pp. 100, 102–4. Annual average employment estimates.

[b]From *Zhenshchiny i deti v SSSR* (Moscow, 1961), pp. 122–24. Annual average employment estimates.

[c]From E. Orlikova, "Zhenskii trud v SSSR," *Planovoe khoziaistvo*, No. 10 (Oct., 1939), 113. Data for 1930 are annual averages, for 1934–37, as of Jan. 1. Data are not strictly comparable

with those for 1929, 1933, and subsequent years, because of branch classification changes. For example, before Jan. 1, 1935, women employed in the Ministry of Railways' repair plants were included in transport, afterward in industry. Slight changes in the construction branch classification also took place.

[d]From *Narodnoe khoziaistvo SSSR v 1962 godu* (Moscow, 1963), pp. 453–54, 459. Annual average employment estimates. The corrected total is from *Vestnik statistiki*, No. 2 (1964), 91.

[e]From *Narodnoe khoziaistvo SSSR v 1956 godu* (Moscow,

1933[a,b]	%	1934[c]	%	1935[c]	%	1936[c]	%	1937[c]	%	1940[a,b]	%	1945[a]	%
6,720	30	7,204	31.7	7,964	33.4	8,492	34.0	9,357	35.4	11,978	38	15,076	55
2,410	31	–	–	–	–	–	–	–	–	4,496	41	4,840	51
–	–	2,274	35.6	2,624	38.3	2,908	38.8	3,298	39.8	–	–	–	–
291	16	454	18.7	450	19.7	402	19.1	488	20.6	359	23	489	32
629	26	605	25.4	672	27.0	628	26.4	545	25.7	593	34	1,310	61
13	7[b]	–	–	–	–	–	–	–	–	57[b]	11	144[b]	38[b]
374	(17)	–	–	–	–	–	–	–	–	932	24[a]	1,547	(29)
276	14	358	15.1	427	17.8	446	17.5	477	18.3	702	21	1,251	40
98	38	–	–	–	–	–	–	–	–	230	48	296	70
884	41	766	40.0	820	(39)	781	(37)	876	(35)	1,463	44	1,686	69
–	–	–	–	478	30.8	530	31.8	640	34.0	(965)	38[a]	–	–
–	–	–	–	342	64.2	251	63.2	236	62.2	(525)	67[e]	–	–
498	71	506[g]	72.2[g]	541	71.2	643	72.0	725	72.4	1,142	76	1,206	85
866	56	859[g]	56.6[g]	941	56.6	1,076	55.9	1,252	56.6	1,748	58	1,934	73
–	–	–	–	–	–	–	–	–	–	–	–	–	–
470	29	499[g]	29.4[g]	522[g]	31.1[g]	–	–	–	–	728	35	1,079	59
–	–	–	–	499	29.9	540	30.5	580	31.0	–	–	–	–
–	–	–	–	–	–	–	–	–	–	–	–	–	–
(285)	(14)	(883)	(27)	(967)	(27)	(1,068)	(28)	(1,116)	(42)	(460)	(18)	(841)	(44)

1958[f]	%	1960[b]	%	1961[a,d]	%	1962[d]	%	1963[g]	%	1964[h]	%
25,610	47[c]	29,300	47	31,609	48	(33,037)	48	(34,557)	49	(35,896)	49
8,814	45	10,140	45	10,681	45	(10,934)	46	(11,276)	45	(11,929)	46
–	–	–	–	–	–	–	–	–	–	–	–
1,335	30	1,500	29	1,544	29	(1,494)	29	(1,519)	29	(1,035)	29
1,906	41	2,768	43	3,170	43	(3,324)	43	(3,386)	43	(3,471)	43
106	9[f]	34	10	–	–	–	–	–	–	–	–
1,945	(31)	2,055	(29)	2,137	(29)	(2,301)	(31)	(2,271)	(29)	(2,367)	(30)
1,525	27	1,580	25	1,630	25	(1,669)	25	(1,710)	25	(1,764)	25
420	63	475	64	507	64	(532)	64	(561)	64	(603)	65
2,790	67	3,100	69	3,532	70	(3,730)	71	(4,006)	73	(4,256)	74
(1,984)	61	–	–	–	–	–	–	–	–	–	–
(806)	84[j]	–	–	–	–	–	–	–	–	–	–
2,613	85	2,952	85	3,151	86	(3,283)	86	(3,382)	86	(3,511)	86
3,607	62[f]	4,082	62	4,438	62	(4,839)	(67)	(5,128)	(62)	(5,504)	(63)
(3,021)	69	–	–	(3,615)	70	(3,865)	70	(4,085)	70	(4,405)	71
(583)	42	–	–	(865)	43	(947)	44	(1,043)	44	(1,099)	44
803	52	811	54	854	54	(879)	(55)	(895)	(56)	(944)	(57)
(634)	49	–	–	(660)	51	(684)	52	(693)	53	(731)	54
(172)	66	–	–	(191)	68	(195)	69	(202)	70	(213)	72
(1,691)	–	(1,858)	(37)	(2,102)	(42)	(2,100)	(40)	(2,694)	(50)	(2,879)	(50)

1957), pp. 204–6.

fFrom *Zhenshchina v SSSR* (Moscow, 1960), pp. 33–35.

gFrom *Narodnoe khoziaistvo SSSR v 1963 godu* (Moscow, 1965), pp. 475–76, 480.

hFrom *Narodnoe khoziaistvo SSSR v 1964 godu* (Moscow, 1965), pp. 546–47, 552.

iFrom *Trud v SSSR* (Moscow, 1936), pp. 25, 360.

jFrom *Narodnoe khoziaistvo SSSR v 1959 godu* (Moscow, 1960), pp. 592–94.

kResidual (total female employment minus reported or estimated employment in the sub-branches of the national economy in each column).

TABLE 101. Percentage of women wage workers, by branch of industry, selected years, 1913–62.*

Branch	1913[a]	1923[b]	1926[b]	Nov., 1927[a]	1928[a]	Jan. 1, 1929[c]	1930[b]	Jan. 1, 1932[d]
All industry	24.5	28.1	28.2	–	28.6	28.8	28.8	32.9
Ferrous metallurgy	–	–	–	–	–	7.1	–	–
Coke-chemical	–	–	–	–	–	–	–	–
Oil refining	–	–	–	–	–	–	–	–
Oil extraction	–	–	–	–	–	–	–	–
Electric power stations	–	–	–	3.0	–	–	–	–
Machine building and metalworking	4.2	12.1	9.2	–	8.9	8.8	12.2	20.7
Agricultural machine building	–	–	–	4.2	–	–	–	–
Locomotive car building	–	–	–	3.6	–	–	–	–
Electrotechnical	–	–	–	18.4	–	–	–	–
Auto-tractor	–	–	–	–	–	–	–	–
Production and other	–	–	–	8.9	–	–	–	–
Metallic wares	–	–	–	–	–	–	–	–
Mineral extraction and processing	21.8	26.1	23.4	–	22.4	–	23.7	25.9
Coal	3.6	11.9	8.3	–	7.6	7.7	9.6	14.6
Peat extraction	–	–	–	–	–	–	–	–
Iron ore	–	–	–	–	–	6.3	–	–
Chemical and fuel refining	–	–	–	–	–	–	–	–
Chemical	39.9	31.2	33.5	–	34.3	–	35.5	38.2
Rubber-asbestos	–	–	–	–	–	57.4	–	–
Rubber	–	–	–	56.7	–	–	–	–
Cement	–	–	–	–	–	–	–	–
Glass	–	–	–	–	–	–	–	–
Chinaware	–	–	–	–	–	–	–	–
Woodworking	9.9	16.0	15.1	–	17.2	–	23.4	29.6
Sawn wood	–	–	–	19.7	–	18.3	–	–
Match	–	–	–	–	–	54.6	–	–
Paper	–	–	–	27.6	–	27.5	–	–
Textile and clothing	55.7	58.7	59.6	–	61.2	–	64.3	69.1
Textile	–	–	–	–	–	–	–	–
Cotton textile	56.6	59.6	60.1	62.6	61.3	61.5	63.7	67.3
Wool	41.7	48.4	48.5	–	49.7	50.3	52.2	58.1
Flax	–	–	–	65.6	–	65.2	–	–
Knitted wear	–	–	–	–	–	–	–	–
Hemp and jute	–	–	–	64.6	–	–	–	–
Clothing (sewn goods)	–	–	–	–	–	63.9	–	–
Leather and fur	–	–	–	11.3	–	12.9	–	–
Shoe	–	–	–	–	–	–	–	–
Food	22.0	23.3	26.0	–	26.4	26.3	28.4	33.3
Bread baking	–	–	–	–	–	–	–	–
Candy	–	–	–	–	–	–	–	–
Meat	–	–	–	–	–	–	–	–
Flour milling and grain cracking	–	–	–	–	–	–	–	–
Tobacco-makhorka	–	–	–	–	–	–	–	–
Canning	–	–	–	–	–	–	–	–
Printing	–	–	–	–	–	22.6	–	–

*–, data not available.

[a]*Zhenshchina v SSSR* (Moscow, 1937), pp. 58, 62, 83–100. Large-scale industry. Data for 1913, 1928, 1932, and 1935 include apprentices; for Nov., 1927, and Oct., 1934—adult wage workers.

[b]*Sotsialistichiskoe stroitel'stvo SSSR* (Moscow, 1934), pp. 323, 346–47. Large-scale industry.

[c]E. Orlikova, "Zhenskii trud v SSSR," *Planovoe khoziaistvo*, No. 10 (1939), p. 114. Large-scale industry, including apprentices.

[d]Central Administration of Economic and Social Statistics of the State Planning Commission of the U.S.S.R., *Socialist Construction in the U.S.S.R.* (Moscow, 1936), p. 381 (in English). Large-scale industry.

July 1, 1932[e]	Jan. 1, 1933[b]	Oct., 1934[a]	July 1, 1935[f]	July 1, 1936[a]	July 1, 1937[g]	July 1, 1938[c]	Nov. 1, 1939[g]	Nov. 1, 1940[e]	May 5, 1950[e]	Jan. 1, 1959[h]	Jan. 1, 1960[f]	Jan. 1, 1962[e]
35.1	35.5	–	39.5	40.1	41.6	42.1	43.4	42.9	46.0	44.2	44.0	45.6
18.7	–	21.8	23.1	23.2	24.1	23.9	24.9	25.2	–	31.0	29.5	29.4
–	–	22.9	–	–	–	–	–	–	–	–	–	–
17.7	–	26.6	–	–	–	–	–	31.5	–	39.4	39.4	38.1
4.4	–	9.6	–	8.4	8.7	–	15.4	–	–	–	–	23.0[i]
11.0	–	21.9	16.7	17.4[c]	16.1	16.8	20.9	22.8	–	30.5	29.4	28.8
21.4	22.8	–	25.8	26.9	28.1	29.7	31.7	31.5	40.0	39.3	38.9	38.9
–	–	27.5	–	–	–	–	–	–	–	–	–	–
–	–	20.4	–	–	–	–	–	–	–	–	–	–
–	–	38.6	–	–	–	–	–	–	–	–	–	–
–	–	30.4	–	–	–	–	–	–	–	–	–	–
–	–	27.0	–	–	–	–	–	–	–	–	–	–
–	–	42.1	–	–	–	–	–	–	–	–	–	–
–	29.1	–	–	35.9	–	–	–	–	–	–	–	–
16.5	17.5	–	24.0	23.6	24.5	24.5	24.8	–	–	–	–	17.4[i]
43.1	–	–	45.5	48.8[c]	50.1	48.4	48.9	–	–	–	–	–
20.7	–	–	23.0	18.5[c]	19.7	21.9	23.6	–	–	–	–	20.8[i]
–	–	–	31.7	33.5[c]	34.2[c]	36.5	–	–	–	–	–	–
36.7	38.9	–	–	41.6	36.3	–	41.3	–	–	–	–	50.6[i]
63.7	–	–	61.3	62.0	61.6	60.2	62.4	–	–	–	–	–
63.7[j]	–	56.9	–	–	–	–	–	–	–	62.0[j]	–	–
21.9	–	–	–	30.7	27.7	–	28.6	28.6	–	37.0	36.1	36.3
34.0	–	39.7	–	–	46.1	–	49.8	–	–	–	–	–
–	–	52.6	–	–	–	–	–	–	–	–	–	–
–	32.0	–	–	39.0	–	–	–	–	–	–	–	–
32.5	–	43.1	39.2	38.7	40.9	44.2	43.9	–	–	–	–	–
58.7	–	–	64.4	63.5[c]	63.5	61.6	64.6	–	–	–	–	–
28.9	–	40.3	41.1	42.4[c]	44.6	44.5	49.4	49.2	–	42.7	42.7	43.9
70.1	69.9	–	–	72.2	–	–	–	72.0	75.5	75.8[j]	76.2	76.6
67.5	–	–	–	–	–	–	–	69.2	–	72.4	72.2	72.9
69.0	66.9	71.2	69.9	70.0	69.8	67.4	68.5	–	–	–	–	72.4[i]
58.9	59.9	63.2	63.1	63.6	64.9	63.8	65.5	–	–	–	–	70.3[i]
69.3	–	69.5	69.6	71.3	70.1	68.5	68.3	–	–	–	–	–
82.6	–	–	84.9	85.1	85.4	85.5	85.5	–	–	–	–	83.6[i]
–	–	68.1	–	–	–	–	–	–	–	–	–	67.2[i]
80.1	–	84.3	82.5	81.9[c]	82.4	82.4	83.4	82.7	–	83.8	85.3	82.0
41.3	–	45.8	55.7	55.7[c]	58.4	57.2 }	58.2	60.6	–	64.3	64.5	62.6
51.3	–	64.1	56.3	57.1[c]	57.9	57.4 }		55.7	–	65.2	66.1	64.1
32.8	35.4	–	44.9	45.5	46.8	47.2	47.2	48.6	50.8	53.1	53.8	54.4
28.3	–	48.4	–	47.8	48.5	–	55.5	57.5	–	68.5	69.1	70.6
53.8	–	64.0	–	65.2	66.1	–	68.6	66.7	–	70.5	70.2	69.8
25.8	–	–	–	40.6	41.9	–	47.8	–	–	–	–	–
18.8	–	–	–	28.2	28.7	–	34.1	–	–	–	–	–
57.3	–	–	–	63.3	64.2	–	65.1	–	–	–	–	–
–	–	–	–	58.5	–	–	–	–	–	–	–	–
40.9	–	57.6	54.0	56.1[c]	57.2	55.5	57.8	–	–	–	–	–

[e]*Zhenshchiny i deti v SSSR* (Moscow, 1963), pp. 106–7. Data for 1932 and 1940 for large-scale industry.

[f]*Zhenshchiny i deti v SSSR* (Moscow, 1961), pp. 126–27.

[g]E. Orlikova, "Sovetskaia zhenshchina v obshchestvennom proizvodstve," *Problemy ekonomiki*, No. 7 (July, 1940), 114. Large-scale industry.

[h]*Zhenshchina v SSSR* (Moscow, 1960), pp. 37–38.

[i]Korneev *et al.* (eds.), *Promyshlennost' v khoziaistvennom komplekse ekonomicheskikh raionov SSSR* (Moscow, 1964), pp. 457, 459.

[j]*Trudovye resursy SSSR (Problemy raspredeleniia i ispol'zovaniia)*, ed. by N. I. Shishkin (Moscow, 1961), pp. 136–37.

TABLE 102. Percentage of women among workers and employees, by republic, selected years, 1933–64.*

Republic	1933[a]	1950[a]	1952[b]	1955[c]	1956	1957	1958[b]	1959	1960[d]	1961[b]	1962[b]	1963[e]	1964[f]
U.S.S.R.	30	47	48	45	—	—	47	—	47	48	48	49	49
R.S.F.S.R.	32	50	51	47	—	—	49	—	50	50	51	51	51
Ukrainian S.S.R.	28	43	44	42	—	—	44	—	45	46	46	47	47
Belorussian S.S.R.	28	45	47	45	—	—	48	—	49	50	50	50	50
Uzbek S.S.R.	27	40	40	38	—	—	40	—	39	39	39	40	40
Kazakh S.S.R.	20	39	40	34	—	—	37	—	38	39	40	41	41
Georgian S.S.R.	25	41	41	41	—	—	41	—	40	41	41	42	42
Azerbaidzhan S.S.R.	24	40	39	38	—	—	38	—	38	38	38	39	39
Lithuanian S.S.R.	–	38	41	41	—	—	42	—	43	44	45	45	46
Moldavian S.S.R.	–	38	41	39	39[g]	41[g]	43	44[g]	43	44	45	45	45
Latvian S.S.R.	–	45	48	46	—	—	47	—	48	49	49	49	51
Kirgiz S.S.R.	21	42	42	40	39[h]	40[h]	41	41[h]	41	42	42	43	43
Tadzhik S.S.R.	23	39	39	36	36[i]	36[i]	38	—	36	37	37	37	37
Armenian S.S.R.	21	39	40	38	—	—	37	—	38	38	39	39	39
Turkmen S.S.R.	19	40	39	36	—	—	37	36[j]	37	38	38	39	39
Estonian S.S.R.	–	47	50	48	—	—	50	—	51	51	51	52	52

*–, not applicable; —, data not available.
[a]*Zhenshchiny i deti v SSSR* (Moscow, 1963), p. 105.
[b]*Narodnoe khoziaistvo SSSR v 1962 godu* (Moscow, 1963), p. 460.
[c]*Narodnoe khoziaistvo SSSR v 1960 godu* (Moscow, 1961), p. 643.
[d]*Zhenshchiny i deti v SSSR* (Moscow, 1961), p. 125.
[e]*Narodnoe khoziaistvo SSSR v 1963 godu* (Moscow, 1965), p. 481.
[f]*Narodnoe khoziaistvo SSSR v 1964 godu* (Moscow, 1965), p. 553.

[g]Tsentral'noe statisticheskoe upravlenie pri Sovete ministrov Moldavskoi SSR, *Zhenshchina SSR* (Kishinev, 1961), p. 17.
[h]Tsentral'noe statisticheskoe upravlenie pri Sovete ministrov Kirgizskoi SSR, *Zhenshchina v Kirgizskoi SSR* (Frunze, 1960), p. 21.
[i]Tsentral'noe statisticheskoe upravlenie pri Sovete ministrov Tadzhikskoi SSR, *Zhenshchina v Tadzhikskoi SSR* (Stalinabad, 1960), p. 19.
[j]Tsentral'noe statisticheskoe upravlenie pri Sovete ministrov Turkmenskoi SSR, *Zhenshchina v Turkmenskoi SSR* (Ashkhabad, 1960), p. 21.

tively high percentage of workers and employees in the Baltic republics. Since the percentage of women workers and employees has nearly doubled in the Central Asian republics since 1933, in this respect the disparity among the republics is not so great as previously.

MAJOR OCCUPATIONS

We have seen that, according to 1959 census data, four fifths of the total of 56.6 million women employed in the labor force were engaged in what is officially termed physical labor. Although the number and proportion of those working in the major sectors of the economy have been discussed, it is helpful to bring together in one table the principal occupational categories in which women engaged in physical labor were employed in 1959. Table 103 shows seventeen broad occupational groups in which more than 200,-000 women were employed. Although other groupings are possible, the major outlines of the over-all picture would not change appreciably with a different classification scheme.

The overwhelming importance of agricul-

tural occupations among those involving physical work is obvious. Nonspecialized agricultural work accounts for one third of the women engaged in physical labor. When the other agricultural occupations are added, agriculture accounts for 63 per cent of all women

TABLE 103. Number and percentage of women employed in major occupations involving physical labor, 1959.[a]

Employment Categories	Thousands of Women	Percentage of age Women
Total engaged in physical labor	45,501.1	51
Nonspecialized agricultural workers	15,932.9	66
Private subsidiary agricultural workers	8,950.9	91
Specialized agricultural workers	3,809.8	38
Communal and household service workers	3,343.3	67
Metal workers	1,304.0	15
Garment workers	1,171.6	90
Textile workers	958.3	85
Construction workers	905.4	18
Nursing (orderlies, nurses, and nursemaids)	868.9	97
Public dining (cooks, waitresses, and barmaids)	703.7	90
Food industry workers	525.2	64
Railway workers	518.9	31
Power station workers	294.4	26
Construction materials industry workers	290.2	54
Operators of materials handling equipment	263.0	44
Woodworking industry workers	246.9	18
Chemical industry workers	226.2	57

[a]Based on *Itogi . . . 1959 goda: SSSR*, pp. 160, 167–70, and *Zhenshchiny i deti v SSSR* (Moscow, 1963), pp. 86–88.

employed in physical labor; hence, the emphasis we have given to women in agriculture in the preceding pages.

Among the remaining employment categories shown in Table 103, only three occupational groupings would be considered women's occupations by American standards—communal and household services, nursing, and public dining.[53] A relatively high percentage of women would also be expected in the garment trades and various occupations in the textile and food industries. The remaining categories, such as metal, construction, and railway work, are not occupations in which many women could be found in the United States or other industrial nations of the West. The high percentage of Soviet women in these occupations reflects the shortage of males of working age and the determination of the regime to maintain high rates of growth with little regard for the social costs. If Soviet women did not do this kind of work, men who are now engaged in more productive activities would have to replace them, with a substantial loss to the economy.

CONCLUSIONS

Among women employed in nonprofessional occupations the characteristic figure today, just as a hundred years ago, is the farm woman working in the field at unskilled tasks —hoeing, raking, loading produce, and so forth. These women still make up a third of all women employed in the socialized sector of the economy. Their importance to the agricultural sector is underscored by the fact that they make up almost two thirds of all unskilled, nonspecialized workers employed in socialized agriculture. If persons engaged in private subsidiary agriculture are added to these, the share of women in the unskilled, nonspecialized agricultural labor force is increased to 73 per cent. This extremely high percentage of women reflects a number of historical influences. For centuries women

have played an important part in unskilled, seasonal agricultural work, working in the field alongside their husbands during the harvest and other peak seasons of labor demand. Although many women in agriculture have acquired specialized skills under the Soviet regime, men have been, for the most part, the principal beneficiaries of advances in Soviet agricultural technique. Men have tended to obtain more training and to acquire the better jobs. Women, with less educational background and professional orientation, have tended to be bypassed. Finally, the large male losses during World War II and the more rapid migration of males into urban employment left many collective farms largely dependent upon female labor after the war. Although some balance between the sexes will be restored with the passage of time, it appears inevitable that for some time women will continue to play a major role in the less attractive kinds of agricultural work. The government apparently has written off these women, many of whom are along in years, because of the poor prospects for an adequate return from the development of their skills or specialized talents.

With industrialization new possibilities for the employment of women opened. In the Tsarist era women already made up a high proportion of workers in the textile industry and the needle trades. In the course of the 1930's their share in a variety of industries, such as paper, food, chemicals, machine building, and metalworking, increased dramatically. As the number of women employed in industry increased fourfold, the share of women in industrial employment rose from 29 to 41 per cent. Between 1940 and 1964 the number of women further increased almost 2.7 times and their share rose to 46 per cent. Again the wartime losses of men led to strong pressures to utilize more women in industry and even in branches where it was considered unhealthy or undesirable for women. Although women are now being shifted out of undesirable types of employment, no indication of a reduction in the proportion of women among industrial workers as a whole is in sight.

---

[53]Among the broad category of communal and household service workers are a number of occupations which are traditionally male—guard, watchman, porter, stoker, fireman, and others.

chapter
10

SEMIPROFESSIONAL AND PROFESSIONAL OCCUPATIONS

THE HIGH percentage of women in semiprofessional and professional occupations is one of the major accomplishments of the Soviet regime. Many women have been provided opportunities to develop and use talents which would otherwise have been wasted. By opening to them professions which traditionally had been dominated by men, the Soviet Union has been among the leaders in the evolution of the status of women—an evolution which is taking place in many other developing countries.

The semiprofessional and professional occupations form a rather heterogeneous group which includes administrators, managers, and supervisory personnel; scientists, engineers, and technicians; educators, doctors, lawyers, accountants, and other persons in occupations we would consider "the professions"; journalists, artists, and performers; and the many categories which we associate with "white-collar workers"—bookkeepers, clerical personnel, and others. We are not, in other words, dealing here with the intelligentsia typical of nineteenth-century Russia—a small, highly cultured, and tightly knit nucleus of intellectuals. The terms semiprofessional and professional as used in the Soviet Union apply broadly to those engaged in "mental work" as opposed to "physical labor." According to the 1959 census, 20.5 million persons were "mental" workers, and of these,

11.1 million, or more than half, were women. Thus women make up more than half of this important segment of the labor force.

The participation of women in semiprofessional and professional occupations has increased substantially since the inauguration of the First Five-Year Plan in 1928. As Table 104 shows, the employment of female specialists with a higher or secondary education increased between 1928 and 1941 from 151,000 to 864,000, and the proportion of women increased from 29 to 36 per cent. This increase in the proportion of women among students and graduates of specialized secondary and higher educational institutions resulted from the opening of all fields of education to women and the imperative demand for trained specialists to carry forward the industrialization drive.

Although the gains in the number of women specialists before World War II were impressive, the largest increase came as a result of the war, when a number of factors combined to increase the proportion of women. First, male war casualties, both military and civilian, were substantially higher than female. Second, the ratio of female to male students, and graduates, rose to a peak during the war period, and remained high for a decade afterward. Third, there were large increases in the number of semiprofessionals and professionals in the fields of education

TABLE 104. Women specialists employed in the economy, with higher or specialized secondary education.[a]

	Jan. 1,	Apr. 1,	July 1,		December 1,							Nov. 15,
	1928	1941	1954	1955	1956	1957	1959	1960	1961	1962	1963	1964
Total number of women specialists (in thousands)..............	151	864	n.a.	3,155	3,777	4,087	4,787	5,189	5,547	5,856	6,099	6,611
With higher education.........	65	312	1,098	1,155	1,396	1,464	1,701	1,865	2,015	2,133	2,234	2,394
With specialized secondary education.....................	86	552	n.a.	1,960	2,381	2,623	3,086	3,324	3,532	3,723	3,865	4,216
Percentage of women among all specialists.....................	29	36	–	61	61	60	59	59	59	58	58	59
With higher education.........	28	34	55	53	53	52	53	53	53	53	52	53
With specialized secondary education.....................	30	37	–	67	66	65	65	63	63	63	62	63

[a]Based on *Zhenshchiny i deti v SSSR* (Moscow, 1961), p. 137; *Zhenshchiny i deti v SSSR* (Moscow, 1963), p. 117; *Vysshee obrazovanie v SSSR* (Moscow, 1961), pp. 52, 66; *Narodnoe khoziaistvo SSSR v 1956 godu* (Moscow, 1957), pp. 210–11; *Narodnoe khoziaistvo SSSR v 1962 godu* (Moscow, 1963), p. 472; *Narodnoe khoziaistvo SSSR v 1963 godu* (Moscow, 1965), p. 492; *Vestnik statistiki*, No. 6 (1956), 91–92, and No. 9 (1965), 86, 92.

and health, fields in which women are heavily represented. As a result of these factors, the number of female specialists increased from 864,000 in 1941 to 3.2 million in 1955 and 6.6 million in 1964. The share of women among the semiprofessionals and professionals was at a peak—of the years for which data are available—in 1955, when women made up three fifths of the specialists. Their share has remained at approximately the same level since then.

FACTORS ACCOUNTING FOR THE HIGH PROPORTION OF WOMEN SPECIALISTS

With educational and occupational doors nearly everywhere opened to women, it is not surprising that the percentage entering the semiprofessional and professional occupations has been large, and, although it is true that few women have attained eminence in science or in other professions, many have had distinguished careers as researchers, teachers, and practitioners. It should be expected, therefore, that ultimately women would make up a proportion of the semiprofessional and professional labor force at least equal to that of their participation in the labor force as a whole. In fact, their participation has been greater.

One of the most important reasons for this was, of course, the impact of the war. The decimation of males in the age group now 35 to 59, from which much of the administrative and professional leadership of a society is normally drawn, has required that large numbers of women step into the breach. Furthermore, many widows or women who would have been married if there had been no war found it necessary to work when they might otherwise have withdrawn or remained outside the labor force. Thus, the participation rate of women has remained higher than it otherwise would have, especially among the older age groups. Nevertheless, the participation of women in "mental" work declines rapidly with age. In the age group 40 to 59 women make up 63 per cent of the population, but only 38 per cent of the semiprofessional and professional employment (see Fig. 26).

The predominance of women specialists must, therefore, be explained by the larger number of women employed in the earlier age groups, particularly in the age group 20 to 29. Although there are only slightly more women than men in the population in this age group, women account for 4.0 million and men for only 2.3 million of the 6.3 million "mental" workers. A part of this 1.7 million difference may be attributed to the large number of young men in this age group who are doing military service. Consistent with this is the sharp increase in the number of professional men employed in the age

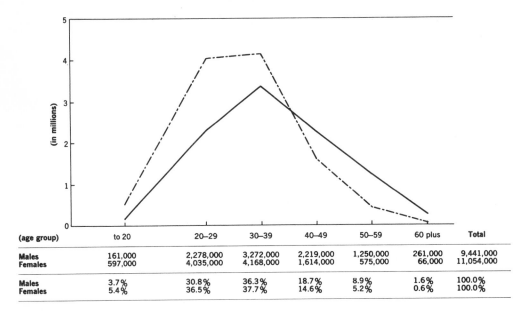

(age group)	to 20	20–29	30–39	40–49	50–59	60 plus	Total
Males	161,000	2,278,000	3,272,000	2,219,000	1,250,000	261,000	9,441,000
Females	597,000	4,035,000	4,168,000	1,614,000	575,000	66,000	11,054,000
Males	3.7%	30.8%	36.3%	18.7%	8.9%	1.6%	100.0%
Females	5.4%	36.5%	37.7%	14.6%	5.2%	0.6%	100.0%

FIG. 26. Age distribution of males and females in semiprofessional and professional occupations, 1959. *Solid line,* males; *broken line,* females. Calculated from *Itogi . . . 1959 goda: SSSR,* pp. 138, 143, 164, 168.

group 30 to 39 despite the substantially smaller number of males in this group because of heavy war losses. The 3.3 million male specialists age 30 to 39 exceed the number in the age group 20 to 29 by one million, while the 4.2 million females represent an increase of only 133,000 over the number in the age group 20 to 29.

At the end of the European phase of the war women made up almost 70 per cent of the enrollment in specialized secondary educational institutions.[1] The percentage then declined but remained at a high level between 1950 and 1955 before finally falling below 50 per cent in 1957. The situation in higher educational enrollment was similar. From a high of 77 per cent in 1945 the percentage of women declined to 53 per cent in 1950 but did not drop below the 50 per cent level until 1957.[2] These high percentages of female enrollment reflect, of course, the relatively large number of females with a higher or specialized secondary education. In the age group 20 to 29, females with a completed higher, an incomplete higher, or a specialized secondary education totaled 3.0 million, while males totaled only 2.0 million. In the age group 30 to 39, females totaled 2.4 million and males 1.8 million.[3] In these two age groups combined, females with specialized training outnumbered males by 1.6 million.

The reason for the larger female enrollments and graduations from specialized secondary and higher educational institutions during the war is obvious. After the war the proportion of male graduates was kept down for a number of reasons. Demobilization was slow, and in most cases it took returning soldiers several years to complete their studies. DeWitt reports that up to 1950 graduating classes were composed largely of women.[4] Mobilization measures connected with the Korean conflict also appear to have delayed

[1]See Table 53, p. 110.
[2]See Table 61, p. 120.

[3]*Itogi . . . 1959 goda: SSSR,* p. 74.
[4]Nicholas DeWitt, *Education and Professional Employment in the U.S.S.R.* (Washington, D.C., 1961), p. 347.

the return to a more equal balance of the sexes. Since 1956, however, male enrollments have exceeded female, and in this regard the effect of the war and its aftermath has finally subsided. The new admission policies of specialized secondary and higher educational institutions appeared to favor males until the most recent changes introduced in 1965.[5] In 1964, males made up 49 per cent of the enrollment in specialized secondary schools and 43 per cent of the enrollment in higher educational institutions. This cannot fail to have an adverse effect upon the proportion of women among professionals in the lower age groups in the near future.

In addition to the special circumstances mentioned above, an underlying factor accounting for the high percentage of women currently employed in occupations requiring "mental" work is the special appeal which many of these occupations have for women. Most types of physical labor on the farm, in the factory, or on a construction site are much less attractive to women in interest, prestige, individual recognition, and especially working conditions than are white-collar or professional jobs in an office, a laboratory, or a school. The relatively low pay of many of these white-collar jobs tends to discourage men who otherwise might be attracted.

As a result of the more attractive nature of "mental" work, women do not withdraw from semiprofessional and professional employment as early as they do from unskilled and manual work. Examination of the age distribution of employed women indicates that in almost every occupation involving mental work the peak employment of women is in the age group 30 to 39, while in occupations involving physical labor the peak is almost invariably in the age group 20 to 29.[6] This difference is due in part to the longer period of training of semiprofessional and professional workers, but employment is high in the

age group 20 to 29 as well. However, the principal reason for the difference is the frequent withdrawal of women engaged in physical work from the labor force at an earlier age—sometimes in their thirties.

Figure 26 shows the age distribution of males and females employed in occupations involving mental work at the time of the 1959 census. The employment of women rises to a peak in the age group 30 to 39 both in absolute and percentage terms and then declines rapidly in the older age groups. In the three younger age groups the employment of women is substantially higher than that of men, while in the three older age groups it is substantially lower. Average employment of women exceeds that of males.[7] Of special interest is the fact that, although female employment shows a later peak for the mental occupations (see Fig. 26) than the physical (see Fig. 23), the decline of the number of those in mental occupations is much more precipitous, once it sets in, than in the physical. On the surface, this would seem to contradict the earlier assertion that women withdraw from "mental" work later than from "physical" labor, but on further examination one might conclude that the data reflect the small number of women in the older age groups in the Soviet Union who are qualified by education or by experience for semiprofessional or professional work. Support for this hypothesis is provided by statistics on the age distribution of females who have acquired a higher or specialized secondary education.

In Table 105 females age 20 and older are divided into five age groups. The table compares the distribution among these five age groups of all females in "mental" employment with the age distribution of females having specialized training. The comparison shows that fewer women in the age groups 20 to 29 and 50 to 59 are actually employed in "mental" work than would be expected if the age distributions of employment and spe-

---

[5] The impact of changing admission policies is discussed in Chapter 6.

[6] See Appendix VII, Fig. 2, and Appendix VIII, Fig. 1.

[7] Appendix VIII, Fig. 1, shows the age distribution of males and females employed in a number of "mental" occupations.

TABLE 105. Age distribution of female "mental" and "physical" workers compared with age distribution of females having specialized training and with the entire female population.[a]

Age Groups	To 20	20–29	30–39	40–49	50–59	60 plus	Total
1. Female "mental" employment (in thousands).	597	4,035	4,168	1,614	575	66	11,054
2. Females with specialized training (in thousands).................................	172	3,008	2,441	963	415	218	7,217
3. Percentage of female "mental" employment ..	–	38.6	39.9	15.4	5.5	0.6	100.0
4. Percentage of females with specialized training	–	42.7	34.6	13.7	5.9	3.1	100.0
(3) as a percentage of (4).................	–	90	115	112	93	19	–
5. Percentage of female "physical" employment..	–	32.8	25.7	23.3	14.1	4.1	100.0
6. Percentage of female population.............	–	25.4	22.7	18.1	15.9	17.9	100.0
(5) as a percentage of (6).................	–	129	113	129	89	23	–

[a]Calculated from Figs. 23 and 25 and from *Itogi . . . 1959 goda: SSSR*, p. 74. Specialized training as used here includes higher, incomplete higher, and completed secondary education.

cialized training were identical. For the age group 60 and above, the comparison is especially striking, with far fewer women being actually employed than would be expected. The data thus indicate—as anticipated—that a substantial number of women with specialized training, in the age group 50 to 59, withdraw from participation in the labor force and that a very high proportion of such women in the age group 60 and over withdraw.

Table 105 also presents a comparison of the age distribution of the total female population, age 20 and over, with the age distribution of females actually engaged in "physical" employment. This comparison also indicates that fewer women in the age group 50 to 59, and far fewer women in the age group 60 and over, remain in actual employment than would be expected if the age distribution of female "physical" workers corresponded exactly to the age distribution of the female population. For these two older age groups, however, the data indicate a slightly less marked withdrawal from the labor force than is true for women with specialized training who have reached age 50.

These statistics show that the rapid decline in the number of women mental workers in the older age groups is primarily due to the sharp decline in the number of women with specialized training in each successive age group. When the declining number of women with specialized education in the older age groups is taken into account, the withdrawal of older female mental workers from the labor force is seen to occur at about the same pace as the withdrawal of physical workers. Older women with specialized educational background do not, therefore, show any significant tendency to prolong their careers. Although they may find their work more interesting, they are not so likely to be under pressure of economic necessity as are physical workers whose family incomes are, on the average, smaller than those of semiprofessional and professional workers, compelling many to continue working when they would prefer to withdraw from the labor force.

Professional women often have husbands with good incomes, which permit them some real freedom of choice. Some, however, are career-oriented and are inclined to continue working after reaching retirement age, a point emphasized by Madame Kovrigina, former Minister of Health of the U.S.S.R., and Mrs. Pergament, an authority on Soviet law, in a conversation with the author. Both felt that professional women often become more involved in their work and that the tempo of their careers picks up in their forties and fifties when family responsibilities have decreased. These are the years when most women engaged in physical labor are beginning to retire and tend garden plots and care for grandchildren so that more vigorous and capable daughters or daughters-in-law with higher earning power are able to enter or remain in the labor force.

As already predicted from the projection of enrollment statistics for women in specialized education, the percentage of women in mental occupations can be expected to fall off in the next decade or so. There are a number of reasons why, given a normal sex ratio in the population in the able-bodied age groups, the government might prefer to invest more heavily in the training and education of men rather than women. The 1959 census showed that the number of males and females was approximately equal up to age 30. At the present time, 1966, the ratio should be approximately equal up to age 37. In another twenty to twenty-five years the ratio will be normal throughout the entire working-age group.[8] Since there is a considerable delay between admission to specialized training institutions and graduation, it is necessary for manpower planners to make adjustments at the present time if they are seeking to increase the role of males in future decades. This is what planners seem to be doing through the changes in admission require-

ments which tend to produce a higher proportion of male students.

WOMEN IN SEMIPROFESSIONAL EMPLOYMENT

The number of women with semiprofessional training who are employed in the Soviet economy has grown rapidly in recent years, increasing, as shown in Table 106, from not quite 2 million in 1955 to 4.2 million in 1964. Technicians increased from 309,060 to 1,014,000, and statisticians, planners, and commodity specialists from 144,000 to 530,000. In both these categories the increase was nearly threefold, while the over-all increase for all semiprofessional groups was slightly less than twofold. The two fields in which the largest number of women are employed, the medical (1,279,000) and educational-cultural (1,026,000) fields, showed a below-average rate of increase. In the former, the number of women increased 90 per cent and in the latter about 60 per cent. As a result, their combined share among specialists with a specialized secondary education declined from 67 to 55 per cent (see Table 107).

In 1955 two thirds of all specialists with a specialized secondary education were women.

---

[8]See Appendix I, Table 2.

TABLE 106. Women specialists with specialized secondary education employed in the economy, by specialty, 1955–57, 1959–64.[a]

Specialty	July 1, 1955	Dec. 1, 1956	Dec. 1, 1957	Dec. 1, 1959	Dec. 1, 1960	Dec. 1, 1961	Dec. 1, 1962	Dec. 1, 1963	Nov. 15, 1964
Total number of female specialists.......	1,960	2,381	2,623	3,086	3,324	3,532	3,723	3,865	4,216
Technicians........................	309	414	499	660	701	816	873	922	1,014
Agronomists, zootechnicians, veterinary personnel, foresters...............	116	117	123	147	155	–	–	–	–
Excluding foresters.................	–	–	119	–	–	166	180	176	196
Statisticians, planners, commodity specialists........................	144	194	217	287	329	375	394	432	530
Legal personnel.....................	7	7	6	5	5	5	5	–	–
Medical personnel (including dentists)....	668	818	895	1,026	1,088	1,118	1,154	1,194	1,279
Teachers, library and cultural enlightenment personnel....................	639	738	773	826	861	902	948	962	1,026
Residual...........................	77	93	110	135	185	150	169	179	171

[a]Figures are expressed in thousands. This table is based on data from *Zhenshchina v SSSR* (Moscow, 1960), p. 59; *Zhenshchiny i deti v SSSR* (Moscow, 1961), p. 139; *Zhenshchiny i deti v SSSR* (Moscow, 1963), p. 120; *Srednee spetsial'noe obrazovanie v SSSR* (Moscow, 1962), p. 42; *Narodnoe khozi-aistvo SSSR v 1956 godu* (Moscow, 1957), p. 211; *Narodnoe khoziaistvo SSSR v 1959 godu* (Moscow, 1960), p. 616; *Narodnoe khoziaistvo SSSR v 1962 godu* (Moscow, 1963), p. 472; *Narodnoe khoziaistvo SSSR v 1963 godu* (Moscow, 1965), p. 492; and *Narodnoe khoziaistvo SSSR v 1964 godu* (Moscow, 1965), p. 566.

TABLE 107. Distribution of women specialists with specialized secondary education employed in the economy, by specialty, 1955–57, 1959–64.[a]

Specialty	July 1, 1955	Dec. 1, 1956	Dec. 1, 1957	Dec. 1, 1959	Dec. 1, 1960	Dec. 1, 1961	Dec. 1, 1962	Dec. 1, 1963	Nov. 15, 1964
Total female specialists..............	100.0	100.0	100.0	100.0	100.0	100.0	100.0	100.0	100.0
Technicians..........................	15.8	17.5	19.0	21.4	21.1	23.1	23.5	23.9	24.1
Agronomists, zootechnicians, veterinary personnel, foresters...............	5.9	5.9	4.7	4.8	4.7	–	–	–	–
Excluding foresters.................	–	–	4.5	–	–	4.7	4.8	4.6	4.7
Statisticians, planners, commodity specialists.........................	7.3	8.4	8.3	9.3	9.9	10.6	10.6	11.2	12.6
Legal personnel.....................	0.4	0.4	0.2	0.1	0.1	0.1	0.1	–	–
Medical personnel (incluing dentists)....	34.1	34.5	34.1	33.2	32.7	31.7	31.0	30.9	30.3
Teachers, library and cultural enlightenment personnel...................	32.6	30.2	29.5	26.8	25.9	25.5	25.5	24.9	24.3
Residual...........................	3.9	4.0	4.2	4.4	5.6	4.3	4.5	4.6	4.0

[a]For the sources of this table, see Table 106, n.

The proportion has declined slightly since that date and now stands at 63 per cent. A number of fields are dominated by women. The proportion among semiprofessional medical personnel—dentists, "medics" (*feldshers*), nurses, medical technicians—is 92 per cent. Among educational and cultural specialists—preschool and elementary schoolteachers, youth leaders—women constitute 83 per cent. Among specialists in the socioeconomic field—planners, statisticians, accountants—the proportion is 76 per cent. These are the major fields of semiprofessional female employment. But, as shown by Table 108, women also constitute a significant proportion of technicians in industry (38 per cent), agronomists and related personnel (44 per cent), and legal personnel (30 per cent).

The proportion of women among semiprofessionals is substantially higher than among professionals. It is also higher than among workers and employees and is even higher than the proportion of women among collective farm workers. Only in the private subsidiary sector is the proportion of women higher than among semiprofessionals. Although the professions offer more attraction in terms of income and status than the semiprofessional occupations, the latter are more readily accessible and require less commitment and talent for success.

The Soviets have not published sufficient

TABLE 108. Percentage of women among all specialists with specialized secondary education employed in the economy, by specialty, 1955–57, 1959–64.[a]

Specialty	July 1, 1955	Dec. 1, 1956	Dec. 1, 1957	Dec. 1, 1959	Dec. 1, 1960	Dec. 1, 1961	Dec. 1, 1962	Dec. 1, 1963	Nov. 15, 1964
Total......................	67	66	65	65	63	63	63	62	63
Technicians.................	38	39	40	39	36	38	38	38	38
Agronomists, zootechnicians, veterinary personnel, foresters	46	40	40	41	41	43	44	43	44
Statisticians, planners, commodity specialists..........	77	77	74	74	74	74	74	70	76
Legal personnel..............	30	30	30	30	30	30	30	–	–
Medical personnel (including dentists)....................	91	91	91	92	92	91	92	92	92
Teachers, library and cultural enlightenment personnel.....	78	79	80	81	81	82	83	82	83

[a]For the sources of this table, see Table 106, n.

data to permit the presentation of a reliable picture of the distribution of semiprofessionals among the labor force, the military, the student, and the nonworking groups. Although the figures for employment in the civilian labor force can be accepted with confidence, published figures on the stock of semiprofessionals with a specialized secondary education are not believed to be reliable. When these figures are inaccurate, large errors in the estimates of the military, student, and nonworking groups can result. It is possible, nevertheless, to estimate these groups for each sex in order to provide a general picture of the way in which persons with a semiprofessional training are utilized. Table 109 shows that women make up almost two thirds of the graduates of specialized secondary institutions who are employed in the civilian labor force, even though their share among total graduates is only 57 per cent. The reason for this difference is the large number of men, more than half of the total or 54 per cent, who are employed in the armed services, who are students, or who are not working, while only 35 per cent of the women fall into these categories. Participation rates of 46 per cent for men and 65 per cent for women both represent much lower rates than are found among graduates of higher educational institutions (see Table 114). The breakdown of men and

women among those in the military, in educational institutions, and those not working is largely conjectural. The greatest uncertainty attaches to the number of men serving in the armed forces. It is estimated than 1 million men or 29 per cent of those with a specialized secondary education are in military service. However, this figure could easily be higher or lower by 100,000 or 200,000, depending upon variations in the estimates of the number of men enrolled in educational institutions and the number not working. If the proportion of men not working were assumed to be 12 per cent—in line with the percentage for all males age 20 to 24 not in the labor force—the estimated number in the armed services would be more than 200,000 higher.[9] More probable, however, is that the total figure for persons with a specialized secondary education of 7.9 million is overstated by several hundred thousands, which would mean that the figure for the military might be only 700,000 or 800,000. Whatever the actual figure, the probable range indicates that the induction of male graduates into the armed services results in a severe drain on male semiprofessional manpower. For our purposes, however, it is sufficient to note that, as a consequence of these circumstances, women with a spe-

[9]See Fig. 11, p. 36.

TABLE 109. Utilization of men and women with specialized secondary education, beginning of 1959.[a]

	Total	Distri-bution	Men	Distri-bution	Women	Distri-bution	Women
	thousands	*%*	*thousands*	*%*	*thousands*	*%*	*%*
Total with specialized secondary education.........	7,870	100	3,414	100	4,456	100	57
In the civilian labor force.....................	4,449	57	1,557	46	2,192	65	49
Not in the civilian labor force.................	3,418	43	1,856	54	1,562	35	46
Armed services...........................	(1,000)	(13)	(1,000)	(29)	–	–	–
Students.................................	(300)	(4)	(200)	(6)	(100)	(2)	33
Not working.............................	(2,118)	(26)	(656)	(19)	(1,462)	(33)	66

[a]Graduates are from *Itogi . . . 1959 goda: SSSR*, p. 82. The total civilian labor force at the end of 1958 is from *Narodnoe khoziaistvo SSSR v 1959 godu* (Moscow, 1960), p. 602. It is assumed that there were no graduates added to the labor force between the end of 1958 and Jan. 15, 1959. The male-female ratio is calculated by interpolation between the ratios for Dec. 1, 1957, and Dec. 1, 1959 (*Narodnoe khoziaistvo SSSR v 1958* [Moscow, 1959], p. 691, and *Narodnoe khoziaistvo SSSR v 1959 godu* [Moscow, 1960], p. 616). The figures in parentheses are very rough estimates of how the specialized secondary school graduates who are not employed in the labor force are allocated.

It is estimated that approximately 40 percent of the daytime enrollment in higher educational institutions consisted of graduates of specialized secondary schools and that two thirds of this number were men. The other estimate concerns the percentage of males in the armed services. It is assumed that the percentage would be higher than that of graduates of higher educational institutions (18.3 per cent) and that the percentage not working would not be far above that for males in the age group 20 to 24 (12 per cent). An estimate of 29 and 19 per cent seemed reasonable on the basis of these assumptions.

cialized secondary education supply a major share of the semiprofessionals in the civilian labor force.

The contribution of the different national and ethnic groups to the number of women in the civilian economy who have a specialized secondary education varies greatly. The most prominent group is the Russians. Women comprise 66 per cent of specialists of Russian nationality; and, although Russian women make up 55.4 per cent of the female population in the U.S.S.R., their share among female specialists employed in the economy is

68.6 per cent.[10] Figures for the Jews are especially striking. Although Jewish women rank twelfth in population, they are fourth in rank among female specialists. Table 110 indicates that their contribution is approximately twice what would be expected from their share in the population. On the other hand, only 54 per cent of all Jewish specialists are women. The Latvians and Estonians also

[10]Specialists with a secondary education are referred to interchangeably as specialists or semiprofessionals in the following discussion.

TABLE 110. Number and percentage of women specialists with specialized secondary education employed in the economy, by nationality, December 1, 1961.[a]

Nationality	Total	Women		Women Specialists of Given Nationality	Women of Given Nationality in Total Female Population
			%	%	%
Total....................	5,609,106	3,531,873	63.0	100.0	100.0
Russians..................	3,670,976	2,421,958	66.0	68.6	55.4
Ukrainians................	885,508	536,858	60.6	15.2	17.9
Belorussians..............	174,534	112,755	64.6	3.2	3.8
Jews......................	143,146	78,089	54.5	2.2	1.1
Tatars....................	88,047	57,158	64.9	1.6	2.4
Georgians.................	70,402	42,306	60.1	1.2	1.2
Armenians.................	60,152	33,451	55.6	0.9	1.2
Uzbeks....................	54,408	13,844	25.4	0.4	2.6
Azerbaidzhani.............	53,419	20,298	38.0	0.6	1.3
Lithuanians...............	47,408	31,256	65.9	0.9	1.1
Kazakhs...................	45,535	15,183	33.3	0.4	1.6
Latvians..................	40,916	25,219	61.6	0.7	0.7
Estonians.................	30,778	19,616	63.7	0.6	0.5
Chuvashi..................	23,512	13,593	57.8	0.4	0.7
Moldavians................	21,733	13,033	60.0	0.4	1.0
Tadzhiks..................	13,830	2,428	17.6	0.1	0.6
Mordvians.................	13,744	7,970	58.0	0.2	0.6
Dagistani.................	12,439	3,924	31.5	0.1	0.4
Komis.....................	12,004	8,507	70.9	0.2	0.2
Turkmen...................	10,961	1,827	16.7	–	0.4
Bashkirs..................	10,764	6,086	56.5	0.2	0.5
Kirgiz....................	10,556	3,373	31.9	0.1	0.4
Ossetians.................	9,689	5,998	61.9	0.2	0.2
Udmurts...................	8,922	5,696	63.8	0.2	0.3
Yakuts....................	6,178	3,092	50.0	0.1	0.1
Buriats...................	5,257	3,185	60.6	0.1	0.1
Maritsi...................	5,236	2,847	54.4	0.1	0.3
Karelians.................	4,021	2,873	71.4	0.1	0.1
Karbardinians.............	3,060	1,842	60.2	–	0.1
Karakalpaks...............	2,231	399	17.9	–	0.1
Others....................	106,946	37,206	34.8	1.1	2.9

[a]Excluding military personnel. This table is based on data from *Srednee spetsial'noe obrazovanie v SSSR* (Moscow, 1962), p. 43, and *Itogi . . . 1959 goda: SSSR*, p. 185. The omission of amounts indicates a negligible figure.

contribute a disproportionately large number of female specialists.

Most of the Transcaucasian and Central Asian ethnic groups account for only a very small proportion of women specialists with a specialized secondary education. Uzbek women, for example, make up 2.6 per cent of the female population of the U.S.S.R. but account for only 0.4 per cent of the specialists. It may also be noted that only 25 per cent of all Uzbek specialists are women. This is by far the smallest proportion of any major nationality group, exceeded only by the Kirgiz and Turkmen, and there is no indication of an increase in recent years in the share of women among specialists with a specialized secondary education in these backward areas where the influence of Moslem culture is still felt.[11] Between 1957 and 1961 the proportion declined from 53 to 49 per cent in the Uzbek republic and from 51 to 50 per cent in the Turkmen republic, while it remained unchanged in the Kazakh, Azerbaidzhan, Kirgiz, and Tadzhik republics.[12] Thus, although the part played by women in the semiprofessional occupations in these republics increased greatly in the past, progress now seems to have come to a halt.

WOMEN SPECIALISTS WITH A HIGHER EDUCATION

The number of women specialists with a higher education employed in the economy increased 33 times from the beginning of 1928 to the end of 1962. The increase was approximately fivefold during the prewar period, the number of women professionals growing from 65,000 at the beginning of 1928 to 312,000 at the beginning of 1941 (see Table 104). By 1928 the growing number of women graduates began to be reflected in the labor force: between 1928 and 1941 the percentage of women specialists with a higher education rose from 28 to 34 per cent. Further increases

[11]The historical and cultural factors which account for such a small proportion among the Moslems have been discussed in Chapter 6.

[12]See Appendix VIII, Table 1.

occurred during and after World War II, so that by 1954 the number of female specialists with a higher education had grown another 350 per cent to over 1 million, and the percentage of women among all specialists with a higher education had increased to 55 per cent. In the past decade the number has more than doubled again, reaching 2.4 million at the end of 1964. The proportion of women has declined slightly, however, to 53 per cent.

The growth in the number of women professionals varied from field to field. By far the largest numerical increase occurred among employed women who were graduates of pedagogical, library, and cultural educational institutes and universities (except geologists, legal personnel, doctors, and economists). Their number rose sevenfold, from 144,000 at the beginning of 1941 to 1,179,000 at the end of 1964 (see Table 111). Unfortunately, a detailed breakdown by specialty and sex has not been published.

The number of female engineers increased tenfold, from 44,000 in 1941 to 460,000 in 1964; a similar phenomenon occurred in the case of female economists, statisticians, and commodity specialists, whose number increased from 18,000 to 191,000. Considerable gains were observed among professional women in agriculture (18,000 to 117,000) and in legal work (3,000 to 25,000). The smallest increase was among women doctors (85,000 to 354,000). In spite of the great increase in numbers of women specialists with a higher education since 1941, the distribution of women among the fields did not change significantly except for an increase in the proportion of women who were engineers and a substantial reduction in the proportion of women who were physicians (see Table 112).

In 1964, as shown in Table 113, the highest percentage of women among specialists with a higher education was found among physicians (74 per cent); graduates of pedagogical and related institutes and universities, except geologists, legal personnel, physicians, and economists (67 per cent); and economists and related professionals (61 per

TABLE 111. Women specialists with higher education employed in the economy, by specialty, 1941, 1954–57, 1959–64.[a]

Specialty	Jan. 1, 1941	Apr. 1, 1954	July 1, 1955	Dec. 1, 1956	Dec. 1, 1957	Dec. 1, 1959	Dec. 1, 1960	Dec. 1, 1961	Dec. 1, 1962	Dec. 1, 1963	Nov. 15, 1964
Total	312	1,098	1,155	1,396	1,464	1,701	1,865	2,015	2,133	2,237	2,394
Engineers (including geologists)	43	152	168	205	233	293	320	379	409	434	460
Agronomists, zootechnicians, veterinarians, foresters	18	55	65	70	74	87	94	100	107	109	117
Economists, economist-statisticians, commodity specialists	18	56	62	76	90	111	113	129	159	171	191
Legal personnel	3	13	15	18	19	21	22	24	25	25	–
Physicians (excluding dentists)	85	214	228	247	260	285	302	315	331	341	354
Teachers and university graduates (except geologists, legal personnel, physicians, economists), library and cultural enlightenment personnel	144	581	606	738	748	837	901	985	1,036	1,096	1,179
Residual	–	37	11	42	40	67	113	83	66	61	93

[a]Figures are expressed in thousands. This table is based on data from *Zhenshchina v SSSR* (Moscow, 1960), p. 58; *Zhenshchiny i deti v SSSR* (Moscow, 1961), p. 138; *Zhenshchiny i deti v SSSR* (Moscow, 1963), p. 118; *Narodnoe khoziaistvo SSSR v 1962 godu* (Moscow, 1963), p. 472; *Narodnoe khoziaistvo SSSR v 1959 godu* (Moscow, 1960), p. 615; *Narodnoe khoziaistvo SSSR v 1956 godu* (Moscow, 1957), p. 210; *Vysshee obrazovanie v SSSR* (Moscow, 1961), pp. 52, 66; *Narodnoe khoziaistvo SSSR v 1963 godu* (Moscow, 1965), p. 492; and *Narodnoe khoziaistvo SSSR v 1964 godu* (Moscow, 1965), p. 566.

TABLE 112. Distribution of women specialists with higher education employed in the economy, by specialty, 1941, 1954–57, 1959–64.[a]

Specialty	Jan. 1, 1941	Apr. 1, 1954	July 1, 1955	Dec. 1, 1956	Dec. 1, 1957	Dec. 1, 1959	Dec. 1, 1960	Dec. 1, 1961	Dec. 1, 1962	Dec. 1, 1963	Nov. 15, 1964
Total	100.0	100.0	100.0	100.0	100.0	100.0	100.0	100.0	100.0	100.0	100.0
Engineers (including geologists)	14.1	13.8	14.6	14.7	15.9	17.2	17.6	18.8	19.2	19.4	19.2
Agronomists, zootechnicians, veterinarians, foresters	5.8	5.0	5.6	5.0	5.0	5.1	5.0	5.0	5.0	4.9	4.9
Economists, economist-statisticians, commodity specialists	5.8	5.1	5.4	5.4	6.2	6.5	6.1	6.4	7.4	7.6	8.0
Legal personnel	1.0	1.2	1.3	1.3	1.3	1.2	1.2	1.2	1.2	1.1	–
Physicians (excluding dentists)	27.2	18.6	19.7	17.7	17.8	16.8	16.2	15.6	15.5	15.2	14.8
Teachers and university graduates (except geologists, legal personnel, physicians, economists), library and cultural enlightenment personnel	46.1	52.9	52.4	52.9	51.1	49.3	48.3	48.9	48.6	49.0	49.3
Radio technology and communcations, art, cinematography, physical culture, sports, and other unspecified specialties	–	3.4	1.0	3.0	2.7	3.9	5.6	4.1	3.1	2.7	3 8

[a]For the sources of this table, see Table 111. The residual is incorporated as "other unspecified specialties."

TABLE 113. Percentage of women among all specialists with higher education employed in the economy, by specialty, 1941, 1954–57, 1959–64.[a]

Specialty	Jan. 1, 1941	Apr. 1, 1954	July 1, 1955	Dec. 1, 1956	Dec. 1, 1957	Dec. 1, 1959	Dec. 1, 1960	Dec. 1, 1961	Dec. 1, 1962	Dec. 1, 1963	Nov. 15, 1964
Total	34	55	53	53	52	53	53	53	53	52	53
Engineers (including geologists)	15	29	28	28	29	30	29	31	31	31	31
Agronomists, zootechnicians, veterinarians, foresters	25	41	41	39	38	39	39	41	42	41	41
Economists, economist-statisticians, commodity specialists	31	59	54	54	57	57	57	59	61	61	63
Legal personnel	15	32	32	32	32	32	32	32	32	32	–
Physicians (excluding dentists)	61	76	76	75	75	75	75	74	75	74	74
Teachers and university graduates (except geologists, legal personnel, physicians, economists), library and cultural enlightenment personnel	49	67	67	66	65	65	65	67	67	67	68

[a]For the sources of this table, see Table 111.

cent). The professionals among whom women were a minority were agricultural specialists and foresters (41 per cent), legal specialists (32 per cent), and engineers (31 per cent). This pattern closely parallels that of female participation among specialists with a specialized secondary education.

A breakdown by field of specialization of women holding advanced degrees has not been published, but information for recent years on their share among doctoral and candidate degree holders is available. The candidate degree (*kandidat nauk*) is roughly comparable to the Ph.D. degree in the United States, while the doctoral degree (*doktor nauk*) is the ultimate degree, usually received a decade or more after the candidate degree, when the recipient has become a mature and seasoned scholar. In the immediate postwar period almost half the recipients of the candidate degree were in their thirties at the time of the award while almost half the recipients of the doctoral degree were in their forties.[13] Table 114 shows that in 1950 only 7 per cent of the small number of holders of doctoral degrees were women.[14] By 1961 the share of women, though it still remained at a low level, had increased by more than half, to 11 per cent. The proportion of women among holders of candidate degrees is substantially larger and rose from 25 per cent in 1950 to 29 per cent in 1959, during which period the total number of candidate degree holders doubled. In 1960 and 1961 no change in the share of women occurred. From these figures, the progressive thinning of the ranks of women from the lower to the higher rungs of the academic ladder is quite apparent.

Among women specialists with a higher education a select group holds academic rank. This does not necessarily mean that these women are employed in an academic institu-

TABLE 114. Women holding doctoral and candidate degrees, 1950 and 1959–61.[a]

Academic Degree	October 1			
	1950	1959	1960	1961
Doctoral degree				
Total number........	8,277	10,530	11,945	11,300
Number of women.....	600	1,100	1,100	1,200
Percentage of women...	7	10	9	11
Candidate degree				
Total number..........	45,530	93,999	98,262	102,500
Number of women.....	11,400	27,200	28,800	29,700
Percentage of women...	25	29	29	29

[a]Based on *Zhenshchiny i deti v SSSR* (Moscow, 1963), p. 129; *Vysshee obrazovanie v SSSR* (Moscow, 1961), p. 205; and *Narodnoe khoziaistvo SSSR v 1962 godu* (Moscow, 1963), p. 582.

tion, although it is true for many. Once a person has been certified in an advanced academic rank, he retains it whether he is employed in a higher educational or research establishment, in an industrial enterprise, in government administration, or in the military service. The academic titles (*uchenoe zvanie*), in descending order, are: academician (*akademik*), corresponding member (*chlen korrespondent*) of an academy of science, professor (*professor*), associate professor (*dotsent*), senior scientific worker (*starshyi nauchnyi sotrudnik*), assistant professor (*assistent*), and junior scientific worker (*mladshyi nauchnyi sotrudnik*). Members of the first two categories are not very numerous and the percentage of women is very small.[15] Almost two thirds of the professors of both sexes are employed in higher educational institutions and more than four fifths of these possess a doctoral degree. Of this group approximately three fourths are the head of a department (*kafedra*). In 1960 women made up 7.3 per cent of the academicians, corresponding members of academies, and professors (see Table 115). Associate professors are even more heavily concentrated than professors in higher educational institutions and almost three quarters of the total are so employed. More than 90 per cent of these have candidate degrees. The proportion of women among this group in 1960 was 17.1 per cent.

---

[13]K. T. Galkin, *Vysshee obrazovanie i podgotovka nauchnykh kadrov v SSSR* (Moscow, 1958), p. 164.

[14]The percentage of women with advanced degrees in the prewar period has not been uncovered. Presumably it was considerably smaller than in the postwar period.

---

[15]See Table 124, p. 207.

TABLE 115. Women scientific workers having academic titles, 1950, 1955, and 1960–64.[a]

Position	Oct. 1, 1950			Oct. 1, 1955			Oct. 1, 1960		
	Number of Women	Percentage Distribution	Percentage of Women	Number of Women	Percentage Distribution	Percentage of Women	Number of Women	Percentage Distribution	Percentage of Women
Total......................	16,569	100.0	26.9	18,711	100.0	27.0	26,271	100.0	28.2
Academicians, corresponding members and professors.....	474	2.9	5.4	555	3.0	6.2	725	2.8	7.3
Associate professors.........	3,226	19.5	14.8	4,807	25.7	16.8	6,171	23.5	17.1
Senior research workers.......	3,450	20.8	30.4	4,434	23.7	30.4	5,761	21.9	28.4
Junior research workers and assistants..................	9,419	56.8	48.0	8,915	47.6	52.0	13,614	51.8	51.0

Senior research workers are found almost exclusively in scientific research establishments, in which more than 93 per cent of them were employed in 1960. Less than 5 per cent were in higher educational institutions, the remaining 2 per cent being employed in government administration and elsewhere. More than 90 per cent of the senior research workers had candidate degrees, and 3 per cent doctoral degrees. The share of women among senior research workers was 28.4 per cent in 1960. The bulk of the junior research workers are employed in scientific research establishments, while the majority of the assistant professors are employed in higher educational institutions. Fewer than a quarter of these have a candidate degree. Among these two lower-ranking groups the share of women is high and was 51 per cent in 1960. As indicated in Table 115, the percentage of women among professors and associate professors has increased markedly in the last ten years, but no distinct trend in the share of women in the other two groups is evident. It is clear from these figures that the percentage of women among the higher academic ranks remains quite low in comparison with what their proportionate share would be.

The contribution of the different nationality groups to women specialists with a higher education who are employed in the civilian economy differs even more widely than their contribution to women with specialized secondary education. Again the Russian nationality supplies by far the largest number, accounting for 63.9 per cent of all women specialists with a higher education employed in the economy (see Table 116). Again, Jewish women have a disproportionately high representation. Although they constitute only 1.1 per cent of the women in the Soviet population, they comprise 7.6 per cent of all employed female specialists with a higher education. Other nationality groups with unusually high representations are the Georgians, Armenians, and Latvians. The small number of women professionals with a higher education from among the Belorussians and Lithuanians is explained by the heavily rural population of their republics. Women of the Central Asian nationalities are also underrepresented, due to the persistence of Moslem traditions. In recent years the proportion of women among specialists with a higher education from these underrepresented groups does not appear to have increased, nor has the all-Union proportion of women changed very much, rising only from 52 per cent in 1957 to 53 per cent in 1961.[16]

The utilization pattern of women with a higher education is shown in Table 117, which gives 1959 census data on the number of men and women with a higher education, on the number of men and women employed in the civilian economy, and on the number of men and women enrolled as graduate students. Some of the figures have been estimated

[16]See Appendix VIII, Table 1; see also Table 116 and n.

Oct. 1, 1961			Nov. 1, 1962			Nov. 1, 1963			Nov. 1, 1964		
Num- ber of Women	Percent- age Dis- tribution	Percent- age of Women	Num- ber of Women	Percent- age Dis- tribution	Percent- age of Women	Num- ber of Women	Percent- age Dis- tribution	Percent- age of Women	Num- ber of Women	Percent- age Dis- tribution	Percent- age of Women
28,000	100.0	28.5	38,000	100.0	31.6	41,400	100.0	32.3	42,900	100.0	32.2
800	2.9	7.8	900	2.4	8.2	900	2.2	7.9	1,000	2.3	8.3
6,700	23.9	17.5	7,300	19.2	18.0	8,000	19.3	18.6	8.800	20.5	19.1
6,000	21.4	28.6	7,100	18.7	29.8	7,600	18.4	29.5	7,900	18.4	29.0
14,500	51.8	50.5	22,700	59.7	50.4	24,999	60.1	52.0	25,200	58.7	52.3

[a]Based on *Vysshee obrazovanie v SSSR* (Moscow, 1961), p. 212; *Narodnoe khoziaistvo SSSR v 1962 godu* (Moscow, 1963), pp. 582–83; *Narodnoe khoziaistvo SSSR v 1963 godu* (Moscow, 1965), pp. 589–90; and *Narodnoe khoziaistvo SSSR v 1964 godu* (Moscow, 1965), pp. 699–700. The percentage of women among the totals is derived from the number and percentage of women of each rank.

TABLE 116. Number and percentage of women specialists with higher education employed in the economy, by nationality, December 1, 1960.[a]

Nationality	Total	Women	Women	Women Specialists of Given Nationality	Women of Given Na- tionality in Total Female Population
			%	%	%
Total..................	3,545,234	1,864,644	52.6	100.0	100.0
Russians...............	2,070,333	1,190,250	57.5	63.8	55.4
Ukrainians.............	517,729	259,146	50.1	13.9	17.9
Jews..................	290,707	141,847	48.8	7.6	1.1
Belorussians...........	95,116	47,686	50.1	2.6	3.8
Georgians.............	88,631	34,691	39.1	1.9	1.2
Armenians.............	74,122	31,927	42.2	1.7	1.2
Tartars...............	51,164	28,411	55.5	1.5	2.4
Azerbaidzhani..........	47,859	15,008	31.4	0.8	1.3
Uzbeks................	46,526	10,756	23.1	0.6	2.6
Kazakhs...............	34,760	10,039	28.9	0.5	1.6
Lithuanians............	30,004	15,029	50.1	0.8	1.1
Latvians...............	24,914	13,924	55.9	0.7	0.7
Estonians.............	19,272	9,975	51.8	0.5	0.5
Chuvashi..............	13,325	5,295	39.7	0.3	0.7
Moldavians............	11,331	5,006	44.2	0.3	1.0
Tadzhiks..............	10,857	1,949	18.0	0.1	0.6
Turkmen..............	10,356	1,544	14.9	0.1	0.4
Kirgiz................	9,451	2,772	29.3	0.1	0.4
Ossetians..............	8,889	3,912	44.0	0.2	0.2
Dagestani..............	7,342	1,756	23.9	0.1	0.4
Bashkirs...............	6,420	2,836	44.2	0.2	0.5
Mordvians.............	6,328	2,762	43.6	0.1	0.6
Komis................	4,352	2,712	62.3	0.1	0.2
Udmurts..............	4,249	2,488	58.6	0.1	0.3
Buriats...............	4,021	1,884	46.9	0.1	0.1
Yakuts................	3,176	1,185	37.3	–	0.1
Maritsi...............	2,577	1,045	40.6	–	0.3
Kabardinians..........	2,336	668	28.6	–	0.1
Karakalpaks...........	2,043	279	13.7	–	0.1
Karelians..............	1,534	864	56.3	–	0.1
Others................	45,510	16,998	37.4	0.9	2.9

[a]Excluding military personnel. This table is based on data from *Vysshee obrazovanie v SSSR* (Moscow, 1961), pp. 67–68; and *Itogi . . . 1959 goda: SSSR*, p. 185; –, a negligible figure. *Narodnoe khoziaistvo SSSR v 1962 godu* (Moscow, 1963), p. 473, gives Dec. 1, 1962, data.

TABLE 117. Utilization of men and women with higher education, beginning of 1959.[a]

	Total	Distribution %	Men	Distribution %	Women	Distribution %	Women %
	thousands	*%*	*thousands*	*%*	*thousands*	*%*	*%*
Graduates of higher educational institutions....	3,778	100.0	1,933	100.0	1,844	100.0	48.8
In the labor force........................	3,381	89.5	1,794	92.8	1,587	86.0	46.9
Armed services..........................	354	9.4	354	18.3	–	–	–
Civilian labor force....................	3,027	80.1	1,440	74.5	1,587	86.0	52.4
Not in the labor force....................	397	10.5	139	7.2	258	14.0	65.0
Full-time graduate students.............	16	0.4	12	0.6	4	0.2	26.0
Not working..........................	381	10.1	127	6.6	254	13.8	66.7

[a]Graduates are from *Itogi . . . SSSR: 1959 goda*, p. 82. The total civilian labor force with a higher education at the end of 1958 is from *Narodnoe khoziaistvo SSSR v 1959 godu* (Moscow, 1960), p. 602. It is assumed that there were no new graduates added to the labor force between the end of 1958 and Jan. 15, 1959. The male-female ratio is calculated by interpolation between the ratios for Dec. 1, 1957, and Dec. 1, 1959, taken from *Narodnoe khoziaistvo SSSR v 1958 godu* (Moscow, 1959), p. 690, and *Narodnoe khoziaistvo SSSR v 1959 godu* (Moscow, 1960), p. 615. The number of males in the labor force was calculated by applying a participation rate of 92.8 per cent to total male graduates. This percentage is the rate for the male population age 25 to 59, an age span which covers 87.5 per cent of the male higher education graduates. The number of full-time postgraduate students (15,532) is from *Narodnoe khoziaistvo SSSR v 1961 godu* (Moscow, 1962), p. 707. The proportion of women is interpolated on the basis of data in Table 111.

by interpolation of male-female ratios.[17] Although the picture cannot be considered accurate in detail, it does present the major characteristics of the pattern of utilization of men and women professionals.

The picture which emerges is one of very high utilization of males in the combined civilian and military labor force (92.8 per cent) and a lower rate of utilization of women (86.0 per cent). The utilization of women is unusually high, however, when compared with the United States or other leading Western countries. Furthermore, because of the large number of male graduates of higher educational institutions serving in the military (an estimated 354,000), the number of males employed in the civilian labor force is actually smaller than the number of females, and the civilian participation rate for males is only 74.5 per cent as compared with 86.0 per cent for women. The percentage of females outside the labor force (14.0 per cent) is twice that of males (7.2 per cent). The only identifiable portion of the men and women not in the labor force are those enrolled in postgraduate training. Out of a total of 15,500, approximately 4,000 were women. The remaining men and women were presumably in temporary or permanent withdrawal from the labor force.

Almost two thirds of the women graduates were concentrated in the age group 25 to 39, yet their participation in the labor force remained high, although these are the years during which a woman's involvement with childbearing and child rearing is greatest.

Of almost equal interest is the large number of men with a higher education who are in the military. The estimated figure of 354,000 is almost a fifth of the males with a higher education. The high retention of females in the labor force can, in a sense, be viewed as permitting such a large number of males to serve in the military without adversely affecting the civilian economy.

CONCLUSIONS

The role of women in the semiprofessional, professional, and administrative labor force has increased greatly since the Revolution and has assumed proportions unequaled elsewhere in the world. Today women make up more than half the labor force employed in "mental" work. About half of the 11 million women in this category have had a specialized secondary or higher education. The proportion of women among specialists with a specialized secondary education is very high, amounting to 63 per cent in recent years. Among professionals with a higher education

[17]See Table 117, n.

the proportion has been 53 per cent. Thus, women form a clear majority of the specialized labor force in the Soviet Union.

Impressive gains were scored by female semiprofessionals and professionals before World War II, but the largest advances were made from 1941 to 1964, when the number of women specialists with a specialized secondary or higher education increased from 864,000 to 6,611,000 and the share of women increased from 36 to 59 per cent. The increase in the number of women specialists with a higher education was particularly impressive, growing almost fivefold from 1928 to 1941 and almost eightfold between 1941 and 1964, making a thirty-sevenfold increase over the thirty-six-year period. During the same years, the proportion of women among those with a higher education employed in the economy increased from 28 to 34 and then to 53 per cent. Health, education, and the statistics-economics field were soon dominated by women specialists.

Interestingly, the predominance of women among persons doing "mental" work must be explained, not by an excess in the age groups over age 35 which suffered the highest male war losses, but by the excess of women in the age group 20 to 34. Indeed, the number of women "mental" workers in this age group exceeds that of men by as much as 2.5 million. Part of this difference is due to the very high female enrollment in specialized secondary and higher educational institutions during and after the war. Also, part (perhaps half) can be explained by the large number of young men in this age group with a specialized secondary or higher education who serve in the military. The availability of trained women makes it possible, of course, for so large a number of male specialists to be enlisted in the military services without serious repercussions on the civilian economy. The rapid decline in the number of women "mental" workers in the older age groups where males predominate is primarily due to the sharp reduction in the number of women possessing specialized training in each successive age group.

With each successive level of educational attainment, the proportion of women declines. Women make up about 30 per cent of the persons holding the candidate degree, for example, but only 10 per cent of those holding doctorates. The importance of women in semiprofessional and professional occupations is greatest, therefore, in the less demanding occupations and least in those requiring greater amounts of education and training. The thinning out of women in the higher ranks of employment is discussed in detail in the following chapter.

chapter
11

PROFESSIONAL ATTAINMENT

MANAGERIAL PERSONNEL, administrators, and specialists, or "leading personnel," form a category used by the Soviets to include persons holding jobs requiring administrative ability or specialized knowledge or skill acquired either through formal training or on-the-job experience. The category is broader than that of engineering-technical personnel, which is included as a major subcategory. Among the persons counted among the "leading personnel" are directors and deputy directors of enterprises and other establishments; heads and deputy heads of divisions and subdivisions of enterprises; and all engineers, technicians, laboratory workers, dispatchers, chief accountants, planners, economists, and the like. The precise occupations in the various sectors of the economy which are included will become clearer as the role of women among the leading personnel of each of these sectors is discussed.[1] It is desirable, however, to take an over-all view of the role of women among the leading personnel throughout the entire economy and in its major branches.

Women have made up an increasing proportion of the administrative, managerial, and specialized personnel, as can be seen from Table 118. In the economy as a whole in 1941, 31 per cent of the leading personnel were women. By 1957 their share had increased to 50 per cent. Gains were made in every field for which information is available. In industrial enterprises the proportion of women among leading personnel was 17 per cent in 1941 and 31 per cent at the end of 1956. In construction organizations the increase was from 9 to 22 per cent. In semi-professional and professional training establishments the share of women among the leading personnel increased from 27 to 39 per cent and in scientific research institutes from 36 to 52 per cent.

The role of women among leading personnel varies widely from branch to branch in the economy. The highest percentages are to be found in public health institutions (88 per cent) and educational-cultural services (66 per cent). In trade and distribution women comprise 46 per cent and in government administration 44 per cent. Much lower proportions are found in industry (31 per cent), transportation and communication (28 per cent), construction (22 per cent), and agriculture (21 per cent).

In most of these branches the percentage of women among the managerial personnel and specialists tends to be substantially less than the percentage of women among workers

---

[1]For a discussion of the survey of Dec. 1, 1956, of "Managerial Personnel and Specialists," see the U.S. Bureau of the Census study prepared by Murray Feshbach, *The Soviet Statistical System: Labor Force Recordkeeping and Reporting Since 1957* (Washington, D.C., 1962), pp. 29–31. The results of this survey are presented in the Soviet tables cited later as referring to "the beginning of 1957."

TABLE 118. Number and percentage of women administrators and specialists employed in the economy, 1941 and 1956.[a]

Branch or Sector	Thousands of Women		Percentage Distribution		Percentage of Women		Percentage of Women among All Workers and Employees
	Jan. 1, 1941	Dec. 1, 1956	Jan. 1, 1941	Dec. 1, 1956	Jan. 1, 1941	Dec. 1, 1956	1956
Total...................	1,694	4,678	100.0	100.0	31	50	45
Agriculture (collective and state farms and other state-operated agricultural enterprises)......................	–	119	–	2.5	–	21	31
Industrial enterprises...............	182	572	10.7	12.2	17	31	45
Construction enterprises............	7	73	0.4	1.6	9	22	30
Transportation and communication....	–	159	–	3.4	–	28	33
Transport......................	–	89	–	1.9	–	21	(29)
Communication.................	–	70	–	1.5	–	46	(63)
Trade and distribution (trade procurement and supply organizations, restaurants, public dining and catering services)........................	–	264	–	5.6	–	46	64
Total, production and distribution.....	–	1,187	–	25.4	–	36	–
Educational-cultural services.........	–	1,645	–	35.3	–	66	67
Preschools and children's institutions	–	68	–	1.5	–	91	–
General education schools.........	–	1,253	–	26.8	–	71	–
Professional and semiprofessional training establishments...........	43	153	2.5	3.3	27	39	–
Cultural services...............	–	150	–	32.1	–	70	–
Editorial offices in publishing.......	–	12	–	0.3	–	32	–
Arts and entertainment...........	–	9	–	0.2	–	33	–
Public health (medical and public health institutions, sanitariums, rest homes, etc.)......................	–	1,085	–	23.2	–	88	85
Research, design and development....	–	261	–	5.6	–	45	(41)
Research institutes................	28	128	1.7	2.7	36	52	–
Project institutes.................	13	72	0.8	1.5	19	43	–
Design institutes.................	–	35	–	0.7	–	38	–
Geological surveying.............	–	26	–	0.6	–	35	–
Government administration, economic management and planning organizations........................	–	500	–	10.7	–	44	50
Total, education, health, research, and government.....................	–	3,941	–	74.6	–	64	–

[a]Based on *Zhenshchina v SSSR* (Moscow, 1960), pp. 45–46; for workers and employees, Table 95. The 1941 data on Project institutes are from "Zhenshchina v SSSR," *Partinaia zhizn'*, No. 4 (Feb., 1960), 59. Figures in parentheses in the last column are estimates based on 1958 figures. The *Zhenshchina* figures are reported as being for the beginning of 1957; actually they refer to Dec. 1, 1956. The format of this and similar tables, which follow, is from DeWitt, *Education and Professional Employment in the U.S.S.R.* (Washington, D.C., 1961), pp. 495 ff.

and employees. The only fields in which this disparity is reversed or reduced are the two in which women dominate—in public health women make up 85 per cent of the workers and employees and 88 per cent of the managerial personnel and specialists, while in educational-cultural services the percentages are 69 and 66, respectively. In trade and distribution the percentage of women workers and employees is also high, but the percentage among leading personnel is substantially lower.

We shall now examine in greater detail the role of women among the leading personnel in each of the fields for which data are available. Our discussion will be divided into two major parts, the first dealing with the "productive" sectors of the economy: agriculture, industry, construction, and distribution; and the second with the "nonproductive" sectors of education, health, research in the applied and pure sciences, and government administration.[2]

PRODUCTION AND DISTRIBUTION ACTIVITIES

A general characteristic of the so-called productive sectors is the smaller proportion of women among managerial personnel and specialists, perhaps as a result of the nature of the work involved. The greater physical demands of the work and a lingering prejudice against participation in it by women still present a barrier. Also, protective legislation in heavy or dangerous occupations, such as mining, reduces women's chances of rising to leading positions in these sectors.

Agriculture. The percentage of women among managerial personnel and specialists in

agriculture is much smaller than their share in agricultural employment. We have already quoted Khrushchev's remark that "It is the men who do the administrating and the women who do the work." At the end of 1956 women made up approximately three fifths of the able-bodied collective farmers and two fifths of the workers and employees, but only one fifth of the leading personnel (see Table 119). At the highest level of administrators of productive units—chairmen of collective farms and directors of state farms and other state agricultural enterprises—few women are to be found. At the end of 1956 fewer than 2 per cent of the chairmen and directors were women. The situation was no different in the 1930's. In 1936 women made up only 1.7 per cent of collective farm chairmen. By 1939 their share had increased slightly to 2.7 per cent.[3] Only during World War II, however, did the number of women chairmen and directors reach significant proportions. At the end of 1940 women chairmen and directors accounted for 2.6 per cent of the total, and by the end of 1943 their share had increased to 14.2 per cent. At the end of 1944, how-

---

[2]The classification of productive and nonproductive sectors is made by the Soviets on the basis of Marx's distinction between the two. Only material production is "productive." Services are not considered productive and are omitted from national income.

[3]E. Orlikova, "Sovetskaia zhenshchina v obshchestvennom proizvodstva," *Problemy ekomomiki*, No. 7 (1940), 120.

TABLE 119. Women administrators and specialists on collective and state farms and in other state agricultural enterprises, by occupation, December 1, 1956.[a]

Occupations	Men and Women		Women		
	Number (thousands)	Percentage Distribution	Number (thousands)	Percentage Distribution	Percentage of Women
Collective farm chairmen and directors of state farms	89.9	15.8	(1.7)	(1.4)	(1.9)
Agronomists	106.2	18.7	42.5	35.7	40
Zootechnicians (livestock specialists)	69.1	12.2	30.4	25.5	44
Veterinarians, veterinary *feldshers*, veterinary technicians	73.9	13.0	13.3	11.1	18
Others, unspecified	227.5	40.1	31.1	26.3	14
Total, on collective and state farms and other state agricultural enterprises	566.7	100.0	119.0	100.0	21

[a]Based on *Zhenshchina v SSSR* (Moscow, 1960), p. 49. Shishkin (*Trudovye resursy SSSR* [Moscow, 1961], p. 140) reports that about 1,000 of the more than 52,000 chairmen and directors of collective and state farms at the beginning of 1960 were women. This percentage (1.9 per cent) is applied to the number of collective and state farms at the end of 1956 (89,900) to derive the estimate of 1,700 women chairmen and directors at the end of 1956. See *Narodnoe khoziaistvo SSSR v 1958 godu* (Moscow, 1959), pp. 494, 514.

ever, the share of women had declined to 11.8 per cent and a year later to 8.1 per cent.[4]

The proportion of women chairmen and directors varied considerably among the different republics at this time, being much lower in the Transcaucasian and Central Asian republics and the Ukraine than in the R.S.F.S.R. and Belorussia, where women made up almost 15 per cent of the total. In the Karelo-Finnish S.S.R. the proportion was 26 per cent.[5] With demobilization after the war, it became government policy to encourage experienced officers to return to their home villages to serve as chairmen. Also, the drive to consolidate farms launched in 1950 may have caused a further shrinkage of opportunities for women, since a man was more likely to emerge as the new chairman when several farms were combined into one.

In contrast with their poor representation among local agricultural administration, women make up a high percentage of agricultural specialists. Among agronomists they account for 46 per cent of the total; among livestock specialists, 44 per cent; and among veterinary doctors and technicians, 18 per cent. These three occupational groups account for almost 75 per cent of the women employed as agricultural managerial and specialized personnel.

Not only Khrushchev but others have remarked that the number of women among leading personnel in agriculture is disproportionately small when compared with their very important role in the total agricultural labor force. As we have seen, the situation has not improved over the years. N. I. Shishkin, a Soviet labor economist, for example, has commented that, "The promotion of women to executive positions in agriculture is taking place on an inadequate scale."[6]

Construction. Between the end of 1940 and the end of 1956 the percentage of women among administrators and specialists in construction enterprises increased sharply, from 9 to 22 per cent (see Table 118). For the next five years no change occurred in the proportional representation of women in this category, although there was a tendency between 1957 and 1962 for women to occupy a progressively smaller role in the most responsible positions.[7]

In jobs involving less supervision or less responsibility, such as staff jobs, women played a more important role (see Table 120). For example, more than 13,000 engineers without administrative responsibility were women, amounting to 31 per cent of the total. Almost as many women worked as chief accountants and head bookkeepers, making up 41 per cent of the total. Among engineer-economists, economists, and planning specialists women numbered 7,500, or 67 per cent of the total. Their share among technicians was 44 per cent.

Access to positions at the highest level in the construction industry seems to be more constricted for women than in other fields. Apart from the nature of construction work, which requires a large measure of personal authority and physical stamina, such work tends to be more peripatetic than other types of employment. Undoubtedly a major deterrent to women rising to the top in the construction field is the difficulty in assigning a woman with a family to a job which would allow the family to stay together. Where both husband and wife are employed in construction work, it should be possible to assign them together to the same project or area, but the husband-and-wife team is the exception.

Although the proportion of women among administrators and specialists in construction has not shown any change in recent years, internal shifts have occurred, resulting in an increase to 5 per cent for the top three administrative categories combined in Table 120, a decline from 19 to 13 per cent among construction foremen, and a drop from 41 to 27

---

[4]Iu. V. Arutiunian, *Sovetskoe krest'ianstvo v gody Velikoi otechestvennoi voiny* (Moscow, 1963), p. 289.

[5]*Ibid.*, pp. 402–4.

[6]*Trudovye resursy SSSR* (Moscow, 1961), ed. by N. I. Shishkin, p. 140.

[7]*Zhenshchiny i deti v SSSR* (Moscow, 1963), p. 124.

TABLE 120. Women administrators and specialists employed in construction enterprises, by occupation, December 1, 1956.[a]

Occupations	Men and Women		Women		
	Number (thousands)	Percentage Distribution	Number (thousands)	Percentage Distribution	Percentage of Women
Heads of construction enterprises, chief engineers, and other leading specialists and their deputies...............	5.0	1.4	0.5	0.7	10
Heads of divisions, offices, and other structural subdivisions of construction enterprises and their deputies..............	25.0	7.6	3.5	4.8	14
Heads of subordinate (nonindependent) construction and construction assembly sections, job supervisors, heads of auxiliary production units and shops and their deputies............................	70.0	21.2	2.1	2.9	3
Heads of laboratories and norm (standard) setting and testing stations.............	1.3	0.4	0.8	1.1	60
Engineers without administrative functions..	42.6	12.9	13.2	18.2	31
Technicians, without administrative functions................................	21.8	6.6	9.6	13.2	44
Construction foremen...................	71.1	21.5	13.5	18.6	19
Expediters and dispatchers..............	1.0	0.3	0.3	0.4	30
Chief accountants and head bookkeepers...	28.8	8.7	11.8	16.2	41
Engineer-economists, economists, and planning specialists......................	11.2	3.4	7.5	10.3	67
Other unspecified construction personnel....	52.7	16.0	9.9	13.6	19
Total................................	330.5	100.0	72.7	100.0	22

[a]Calculated from *Zhenshchina v SSSR* (Moscow, 1960), p. 48. The source reports that women made up 1 per cent of the heads of construction enterprises, etc., but this would be inconsistent with the remainder of the table. Therefore, it is assumed that the figure should be 10 per cent.

per cent in the case of chief accountants and head bookkeepers.

Other "Productive" Fields. No detailed information is available about the role of women among the leading personnel of other "productive" sectors of the economy. From data presented in Table 118 we have seen that women accounted for 21 per cent of the administrators and specialists employed in transportation, 42 per cent in communications, and 46 per cent in trade and distribution. In each instance the proportion of women among the leading personnel is substantially less than among workers and employees as a whole. Thus, the progressively smaller role of women in the most responsible positions observed in other branches of the economy characterizes these as well. Even in those branches of communications and of trade and distribution where the proportion of women in the labor force is almost two thirds, women comprise less than half of the leading personnel.

WOMEN ADMINISTRATORS AND SPECIALISTS IN THE PROFESSIONS

Fields included in the so-called "nonproductive" sector of the economy are education and the arts, health, scientific research, and government. The leading personnel in these categories form the professional elite of the Soviet Union, and the role of women in these fields is, therefore, of unusual interest. It should be noted at the outset that their role is large. As we saw in Table 118, women make up 64 per cent of the leading personnel in this nonproductive sector of the economy, and it is here that three fourths of the women administrators and specialists are employed. However, the high percentage of women among administrators and specialists in the "nonproductive" sectors mentioned above should not be contrasted with the lower percentage we have found among the "productive" sectors without some qualifications. As the following discussion will show, although the proportion of women among specialists in the "nonproductive" sector is high, the proportion among administrators differs little from that in the "productive" sectors of the economy.

Education and Cultural Services. Women play a very important role in education and culture, making up two thirds of the administrators and specialists employed in these fields on December 1, 1956 (see Table 118). In the cultural field women made up 70 per cent of the leading personnel providing cultural services, 33 per cent of those in the entertainment field, and 32 per cent of those engaged in editorial work at publishing houses, newspapers, magazines, and the like. In the educational field the role of women is negatively correlated with the educational level at which the women are employed. In preschool and children's institutions the share of women is 91 per cent. In general education schools it declines to 71 per cent, and in institutions providing semiprofessional and professional training it is reduced further to 39 per cent.

Since the bulk of employment is in general education schools where the proportion of women is high, more than three fourths of the women administrators and teachers were employed in these schools on December 1,

1956. In 1955 a little less than a quarter of these women had a higher education and a little more than a quarter were graduates of two-year teachers' institutions.[8] Therefore, a large number of teachers, primarily those teaching the lower grades, did not have special teacher training.

The percentages of women administrators and teachers in elementary and secondary schools for selected years are shown in Table 121. A substantial increase in the percentage of women in all positions can be observed between the prewar and postwar period. Even more striking is the persistent decrease in the percentage of women school directors as one moves upward from primary schools (72 per cent in 1964–65) to seven- and eight-year schools (24 per cent) and to secondary schools (20 per cent). A similar but less marked decrease in the proportion of women teachers may be observed as one moves upward through the grades from grades 1 to 4

---

[8]Nicholas DeWitt, *Education and Professional Employment in the U.S.S.R.* (Washington, D.C., 1961), p. 523. It is assumed that the percentages he gives for all primary and secondary school-teachers and administrators apply also to women. In fact, the percentage of women with special training is probably smaller than for men.

TABLE 121. Percentage of women administrators and teachers in elementary and secondary schools of the Ministry of Education and Ministry of Transportation, 1940–41, 1950–51, 1955–56, 1958–64.[a]

Positions	Beginning of School Year									
	1940–41	1950–51	1955–56	1958–59	1959–60	1960–61	1961–62	1962–63	1963–64	1964–65
Percentage of women teachers (including school directors)	60	70	70	70	70	70	70	69	69	69
Primary school directors	47	61	69	69	69	69	71	71	72	72
7-yr. and 8-yr. school directors	12	20	22	22	23	23	24	24	24	24
Secondary school directors	13	21	21	20	20	20	20	20	20	20
Heads of 7-yr. and 8-yr. school training units	32	47	50	53	54	54	56	57	56	57
Heads of secondary school training units	30	51	52	52	53	53	49	46	44	44
Teachers (excluding school directors)	66	75	–	74	–	73	73	–	–	–
Grades 1–4	–	84	86	87	88	87	87	87	87	87
Grades 5–7	–	74	74	75	76	76	76	76	75	76
Grades 8–11	–	67	70	68	67	67	68	67	67	68
Music, singing, physical culture, and work teachers	17	19	30	26	27	26	27	27	28	28

[a]Based on *Zhenshchiny i deti v SSSR* (Moscow, 1963), p. 127; *Narodnoe khoziaistvo SSSR v 1956 godu* (Moscow, 1957), p. 247; *Narodnoe khoziaistvo SSSR v 1959 godu* (Moscow, 1960), p. 735; *Narodnoe khoziaistvo SSSR v 1962 godu* (Moscow, 1963), p. 557; *Narodnoe khoziaistvo SSSR v 1963 godu* (Moscow, 1965), p. 561; and *Narodnoe khoziaistvo SSSR v 1964 godu* (Moscow, 1965), p. 673.

(87 per cent in 1964–65) to grades 5 to 7 (76 per cent) to grades 8 to 11 (68 per cent).

Substantial variations in the percentage of women administrators and teachers in elementary and secondary schools exist among the various republics. In recent years the percentages have been above the national average in the R.S.F.S.R. and the Baltic republics and consistently and substantially below it in the Central Asian republics and Azerbaidzhan. The lowest percentage has been in the Tadzhik Republic, where only a third of the administrators and teachers of elementary and secondary schools were women in 1961. Women made up less than half such personnel in the Turkmen, Uzbek, and Azerbaidzhan republics (see Table 122). This is the same pattern of backwardness already noted where the influence of Moslem customs persists. Although little improvement has been apparent in these republics in the past five years, the gains made since the prewar period are significant. The share of women among administrators and teachers of elementary and secondary schools was only 18 per cent in the Turkmen, 21 per cent in the Tadzhik, and 36 per cent

in the Kirgiz republic. Present levels are substantially above these.[9]

The proportion of women among administrators, teachers, and other specialists in specialized secondary schools and higher educational institutions is substantially less than at the primary and secondary level. At the end of 1956 women comprised 39 per cent of this group of leading personnel (see Table 123). Three fifths of this 39 per cent were academic personnel in the ranks engaged primarily in teaching—heads of departments, professors, associate professors, instructors, and assistants. Among this academic group as a whole the proportion of women was 41 per cent. The share of women among leading personnel in laboratory and library work was higher,

---

[9] *Zhenshchina v Turkmenskoi SSR* (Ashkhabad, 1960), p. 49; *Zhenshchina v Tadzhikskoi SSR* (Stalinabad, 1960), p. 36; and *Zhenshchina v Kirgizskoi SSR* (Frunze, 1960), p. 48. In the latter two republics the share of women was 29 and 50 per cent, respectively, in the 1950–51 academic year, indicating that, as in the other republics, most of the increase in the share of women since the prewar period had occurred by 1950.

TABLE 122. Number and percentage of women administrators and teachers in elementary and secondary schools of the Ministry of Education, by republic, beginning of school years, 1958–59, 1960–61, 1961–62.[a]

Republic	1958–59		1960–61		1961–62	
	thousands	%	*thousands*	%	*thousands*	%
U.S.S.R.	1,189	70	1,263	69	1,343	70
R.S.F.S.R.	684	77	723	76	766	76
Ukrainian S.S.R.	234	71	248	70	268	70
Belorussian S.S.R.	56	69	58	68	60	68
Uzbek S.S.R.	31	41	34	41	37	40
Kazakh S.S.R.	47	60	54	62	60	62
Georgian S.S.R.	32	61	34	61	35	61
Azerbaidzhan S.S.R.	17	44	19	44	20	44
Lithuanian S.S.R.	17	73	18	73	18	73
Moldavian S.S.R.	14	62	16	63	17	63
Latvian S.S.R.	13	76	14	76	15	77
Kirgiz S.S.R.	11	53	12	54	12	53
Tadzhik S.S.R.	7	33	7	33	8	32
Armenian S.S.R.	10	53	11	54	12	55
Turkmen S.S.R.	5	38	6	39	6	39
Estonian S.S.R.	8	81	9	79	9	79

[a]Based on *Zhenshchina v SSSR* (Moscow, 1960), p. 52; *Zhenshchiny i deti v SSSR* (Moscow, 1961), p. 150; and *Zhenshchiny i deti v SSSR* (Moscow, 1963), p. 128.

TABLE 123. Women administrators, teachers, and other specialists in educational institutions training specialized manpower, by occupation, December 1, 1956.[a]

Occupations	Men and Women		Women		
	Number (thousands)	Percentage Distribution	Number (thousands)	Percentage Distribution	Percentage of Women
Directors, rectors, and heads of institutions; heads of study or research subdivisions, deans of faculties, heads of branches, and their deputies...........	32.7	8.4	4.9	3.2	15
Heads of departments, professors, associate professors, instructors, and assistants.	220.0	56.3	90.2	59.2	41
Heads of laboratories, study offices, and libraries.............................	10.8	2.8	7.0	4.6	65
Senior laboratory personnel and laboratory technicians......................	47.9	12.2	32.1	21.0	67
Other unspecified instructional and academic personnel......................	79.6	20.3	18.3	12.0	23
Total.................................	391.0	100.0	152.5	100.0	39

[a]Calculated from *Zhenshchina v SSSR* (Moscow, 1960), p. 53.

amounting to approximately two thirds. However, among heads of institutions, deans, and other top academic administrators it was only 15 per cent.

If one considers only the data for women in higher educational institutions, a similar picture emerges, except that the reduction in the proportion of women in the higher academic ranks is even sharper. Examination of Table 124 reveals that in 1960 only 5.3 per cent of the directors and their academic deputies were women. Among deans the proportion was 8.9 per cent. Among heads of departments the share rose to 12.3 per cent, and at the level of associate professor the proportion had doubled to 24.4 per cent.

If we compare the percentage distribution of women among the academic positions and ranks with the percentage distribution of men, we find the probability that a woman will be a director or deputy director of a higher educational institution to be one tenth that for a man. The probability that she will be a dean is less than a fifth, and that she will be the

TABLE 124. Women scientific workers in higher educational institutions, 1950, 1955, and 1960.[a]

Position	Oct. 1, 1950			Oct. 1, 1955			Oct. 1, 1960		
	Number of Women	Percentage Distribution	Percentage of Women	Number of Women	Percentage Distribution	Percentage of Women	Number of Women	Percentage Distribution	Percentage of Women
Directors, deputy directors for training and scientific work........	95	0.3	4.8	96	0.2	5.1	109	0.2	5.3
Deans.................	142	0.5	6.6	193	0.5	8.5	256	0.5	8.9
Heads of departments...	1,550	5.5	11.3	1,983	5.0	12.9	2,083	4.2	12.3
Professors............	110	0.4	8.5	125	0.3	8.7	164	0.3	10.6
Associate professors.....	2,464	8.7	21.3	4,367	11.1	22.9	6,342	12.8	24.4
Other positions........	23,951	84.6	42.9	32,632	82.9	41.3	40,448	82.0	41.4
Total.................	28,312	100.0	32.7	39,396	100.0	33.1	49,402	100.0	33.6

[a]Based on *Vysshee obrazovanie v SSSR* (Moscow, 1961), pp. 208, 212.

head of the department, about three tenths.[10]

The proportion of women among the academic personnel of higher educational institutions varies widely from field to field. No current data are available, but the distribution in 1947 is shown in Figure 27. The general pat-

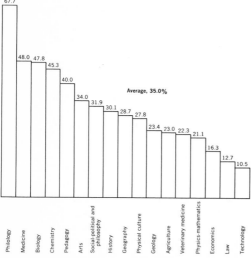

FIG. 27. Percentage of women among the teaching staffs of higher educational institutions, by field, 1947. Based on Sinetskii, *op. cit.*, pp. 138–39. The fields are as shown in Sinetskii. Philology includes literature and foreign languages.

tern revealed in the diagram probably persists to the present. It shows that among the various disciplines in higher educational institutions women predominate in one field— philology (67.7 per cent). In four other fields—medicine (48.0 per cent), biology (47.8 per cent), chemistry (45.3 per cent) and pedagogy (40.0 per cent)—they make up between 40 and 50 per cent of the academic personnel. The smallest proportion of women —approximately 10 to 20 per cent—is to be

found in technology (10.5 per cent), law (12.7 per cent), economics (16.3 per cent), and the combined field of physics and mathematics (21.1 per cent).[11] Clearly, the proportion of women in the sciences, particularly life sciences, is impressively large. But even in the physical sciences and technology the proportion of women is large in comparison with that in other countries.

Medicine and Health. The percentage of women physicians increased from 10 per cent in 1913 to 76 per cent in 1950—a proportion unequaled anywhere else in the world. The percentage of women among administrators and specialists in medicine and health is even higher—88 per cent at the end of 1956. Enrollment trends indicate, however, that the proportion of women physicians will decline in the future as the government pursues policies aimed at promoting a more equal balance between the sexes.

After the Revolution women flocked into the medical schools: by 1928 the number of women physicians was 15 times the pre-World War I level, and women comprised 45 per cent of the total (see Table 125). By 1940 the number had tripled again, and the proportion of women had increased to 60 per cent. Graduations of women physicians during the 1940's more than doubled the total by 1950. Since then the share of women has remained in the neighborhood of 75 per cent.

In contrast to some of the other professions, the regional distribution of women physicians is relatively uniform. In 1961 women made up 74 per cent of all physicians in the Soviet Union. The percentage ranged from a high of 78 per cent in the R.S.F.S.R. to a low of 55 per cent in the Turkmen S.S.R., but, excluding the latter republic, the lowest percentage of women physicians was 62 per cent in the Tadzhik and Moldavian republics (see Table 126). Other republics in which Moslem traditions persist also show relatively low percentages of women physicians.

---

[10]The percentage distribution of men among the various positions and ranks was calculated from *Vysshee obrazovanie v SSSR* (Moscow, 1961), pp. 209 and 212. Of the males, 1.9 per cent were heads of higher educational institutions or their deputies, 2.7 per cent were deans, and 15.2 per cent were heads of departments in 1960.

[11]A. Ia. Sinetskii, *Professorsko-prepodavatel'skie kadry vysshei shkoly SSSR* (Moscow, 1950), pp. 138–39.

Campus Bookstore

672 - 7360

900 Riverside Drive
St. Lambert, Quebec
J4P 3P2

HOURS:

September - May
(excluding holidays)
Monday   -   Friday
9:00 a.m. -   12 noon
1:30 p.m. -   3:30 p.m.

Summer School -as posted

Closed on Saturdays &
    Sundays

REFUND POLICY

TEXTBOOKS
A full refund will be given
up to 3 weeks after classes
start, if the following
conditions are met:

- have withdrawn from a
  course (Academic note
  must be presented)
- returns must be
  accompanied by a sales
  receipt
- text is in mint condition

SUPPLIES & SUNDRIES

No returns. All sales final

DEFECTIVE MERCHANDISE

Returnable for refund or
exchange

There will be no exceptions
to the above policy.

The Campus Bookmark

The distribution and proportion of women among the different levels of the medical and health profession may be seen in Table 127, which shows the number and proportion of women administrators and specialists in medi-

TABLE 125. Number of physicians, women physicians, and percentage of women, selected years, 1913–63.[a]

End of Year	Total (thousands)	Women (thousands)	Percentage of Women
1913[b].......	23.2	2.3	10
1913[c].......	19.8	1.9	10
1928........	63.2	28.4	45
1930........	(67.8)	30.5	45
1934........	(85.7)	42.0	49
1935........	(90.2)	42.4	47
1937........	103.7	52.8	51
1940........	141.8	85.4	60
1950........	247.3	189.0	76
1955........	310.2	234.3	76
1956........	329.4	246.7	75
1957........	346.0	260.2	75
1958........	361.5	272.3	75
1959........	379.5	286.1	75
1960........	401.6	302.1	75
1961........	425.7	315.9	74
1962........	445.1	333.1	75
1963........	466.0	348.6	75

[a]Excluding physicians in the military service and all dentists. Calculated from *Zhenshchiny i deti v SSSR, statisticheskii sbornik* (Moscow, 1963), p. 125; *Narodnoe khoziaistvo SSSR v 1962 godu, statisticheskii ezhegodnik* (Moscow, 1963), p. 617; *Zhenshchina v SSSR* (Moscow, 1937), p. 110; and *Vestnik statistiki*, No. 2 (1964), 93.
[b]Current boundaries.
[c]Revised boundaries (until Sept. 17, 1939).

cal and health-care establishments on December 1, 1956. Among this broad group of physicians, dentists, medics (*feldshers*), midwives, technicians, and others, the share of women was 88 per cent. The largest occupational group—a semiprofessional one—consists of medics, midwives, and medical nurses. Women in this group numbered 761,000, comprising 70 per cent of the women in the medical field and 93 per cent of all persons employed as semiprofessionals in medicine. Women physicians without administrative functions make up the second largest group, numbering 156,000 at the end of 1956. Their share in the total of this group was 82 per cent. Among laboratory technicians, another semiprofessional group, the share of women was 94 per cent.

Among administrative personnel the proportion of women declines. Among the heads of divisions in medical establishments and of offices and laboratory chiefs the share was 73 per cent, and among heads of medical establishments, deputy chiefs, and head physicians 57 per cent. Thus, in a field dominated by women the percentage of the administrative posts held by women is substantially below their proportionate share, but of course much higher than in other areas. It is doubtful that

TABLE 126. Number of physicians, women physicians, and percentage of women, by republic, 1958, 1959, 1960, and 1961.[a]

Republic	Total (thousands)				Women (thousands)				Percentage of Women			
	1958	1959	1960	1961	1958	1959	1960	1961	1958	1959	1960	1961
U.S.S.R...............	361.5	379.5	401.6	425.7	272.3	286.1	302.1	315.9	75	75	75	74
R.S.F.S.R..............	−	220.8	233.1	246.6	165.3	174.3	184.2	193.6	78	79	79	78
Ukrainian S.S.R.........	−	75.5	80.1	84.6	52.7	55.1	58.6	59.1	73	73	73	70
Belorussian S.S.R.......	−	10.8	11.8	12.6	7.1	7.5	8.2	8.6	71	69	69	68
Uzbek S.S.R............	−	10.6	11.3	12.6	6.7	6.8	7.3	8.0	68	64	65	64
Kazakh S.S.R...........	−	12.5	13.4	14.7	8.7	9.8	9.7	10.8	76	78	72	74
Georgian S.S.R.........	−	13.0	13.5	13.7	8.2	8.1	8.5	8.7	64	62	63	64
Azerbaidzhan S.S.R......	−	8.4	8.7	9.1	5.3	5.6	5.8	6.1	67	67	66	67
Lithuanian S.S.R........	−	4.6	4.8	5.0	3.0	3.1	3.3	3.6	70	68	69	71
Moldavian S.S.R........	−	3.8	4.1	4.5	2.3	2.4	2.5	2.8	66	62	62	62
Latvian S.S.R...........	−	5.1	5.4	5.7	3.6	3.8	3.9	4.0	74	74	72	69
Kirgiz S.S.R...........	−	2.8	3.2	3.4	1.7	1.9	2.0	2.2	63	67	63	64
Tadzhik S.S.R..........	−	2.3	2.4	2.6	1.4	1.4	1.5	1.6	67	63	63	62
Armenian S.S.R........	−	4.0	4.2	4.6	2.9	2.8	3.0	3.0	75	70	70	66
Turkmen S.S.R.........	−	2.6	2.8	3.0	1.6	1.6	1.7	1.7	60	59	59	55
Estonian S.S.R.........	−	2.7	2.8	3.0	1.8	1.9	1.9	2.1	70	70	69	71

[a]Based on *Zhenshchina v SSSR* (Moscow, 1960), p. 62; *Zhenshchiny i deti v SSSR* (Moscow, 1961), p. 148; *Zhenshchiny i deti v SSSR* (Moscow, 1963), p. 126; and *Zdravookhranenie v SSSR* (Moscow, 1960), p. 79.

TABLE 127. Women administrators and specialists in medical and health-care establishments, by occupation, December 1, 1956.[a]

Occupations	Men and Women		Women		
	Number (thousands)	Percentage Distribution	Number (thousands)	Percentage Distribution	Percentage of Women
Heads of medical establishments, chief physicians, and deputy chiefs	44.4	3.6	25.3	2.3	57
Heads of divisions in medical establishments and of offices and laboratory chiefs	44.2	3.5	32.3	33.0	73
Physicians of all specialties (except dentists) who are not heads of divisions above or chief physicians	190.1	15.5	155.9	14.4	82
Dentists	21.8	1.8	18.1	1.7	83
Laboratory technicians	44.6	3.6	41.9	3.8	94
Medics (*feldshers*), midwives, and medical nurses	818.6	66.4	761.3	70.2	93
Heads of medical aid stations attached to enterprises	26.4	2.1	20.3	1.9	77
Heads of apothecaries (prescription druggists)	2.3	0.2	1.8	0.2	80
Pharmacists and pharmaceutical chemists	5.8	0.5	5.3	0.5	92
Other unspecified medical personnel	34.2	2.8	42.6	2.0	65
Total	1,232.4	100.0	1,084.5	100.0	88

[a]Calculated from *Zhenshchina v SSSR* (Moscow, 1960), p. 50.

discrimination accounts significantly for the smaller share of women in the top echelons. As Mark Field has remarked in his study of the medical profession, "Women often are not able to devote themselves fully to a career and have a smaller chance to rise in the medical hierarchy than their male colleagues."[12] A survey of physicians referred to in the journal of the U.S.S.R. Ministry of Health during several months of the postwar period led Field to the following conclusions:

Among physicians holding high rank, four out of five are men, when in the profession at large four out of five physicians are women. Among male physicians, eight out of ten hold a high rank, but among women only half that number hold such a rank. By chance alone, the possibility for a woman doctor to rise in the medical ladder appears to be somewhat poorer than that of her male colleague, and her chances of being rated as competent as a man seem to be correspondingly small. It was also my impression, when I was in the Soviet Union, that most of the high administrative and clinical posts were held by men

rather than by women, with the notable exception of the Minister of Health of the U.S.S.R.[13]

Based on the data in Table 127, the probability that a woman physician or dentist will be the head of a medical establishment, a chief physician, or a deputy is about one in ten, whereas the probability that a male physician would occupy such a position is almost three in ten. The probability that a woman will hold a position in the next echelon is approximately one in seven, while for a man it is a little better than one in six. Thus, even in the Soviet Union where the situation is much more favorable to a woman physician than in any other part of the world, a woman physician faces more obstacles than a man in the pursuit of high position.

Research, Development, and Design. Many women administrators and specialists are employed in research, development, and design establishments. Altogether, 261,000 women were employed in research institutes, 73,000 in project-making institutes, 35,000 in design

[12]Mark G. Field, *Doctor and Patient in Soviet Russia* (Cambridge, Mass., 1957), p. 193.

[13]*Ibid.*, p. 194.

institutes, and 26,000 in geological surveying activities (see Table 118).

The role of women among administrators and specialists in research institutes is shown by Table 128. According to DeWitt,[14] these institutes are divided into two categories: institutes under the auspices of the Soviet academies of science, conducting both theoretical and applied research, and those institutes sponsored by state committees or regional economic councils, dealing mainly with technological research on design and the testing of products and processes. The share of women among the leading personnel in all these institutes was 52 per cent. Their share among laboratory technicians and technicians without administrative responsibility was substantially higher (78 and 64 per cent), while their proportion among scientific research personnel was 50 per cent. The percentage of engineers in research institutes who were women (40 per cent) was above the average for all engineers employed in the economy (29 per cent), indicating a greater preference

for or suitability of women for engineering work in research institutes rather than in industrial or other enterprises.

Among the top echelon the percentage of women shrinks, although not so drastically as in several other fields which we have examined. In the more responsible administrative positions (the top four categories in Table 128) the proportion of women varies from one third to one sixth. The probability that a woman administrator or specialist employed in a research institution would be in the highest echelon is one fourth that for a man.[15]

In project-making and design organizations, which are more closely aligned to practical design and production problems, the over-all proportion of women among administrators and specialists is smaller than in research institutions, amounting to 41 per cent on December 1, 1956 (see Table 129). The pro-

---

[14]*Op. cit.,* pp. 525, 526.

[15]On the basis of the data in Table 128, it can be calculated that 6.3 per cent of the males are in the highest echelon, while only 1.2 per cent of the females have achieved this rank.

TABLE 128. Women administrators and specialists in research institutions, by occupation, December 1, 1956.[a]

Occupations	Men and Women		Women		
	Number (thousands)	Percentage Distribution	Number (thousands)	Percentage Distribution	Percentage of Women
Heads, directors, and deputies of research and research and development establishments, chairmen of research boards, and leading specialists............	8.8	3.5	1.4	1.2	16
Heads of structural subdivisions in research establishments and their deputies......................	20.5	8.4	4.3	3.4	21
Heads of branch divisions (affiliates) and their deputies.	1.5	0.6	0.5	0.3	34
Heads of experimental plants, testing enterprises, experimental establishments, their shops, shifts and units, and their deputies........................	3.3	1.3	0.5	0.3	15
Heads of research expeditions, surveying parties, and expedition teams, and their deputies..............	0.7	0.3	0.2	0.2	28
Research (academic) personnel (*nauchnye rabotniki*)....	58.2	23.7	29.1	22.8	50
Engineers without administrative duties.............	50.5	20.6	20.2	15.8	40
Technicians without administrative duties...........	45.2	18.4	28.9	22.6	64
Laboratory technicians............................	35.5	14.5	27.7	21.7	78
Chief accountants and head bookkeepers...........	4.6	1.9	2.8	2.2	61
Other leading research and administrative personnel, unspecified...................................	16.8	6.8	12.1	9.5	72
Total..	245.6	100.0	127.7	100.0	52

[a]Calculated from *Zhenshchina v SSSR* (Moscow, 1960), p. 54.

TABLE 129. Women administrators and specialists employed in project-making and design organizations, by occupation, December 1, 1956.[a]

Occupations	Men and Women		Women		
	Number (thousands)	Percentage Distribution	Number (thousands)	Percentage Distribution	Percentage of Women
Heads and deputy heads of project-making and design organizations, chief engineers, and other leading specialists..................................	18.8	7.2	1.5	1.4	8
Heads of divisions, sections, design teams, and other structural subdivisions of design and project-making organizations, and their deputies................	32.4	12.4	5.5	5.1	17
Engineers without administrative duties.............	115.5	44.2	46.2	43.1	40
Technicians without administrative duties...........	74.8	28.6	45.6	42.6	61
Chief accountants and head bookkeepers............	3.2	1.2	2.1	2.0	66
Engineer-economists, economists, and planning specialists.......................................	4.2	1.6	3.1	2.9	73
Other design and project-making personnel, unspecified...	12.3	4.8	3.1	2.9	25
Total...	261.2	100.0	107.1	100.0	41

[a]Calculated from *Zhenshchina v SSSR* (Moscow, 1960), p. 55.

portion of women among those occupying the most responsible jobs is also more restricted. The probability that a woman would be employed in the highest echelon is only one eighth that of a man.[16]

Research Workers in Scientific Research Institutions of All Types. An important category of specialists cuts across all the branches of the economy and professions we have been discussing. These are the scientific research workers (*nauchnye rabotniki*) who comprise the group of specialists, other than those employed in academic institutions, who are most directly involved in the Soviet Union's research effort. This group is divided among three main categories of scientific workers: scientific-administrative personnel, senior scientific workers (*starshie nauchnye sotrudniki*), and junior scientific workers (*mladshie nauchnye sotrudniki*). In Table 130 we find that the proportion of the first group who are women has been in the neighborhood of 20 per cent in the past decade. Among senior scientific workers the propor-

[16]On the basis of the data in Table 129, it can be calculated that 11.2 per cent of the males are in the higher echelons, while only 1.4 per cent of the females have achieved this rank.

tion has been more than a third; among the lower ranks, more than one half. Over the past decade the proportion of women in each category has declined slightly, but remains at an impressive level.

There is, however, the same tendency which we have observed in other fields for women to occupy a progressively smaller role in the more responsible positions. If one considers the probability of a woman scientific worker's reaching the top echelon of scientific-administrative personnel, one finds that in 1960 it was one in ten while for a man it was a little better than one in four. Thus, the prospects for a man were almost three times better than for a woman. Although there is no assurance that probabilities based on past achievement patterns accurately reflect the prospects of a girl's entering scientific research work today, the slight downward trend in the percentage of women in the highest echelon is not encouraging. At the same time, the prospects of a Soviet woman's reaching the prestige position of senior scientific worker are immeasurably better than in other societies, including those most advanced economically and socially.

The rapid increase in the absolute number of women scientific workers in research in-

TABLE 130. Women scientific workers in scientific researc h institutes, enterprises, and other organizations, 1950, 1955, and 1960.[a]

Place and Position	Oct. 1, 1950			Oct. 1, 1955			Oct. 1, 1960		
	Number of Women	Percent-age Dis-tribution	Percent-age of Women	Number of Women	Percent-age Dis-tribution	Percent-age of Women	Number of Women	Percent-age Dis-tribution	Percent-age of Women
Scientific research institutes									
Scientific-administrative personnel......	4,768	15.9	23.6	5,120	12.7	23.2	7,442	9.6	18.2
Senior scientific workers...........	6,047	20.3	37.2	7,955	19.7	36.1	13,516	17.4	35.3
Other positions.......	19,039	63.8	55.9	27,254	67.6	52.1	56,796	73.0	47.0
Total..............	29,854	100.0	42.4	40,329	100.0	41.8	77,754	100.0	38.9
Enterprises and other organizations									
Total..............	(833)	100.0	15.1	(2,865)	100.0	34.4	(1,574)	100.0	21.9

[a]Calculated from *Vysshee obrazovanie v SSSR* (Moscow, 1961), pp. 208, 212.

stitutes is also worthy of note. In the five years from 1950 to 1955 the number rose 35 per cent while from 1955 to 1960 the increase of 93 per cent represented a near doubling. The rapid increase during this period was primarily a consequence of the impressive growth of female enrollment in higher educational institutions between 1945 and 1955. Since 1955 the enrollment of females has leveled off, but the rate of increase of women scientific workers had not shown any tendency to decline up to 1964.[17]

WOMEN IN THE PARTY LEADERSHIP AND GOVERNMENT

Since the Communist Party's role is crucial in shaping and carrying out the social and economic policies of the Soviet Union, the part women play in the leadership of the Communist Party is a particularly significant index of the ultimate importance of women in the leadership of Soviet society. The role of women in the party throughout its history has been far smaller than their contribution generally to the social and economic life of the Soviet Union would warrant. Their influence

has been largely in the lower ranks of the party hierarchy rather than in the upper reaches, which have remained almost exclusively male.

During the 1920's the proportion of women in the party steadily increased, rising from 8.2 per cent in January, 1924, when special efforts to bring women into the party were initiated,[18] to 15.9 per cent in July, 1932. The proportion remained fairly constant during the 1930's, declining slightly to 14.9 per cent in 1941. During the war and immediately afterward, the role of women widened substantially, as positions formerly held by men devolved upon women. By January 1, 1945, the number of women had increased to 17.0 per cent of the party membership and by July 1, 1950 to 20.7 per cent.[19] The proportion of women remained at approximately one fifth through 1961.[20] More recent figures are not yet available.

---

[17]See Appendix VIII, Table 3, which gives figures for all women scientific workers at higher educational institutions and at research and other establishments.

[18]G. Gromova, "Sovetskie zhenshchiny v upravlenii gosudarstvom," *Sovety deputatov trudiashchikhsia*, No. 5 (Nov., 1957), 23.

[19]Merle Fainsod, *How Russia Is Ruled* (rev. ed.; Cambridge, Mass., 1963), pp. 254, 265, 271.

[20]*Ezhegodnik Bol'shoi Sovetskoi entsiklopedii, 1957* (Moscow, 1957), p. 9; *1960*, p. 11; and *1962*, p. 17; *Pravda* (Feb. 17, 1956, and Jan. 30, 1959); and *Sovetskaia Rossiia* (Oct. 21, 1961).

More important than the over-all percentage of women in the party is, of course, their role in higher party circles. As Table 131 indicates, the representation of women on the Central Committee of the party has been much smaller than in the party as a whole. A small increase above the infinitesimal levels of the 1920's and 1930's has occurred in the representation of women during the past twelve years—largely at the prompting of Khrushchev. It was also under Khrushchev that the first woman, Ekaterina Furtseva, was admitted to the Presidium. Nonetheless, in spite of these recent gains, women play an extremely limited role in the top party leadership.

TABLE 131. Number and percentage of women among the membership of the Central Committee of the Communist Party of the U.S.S.R.[a]

	1924	1934	1939	1941	1952	1956	1961
Number......	2	3	3	2	7	10	10
Percentage....	2.4	2.2	2.2	1.5	3.1	3.9	3.1

[a]This table is based on the following sources: for 1924, Institute Marksisma-Leninizma pri TsK KPSS, *Trinadtsatyi s"ezd RKP(b)—stenograficheskii otchet* (Moscow, 1963), pp. 711–12; for 1934, Vsesoiuznaia kommunisticheskaia partiia (bol'-shevikov), *XVII s"ezd Vsesoiuznoi kommunisticheskaia partii (b)—stenograficheskii otchet* (Moscow, 1934), pp. 680–81; for 1939–56, "Zhenshchiny sredi sovetskoi elity," *Sotsialisticheskii vestnik*, Sbornik No. 1 (April, 1964), p. 74; the percentage for 1956 has been corrected from 4.0 per cent; for 1961, *Pravda* (Nov. 1, 1961) and *Deputaty Verkhovnogo Soveta SSSR, shestoi sozyv* (Moscow, 1962).

The representation of women in high governmental posts is also disproportionately small. Nevertheless, compared with other countries, the role of Soviet women in government is impressive. In 1957, 103 women were among the members of the U.S.S.R. and Union republic governments. Four of these were vice-chairmen of Councils of Ministers, twenty-five were ministers, and seventy-four served as deputy ministers.[21] Among these women were Maria Kovrigina, at the time Minister of Health of the U.S.S.R.; Agrippina Krachun, formerly Minister of Education of

the Moldavian S.S.R. and then Vice-Chairman of the republic's Council of Ministers in charge of education, culture, and health; Nonna Muravyova, Minister of Social Security of the R.S.F.S.R.; Tatiana Zueva, Minister of Culture of the R.S.F.S.R.; Larissa Stepanian, Minister of Finance of the Armenian S.S.R.; Emiliia Veinberg, Minister of Justice of the Latvian S.S.R.; and Kurban-gozel Alieva, Minister of Light Industry of the Turkmen S.S.R.[22] More recently Ekaterina Furtseva has been Minister of Culture of the U.S.S.R. in addition to serving on the Presidium of the party.[23] As a rule, women are more likely to be found in ministerial posts in the Union republics, particularly in Transcaucasia and Central Asia, than they are in the U.S.S.R. Indeed, it would appear that a deliberate effort has been made to bring women into prominent positions in public life in the less developed republics. However, despite this effort, even here the over-all participation of women in the higher levels of government remains very small.[24]

CONCLUSIONS

Although the prospects for a woman entering and succeeding in a professional career in the Soviet Union appear to be much more favorable than in the United States or in other Western countries, the prospects for advancement are not equally favorable. The proportion of women in the administrative and professional jobs, although much higher now than before World War II, tends to decrease with each successive increase in rank, even in such fields as education and health, where the role of women is dominant. The same pattern holds in the fields of science and technology where women are less important. There appears to be an undeniable tendency

---

[21]"Meet Ten Women Ministers," *Soviet Woman*, No. 1 (Jan., 1957), 6. These figures do not include women in high office in the autonomous republics.

[22]*Ibid.*, pp. 6–7.

[23]At the present time she maintains only the ministerial post.

[24]Data on the proportion of women in the Supreme Soviet of the U.S.S.R. are not presented, although often stressed by the Soviets, because this body serves more ritual than real functions.

for female specialists in all fields to congregate in the lower and middle echelons. Perhaps the most striking instance of this is the small number of women among the party professionals, but it holds to a lesser degree in all other areas of activity.

To what extent the smaller proportion of women in the higher administrative and professional echelons may be due to innate rather than to socially or culturally determined factors is a question which cannot be answered easily. The Soviets do not appear to have done research on the subject. Psychological studies on the differences in intellectual capacity between the sexes would not be in keeping with existing policies and attitudes. Nor does research on the effect of various social or environmental factors on the achievement of women seem to have been undertaken. Nevertheless, the question of the productivity of women and of the factors which affect it merits the investigation and discussion which will be undertaken in the next chapter. Such an analysis is essential if we are to gain insight into how successfully the Soviets are utilizing their professional women. If they are as competent and as productive as men, yet are not employed in positions commensurate with their capacities, wasteful use is being made of them. If, on the other hand, their competence or productivity is less, there is an economic rationale for the employment of a smaller proportion of women in the higher ranks.

chapter
12

ACHIEVEMENTS IN SCIENCE AND TECHNOLOGY

DESPITE THE GAPS in the record of female achievement which were apparent in the preceding chapter, the quantitative importance of women as a manpower resource in the professions, particularly in science and technology, is clear. What is less clear—but no less important—is the achievement of Soviet professional women compared with that of men holding the same or comparable professional rank. This aspect of the contribution of Soviet women can be determined in a number of ways: on the basis of such indices as honors bestowed and other extraordinary forms of recognition, bibliographic analyses of the contribution of women to scholarly research, and occupancy of positions that give scope for unusual abilities and influence. Less susceptible of measurement are the extent to which women are indispensable in given professions, either because of their numerical representation or of some quality they bring to their work, the influence they have on trends and developments within each profession and society at large, and the attitudes which promote or restrict the potential contribution of professional women.

The discussion which follows will be limited to an assessment of the first, and more easily measurable, type of achievement. It will not reflect the intellectual achievements which may have gone unrecognized, but will indicate the evaluation placed on achievement by the Soviet system itself.

WOMEN IN THE ACADEMIES OF SCIENCES

One of the principal forms of recognition for outstanding achievement in scientific, engineering, and scholarly fields in the Soviet Union is election to one of the academies of sciences and appointment to key posts within the academies and their institutes. The number of women so recognized will give some indication of how far women scientists can rise in these areas of intellectual and professional activity.

The Academy of Sciences of the U.S.S.R. occupies a special position in Soviet scientific research. In a hierarchical and planned society it stands at the apex of the entire scientific effort, and the academicians and corresponding members of the Academy form the elite "general staff" of the army of scientific workers. Somewhat below the Academy of Sciences of the U.S.S.R., but with some overlapping of personnel, are the academies of the Union republics and specialized academies, such as the Academy of Medical Sciences and the Academy of Social Sciences. Closely related to them in function and status are the research-oriented higher educational institutions, such as Leningrad State University and Bauman Higher Technical School, where many academicians and corresponding members may be found on the staffs. The majority of academicians and corresponding members are also professors and over 100 of them teach in Moscow and Leningrad higher educational institutions on a full- or part-time basis.[1]

Within the interlocking directorate of Soviet science there is a complex hierarchy. The status of each person is determined by a combination of the three interrelated systems of ranks in the academies. First, there are the scientific titles: academician, corresponding member, senior research worker, junior research worker, and assistant. Second, there are administrative ranks. The highest position is that of president of the Academy of Sciences of the U.S.S.R. Below him are the four vice-presidents, the chief scientific secretary, and the heads of the fifteen departments into which the Academy has been recently divided.[2] These, plus a dozen other elected members, make up the presidium of the Academy, the body in which the general assembly of the Academy vests its authority between meetings. Below this top policy-making group come the various departments, councils, and other agencies of the Academy. Within each department is a small replica, with slight variations, of the hierarchy of the Academy. The heads of the departments (academician-secretaries) and the governing bureau represent the top policy-making group, while the principal operating units are the research institutes and laboratories. In addition, most departments have a number of independent commissions examining special problems. The directors of the research institutes and laboratories and the chairmen of the various commissions together make up the lower administrative rank.

In general, academicians have greater status than corresponding members of the Academy, but this is not always true. Among both groups, administrative position and scientific rank are critical in determining a person's weight in scientific affairs. Many academicians lack administrative functions and some have, in effect, been shunted to the side lines for reasons of age, health, or ideology. Active corresponding members carry much more weight than the academicians who have been bypassed. The determinants of rank in descending order among the top echelon of the Academy have been summarized by Alexander Vucinich as follows:

(1) Those who hold the administrative positions which by law or tradition are a monopoly of the academicians. Here belongs the top administrative level of the Academy, including the academicians-secretaries of the eight [now fifteen] departments and the chairmen of the various councils.
(2) Those who hold the administrative positions which by law or tradition are a monopoly of both academicians and corresponding members. Here belong the deputy department heads and chairmen of the larger commissions.
(3) Those who hold positions that are open not only to the corresponding members but also to senior research associates with doctorates. Here belong the directors and deputy directors of institutes, the chairmen of small commissions, the heads of sections, and the members of editorial boards.
(4) Those who have no administrative responsibility; . . . most of these are academicians in title alone. The most unenviable position is held by the victims of ideological warfare, the champion of ideas which have been found incompatible with the official thought currents.[3]

The full and corresponding members of the academies of sciences of the Union republics occupy a *de facto* subordinate position to the

---

[1] Alexander Vucinich, *The Soviet Academy of Sciences* (Stanford, 1956), p. 94.

[2] The divisions include the following: mathematics; general and applied physics; nuclear physics; physical-technical problems of energetics; earth sciences; mechanics and control processes; general and technical chemistry; physical chemistry and the technology of inorganic materials; biochemistry, biophysics, and the chemistry of physiologically active compounds; physiology; general biology; history; philosophy and law; economics; and literature and language. For a description of the current organization of the Academy, see *Pravda* (July 5, 1963); translated in *The Current Digest of the Soviet Press* (July 31, 1963), pp. 19–20.

[3] Vucinich, *op. cit.*, p. 94.

members of the U.S.S.R. Academy. Some full members of republican academies are also corresponding members of the U.S.S.R. Academy, but there can be no doubt that the latter carry more weight and prestige in Soviet science than do the members of republic academies. As Vucinich points out, many more promotions to full membership in the U.S.S.R. Academy come from among the corresponding members of the U.S.S.R. Academy than from among the full members of the republican academies.

Although the most outstanding scientists usually have had sufficient executive talent to hold high administrative posts, it cannot be said that the highest-ranking administrators in the academies have also been the most outstanding scholars. Despite the emphasis on scholarly distinction in the selection of members, scientific "politicians" of mediocre caliber, and even scientists of dubious reputation, such as Lysenko, have gained admission to the Academy and occasionally wielded great power. Conversely, particularly during the Stalin era, scientists of great capacity and talent but of an ideological persuasion unacceptable to the regime have been destroyed or deprived of the means and authority to carry out their work effectively. Allowing for these considerations, it can still be said that the U.S.S.R. and republican academies represent fairly accurately the elite of Soviet science, and the position of a scientist within an academy reflects to a considerable degree his, or her, status as a productive contributor to the advancement of science.

Up to the present time, no woman has ever served as president, vice-president, chief scientific secretary, or member of the presidium of the Academy of Sciences of the U.S.S.R. Nor has any woman headed one of the fifteen departments into which the Academy is divided or been one of the deputy department secretaries or even a member of a departmental bureau. Thus, no woman has even figured among the most powerful policy makers and administrators of Soviet science.

A small number of women have been elected full or corresponding members of the Academy. At the present time there are three academicians: Lena Shtern, a physiologist (born 1878, elected 1939); Melitsia Nechkina, a historian and archeologist (born 1901, elected 1958); and Pelagair Kochina, a specialist in hydromechanics and the theory of filtration (born 1899, elected 1958). Lena Shtern, now quite old, seems to have passed into academic oblivion, since she is seldom mentioned outside official listings. According to Vucinich, she has been officially "forgotten" along with a dozen other members of the Academy, and no reference to her contributions is ever made.[4] Galkin also omits her in his discussion of leading women scientists, but mentions the other two.[5]

Among the corresponding members of the Academy there were eight women in 1960: Ekaterina Blinova, a geophysicist (born 1903, elected 1953); Aleksandra Novoselova, a general and inorganic chemist (born 1900, elected 1953); Rakhil Freidlina, an organic chemist (born 1906, elected 1958); Nina Pigulevskaia, an Oriental and Byzantine historian (born 1894, elected 1946); Kamila Trever, an art historian (born 1892, elected 1943); Revekka Levina, an economist (born 1899, elected 1939); Maria Smit-Fal'kner, an economist (born 1878, elected 1939); and Varvara Adrainova-Perets, an authority on Russian literature (born 1886, elected 1943). Several of these, such as the two women economists, are seldom heard of, never publish, and appear to be completely outside the main stream of economics at the present time.

Prior to 1939, when Lena Shtern was elected, there were no women academicians.[6] Although there had been two women corresponding members in 1925, they had vanished by 1939. In 1940 the proportion of women academicians was 0.8 per cent, and the proportion of women corresponding members was 2.1 per cent. Since 1940 only a slight in-

---

[4] *Ibid.*, p. 92.

[5] K. Galkin, *The Training of Scientists in the Soviet Union* (Moscow, 1959), pp. 125–26.

[6] Akademiia nauk SSSR, *Spravochnik kalendar' na 1940 god* (Moscow, Leningrad, 1940).

crease has occurred. At present 2 per cent of the academicians and 2.6 per cent of the corresponding members are women, and they are among the least influential members, judging by the infrequent reports of their scientific activities and the small role they play in the intermediate and higher administrative levels of the Academy. No women were added on June 29, 1962, at the election of thirteen academicians and twenty-five corresponding members.[7]

On June 8 and 9, 1964, new nominations for election to membership in the Academy were made. Among the 112 persons proposed for election to full membership in the Academy was one woman, Nina Pigulevskaia, who was already a corresponding member of the Academy.[8] Of the 470 persons proposed for election to corresponding membership in the Academy, 16, or 3.4 per cent, were women.[9]

Of these sixteen women nominees none was among the twenty-eight elected to full membership in the Academy, and only one, Agniia Desnitskaia, a linguist, was among the fifty-one elected to corresponding membership. As a result, no improvement in the representation of women in the Academy occurred.[10]

If we turn to the fourteen republican academies, we find a slightly better representation of women. In 1962 there were nine full members and twenty corresponding members of these academies (2.1 and 4.3 per cent, respectively).[11] Two women representative of those elected to the republican academies are Lydia Lelin and Alma Tomingas. A doctor of chemistry, Lydia Lelin, was elected a full member of the Latvian Academy of Sciences in 1941. She has been head of a department at the

---

[7]*Pravda* (June 30, 1962).

[8]*Izvestiia* (June 8, 1964).

[9]*Ibid.* and *Izvestiia* (June 9, 1964). The nominees included Olga Aleksandrovna Ladyzhenskaia, professor and doctor of physical-mathematical sciences and head of a laboratory in the Leningrad branch of the Institute of Mathematics of the Academy of Sciences; Zinaida Vasil'evna Ershova, professor and doctor of technical science and head of a department of the Kurchatov Institute of Atomic Energy; Mariia Al'fredovna Glazovskaia, professor and doctor of geography and head of a department of Moscow State University; Olga Arsen'evna Oleinik, professor and doctor of physical-mathematical sciences at Moscow State University; Natalia Alekseevna Bakh, professor and doctor of chemical sciences and director of a laboratory of the Intsitute of Electro-Chemistry of the Academy of Sciences; Nina Petrovna Luzhnaia, professor and doctor of chemical sciences and director of a laboratory of the Kurnakov Institute of General and Inorganic Chemistry of the Academy of Sciences; Nailia Urzagulovna Bazanova, academician of the Kazakh Academy of Sciences, professor and doctor of biological sciences and director of a department of the Alma-Ata Zooveterinary Institute; Esfir' Borisovna Genkina, professor and doctor of history and senior research worker at the Institute of History of the Academy of Sciences; Aleksandra Dmitrievna Liublinskaia, professor and doctor of history and senior scientific worker at the Leningrad department of the In-

stitute of History of the U.S.S.R.; Sophia Aleksandrovna Yanovskaia, professor and doctor of physical-mathematical sciences at Moscow State University; Olimpiada Vasil'evna Kozlova, professor and doctor of economics and rector of the Moscow Engineering-Economics Institute; Agniia Vasil'evna Desnitskaia, professor and doctor of philology and deputy director of the Institute of Linguistics of the Academy of Sciences; Olga Ivanova Moskal'skaia, professor and doctor of philology at the Moscow Pedagogical Institute of Foreign Languages; Vera Ivanovna Tsintsius, professor and doctor of philology and senior research worker at the Leningrad department of the Institute of Languages of the Academy of Sciences; Ekaterina Aleksandrovna Radkevich, doctor of geology and director of the Far Eastern Geological Institute of the Far Eastern Department of the Siberian Department of the Academy of Sciences; and Kira Arked'evna Sokolevskaia, professor and doctor of biology and director of the Central Siberian Botanical Garden of the Siberian Department of the Academy of Sciences.

[10]*Vestnik Akademii nauk SSSR*, No. 8 (Aug., 1964), 8–11.

[11]Akademiia nauk SSSR, *Akademii nauk soiuznikh respublik—spravochnik na 1962 g.* (Moscow, 1962). Some discrepancies in detail have been noted between the data derived from an examination of this volume and the publication *Prominent Personnel of the Academies of Sciences of the USSR and Union Republics*, prepared by the Research Section of the Institute for the Study of the U.S.S.R., Munich, December, 1962, published in 1963. Such differences would not alter the percentages significantly.

Latvian State University since 1946 and has simultaneously directed the laboratory of physical chemistry at the Academy. She is the author of more than 200 scientific papers. Alma Tomingas, a doctor of pharmacology, was elected a full member of the Estonian Academy of Sciences in 1946 when she also was awarded the title of Merited Scientific Worker of Estonia. She is a professor and heads the department of pharmacology at Tartu University.[12] It should be noted that Varvara Adrainova-Perets, a specialist in the field of Russian literature, is a corresponding member of both the Ukrainian and the U.S.S.R. academies.

Women members of academies are not confined to the European part of the Soviet Union. In fact, they are very poorly represented in the academies of Moldavia, Belorussia, and the Baltic republics. In Transcaucasia and Central Asia, in contrast, their representation is slightly above average, suggesting that the election of women to the academies of sciences in these areas may have been encouraged by the central government, since we have already seen that the local cultural pattern militates against female intellectual achievement.[13]

Women are represented only to a limited extent at the intermediate administrative levels of the academies. Although the proportion of women among scientific workers of the various academies is close to 40 per cent, no woman served as a director of an institute of the Academy of Sciences of the U.S.S.R., and only five were deputy directors. There is no significant female representation in the administration of the U.S.S.R. Academy until we descend to the position of scientific secretary of an institute, where in 1960, 21 per cent of the occupants were women.[14]

In the 204 institutes and observatories of the academies of sciences of the Union republics, four directors were women, according to the handbook for 1957–58.[15] Only eight women served as deputy directors for scientific work, and none as deputy directors for administration. Since many institutes had more than one deputy director in addition to the deputy director for administration, women accounted for less than 4 per cent of the deputies concerned with scholarly work. Only at the level of scientific secretary did they account for a substantial share (23 per cent).[16]

No women served as chairmen of the fifty committees, councils, and commissions of the U.S.S.R. Academy in 1960. Two women served as deputy chairmen, but neither was a sole deputy chairman. Seven of the scientific secretaries were women, however.[17] Comparable data for the republic academies of sciences are lacking.

Among the departments of the Academy, the Department of Technical Sciences seems to be the unassailable domain of men, and women play no role in it. There is token representation of women among the other departments, with some concentration in the Departments of Chemical and Biological Sciences, which, as has been noted previously, are the scientific disciplines in which the highest proportion of women is to be found.

The role of women in the specialized academies of sciences is also limited. In spite of the high proportion of women active in the field of medicine and medical research, in 1959 only 3 of the 91 academicians and 9 of the 135 corresponding members of the Academy of Medical Sciences of the U.S.S.R. were women.[18] The proportion of women had in-

---

[12]Galkin, *The Training of Scientists,* p. 129.

[13]In the Kirgiz Academy, for example, 2 of the 24 full members and 3 of the 20 corresponding members were women.

[14]Akademiia nauk SSSR, *Akademiia nauk SSSR—spravochnik na 1960 god* (Moscow, 1960), and *Zhenshchiny i deti v SSSR* (Moscow, 1961), p. 154.

[15]Akademiia nauk SSSR, *Akademiia nauk Soiuznykh Respublik—spravochnik na 1957–1958* (Moscow, 1957).

[16]*Ibid.*

[17]*Akademiia nauk SSSR—spravochnik na 1960 god* (Moscow, 1960).

[18]A list of the membership of the Academy of Medical Sciences for 1959 may be found in Galina V. Zarechnak, *Academy of Medical Sci-*

creased slightly by 1964, however, when 4 of the 104 academicians and 13 of the 142 corresponding members of the Academy were women.[19] In the Academy of Pedagogical Sciences of the R.S.F.S.R. in 1958, there were 2 women among the 30 academicians and 9 among the 66 corresponding members.[20] In 1958 only 2 of the 70 academicians and none of the 73 corresponding members of the Academy of Agricultural Sciences were women,[21] but by 1961 one woman had been elected a corresponding member.[22] In 1962 none of the 65 academicians and only 1 of the 107 corresponding members of the Academy of Construction and Architecture of the U.S.S.R. were women.[23] In the Academy of Arts of the U.S.S.R. there were no women among the 44 academicians but 5 among the 63 corresponding members in 1964.[24]

Few women can be found heading the research institutes of these specialized academies. Of the 28 institutes of the Academy of Medical Sciences, only 3 are known to be headed by women (1 undetermined). Of the 21 institutes of the Academy of Agricultural Sciences, none are known to be headed by women (2 undetermined), and of the 11 in-stitutes of the Academy of Construction and Architecture, none are headed by women.[25]

These data show clearly that women have not achieved high status in the Soviet scientific hierarchy despite the putative equality of the sexes and the large number of women who obtain scientific training in the U.S.S.R. During visits to the Soviet Union in 1962 and 1965 the author explored the hypothesis that lingering prejudice explains in part the small representation of women. None of the Soviet scientists approached on the subject felt prejudice was a factor, but few denied that political influence and personal contacts played a role in election to the academies. This was not to imply that the scientific qualifications of the members were not high, merely that many scientists outside the academies might be equally or better qualified. It was felt that male candidates for election were more likely to be personally acquainted with the electing academicians than women, with the result that men have a built-in advantage which is not the result of prejudice but has the same effect. The same principle would apply to appointments to top administrative posts. Even granting a degree of bias, the role of women in the upper echelons of the academies is so limited that one is forced to conclude that other factors must be much more important.[26]

One of the factors which should not be overlooked is that most academicians are mature scholars who obtained their higher education several decades ago when the proportion of women receiving postgraduate training was small. The average age of male academicians in 1960 was a little more than 64 years, while the average age of the three women academicians was 67; for corresponding members the averages were close to 58 and 59 years, respectively. The average age

---

ences of the USSR: History and Organization, 1944–1959 (Public Health Monograph, No. 63; Washington, D.C., 1960), pp. 44–48.

[19]Akademiia meditsinskikh nauk SSSR, *Spravochnik na 1964 god* (Moscow, 1964).

[20]Akademiia pedagogicheskikh nauk RSFSR, *Spravochnik na 1958 god* (Moscow, 1958).

[21]Vsesoiuznaia ordena Lenina Akademiia sel'-skokhoziaistvennykh nauk imeni V. I. Lenina, *Spravochnik* (Moscow, 1958).

[22]A list of the membership of the Academy of Agricultural Sciences may be found in *A Guide to the Soviet Academies* (May, 1961), pp. 72–78. Of the 63 academicians, the sex of 3 could not be determined, and of the 75 corresponding members, the sex of 23 could not be determined. These 26 had ambiguous name endings and could not be identified readily in other sources, such as *Who's Who in the USSR, 1960/1961*. Some of these may be women, but the probabilities appear to be low.

[23]Akademiia stroitel'stva i arkhitektury SSSR, *Spravochnik na 1962 god* (Moscow, 1962).

[24]Akademiia khudozhestv Soiuza SSR (Moscow, 1964).

---

[25]The sources are the same as cited above for the various specialized academies.

[26]A case can be made that, in view of the official position on the equality of men and women, the election of qualified women might be actively sought in order to avoid embarrassment at the discrepancy between high-principled policy and actual practice.

at which both men and women academicians were elected was 52 years; for male corresponding members it was close to 50 and for women close to 49 years.[27] As a result, these men and women who are members of the Academy received their education in the 1920's, when the percentage of women enrolled in higher educational institutions, particularly in the fields of science and technology, was much smaller than it is today. This fact alone accounts in part for the underrepresentation of women in the Academy. As the school years of the age group from which members are usually selected move into the 1940's and 1950's, when the proportion of women in higher educational institutions was several times higher than in the 1920's, some increase in the proportion of women in the Academy can be expected.

WOMEN LENIN PRIZE WINNERS

Another indicator of achievement in science and technology is the annual award of Lenin prizes in science, technology, and the arts. These prizes confer upon the recipients not only honor and prestige but also substantial financial rewards. Although awards in the social sciences and the arts are often made for polemical work which is of little real merit, the awards in the physical and natural sciences and technology, where ideology is less important, are made on more objective grounds. During the years 1957 through 1964 there were 57 awards in the sciences, 62 in technology, and 45 in the arts.[28] Awards in

the field of technology are almost invariably made to groups of persons, and this is also the usual pattern in the sciences. As a result, more than a hundred persons may be among the recipients of the science and technology prizes each year. In the arts, however, individual awards are usual.

In the eight-year period, nineteen women have been among the winners: Olga Bazkevskaia, member of the Atomic Energy Institute of the U.S.S.R. Academy of Sciences and one of twelve from the Institute, for research work on powerful impulse discharges in gas for obtaining high-pressure plasma; Elena Solinevich, doctor of medical sciences, for her work "Rikettsiae and Rickettsial Diseases," published in 1956; Valentina Mamontova, head of a laboratory at the Southeastern Agricultural Research Institute and one of a group of three, for the development of high-yield strains of winter and spring wheat and barley; Dina Gaba, a junior research worker, for assisting in the development of capillary methods of studying microorganisms; Valentina Nokitina, a junior scientific worker, for her work in a team of five who perfected an operation for restoring the hearing of victims of otosclerosis; Inna Kazanskaia, a laboratory head at the All-Union Research and Design Institute of Metallurgical Machine Building, for her work in a team of seven who developed a complex of mills for rolling graduated cylindrical sections; Varvara Saulina, head of a group of eight at the Tire Industry Research Institute, for working out the processes and industrial technology for the production of high-dispersal carbon black from liquid hydrocarbons; Krestina Ivasheva, one of a group of five engineers of the State Design Institute for Communal Economy, Roads, and Transportation, for the construction of a bridge across the Yenesei river at Krasnoiarsk; Mindanora Ivanova, deputy di-

---

[27] Akademiia nauk SSSR, *Akademiia nauk SSSR—spravochnik na 1960 god* (Moscow, 1960). A survey of seven republican academies, using data from the handbook, *Akademii nauk soiuznykh respublik—spravochnik na 1957–1958 gody,* indicates that members tend to be older and to have been elected at an older age in the Baltic republics and to be younger and to have been elected at a younger age in the Central Asian republics. The women members in the Central Asian republics tend to be younger both in present age and in age at election.

[28] *Pravda* and *Izvestiia,* various issues (1957–64). Award winners have been announced on or around the beginning of the third week in April

since 1957, when the awards in their present form were initiated. The awards were previously known as Stalin prizes and were discontinued after Stalin's death. Science includes the social sciences and the arts include literature.

rector of the Tatar Petroleum Institute and one of a group of twelve, for a new system of working oil deposits with intracontour flooding and the application of this method at the Romashkin oil deposit; Sofia Belkina and Tatiana Osyko, geologists, for their work in a team of thirteen who located the Borezova gas region; Tatiana Berends and Tamara Yefremova, senior engineers, and Agnia Tagayevskaia, a junior scientific worker, for their contribution in a team of seven at the Institute for Automatic Equipment and Remote Control to the development of a universal system of pneumatic components for industrial automation; Maria Bordonos, senior scientific research worker at the Ukrainian Academy of Agricultural Sciences, and Olga Kolomiets, manager of the sugar beet selection department of the Belaia Tsverkov Experimental Selection Station, both members of a group of six, for producing a new single-seed form of sugar beet; Vera Pashennaia, for her work as an actress; and Galina Ulanova and Maia Plisetskaia, each for her achievement in the ballet. Thus women accounted for 4 of the 141 individuals winning prizes in the sciences, for 12 of the 481 winners in technology, and for 3 of 51 in the arts.

The percentage of women nominated for these awards is also small. Of nearly 1,000 names submitted in 1962, in the first step of the nomination procedure, only 23, or 2.3 per cent, were women. In the second step in the selection process, the number was reduced to around 400, which included 23 women. Only 2 women remained among the 121 final award winners.[29]

WOMEN SCHOLARS AND SCIENTISTS IN HIGHER EDUCATIONAL INSTITUTIONS AND RESEARCH INSTITUTES

In higher educational institutions and in the research institutes of the academies there are many women scientists who make a significant

contribution by active work in scientific administration or scholarly research, either as an adjunct to their responsibilities as teachers in higher education or as a full-time occupation at a research institute or laboratory of the academies of sciences. In interpreting the statistics presented later in this chapter, it may be of some interest to gain an impression of the background of a few women representative of this professional group.

In 1947 women made up 5.7 per cent of the directors or deputy directors of higher educational institutions and 9.9 per cent of the heads of departments.[30] More recently, 11 women were directors or deputy directors for scientific or educational work at higher educational institutions, 46 were deans of faculties, and 505 were heads of departments.[31] For example, Olympiada V. Kozlova, the daughter of a Volga fisherman, has been director of the Moscow Engineering-Economic Institute since the beginning of the 1950's. She began work as a machinist, became interested in the economic side of factory operation, and decided to resume her schooling. After completing a postgraduate course at the Higher Pedagogical Institute, she received her candidate degree in economics in 1946 and more recently was awarded her doctorate. As director, she supervises the training of thousands of engineer-economists. She has also done much political work and has represented her country abroad.[32] Recently she was nominated for election as a corresponding member of the Academy of Sciences of the U.S.S.R.[33] A few women of the Central Asian nationality groups have become directors or rectors of higher educational institutions. The most noted of these, Bibi Pal'vanova, a Turkmen woman, is the only woman to head a Soviet university. In addition to being rector of the Ashkhabad State University, she

---

[29]*Pravda* (Dec. 19, 1961, Feb. 16, 1962, and April 22, 1962).

[30]A. Ia. Sinetskii, *Professorsko-prepodavatel'- skie kadry vysshei shkoly SSSR* (Moscow, 1950), p. 138.

[31]Galkin, *The Training of Scientists*, p. 126.

[32]*Ibid.;* also, a personal interview with Mrs. Kozlova.

[33]*Izvestiia* (June 9, 1964).

is a corresponding member of the Turkmen Academy of Sciences and professor and doctor of history. She has written on the emancipation of women in the Turkmen and Central Asian republics and has also played an active role i nthe emancipation process. M. A. Khadzhinova, an Uzbek woman, is director of the Tashkent Textile Institute. She received her candidate degree in 1946 and her doctorate in 1958 and has more than fifteen published scientific works to her credit.[34] Illustrative of the women who serve as deputy directors of higher educational institutions is T. V. Alekseeva, who has been working for many years as Deputy Director for Scientific Work and Education at the Siberian Motor and Highways Institute. K. M. Olshanova has been Deputy Director for Education at the Moscow Chemico-Technological Institute of the Meat Industry since 1953, while G. A. Osipova has been Deputy Director for Education at the Gorky Institute of Civil Engineering since 1954.[35]

In 1947, 35 per cent of the teaching staffs of all higher educational institutions were women.[36] Their share among professors was 4.7 per cent; *dotsents,* 16.4 per cent; and assistants, 42.8 per cent. Although the percentage of women remained small in the higher ranks, there was a sharp increase from the beginning of the First Five-Year Plan, when women made up only 1.1 per cent of the professors and 4.2 per cent of the *dotsents.*[37] During this period the proportion of women of all ranks almost doubled (see Table 132).

The proportion of women has varied considerably among the teaching staffs of different types of institutions. Table 132 shows that in 1927 the proportion of women was above average at institutions in the fields of the arts, education, and health and also at the universities. In 1947 the proportion remained above average at institutions in the fields of education and health while the proportion teaching

TABLE 132. Percentage of women among the teaching staffs of different types of higher educational institutions, 1927 and 1947.[a]

Type of Institution	Percentage of Women	
	1927	1947
Industrial and construction.....	5.8 }	24.1
Transport and communication..		21.0
Agricultural..................	16.5	28.4
Economic....................	4.5 }	28.1
Legal.......................		44.7
Education...................	23.0	39.0
Arts........................	20.6	32.7
Medical and health...........	25.1	47.8
University..................	26.3	–
Total......................	18.5	35.0

[a]Based on Sinetskii, *op. cit.,* pp. 61, 137.

in institutions devoted to the arts dropped below average and the proportion in legal institutions rose above average. The proportion of women on the staffs of universities was not given for 1947. Data for individual universities a decade later suggest that the role of women on the staffs of universities continues to be important and above the average for all higher educational institutions.

By the end of 1957 there were on the teaching staff of 2,224 at Moscow State University a total of 944 women. Of this number, 29 were professors, 146 were associate professors, and 24 were senior scientific workers. Of the 625 women among a teaching staff of 1,293 at the Leningrad State University, 12 were professors, 132 were associate professors, and 3 were senior scientific workers. At Saratov State University there were 197 women among the 381 staff members; 3 were professors, and 22 were associate professors. The 412 teachers at Tartu State University included 126 women, of whom 4 were professors and 9 were associate professors. At Kazan State University, 94 of the 332 on the teaching staff were women; 2 were professors and 23, associate professors.[38]

An examination of female representation on the staffs of the universities in Transcau-

---

[34]Galkin, *The Training of Scientists,* p. 126.
[35]*Ibid.*
[36]Sinetskii, *op. cit.,* p. 137.
[37]*Ibid.,* p. 140.

[38]Galkin, *The Training of Scientists,* pp. 127–28. For examples of women scientists at universities, see Appendix IX.

casia and Central Asia reveals somewhat smaller numbers than those in the European U.S.S.R. At the end of 1957, 124 of the 494 teachers at the Tbilisi State University were women; 5 were professors and 36, associate professors. At Erevan State University, 116 of the 404 members of the teaching staff were women; 2 were professors and 26, associate professors. Tadzhik State University numbered 45 women among its staff of 70; 1 was a professor and 5 were associate professors. At Azerbaidzhan State University, with its staff of 324, there were 124 women, including 1 professor and 15 associate professors. The teaching staff at Kazakh State University included 1 professor and 32 associate professors among the 122 women, out of a total staff of 270. Uzbek State University had 81 women on its teaching staff of 301, of whom 8 were associate professors. A total of 134 women were members of Central Asian University's teaching staff of 432; 3 were professors and 48, associate professors.[39]

The life and scientific career of Kadich Salaimanova, an Uzbek woman, illustrates the upward mobility which education has provided the young women of Central Asia. She was born in 1916, the daughter of an office clerk. After graduating from the Tashkent Institute of Government and Law in 1935, she was made a judge of the Supreme Court in her republic for four years. In 1939 she began graduate study at the Moscow Law Institute, which she completed in 1941. She then started to teach and do research work at the Tashkent Law Institute as a junior instructor. After defending her candidate dissertation in 1945, she was appointed head of the department of criminal law. Five years later she successfully defended a doctoral dissertation and obtained a professorship in 1952. She was then appointed director of the Tashkent Law Institute. Since 1956 she has been Minister of Justice in her republic. She continues to teach and to do research in her capacity as professor at the Central Asian State University. She has published more than

fifteen treatises. For her scientific and pedagogical services she has been awarded the honorable title of Merited Scientific Worker of her republic.[40]

Another illustrative case is that of Sarandjan Yusupova, who was born into the family of a Tadzhik farm laborer. She graduated in 1935 from Tadzhik State University, where she began teaching. In 1939 she received the candidate degree in the field of geology and mineralogy, and in 1948 received her doctorate. Since 1949 she has been head of the university's department of geology. She has written several scientific works.[41]

Women scholars are also to be found in research institutes of the academies of sciences and other organizations. A woman who had already achieved considerable scientific prominence in her early thirties is Alla Masevich, doctor of physical-mathematical sciences, who now is deeply involved in the Soviet space program as vice-chairman of the Astronomical Council of the Academy of Sciences of the U.S.S.R.

An interview with two women research chemists at the Institute of High Molecular Compounds of the U.S.S.R. Academy of Sciences in Leningrad provided insights into the part played by women scientists in the research work of such an institute.[42] Galina Belonovskaia completed her undergraduate work at the Leningrad Chemical-Technological Institute in 1938 and worked there until 1942. During the war she was employed as a senior chemical engineer and then joined the Institute of High Molecular Compounds when it was founded in 1949. Among the staff members are 180 women research workers with a higher education, accounting for between a third and two fifths of the professional staff; 2 have doctor's degrees, 12 have

[39]Galkin, *The Training of Scientists,* p. 128.

[40]*Ibid.,* pp. 128–29.

[41]*Ibid.,* p. 129.

[42]Supplementary details were obtained from an article published by one of the women, Galina Belonovskaia, "Khimiia—cheloveku," in *Zhenshchiny goroda Lenina,* ed. by E. A. Giliarova, M. N. Popova, M. Ia. Razumova, and M. G. Savchenko (Leningrad, 1963), pp. 326–32.

candidate degrees and hold the rank of senior research worker, and 25 have candidate degrees with the rank of junior research worker. Mrs. Belonovskaia completed her candidate degree under the supervision of Elina Tiniakova, a senior scientific worker, who has become one of the leading figures at the institute.

Elina Tiniakova was trained at the Institute of Fine Chemical Technology in Moscow. After working at the Yaroslav Synthetic Rubber Plant she returned to the institute as a graduate student to complete her candidate degree. Since coming to the Institute of High Molecular Compounds, she has worked with B. A. Dolgopolsk, a corresponding member of the Academy of Sciences, and originated the theory of redox reactions in the process of polymerization. She is the author of forty publications and has six patents to her credit. Recently she and Dolgopolsk completed development of a new type of rubber, carboxylic rubber, whose properties are superior to other synthetic rubbers and in many respects not inferior to those of natural rubber.[43]

Nina Siderova, the other woman interviewed, is in charge of the graduate student program, heads a research group, and is secretary of the institute's party organization. She completed her candidate dissertation under the supervision of a corresponding member of the Academy of Sciences, S. N. Danilov, and received her degree in 1952. After completing a number of projects in cellulose and hydrocarbon chemistry, she became a senior scientific worker in 1960. She is now working on an important project in the field of biological polymers (proteins and nucleic acids), which is headed by Professor S. E. Bresler. In connection with this work she spent a year in France. She holds a most respected position at the institute because of her activities.[44]

Other women at the institute mentioned by Mrs. Belonovskaia include Marina Glinkina,

a member of the older generation of women scientists. Since 1935 she has worked in various institutes of the U.S.S.R. Academy of Sciences. Before the war she took part in several projects on the physics and chemistry of polymers, protein chemistry, and antibiotics. During the war she organized a laboratory to produce a new antibiotic for protection against gangrene, which was used in the surgical divisions of Leningrad hospitals. After the blockade was broken in 1944 she returned to work at the Physico-Technical Institute of the Academy of Sciences and together with Professor S. E. Bresler achieved a series of successes in the field of protein chemistry. At present Mrs. Glinkina is a senior scientific worker in the laboratory of Professor G. V. Sasonov and is working on the catalytic transformation of proteins and model substances on ion-exchange series aimed at creating a general theory of the interaction of organic ions with polyelectrolytes. On the basis of this theory, methods of propagation and isolation of organic ions are already being developed and placed into industrial production.[45]

Reference could be made to many other productive women scientists, but those mentioned above are sufficient to indicate a certain pattern in the role played by women research scholars which is consistent with the pattern revealed by the statistics presented in the last chapter. The activities of the women at the Institute of High Molecular Compounds in Leningrad are a clear illustration. Although these women are doing important research, all are working in collaboration with or under the direction of men who have greater professional distinction. The real guidance of the research appears to be firmly in the hands of men.

---

[43]*Ibid.*, p. 328.
[44]*Ibid.*, p. 329.

[45]*Ibid.*, pp. 230–31. Among the substances introduced into industry is a series of medical compounds—antibiotics (penicillin, tetracycline, Terramycin, etc.), vitamins (B_{12}, etc.), hormones, and other compounds.

WOMEN AS CONTRIBUTORS TO SCIENTIFIC AND SCHOLARLY LITERATURE

One indication of the achievement of women in the middle ranks of research scholars is their contribution to the literature of their field. With some allowance for a slight degree of uncertainty in Slavic names and for a much larger degree in those of other linguistic origins, an analysis to determine the amount of published research by women is made possible by the use of separate surname suffixes for women throughout the Soviet Union. The method followed has been to count the number of clearly male and female contributors of substantive articles to leading professional journals in fields for which information on the percentage of women professionals is known.[46] In instances where two, three, or four or more authors were listed, fractional credit was given to each author. The percentage of contributions by women was then compared with the proportion of women in a given field.

The findings are summarized in Table 133, which shows the proportion of women in the professional fields, when it is known or can be estimated with considerable accuracy, and

[46]For a list of the journals, see Appendix IX. It would be desirable to expand the study to include monographs and books, but time and resources were not available.

the proportion of women contributors to journals in these fields. It will be noted immediately that the latter proportion is substantially below the former. This is particularly marked in engineering and in the combined field of economics, statistics, and trade, where the inclusion of trade specialists injects a non-scholarly element which may bias the results. It should be noted, however, that in the case of engineering, in the two decades since 1940, the increase in the percentage of articles contributed has been greater than the increase in the percentage of women engineers. The same is true of veterinarians and physicians. The improvement in the ratios is not sufficient, however, to permit any definite conclusions regarding the over-all trend in the scholarly productivity of women as measured by publications.[47]

[47]On the basis of handbooks listing zoologists and botanists (Akademiia nauk SSSR, *Zoologi Sovetskogo Soiuza: spravochnik* [Moscow, Leningrad, 1961]; and Obshchestva Ispytatelei Prirody, *Slovar' Russkie botaniki* [Moscow, 1952]), it has been possible to arrive at the estimates of the proportion of women in these two professional subgroups which are believed to be quite accurate. These were 44 and 47 per cent, respectively. Women are estimated to have contributed 22 per cent of the articles in the field of zoology in 1940, 32 per cent in 1950, and 31 per cent in 1960. In botany the percentages are estimated to have been 40, 37, and 42 per cent, respectively. See Appendix IX for the journals employed in making the estimates.

TABLE 133. Percentage of women with higher education in various specialties compared with percentage of articles in related professional journals contributed by women.[a]

Specialists	1940				1960			
	Percentage of Women in Specialty	Percentage of Articles by Women	Ratio	Sample Size	Percentage of Women in Specialty	Percentage of Articles by Women	Ratio	Sample Size
Engineers, including geology....	15	4	0.27	(868)	29	9	0.31	(1,877)
Agronomists, zootechnicians, veterinarians, and foresters...	25	15	0.60	(430)	39	24	0.62	(676)
Agronomists...............	n.a.	16	–	(156)	41	25	0.61	(345)
Veterinarians...............	16	6	0.38	(274)	31	16	0.52	(331)
Economists, statisticians, and trade specialists............	31	9	0.29	(168)	57	12	0.21	(447)
Judges, procurators, and lawyers	15	6	0.40	(121)	32	10	0.36	(203)
Physicians, excluding dentists...	60	24	0.40	(203)	75	39	0.52	(549)

[a]See Appendix X and *Vysshee obrazovanie v SSSR* (Moscow, 1961), p. 66.

An objection to our approach might be that the group of professionals in each specialty is too broad and may include many men and women who neither reach nor aspire to the level at which writing is expected or required. Engineers, statisticians, and trade specialists would illustrate this point. However, since the relative interests and probabilities of publication by men and by women are precisely what we are trying to measure, this objection is not entirely valid.

It is possible, however, to take this objection into account by limiting our comparison to men and women who, by the nature of their work, are likely to publish. Figures have been collected by A. Ia. Sinetskii, an expert on Soviet academic personnel, showing the percentages of women on the professional staffs of higher educational institutions in 1947 for each field of specialization—women who are, of course, expected to publish. A considerable volume of publications is also produced by the staffs of research institutes. Unfortunately, the data necessary to include them in our comparison are lacking. Therefore, the comparison in Table 134 may err somewhat by their absence.

Table 134, which compares the percentage of women in each field on the staffs of higher educational institutions in 1947 with estimates of the contribution of women to the literature of the various disciplines in 1940, 1950, and 1960, shows that on the average women have contributed only about half as many articles as their proportion in numbers should call for. The scholarly productivity of women measured in terms of articles contributed was, therefore, about half that of men. However, wide variations exist among the different fields of specialization. Using the 1950 contributions, we find that women were the least productive, relatively, in the fields of social-political and philosophical subjects (0.19), physical culture (0.25), veterinary medicine

TABLE 134. Percentage of women on the professional staffs of higher educational institutions in 1947 compared with percentage of articles in professional journals contributed by women in 1940, 1950, and 1960.[a]

| | 1947 | 1940± | | 1950± | | 1960± | |
Discipline	Percentage of Women in Field	Percentage of Articles by Women	Sample Size	Percentage of Articles by Women	Sample Size	Percentage of Articles by Women	Sample Size
Physics-mathematics	21.1	11	(247)	11	(653)	7	(1270)
Chemistry	45.3	26	(206)	32	(222)	40	(320)
Biology	47.8	26	(384)	31	(435)	36	(565)
Geology	23.4	9	(186)	23	(141)	25	(315)
Engineering	10.5	4	(868)	5	(2203)	9	(1877)
Agriculture	23.0	14	(156)	25	(294)	21	(409)
Veterinary medicine	22.3	6	(274)	7	(302)	16	(331)
Medicine	48.0	24	(203)	37	(488)	39	(549)
Physical culture	27.6	9	(127)	7	(174)	13	(115)
Social-political and philosophy	31.0	8	(131)	6	(145)	10	(180)
Economics	16.3	9	(168)	12	(288)	11	(447)
History	30.1	21	(154)	15	(178)	14	(188)
Geography	28.7	9	(105)	15	(194)	12	(125)
Philology	67.7	24	(134)	29	(120)	21	(227)
Arts	34.0	11	(216)	28	(197)	37	(207)
Law	12.7	6	(121)	7	(123)	10	(203)
Pedagogy	40.0	22	(294)	20	(348)	26	(639)
Total	35.0	16	(3974)	19	(6505)	19	(7967)

[a]The percentage of women in each field is from A. Ia. Sinetskii, *Professorsko-prepodavatel'skie kadry vysshei shkoly SSSR* (Moscow, 1950), p. 130. See Appendix X for the remaining sources. The average percentages for 1940, 1950, and 1960 were calculated by weighting the percentage of articles contributed by women in each field by the number of persons in the field who were on the professional staffs of higher educational institutions in 1960 and 1950, in *Vysshee obrazovanie v SSSR* (Moscow, 1961), p. 204. The 1950 weights were also employed in the 1940 calculation. ±, indicates that articles published in years before or after the main year may have been included in the sample in order to enlarge it to a sufficient size for significant results.

(0.31), and philology (0.43). Women appear to have been most productive in the areas of agriculture (1.09), geology (0.98), and the arts (0.82). In these three fields women contributed to the professional literature roughly in proportion to their share of the staffs in each field. These results should be interpreted with caution, however, since in fields such as agriculture and geology the percentage of women employed as professionals in research institutions appears to be higher than in higher educational institutions.[48] As an illustration of the problem, if the percentage of women on the staffs of engineering research institutes in 1960 were twice that of higher educational institutions, the proportion of women in the combined group responsible for most scholarly publications would be approximately 16 per cent. When this figure is compared with the 9 per cent contribution of women to engineering articles in 1960, the productivity of women appears to be significantly less than if the comparison were made with the proportion of women in higher educational institutions alone, 10.5 per cent. Thus, in fields where the proportion and number of women in research institutions substantially exceed those of the staffs of higher educational institutions, the scholarly productivity of women at the higher educational institutions is exaggerated in the table.

It is also interesting to note the fields in which women make the greatest contribution to scholarly literature. In chemistry, where a high proportion of women are employed, the

proportion of articles contributed by women has risen from 26 to 40 per cent in the twenty-year span from 1940 to 1960. The percentage has been almost as high in the fields of medicine and biology, which are very popular with women. The arts are another area in which women are now making a major contribution to the literature. Future trends in these and other fields will undoubtedly depend heavily upon trends in the proportion of women being graduated in these fields. Since the proportion of women receiving a higher education has declined over the past decade, it is quite possible that there will be no significant improvement in the proportion of scholarly publication by women.

FACTORS AFFECTING THE SCHOLARLY PRODUCTIVITY OF WOMEN

A number of factors appear to be responsible for the smaller contribution which women make to scholarly research. First, we shall examine critically the common belief that the capacity of women for scholarly work or scientific research is less than that of men. Secondly, we shall consider the influence of motivation upon the performance of women. An estimate of the effect on the productivity of women of time lost in the course of their working career by virtue of their being women will then be estimated. Finally, we shall consider the effect on the efficient utilization of manpower resources of difficulties in assigning women to appropriate positions because of family and other considerations.

The Academic Capabilities of Women. In view of the occasional doubts still expressed regarding the capacity of women for scientific or other intellectual pursuits, it is desirable to consider the academic performance of women and to examine some of the findings regarding the capacity of women for creative work in science and other fields. The question which we are raising would scarcely be intelligible to a Soviet student or educator. They are so accustomed to women's participating effectively in all fields of study and at all

---

[48]The total number of women employed as professionals in research institutions exceeded that of women in higher educational institutions by 57 per cent on Oct. 1, 1960. However, in 1950, which is closer to the date for which the percentages of women by field are given in Table 134, the excess was only 5 per cent. Unfortunately, the excess at this time is not available by field of specialization. The percentage in Table 133 for agriculture, for example, suggests that the proportion of women in research institutions is higher than in higher educational institutions. In the field of geology scattered reports from visitors to universities and research institutes suggest that a similar situation exists.

levels of learning that the possibility of sex differences usually has not occurred to them. This confidence in the intellectual capacity of women appears to be borne out by the academic records of students.

In the mid-1930's women received a slightly higher percentage of "outstanding" (*otlichno*) marks than men on the *gostekhekzamen,* an examination for the certification of semiprofessionals in various occupational fields. Table 135 shows the performance of women relative to men in four different areas. On the whole, they did a bit better despite the technical nature of the specialties involved.

TABLE 135. Percentage of students receiving "outstanding" on their *gostekhekzamen,* January, 1936.[a]

Field	Men	Women
Machine building............	40	39
Metallurgy..................	50	52
Coal industry...............	55	62
Textile industry.............	41	55
Total.....................	44	49

[a]Based on *Zhenshchina v SSSR* (Moscow, 1937), p. 27.

Recently two English women engineers had an opportunity to scan class lists while visiting secondary schools in the U.S.S.R. and found that the performance of girls was comparable to that of boys in mathematics and physics. They also discovered that over a ten-year period the share of academic prizes won by the girls was proportionate to their numbers. At the Kharkov Polytechnical Institute they found some sex differences in entrance examination scores in various fields. Girls performed slightly better than boys in physics, chemistry, and foreign languages, while the boys did better in mathematics and the Russian language.[49] Both sexes are exposed to essentially the same educational experiences, and the curricula in the sciences are the same throughout the entire U.S.S.R. at the secondary school level.

The educational reform of 1958 increased the share of applied and vocational skill sub-

jects for boys and girls from about a quarter to a third of the instruction hours, a 60 per cent increase. At the same time the lengthening of the curriculum from ten to eleven years resulted in almost an 18 per cent increase in total instruction hours. In grades 9 to 11, a basic course on production fundamentals was given which is oriented toward either agriculture or industry. In addition to courses which apply the knowledge the student has learned in his science courses, the student also acquired on-the-job training in some trade. Souter and Winslade observed that "Schoolgirls appear to have no inhibitions about tackling technical work and the technical streams of secondary schools have between 40 and 45 per cent girls. These girls show a great deal of enthusiasm for all types of technical work and, indeed, in some schools at least, they have the reputation of being more accurate with machine tools than are the boys."[50] Some sex differences in the choice of on-the-job training was evident, however, at the schools visited by the author in 1962.

On August 13, 1964, it was announced that the Soviets would return to the ten-year school. Although it was asserted that the decree did not mean that polytechnical education, the cornerstone of the 1958 reform, was being abandoned, it seems clear that "production training" must be reduced to token proportions. As a result there should be less differentiation between the sexes stemming from "production training" in the future than in the recent past. Whatever the implications of the new reform, if in fact girls are not naturally averse to technical skills and are as capable as boys in their performance, one can hardly argue that, up to the time of puberty at least, there are inherent female deficiencies in these fields.

The performance of girls in higher educational institutions also is reported to be comparable to that of boys. A British observer of Soviet education has stated that "There is not the slightest evidence that girls are any worse at scientific or mathematical subjects

[49]L. S. Souter and R. Winslade, *Women Engineers in the U.S.S.R.* (London, 1960), p. 15.

[50]*Ibid.*

than boys."[51] The findings of Souter and Winslade reinforce this view:

. . . it was the general view that the young women were, on an average, just as capable at their studies, if not slightly more so than the young men. In the few cases for which the pass marks were actually quoted, the proportion of girls in the various grades of marks were certainly in proportion to their numbers . . . Kharkov Polytechnic [Institute] was an example of an institute where the girls put up a better average performance than the boys; a greater proportion of the "excellent" diplomas go to girls and more girls than boys receive the extra stipends of 75 roubles per month.[52]

A number of teachers with whom the author spoke felt that girls were more diligent in their studies than the boys, but they believed that this greater application was coupled with more learning "by the book." The boys, on the other hand, were less systematic and tended to show greater imagination and originality. Again Souter and Winslade's questioning elicited similar observations. They make the following comment:

While there was a slight disagreement as to whether the girls are just as capable or more capable than boys and whether or not they achieve just as good or slightly better results than boys, there was complete unanimity that these results are achieved by a different method of approach. The girls are more conscientious, diligent and persevering than the boys; they are more even and systematic in their studies, while the boys have ups and downs . . . working hard at the subjects they like and neglecting the subjects they don't. Some institutes felt that this difference is marked only in the first three years of study.[53]

Questioning of Soviet teachers and scientists concerned with graduate training confirmed the view that the basic intellectual capacity of women for scientific work is equal to that of men. Sharp differences in scientific

talent were admitted to exist, of course, but these, it was pointed out, cut across the sexes. For an explanation of the smaller proportion of women continuing for advanced degrees than graduated from higher educational institutions, it was felt one had to look elsewhere, to differences in motivation, distractions, and traditional expectations. As women reach their twenties and thirties, these factors may play a more important role in determining their accomplishment than when they were schoolgirls.

Nevertheless, recent research suggests that there may be some underlying differences between the sexes in their ability to cope with certain types of abstract or complex problems.[54] These findings prompt Eleanor Maccoby to suggest that "women on the average develop a somewhat different way of handling incoming information—that their thinking is less analytic, more global, and more preservative—and that this kind of thinking may serve them very well for many kinds of functioning but that it is not the kind of thinking most conducive to high-level intellectual productivity, especially in science."[55] She hastens to add, however, that there are many women who think analytically, and many men who do not, but maintains that there are consistent

---

[51]"New Minds for the New World," *New Statesman and Nation* (Sept. 8, 1956), p. 279.

[52]Souter and Winslade, *op. cit.*, p. 15.

[53]*Ibid.*, p. 16.

[54]See Jerome Kagan, Howard A. Moss, and Irving E. Siegel, "The Psychological Significance of Styles of Conceptualization," in *Basic Cognitive Processes in Children*, ed. by J. C. Wright and Jerome Kagan (Monogr. Soc. Res. Child Development, 23; No. 86, 1963); H. Gutzkow, "An Analysis of the Operation of Sex in Problem-Solving Behavior," *Journal of Genetic Psychology*, XLV (1951), 219–44; E. J. Sweeney, *Sex Differences in Problem-Solving* (unpublished dissertation; Stanford University, 1953); H. A. Witkin, Helen B. Lewis, M. Herzman, Karen Machover, Pearl B. Meissner, and S. Wapner, *Personality through Perception* (New York, 1954); and H. A. Witkin, R. B. Dyk, H. E. Faterson, D. R. Goodenough, and S. A. Karp, *Psychological Differentiation* (New York, 1962); the last two works are cited by Eleanor E. Maccoby, "Woman's Intellect," in *The Potential of Women*, ed. by Seymour M. Farber and Roger H. L. Wilson (New York, 1963), pp. 29–30.

[55]Maccoby, *op. cit.*, p. 30.

differences in the average performance of the two sexes.

Why do some people develop more analytical modes of thought than others? Research on this subject is in its infancy, but suggests that the key lies within the extent to which a child is encouraged to assume initiative, take responsibility, and solve problems by himself. Overprotected children, both boys and girls, have been found to be less proficient at analytical thinking. A researcher working on this problem is reported to have said that a girl must be a "tomboy" at some point in her childhood in order to become an intellectual person.[56]

Thus far this research seems to indicate that intellectual performance does not develop according to its own inner laws but is responsive to some degree to the external environment. Furthermore, the development of certain intellectual capacities may depend on the development of certain personality traits. Therefore, a home or cultural environment may discourage the full development of women's analytical ability. In discussing this problem, Eleanor Maccoby makes the following judgment:

Suppose a girl does succeed in maintaining, throughout her childhood years, the qualities of dominance, independence, and active striving that appear to be requisites for good analytic thinking. In so doing, she is defying the conventions concerning what is appropriate behavior for her sex. She may do this successfully, in many ways, but I suggest that it is a rare intellectual woman who will not have paid a price for it: a price in anxiety. And I hazard the guess that it is this anxiety which helps account for the lack of productivity among those women who do make intellectual careers.[57]

These comments raise many questions. Certainly Soviet society has lowered many of the barriers against women intellectuals which previously existed in Russia. The atmosphere is conducive for capable women to enter the professions, yet the full potential of Soviet women in the realm of scholarship and research does not appear to have been fully realized. Some of the reasons for this failure, such as the distractions of a home and family, were discussed in Chapter 5. Others will be touched upon in this chapter.

The Motivation of Professional Women. Cultural anthropology has demonstrated that intellectual and other motivation is conditioned by the culture or subculture in which a person lives. We must, therefore, ask what qualities are encouraged in women in Soviet society and in what direction they are urged to apply them.[58]

Our own industrial culture does not encourage a young woman to direct her energy, application, and ambition toward a creative, professional career. The American woman's orientation is more toward a family and a home. Her initial employment is likely to be considered a way station between school and marriage. The housewife image is extolled daily by all the mass media. With rare exceptions it is in this role that she will seek fulfillment. As Marya Mannes has stated, "Irresistibly, the American girl is formed in this image from childhood, and by the time she is going steady at twelve her future is so clearly indicated that only exceptional will and courage can change it."[59] In the Soviet Union, on the other hand, the regime has made major efforts to develop a career orientation among girls and young women. The mass media in the Soviet Union extol the accomplishments of women scientists and other professional women. The image of the hardworking, productive, and patriotic professional

---

[56]*Ibid.,* p. 33. Research is cited on environmental factors affecting intelligence: D. M. Levy, *Maternal Overprotection* (New York, 1943); I. W. Sontag, C. T. Baker, and Virginia A. Nelson, *Mental Growth and Personality Development: A Longitudinal Study* (Monogr. Soc. Res. Child Development, 23; No. 68, 1958); and her own work.

[57]*Op. cit.,* pp. 36–37.

[58]For an interesting discussion of these problems, see Ethel M. Albert, "The Roles of Women: Questions of Values," in Faber and Wilson, *op. cit.,* pp. 105–15.

[59]Marya Mannes, "The Problem of Creative Women," in Faber and Wilson, *op. cit.,* p. 121.

woman is constantly held up before the eyes of young girls. As a result, to aspire to follow in the footsteps of a famous woman scientist, physician, or engineer is perfectly natural for a girl growing up in the Soviet Union today.

Although the regime has been quite successful in altering popular attitudes, conflicts still remain between the role of a woman as a wife and mother and that as a professional. Professional women cannot completely escape the special responsibilities of being women. They must be thinking of shopping, of an ailing parent, and of husbands and children. Marya Mannes has posed the conflict succinctly, "No woman with any heart can compose a paragraph when her child is in trouble or her husband ill; forever they take precedence over the companions of her mind. In this as in many other things, the creative woman has a tougher time than the creative man."[60] Of course, men are not unconcerned about their family's welfare, but in the Soviet Union domestic matters inevitably remain primarily the responsibility of women despite their involvement in the labor force. Unless a far greater transformation occurs in the family and in the relationships within the family, most women will remain more deeply involved in family concerns than men.

There appears to be a tendency, borne out by the author's interviews, for Soviet women to shy away from the more responsible jobs, which require a total commitment of time and energy, even though their training and experience might fully qualify them. As a woman director of a hospital commented in an interview, "My job as director does not end with the end of the day. It's with me all the time." Women in less responsible positions, she pointed out, can leave their work behind them at the end of the day. Similarly, the sustained intellectual concentration which is required for first-rank creative work in the arts and sciences may not be possible for many women who possess the training and capability for it but who are simply unable to escape the endless distractions and worries of caring for a

husband and children. For many women the price of excelling in their profession is simply too high a price to pay, and the more responsible positions are left to men who are eager to take them.

Working Time Lost by Women. Another factor, related to motivation, which affects the productivity of a professional woman is the time lost through pregnancy, child care, and other family responsibilities. Although precise data on the total number of hours of work spent by men and women over their working life are not available, it is possible to construct some estimates which suggest that the difference is not insignificant in quantitative terms. Qualitatively, it may be of even greater significance, since the time lost for childbearing and child rearing is likely to come at times which are particularly important for a professional career.

Under present legislation, a Soviet woman loses a minimum of sixteen weeks from her job for each child she bears. If we assume that the typical professional woman has two children, she will lose a minimum of thirty-two weeks of work over her working career. However, the loss of a full year would be a more realistic estimate, since many women take extra time off when they bear children. Caring for a family also results in more time off from the job for a woman than for a man because it is the woman, as wife and mother, who cares for the sick and looks after the children when other arrangements fail. Scattered reports indicate that a woman loses five to seven more working days a year than a man for these reasons. Women also take more sick leave because of menstrual difficulties, abortions, and other health problems.[61] Altogether, these additional losses of work time over the working life of a woman add up to almost a year. If we assume an average working life of thirty-five years for a

---

[60] *Ibid.*, p. 125.

[61] See, for example, V. D. Patrushev, *Intensivnost' truda pri sotsializme* (Moscow, 1963), p. 132; and R. E. Fakiolas, "Work Attendance in Soviet Industry," *Soviet Studies*, No. 4 (April, 1963), 367–70.

professional woman, the loss of two years' work time amounts to nearly 6 per cent of a woman's working life.

Data on the average working life of professional women and men are lacking, but there can be no doubt that women tend to withdraw from the semiprofessional and professional labor force at an earlier age than men.[62] The earlier retirement age for women, normally age 55 as opposed to age 60 for men, is unquestionably a significant factor, but women begin to withdraw from the labor force more rapidly than men at even earlier ages. Participation rates presented in Chapter III indicate that a significant decline in women's participation begins in the age group 50 to 55. Data on the participation rates of male and female graduates of higher educational institutions in the national economy[63] provide further insight into the difference between the length of the working life of professional men and women. In 1959 the participation rate of men was approximately 93 per cent, and that of women, 86 per cent. The discrepancy is deceptively small, however, because in 1959 so few women with a higher education were in the older age groups, where the participation rates are lower. Indeed, 72 per cent of all female graduates were younger than age 40 in 1959, and it is in these younger age groups that the participation rate is highest. Therefore, as the percentage of female graduates in the older age groups increases, the average participation rate for female graduates should be reduced, and a greater withdrawal of professional women from the labor force should become apparent.

If we add to the present lower participation rate of women (8 per cent) the nearly 6 per cent loss in a woman's working life due to childbearing, family care, and incapacitation, we arrive at an estimate of the differential between the quantitative contribution of a woman and a man over a lifetime of work.

This estimate indicates that over her lifetime a woman with professional training may be expected to contribute at least 13 to 14 per cent less work than a man.

Assignment Problems and Economic Planning Difficulties. From both a political and an economic point of view, control over the appointment of specialized and professional personnel is of vital importance to the operation of the Soviet system. Through their important functions the members of the Soviet intelligentsia form a vital link in the chain of party control. Hence the great concern of the party for the ideological commitment of this elite group, particularly for the educators, scientists, and technicians who play a strategic role in the Soviet industrial economy.

As indicated in an earlier chapter, indirect control can be exercised by manipulating a system of incentives and rewards. At two points in a person's career, however, the regime intervenes in a rather direct manner. This is in the assignment of jobs to graduates of vocational, semiprofessional, and professional schools and in the appointment of persons to administrative or other posts in which the party has a direct interest. The categories of jobs which may be filled only with the party's consent are called the *nomenklatura*.

After a person has fulfilled his initial employment obligation after graduation, but before he has advanced to positions included in the *nomenklatura* of the party, he is not likely to be singled out by the party or government through a change of position or location. A person cannot rise very high in the economic hierarchy without, however, being employed in a position which falls within the *nomenklatura* of the party. Hence, an intelligent, ambitious person's fitness in the eyes of the party will inevitably be scrutinized and weighed. The higher the position, the higher the party body which will be concerned in making a decision. The party maintains files which it employs to search out and recruit the talents and political morality required for a given position.

The functioning of the *nomenklatura* system has been concisely described by DeWitt:

---

[62]See Fig. 26, p. 186.
[63]See Table 117, p. 198.

These procedures are applied to all segments of the Soviet labor force. School directors cannot be appointed without the consent of the regional committees of the party. Directors of higher educational establishments, deans of universities, and heads of research institutes, if they are important enough, are all appointed with the consent of the republic or all-union central committees of the party. Presidents of Soviet academies of science cannot be "elected" or hold these jobs unless they are cleared by the Central Committee of the Communist Party of the Soviet Union. Thus party control permeates the entire Soviet system; for any job of responsibility a person needs party clearance.[64]

As a specialist begins a professional career and as he or she is promoted to positions of greater responsibility, the question of his or her sex will be weighed consciously in connection with an assignment. As we shall see, despite legal equality of the sexes, the question of sex cannot be ignored in making assignments. It is the general rule that separation of husband and wife, whenever practicable, should be avoided. Even at a fairly early stage of a woman's career, when her destiny is more her own rather than the party's, her willingness to accept a promotion to a more interesting or demanding job may be entirely conditional upon its location if she is married. Thus, the limited mobility of married women undoubtedly deprives them of opportunities for career advancement which are open to a man. Furthermore, if the husband's career dictates where the family lives, the wife's career may suffer from absence of opportunity to use her skills or, if moves are required, from the disruption of continuity in her career.

Since young women constitute a very high percentage of the graduating semiprofessionals and physicians, the best illustrations of assignment difficulties come from the field of medicine. A proper distribution of medical personnel in relation to population has required that many young women be dispatched to remote parts of the Soviet Union each year. The assignment task is made more difficult by the fact that some of these young women may be married and their assignment cannot properly be made apart from their husbands. Furthermore, remote rural appointments are even less desirable for young women than for young men. Working conditions are likely to be difficult, and the young, inexperienced physician may be completely isolated and unable to obtain advice or assistance. Opportunities for finding an acceptable husband may be extremely limited. The poor living conditions are harder on a woman than a man. According to regulations, rural physicians must be provided with housing, light, and fuel by the local organs of the republican health ministries, but in practice they are often forced to live in peasant huts or sleep in hospital offices or consultation rooms.[65]

In *Doctor and Patient in Soviet Russia*, Field cites a classic example of resistance to an assignment, "The Case History of Dr. Lisitsyna's Illness," which appeared in *Komsomolskaia Pravda*. When Dr. Olga Lisitsyna of the Voronezh Medical Institute learned that she was being assigned to work in Kemerovo, 2,000 miles to the east in eastern Siberia, she fell ill. Her parents then began a campaign to permit her to stay in town, first on the grounds that she was suffering from malaria. Then her mother, an X-ray specialist, found her to be suffering from secondary anemia and asked that she be allowed to remain. When this attempt failed, her father, who was manager of a nursery growing fruit trees, pulled strings in Moscow, claiming that the departure of his daughter would adversely affect horticulture in the Voronezh area. Despite intervention at a high level, this attempt failed. The mother then considered having her daughter adjudged insane, but gave up the idea in the face of required hospitalization and observation. At the time the article was published, twenty-

---

[64]Nicholas DeWitt, *Education and Professional Employment in the U.S.S.R.* (Washington, D.C., 1961), p. 465.

[65]See Mark G. Field, *Doctor and Patient in Soviet Russia* (Cambridge, Mass., 1957), p. 84.

five-year-old Olga continued to remain idle, hoping that intercession at still higher levels might prevail.[66]

Although it is said that some women physicians may marry before completing their studies to avoid remote assignments, they are not always successful in this ruse. Sometimes the husband is sent to the same area if work is available, but this may be difficult to arrange.[67] Sometimes husbands and wives try to arrange to be assigned separately and then reassigned in an effort to end with an assignment to the same place, but when a woman is married to a man in the same profession, it may be difficult to assign both to the same locality because of limited openings for specialized skills. Since the regime cannot ignore the dislocations to family life which an inflexible allocation would entail, some flexibility has to be permitted at the expense of the system.

At a later point, when the husband or wife is employed at levels in which the party has an interest, the wife will continue to be at a disadvantage. In considering a woman for a responsible post, her family obligations will undoubtedly enter into the evaluation. If there is a desirable position in the Novosibirsk Branch of the Academy of Sciences, for example, a woman whose husband has a good job in Moscow is not so likely to take it, even if it represents a promotion, as a man in the reverse situation. The woman would be more likely to stay on in Moscow at her old job in order not to disrupt her family or her husband's career.

CONCLUSIONS

Although no perfect means can be devised to measure the achievement or productivity of professional women, such indexes as we have

presented here show a consistently lower level of achievement and productivity on the part of women. The discrepancy between the sexes is greatest at the highest levels of scholarly achievement. No women are to be found in the upper reaches of the direction of the Academy of Sciences of the U.S.S.R. Only a few are to be found among the full and corresponding members of the Academy. Similarly, few women are employed in key positions in the many research institutes of the Academy. Another measure of professional success, the receipt of Lenin prizes, yields similar results. Women have made up only a small proportion of the prize winners and have usually appeared among the winners as members of sizable research teams. As contributors of scholarly articles women make a better showing. Nevertheless, their contributions have been only about half as large as their numbers would suggest.

From the evidence of the indicators, supplemented by information on the role women play in research institutes and higher educational institutions, we must conclude that the scholarly achievement and productivity of women are, on the whole, considerably lower than those of men. This is hardly a startling conclusion, but it is one of great practical significance for the effective and efficient development and utilization of Soviet professional manpower.

We have touched upon some of the reasons that women have been less productive than men in the sciences or other professions. Some of the inhibiting factors, such as lost work time, interrupted careers, and assignment difficulties, cannot readily be eradicated. Others, involving the intellectual development of girls and their career motivations, can undoubtedly be improved; great progress has already been made in the Soviet Union in altering the image of a woman's role in society. The intellectual, career-oriented girl in the Soviet Union today will find much support and social approbation compared with the situation only a few decades ago. It appears, however, that conflicts between career

---

[66]For a fuller description of the case, see Field, *op. cit.,* pp. 84–85, or *Komsomolskaia Pravda* (Sept. 2, 1951). A translation appears in the *Current Digest of the Soviet Press,* III, No. 41 (1951), 5.

[67]Field, *op. cit.,* pp. 91–96, gives several illustrations of the ineptness of the Soviet bureaucracy in handling cases of this sort.

and marriage and motherhood will remain for some time to come, since the greater involvement of a woman in her family is not likely to be eradicated. Nevertheless, through provision of more child-care facilities and lightening the burden of housework, women should find the family side of life draining away less vital energy.

It would seem probable that over the years the professional productivity of women will increase as their full potential for creative work is more fully realized. As this increase occurs, a higher proportion of women should appear in the upper reaches of scholarly activity. In the meantime, the efficient use of scholarly manpower resources dictates that males fill most of the higher posts. Nevertheless, although as yet the potential of Soviet women is imperfectly realized, the Soviet Union today appears to lead the rest of the world in making use of the creative talents of women.

chapter
13

SUMMARY AND CONCLUSIONS

ALTHOUGH THE FOCUS of this study has been on the role of women in Soviet science and technology, it has been necessary to discuss women in a much broader context. The complexity of the interrelationship of the roles of woman, as wife, mother, consumer, and producer, makes it difficult simply to summarize or to characterize Soviet policy toward women in the Russian economy as a whole or in any part of it. These varied roles so interact that Soviet policy in one area may have unintended repercussions on the way in which women perform in other areas. There is still little evidence that Soviet planners have managed to achieve a single, coherent, over-all policy with respect to the economic utilization of women but, rather, that they have several imperfectly co-ordinated and sometimes contradictory policies. An attempt will now be made, nevertheless, to summarize, interpret, and evaluate Soviet experience in the utilization of women in the economy, particularly in the fields of science and technology.

To begin with, war, revolution, and political repression over the past five decades drastically altered the sex ratio in the Soviet Union in favor of women. In 1897, with a sex ratio of 99 males per 100 females, there was near balance between the sexes in the Russian population. But in 1926, as a result of World War I and the Civil War, there were 5 million fewer males than females, and the sex ratio was 94. The census of 1939 reported 7 mil-

lion fewer males than females and a further decline in the sex ratio to 92. These changes reflected the impact of collectivization and the purges, in which more men than women were killed. But by far the most drastic change came with World War II, which decimated the adult male population. The 1959 census reported 114.8 million females and 94 million males, a deficit of 20.8 million males. By calculating backward, with published birth rates and certain assumptions about the distribution of mortality by sex, it can be estimated that in 1946 there were 26 million fewer males than females in the adult population and that the sex ratio for the entire population was only 74 males per 100 females. The tremendous imbalance of the late 40's and early 50's was moderated by time, and by 1959 the sex ratio had risen to 83. At the present time the imbalance in the sexes is confined to the age groups over 35, but it is estimated that not until 1980 will the sex ratio be 92, or at the level prior to the outbreak of World War II.

Irregularities in the Soviet population pyramid caused by war and other vicissitudes are so great that many decades will be required to moderate them. Although the male deficit is now confined to the older age groups, the manpower shortage continues for other reasons. Most important, the birth rate during and immediately after the war was unusually low. As a result, during the past half dozen years additions to the labor force have been small and the pressure to utilize women, which was so insistent in the decade following the war, has continued up to the present. Furthermore, the shrunken generation of war babies is now entering the childbearing age, and, therefore, the annual number of births is significantly reduced. In another generation, these small numbers will in turn keep additions to the labor force and to the population below the normal level. Thus, irregularities in the population pyramid will be perpetuated through several generations.

The present population policy of the government is aimed at maintaining or increasing the rate of growth in population, because a large and rapidly growing population is viewed as an asset rather than a liability. Certain programs, such as family allowances and medals for mothers of large families, are designed to increase the birth rate. On the other hand, in 1955, the government felt obliged once again to legalize abortion because of pressures from women and from the medical profession which was concerned with the large number of illegal abortions performed under unsafe circumstances. Continuing concern over the high rate of abortion has led to increased efforts to develop and distribute effective contraceptive devices. The combined effect of legalized abortions and more effective contraception will be, of course, to reduce the birth rate at the same time other measures are being taken to increase it. Nevertheless, in spite of these contradictions in Soviet population policy, the intent of the government is to increase fertility. Thus far, however, the results are not impressive.

Demographic factors have played, and will continue to play, an important part in determining the role of women in the Soviet economy. The present high rate of participation of women in the Soviet labor force is not without precedent, however. In 1926, when the country was largely agricultural, almost every woman participated in economic activity outside the home for a part of the year. What is unique in the Soviet situation today is the very high rate of participation by women in the economy of a country so in-dustrially advanced. At the present time, the Soviet participation rate of close to 70 per cent in the working ages is almost twice as high as the rate in the United States. This high rate has been maintained despite a major structural shift in the population away from rural areas, where the participation rate has always been very high, into urban areas where the participation rate initially was much lower. Since 1926, however, the participation rate of urban women age 16 to 59 has increased from 40 to 67 per cent. This increase has almost completely offset the decline in the average participation rate which would otherwise have occurred as the industrialization process proceeded.

Although rates of female participation in the labor force are high in all regions of the U.S.S.R., variations occur which are usually related to the degree of urbanization, the influence of Moslem traditions, and the size of the male deficit. Since urbanization and Moslem traditions tend to lower the rate, while the shortage of men tends to raise it, the rate reaches its extreme high in largely rural and traditionally Christian republics which were badly hit by the war, such as Belorussia, and its extreme low in the more urbanized of the traditionally Moslem republics, such as Azerbaidzhan. Another factor which affects the local rates of female participation, but about which little statistical information is available, is the lack of employment opportunity near women's homes or in particular specialties.

The continuance of a high rate of female participation at all ages, even through the childbearing and child-rearing ages, is another distinctive Soviet characteristic. In the age group 20 to 39, which encompasses the most important childbearing and child-rearing ages, approximately 80 per cent of the women are employed, a remarkably high rate for a country as advanced industrially as the Soviet Union. Women begin to withdraw from employment in the socialized sector of the economy as they approach the retirement age, but many older women continue to work on private agricultural plots.

In the United States and other highly developed countries the pattern is quite different. Although in the United States 45 per cent of the women in their early twenties are employed, many of these women withdraw from the labor force when they begin to have children. Only 33 per cent remain employed in their later twenties. The participation rate then climbs to a second peak for women in their forties and early fifties when their children are able to fend for themselves. In the age groups under 40 and over 65, the participation rate of Soviet women is approximately double that of American women. In the age group 40 to 65 it exceeds the American by a little more than 50 per cent.

The male population deficit in the older age groups, coupled with high female participation rates, has resulted in a substantial majority of women in the Soviet labor force age 35 and older. This is a crucial age group for any economy, since it is from this group that the leadership of an economy and of a society is normally drawn. This special circumstance has made the effective utilization of women since World War II even more vital for the Soviet Union than numbers alone would suggest.

If the present high proportion of working women in the Soviet Union is examined in terms of the gradual restoration of a normal male-female ratio in the population, the share of women in the total employment of the future is not likely to increase above the present 52 per cent. In the United States and other developed countries, on the other hand, there is still ample room for growth in the employment of women. The President's Commission on the Status of Women projects a level of 34 per cent for the United States in 1970.[1] Given circumstances more favorable to working women, still further increases would be a possibility.

In the Soviet Union economic pressures compelling women to work to make ends

meet play a major role in keeping women in the labor force. The shortage of men has left many women without husbands, and they must work to support themselves and their families. Furthermore, for many families a single pay check provides only a bare subsistence, and many married women feel they must work in order to maintain an acceptable standard of living. Also, government and party action has altered social custom and public attitudes toward the employment of women. At the present time, few fields are considered inaccessible, and a woman is actually likely to feel defensive if she does not have a job. The regime has been particularly successful in opening the fields of science and technology to women. Attitudes toward women participating in these fields have so radically changed that they are freely accepted everywhere—except in work considered detrimental to their health.

The policies of the Soviet regime on the employment of women, protection on the job, and maternity benefits have been embodied in extensive legislation and executive orders issued since the Revolution. Often the legislation has not been enforced, particularly during the war emergency when women were in fact employed in many occupations from which by the existing law they were excluded for reasons of health. At the present time, however, the legal provisions concerning Soviet women are generally enforced, and in this respect the Soviet Union is among the more enlightened countries of the world.

Another factor affecting the participation of women in the labor force is the burden of family responsibilities. Although adequate data are lacking, the participation rate of Soviet women appears to decline, as is normally the case everywhere, as the number of their children increases. We have seen, however, that the Soviet participation rate holds up remarkably well, even in the face of this burden, throughout the childbearing and child-rearing ages. This is possible partly because the varied child-care facilities provided in the Soviet Union free several millions of women with young children for employment outside

---

[1] President's Commission on the Status of Women, *American Women* (Washington, D.C., 1963), p. 28.

the home. As has been pointed out, the demand for the services of these institutions continues to outrun the supply. According to estimates, approximately 12 per cent of the children of nursery age and 20 per cent of the children of kindergarten age can be accommodated in permanent child-care facilities. Substantially more can be accommodated in seasonal summer facilities. Most of the permanent facilities are concentrated in urban centers, and the seasonal facilities in the countryside. In a major city such as Moscow, almost half the children of nursery and kindergarten age are cared for in child-care centers, but in most communities there are long lists of children waiting to be admitted.

Although the government has allocated substantial investment funds over the years to the expansion of child-care facilities, it has been unwilling to assign to this program sufficient resources to satisfy demand. On the contrary, it has chosen to compel most working women to make their own arrangements—with members of their families or outside help—for the care of their young children. This policy can hardly be considered beneficial to the working mothers. From the standpoint of the regime's overriding goal of economic growth, however, the imposition of hardship on the working mother and a slightly lower rate of participation of women in the labor force have apparently been considered preferable to the diversion of investment funds and other resources to additional child-care facilities.

More information than is presently available would be required to judge whether the government's policy has struck the correct balance, given its schedule of priorities. It is equally difficult to pass judgment on party and governmental thinking with respect to housing, consumers' goods, and the provision of services to relieve women of some of the burden of housework. Such a judgment would require an assessment of whether or not a larger investment in labor-saving devices for the home would encourage a sufficiently larger number of women to enter the labor force, or would sufficiently increase the productivity

of those already in the labor force, to offset the negative effect on the rate of growth which a diversion of resources to the consumer sector would entail. One would also need to assess the effect of such improvements on fertility rates and the long-run supply of labor. Until more data are available, these questions cannot be conclusively answered.

As the Soviet economy has passed through successive stages of development, there have, of course, been changes in the pattern of priorities. What was conceived as correct strategy during the period of forced industrialization under Stalin does not appear applicable today, at a higher stage of economic development when emphasis on producers' goods production is no longer so important. As a result, conditions in the Soviet Union are now favorable to greater investments in housing, production of consumers' goods, and child-care facilities with the aim of lightening the burden on women. Apparently the government expects to sustain or to increase the participation rate of women in this fashion rather than through the more Draconic policies pursued in the past.

Education was the first step by which Soviet women were enabled to equip themselves for a broader and more productive participation in the Soviet economy. Dramatic progress has been made in raising the educational levels of the population, and women have been, perhaps, the principal beneficiaries of this process. For all practical purposes, illiteracy among women has been wiped out except among the older generation and in some of the more stubbornly backward areas of the country. The most striking improvements have been realized by women in rural areas and in some of the less developed republics where, in the past, Moslem traditions barred women from acquiring an education. It should not be overlooked, however, that a third of the persons in prime working ages still have less than a four-year education, and that two thirds of this group are women. It appears that the government has never intended to provide the bulk of the older female population with more than the minimal educational requirements for "functional" literacy. These older women apparently were written off at the start as prospects for the development of special skills.

By concentrating its efforts on the younger age groups during the past four decades, the Soviet government has succeeded in raising substantially the level of educational attainment of millions of young men and women in those occupational fields critical for economic growth and development. Great numbers of younger women have been given on-the-job training in industry and have become an important element in the industrial labor force. Similarly, many young women have been afforded a specialized secondary or higher educational training in science and technology and in other key fields for economic development. Girls have been as well prepared as boys for admission to the scientific or technical faculties of specialized secondary and higher educational institutions because the curricula at the lower educational levels were made uniform for both sexes. Initially, minimum quotas were set for women to encourage their enrollment, and other efforts were made to increase female matriculation, especially in scientific and technical disciplines. As a result, women have had opened to them many of the more interesting and attractive occupations from which they had previously been excluded. This has been a major positive accomplishment of the Soviet regime.

The remarkable success of the Soviet Union in attracting women to the fields of science and technology is apparent from the statistics on education which we have surveyed. The great demand for women with scientific and technological training which arose in the 1930's initiated the impressive increase in the proportion of women enrolled in these fields. Although comprehensive statistics on the proportion of women enrolled in specific fields of science and technology are not available, such data as we do have show that women make up approximately three quarters of the enrollment in courses in the technology of food and consumers' goods production and approximately three fifths of those studying chemical engineering, hydrology, meteorology, geodesy, and cartography. In fields such as mining engineering, transportation, and machine building, on the other hand, only a fifth to a sixth of the students are women. But 53 per cent of the medical students and 25 per cent of the agricultural students are women, both percentages having dropped sharply in recent years. It is estimated that at Soviet universities three fourths to four fifths of the students enrolled in biology, more than two thirds of those in chemistry, two fifths to a half in mathematics, and a quarter to two fifths in physics, geology, and the agricultural sciences are women. In comparison with other countries of the world, these are strikingly high percentages.

It should be emphasized that the choice of a specific field of study by young Soviet men and women is not decided by the state. The percentage of men and women enrolled in each discipline is a fairly faithful reflection of the relative attraction of a field. Initially, the proportion of women grew in all fields, but by no means to the same degree. Certain disciplines, such as medicine, came to be dominated by women; others, such as architecture, by men. In recent years, however, more men have been attracted to medicine— a tendency which has been reinforced by the fact that today men seem to be given admission preference. There have, then, been shifts in the attitudes of young men and women toward certain fields, with resulting shifts over the years in the proportion of women enrolled. To what extent these shifts are a function of altered admission policies and to what extent they depend on changes in individual preferences are matters for conjecture.

There has been a major shift in the overall proportion of women enrolled in specialized secondary and higher education since World War II. During and immediately after the war, the proportion of women enrolled reached its peak. In the past decade, however, the proportion of women has declined— slightly in specialized secondary education and sharply in higher education. This decline has occurred in every field, but is particularly pronounced in medicine, agriculture, and the socioeconomic disciplines. The immediate causes limiting the proportion of women in higher education have been changes in the organization of the secondary school system and more especially in the regulations governing admission to higher educational institutions. Although equality of the sexes remains the stated policy of the Soviet regime, actual admission policies indicate an increasing departure from this principle. Although we cannot be certain that the reduction in the proportion of female enrollment has in fact stemmed from considerations of efficiency, such a reduction does admit of justification on economic grounds. In fields such as medicine, an excessively high proportion of women (from the standpoint of efficient utilization) was permitted to receive training. The government is now eager to restore a more desirable balance of the sexes. In other fields also, where the proportion of women was always lower, the proportion is being further reduced in the interest of efficiency, since the productivity of professional women in most fields tends to be less than that of men.

Even though education has prepared many Soviet women for professional careers, most Soviet women are still engaged in heavy, unskilled work. According to 1959 census data, four fifths of the total 56 million women employed in the labor force were engaged in what is officially termed "physical" labor, and of these the majority were employed in agricultural occupations. Nonspecialized agricultural work alone accounts for one third of the women engaged in physical labor. Typically, women are the field workers and livestock tenders, while men handle the skilled mechanical and construction work and serve as administrators. When the other more skilled agricultural occupations are included, agriculture accounts for 63 per cent of all women employed in physical labor. The large number of women still working in the fields, in spite of Soviet industrial advances, is one of the distinctive features of the Soviet economy.

Women have also come to play an im-portant role in the nonagricultural sectors of the economy—particularly in industry and in the service sector. Throughout a wide range of occupations the percentage of women is substantially higher than that in the United States. Only in such traditional areas of female employment as secretarial, sales, and clerical work and nursing are the American percentages equally high. A high percentage of women is employed in communal and household services and in public dining, and women are relatively well represented in the garment trades and in various occupations in the textile and food industries. Large numbers of women may also be found in metalwork, construction, and transportation. Although most of the industrial and unskilled occupations have little intrinsic appeal for women, for those who lack training or talent for professional work they offer an opportunity to supplement the family income. Also, the high percentage of Soviet women in such occupations dramatically reflects the shortage of males of working age and the determination of the regime to maintain high rates of economic growth at the cost, if necessary, of individual welfare.

Perhaps even more distinctive than the high over-all participation rate of Soviet women, and the vital role they play in the older age groups of the labor force, is their heavy representation in white-collar occupations and the professions. This is the bright side of the employment picture for Soviet women. The role of women in white-collar occupations has increased greatly since the Revolution and has assumed proportions unequaled elsewhere in the world. Today, women comprise more than half the labor force employed in "mental" work. About half of the 11 million women in this category have had a specialized secondary or higher education. The proportion of women among specialists with a specialized secondary education is very high, amounting to 63 per cent in recent years. Among professionals with a higher education, the proportion is 53 per cent. Thus, women form a clear majority of the semiprofessional and professional labor force in the Soviet Union. The woman physician, engineer, research worker, or technician is a commonplace. American women, in contrast, make up very small minorities in most professions, the only exception being teaching; and in such fields as engineering, physics, and medicine, the professional woman is a rarity. For example, while women comprise only 7 per cent of the physicians in the United States, they make up 75 per cent of the total in the Soviet Union. In engineering, the contrast is even more striking; over a quarter of a million Soviet women are engineers, and make up a third of the profession,[2] while in the United States, female engineers account for less than 1 per cent of the total.[3] The number of women in the natural sciences in the Soviet Union is also substantial, although the proportion of women varies considerably from field to field, tending to be higher in the biological sciences and chemistry and lower in a field such as physics.

In 1947, the only year for which data are available, women made up 35 per cent of the staffs of Soviet higher educational institutions, while in the United States they constituted 22 per cent in 1954–55.[4] In the Soviet Union, 68 per cent of the philologists[5] were women, 48 per cent of the teachers of medicine and biology, 45 per cent of the chemists, and 40 per cent of the education teachers. In the remaining fields, the proportion of women lay below the average of 35 per cent for all fields combined. For example, 34 per cent of the staffs in the arts were women, 30 per cent of the historians, 29 per cent of the geographers, 23 per cent of the geologists, 21 per cent of the physicists and mathematicians, 16 per cent of the economists, and 11 per cent of the engineers. U.S. statistics, while they do not follow exactly the Soviet classification of occupations, nevertheless present interesting comparisons. In 1954–55, 40 per cent of education teachers in colleges and universities were women; 28 per cent of those in English, journalism, and foreign languages; 27 per cent in the fine arts; 20 per cent in business and commerce; 14 per cent in mathematics; 11 per cent in the social sciences; 10 per cent in agriculture and the biological sciences; 6 per cent in the physical sciences; and less than 1 per cent in engineering and architecture.[6] As these figures reveal, only in education, and to a lesser degree in the arts, are the percentages of women at all comparable in the two countries. In all other corresponding fields, the Soviet percentages are substantially higher, evincing the success of the Soviets in utilizing the talents of women in fields which in the United States and other western countries remain almost exclusively male domains.

Although the prospects for a woman's embarking upon a professional career in the Soviet Union are much more favorable than in the United States or other Western countries, the prospects for her professional advancement are not so happy; for the proportion of Soviet women in the higher professional echelons tends to decrease as the rank advances. This phenomenon can be observed even in fields, such as education and health, where women predominate. In the former, the proportion of women primary school directors in the Soviet Union is almost identical to the percentage of women teachers, but the percentage declines sharply from 72 per cent for primary school directors to 24 per cent for eight-year school directors and 20 per cent for secondary school directors. A similar attrition occurs in higher education, where in 1960 women comprised 41 per cent of the assistant professors and other lower-level professionals, 24 per cent of the associate professors, 11 per cent of the professors, 12 per cent of the department heads, 9 per cent of the deans, and only 5 per cent of the deputy directors and directors. In medicine and health, although women make up 75 per cent of the medical profession, they account for

---

[2] Tsentral'noe statisticheskoe upravlenie pri Sovete ministrov SSSR, *Zhenshchiny i deti v SSSR* (Moscow, 1961), p. 109.

[3] National Science Foundation, *Women in Scientific Careers* (Washington, D.C., 1961), p. 9.

[4] *Ibid.* and Sinetskii, *op. cit.,* p. 130.

[5] "Philologist" is the common Soviet term for a teacher of languages and literature.

---

[6] National Science Foundation, *op. cit.,* p. 9.

only 57 per cent of the directors, deputy directors, and chief physicians of medical establishments. In research institutions where women make up half the scientific workers (*nauchnye rabotniki*), they account for about a third of heads and deputy heads of branches, 21 per cent of the division heads and their deputies, and 16 per cent of the directors and their deputies and other top administrative personnel. This pattern of declining representation of women as rank increases is repeated in all other fields for which data are available.

The lodging of a disproportionate share of women in the lower and intermediate professional levels suggests that the Soviet government is not receiving so high a return on its educational investment in women as in men, since Soviet professional women with comparable educational training show, on the whole, a lower level of achievement than men. Further evidence of this is provided by various indexes of scholarly productivity. For example, among the top Soviet scientists—full and corresponding members of the Academies of Sciences—very few women are to be found. Women also make up a very small proportion of the recipients of Lenin prizes. An extensive survey of scholarly publications gives further unmistakable evidence that the scholarly productivity of women is lower than that of men. In a comparison of the proportion of women in various specialties on the staffs of higher educational institutions with the proportion of scholarly articles contributed in each field by women, it was found that on the average women contributed about half as many articles as would be expected from their numbers.

The Soviets have done little or no research on the possible effects of various social or environmental factors on the achievement of women. To what extent their lower productivity and their smaller proportions at the higher administrative and professional levels may be due to innate rather than to socially or culturally determined factors is a question that cannot be easily answered. Unlike the woman farmer or factory worker doing a routine job, the Soviet professional woman is likely to derive considerable satisfaction from her work and to be seriously interested in it. But even though her motivation is high, the obstacles to achievement are considerable. Some of the important factors inhibiting a woman's productivity are lost work time and distractions due to family responsibilities, the interruption of a career because of childbearing, and job assignment difficulties. Such factors cannot, of course, readily be eradicated. Other conditions which involve the intellectual development of girls and their career motivations can perhaps be improved. Great progress has already been made in altering the image of a woman's role in society. The intellectual, career-oriented girl in the Soviet Union today can find much support and social approval compared with the girl of only a few decades ago. It appears, however, that conflicts between career and marriage and motherhood will remain for some time to come, since the greater involvement of a woman with her family is not susceptible of drastic change even in Soviet society. If the regime should choose to divert a greater proportion of its investment funds toward the provision of child-care facilities and consumers' goods to lighten the burden of housework, women would be thereby relieved of some of the drain on their creative energies caused by family responsibilities, and their productivity should increase accordingly.

It is evident from this survey that the Soviet regime has a very different attitude toward women from that of a largely unplanned, individualistic society such as our own. Reflecting a philosophy which conceives of the individual's welfare as the basic social goal, our society views the education of women, as well as that of men, to be desirable as an end in itself. Although much of our education is career-oriented, the failure of a young woman after her marriage to pursue a career for which she has been trained does not mean that her education is considered wasted. The raising of a family is considered in itself a sufficient contribution to the welfare of society and is not normally viewed as a distraction from which a woman should, if possible, be relieved so that she can pursue a "productive" career. In contrast, the Soviets see women as an economic asset or resource, to be developed and exploited as effectively as possible. This attitude reflects, of course, the regime's overriding goal of promoting economic development, a goal which has governed Soviet economic policies since the late 1920's. Concurrently, the regime has been concerned with the enlargement of women's rights and with freeing women from all forms of repression and discrimination. This idealistic motif in Soviet policy cannot be denied, but it must be viewed in the proper perspective.

As we have seen, Soviet policy toward women is complex and sometimes contradictory. However, if the predominance of the economic motive in determining Soviet policies toward women is recognized and borne in mind, many of the apparent contradictions can be better understood. It is true that, on occasion, policies inspired by idealism have coincided with those motivated by strictly material considerations, but wherever they diverge, the Soviets have consistently chosen to pursue the economic rather than the idealistic goal. In the first years following the Revolution, for example, the regime was altruistically concerned with securing women's rights and bringing about a greater equality of the sexes. A great deal of legislation was passed to these ends, and the percentage of women in specialized secondary and higher educational institutions, as well as the percentage employed in industry and other branches of the economy, increased significantly during the 1920's and 1930's. But women were perhaps too successful in securing "equality." Too much equality can become a burden to women whose physiological function of motherhood makes impossible their avoidance of heavy responsibilities over and above those imposed by their work. Soviet time-use studies show clearly that the total burden of employment in the labor force and in the home falls much more heavily upon

women than upon men. Although Soviet legislation recognizes that physiological differences necessitate certain safeguards to a woman's health and welfare, the laxity of enforcement and even the suspension of some of these safeguards during various periods of Soviet history suggest that the goal of greater production has more often than not overridden the altruistic concern for protection. Naturally, even under the most extreme pressures, the regime cannot afford a complete abandonment of safeguards and protective measures, since the effective utilization of women as producers depends to a considerable degree upon the reduction of the conflicts which arise from the woman's competing roles as wife and mother. But if the regime had consistently placed women's welfare ahead of production in its scale of priorities, there would be concrete evidence of this in a greater abundance of child-care facilities and a more conscientious enforcement of protective legislation. Similarly, if equality of educational opportunity between the sexes had been of primary concern, admissions regulations and other factors which have contributed to the decline over the past decade in the proportion of women among students in higher education would have been altered when the decline first became evident. Failure to alter them until recently is evidence that the regime in fact preferred the efficient use of its limited higher educational facilities to the social ideal of equality. Apparently realizing that a woman is not likely to be so economically productive as a man in the course of a lifetime, Soviet planners opted for productivity as a social goal and chose accordingly to restrict access to higher education to a smaller proportion of women. It remains to be seen whether the recent modifications in admission requirements are sufficient to redress the balance between the sexes and to permit the percentage of women in higher education to rise to a level proportionate with the percentage of women in the college age population as a whole.

In a totalitarian society such as the Soviet Union, many options are open to the regime in pursuing its policies which are not available to a government responsive to the public will. The party, both directly and through the government, exercises a decisive influence on almost every aspect of economic and social behavior. As we have seen, certain of the policies adopted may be mutually counter-productive—as are, for instance, those aimed simultaneously at the achievement of a higher birth rate and a greater participation of women in the labor force. Others may be in conflict with deep-seated beliefs and customs and may make slow headway—as, for example, the higher education of women in Central Asia, where the traditional subservience of women leads to the early withdrawal of girls from school. For the most part, however, through its control of the means of mass communication and education, the regime has succeeded in achieving acceptance of the new attitudes toward female participation in the labor force, particularly in sectors and occupations which had previously been all but closed to women.

To a society such as our own, which does not tap more than a fraction of the full economic potential of its women, both a lesson and a challenge are implied in the success of the Soviets in developing skilled and capable professional women, particularly in the fields of science and technology. Indeed, Soviet numerical superiority in certain scientific and technological fields is due entirely to the employment of a large number of women in these fields. Although it has been pointed out that the achievement of Soviet women, on the average, falls short of that of men, there can be no doubt that many talents and skills which would have been neglected in another society have been developed and utilized in the Soviet Union and that Soviet policies have made of women one of the major sources of economic strength. Indeed, the imbalance of the sexes in the Soviet population, particularly in the mature age groups, has made the effective participation of women in all sectors of the economy essential to its development. In other, more advanced, societies, this urgent need for the services of women does not arise. The Soviet example proves, however, that a large reservoir of female talent in the United States and other Western countries remains untapped or underdeveloped. Although the tools and mechanisms required to exploit this potential may not be so readily available to our governments, nor the motivation to exploit it so pressing, it is clear that our own society could go much farther than it presently does toward a full utilization of its womanpower. Indeed, the question might be raised whether we can really afford—not only from the standpoint of the national interest, but also from that of the welfare of women as individuals—to neglect their potential contribution of talent and intellect and to leave them so largely at the margin of our economic life.

Appendixes

appendix

I

DEMOGRAPHIC TABLES

TABLE 1. Population of the Soviet Union, by age and sex, 1897–1959.[a]

Age Group	January 28, 1897			December 17, 1926			January 17, 1939		
	Both Sexes	Males	Females	Both Sexes	Males	Females	Both Sexes	Males	Females
All ages...........	125,640	62,477	63,163	147,028	71,043	75,985	170,557	81,695	88,862
Under 5...........	18,880	9,413	9,466	22,322	11,238	11,085	20,780	10,555	10,225
5 to 9.............	15,460	7,718	7,742	15,270	7,650	7,620	18,332	9,197	9,135
10 to 14...........	13,969	7,030	6,939	17,091	8,643	8,448	22,360	11,199	11,161
15 to 19...........	12,485	6,065	6,421	16,977	8,133	8,844	15,201	7,551	7,650
20 to 24...........	10,729	5,373	5,356	13,813	6,712	7,101	14,223	7,140	7,083
25 to 29...........	9,632	4,773	4,860	12,038	5,490	6,547	16,687	8,112	8,575
30 to 34...........	8,277	4,055	4,222	9,065	4,297	4,768	13,943	6,656	7,287
35 to 39...........	7,529	3,839	3,690	8,453	3,994	4,458	11,583	5,267	6,316
40 to 44...........	6,477	3,194	3,283	6,955	3,393	3,562	8,475	3,904	4,571
45 to 49...........	5,230	2,680	2,550	5,907	2,893	3,015	6,862	3,176	3,686
50 to 54...........	4,814	2,294	2,521	5,041	2,343	2,698	5,776	2,526	3,250
55 to 59...........	3,507	1,817	1,690	4,205	1,887	2,318	5,148	1,959	3,189
60 to 64...........	3,473	1,666	1,807	3,835	1,709	2,126	4,283	1,772	2,511
65 to 69...........	1,936	998	938	2,564	1,157	1,407	3,064	1,233	1,831
70 to 74...........	1,655	768	887	1,703	722	981	2,080	788	1,292
75 and over........	1,536	770	766	1,701	731	969	1,760	660	1,100
Age unknown.......	50	26	25	89	50	38	–	–	–
Broad age groups									
Under 16.........	50,933	25,477	25,456	58,323	29,339	28,984	65,105	32,760	32,345
16 to 34..........	38,498	18,949	19,550	48,252	22,824	25,428	56,421	27,650	28,771
35 to 59..........	27,557	13,823	13,734	30,561	14,510	16,051	37,844	16,832	21,012
60 and over.......	8,601	4,203	4,399	9,803	4,319	5,483	11,187	4,453	6,734
16 to 59..........	56,055	32,772	33,283	78,813	37,334	41,479	94,265	44,482	49,783

TABLE 1. Population of the Soviet Union, by age and sex, 1897–1959.[a]—*continued*

Age Group	January 1, 1946			January 1, 1950			January 15, 1959		
	Both Sexes	Males	Females	Both Sexes	Males	Females	Both Sexes	Males	Females
All ages............	176,000	75,015	100,985	180,342	78,001	102,341	208,827	94,050	114,777
Under 5............	13,936	7,084	6,852	18,472	9,414	9,058	24,326	12,434	11,892
5 to 9.............	22,813	11,360	11,453	13,642	6,859	6,765	22,037	11,206	10,831
10 to 14............	18,434	9,124	9,310	21,717	10,776	10,941	15,309	7,755	7,554
15 to 19............	20,229	9,517	10,712	18,241	9,004	9,237	16,499	8,279	8,220
20 to 24............	15,465	6,494	8,971	19,954	9,213	10,741	20,343	10,056	10,287
25 to 29............	10,826	4,122	6,704	13,242	5,353	7,889	18,190	8,917	9,273
30 to 34............	12,632	4,884	7,748	10,574	4,055	6,519	18,999	8,611	10,388
35 to 39............	12,534	4,938	7,596	12,611	4,860	7,751	11,590	4,528	7,062
40 to 44............	10,626	3,861	6,765	11,531	4,517	7,014	10,408	3,998	6,410
45 to 49............	8,761	3,115	5,646	9,788	3,404	6,384	12,264	4,706	7,558
50 to 54............	7,167	2,700	4,467	7,854	2,788	5,066	10,447	4,010	6,437
55 to 59............	6,422	2,293	4,129	6,364	2,322	4,042	8,699	2,906	5,793
60 to 64............	5,502	1,897	3,605	5,619	1,907	3,712	6,697	2,348	4,349
65 to 69............	4,244	1,447	2,797	4,395	1,462	2,933	5,039	1,751	3,288
70 to 74............	3,195	1,098	2,097	3,087	997	2,090	3,805	1,273	2,532
75 and over.........	3,214	1,081	2,133	3,269	1,070	2,199	4,167	1,268	2,899
Age unknown.......	–	–	–	–	–	–	8	4	4
Broad age groups									
Under 16.........	58,917	29,390	29,527	57,262	28,745	28,517	63,496	32,317	31,179
16 to 34..........	55,418	23,195	32,223	58,562	25,929	32,633	72,207	34,941	37,266
35 to 59..........	45,510	16,907	28,603	48,148	17,891	30,257	53,408	20,148	33,260
60 and over.......	16,155	5,523	10,632	16,370	5,436	10,934	19,708	6,640	13,068
16 to 59..........	100,928	40,102	60,826	106,710	43,820	62,890	125,615	55,089	70,526

[a]Figures are expressed in thousands; they relate to the *de facto* territory on the respective dates. This table is based on figures compiled from the following sources for the following dates: for Jan. 28, 1897, Tsentral'nyi statisticheskii komitet, *Obshchii svod po imperii resul'tatov razrabotki dannykh pervoi vseobshchei perepisi naseleniia* (St. Petersburg, 1905), I, 46–48; for Dec. 17, 1926, Gosplan SSSR, *Vsesoiuznaia perepisi naseleniia 1926 goda:* tom LI, *Soiuz Sovetskikh Sotsialisticheskikh Respublik* (Moscow, Leningrad, 1931), pp. 56–58; for Jan. 17, 1939, Michael K. Roof, unpublished working paper (Library of Congress, Washington, D.C., 1964); for Jan. 1, 1946, an estimate was obtained by "reviving" the 1950 population to 1946; for Jan. 1, 1950, James W. Brackett, "Demographic Trends and Population Policy in the Soviet Union," in Joint Economic Committee of the United States Congress, *Dimensions of Soviet Economic Power* (Washington, D.C., 1962), pp. 564–65; for Jan. 15, 1959, figures are based on the distribution appearing in *Itogi . . . 1959 goda: SSSR* (*Svodnyi tom*) (Moscow, 1962), p. 52, and in other official sources.

TABLE 2. Projected population of the Soviet Union, January 1, 1970 and 1980.[a]

Age Group	Series	1970 Both Sexes	Males	Females	1980 Both Sexes	Males	Females
All ages	A	244,812	113,557	131,255	279,425	132,917	146,508
	B	243,247	112,753	130,494	272,567	129,395	143,172
	C	240,376	111,278	129,098	260,810	123,357	137,453
	D	238,550	110,340	128,210	251,983	118,823	133,160
Under 5	A	23,048	11,838	11,210	27,738	14,257	13,481
	B	21,664	11,127	10,537	24,767	12,730	12,037
	C	19,155	9,838	9,317	19,815	10,185	9,630
	D	17,510	8,993	8,517	15,850	8,147	7,703
5 to 9	A	24,132	12,383	11,749	24,730	12,704	12,026
	B	23,951	12,290	11,661	22,396	11,505	10,891
	C	23,589	12,104	11,485	18,444	9,475	8,969
	D	23,408	12,011	11,397	15,391	7,907	7,484
10 to 14	A	24,211	12,378	11,833	22,886	11,740	11,146
	B				21,513	11,036	10,477
	C				19,021	9,758	9,263
	D				17,392	8,922	8,470
15 to 19	A	22,408	11,395	11,013	24,045	12,326	11,719
	B				23,865	12,234	11,631
	C				23,504	12,049	11,455
	D				23,324	11,957	11,367
20 to 24		17,308	8,767	8,541	24,093	12,310	11,783
25 to 29		13,904	6,967	6,937	22,252	11,289	10,963
30 to 34		21,062	10,382	10,680	17,146	8,653	8,493
35 to 39		17,455	8,542	8,913	13,719	6,845	6,874
40 to 44		18,908	8,643	10,265	20,690	10,141	10,549
45 to 49		12,404	4,940	7,464	16,985	8,243	8,742
50 to 54		9,703	3,624	6,079	18,129	8,172	9,957
55 to 59		11,180	4,131	7,049	11,650	4,526	7,124
60 to 64		9,674	3,546	6,128	8,786	3,144	5,642
65 to 69		7,604	2,396	5,208	9,551	3,323	6,228
70 to 74		5,381	1,689	3,692	7,536	2,561	4,975
75 and over		6,430	1,936	4,494	9,489	2,683	6,806
Broad age groups							
Under 16	A	76,127	39,011	37,116	80,040	41,102	38,938
	B	74,562	38,207	36,355	73,182	37,580	35,602
	C	71,691	36,732	34,959	61,425	31,542	29,883
	D	69,865	35,794	34,071	52,598	27,008	25,590
16 to 34		69,846	35,099	34,747	82,850	48,177	40,673
35 to 59		69,650	29,880	39,770	81,173	37,927	43,246
60 and over		29,089	9,567	19,522	35,362	11,711	23,651
16 to 59		139,496	64,979	74,517	164,023	80,104	83,919

[a]Figures are expressed in thousands. This table is based on data from U.S. Department of Commerce, Bureau of the Census, Foreign Demographic Analysis Division, *Estimates and Projections of the Population of the U.S.S.R. and of the Communist Countries of Eastern Europe, by Age and Sex* (Washington, D.C., April, 1964).

The four projection series designated A, B, C, and D differ mainly with respect to fertility and apply only to persons born in 1964 or after. The specific assumptions are as follows:

Mortality: All series assume that mortality will decline and that migration will be negligible.

Fertility: Series A, that the gross reproduction rate (GRR) will rise from its level of 126 in 1963 to 130 in 1964 and that it will continue to rise by a constant annual amount until 1974, after which it will stabilize at 140; Series B, that the GRR will remain constant at 125 throughout the projection period; Series C, that the GRR will decline to 115 in 1964 and that it will continue to decline by a constant annual amount until 1974, after which it will stabilize at 100; Series D, that the GRR will decline to 110 in 1964 and will continue to decline by a constant annual amount until 1974, after which it will stabilize at 80.

TABLE 3. Family members living together, by family size, urban and rural residence, age, and sex, 1959.[a]

Age, Sex, and Residence	Total No. of Family Members	Number of Family Members in Families with								
		2 members	3 members	4 members	5 members	6 members	7 members	8 members	9 members	10 or more members
Urban and rural both sexes										
All ages	186,797	26,157	39,233	43,747	33,812	21,636	11,466	5,840	2,720	2,186
Under 10	45,896	1,439	6,800	11,593	10,347	7,428	4,243	2,213	1,031	802
10 to 19	27,463	2,485	5,231	6,234	5,275	3,678	2,211	1,248	619	482
20 to 24	13,922	2,354	3,923	3,062	2,029	1,226	622	343	179	184
25 to 29	16,296	2,092	4,708	4,375	2,637	1,370	590	263	123	138
30 to 34	17,410	1,831	3,923	5,031	3,448	1,839	786	321	127	104
35 to 39	10,637	1,308	2,093	2,844	2,097	1,226	606	277	112	74
40 to 44	9,436	1,700	2,093	2,187	1,555	938	508	263	115	77
45 to 49	11,336	2,485	2,746	2,406	1,690	1,010	524	270	121	84
50 to 54	9,480	2,485	2,354	1,859	1,353	757	360	175	76	61
55 to 59	7,742	2,354	1,831	1,422	1,014	613	279	124	57	48
60 and over	17,179	5,624	3,531	2,734	2,367	1,551	737	343	160	132
Median age	26.9	44.6	28.9	26.1	23.2	19.2	16.7	15.7	15.3	16.0
Urban and rural males										
All ages	83,131	9,809	17,001	20,014	15,621	10,133	5,422	2,774	1,303	1,054
Under 10	23,277	654	3,531	5,906	5,275	3,750	2,130	1,110	517	404
10 to 19	13,326	1,177	2,485	3,062	2,570	1,803	1,081	606	305	237
20 to 24	5,574	915	1,569	1,203	811	505	262	153	79	77
25 to 29	7,878	1,046	2,354	2,078	1,217	649	279	124	60	71
30 to 34	7,754	654	1,831	2,297	1,555	829	344	139	54	51
35 to 39	4,050	262	654	1,203	947	541	262	109	42	30
40 to 44	3,632	392	654	984	744	433	229	117	49	30
45 to 49	4,645	654	1,046	1,094	811	505	278	146	67	44
50 to 54	3,786	654	915	765	609	361	180	95	43	33
55 to 59	2,798	785	654	547	338	252	115	58	27	22
60 and over	6,411	2,485	1,308	875	744	505	262	117	60	55
Median age	24.5	42.6	26.9	24.3	19.9	17.3	15.4	14.6	14.4	15.2
Urban and rural females										
All ages	103,666	16,348	22,232	23,733	18,191	11,503	6,044	3,066	1,417	1,132
Under 10	22,619	785	3,269	5,687	5,072	3,678	2,113	1,103	514	398
10 to 19	14,137	1,308	2,746	3,172	2,705	1,875	1,130	642	314	245
20 to 24	8,348	1,439	2,354	1,859	1,218	721	360	190	100	107
25 to 29	8,418	1,046	2,354	2,297	1,420	721	311	139	63	67
30 to 34	9,656	1,177	2,092	2,734	1,893	1,010	442	182	73	53
35 to 39	6,587	1,046	1,439	1,641	1,150	685	344	168	70	44
40 to 44	5,804	1,308	1,439	1,203	811	505	279	146	66	47
45 to 49	6,691	1,831	1,700	1,312	879	505	246	124	54	40
50 to 54	5,694	1,700	1,439	1,094	744	396	180	80	33	28
55 to 59	4,944	1,569	1,177	875	676	361	164	66	30	26
60 and over	10,768	3,139	2,223	1,859	1,623	1,046	475	226	100	77
Median age	29.0	46.8	30.9	27.5	25.4	21.4	18.0	16.7	16.2	16.9

Urban *both sexes*										
All ages	85,997	13,205	21,121	22,454	14,791	7,800	3,560	1,674	771	621
Under 10	19,371	792	3,943	5,894	4,201	2,366	1,145	557	265	208
10 to 19	12,220	1,122	2,535	3,256	2,455	1,430	732	373	180	137
20 to 24	6,654	1,387	1,971	1,403	887	507	249	130	61	59
25 to 29	8,068	1,255	2,816	2,077	1,065	481	198	90	41	45
30 to 34	9,166	1,122	2,535	2,863	1,568	676	239	94	37	32
35 to 39	5,503	792	1,196	1,684	1,006	455	178	71	30	20
40 to 44	4,903	924	1,267	1,291	799	390	168	77	34	24
45 to 49	5,589	1,255	1,478	1,291	799	416	194	88	39	29
50 to 54	4,539	1,255	1,197	954	591	299	137	62	25	19
55 to 59	3,431	1,122	845	618	444	234	97	40	17	14
60 and over	6,553	2,179	1,338	1,123	976	546	223	92	42	30
Median age	27.9	40.7	28.7	26.6	24.2	21.0	18.7	17.5	16.8	17.5
Urban *males*										
All ages	38,184	5,018	9,293	10,329	6,804	3,614	1,673	789	366	298
Under 10	9,884	396	2,042	3,031	2,130	1,196	575	279	131	104
10 to 19	5,792	462	2,197	1,572	1,183	689	356	178	88	67
20 to 24	2,511	529	704	505	355	208	102	57	27	24
25 to 29	3,835	595	1,408	954	473	221	96	44	21	23
30 to 34	4,173	396	1,197	1,347	740	312	107	42	16	16
35 to 39	2,105	198	422	730	444	195	71	27	10	8
40 to 44	2,003	264	422	617	385	182	76	33	15	9
45 to 49	2,383	396	563	617	414	208	102	46	21	16
50 to 54	1,875	396	493	449	266	143	71	33	14	10
55 to 59	1,286	396	352	225	148	91	41	19	8	6
60 and over	2,337	990	493	282	266	169	76	31	15	15
Median age	26.2	38.3	27.4	25.3	21.3	18.9	17.3	16.8	15.9	16.7
Urban *females*										
All ages	47,813	8,187	11,828	12,125	7,987	4,186	1,887	885	405	323
Under 10	9,487	396	1,901	2,863	2,071	1,170	570	278	134	104
10 to 19	6,428	660	1,338	1,684	1,272	741	376	195	92	70
20 to 24	4,143	858	1,267	898	532	299	147	73	34	35
25 to 29	4,233	660	1,408	1,123	592	260	102	46	20	22
30 to 34	4,993	726	1,338	1,516	828	364	132	52	21	16
35 to 39	3,398	594	845	954	562	260	107	44	20	12
40 to 44	2,900	660	774	674	414	208	92	44	19	15
45 to 49	3,206	859	915	674	385	208	92	42	18	13
50 to 54	2,664	859	704	505	325	156	66	29	11	9
55 to 59	2,145	726	493	393	296	143	56	21	9	8
60 and over	4,216	1,189	845	841	710	377	147	61	27	19
Median age	29.5	41.5	30.4	27.7	26.0	23.0	19.9	18.4	17.4	18.2

TABLE 3. Family members living together, by family size, urban and rural residence, age, and sex, 1959.ᵃ—continued

Age, Sex, and Residence	Total No. of Family Members	Number of Family Members in Families with								
		2 members	3 members	4 members	5 members	6 members	7 members	8 members	9 members	10 or more members
Rural *both sexes*										
All ages	100,799	12,951	18,111	21,292	19,022	13,837	7,906	4,166	1,949	1,565
Under 10	26,378	583	2,838	5,642	6,163	5,051	3,083	1,656	767	595
10 to 19	15,354	1,360	2,656	3,088	2,853	2,260	1,479	875	440	343
20 to 24	7,303	1,036	1,932	1,650	1,141	715	373	213	117	126
25 to 29	8,232	842	1,932	2,236	1,598	899	384	167	82	92
30 to 34	8,306	712	1,449	2,182	1,826	1,199	553	224	89	72
35 to 39	5,315	583	845	1,224	1,103	784	429	208	84	55
40 to 44	4,521	777	905	905	761	530	328	182	80	53
45 to 49	5,658	1,166	1,268	1,118	875	577	339	177	82	56
50 to 54	4,893	1,165	1,147	959	723	461	226	120	52	40
55 to 59	4,399	1,295	1,026	745	609	369	192	89	39	35
60 and over	10,440	3,432	2,113	1,543	1,370	992	520	255	117	98
Median age	25.8	47.5	29.2	25.6	22.2	18.3	15.9	14.9	14.7	15.5
Rural *males*										
All ages	44,932	4,792	7,667	9,688	8,826	6,526	3,750	1,989	937	757
Under 10	13,396	324	1,449	2,874	3,120	2,560	1,547	833	388	301
10 to 19	7,586	648	1,328	1,544	1,407	1,107	734	432	217	169
20 to 24	3,042	453	785	692	457	300	158	94	50	53
25 to 29	4,003	389	1,026	1,065	761	415	181	78	41	47
30 to 34	3,646	259	604	1,011	837	530	237	94	39	35
35 to 39	2,085	130	241	532	494	369	181	83	32	23
40 to 44	1,677	130	241	373	381	254	158	83	35	22
45 to 49	2,103	259	423	426	380	277	170	94	45	29
50 to 54	1,897	323	423	373	304	230	124	68	30	22
55 to 59	1,536	388	362	266	228	138	79	42	17	16
60 and over	3,961	1,489	785	532	457	346	181	88	43	40
Median age	22.4	46.2	26.3	23.1	19.2	16.4	14.5	13.7	13.7	14.6
Rural *females*										
All ages	55,867	8,159	10,444	11,604	10,196	7,311	4,156	2,177	1,012	808
Under 10	12,982	259	1,389	2,768	3,043	2,491	1,536	823	379	294
10 to 19	7,768	712	1,328	1,544	1,446	1,153	745	443	223	174
20 to 24	4,261	583	1,147	958	684	415	215	119	67	73
25 to 29	4,229	453	906	1,171	837	484	203	89	41	45
30 to 34	4,660	453	845	1,171	989	669	316	130	50	37
35 to 39	3,230	453	604	692	609	415	248	125	52	32
40 to 44	2,844	647	664	532	380	276	170	99	45	31
45 to 49	3,555	907	845	692	495	300	169	83	37	27
50 to 54	2,996	842	724	586	419	231	102	52	22	18
55 to 59	2,863	907	664	479	381	231	113	47	22	19
60 and over	6,479	1,943	1,328	1,011	913	646	339	167	74	58
Median age	28.5	47.9	32.7	27.3	24.5	20.1	17.3	16.0	15.7	16.3

ᵃFor a discussion of this table, see p. 27. Figures are expressed in thousands. This table is based on figures from the national census of Jan. 15, 1959; see *Itogi . . . 1959 goda: SSSR*, pp. 242–43, 245–47.

Table 4. Family members living together, by family size, urban and rural residence, broad age groups, and sex, 1959.[a]

Age, Sex, and Residence	Total No. of Family Members	Number of Family Members in Families with								
		2 members	3 members	4 members	5 members	6 members	7 members	8 members	9 members	10 or more members
Urban and rural										
both sexes										
All ages	186,797	26,157	39,233	43,747	33,812	21,636	11,466	5,840	2,720	2,186
Under 20	73,359	3,924	12,031	17,827	15,622	11,106	6,454	3,461	1,650	1,284
20 to 59	96,259	16,609	23,671	23,186	15,823	8,979	4,275	2,036	910	770
60 and over	17,179	5,624	3,531	2,734	2,367	1,551	737	343	160	132
males										
All ages	83,131	9,809	17,001	20,014	15,621	10,133	5,422	2,774	1,303	1,054
Under 20	36,603	1,831	6,016	8,968	7,845	5,553	3,211	1,716	822	641
20 to 59	40,117	5,493	9,677	10,171	7,032	4,075	1,949	941	421	358
60 and over	6,411	2,485	1,308	875	744	505	262	117	60	55
females										
All ages	103,666	16,348	22,232	23,733	18,191	11,503	6,044	3,066	1,417	1,132
Under 20	36,756	2,093	6,015	8,859	7,777	5,553	3,243	1,745	828	643
20 to 59	56,142	11,116	13,994	13,015	8,791	4,904	2,326	1,095	489	412
60 and over	10,768	3,139	2,223	1,859	1,623	1,046	475	226	100	77
Urban										
both sexes										
All ages	85,997	13,205	21,121	22,454	14,791	7,800	3,560	1,674	771	621
Under 20	31,591	1,914	6,478	9,150	6,656	3,796	1,877	930	445	345
20 to 59	47,853	9,112	13,305	12,181	7,159	3,458	1,460	652	284	242
60 and over	6,553	2,179	1,338	1,123	976	546	223	92	42	34
males										
All ages	38,184	5,018	9,293	10,329	6,804	3,614	1,673	789	366	298
Under 20	15,676	858	3,239	4,603	3,313	1,885	931	457	219	171
20 to 59	20,171	3,170	5,561	5,444	3,225	1,560	666	301	132	112
60 and over	2,337	990	493	282	266	169	76	31	15	15
females										
All ages	47,813	8,187	11,828	12,125	7,987	4,186	1,887	885	405	323
Under 20	15,915	1,056	3,239	4,547	3,343	1,911	946	473	226	174
20 to 59	27,682	5,942	7,744	6,737	3,934	1,898	794	351	152	130
60 and over	4,216	1,189	845	841	710	377	147	61	27	19
Rural										
both sexes										
All ages	100,799	12,951	18,111	21,292	19,022	13,837	7,906	4,166	1,949	1,565
Under 20	41,732	1,943	5,494	8,730	9,016	7,311	4,562	2,531	1,207	938
20 to 59	48,627	7,576	10,504	11,019	8,636	5,534	2,824	1,380	625	529
60 and over	10,440	3,432	2,113	1,543	1,370	992	520	255	117	98
males										
All ages	44,932	4,792	7,667	9,688	8,826	6,526	3,750	1,989	937	757
Under 20	20,982	972	2,777	4,418	4,527	3,667	2,281	1,265	605	470
20 to 59	19,989	2,331	4,105	4,738	3,842	2,513	1,288	636	289	247
60 and over	3,961	1,489	785	532	457	346	181	88	43	40
females										
All ages	55,867	8,159	10,444	11,604	10,196	7,311	4,156	2,177	1,012	808
Under 20	20,750	971	2,717	4,312	4,489	3,644	2,281	1,266	602	468
20 to 59	28,638	5,245	6,399	6,281	4,794	3,021	1,536	744	336	282
60 and over	6,479	1,943	1,328	1,011	913	646	339	167	74	58

[a]Figures are expressed in thousands. Data from the census of Jan. 15, 1959, as presented in Table 3 above, are the source of this table.

257

TABLE 5. Percentage of family members living together, by family size, urban and rural residence, broad age groups, and sex, 1959.[a]

Age, Sex, and Residence	Percentage of Family Members in Families with								
	2 members	3 members	4 members	5 members	6 members	7 members	8 members	9 members	10 or more members
Urban *both sexes*									
All ages...................	15.9	24.6	26.1	17.2	9.1	4.1	1.9	0.9	0.7
Under 20..................	6.1	20.5	29.0	21.1	12.0	5.9	2.9	1.4	1.1
20 to 59..................	19.0	27.8	25.5	15.0	7.2	3.0	1.4	0.6	0.5
60 and over...............	33.3	20.4	17.1	14.9	8.3	3.4	1.4	0.7	0.5
Urban *males*									
All ages...................	13.1	24.3	27.0	17.8	9.5	4.4	2.1	1.0	0.8
Under 20..................	5.5	20.7	29.4	21.1	12.0	5.9	2.9	1.4	1.1
20 to 59..................	15.7	27.6	27.0	16.0	7.7	3.3	1.5	0.6	0.6
60 and over...............	42.4	21.1	12.1	11.4	7.2	3.3	1.3	0.6	0.6
Urban *females*									
All ages...................	17.1	24.7	25.4	16.7	8.8	3.9	1.9	0.8	0.7
Under 20..................	6.6	20.4	28.6	21.0	12.0	5.9	3.0	1.4	1.1
20 to 59..................	21.5	28.0	24.3	14.2	6.8	2.9	1.3	0.5	0.5
60 and over...............	28.2	20.0	20.0	16.9	8.9	3.5	1.5	0.6	0.5
Rural *both sexes*									
All ages...................	12.9	18.0	21.1	18.9	13.7	7.8	4.1	1.9	1.6
Under 20..................	4.7	13.2	20.9	21.6	17.5	10.9	6.1	2.9	2.2
20 to 59..................	15.6	21.6	22.7	17.7	11.4	5.8	2.8	1.3	1.1
60 and over...............	32.9	20.2	14.8	13.1	9.5	5.0	2.5	1.1	0.9
Rural *males*									
All ages...................	10.7	17.1	21.6	19.6	14.5	8.3	4.4	2.1	1.7
Under 20..................	4.6	13.2	21.1	21.6	17.5	10.9	6.0	2.9	2.2
20 to 59..................	11.7	20.5	23.7	19.2	12.6	6.4	3.2	1.5	1.2
60 and over...............	37.6	19.8	13.4	11.6	8.7	4.6	2.2	1.1	1.0
Rural *females*									
All ages...................	14.6	18.7	20.8	18.3	13.1	7.4	3.9	1.8	1.4
Under 20..................	4.7	13.1	20.8	21.6	17.6	11.0	6.1	2.9	2.2
20 to 59..................	18.3	22.3	21.9	16.7	10.6	5.4	2.6	1.2	1.0
60 and over...............	30.0	20.5	15.6	14.1	10.0	5.2	2.6	1.1	0.9

[a]Total percentage of total number of family members in each category is 100.0. Data from the census of Jan. 15, 1959, as presented in Table 3 above, are the source of this table.

appendix

II

POPULATION AND EMPLOYMENT, BY SEX AND AGE, BY REPUBLIC, 1959

METHODS OF ESTIMATING POPULATION

The U.S.S.R. volume of the 1959 census gives the distribution of the population of the U.S.S.R. as a whole and of each republic by age and sex on January 15, 1959.[1] Some further data on individual republics is available in the census volumes for each republic. The age breakdown in each instance is by ten-year age groups to age 20, five-year age groups to age 60, a ten-year age group from ages 60 to 70, and a single age group for age 70 or more. A breakdown of the age group 60 to 69 into two five-year groups is given, however, in the education statistics of the U.S.S.R. and of each republic. These data may be found in the various census volumes.[2] In order to construct population pyramids with five-year age groups to age 80, it was necessary first to divide the population in each of the ten-year age groups (0 to 9, 10 to 19) into two five-year age groups. The division for the U.S.S.R. as a whole was made on the basis of the following

proportions[3] in each five-year group: for males age 0 to 9, 52.6 per cent in the age group 0 to 4, 47.4 per cent in the age group 5 to 9; for males age 10 to 19, 48.4 per cent in the age group 10 to 14, 51.6 per cent in the age group 15 to 19. For the oldest ten-year age group (70 to 79), the first five-year group (70 to 74) for males and females was taken from Brackett's study, and the second was calculated as a residual. Further refinement of these estimates, while desirable, was not felt to be necessary, since the contribution of these age groups to the labor force was not very significant. The proportions in the five-year subgroups for the U.S.S.R. were used for estimating the numbers of males and females in the age groups 0 to 4, 5 to 9, 70 to 74, and 75 to 79 in all republics except those in Transcaucasia, Central Asia, and Kazakhstan. For these areas, where the mortality rate for children tends to be higher than in other areas of the U.S.S.R., the following estimate from data for Kazakhstan[4] was employed: 54.3 per

---

[1] Tsentral'noe statisticheskoe upravlenie pri Sovete ministrov SSSR, *Itogi Vsesoiuznoi perepisi naseleniia 1959 goda: SSSR* (Moscow, 1962), Table 15, pp. 54–71.

[2] *Ibid.*, Table 20, p. 74. (See also Table 20 in the census volumes for the republics, which are listed in the bibliography.)

[3] Derived from figures presented by James W. Brackett, "Demographic Trends and Population Policy in the Soviet Union," in Joint Economic Committee of the United States Congress, *Dimensions of Soviet Economic Power* (Washington, D.C., 1962), pp. 555–56.

[4] Derived from data on Kazakhstan in *Narodnoe khoziaistvo Kazakhstana*, No. 3 (1961), 72, where the numbers of children under age 3, age 3 to 6, and age 7 to 10 are listed.

cent of the males age 0 to 9 in the age group 0 to 4 and 54.1 per cent of the females. These percentages were then adjusted for male-female differences according to the population estimates by one-year age groups for the U.S.S.R. as a whole which were made by Brackett.[5]

In breaking down the age group 10 to 19, three sets of proportions were employed. The first, which was applied to the R.S.F.S.R., Ukraine, and Belorussia, was based on the following census data from the R.S.F.S.R.:[6] 48.7 per cent in the age group 10 to 14 and 51.3 per cent in the age group 15 to 19. These average figures were then adjusted for each sex according to the differences in the proportions for the U.S.S.R. as a whole.[7] The resulting percentages were: for males age 10 to 14, 49.1 per cent; age 15 to 19, 50.9 per cent; for females age 10 to 14, 48.3 per cent; age 15 to 19, 51.7 per cent.

The second set of proportions, which was applied to Lithuania, Latvia, Estonia, and Moldavia, was based on figures giving the number of males and females age 15 to 19 in Lithuania.[8] The proportion of the age group 10 to 19 was readily calculated. This proportion was then adjusted for each sex according to the differences in the proportions for the U.S.S.R. as a whole.[9] The resulting percentages were as follows: for males age 10 to 14, 49.2 per cent; age 15 to 19, 50.8 per cent; for females age 10 to 14, 48.0 per cent; age 15 to 19, 52.0 per cent.

The third set of proportions, which was applied to Kazakhstan and the Transcaucasian and Central Asian republics, was derived in a similar fashion from the same type of data for Kazakhstan.[10]

Where data were given in the republic census volumes on population in the age group 70 to 79, the division was made as 62.5 and 37.5 per cent in the age groups 70 to 74 and 75 to 79 for males, and 57 and 43 per cent for females.

In the absence of sufficient computational resources, no attempt was made to reconcile the sum of the estimates of republic population for the two older age groups with the total for the U.S.S.R. The differences are not sufficiently large to distort the picture we are trying to present. With more time and resources, it would be desirable to reconcile the whole with the sum of the parts.

METHODS OF ESTIMATING EMPLOYMENT

The employment pyramids represent estimates based upon census data in the U.S.S.R. volume and in the republic census volumes, which give the age distribution by sex of the population employed in the socialized and private independent sector, including those employed in the military;[11] they are also based on figures for those employed in the private subsidiary sector.[12] The age distribution given for the former category is broken down into: age 0 to 20, three ten-year age groups, two five-year groups, and age 60 and above. The age breakdown for persons in the private subsidiary sector is very poor, giving figures only for the total and for those in the able-bodied age groups.

Estimates of employment in the first category by five-year age groups were made as follows. It was assumed for practical purposes that all males and females under age 20 who were employed were in the age group 15 to 19. Employment by five-year age groups up to age 50, when employment in five-year groups is given, was estimated by interpolating five-year participation rates for males and females and applying these rates to the male

[5]*Op. cit.*, pp. 555–56.

[6]Tsentral'noe statisticheskoe upravlenie pri Sovete ministrov SSSR, *Narodnoe khoziaistvo RSFSR v 1960 godu* (Moscow, 1961), p. 43.

[7]Again, as estimated by James W. Brackett, *op. cit.*, pp. 555–56.

[8]From Tsentral'noe statisticheskoe upravlenie pri Sovete ministrov Litovskoi SSR, *20 let sovetskoi Litvy* (Vilnius, 1960), p. 82.

[9]Again, from figures in Brackett, *op. cit.*, pp. 555–56.

[10]From *Narodnoe khoziaistvo Kazakhstana, loc. cit.*

[11]*Itogi . . . 1959 goda: SSSR*, Tables 42, 43, 47, 48, pp. 132–45, 161–70 (and corresponding tables in the republic volumes).

[12]*Ibid.*, Tables 30 and 32, pp. 96–99 (and corresponding tables in the republic volumes).

and female population in each five-year group. Certain adjustments were made, however, to avoid absurdities from the slavish interpolation of rates in the critical early and late age groups. In calculating the rate for age 20 to 24 the interpolated rate for the age group 30 to 34 was assumed to apply as well to the age group 25 to 29. Then the age group 20 to 24 was calculated as a residual. This method prevented the overly sharp drop in participation in the age group 25 to 29 which would have resulted from straight interpolation. In the age groups 40 to 44 and 45 to 49, where the participation rate, particularly for women, begins to fall, conversion back to employment figures from the interpolated five-year rates sometimes resulted in discrepancies between the sum of the estimated five-year employment figures and the ten-year total given in the census. When this occurred, the residual was distributed, two thirds to the age group 45 to 49 and one third to the age group 40 to 44. Again, in most cases, the effect was to give the participation curve a more likely shape where it was beginning to decline fairly sharply.

For the U.S.S.R. and most republics, employment in the age group 60 and above was arbitrarily distributed among these four groups as follows: 60, 25, 10, and 5 per cent. This meant that all persons were assumed to be out of the labor force in the socialized and private independent sector by age 70. In some republics, such as Belorussia and Georgia, where many old persons continue to work, it was necessary to assume that a higher percentage worked in the older age groups and that some persons continued working in this sector beyond age 70. Since the figures involved at this end of the distribution are small, use of these rough estimates was felt justified. Furthermore, unless one admits the possibility of an increase in the participation rate in these oldest groups, the estimates are closely controlled by the totals.

Estimates of the distribution of persons employed in private subsidiary agriculture were made separately for males and females. The number of males is small, of course, and it was estimated that 10 per cent of the total

employed in the working-age groups was employed in each of the five-year age groups from age 20 to 59. It was estimated that 5 per cent of this group was in the age group 15 to 19, 15 per cent in the age group 50 to 54, and 20 per cent in the age group 55 to 59. The older males were distributed for the U.S.S.R. and most republics in the following proportions: 25, 35, 25, and 10 per cent in the four five-year age groups between age 60 and 80; 5 per cent were assumed to be age 80 and over. Females working in private subsidiary agriculture were numerous and their estimation more critical. It was assumed that 7 per cent of the women working in this sector were in the age group 15 to 19. Up to age 45 it was assumed that the percentage varied about 10 per cent for each five-year group—1 or 2 per cent higher or lower, depending upon whether or not the age group was a large one. At age 45 it was assumed that women began to enter the private subsidiary sector in greater numbers as they withdrew from the socialized sector. Therefore, it was assumed that 18 and 22 per cent were employed in the age groups 45 to 49 and 50 to 54, respectively. The older females (from age 55) were distributed in most instances in the following percentages: 35, 30, 20, 10, and 4 per cent in the five five-year age groups between age 60 and 80. In some republics, such as Belorussia, it was necessary to assume that more women in the older age groups worked and that more women over age 80 continued to work on their plots of land. Since these estimates were constructed, the Soviet demographer B. Ts. Urlanis has published estimates of his own of the extent of involvement of women in the private subsidiary agriculture of the U.S.S.R. in the age groups 16 to 19, 20 to 29, 30 to 39, 40 to 49, 50 to 54, 55 to 59, and 60 and over.[13] His estimates and my own do not appear to differ greatly.

Although the general outline of the employment pyramids is firmly based on census data, the details of their precise shapes, particularly in the older age groups, can only be

[13]B. Ts. Urlanis, *Dinamika i struktura naseleniia SSSR i SShA* (Moscow, 1964), pp. 44–45.

approximated. It was felt, however, that sensible estimates permitted a better understanding of participation in the Soviet labor force by age and by sex than would be possible with no estimates at all. Further refinements would, of course, be desirable.

TABLE 1. Population and employment, by sex and by age, 1959, R.S.F.S.R.[a]

Age	Males			Females		
	Total	Employed	Participa-tion Rate	Total	Employed	Participa-tion Rate
			%			%
0 to 4	6,895	–	–	6,621	–	–
5 to 9	6,214	–	–	6,038	–	–
10 to 14	4,329	–	–	4,183	–	–
15 to 19	4,487	2,869	64	4,478	2,755	62
20 to 24	5,794	5,180	89	5,758	4,755	83
25 to 29	5,251	4,933	94	5,340	4,307	81
30 to 34	5,051	4,774	95	6,052	4,798	79
35 to 39	2,474	2,362	96	3,949	3,089	78
40 to 44	2,356	2,216	94	3,821	2,906	76
45 to 49	2,682	2,444	91	4,485	3,286	73
50 to 54	2,168	1,866	86	3,797	2,569	68
55 to 59	1,481	1,156	78	3,270	1,532	47
60 to 64	1,162	774	67	2,427	955	39
65 to 69	847	382	45	1,817	545	30
70 to 74	615	150	24	1,346	257	19
75 to 79	369	66	18	1,015	109	12
All ages	52,425	29,172	56	65,110	27,863	43

[a]Figures are expressed in thousands.

TABLE 2. Population and employment, by sex and by age, 1959, Ukrainian S.S.R.[a]

Age	Males			Females		
	Total	Employed	Participa-tion Rate	Total	Employed	Participa-tion Rate
			%			%
0 to 4	2,120	–	–	2,019	–	–
5 to 9	1,910	–	–	1,847	–	–
10 to 14	1,598	–	–	1,563	–	–
15 to 19	1,656	1,093	66	1,673	1,136	68
20 to 24	2,012	1,792	89	2,096	1,732	83
25 to 29	1,612	1,520	94	1,739	1,408	81
30 to 34	1,680	1,596	95	2,149	1,702	79
35 to 39	1,001	962	96	1,587	1,212	76
40 to 44	813	772	95	1,355	1,019	75
45 to 49	1,045	963	92	1,712	1,285	75
50 to 54	917	807	88	1,435	1,008	70
55 to 59	682	567	83	1,265	853	68
60 to 64	549	461	84	952	576	61
65 to 69	414	280	68	753	326	43
70 to 74	288	123	19	511	143	28
75 to 79	173	25	15	386	52	13
All ages	18,575	29,172	56	23,294	12,452	54

[a]Figures are expressed in thousands.

TABLE 3. Population and employment, by sex and by age, 1959, Belorussian S.S.R.[a]

Age	Males			Females		
	Total	Employed	Participa-tion Rate	Total	Employed	Participa-tion Rate
			%			%
0 to 4..............	474.3	–	–	452.9	–	–
5 to 9..............	427.4	–	–	413.1	–	–
10 to 14............	319.7	–	–	318.8	–	–
15 to 19............	331.4	204.4	62	341.3	227.2	67
20 to 24............	349.5	309.5	89	401.6	341.6	85
25 to 29............	339.6	320.0	94	390.0	341.9	88
30 to 34............	286.5	271.9	95	390.0	357.2	92
35 to 39............	176.5	169.7	96	272.4	249.1	91
40 to 44............	126.3	120.0	95	211.8	180.5	85
45 to 49............	160.0	150.0	94	261.8	230.1	88
50 to 54............	159.5	148.1	93	234.1	206.1	88
55 to 59............	125.6	114.1	91	228.7	200.4	86
60 to 64............	101.9	93.1	91	172.6	128.0	74
65 to 69............	81.2	69.3	85	144.8	92.9	64
70 to 74............	60.2	37.6	62	112.1	65.6	59
75 to 79............	36.1	13.2	37	67.2	17.0	25
All ages..........	3,581.0	2,020.9	56	4,473.6	2,637.6	59

[a]Figures are expressed in thousands.

TABLE 4. Population and employment, by sex and by age, 1959, Kazakh S.S.R.[a]

Age	Males			Females		
	Total	Employed	Participa-tion Rate	Total	Employed	Participa-tion Rate
			%			%
0 to 4..............	714.8	–	–	689.1	–	–
5 to 9..............	601.5	–	–	584.6	–	–
10 to 14............	375.9	–	–	348.0	–	–
15 to 19............	394.3	240.8	61	377.0	211.9	56
20 to 24............	508.9	457.0	90	483.3	344.8	71
25 to 29............	377.2	356.9	95	359.9	254.9	71
30 to 34............	370.0	352.6	95	422.4	292.1	69
35 to 39............	181.7	175.0	96	265.8	182.5	69
40 to 44............	167.2	158.1	95	240.8	164.4	68
45 to 49............	178.1	163.3	91	253.0	172.9	68
50 to 54............	153.6	133.7	87	213.0	143.7	68
55 to 59............	110.9	89.4	81	211.6	79.3	38
60 to 64............	97.2	77.7	80	152.7	45.3	30
65 to 69............	78.2	38.5	49	112.8	26.9	24
70 to 74............	56.8	18.1	32	76.0	12.9	17
75 to 79............	34.1	8.5	25	57.3	5.3	9
All ages..........	4,422.2	2,269.6	51	4,887.7	1,936.9	40

[a]Figures are expressed in thousands.

TABLE 5. Population and employment, by sex and by age, 1959, Georgian S.S.R.[a]

Age	Males			Females		
	Total	Employed	Participation Rate	Total	Employed	Participation Rate
			%			%
0 to 4.............	240.7	–	–	230.2	–	–
5 to 9.............	202.5	–	–	195.4	–	–
10 to 14...........	158.4	–	–	157.1	–	–
15 to 19...........	166.1	84.5	51	170.1	81.7	48
20 to 24...........	185.0	150.3	81	214.6	144.0	67
25 to 29...........	174.3	162.1	93	192.0	132.7	69
30 to 34...........	171.9	161.8	94	191.7	136.5	71
35 to 39...........	87.6	85.6	98	133.6	98.8	74
40 to 44...........	73.2	69.8	95	114.9	85.6	75
45 to 49...........	83.7	78.4	94	113.9	87.6	77
50 to 54...........	73.7	68.1	92	97.9	78.4	80
55 to 59...........	61.8	56.2	91	109.9	80.6	73
60 to 64...........	53.6	48.5	90	80.5	53.6	67
65 to 69...........	45.5	37.2	82	56.2	37.8	67
70 to 74...........	39.0	28.9	74	47.7	25.5	49
75 to 79...........	23.4	8.3	35	36.0	12.2	34
All ages..........	1,856.3	1,045.2	56	2,178.7	1,055.0	48

[a]Figures are expressed in thousands.

TABLE 6. Population and employment, by sex and by age, 1959, Azerbaidzhan S.S.R.[a]

Age	Males			Females		
	Total	Employed	Participation Rate	Total	Employed	Participation Rate
			%			%
0 to 4.............	301.3	–	–	287.1	–	–
5 to 9.............	253.6	–	–	243.5	–	–
10 to 14...........	144.4	–	–	136.3	–	–
15 to 19...........	151.6	69.7	46	147.6	72.3	49
20 to 24...........	189.6	159.7	84	207.2	142.2	69
25 to 29...........	170.7	160.1	94	172.2	118.5	69
30 to 34...........	141.1	134.2	95	146.3	99.1	68
35 to 39...........	65.7	64.5	98	92.7	64.0	69
40 to 44...........	51.6	49.8	97	78.2	55.3	71
45 to 49...........	67.0	63.4	95	86.8	60.4	70
50 to 54...........	54.6	50.7	93	76.6	50.3	66
55 to 59...........	42.4	37.5	88	78.8	45.1	57
60 to 64...........	40.7	35.5	87	59.1	28.1	48
65 to 69...........	29.6	25.1	85	39.7	18.8	47
70 to 74...........	21.8	12.4	57	32.1	11.5	36
75 to 79...........	13.1	4.1	31	24.2	3.4	14
All ages..........	1,756.6	866.7	51	1,941.2	769.0	40

[a]Figures are expressed in thousands.

TABLE 7. Population and employment, by sex and by age, 1959, Lithuanian S.S.R.[a]

Age	Males			Females		
	Total	Employed	Participa-tion Rate	Total	Employed	Participa-tion Rate
			%			%
0 to 4	135.4	–	–	130.3	–	–
5 to 9	122.0	–	–	118.9	–	–
10 to 14	112.3	–	–	110.6	–	–
15 to 19	116.0	68.4	59	119.8	64.2	54
20 to 24	111.0	93.5	84	123.4	98.4	80
25 to 29	112.0	104.8	94	127.0	97.1	77
30 to 34	94.4	89.2	95	124.7	93.6	75
35 to 39	71.2	68.3	96	95.6	70.7	74
40 to 44	49.2	46.7	95	69.6	54.1	78
45 to 49	57.4	54.2	94	85.4	68.7	80
50 to 54	85.4	80.1	94	83.2	65.1	78
55 to 59	55.9	51.1	91	78.3	59.7	76
60 to 64	46.4	42.6	92	66.6	48.5	73
65 to 69	33.3	28.6	86	48.5	25.2	52
70 to 74	20.4	15.4	76	34.9	11.4	33
75 to 79	12.3	5.4	44	26.4	5.1	19
All ages	1,244.7	748.3	60	1,466.8	761.8	52

[a]Figures are expressed in thousands.

TABLE 8. Population and employment, by sex and by age, 1959, Moldavian S.S.R.[a]

Age	Males			Females		
	Total	Employed	Participa-tion Rate	Total	Employed	Participa-tion Rate
			%			%
0 to 4	199.1	–	–	191.0	–	–
5 to 9	179.4	–	–	174.2	–	–
10 to 14	110.8	–	–	114.7	–	–
15 to 19	114.4	87.8	77	124.3	107.1	86
20 to 24	117.7	108.5	92	143.7	130.4	91
25 to 29	109.1	105.4	97	127.4	112.6	88
30 to 34	103.2	99.7	97	127.4	109.6	86
35 to 39	86.5	84.1	97	111.1	92.9	84
40 to 44	61.7	60.1	97	78.5	66.2	84
45 to 49	71.7	69.2	97	86.0	72.8	85
50 to 54	55.0	52.5	96	64.7	54.5	84
55 to 59	43.1	40.6	94	66.9	54.9	82
60 to 64	31.7	27.4	86	49.7	38.6	78
65 to 69	20.5	16.5	80	36.4	19.2	53
70 to 74	15.3	11.6	76	25.1	8.5	34
75 to 79	9.2	4.9	53	18.9	3.8	20
All ages	1,333.8	768.3	58	1,550.7	871.1	56

[a]Figures are expressed in thousands.

TABLE 9. Population and employment, by sex and by age, 1959, Kirgiz S.S.R.[a]

Age	Males			Females		
	Total	Employed	Participa-tion Rate	Total	Employed	Participa-tion Rate
			%			%
0 to 4.............	168.1	–	–	162.0	–	–
5 to 9.............	141.4	–	–	137.4	–	–
10 to 14...........	79.3	–	–	72.4	–	–
15 to 19...........	83.1	42.2	51	78.5	38.3	49
20 to 24...........	85.8	75.9	89	93.4	72.0	77
25 to 29...........	86.0	80.1	93	90.4	68.8	76
30 to 34...........	80.2	76.2	95	87.7	68.0	78
35 to 39...........	42.1	40.6	96	61.0	46.5	76
40 to 44...........	32.2	30.4	94	47.4	34.8	73
45 to 49...........	37.0	34.1	92	49.7	36.8	74
50 to 54...........	30.4	27.1	89	41.9	29.0	69
55 to 59...........	26.6	23.0	87	52.3	30.1	58
60 to 64...........	26.5	23.1	87	41.0	18.1	44
65 to 69...........	22.5	16.9	75	31.2	10.7	34
70 to 74...........	16.5	9.6	58	19.6	5.1	26
75 to 79...........	9.9	3.4	34	14.7	2.2	15
All ages.........	974.6	482.6	50	1,091.2	460.4	42

[a]Figures are expressed in thousands.

TABLE 10. Population and employment, by sex and by age, 1959, Tadzhik S.S.R.[a]

Age	Males			Females		
	Total	Employed	Participa-tion Rate	Total	Employed	Participa-tion Rate
			%			%
0 to 4.............	168.3	–	–	161.7	–	–
5 to 9.............	141.6	–	–	137.2	–	–
10 to 14...........	83.2	–	–	69.1	–	–
15 to 19...........	87.4	48.0	55	74.9	45.9	61
20 to 24...........	83.0	73.9	89	97.6	81.4	83
25 to 29...........	83.0	77.1	93	90.9	73.8	81
30 to 34...........	78.2	75.6	97	78.3	61.3	78
35 to 39...........	43.5	43.0	99	56.2	42.9	76
40 to 44...........	31.5	30.4	97	43.8	33.1	76
45 to 49...........	35.1	33.4	95	39.2	29.4	75
50 to 54...........	32.1	30.2	94	37.6	25.1	67
55 to 59...........	28.9	26.6	92	41.4	21.2	51
60 to 64...........	25.2	20.9	83	33.9	13.2	39
65 to 69...........	18.4	14.5	79	21.7	7.7	35
70 to 74...........	12.6	8.0	63	14.0	3.7	26
75 to 79...........	7.6	2.8	37	10.6	1.6	15
All ages.........	964.4	484.4	50	1,015.5	440.3	43

[a]Figures are expressed in thousands.

TABLE 11. Population and employment, by sex and by age, 1959, Armenian S.S.R.[a]

Age	Males			Females		
	Total	Employed	Participa- tion Rate	Total	Employed	Participa- tion Rate
			%			%
0 to 4...............	142.3	–	–	135.0	–	–
5 to 9...............	119.8	–	–	114.6	–	–
10 to 14...............	68.3	–	–	65.2	–	–
15 to 19...............	71.6	33.7	47	70.6	33.0	47
20 to 24...............	87.8	71.5	81	99.8	67.4	68
25 to 29...............	81.4	76.4	94	85.8	56.9	66
30 to 34...............	76.9	73.1	95	81.4	53.6	66
35 to 39...............	30.7	30.5	99	41.8	28.4	68
40 to 44...............	22.9	22.2	97	34.1	24.2	71
45 to 49...............	30.5	28.9	95	39.6	29.2	74
50 to 54...............	28.7	26.3	92	36.2	24.6	68
55 to 59...............	21.7	19.2	89	34.7	19.0	55
60 to 64...............	18.0	15.5	86	24.0	12.5	52
65 to 69...............	14.8	11.1	75	19.6	7.1	36
70 to 74...............	12.3	5.9	48	15.2	3.3	22
75 to 79...............	7.4	2.1	28	11.4	1.4	12
All ages............	842.4	417.2	50	920.6	360.6	39

[a]Figures are expressed in thousands.

TABLE 12. Population and employment, by sex and by age, 1959, Turkmen S.S.R.[a]

Age	Males			Females		
	Total	Employed	Participa- tion Rate	Total	Employed	Participa- tion Rate
			%			%
0 to 4...............	127.0	–	–	122.5	–	–
5 to 9...............	106.9	–	–	103.9	–	–
10 to 14...............	61.3	–	–	53.6	–	–
15 to 19...............	64.2	33.6	52	58.1	28.0	48
20 to 24...............	66.6	59.0	89	68.7	48.9	71
25 to 29...............	62.1	59.3	96	64.5	44.7	69
30 to 34...............	57.3	54.4	95	62.5	42.8	69
35 to 39...............	32.0	31.0	97	46.0	33.6	73
40 to 44...............	26.3	25.5	97	37.0	26.4	71
45 to 49...............	28.8	27.2	94	37.3	27.4	74
50 to 54...............	24.4	22.4	92	31.2	21.7	70
55 to 59...............	20.5	18.0	88	33.9	17.6	52
60 to 64...............	18.9	14.1	83	25.5	10.5	41
65 to 69...............	13.6	9.4	69	16.4	6.2	38
70 to 74...............	10.2	6.7	66	10.8	2.9	27
75 to 79...............	6.1	2.8	46	8.2	1.2	15
All ages............	730.3	362.2	50	786.0	322.9	41

[a]Figures are expressed in thousands.

TABLE 13. Population and employment, by sex and by age, 1959, Estonian S.S.R.[a]

Age	Males			Females		
	Total	Employed	Participa-tion Rate	Total	Employed	Participa-tion Rate
			%			%
0 to 4...............	50.9	–	–	48.3	–	–
5 to 9...............	45.9	–	–	44.1	–	–
10 to 14..............	41.8	–	–	40.0	–	–
15 to 19..............	43.2	20.9	48	43.3	17.0	39
20 to 24..............	49.5	43.5	88	49.2	37.4	76
25 to 29..............	49.4	46.4	94	53.6	39.8	74
30 to 34..............	42.2	40.0	95	56.2	41.0	73
35 to 39..............	29.8	28.6	96	45.8	33.3	73
40 to 44..............	25.8	24.4	95	36.5	27.6	76
45 to 49..............	31.9	29.7	93	46.0	35.0	76
50 to 54..............	29.8	27.2	91	43.8	32.2	74
55 to 59..............	26.5	23.3	88	42.1	28.0	67
60 to 64..............	19.5	14.7	75	35.9	21.6	60
65 to 69..............	15.6	10.6	68	31.1	10.4	33
70 to 74..............	11.4	7.2	63	23.8	4.6	19
75 to 79..............	6.8	2.0	29	17.9	2.1	12
All ages............	525.1	318.5	60	671.7	330.0	49

[a]Figures are expressed in thousands.

appendix
III

CHILD-CARE FACILITIES
AND TIME BUDGETS

TABLE 1. Number of children in nurseries of all jurisdictions, by republic, 1940–64.[a]

Republic	1940	1950	1952	1955	1958	1959	1960	1961	1962	1963	1964
U.S.S.R.	859.5	776.7	796.0	907.2	1,134.9	1,208.4	1,260.2	1,323.2	1,371.8	1,490.8	1,494.5
R.S.F.S.R.	563.1	502.7	516.5	584.5	735.5	794.7	837.8	892.2	932.9	1,030.0	1,041.5
Ukrainian S.S.R.	161.3	125.1	126.1	144.6	174.6	179.9	188.8	197.1	208.0	216.4	217.1
Belorussian S.S.R.	21.4	11.7	12.5	15.9	21.3	24.0	25.4	27.2	27.8	32.4	32.4
Uzbek S.S.R.	44.5	42.6	43.8	49.2	63.2	63.3	64.2	64.0	57.9	60.0	56.8
Kazakh S.S.R.	17.9	25.3	26.1	32.9	49.2	53.4	55.5	56.7	59.0	61.1	57.4
Georgian S.S.R.	10.9	13.9	13.8	14.7	14.7	15.0	14.1	14.5	14.7	13.4	14.2
Azerbaidzhan S.S.R.	15.2	12.1	11.2	12.1	13.7	14.5	13.6	12.8	12.7	12.9	12.5
Lithuanian S.S.R.	0.2	2.1	2.5	3.3	4.3	4.5	4.7	5.4	5.3	5.5	5.7
Moldavian S.S.R.	1.8	4.2	4.8	6.5	8.0	8.4	8.7	9.2	8.7	9.7	8.8
Latvian S.S.R.	0.2	3.3	3.8	4.9	5.7	6.0	5.9	5.7	6.2	6.7	7.0
Kirgiz S.S.R.	2.8	5.0	4.9	5.7	7.9	9.2	10.0	10.1	11.0	12.5	12.2
Tadzhik S.S.R.	5.9	6.2	6.3	7.2	9.2	8.2	7.7	8.0	8.2	9.0	8.4
Armenian S.S.R.	4.1	4.2	4.4	4.9	5.9	5.4	3.0	3.2	2.2	2.3	2.1
Turkmen S.S.R.	10.0	15.6	16.0	16.5	17.2	17.2	16.0	12.1	12.2	13.3	12.9
Estonian S.S.R.	0.2	2.7	3.3	4.3	4.5	4.7	4.8	5.0	5.0	5.6	5.5

[a]Figures are expressed in thousands, as of the end of each specified year. This table was compiled from figures presented in *Zhenshchiny i deti v SSSR* (Moscow, 1963), p. 134; *Narodnoe khoziaistvo SSSR v 1961 godu* (Moscow, 1962), p. 749; *Narodnoe khoziaistvo SSSR v 1962 godu* (Moscow, 1963), p. 622; and *Narodnoe khoziaistvo SSSR v 1964 godu* (Moscow, 1965), p. 472. Figures for 1963 and 1964 are not entirely compatible with the previous series. In 1962, the latest year in which the two series overlap, the new series was 96,000 larger. Children of nursery age in nursery-kindergartens are not included in either series.

TABLE 2. Children's summer playgrounds, 1927–59.[a]

Year	Total		Town		Country	
	Playgrounds	Children	Playgrounds	Children	Playgrounds	Children
1927	3,467	192,877	1,665	126,191	1,802	66,686
1932	93,136	4,034,632	10,846	674,186	82,290	3,360,446
1937	71,636	2,257,839	5,256	254,059	66,380	2,003,780
1940	31,593	1,175,130	4,366	232,782	27,227	942,348
1945	63,867	2,112,932	3,988	316,328	59,879	1,796,604
1946	44,090	1,394,899	3,709	266,406	40,381	1,128,493
1947	36,590	1,439,153	4,861	508,444	31,729	930,709
1948	38,863	1,121,678	3,416	283,576	35,447	838,102
1949	39,673	1,021,253	3,318	241,367	36,355	779,886
1950	37,482	966,665	2,399	236,921	35,083	729,744
1951	29,083	847,972	2,053	226,447	27,030	621,525
1952	25,781	867,723	1,763	167,583	24,018	700,140
1953	24,673	767,346	1,461	133,787	23,212	633,559
1954	25,982	811,959	1,439	123,265	24,543	688,694
1955	27,267	970,655	1,651	155,853	25,616	814,802
1956	29,277	1,060,300	n.a.[b]	n.a.	n.a.	n.a.
1957	32,421	1,228,800	n.a.	n.a	n a.	n.a.
1958	33,574	1,335,900	n.a.	n.a.	n.a.	n.a.
1959	38,549	1,553,700	n.a.	n.a.	n.a.	n.a.

[a]Based on Tsentral'noe statisticheskoe upravlenie pri Sovete ministrov, *Kul'turnoe stroitel'stvo SSSR* (Moscow, 1956), p. 193; and *Narodnoe khoziaistvo SSSR v 1959 godu* (Moscow, 1960), pp. 738–39.
[b]No data available.

TABLE 3. Distribution of kindergartens, by departmental subordination, 1937–55.[a]

Year[b]	Total		Departments of Public Education		Other Departments and Organizations		Collective Farms	
	Kinder-gartens	Enrollment	Kinder-gartens	Enrollment	Kinder-gartens	Enrollment	Kinder-gartens	Enrollment
1937	24,535	1,045,289	7,220	335,541	12,570	573,762	4,745	135,986
1940	23,999	1,171,507	8,762	451,381	12,883	649,240	2,354	70,886
1945	28,436	1,471,036	9,926	531,335	17,404	910,018	1,106	29,683
1946	27,662	1,283,230	10,165	491,598	16,680	769,791	817	21,841
1947	27,246	1,253,621	10,197	486,207	16,358	749,514	691	17,900
1948	26,143	1,054,657	10,017	414,077	15,695	630,846	431	9,734
1949	25,499	1,088,561	9,787	418,920	15,240	659,790	472	9,851
1950	25,624	1,168,779	9,928	445,945	15,275	711,396	421	11,438
1951	26,337	1,256,948	10,130	482,482	15,747	759,798	460	14,668
1952	27,140	1,352,550	10,300	510,232	16,337	826,844	503	15,474
1953	28,258	1,438,307	10,611	535,348	17,140	887,188	507	15,771
1954	29,896	1,577,398	10,929	574,700	18,369	983,421	598	19,277
1955	31,596	1,730,941	11,244	609,216	19,510	1,091,343	842	30,382

[a]Based on *Kul'turnoe stroitel'stvo SSSR* (Moscow, 1956), p. 192.   [b]As of the end of each year.

TABLE 4. Distribution of summer playgrounds, by departmental subordination, 1955.[a]

	Total	Departments of Public Education			Other De-partments	Collective Farms
		Total	Preschool Age	School Age		
Playgrounds	27,267	2,325	533	1,792	493	24,449
Enrollment	970,655	171,319	21,072	150,247	27,990	771,346
Children age 3–7	564,799	26,750	19,294	7,456	14,370	523,679

[a]Based on *Kul'turnoe stroitel'stvo SSSR* (Moscow, 1956), p. 193.

TABLE 5. Children's establishments (other than schools) under the Ministries of Education and the Ministry of Railways in the U.S.S.R. and the Union republics on January 1, 1956.[a]

Republic	Young Technicians' Centers	Young Naturalists' Centers	Excursion and Tourist Stations	Pioneer Palaces and Houses	Children's Stadiums	Children's Parks
U.S.S.R.	258	214	135	2,382	33	135
Under Ministries of Education						
R.S.F.S.R.	112	101	63	1,187	12	84
Ukrainian S.S.R.	53	36	27	493	4	3
Belorussian S.S.R.	2	12	7	51	2	–
Uzbek S.S.R.	16	18	10	53	5	2
Kazakh S.S.R.	15	16	15	216	3	17
Georgian S.S.R.	9	3	1	62	–	5
Azerbaidzhan S.S.R.	4	2	1	76	–	9
Lithuanian S.S.R.	3	3	1	41	–	–
Moldavian S.S.R.	6	6	1	62	–	–
Latvian S.S.R.	4	2	1	9	–	1
Kirgiz S.S.R.	–	–	–	6	–	2
Tadzhik S.S.R.	6	4	–	18	–	5
Armenian S.S.R.	1	3	3	36	–	–
Turkmen S.S.R.	6	3	4	52	5	5
Estonian S.S.R.	–	3	1	14	2	2
Under Ministry of Railways	21	2	0	6	–	–

[a]In addition, there are over 800 children's sports schools and 30 children's railways in the U.S.S.R. This table is based on *Kul'turnoe stroitel'stvo SSSR* (Moscow, 1956), p. 188.

TABLE 6. Number of Pioneer camps in the U.S.S.R. and the Union republics, 1950–64.[a]

Republic	1950	1952	1953	1954	1955	1956	1957	1958	1959	1960	1961	1962	1963	1964
U.S.S.R.	8,103	8,604	8,327	8,096	7,964	7,660	7,577	7,540	7,438	7,626	7,797	7,916	7,808	8,041
R.S.F.S.R.	5,562	5,870	5,577	5,363	5,227	4,974	4,917	4,963	4,943	5,140	5,288	5,365	5,290	5,444
Ukrainian S.S.R.	1,508	1,592	1,596	1,591	1,598	1,570	1,546	1,525	1,430	1,393	1,371	1,366	1,285	1,295
Belorussian S.S.R.	264	257	253	251	249	256	241	221	223	232	238	241	259	273
Uzbek S.S.R.	94	108	118	114	121	120	119	111	111	117	115	129	128	138
Kazakh S.S.R.	243	287	298	295	315	297	307	265	280	282	291	322	334	359
Georgian S.S.R.	107	120	121	121	116	105	113	115	93	85	94	86	89	94
Azerbaidzhan S.S.R.	78	77	76	76	69	71	70	79	75	80	85	87	91	92
Lithuanian S.S.R.	29	33	35	41	42	42	46	46	52	49	46	50	56	64
Moldavian S.S.R.	28	30	27	33	30	21	21	20	28	30	30	32	34	36
Latvian S.S.R.	38	43	43	44	43	41	41	42	44	48	51	53	59	63
Kirgiz S.S.R.	38	50	47	43	42	46	41	45	45	46	53	47	43	49
Tadzhik S.S.R.	11	21	22	24	20	20	21	22	23	22	26	28	29	24
Armenian S.S.R.	57	62	57	47	45	45	39	37	36	41	42	43	43	41
Turkmen S.S.R.	12	16	19	17	16	19	19	17	21	23	24	23	24	23
Estonian S.S.R.	34	38	38	36	31	33	36	32	34	38	43	44	44	46

[a]This table is based on *Kul'turnoe stroitel'stvo SSSR* (Moscow, 1956), pp. 196–97; *Narodnoe khoziaistvo SSSR v 1959 godu* (Moscow, 1960), pp. 738–39; *Narodnoe khoziaistvo SSSR v 1962 godu* (Moscow, 1963), pp. 558–59; and *Narodnoe khoziaistvo SSSR v 1964 godu* (Moscow, 1965), pp. 674–75.

TABLE 7. Number of children attending Pioneer camps in the Union republics, 1950-64.[a]

Republic	1950	1953	1954	1955	1956	1957	1958	1959	1960	1961	1962	1963	1964
U.S.S.R.	2,409,937	2,559,661	2,609,941	2,644,422	2,770,800	2,963,300	3,081,800	3,283,500	3,571,000	3,889,200	4,144,400	4,369,200	4,686,200
R.S.F.S.R.	1,695,371	1,805,895	1,838,513	1,857,322	1,949,300	2,088,400	2,167,100	2,314,900	2,506,400	2,738,800	2,911,800	3,058,700	3,267,100
Ukrainian S.S.R.	405,736	432,651	444,467	449,629	469,600	490,200	522,200	541,900	587,200	620,800	656,500	683,200	730,200
Belorussian S.S.R.	64,114	61,764	61,433	61,357	65,100	68,100	71,900	79,200	90,900	98,800	106,300	119,600	129,800
Uzbek S.S.R.	39,955	37,890	40,268	43,860	45,500	51,000	49,800	55,600	64,300	71,500	79,800	83,400	91,600
Kazakh S.S.R.	58,483	61,196	57,851	68,971	73,800	82,400	77,500	87,500	101,300	116,000	133,400	148,200	176,600
Georgian S.S.R.	31,192	34,596	37,469	36,595	34,900	40,100	38,800	37,300	36,600	41,600	37,000	40,500	44,400
Azerbaidzhan S.S.R.	31,699	29,536	30,542	29,229	30,600	33,400	34,600	34,300	35,700	38,200	41,400	41,400	41,500
Lithuanian S.S.R.	11,336	11,745	14,070	14,386	15,100	16,400	17,800	20,900	21,500	22,800	25,100	28,500	31,800
Moldavian S.S.R.	8,343	8,868	9,824	9,488	9,200	10,700	11,000	12,900	14,700	16,600	19,400	22,200	23,200
Latvian S.S.R.	14,395	20,003	21,636	21,724	20,400	21,400	22,600	24,300	26,600	28,200	29,800	30,800	31,000
Kirgiz S.S.R.	9,307	12,440	12,243	12,800	14,300	14,800	16,900	18,800	23,400	26,900	29,500	31,400	37,000
Tadzhik S.S.R.	4,204	7,307	7,738	7,450	7,800	9,100	11,700	12,500	14,200	14,100	16,800	20,300	18,600
Armenian S.S.R.	16,770	16,653	14,622	13,398	14,700	15,100	17,000	17,200	18,600	21,500	22,900	24,000	25,400
Turkmen S.S.R.	8,171	6,880	6,876	7,370	8,100	8,500	8,400	10,300	12,100	13,700	14,700	15,800	16,400
Estonian S.S.R.	10,861	12,237	12,389	10,763	12,400	13,700	14,500	15,900	17,500	19,700	20,000	21,200	21,600

[a]For the sources on which this table is based, see preceding table, n.

TABLE 8. Number of children in kindergartens of all jurisdictions, by republic, 1940-64.[a]

Republic	1940	1950	1953	1955	1956	1957	1958	1959	1960	1961	1962	1963	1964
U.S.S.R.	1,171.5	1,168.8	1,438.3	1,730.9	1,882.0	2,095.1	2,354.1	2,671.1	3,115.1	3,622.5	4,171.7	4,813.0	5,496.0
R.S.F.S.R.	751.9	829.8	1,028.3	1,226.4	1,326.9	1,474.6	1,653.8	1,868.8	2,149.7	2,458.6	2,774.7	3,140.5	3,522.0
Ukrainian S.S.R.	172.2	155.8	185.0	219.1	236.7	261.2	292.2	330.7	399.4	479.0	573.6	702.9	841.3
Belorussian S.S.R.	45.5	19.9	25.3	34.2	37.8	42.8	48.1	57.6	70.4	85.2	102.1	121.5	143.4
Uzbek S.S.R.	33.7	30.2	38.1	55.6	68.6	70.1	81.1	93.4	112.5	138.1	167.9	185.3	204.6
Kazakh S.S.R.	21.4	26.7	33.7	44.1	48.3	64.9	74.0	88.8	111.1	146.1	185.1	241.7	292.6
Georgian S.S.R.	38.7	24.0	27.1	30.6	32.2	33.7	36.6	40.7	46.3	51.0	56.7	65.6	72.5
Azerbaidzhan S.S.R.	43.8	21.9	23.6	26.2	27.1	29.9	32.9	36.8	40.2	45.6	50.9	58.2	67.1
Lithuanian S.S.R.	13.3	6.5	8.0	9.3	10.0	11.0	12.4	13.9	16.0	18.4	24.3	29.3	35.6
Moldavian S.S.R.	3.0	4.2	6.4	8.9	9.6	11.1	13.1	15.8	19.8	25.8	34.4	41.0	49.7
Latvian S.S.R.	5.5	7.0	10.0	11.7	12.1	13.1	14.8	16.6	19.6	23.3	28.6	33.3	39.7
Kirgiz S.S.R.	3.7	6.6	8.0	10.8	13.0	14.8	18.8	21.4	26.2	30.6	35.2	40.0	49.6
Tadzhik S.S.R.	3.1	5.2	7.0	9.6	10.8	13.6	15.8	19.3	23.3	27.9	30.7	34.8	39.4
Armenian S.S.R.	14.5	10.3	10.5	13.2	14.5	16.7	19.2	22.8	29.8	35.7	41.3	46.3	53.8
Turkmen S.S.R.	16.0	15.3	20.6	23.1	25.3	27.5	29.0	30.6	34.8	38.1	43.9	47.3	54.5
Estonian S.S.R.	5.2	5.4	6.7	8.0	9.1	10.1	12.3	13.9	16.0	19.1	22.3	25.3	30.5

[a]Figures are expressed in thousands, as of the end of each specified year. This table is based on Zhenshchiny i deti v SSSR (Moscow, 1963), p. 135; Narodnoe khoziaistvo SSSR v 1958 godu (Moscow, 1959), pp. 822-23; Narodnoe khoziaistvo SSSR v 1961 godu (Moscow, 1962), pp. 686-87; Kul'turnoe stroitel'stvo SSSR (Moscow, 1956), p. 192; Narodnoe khoziaistvo SSSR v 1962 godu (Moscow, 1963), p. 561; and Narodnoe khoziaistvo SSSR v 1964 godu (Moscow, 1965), p. 667. For the years after 1958 enrollment in combined nursery-kindergartens is included.

TABLE 9. Number of children's summer playgrounds in the Union republics, 1950–59.[a]

Republic	1950	1953	1954	1955	1956	1957	1958	1959
U.S.S.R.	38,451	24,673	25,982	27,267	29,277	32,421	33,574	38,549
R.S.F.S.R.	10,772	8,597	12,146	13,100	14,118	14,630	15,638	19,147
Ukrainian S.S.R.	16,664	3,618	3,510	4,862	5,423	8,546	8,928	10,601
Belorussian S.S.R.	140	114	94	156	182	146	192	242
Uzbek S.S.R.	6,089	7,411	5,338	4,422	4,337	3,817	4,324	4,191
Kazakh S.S.R.	2,667	1,640	1,841	1,859	2,351	2,533	1,809	1,710
Georgian S.S.R.	32	11	–	–	–	–	–	–
Azerbaidzhan S.S.R.	616	416	431	336	383	239	181	258
Lithuanian S.S.R.	39	54	20	31	20	17	12	12
Moldavian S.S.R.	301	1,530	1,713	1,718	1,722	1,712	1,731	1,729
Latvian S.S.R.	12	372	–	–	–	38	128	122
Kirgiz S.S.R.	355	296	370	361	393	409	342	272
Tadzhik S.S.R.	42	56	60	48	83	69	74	84
Armenian S.S.R.	381	261	209	199	174	134	97	76
Turkmen S.S.R.	360	141	149	138	68	123	115	102
Estonian S.S.R.	12	156	101	37	23	8	3	3

[a]Based on *Kul'turnoe stroitel'stvo SSSR* (Moscow, 1956), pp. 194–95; and *Narodnoe khoziaistvo SSSR v 1959 godu* (Moscow, 1960), pp. 738–39.

TABLE 10. Number of children attending summer playgrounds in the Union republics, 1950–59.[a]

Republic	1950	1953	1954	1955	1956	1957	1958	1959
U.S.S.R.	983,600	767,346	811,959	970,655	1,060,300	1,228,800	1,335,900	1,553,700
R.S.F.S.R.	323,319	242,552	298,338	377,702	417,600	470,800	567,800	716,200
Ukrainian S.S.R.	345,333	136,072	133,294	196,342	218,100	328,100	341,700	406,800
Belorussian S.S.R.	13,562	9,448	6,428	7,438	9,200	8,200	8,700	9,800
Uzbek S.S.R.	131,200	143,082	128,343	121,817	125,700	128,700	130,800	130,700
Kazakh S.S.R.	57,857	55,498	61,080	70,055	82,300	87,800	71,200	74,900
Georgian S.S.R.	2,193	438	–	–	–	–	–	–
Azerbaidzhan S.S.R.	40,193	28,702	25,995	18,590	24,100	16,500	20,600	22,400
Lithuanian S.S.R.	1,862	2,424	396	1,003	400	300	200	300
Moldavian S.S.R.	13,030	102,802	117,388	139,738	141,800	141,900	144,100	144,800
Latvian S.S.R.	126	4,364	–	–	–	700	1,900	3,200
Kirgiz S.S.R.	19,315	16,291	18,312	16,461	20,700	23,100	26,800	22,100
Tadzhik S.S.R.	4,837	4,733	5,176	4,804	6,900	6,700	7,400	8,400
Armenian S.S.R.	14,704	9,426	5,977	5,805	5,000	3,600	2,900	2,700
Turkmen S.S.R.	15,940	9,400	9,783	10,284	8,100	12,300	11,700	11,300
Estonian S.S.R.	246	2,114	1,449	616	400	100	100	100

[a]For the source of this table, see Table 9, n.

TABLE 11. Children's homes, 1940–55.[a]

Republic	Number of Homes					Number of Resident Children				
	1940	1950	1953	1954	1955	1940	1950	1953	1954	1955
U.S.S.R.	2,967	6,543	5,494	4,972	4,461	324,220	635,913	457,882	419,245	381,185
Under Ministries of Education	2,967	5,799	4,991	4,555	4,099	324,220	592,395	426,620	392,998	357,586
R.S.F.S.R.	1,721	3,751	3,269	2,993	2,685	187,217	360,115	260,733	240,918	218,146
Ukrainian S.S.R.	553	821	728	685	621	68,774	99,938	73,038	69,222	64,230
Belorussian S.S.R.	181	297	289	279	250	14,820	35,645	29,365	27,279	24,810
Uzbek S.S.R.	104	260	140	111	101	11,769	22,709	10,614	9,175	8,592
Kazakh S.S.R.	140	170	146	123	109	17,949	21,554	13,945	11,837	10,316
Georgian S.S.R.	35	48	50	47	38	2,697	4,547	3,969	3,555	3,039
Azerbaidzhan S.S.R.	43	86	69	57	48	4,172	8,137	5,278	4,198	3,524
Lithuanian S.S.R.	64	38	39	39	41	4,374	3,827	4,805	4,229	4,434
Moldavian S.S.R.	3	113	71	54	49	521	13,038	7,482	5,954	5,027
Latvian S.S.R.	20	40	38	38	38	1,284	3,463	3,727	3,884	3,953
Kirgiz S.S.R.	18	43	34	28	26	2,657	5,449	3,577	3,012	2,773
Tadzhik S.S.R.	23	35	27	22	20	2,546	3,849	3,087	2,692	2,323
Armenian S.S.R.	14	33	24	17	14	1,584	4,298	2,364	1,881	1,548
Turkmen S.S.R.	21	29	31	26	24	2,212	3,187	2,511	2,239	2,076
Estonian S.S.R.	27	35	36	36	35	1,644	2,639	2,845	2,923	2,795
Under other ministries and departments	–	744	503	417	362	–	43,518	31,262	26,247	23,599
Children's homes attached to kindergartens	–	202	58	35	30	–	5,454	1,402	935	769

[a]Including boarding schools for children with physical defects. This table is based on *Kul'turnoe stroitel'stvo SSSR* (Moscow, 1956), p. 198.

TABLE 12. Time budgets of male and female workers in the U.S.S.R. in 1922 and at the beginning of 1960.[a]

	1922		At the Beginning of 1960											
	Moscow, Petrograd, Ivanovo-Voznesensk		Krasnoiarsk Krai						City of Krasnoiarsk					
			8-hr work day		7-hr work day		6-hr work day		8-hr work day		7-hr work day		6-hr work day	
Time Use	M	F	M	F	M	F	M	F	M	F	M	F	M	F
Total number of budgets	145	—	1,722	804	804	462	744	324	534	306	192	156	54	102
Socially useful labor time	9.44	9.07	10.64	9.91	9.50	8.90	9.10	8.29	9.76	9.29	8.47	8.41	7.68	7.66
Productive working time	8.61	8.49	9.10	8.75	7.61	7.53	7.00	6.85	8.23	7.94	7.04	7.14	5.95	6.18
In state production	8.54	8.15	8.07	8.10	7.07	6.97	6.46	6.20	7.75	7.56	7.04	6.85	5.93	5.95
In private household production	0.07	0.34	1.03	0.65	0.54	0.56	0.54	0.65	0.48	0.38	—	0.29	0.02	0.23
Nonworking time connected with the job	0.83	0.58	1.54	1.16	1.89	1.37	2.10	1.44	1.53	1.35	1.43	1.27	1.73	1.48
Idle time	—	—	0.11	0.05	0.05	0.03	0.09	0.03	0.10	0.08	0.06	0.07	0.07	0.01
Travel to and from work	—	—	0.95	0.69	1.18	0.94	1.51	0.89	0.87	0.75	0.74	0.84	0.83	0.91
Personal care before and after work	0.83	0.58	0.24	0.22	0.45	0.30	0.41	0.47	0.26	0.22	0.34	0.21	0.43	0.52
Lunch break (except eating time)	—	—	0.24	0.20	0.21	0.10	0.09	0.05	0.30	0.30	0.29	0.15	0.40	0.04
Time spent on household chores	1.41	4.40	1.36	3.64	1.92	4.65	1.95	4.88	1.64	3.80	1.86	4.79	2.45	3.63
Shopping	0.20	0.60	0.27	0.68	0.42	0.69	0.45	0.75	0.37	0.72	0.28	0.72	0.56	0.67
Preparation of food	0.73	1.90	0.23	1.36	0.25	1.49	0.31	1.57	0.34	1.41	0.41	1.66	0.08	1.05
Cleaning	0.29	0.60	0.33	0.58	0.43	0.74	0.25	0.60	0.35	0.55	0.36	0.76	0.26	0.54
Sewing, laundering, and care of shoes	0.08	0.70	0.07	0.47	0.13	0.80	0.10	0.69	0.06	0.61	0.11	0.73	0.92	0.43
Care of children	0.11	0.60	0.30	0.41	0.53	0.79	0.62	1.07	0.37	0.41	0.59	0.73	0.23	0.68
Other	—	—	0.16	0.14	0.16	0.14	0.22	0.20	0.15	0.10	0.11	0.08	0.40	0.26
Time spent on physiological needs	10.20	8.49	9.36	8.50	9.09	8.47	9.14	8.30	9.32	8.15	9.59	8.84	10.07	8.68
Eating	1.57	1.18	1.18	0.92	1.08	1.02	1.08	0.83	1.30	0.91	1.29	1.05	1.18	0.81
Personal care	0.65	0.58	0.64	0.69	0.64	0.60	0.58	0.50	0.61	0.52	0.68	0.69	0.88	0.54
Sleep	7.98	6.73	7.54	6.89	7.37	6.85	7.54	6.97	7.41	6.72	7.62	7.10	8.01	7.33
Free Time	2.95	2.04	2.64	1.95	3.49	1.98	3.81	2.53	3.28	2.76	4.08	1.96	3.79	4.03
Studies and raising qualifications	0.82	0.75	0.38	0.38	0.73	0.42	0.86	0.69	0.88	0.55	1.00	0.46	1.06	1.20
Individual studies	—	—	0.76	0.43	0.96	0.39	1.03	0.57	0.83	0.25	1.11	0.38	0.94	0.91
Civic activities	0.25	0.23	0.02	0.03	0.02	0.05	0.03	0.14	0.03	0.20	—	0.08	0.04	0.43
Amusement	—	—	1.16	0.89	1.47	0.92	1.47	1.00	1.26	0.85	1.64	0.92	0.87	1.35
Physical culture and sports	0.95	1.01	0.13	0.01	0.08	0.04	0.15	—	0.03	0.01	0.12	0.01	0.68	0.01
Hobbies and amateur interests	—	—	0.02	0.01	0.07	0.01	0.02	0.02	0.01	—	0.05	0.01	0.07	0.01
"Inactive rest"	0.93	0.05	0.17	0.20	0.16	0.15	0.25	0.11	0.24	0.90	0.16	0.10	0.13	0.12
Total	24.00	24.00	24.00	24.00	24.00	24.00	24.00	24.00	24.00	24.00	24.00	24.00	24.00	24.00

[a] Figures express hours per day. This table is based on V. D. Patrushev, Intensivnost' truda pri sotsializme (Moscow, 1963), pp. 215–17.

275

appendix
IV

EDUCATION OF WOMEN

TABLE 1. Percentage of girls in primary, seven-year, and secondary schools, by republic, 1955–56.[a]

Republic	Urban and Rural				Urban				Rural			
	All Grades	Grades			All Grades	Grades			All Grades	Grades		
		1–4	5–7	8–10 (11)[b]		1–4	5–7	8–10 (11)[b]		1–4	5–7	8–10 (11)[b]
U.S.S.R.	49.6	47.9	48.7	55.4	51.2	48.3	50.2	58.2	48.3	47.7	47.8	51.9
Schools under the Ministries of Education												
R.S.F.S.R.	50.7	48.2	49.5	59.2	51.9	48.5	50.5	60.3	49.6	47.9	48.8	57.6
Ukrainian S.S.R.	49.4	48.4	48.1	54.3	50.8	48.4	49.3	56.1	48.7	48.4	47.6	52.6
Belorussian S.S.R.	49.0	47.3	47.9	55.9	51.2	48.1	49.1	57.8	48.3	47.0	47.6	54.5
Uzbek S.S.R.	43.7	47.0	44.9	32.6	48.1	47.7	48.9	48.0	42.1	46.7	43.6	25.7
Kazakh S.S.R.	48.0	46.9	49.2	49.6	50.1	47.5	51.8	53.9	46.9	46.6	47.9	46.1
Georgian S.S.R.	49.7	48.3	48.3	53.4	51.6	48.3	51.6	55.5	48.7	48.3	47.0	51.8
Azerbaidzhan S.S.R.	45.1	46.6	44.9	41.5	48.2	47.0	48.3	50.8	43.0	46.3	42.9	33.5
Lithuanian S.S.R.	50.6	47.1	52.2	61.4	52.1	48.3	51.2	61.2	49.7	46.5	52.8	61.7
Moldavian S.S.R.	49.4	48.8	49.1	53.9	50.6	48.8	50.3	55.9	49.1	48.7	49.0	52.8
Latvian S.S.R.	51.2	47.3	51.5	62.5	52.7	48.1	51.9	62.4	49.4	46.6	51.1	62.7
Kirgiz S.S.R.	45.9	47.7	44.5	42.8	49.5	48.5	48.5	53.0	44.3	47.5	43.1	36.1
Tadzhik S.S.R.	42.3	45.9	40.4	30.4	44.9	46.2	44.6	42.2	41.4	45.9	39.1	21.8
Armenian S.S.R.	47.5	45.5	47.6	51.6	50.5	46.9	50.2	58.0	45.4	44.5	46.2	46.2
Turkmen S.S.R.	45.7	47.4	46.5	37.7	46.3	47.3	47.1	42.0	45.3	47.4	46.2	33.7
Estonian S.S.R.	50.5	47.3	50.8	61.8	52.2	48.2	51.4	61.7	48.3	46.3	50.3	62.7
Schools under the Ministry of Railways	50.8	48.1	50.0	57.6	50.8	48.1	50.0	57.6	–	–	–	–

[a]At the beginning of the school year. Figures express percentage of the total number of pupils. This table is based on data from *Kul'turnoe stroitel'stvo SSSR* (Moscow, 1956), pp. 176–77.

[b]During the period 1959 to 1966 the general secondary school was supposed to include an eleventh year of study.

TABLE 2. Number and percentage of women enrolled in regular and correspondence courses in higher educational institutions, by nationality, 1959 and 1960.[a]

Nationality	1959			1960		
	Total	Women	Women	Total	Women	Women
			%			%
Total..............	2,266,979	1,019,114	45	2,395,545	1,041,645	43
Russians...........	1,384,389	668,782	48	1,479,520	682,048	46
Ukrainians.........	320,865	140,941	44	343,618	145,089	42
Belorussians........	58,954	24,815	42	63,720	25,185	40
Uzbeks............	47,712	12,133	25	53,530	13,219	25
Kazakhs...........	35,158	10,706	30	40,787	12,900	32
Georgians..........	44,186	19,737	45	48,461	21,964	45
Azerbaidzhani......	27,470	7,597	28	28,493	7,856	28
Lithuanians........	24,047	10,811	45	25,829	12,051	47
Moldavians........	10,590	4,581	43	11,995	5,356	45
Latvians...........	15,952	7,885	49	16,477	7,836	48
Kirgiz............	9,167	2,926	32	9,905	2,878	29
Tadzhiks...........	10,808	1,792	17	11,928	1,900	16
Armenians.........	34,814	14,205	41	36,739	14,667	40
Turkmen...........	9,053	1,881	21	9,480	1,947	21
Estonians..........	12,500	5,994	48	12,914	6,184	48
Jews..............	–	–	–	77,177	31,564	41
Tatars.............	–	–	–	39,892	17,517	44
Chuvashi..........	–	–	–	8,133	2,759	34
Dagestani..........	–	–	–	7,366	1,905	26
Bashkirs...........	–	–	–	6,284	2,441	39

[a]At the beginning of the academic year. This table is based on data from *Vysshee obrazovanie v SSSR* (Moscow, 1961), pp. 87, 128–57.

TABLE 3. Number and percentage of women enrolled in regular and correspondence courses in higher educational institutions, by republic, 1958, 1959, and 1960.[a]

Republic	1958		1959		1960	
	Number	%	Number	%	Number	%
U.S.S.R.................	1,018,484	46.7	1,019,114	45.0	1,041,645	43.5
R.S.F.S.R...............	658,676	48.2	657,512	46.4	668,460	44.7
Ukrainian S.S.R.........	171,759	45.1	173,355	43.2	174,362	41.7
Belorussian S.S.R........	23,974	42.1	23,986	42.2	24,594	41.5
Uzbek S.S.R.............	35,070	39.8	34,100	37.0	36,235	35.8
Kazakh S.S.R............	32,518	49.9	32,917	46.9	35,357	45.8
Georgian S.S.R..........	23,447	48.7	23,911	46.8	26,333	46.8
Azerbaidzhan S.S.R.......	12,439	34.6	11,771	34.0	12,154	33.7
Lithuanian S.S.R.........	11,613	47.7	11,863	46.6	12,941	48.4
Moldavian S.S.R.........	7,643	47.1	8,168	45.3	8,722	45.4
Latvian S.S.R............	9,925	54.1	9,860	52.1	9,757	45.2
Kirgiz S.S.R.............	6,722	42.4	7,231	42.3	7,308	42.0
Tadzhik S.S.R...........	5,376	29.0	5,655	30.0	5,878	29.5
Armenian S.S.R..........	8,267	42.1	7,792	40.7	8,270	41.0
Turkmen S.S.R..........	5,070	39.2	4,824	37.8	4,826	36.7
Estonian S.S.R...........	5,985	49.5	6,169	47.9	6,448	47.7

[a]At the beginning of the academic year. This table is based on data from *Vysshee obrazovanie v SSSR* (Moscow, 1961), p. 127.

TABLE 4. Number and percentage of women in secondary specialized educational institutions, by republic, 1958–61.[a]

Republic	1958		1959		1960		1961	
	Number	%	Number	%	Number	%	Number	%
U.S.S.R.	874,682	47	880,683	46	965,400	47	1,139,721	48
R.S.F.S.R.	563,428	49	586,855	49	622,251	49	733,589	50
Ukrainian S.S.R.	153,529	41	156,249	43	171,861	43	203,363	45
Belorussian S.S.R.	27,540	49	28,691	50	32,427	52	39,023	53
Uzbek S.S.R.	18,901	35	15,592	29	17,532	33	21,278	34
Kazakh S.S.R.	34,850	46	37,345	46	39,904	46	45,525	47
Georgian S.S.R.	10,500	39	10,201	38	9,604	37	10,936	38
Azerbaidzhan S.S.R.	7,780	30	7,656	30	8,522	32	10,719	35
Lithuanian S.S.R.	11,811	50	13,404	48	15,715	49	18,996	50
Moldavian S.S.R.	7,549	48	7,578	47	7,950	46	9,608	48
Latvian S.S.R.	11,688	50	11,545	48	12,021	49	13,712	49
Kirgiz S.S.R.	7,028	45	6,576	40	6,955	40	8,161	42
Tadzhik S.S.R.	4,550	37	4,107	36	4,428	37	5,006	37
Armenian S.S.R.	4,904	35	4,554	33	5,021	34	6,380	36
Turkmen S.S.R.	4,687	35	4,311	34	4,215	34	4,903	35
Estonian S.S.R.	5,937	47	6,019	45	6,994	45	8,519	46

[a]At the beginning of the academic year. This table is based on data from *Srednee spetsial'noe obrazovanie v SSSR* (Moscow, 1952), p. 93.

appendix

V

GRADUATE DEGREES

TABLE 1. Number and distribution of candidate degrees awarded by field, sample coverage, and estimated percentage of women.[a]

Field	1936–37				1956–58			
	Total	Distri-bution	Sample Cover-age	Women	Total	Distri-bution	Sample Cover-age	Women
		%	%	%		%	%	%
Basic science	836	26.3	66.4	23.8	2,585	19.9	66.0	38.3
Physics, mathematics	247	7.8	66.0	6.1	632	4.9	61.6	23.1
Chemistry	221	6.9	66.5	25.9	566	4.4	67.8	52.6
Biology	308	9.7	65.3	36.8	433	3.3	71.6	66.5
Geology	60	1.9	73.3	22.7	333	2.6	71.2	27.0
Applied science	2,077	65.3	59.9	19.0	6,492	49.9	65.7	31.4
Technology	568	17.9	67.4	4.4	3,176	24.4	66.3	18.5
Agriculture, veterinary medicine	461	14.5	65.7	19.5	1,908	14.7	66.0	36.3
Medicine	1,048	32.9	53.3	28.6	1,408	10.8	64.1	54.4
Total	2,913	91.5	61.8	20.4	9,077	69.8	65.8	33.4
Social science, humanities	269	8.5	60.2	21.0	3,924	30.2	65.2	31.5
Economics	49	1.5	57.1	10.7	878	6.8	65.3	22.0
History	46	1.4	63.0	17.2	917	7.1	63.7	27.2
Literature, linguistics	67	2.1	55.2	27.0	908	7.0	63.8	45.9
Pedagogy	56	1.8	62.5	28.6	256	6.0	69.9	41.3
Total, all fields	3,182	100.0	61.7	20.5	13,001	100.0	65.6	32.8

TABLE 1. Number and distribution of candidate degrees awarded by field, sample coverage, and estimated percentage of women.[a]—*continued*

Field	1959–61				1962–64			
	Total	Distri-bution	Sample Cover-age	Women	Total	Distri-bution	Sample Cover-age	Women
		%	%	%		%	%	%
Basic science	3,302	18.3	62.4	33.6	3,571	24.9	63.8	25.5
Physics, mathematics	1,085	6.0	56.8	15.3	779	5.4	62.7	16.8
Chemistry	836	4.6	65.3	50.7	496	3.5	67.5	38.2
Biology	519	2.9	60.5	52.2	427	3.0	60.6	53.2
Geology	862	4.8	67.9	26.8	479	3.3	66.8	26.9
Applied science	6,604	57.4	64.0	30.1	7,723	53.9	65.5	30.1
Technology	5,003	27.7	64.8	15.8	2,962	20.7	65.5	12.4
Agriculture, veterinary medicine	2,520	13.9	62.2	33.1	1,529	10.7	65.9	28.6
Medicine	2,861	15.8	64.2	52.7	3,232	22.5	65.3	47.0
Total	9,906	75.7	66.8	30.9	11,294	70.8	64.9	28.7
Social science, humanities	4,395	24.3	66.0	27.2	3,044	21.2	67.7	25.3
Economics	1,100	6.1	60.9	16.4	863	6.0	65.5	15.9
History	932	5.2	66.6	18.3	630	4.4	68.6	20.4
Literature, linguistics	915	5.1	67.3	49.2	599	4.2	64.3	44.2
Pedagogy	409	2.3	71.9	35.7	243	1.7	69.5	35.5
Total, all fields	18,081	100.0	64.2	30.0	14,338	100.0	65.5	27.9

TABLE 1. Number and distribution of candidate degrees awarded by field, sample coverage, and estimated percentage of women.[a]—*continued*

[a]This table is compiled from the following sources:

Leningradskii ordena Lenina Gosudarstvennyi Universitet imeni A. A. Zhdanova: Nauchnaia Biblioteka imeni M. Gor'kogo, *Dissertatsii, zashchishchennie v Leningradskom ordena Lenina Gosudarstvennom Universitete imeni A. A. Zhdanova v 1934–1954 gg.* (Leningrad, 1955).

Ministerstvo iustitsii RSFSR, *Kodeks zakonov o brake, sem'e i opeke RSFSR* (Moscow, 1950).

Ministerstvo kul'tury RSFSR, Gosudarstvennaia ordena Lenina Biblioteka SSSR imeni V. I. Lenina, *Katalog kandidatskikh dissertatsii, postupivshikh v Biblioteku imeni V. I. Lenina* (Moscow, 1956), Vol. 1.

———, *Katalog kandidatskikh dissertatsii, postupivshikh v Biblioteku imeni V. I. Lenina* (Moscow, 1957), Vol. 2.

———, *Katalog kandidatskikh dissertatsii, postupivshikh v Biblioteku imeni V. I. Lenina* (Moscow, 1958), Vol. 3.

———, *Katalog kandidatskikh dissertatsii, postupivshikh v Biblioteku imeni V. I. Lenina* (Moscow, 1957), Vol. 4.

———, *Katalog kandidatskikh dissertatsii, postupivshikh v Biblioteku imeni V. I. Lenina i Gosudarstvennuiu Tsentral'nuiu Nauchnuiu Meditsinskuiu Biblioteku: v 1-m polugodie 1957 goda* (Moscow, 1958).

———, *Katalog kandidatskikh dissertatsii, postupivshikh v Biblioteku imeni V. I. Lenina i Gosudarstvennuiu Tsentral'nuiu Nauchnuiu Meditsinskuiu Biblioteku: vo 2-om polugodie 1957 goda* (Moscow, 1958).

———, *Katalog kandidatskikh i doktorskikh dissertatsii, postupivshikh v Biblioteku imeni V. I. Lenina i Gosudarstvennuiu Tsentral'nuiu Nauchnuiu Meditsinskuiu Biblioteku: v 1-m polugodie 1958 goda* (Moscow, 1959).

———, *Katalog kandidatskikh i doktorskikh dissertatsii, postupivshikh v Biblioteku imeni V. I. Lenina i Gosudarstvennuiu Tsentral'nuiu Nauchnuiu Meditsinskuiu Biblioteku: vo 2-om polugodie 1958 goda* (Moscow, 1959).

———, *Katalog kandidatskikh i doktorskikh dissertatsii, postupivshikh v Biblioteku imeni V. I. Lenina i Gosudarstvennuiu Tsentral'nuiu Nauchnuiu Meditsinskuiu Biblioteku: v 1-m polugodie 1959 goda* (Moscow, 1959).

———, *Katalog kandidatskikh i doktorskikh dissertatsii, postupivshikh v Biblioteku imeni V. I. Lenina i Gosudarstvennuiu Tsentral'nuiu Nauchnuiu Meditsinskuiu Biblioteku: vo 2-om polugodie 1959 goda* (Moscow, 1960).

———, *Katalog kandidatskikh i doktorskikh dissertatsii, postupivshikh v Biblioteku imeni V. I. Lenina i Gosudarstvennuiu Tsentral'nuiu Nauchnuiu Meditsinskuiu Biblioteku: v 1-m kvartale 1960 goda* (Moscow, 1960).

———, *Katalog kandidatskikh i doktorskikh dissertatsii, postupivshikh v Biblioteku imeni V. I. Lenina i Gosudarstvennuiu Tsentral'nuiu Nauchnuiu Meditsinskuiu Biblioteku: vo 2-om kvartale 1960 goda* (Moscow, 1960).

———, *Katalog kandidatskikh i doktorskikh dissertatsii, postupivshikh v Biblioteku imeni V. I. Lenina i Gosudarstvennuiu Tsentral'nuiu Nauchnuiu Meditsinskuiu Biblioteku: v 3-m kvartale 1960 goda* (Moscow, 1961).

———, *Katalog kandidatskikh i doktorskikh dissertatsii, postupivshikh v Biblioteku imeni V. I. Lenina i Gosudarstvennuiu Tsentral'nuiu Nauchnuiu Meditsinskuiu Biblioteku: v 4-m kvartale 1960 goda* (Moscow, 1961).

———, *Katalog kandidatskikh i doktorskikh dissertatsii, postupivshikh v Biblioteku imeni V. I. Lenina i Gosudarstvennuiu Tsentral'nuiu Nauchnuiu Meditsinskuiu Biblioteku: v 1-m kvartale 1961 goda* (Moscow, 1961).

———, *Katalog kandidatskikh i doktorskikh dissertatsii, postupivshikh v Biblioteku imeni V. I. Lenina i Gosudarstvennuiu Tsentral'nuiu Nauchnuiu Meditsinskuiu Biblioteku: vo 2-om kvartale 1961 goda* (Moscow, 1961).

———, *Katalog kandidatskikh i doktorskikh dissertatsii, postupivshikh v Biblioteku imeni V. I. Lenina i Gosudarstvennuiu Tsentral'nuiu Nauchnuiu Meditsinskuiu Biblioteku: v 3-m kvartale 1961 goda* (Moscow, 1962).

———, *Katalog kandidatskikh i doktorskikh dissertatsii, postupivshikh v Biblioteku imeni V. I. Lenina i Gosudarstvennuiu Tsentral'nuiu Nauchnuiu Meditsinskuiu Biblioteku: v 4-m kvartale 1961 goda* (Moscow, 1962).

———, *Katalog kandidatskikh i doktorskikh dissertatsii, postupivshikh v Biblioteku imeni V. I. Lenina i Gosudarstvennuiu Tsentral'nuiu Nauchnuiu Meditsinskuiu Biblioteku: v 1-m kvartale 1962 goda* (Moscow, 1962).

———, *Katalog kandidatskikh i doktorskikh dissertatsii, postupivshikh v Biblioteku imeni V. I. Lenina i Gosudarstvennuiu Tsentral'nuiu Nauchnuiu Meditsinskuiu Biblioteku: vo 2-om kvartale 1962 goda* (Moscow, 1962).

———, *Katalog kandidatskikh i doktorskikh dissertatsii, postupivshikh v Biblioteku imeni V. I. Lenina i Gosudarstvennuiu Tsentral'nuiu Nauchnuiu Meditsinskuiu Biblioteku: v 3-m kvartale 1962 goda* (Moscow, 1963).

———, *Katalog kandidatskikh i doktorskikh dissertatsii, postupivshikh v Biblioteku imeni V. I. Lenina i Gosudarstvennuiu Tsentral'nuiu Nauchnuiu Meditsinskuiu Biblioteku: v 4-m kvartale 1962 goda* (Moscow, 1963).

———, *Katalog kandidatskikh i doktorskikh dissertatsii, postupivshikh v Biblioteku imeni V. I. Lenina i Gosudarstvennuiu Tsentral'nuiu Nauchnuiu Meditsinskuiu Biblioteku: v 1-m kvartale 1963 goda* (Moscow, 1963).

———, *Katalog kandidatskikh i doktorskikh dissertatsii, postupivshikh v Biblioteku imeni V. I. Lenina i Gosudarstvennuiu Tsentral'nuiu Nauchnuiu Meditsinskuiu Biblioteku: vo 2-om kvartale 1963 goda* (Moscow, 1964).

Moskovskii Gosudarstvennii Universitet imeni M. V. Lomonosova, Nauchnaia Biblioteka imeni A. M. Gor'kogo, *Doktorskie i kandidatskie dissertatsii, zashchishchennie v Moskovskom Gosudarstvennom Universitete s 1934 po 1954 gg* (Moscow, 1956).

———, *Doktorskie i kandidatskie dissertatsii, zashchishchennie v Moskovskom Gosudarstvennom Universitete s 1934 po 1954 gg* (2d ed.; Moscow, 1957).

———, *Doktorskie i kandidatskie dissertatsii, zashchishchennie v Moskovskom Gosudarstvennom Universitete s 1934 po 1954 gg.* (3d ed.; Moscow, 1960).

Vsesoiuznaia knizhnaia palata, *Ezhegodnik dissertatsii, 1936 god* (Moscow, 1938).

———, *Ezhegodnik dissertatsii, 1937 god* (Moscow, 1940).

———, *Knizhnaia letopis': dopolnitel'nyi vypusk*, No. 1 (Moscow, 1964).

———, *Knizhnaia letopis': dopolnitel'nyi vypusk*, No. 2 (Moscow, 1964).

———, *Knizhnaia letopis': dopolnitel'nyi vypusk*, No. 3 (Moscow, 1964).

———, *Knizhnaia letopis': dopolnitel'nyi vypusk*, No. 4 (Moscow, 1964).

TABLE 2. Number and distribution of doctoral degrees awarded by field, sample coverage, and estimated percentage of women.[a]

Field	1936–37				1956–58			
	Total	Distri-bution	Sample Cover-age	Women	Total	Distri-bution	Sample Cover-age	Women
		%	%	%		%	%	%
Basic science........................	93	18.3	57.0	15.1	162	26.7	66.7	8.3
Physics, mathematics................	28	5.4	46.4	7.7	45	7.4	64.4	0.0
Chemistry........................	12	2.4	66.7	12.5	23	3.8	73.9	17.6
Biology...........................	38	7.5	55.3	23.8	21	3.5	66.7	28.6
Geology..........................	15	3.0	73.3	9.1	28	4.6	67.9	10.5
Applied science.....................	399	78.4	59.6	8.4	316	52.1	69.3	15.5
Technology.......................	59	11.6	67.9	0.0	157	25.9	71.3	3.6
Agriculture, veterinary medicine......	15	3.0	73.3	0.0	93	15.3	68.8	12.5
Medicine.........................	325	63.8	57.5	10.7	66	10.9	65.2	51.2
Total............................	492	96.7	59.1	9.6	478	78.9	68.4	13.1
Social science, humanities.............	17	3.3	70.6	8.3	128	21.1	63.3	19.8
Economics........................	3	0.6	66.7	50.0	27	4.5	63.0	11.8
History..........................	6	1.2	66.7	0.0	17	2.8	58.8	10.0
Literature, linguistics...............	5	1.0	8.0	0.0	39	6.4	49.0	37.5
Pedagogy........................	1	0.2	100.0	0.0	8	1.3	62.5	40.0
Total, all fields.....................	509	100.0	59.6	9.6	606	100.0	66.8	14.8

TABLE 2. Number and distribution of doctoral degrees awarded by field, sample coverage, and estimated percentage of women.[a]—*continued*

Field	1959–61				1962–64			
	Total	Distri-bution	Sample Cover-age	Women	Total	Distri-bution	Sample Cover-age	Women
		%	%	%		%	%	%
Basic science........................	364	22.5	66.2	15.4	291	21.4	65.6	16.8
Physics, mathematics................	113	7.0	61.1	4.3	58	4.3	67.2	7.7
Chemistry........................	71	4.4	63.4	17.8	24	1.8	62.5	40.0
Biology...........................	70	4.3	71.4	36.0	42	3.1	61.9	30.8
Geology..........................	110	6.8	70.0	10.4	63	4.6	61.9	23.1
Applied science.....................	955	58.9	66.9	18.9	757	55.8	67.8	26.3
Technology.......................	382	23.6	67.8	4.2	196	14.4	71.4	23.6
Agriculture, veterinary medicine......	217	13.4	70.5	11.1	132	9.7	69.7	13.0
Medicine.........................	356	22.0	63.8	41.0	429	31.6	65.5	42.3
Total............................	1,319	81.4	66.8	18.0	1,048	77.2	67.2	23.7
Social science, humanities.............	302	18.6	60.9	16.3	309	22.8	57.3	11.3
Economics........................	63	3.9	55.6	5.7	70	5.2	60.0	11.9
History..........................	74	4.6	67.6	20.0	89	6.6	48.3	9.3
Literature, linguistics...............	74	4.6	53.7	20.6	50	3.7	56.0	14.3
Pedagogy........................	13	0.8	76.9	30.0	19	1.4	78.9	20.0
Total, all fields.....................	1,621	100.0	65.6	17.7	1,357	100.0	64.9	21.2

[a]For the source of this table, see note to Appendix V, Table 1, and Gosudarstvennaia ordena Lenina Biblioteka SSSR im. V. I. Lenina, *Bibliografiia dissertatsii: Doktorskie dissertsii za* *1941–1944 gg.* (Moscow, 1946), and *Bibliografiia dissertatsii: Doktorskie dissertatsii za 1945 g.* (Moscow, 1947).

appendix
VI
EDUCATIONAL ATTAINMENT

TABLE 1. Percentage of literacy of the urban and rural population, age 9–49, by sex and by republic, 1897, 1926, 1939, and 1959.[a]

Republic	Total				Male				Female			
	1897	1926	1939	1959	1897	1926	1939	1959	1897	1926	1939	1959
Total population												
R.S.F.S.R..............	29.6	60.9	89.7	98.5	44.4	77.1	96.0	99.3	15.4	46.4	83.9	97.7
Ukrainian S.S.R...........	27.9	63.6	88.2	99.1	41.7	81.1	93.9	99.6	14.0	47.2	82.9	98.8
Belorussian S.S.R........	32.0	59.7	80.8	99.0	43.5	79.1	90.7	99.5	20.7	41.3	71.4	98.6
Uzbek S.S.R.............	3.6	11.6	78.7	98.1	5.6	15.3	83.6	99.0	1.2	7.3	73.3	97.3
Kazakh S.S.R............	8.1	25.2	83.6	96.9	12.0	35.4	90.3	98.8	3.6	14.5	75.8	95.1
Georgian S.S.R..........	23.6	53.0	89.3	99.0	29.1	61.2	93.4	99.4	17.1	44.6	85.2	98.6
Azerbaidzhan S.S.R......	9.2	28.2	82.8	97.3	13.1	36.1	88.8	98.8	4.2	19.2	76.1	96.0
Lithuanian S.S.R.........	54.2	–	76.7	98.5	57.1	–	78.7	98.9	51.4	–	75.0	98.1
Moldavian S.S.R.........	22.2	–	45.9	97.8	31.2	–	59.0	99.1	12.7	–	33.1	96.6
Latvian S.S.R............	79.3	–	92.7	99.0	80.5	–	94.6	99.4	78.9	–	91.0	98.8
Kirgiz S.S.R.............	3.1	16.5	79.8	98.0	5.0	23.9	84.9	99.0	0.8	8.4	74.4	97.0
Tadzhik S.S.R............	2.3	3.8	82.8	96.2	3.9	6.4	87.4	98.0	0.3	0.9	77.5	94.6
Armenian S.S.R..........	9.2	38.7	83.9	98.4	14.5	53.7	92.7	99.2	2.9	22.7	74.7	97.6
Turkmen S.S.R...........	7.8	14.0	77.7	95.4	11.5	18.3	83.0	97.7	2.7	8.8	71.9	93.4
Estonian S.S.R...........	96.2	–	98.6	99.6	96.0	–	98.9	99.7	96.3	–	98.3	99.5
Urban population												
R.S.F.S.R..............	61.1	85.0	94.9	98.8	71.0	91.9	98.1	99.6	48.5	78.4	91.8	98.2
Ukrainian S.S.R...........	53.9	82.1	94.2	99.1	65.1	90.0	97.6	99.7	40.8	74.2	91.0	98.7
Belorussian S.S.R........	59.9	85.7	93.8	99.1	68.4	91.9	97.2	99.6	50.2	79.1	90.6	98.7
Uzbek S.S.R.............	15.9	39.8	86.8	98.0	22.5	49.6	90.4	99.0	6.6	28.6	82.8	97.1
Kazakh S.S.R............	34.7	61.0	87.5	96.9	43.5	70.3	93.4	98.7	23.8	51.6	80.8	95.2
Georgian S.S.R..........	56.5	80.3	94.7	99.0	59.6	84.6	96.9	99.5	51.0	75.8	92.6	98.5
Azerbaidzhan S.S.R......	31.9	58.7	89.1	97.3	40.7	68.9	94.4	99.0	19.2	47.0	83.7	95.8
Lithuanian S.S.R.........	62.9	–	83.9	98.9	68.6	–	84.9	99.3	56.0	–	82.9	98.5
Moldavian S.S.R.........	45.6	–	70.9	96.9	58.4	–	80.3	98.6	31.4	–	61.7	95.5
Latvian S.S.R............	81.1	–	96.1	99.4	83.6	–	97.1	99.6	78.4	–	95.2	99.2
Kirgiz S.S.R.............	13.2	41.3	85.6	97.9	18.9	50.3	89.5	99.1	6.0	31.0	81.0	96.8
Tadzhik S.S.R............	9.8	19.5	86.8	95.7	15.7	29.2	90.5	97.9	2.9	6.6	82.2	93.7
Armenian S.S.R..........	38.9	68.8	91.9	98.3	48.7	76.7	96.3	99.2	21.9	59.6	87.2	97.6
Turkmen S.S.R...........	49.3	65.6	85.4	95.7	52.4	73.8	89.4	98.1	37.1	54.4	81.0	93.5
Estonian S.S.R...........	95.3	–	99.3	99.7	94.4	–	99.5	99.8	96.2	–	99.1	99.6
Rural population												
R.S.F.S.R..............	24.6	55.0	86.7	98.0	39.5	73.3	94.8	99.1	11.0	38.8	79.3	97.1
Ukrainian S.S.R...........	23.5	58.7	85.0	99.1	37.4	78.6	91.9	99.5	9.8	40.3	78.5	98.9
Belorussian S.S.R........	28.1	53.7	77.1	99.0	39.7	75.9	88.9	99.4	17.0	33.3	65.8	98.6
Uzbek S.S.R.............	1.1	3.5	76.1	98.2	1.9	5.5	81.4	98.9	0.2	1.2	70.2	97.5
Kazakh S.S.R............	6.3	21.6	81.9	96.8	9.9	31.9	89.1	98.7	2.3	10.6	73.7	95.0
Georgian S.S.R..........	15.6	43.7	86.5	99.0	19.8	53.0	91.6	99.3	11.0	34.3	81.3	98.7
Azerbaidzhan S.S.R......	4.6	13.7	78.5	97.4	7.2	20.5	85.3	98.7	1.5	5.8	70.6	96.1
Lithuanian S.S.R.........	52.6	–	74.4	98.2	54.7	–	76.6	98.6	50.7	–	72.5	97.9
Moldavian S.S.R.........	17.7	–	41.7	98.0	25.9	–	55.4	99.3	9.2	–	28.4	97.0
Latvian S.S.R............	79.1	–	90.8	98.5	79.1	–	93.2	99.0	79.1	–	88.5	98.1
Kirgiz S.S.R.............	2.3	13.0	78.3	98.1	3.9	20.1	83.7	99.0	0.4	5.3	72.7	97.2
Tadzhik S.S.R............	1.8	2.0	81.8	96.5	3.2	3.6	86.6	98.0	0.2	0.3	76.5	95.1
Armenian S.S.R..........	5.7	30.5	80.1	98.4	9.7	47.0	90.9	99.3	1.1	13.3	68.8	97.6
Turkmen S.S.R...........	2.5	4.6	73.2	95.2	4.1	7.6	79.2	97.3	0.6	1.3	66.5	93.2
Estonian S.S.R...........	96.3	–	98.2	99.4	96.4	–	98.6	99.4	96.3	–	97.8	99.4

[a]Based on figures from *Itogi . . . 1959 goda: SSSR*, p. 89.

TABLE 2. Educational level of the urban and rural population, by age and sex, 1959.[a]

Urban and Rural Population by Age Group	Higher Education		Incomplete Higher, Secondary, Incomplete Secondary, and 7-yr. Education		Incomplete 7-yr. and Elementary Education		Less than 4-yr. Education	
	Males	Females	Males	Females	Males	Females	Males	Females
Total								
10 and over........	27	20	365	318	377	258	227	374
10–19............	0	0	363	428	401	349	236	223
20–24............	10	16	610	676	342	235	38	73
25–29............	38	49	370	394	507	404	85	152
30–34............	38	41	453	475	433	360	76	124
35–39............	59	41	495	425	338	317	108	217
40–44............	53	25	383	231	379	269	198	475
45–49............	48	16	235	115	361	188	356	680
50–54............	48	14	176	96	323	171	453	719
55–59............	46	12	148	76	300	133	507	780
60–64............	31	10	111	58	271	108	586	824
65–69............	21	7	82	41	244	89	653	863
70 and over......	12	3	50	26	172	60	766	911
Urban								
10 and over........	45	35	442	420	358	252	183	293
10–19............	0	0	406	493	385	319	342	188
20–24............	15	22	671	783	293	165	21	31
25–29............	56	76	437	495	457	350	50	79
30–34............	55	65	510	574	392	296	43	65
35–39............	89	68	574	544	280	265	58	123
40–44............	78	43	469	345	340	286	113	326
45–49............	77	31	325	200	363	247	235	522
50–54...........	86	27	271	174	338	230	305	569
55–59............	88	25	242	149	317	189	353	638
60–64............	67	21	200	116	305	162	428	672
65–69............	49	15	160	86	295	140	496	759
70 and over......	33	8	107	57	236	100	624	835
Rural								
10 and over........	9	6	289	219	396	264	247	509
10–19............	0	0	325	368	414	377	261	255
20–24............	5	9	543	549	396	319	56	123
25–29............	17	20	295	287	564	462	124	172
30–34............	16	13	384	360	483	435	117	192
35–39............	27	10	411	295	399	375	163	320
40–44............	23	5	275	111	426	251	276	633
45–49............	14	2	132	34	358	132	496	832
50–54............	10	2	81	24	309	116	600	858
55–59............	9	2	65	18	285	89	641	891
60–64............	5	1	46	14	246	68	703	917
65–69............	3	1	34	10	212	55	751	934
70 and over......	2	0.3	21	6	141	35	836	959

[a]Figures represent number of persons per thousand. This table is based on data from *Itogi . . . 1959 goda: SSSR*, pp. 75, 77, 79.   The last two columns are calculated as residuals.

TABLE 3. Educational level of the urban and rural population, by age and sex, 1959.[a]

Urban and Rural Population by Age Group	Total Population		Higher Education		Incomplete Higher Education		Specialized Secondary Education	
	Males	Females	Males	Females	Males	Females	Males	Females
Total								
10 and over..............	70,442,003	92,022,285	1,933,226	1,844,309	819,792	918,047	3,414,090	4,456,324
10–19.................	16,066,487	15,742,163	37	15	13,781	19,080	80,973	153,223
20–24.................	10,055,978	10,287,050	99,394	162,612	258,877	362,604	655,880	1,137,982
25–29.................	8,916,969	9,273,160	336,991	455,158	100,432	150,239	562,933	739,112
30–34.................	8,611,011	10,387,888	324,244	421,965	120,885	135,575	612,402	828,205
35–39.................	4,528,310	7,062,169	268,208	286,330	97,289	113,274	423,164	656,501
40–44.................	3,998,239	6,409,856	213,031	157,456	67,626	46,423	362,765	385,590
45–49.................	4,705,761	7,557,730	223,632	123,493	57,887	27,901	297,206	222,659
50–54.................	4,010,114	6,436,620	193,312	88,829	41,998	20,402	178,822	131,199
55–59.................	2,905,486	5,793,368	132,747	67,745	28,430	19,003	101,997	87,525
60–64.................	2,347,564	4,348,691	73,889	42,002	18,425	14,067	64,740	55,182
65–69.................	1,751,358	3,288,632	36,844	21,623	8,991	6,092	38,069	30,440
70 and over............	2,540,685	5,430,604	30,780	17,028	5,140	3,356	34,942	28,556
Urban								
10 and over..............	35,172,835	45,109,428	1,594,870	1,574,521	630,115	701,454	2,334,592	3,111,531
10–19.................	7,518,897	7,539,181	21	10	13,207	18,431	54,453	92,081
20–24.................	5,294,947	5,596,908	77,634	121,193	243,138	333,716	442,918	747,947
25–29.................	4,693,941	4,810,916	263,648	367,235	69,647	88,532	375,520	515,695
30–34.................	4,701,605	5,567,673	259,301	359,060	82,927	79,882	399,468	575,796
35–39.................	2,352,370	3,686,889	209,407	250,493	57,903	71,529	265,919	444,374
40–44.................	2,219,355	3,294,639	172,844	141,293	41,255	32,446	251,807	284,898
45–49.................	2,518,349	3,702,884	192,434	113,832	39,878	22,375	225,032	182,778
50–54.................	2,003,762	3,090,701	172,770	82,501	32,499	16,901	140,371	107,343
55–59.................	1,358,958	2,537,063	119,209	63,214	22,747	16,514	78,593	69,761
60–64.................	995,338	1,871,267	66,460	39,402	15,310	12,621	48,511	44,086
65–69.................	674,249	1,332,501	33,349	20,304	7,468	5,488	27,701	24,147
70 and over............	839,415	2,077,358	27,713	15,955	4,120	3,003	24,189	22,557
Rural								
10 and over..............	35,269,168	46,912,857	338,356	269,788	186,677	216,593	1,079,498	1,344,793
10–19.................	8,547,590	8,202,982	16	5	574	649	26,520	61,142
20–24.................	4,761,031	4,690,142	21,760	41,419	15,739	28,888	212,962	390,035
25–29.................	4,223,028	4,462,244	73,343	87,923	30,785	61,707	187,413	223,417
30–34.................	3,909,406	4,820,215	64,943	62,905	37,958	55,693	212,934	252,409
35–39.................	2,175,970	3,375,280	58,801	35,837	39,386	41,745	157,245	212,127
40–44.................	1,778,884	3,115,217	40,187	16,163	26,371	13,977	110,958	100,692
45–49.................	2,187,415	3,854,846	31,198	9,661	18,009	5,526	72,174	39,881
50–54.................	2,006,352	3,345,919	20,542	6,328	9,499	3,501	38,451	23,856
55–59.................	1,546,528	3,256,305	13,538	4,531	5,683	2,489	23,404	17,764
60–64.................	1,352,226	2,477,424	7,429	2,600	3,115	1,446	16,229	11,096
65–69.................	1,077,109	1,956,131	3,495	1,319	1,523	604	10,368	6,293
70 and over............	1,701,270	3,353,246	3,067	1,073	1,020	353	10,753	5,999

Urban and Rural Population by Age Group	General Secondary Education		Incomplete Secondary and 7-yr. Education		Incomplete 7-yr. and Elementary Education		Less than 4-yr. Education	
	Males	Females	Males	Females	Males	Females	Males	Females
Total								
10 and over........	4,407,570	5,528,060	17,069,779	18,315,996	26,546,080	23,761,488	16,099,533	34,355,668
10–19..........	1,055,202	1,494,395	4,682,331	5,068,864	6,438,111	5,496,939	3,796,052	3,509,647
20–24..........	1,365,965	1,602,320	3,856,911	3,852,245	3,439,816	2,422,268	379,135	747,019
25–29..........	364,691	356,765	2,267,980	2,412,206	4,525,817	3,747,568	758,125	1,412,112
30–34..........	413,185	546,700	2,750,676	3,421,330	3,733,045	3,747,410	656,574	1,786,703
35–39..........	355,487	477,644	1,367,642	1,754,629	1,527,757	2,240,878	488,766	1,532,913
40–44..........	218,380	209,152	881,760	840,498	1,513,335	1,724,009	791,342	3,046,728
45–49..........	180,316	185,756	571,969	434,313	1,698,188	1,422,735	1,676,566	5,140,873
50–54..........	158,013	200,307	325,668	267,149	1,296,392	1,099,691	1,815,909	4,629,043
55–59..........	122,039	195,740	176,957	136,613	871,219	769,909	1,472,097	4,516,833
60–64..........	82,768	119,249	95,089	62,440	636,431	471,627	1,376,222	3,584,124
65–69..........	47,199	65,499	50,151	31,378	426,633	294,149	1,143,471	2,839,451
70 and over......	44,137	74,406	42,003	33,899	438,409	323,731	1,945,274	4,949,628
Urban								
10 and over........	3,120,368	4,305,199	9,445,901	10,808,555	12,578,023	11,382,257	6,469,918	13,171,043
10–19..........	748,207	1,124,607	2,237,058	2,485,358	2,896,893	2,401,794	2,569,893	1,416,900
20–24..........	890,963	1,175,991	1,975,493	2,122,983	1,552,425	924,072	112,376	171,006
25–29..........	254,981	263,601	1,349,421	1,510,779	2,146,029	1,685,853	234,695	379,221
30–34..........	294,109	416,112	1,620,290	2,125,925	1,844,906	1,649,187	200,604	361,711
35–39..........	249,860	374,452	775,482	1,116,281	659,174	975,671	135,435	454,089
40–44..........	163,287	178,392	584,662	639,072	755,663	943,200	249,797	1,075,338
45–49..........	143,460	168,713	410,934	366,657	915,054	913,836	591,557	1,934,693
50–54..........	130,821	184,915	239,177	228,797	676,795	710,647	611,329	1,759,597
55–59..........	101,864	180,308	126,162	112,630	430,133	479,274	480,250	1,615,362
60–64..........	68,987	110,168	66,294	50,110	303,516	303,361	426,260	1,257,519
65–69..........	38,755	60,019	34,039	24,333	198,715	186,677	334,222	1,011,533
70 and over......	34,963	67,849	26,588	25,446	198,342	208,474	523,500	1,734,074
Rural								
10 and over........	1,287,202	1,222,861	7,623,878	7,507,441	13,968,057	12,379,231	8,781,247	23,705,446
10–19..........	306,995	369,788	2,445,273	2,583,506	3,541,218	3,095,145	2,226,994	2,092,748
20–24..........	475,002	426,329	1,881,418	1,729,262	1,887,391	1,458,196	266,759	576,013
25–29..........	109,710	93,164	918,559	901,427	2,379,788	2,061,715	523,430	768,575
30–34..........	119,076	130,588	1,130,386	1,295,405	1,888,139	2,098,223	455,970	924,722
35–39..........	105,627	103,192	592,160	638,348	868,583	1,265,207	354,168	1,078,824
40–44..........	55,093	30,760	297,098	201,426	757,672	780,809	491,505	1,971,390
45–49..........	36,856	17,043	161,035	67,656	783,134	508,899	1,085,009	3,206,180
50–54..........	27,192	15,392	86,491	38,352	619,597	389,044	1,204,580	2,869,446
55–59..........	20,175	15,432	50,795	23,983	441,086	290,635	991,847	2,901,471
60–64..........	13,781	9,081	28,795	12,330	332,915	168,266	949,962	2,272,605
65–69..........	8,444	5,480	16,112	7,045	227,918	107,472	809,249	1,827,918
70 and over......	9,174	6,557	15,415	8,453	240,067	115,257	1,421,774	3,215,554

ªBased on data from *Itogi . . . 1959 goda: SSSR*, pp. 74–79.
The last two columns are calculated as residuals.

TABLE 4. Educational level of the urban and rural population, by age and sex, 1959. [a]

Urban and Rural Population by Age Group	Higher Education		Incomplete Higher Education		Specialized Secondary Education		General Secondary Education		Incomplete Secondary and 7-yr. Education		Elementary and Incomplete 7-yr. Education		Less than 4-yr. Education	
	M	F	M	F	M	F	M	F	M	F	M	F	M	F
Total 10 and over	27	20	12	10	48	48	63	60	242	199	377	258	227	374
10–19	—	—	—	1	5	10	66	95	291	322	401	349	236	223
20–24	10	16	26	35	65	111	136	156	383	374	342	235	38	73
25–29	38	49	11	16	63	80	41	38	254	260	508	404	85	152
30–34	38	41	14	13	71	80	48	53	319	329	434	361	76	124
35–39	59	41	21	16	93	93	29	68	302	248	337	317	108	217
40–44	53	25	17	7	91	60	55	33	221	131	379	269	198	475
45–49	48	16	12	4	63	29	38	25	122	57	361	188	356	680
50–54	48	14	10	3	45	20	39	31	81	42	323	171	453	719
55–59	46	12	8	3	35	15	42	34	61	24	300	133	507	780
60–64	31	10	5	3	28	13	35	27	41	14	271	108	586	874
65–69	21	7	2	2	22	9	27	20	29	10	244	89	653	863
70 and over	12	3	2	1	14	5	17	14	16	6	173	60	766	911
Urban 10 and over	45	35	18	16	66	69	89	95	269	240	358	252	183	296
10–19	—	—	2	2	7	12	100	149	298	350	385	319	342	188
20–24	15	22	46	60	84	134	168	210	373	379	293	165	21	31
25–29	56	76	15	18	80	107	54	55	287	314	457	350	50	79
30–34	55	64	18	14	85	103	63	75	345	382	392	296	43	65
35–39	89	68	25	19	113	121	106	102	330	303	280	265	58	123
40–44	78	43	19	10	113	86	74	54	263	194	340	286	113	326
45–49	76	31	16	6	89	49	57	46	163	99	363	247	235	522
50–54	86	27	17	5	70	35	65	60	119	74	338	230	305	569
55–59	88	25	15	7	58	27	75	71	93	44	317	189	353	638
60–64	67	21	17	7	49	24	69	59	67	27	305	162	428	672
65–69	49	15	11	4	41	18	57	45	50	18	295	140	496	759
70 and over	33	8	5	1	29	11	42	33	32	12	236	100	624	835
Rural 10 and over	10	6	5	5	31	29	36	26	216	160	396	264	247	549
10–19	—	—	—	—	3	7	36	45	286	315	414	377	261	255
20–24	5	9	3	6	45	83	100	91	395	369	396	319	56	123
25–29	17	20	7	14	44	50	26	21	218	202	564	462	124	172
30–34	17	13	10	12	54	52	30	27	289	269	483	435	117	192
35–39	27	11	18	12	72	63	49	31	272	189	399	375	163	320
40–44	23	5	15	4	62	32	31	10	167	65	426	251	276	633
45–49	14	3	8	1	33	10	17	4	74	18	358	132	496	832
50–54	10	2	5	1	19	7	14	5	43	11	309	116	600	858
55–59	8	1	4	1	15	5	13	5	33	7	285	89	641	891
60–64	5	1	2	1	12	4	10	4	21	5	246	68	703	917
65–69	3	—	1	—	10	3	8	3	15	4	212	55	751	934
70 and over	2	—	1	—	6	2	5	2	9	3	141	34	836	959

[a] Calculated from Appendix VI, Table 3. Figures represent the number of persons per thousand. The last two columns are calculated as residuals.

TABLE 5. Educational level of the population, by nationality and sex, 1939 and 1959.[a]

	Higher and Secondary Education[b]			Increase (1959 over 1939)
	1939	1959		
Nationality and Sex	Total	Total	Employed	
				times
Total	83	281	433	3.4
Males	97	291	434	3.0
Females	71	271	431	3.8
Russian	88	295	460	3.4
Males	99	295	441	3.0
Females	77	295	480	3.8
Ukrainian	87	289	115	3.3
Males	108	320	440	3.0
Females	68	263	389	3.9
Belorussian	75	247	341	3.3
Males	95	267	361	2.8
Females	56	230	319	4.1
Uzbek	15	208	399	14.0
Males	21	254	436	11.0
Females	6	165	348	27.0
Kazakh	22	182	360	8.3
Males	37	235	414	6.4
Females	6	133	265	22.0
Georgian	137	375	520	2.7
Males	153	381	546	2.5
Females	121	369	490	3.0
Azerbaidzhan	49	242	427	4.9
Males	76	302	511	4.0
Females	21	184	317	8.8
Lithuanian	68	170	222	2.5
Males	88	171	212	1.9
Females	48	170	234	3.5
Moldavian	39	155	227	4.0
Males	47	181	266	3.9
Females	32	132	191	4.1
Latvian	148	369	502	2.5
Males	180	377	493	2.1
Females	119	362	512	3.0
Kirgiz	9	199	373	22.0
Males	15	253	442	17.0
Females	3	150	290	50.0
Tadzhik	12	201	379	17.0
Males	19	247	414	13.0
Females	4	157	330	39.0
Armenian	113	323	524	2.9
Males	134	331	530	2.5
Females	92	315	516	3.4
Turkmen	14	242	478	17.0
Males	24	281	501	12.0
Females	3	205	445	68.0
Estonian	137	307	417	2.2
Males	152	301	399	2.0
Females	124	309	436	2.5

[a]Based on Tsentral'noe statisticheskoe upravlenie pri Sovete ministrov SSSR, *Srednee spetsial'noe obrazovanie v SSSR* (Moscow, 1962), pp. 23–24.

[b]Including those with incomplete higher or incomplete secondary eduation. Figures represent the number of persons per thousand.

TABLE 6. Educational level of the urban and rural population, by age, sex, and republic, 1959.[a]

Republic	Higher Education Total	Males	Females	F %	Incomplete Higher Education Total	Males	Females	F %	Specialized Secondary Education Total	Males	Females	F %
Total												
U.S.S.R.	3,777,535	1,933,226	1,844,309	48.8	1,737,839	819,792	918,047	52.8	7,870,414	3,414,090	4,456,324	56.6
R.S.F.S.R.	2,265,940	1,128,529	1,113,741	50.0	1,015,506	458,174	557,332	54.9	4,829,040	2,036,408	2,792,632	57.8
Ukrainian S.S.R.	715,438	368,514	346,924	48.5	322,666	152,676	169,990	52.7	1,545,032	691,747	853,285	55.2
Belorussian S.S.R.	95,658	48,062	47,596	49.8	60,104	27,123	32,981	54.9	247,154	99,618	147,536	59.6
Uzbek S.S.R.	104,913	62,336	42,577	40.6	66,206	39,112	27,084	40.9	180,185	95,986	84,199	46.7
Kazakh S.S.R.	113,958	64,689	49,269	43.2	62,854	31,516	31,338	49.8	293,339	139,222	154,117	52.5
Georgian S.S.R.	153,418	81,731	71,687	46.7	42,569	21,649	20,920	49.2	173,354	70,476	102,878	59.3
Azerbaidzhan S.S.R.	77,244	45,697	31,547	40.8	33,834	20,162	13,672	40.4	115,455	59,652	55,803	48.3
Lithuanian S.S.R.	35,389	18,597	16,792	47.4	20,258	9,511	10,747	53.1	66,091	26,681	39,410	59.6
Moldavian S.S.R.	29,531	15,299	14,232	48.2	16,462	8,193	8,269	50.2	66,188	27,818	38,370	58.0
Latvian S.S.R.	44,404	20,693	23,711	53.4	25,359	11,487	13,872	54.7	100,998	45,529	55,469	54.9
Kirgiz S.S.R.	27,194	15,152	12,042	44.3	16,625	9,398	7,227	43.5	58,737	28,703	30,034	51.1
Tadzhik S.S.R.	20,682	12,467	8,215	39.7	13,085	8,497	4,588	35.1	46,476	25,993	20,483	44.1
Armenian S.S.R.	48,772	26,969	21,803	44.7	19,038	10,197	8,841	46.4	49,009	21,368	27,641	56.4
Turkmen S.S.R.	19,811	12,029	7,782	39.3	10,037	6,121	3,916	39.0	42,591	21,917	20,674	48.5
Estonian S.S.R.	25,183	12,462	12,721	50.5	13,236	5,966	7,270	54.9	56,765	22,972	33,793	59.5
Urban												
U.S.S.R.	3,169,391	1,594,870	1,574,521	49.7	1,331,569	630,115	701,454	52.7	5,446,123	2,334,592	3,111,531	57.2
R.S.F.S.R.	1,939,004	959,545	979,459	50.5	801,480	368,759	432,721	54.0	3,418,993	1,449,057	1,969,936	57.6
Ukrainian S.S.R.	603,388	307,863	295,525	49.0	247,262	121,560	125,702	50.8	1,087,272	484,487	602,785	55.4
Belorussian S.S.R.	73,294	36,054	37,240	50.8	38,731	18,027	20,704	53.5	149,373	59,145	90,228	60.4
Uzbek S.S.R.	80,914	43,939	36,975	45.7	46,256	24,166	22,090	47.8	114,807	51,732	63,075	54.9
Kazakh S.S.R.	82,495	44,381	38,114	46.2	42,303	19,368	22,935	54.2	173,737	78,691	95,046	54.7
Georgian S.S.R.	119,846	62,062	57,784	48.2	32,450	16,228	16,222	50.0	98,668	38,204	60,464	61.3
Azerbaidzhan S.S.R.	65,823	36,637	29,186	44.3	25,678	13,935	11,743	45.7	78,766	35,151	43,555	55.3
Lithuanian S.S.R.	30,727	15,997	14,730	47.9	15,796	7,810	7,986	50.6	46,019	18,449	27,570	59.9
Moldavian S.S.R.	21,635	10,914	10,721	49.6	9,970	4,913	5,057	50.7	34,773	13,956	20,817	59.9
Latvian S.S.R.	39,286	18,146	21,140	53.8	20,358	9,421	10,937	53.7	75,987	34,066	41,921	55.2
Kirgiz S.S.R.	18,831	9,796	9,035	48.0	9,447	4,712	4,735	50.1	32,995	14,780	18,215	55.2
Tadzhik S.S.R.	16,046	8,814	7,232	45.1	8,211	4,540	3,671	44.7	28,165	12,505	15,660	55.6
Armenian S.S.R.	40,859	21,586	19,273	47.2	15,709	7,930	7,779	49.5	33,065	13,195	19,870	60.1
Turkmen S.S.R.	15,563	8,473	7,090	45.6	7,200	3,764	3,436	47.7	32,552	14,495	18,057	55.5
Estonian S.S.R.	21,680	10,663	11,017	50.8	10,718	4,982	5,736	53.5	41,011	16,679	24,332	59.3
Rural												
U.S.S.R.	608,144	338,356	269,788	44.4	406,270	189,677	216,593	53.3	2,424,291	1,079,498	1,344,793	55.5
R.S.F.S.R.	326,936	168,984	157,952	48.3	214,026	89,415	124,611	58.2	1,410,047	587,351	822,696	58.3
Ukrainian S.S.R.	112,050	60,651	51,399	45.9	75,404	31,116	44,288	58.7	457,760	207,260	250,500	54.7
Belorussian S.S.R.	22,364	12,008	10,356	46.3	21,373	9,096	12,277	57.4	97,781	40,473	57,308	58.6
Uzbek S.S.R.	23,999	18,397	5,602	23.3	19,950	14,956	4,994	25.0	65,378	44,254	21,124	32.3
Kazakh S.S.R.	31,463	20,308	11,155	35.5	20,551	12,148	8,403	40.9	119,602	60,531	59,071	49.4
Georgian S.S.R.	33,572	19,669	13,903	41.4	10,119	5,421	4,698	46.4	74,686	32,272	42,414	56.8
Azerbaidzhan S.S.R.	11,421	9,060	2,361	20.7	8,156	6,227	1,929	23.7	36,749	24,501	12,248	33.3
Lithuanian S.S.R.	4,662	2,600	2,062	44.2	4,462	1,701	2,761	61.9	20,072	8,232	11,840	59.0
Moldavian S.S.R.	7,896	4,385	3,511	44.5	6,492	3,280	3,212	49.5	31,415	13,862	17,553	55.9
Latvian S.S.R.	5,118	2,547	2,571	50.2	5,001	2,066	2,935	58.7	25,011	11,463	13,548	54.2
Kirgiz S.S.R.	8,363	5,356	3,007	36.0	7,178	4,686	2,492	34.7	25,742	13,923	11,819	45.9
Tadzhik S.S.R.	4,636	3,653	983	21.2	4,874	3,957	917	18.8	18,311	13,488	4,823	26.3
Armenian S.S.R.	7,913	5,383	2,530	32.0	3,329	2,267	1,062	31.9	15,944	8,173	7,771	48.7
Turkmen S.S.R.	4,248	3,556	692	16.3	2,837	2,357	480	16.9	10,039	7,422	2,617	26.1
Estonian S.S.R.	3,503	1,799	1,704	48.6	2,518	984	1,534	60.9	15,754	6,293	9,461	60.1

	General Secondary Education				Incomplete Secondary and 7-yr. Education				Incomplete 7-yr. and Elementary Education			
Republic	Total	Males	Females	F %	Total	Males	Females	F %	Total	Males	Females	F %
Total												
U.S.S.R.	9,935,630	4,407,570	5,528,060	55.6	35,385,775	17,069,779	18,315,996	51.8	50,307,568	26,546,080	23,761,488	47.2
R.S.F.S.R.	5,286,132	2,200,529	3,085,603	58.4	19,773,063	9,271,714	10,501,349	53.1	29,799,353	16,090,497	13,708,856	46.0
Ukrainian S.S.R.	2,181,435	981,910	1,199,525	55.0	7,923,559	3,903,710	4,019,819	50.7	10,160,740	5,178,374	4,982,366	49.0
Belorussian S.S.R.	330,415	146,145	184,270	55.8	1,176,343	572,102	604,241	51.4	2,159,512	1,113,842	1,045,670	48.4
Uzbek S.S.R.	376,939	236,099	140,840	37.4	1,273,370	655,089	618,281	48.7	1,192,921	594,156	598,765	50.2
Kazakh S.S.R.	377,997	194,948	183,049	48.4	1,480,985	777,294	703,691	47.5	1,948,846	1,035,789	913,057	46.8
Georgian S.S.R.	436,660	185,718	250,942	57.5	618,126	306,369	311,757	50.4	689,418	351,651	337,767	48.9
Azerbaidzhan S.S.R.	214,785	119,235	95,550	44.5	603,215	319,610	283,605	47.0	579,181	291,601	287,580	49.6
Lithuanian S.S.R.	89,908	39,208	50,700	56.4	299,795	140,244	159,551	53.2	833,614	421,330	412,284	49.4
Moldavian S.S.R.	74,633	33,811	40,822	54.7	377,300	201,414	175,886	46.6	685,030	365,457	319,573	46.6
Latvian S.S.R.	132,929	49,540	83,389	62.7	462,936	211,713	251,223	54.3	606,830	282,679	324,151	53.4
Kirgiz S.S.R.	86,792	49,629	37,163	42.8	308,203	160,015	148,188	48.1	348,390	179,613	168,777	48.4
Tadzhik S.S.R.	66,051	42,079	23,972	36.3	299,949	160,359	139,590	46.5	305,021	159,275	145,746	47.7
Armenian S.S.R.	143,736	66,159	77,577	54.0	296,335	153,025	143,310	48.4	310,449	160,409	150,040	48.3
Turkmen S.S.R.	58,348	34,563	23,785	40.8	277,448	139,214	138,234	49.8	215,471	112,496	102,975	47.7
Estonian S.S.R.	78,870	27,997	50,873	64.5	215,148	97,877	117,271	54.5	472,792	208,911	263,881	55.8
Urban												
U.S.S.R.	7,425,567	3,120,368	4,305,199	58.0	20,254,456	9,445,901	10,808,555	53.4	23,960,280	12,578,023	11,382,257	47.5
R.S.F.S.R.	4,161,573	1,675,413	2,486,160	59.7	12,435,870	5,691,927	6,743,943	54.2	15,507,673	8,254,896	7,252,777	46.8
Ukrainian S.S.R.	1,657,268	717,034	940,234	56.7	4,228,357	2,020,294	2,208,063	52.2	4,395,758	2,264,299	2,131,459	48.5
Belorussian S.S.R.	211,930	88,717	123,213	58.1	521,572	235,581	285,991	54.8	586,265	293,242	293,023	50.0
Uzbek S.S.R.	200,647	106,100	94,547	47.1	470,044	229,401	240,643	51.2	496,184	249,357	246,827	49.7
Kazakh S.S.R.	234,842	112,302	122,540	52.2	757,793	377,770	380,023	50.1	886,596	478,640	407,956	46.0
Georgian S.S.R.	283,843	116,906	166,937	58.8	279,774	135,746	144,028	51.5	278,659	140,521	138,138	49.6
Azerbaidzhan S.S.R.	149,125	75,333	73,792	49.5	308,747	157,983	150,764	48.8	303,831	157,543	146,288	48.1
Lithuanian S.S.R.	72,357	31,365	40,992	56.7	182,985	83,630	99,355	54.3	303,642	150,420	153,222	50.5
Moldavian S.S.R.	50,053	21,304	28,749	57.4	115,830	56,643	59,187	51.1	147,045	75,339	71,706	48.8
Latvian S.S.R.	109,379	39,727	69,652	63.7	295,019	133,381	161,638	54.8	304,036	137,829	166,207	54.7
Kirgiz S.S.R.	48,068	24,324	23,744	49.4	124,356	60,486	63,870	51.4	134,097	70,438	63,659	47.5
Tadzhik S.S.R.	39,697	22,076	17,621	44.4	104,725	52,803	51,922	49.6	119,892	62,204	57,688	48.1
Armenian S.S.R.	103,588	45,952	57,636	55.6	154,605	78,823	75,782	49.0	151,053	79,415	71,638	47.4
Turkmen S.S.R.	38,327	20,923	17,404	45.4	127,019	63,967	63,052	49.6	122,859	64,708	58,151	47.3
Estonian S.S.R.	64,870	22,892	41,978	64.7	147,760	67,466	80,294	54.3	222,690	99,172	123,518	55.5
Rural												
U.S.S.R.	2,510,063	1,287,202	1,222,861	48.7	15,131,319	7,623,878	7,507,441	49.6	26,347,288	13,968,057	12,379,231	47.0
R.S.F.S.R.	1,124,559	525,116	599,443	53.3	7,337,193	3,579,787	3,757,406	51.2	14,291,680	7,835,601	6,456,079	45.0
Ukrainian S.S.R.	524,167	264,876	259,291	49.5	3,695,202	1,883,446	1,811,756	49.0	5,764,982	2,914,075	2,850,907	49.5
Belorussian S.S.R.	118,485	57,428	61,057	51.5	654,771	336,521	318,250	48.6	1,573,247	820,600	752,647	47.8
Uzbek S.S.R.	176,292	129,999	46,293	26.3	803,326	425,688	377,638	47.0	696,737	344,799	351,938	50.5
Kazakh S.S.R.	143,155	82,646	60,509	42.3	723,192	399,524	323,668	44.8	1,062,250	557,149	505,101	47.6
Georgian S.S.R.	152,817	68,812	84,005	55.0	338,352	170,623	167,729	49.6	410,759	211,130	199,629	48.6
Azerbaidzhan S.S.R.	65,660	43,902	21,758	33.1	294,468	161,627	132,841	45.1	275,350	134,058	141,292	51.3
Lithuanian S.S.R.	17,551	7,843	9,708	55.3	116,810	56,614	60,196	51.5	529,972	270,910	259,062	48.9
Moldavian S.S.R.	24,580	12,507	12,073	49.1	261,470	144,771	116,699	44.6	537,985	290,118	247,867	46.1
Latvian S.S.R.	23,550	9,813	13,737	58.3	167,917	78,332	89,585	53.4	302,794	144,850	157,944	52.2
Kirgiz S.S.R.	38,724	25,305	13,419	34.7	183,847	99,529	84,318	45.9	214,293	109,175	105,118	49.1
Tadzhik S.S.R.	26,354	20,003	6,351	24.1	195,224	107,556	87,668	44.9	185,129	97,071	88,058	47.6
Armenian S.S.R.	40,148	20,207	19,941	49.7	141,730	74,202	67,528	47.6	159,396	80,994	78,402	49.2
Turkmen S.S.R.	20,021	13,640	6,381	31.9	150,429	75,247	75,182	50.0	92,612	47,788	44,824	48.4
Estonian S.S.R.	14,000	5,105	8,895	63.5	67,388	30,411	36,977	54.9	250,102	109,739	140,363	56.1

ᵃBased on data from *Itogi . . . 1959 goda: SSSR*, pp. 82–84.

TABLE 7. Educational level of the population, by socioeconomic group, age, and sex, 1959.[a]

Socioeconomic Group and Age	Higher, Incomplete Higher, and Specialized Secondary Education		General Secondary Education		Incomplete Secondary and 7-yr. Education		Incomplete 7-yr. and Elementary Education		Less than 4-yr. Education	
	M	F	M	F	M	F	M	F	M	F
Workers										
Total population....	16	12	42	36	209	171	332	244	401	537
10 and over........	21	15	55	46	276	218	438	310	210	411
10–19.............	5	4	75	98	302	340	395	342	223	216
20–24.............	41	51	122	142	427	458	379	282	31	67
25–29.............	21	23	34	25	290	289	579	512	76	121
30–34.............	22	20	33	28	348	346	527	473	70	133
35–39.............	32	22	55	36	355	264	444	423	114	255
40–44.............	34	13	34	13	241	115	485	335	206	524
45–49.............	24	6	22	8	123	45	450	229	381	712
50–54.............	18	4	21	10	78	32	397	205	486	749
55–59.............	15	2	20	9	54	18	357	156	554	815
60–64.............	11	2	16	7	34	11	312	124	627	866
65–69.............	8	1	13	5	25	8	279	102	675	884
70 and over........	4	–	9	4	15	5	202	67	770	724
Employees										
Total population....	295	263	98	126	160	205	139	125	308	281
10 and over........	392	317	130	151	213	246	185	151	80	145
10–19.............	18	43	93	177	218	256	412	324	259	200
20–24.............	544	486	243	253	165	228	44	28	4	5
25–29.............	623	513	98	92	192	296	82	88	5	11
30–34.............	490	396	118	119	297	384	89	91	6	10
35–39.............	499	426	153	152	263	304	79	97	6	21
40–44.............	473	363	117	108	255	277	138	172	17	80
45–49.............	463	284	109	123	203	194	185	216	40	183
50–54.............	433	221	130	162	168	148	208	225	61	244
55–59.............	396	187	151	188	144	89	228	204	81	332
60–64.............	346	158	152	154	115	53	260	193	127	442
65–69.............	305	118	140	120	96	37	277	177	182	548
70 and over........	224	60	111	84	63	24	252	137	350	695
Collective farmers										
Total population....	10	4	24	14	148	112	285	209	533	661
10 and over........	13	5	33	18	203	139	390	260	361	588
10–19.............	1	2	42	43	312	335	402	375	243	245
20–24.............	30	26	118	76	386	367	398	372	68	159
25–29.............	20	11	22	12	201	171	598	515	159	291
30–34.............	25	10	18	13	266	232	530	497	161	248
35–39.............	32	9	28	14	252	160	465	424	223	393
40–44.............	28	5	17	4	131	43	465	245	359	703
45–49.............	15	2	8	1	49	10	347	118	581	869
50–54.............	8	1	5	1	27	6	291	104	669	888
55–59.............	5	–	5	1	20	5	271	82	699	912
60–64.............	3	–	4	1	14	4	234	61	745	944
65–69.............	2	–	3	–	11	3	202	49	782	948
70 and over........	1	–	2	–	7	2	134	29	856	969

[a]Figures represent the number of persons per thousand. This table is based on data from *Itogi . . . 1959 goda: SSSR*, pp. 113–14. The last two columns are calculated as residuals.

TABLE 8. Educational level of persons employed in various branches of the economy, 1959.[a]

Branch of the Economy	Higher Education		Incomplete Higher and specialized Secondary Education		General Secondary, Incomplete Secondary, and 7-yr. Education		Incomplete 7-yr. and Elementary Education		Less than 4-yr. Education	
	M	F	M	F	M	F	M	F	M	F
Total economy (except private subsidiary agriculture)	34	32	69	84	331	315	386	272	180	297
Industry	22	17	65	61	395	470	409	301	109	151
Production of electrical and thermal power...	29	30	82	105	411	461	386	250	92	154
Coal mining	16	9	61	49	379	439	435	309	109	194
Crude petroleum production	41	46	68	114	386	442	377	239	128	159
Extraction of other fuels	11	5	41	46	310	285	515	381	123	283
Petroleum refining	39	59	100	153	464	474	327	217	70	97
Coke and coke chemicals	32	38	79	75	406	441	391	279	92	167
Other fuel processing	27	34	76	90	405	410	422	317	70	149
Iron ore mining	29	23	73	73	414	469	395	275	89	161
Ferrous metallurgy	30	23	67	68	422	473	399	288	82	148
Mining of light metal ores	28	24	70	75	365	428	418	298	119	175
Light metal metallurgy	32	29	75	86	387	453	412	280	94	152
Machine building and metal working	33	27	87	87	471	512	353	263	66	111
Mining, chemical	24	25	73	76	374	417	406	308	123	174
Chemical industry	34	38	77	90	396	469	402	277	91	126
Mining of minerals for construction	12	9	46	51	330	376	461	343	151	221
Construction materials industry	14	11	50	51	349	385	447	344	140	209
Glass, china, and pottery industry	17	13	48	51	382	456	448	321	105	159
Timber enterprises	7	6	31	46	279	310	531	382	152	266
Paper and woodworking industries	9	9	35	44	348	383	467	352	141	212
Publishing	28	20	81	63	549	608	288	236	4	73
Textile industry (including knitted goods and felt)	14	8	52	38	383	457	422	334	129	163
Garment industry	11	4	51	38	398	554	397	301	143	103
Leather, fur, and shoe industry	10	10	35	48	330	488	446	320	179	144
Food industry (except meat, fish, and milk)....	15	14	45	53	339	435	409	303	192	195
Meat and milk industry	16	19	56	66	352	471	423	287	153	157
Fish	11	16	75	56	309	350	399	324	206	254
Other branches of industry	21	12	65	51	427	468	377	314	110	155
Administration of industry (trusts, offices, etc.).	144	109	164	171	356	474	257	130	79	116
Construction	29	31	59	74	363	423	438	310	111	162
Construction and capital repairs of buildings and equipment	20	15	55	60	366	428	445	327	114	170
Drilling	35	38	72	109	395	473	398	218	100	162
Planning	512	301	244	293	160	348	71	34	13	24
Agriculture	5	2	20	9	258	198	415	310	302	481
State farms	10	5	29	16	265	233	436	332	260	414
Collective farms	2	1	14	6	249	192	411	308	324	493
Repair technical stations, machine tractor stations, machine livestock stations, and drainage stations	17	32	50	110	417	406	435	228	81	224
Other agricultural enterprises, independent or subordinated to enterprises, establishments, or organizations	15	14	46	43	210	247	425	317	304	379
Organizations serving agriculture and veterinary establishments	140	145	235	240	260	299	233	163	132	153
Administration of agriculture (trusts, offices, etc.)	148	177	171	216	311	361	282	123	88	123
Private farming	0.4	0.2	3	2	95	65	278	188	623.6	744.8

TABLE 8. Educational level of persons employed in various branches of the economy, 1959.[a]—*continued*

Branch of the Economy	Higher Education		Incomplete Higher and Specialized Secondary Education		General Secondary, Incomplete Secondary, and 7-yr. Education		Incomplete 7-yr. and Elementary Education		Less than 4-yr. Education	
	M	F	M	F	M	F	M	F	M	F
Forestry	30	25	71	57	219	260	443	311	238	347
Transportation	13	13	64	60	398	458	415	291	110	188
Railway transport	14	13	58	55	381	442	403	300	144	190
Water transport	29	25	141	67	416	387	325	299	89	222
Urban electric transport	20	7	76	39	497	524	335	315	72	115
Automobile transport	6	11	39	79	440	581	461	221	4	108
Air transport	31	48	288	140	425	510	199	163	57	139
Main pipeline transport	33	25	81	116	373	476	400	247	113	146
Road construction and maintenance	12	9	60	62	279	298	448	366	201	265
Timber floating	8	7	34	44	276	331	529	366	153	252
Communications	17	9	92	76	491	679	321	184	79	62
Trade and public dining	19	14	68	96	376	515	358	237	179	148
Trade enterprises and institutions	20	19	69	122	372	538	358	196	181	125
Public feeding	13	4	64	42	402	468	353	322	168	164
Procurements	9	9	43	58	342	426	395	265	211	142
Material-technical supply	23	26	75	100	366	500	390	216	146	168
Other branches of material production	186	158	155	132	322	451	205	130	142	129
Publishing, editing, telegraph agents	316	203	240	160	349	492	71	81	24	64
Housing	10	5	54	44	295	284	434	302	207	385
Communal services	11	6	50	29	322	294	425	297	192	374
Hotels and homes for transients	24	9	68	41	348	359	380	340	180	251
Baths, laundries, and barbers	4	1	27	17	316	337	433	367	220	288
Other	13	8	54	34	323	266	424	259	186	433
Health, physical culture, and social security	172	97	197	328	244	242	256	187	131	146
Medical and preventive medical institutions	190	99	212	336	222	238	246	183	130	144
Other health institutions	53	45	68	178	317	318	379	260	183	199
Social security institutions	27	17	64	90	324	333	399	326	186	244
Stadiums, beaches, and other physical-culture institutions and organizations	94	76	178	108	456	342	205	242	67	242
Education	272	189	291	374	257	200	118	113	62	124
Higher educational institutions	585	415	90	114	182	244	104	114	39	113
Specialized secondary educational institutions	357	313	179	132	223	225	163	146	78	184
General education schools	284	223	411	458	167	120	77	84	61	115
Other educational institutions and courses	123	150	283	170	363	332	176	164	55	184
Institutions for the care of children	41	39	126	314	292	295	326	206	215	146
Cultural-educational institutions	60	89	149	270	576	407	167	115	48	119
Science and science service	209	219	143	194	333	366	251	126	64	95
Scientific and scientific research institutions (including auxiliary organizations servicing the scientific institutions)	293	255	135	171	306	336	204	129	62	109
Design and planning organizations (except those serving construction), geological prospecting work, hydrometeorological service (except for agriculture and transport)	139	162	150	231	355	413	290	122	66	72
Art	79	84	128	149	542	472	218	184	33	111
Credit and state insurance	72	63	178	244	416	568	214	71	120	54
Administration	142	112	147	162	427	498	223	110	61	118
Party, Komsomol, trade union, co-operative and other social organizations	177	108	260	209	408	459	111	100	44	124

[a]Based on data from *Itogi . . . 1959 goda: SSSR*, pp. 125–28. Figures represent the number of persons per thousand employed in the occupational area given. The last two columns are calculated as residuals.

NONPROFESSIONAL OCCUPATIONS

TABLE 1. Number and percentage of women in various "physical" occupations, 1926, 1939, and 1959.[a]

Occupation	1926		1939		1959	
		%		%		%
Total number employed (excluding private subsidiary economy)...............	–	–	34,102.1	43	47,604.6	48
Employed in primarily physical labor................................	–	–	29,469.4	45	36,550.2	46
Employed at power installations and working with hoisting-transport machines.	1.8	1	134.6	23	557.4	32
Metallurgical and metal workers...........................	32.1	3	522.1	12	1,450.1	16
Lathe operators..........................	1.5	2	57.6	13	136.5	15
Other machine tool operators.......................	3.7	18	146.5	48	300.1	48
Forge and press operators........................	2.8	32	30.3	55	83.7	64
Mechanics, machine-setters, equipment regulators.....................	0.1	1	11.1	4	33.1	6
Chemical workers..............................	20.8	48	95.6	46	226.2	57
Employed in production of construction materials, glass, and chinaware.......	–	–	96.6	40	290.2	54
Woodworkers..............................	–	–	156.4	16	246.9	18
Paper workers................................	–	–	12.3	56	22.5	62
Printing workers.............................	18.7	22	91.9	56	147.5	70
Textile workers.............................	523.8	69	805.0	76	958.3	85
Garment workers............................	205.3	54	555.3	76	1,171.6	90
Leather workers............................	–	–	59.5	30	72.9	50
Shoe workers..............................	–	–	90.3	18	144.7	39
Food workers..............................	64.4	21	273.7	40	525.2	64
Construction workers.........................	–	–	120.3	5	905.4	18
Agricultural occupations.......................	35,511.0	50	20,159.6	58	19,742.7	58
Heads of livestock and poultry farms.........	–	–	41.4	21	22.3	16
Brigadiers of field brigades................	–	–	27.0	5	22.7	9
Brigadiers of livestock brigades.............	–	–	12.3	12	11.8	16
Other brigadiers.........................	–	–	13.7	7	16.5	6
Field-team leaders.......................	–	–	392.8	84	136.5	87
Cattle farm workers, milkmaids, stablemen and grooms, swineherds, poultry workers..............	5.5	–	1,269.0	41	2,712.8	66
Orchard and vineyard workers, vegetable and melon growers.............	–	–	100.1	54	123.0	64
Irrigation workers........................	–	–	3.1	12	3.0	15
Other occupations and nonspecialized workers.......................	–	–	18,247.9	62	16,553.1	59
Forestry workers.............................	–	–	11.1	10	66.0	29
Fishing and fishbreeding workers.................	–	–	28.6	15	18.9	15
Water transport workers........................	–	–	11.9	7	38.7	16
Railroad workers.............................	–	–	174.8	19	518.9	31
Automotive transport and urban electrical transport workers................	–	–	69.0	9	189.2	6
Chauffeurs...............................	–	–	20.3	3	22.3	0.7
Trolley, subway, trolley-bus drivers....................	0.3	3	7.0	35	21.3	57
Bus, trolley, and trolley-bus conductors.......................	5.8	48	34.8	91	113.1	94
Postal workers, letter carriers.......................	–	–	75.3	42	177.2	73
Public dining workers..........................	–	–	473.9	82	703.7	90
Cooks.................................	–	–	273.9	77	457.6	88
Waitresses..............................	–	–	174.0	94	179.5	98
Communal and household service personnel.........................	–	–	2,280.5	50	3,343.3	67
Orderlies, nurses, nursemaids...........................	–	–	410.2	96	868.9	97

[a]Absolute figures are expressed in thousands; –, no data available. The following sources were used in compiling this table: *Itogi . . . 1959 goda: SSSR*, pp. 167–70; *Zhenshchiny i deti v SSSR* (Moscow, 1961), pp. 114–19; and *Zhenshchiny i deti v SSSR* (Moscow, 1963), pp. 94–99.

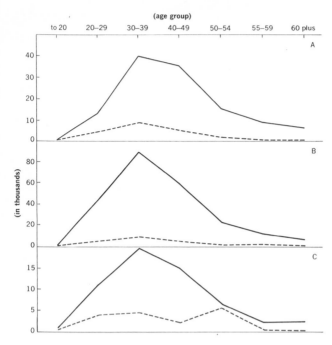

FIG. 1. Age distribution of males and females employed in various agricultural occupations, January 15, 1959. *Solid lines,* males; *broken lines,* females. *A,* heads of livestock sub-farms; *B,* heads of field brigades; *C,* heads of livestock brigades. Calculated from *Itogi . . . 1959 goda: SSSR,* Tables 42, 43, 47, 48, pp. 132–45, 161–70.

TABLE 2. MTS mechanized personnel, by age and sex, 1948 and 1950.[a]

Date and Age Group	Combine Drivers				Tractor Drivers				Brigadiers of Tractor Brigades and Their Assts.			
	Total	M	F	F	Total	M	F	F	Total	M	F	F
				%				%				%
May 1, 1948												
To 17	49	49	–	–	2,809	2,750	59	2.1	28	27	1	3.6
17	146	144	2	1.4	10,378	10,270	108	1.0	41	39	2	4.9
18	761	736	25	3.3	31,965	31,437	528	1.7	207	202	5	2.4
19	2,670	2,534	136	5.4	63,548	61,987	1,561	2.5	1,005	988	17	1.7
20–25	17,083	13,692	3,391	19.9	201,086	181,049	20,037	10.0	15,591	15,004	587	3.8
26–35	30,831	27,718	3,113	10.1	190,041	177,495	12,546	6.6	60,511	59,535	976	1.6
36–49	27,285	26,935	350	12.8	108,641	107,369	1,272	1.2	58,897	58,729	168	0.3
50–54	1,616	1,599	17	1.1	5,899	5,875	24	0.4	2,725	2,723	2	0.1
55–59	290	286	4	1.4	808	807	1	0.1	251	251	–	–
60 and over	74	74	–	–	193	193	–	–	60	60	–	–
Total	80,805	73,767	7,038	8.7	615,368	579,232	36,136	5.9	139,316	137,558	1,758	1.3
May 5, 1950												
To 17	44	44	–	–	4,154	4,119	34	0.8	8	8	–	–
17	188	185	3	1.6	14,825	14,766	129	0.9	48	48	–	–
18	743	742	1	0.1	42,843	42,229	614	1.4	262	252	10	3.8
19	2,711	2,674	37	1.4	80,221	78,831	1,390	1.7	1,219	1,194	25	2.1
20–25	21,884	20,481	1,403	6.4	249,134	237,314	11,820	4.7	19,092	18,534	558	2.9
26–35	37,959	34,990	2,969	7.8	215,993	203,175	12,818	5.9	58,234	57,051	1,183	2.0
36–49	38,460	31,889	571	1.5	142,079	140,441	1,638	1.2	75,094	74,805	289	0.4
50–54	2,748	2,735	13	0.5	9,252	9,182	70	0.8	3,698	3,688	10	0.3
55–59	525	525	–	–	1,273	1,266	7	0.5	444	442	2	0.5
60 and over	101	99	2	2.0	87	87	–	–	81	81	–	–
Total	105,363	100,364	4,999	4.7	759,931	731,410	28,521	3.8	158,180	156,103	2,077	1.3

[a]Based on Iu. V. Arutiunian, *Mekhanizatory sel'skogo khoziaistvo SSSR v 1929–1957 gg. (Formirovanie kadrov mas-* *sovykh kvalifikatsii)* (Moscow, 1960), pp. 295, 298.

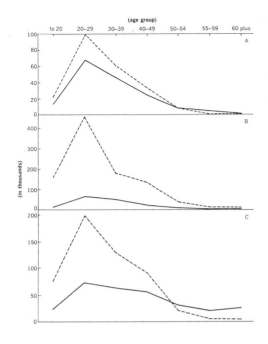

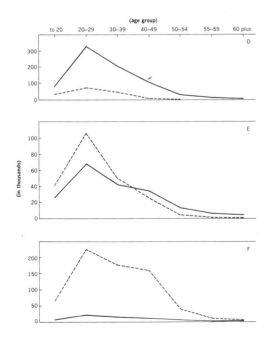

Fig. 2. Age distribution of males and females employed in various "physical" occupations, January 15, 1959. *Solid lines,* males; *broken lines,* females. *A,* chemical workers; *B,* textile workers; *C,* food industry workers; *D,* lathe operators; *E,* painters; *F,* public dining workers. Compiled from data in *Itogi . . . 1959 goda: SSSR,* Tables 42, 43, 47, 48, pp. 132–45, 161–70.

TABLE 3. Persons occupied in private subsidiary agriculture, by republic, age, and sex, January 15, 1959.[a]

	Males and Females			Males			Females		
Republic	Total	Able-bodied Age Group	Over- and Underaged	Total	Able-bodied Age Group	Over- and Underaged	Total	Able-bodied Age Group	Over- and Underaged
U.S.S.R.	9,864,801	5,035,481	4,829,320	913,903	213,087	700,816	8,950,898	4,822,394	4,128,504
R.S.F.S.R.	4,931,757	2,713,460	2,218,327	323,551	69,859	253,692	4,608,236	2,643,601	1,964,635
Ukrainian S.S.R.	2,576,361	1,062,314	1,514,047	282,252	62,565	219,687	2,294,109	999,749	1,294,360
Belorussian S.S.R.	460,592	195,303	265,289	49,793	10,780	39,013	410,799	184,523	226,276
Uzbek S.S.R.	321,430	150,727	170,703	70,825	17,464	53,361	250,605	133,263	117,342
Kazakh S.S.R.	474,260	343,509	130,751	32,603	8,246	24,995	441,657	335,901	105,756
Georgian S.S.R.	248,936	137,416	111,520	38,213	13,511	24,702	210,723	123,905	86,818
Azerbaidzhan S.S.R.	113,721	66,409	47,312	13,079	5,183	7,896	100,642	61,226	39,416
Lithuanian S.S.R.	158,752	76,668	82,084	20,642	5,576	15,066	138,110	71,092	67,018
Moldavian S.S.R.	87,959	41,061	46,898	8,213	2,088	6,125	79,746	38,973	40,773
Latvian S.S.R.	98,416	41,019	57,397	12,121	2,263	9,858	86,295	38,753	47,539
Kirgiz S.S.R.	108,649	51,474	57,175	18,294	3,142	15,152	90,355	48,332	42,023
Tadzhik S.S.R.	99,769	61,094	38,675	13,439	3,656	9,783	86,330	57,438	28,892
Armenian S.S.R.	75,563	44,013	31,550	8,813	2,644	6,169	66,750	41,369	25,381
Turkmen S.S.R.	74,843	40,850	33,993	16,278	5,645	10,663	58,565	35,205	23,360
Estonian S.S.R.	33,763	10,164	23,599	5,787	1,103	4,684	27,976	9,061	18,915

[a]Calculated from *Itogi . . . 1959 goda: SSSR*, Tables 30, 32,
pp. 96–99; Tables 30, 32, in each republic census volume.

TABLE 4. Persons occupied in private subsidiary agriculture, by republic, sex, and urban and rural location, January 15, 1959.[a]

	Urban and Rural			Urban			Rural		
Republic	Total	Males	Females	Total	Males	Females	Total	Males	Females
U.S.S.R.	9,864,801	913,903	8,950,898	1,072,493	58,372	1,014,121	8,792,308	855,531	7,936,777
R.S.F.S.R.	4,931,787	323,551	4,608,236	487,691	18,469	469,222	4,444,096	305,082	4,139,014
Ukrainian S.S.R.	2,576,361	202,252	2,294,109	347,362	17,551	329,811	2,228,999	264,701	1,964,298
Belorussian S.S.R.	460,592	49,793	410,799	44,171	2,792	41,379	416,421	47,001	369,420
Uzbek S.S.R.	321,430	70,825	250,605	16,080	2,513	13,567	305,350	68,312	237,038
Kazakh S.S.R.	474,260	32,603	441,657	59,608	4,298	55,310	414,652	28,305	386,347
Georgian S.S.R.	248,936	38,213	210,723	27,722	3,504	24,218	221,214	34,709	186,505
Azerbaidzhan S.S.R.	113,721	13,079	100,642	17,773	7,811	15,962	95,948	11,268	84,680
Lithuanian S.S.R.	158,752	20,642	138,110	11,472	1,427	10,045	147,280	19,215	128,065
Moldavian S.S.R.	87,959	8,213	79,746	6,928	390	6,538	81,031	7,823	73,208
Latvian S.S.R.	98,416	12,721	86,295	12,481	1,437	11,044	85,935	10,684	75,251
Kirgiz S.S.R.	108,649	18,294	90,355	10,689	1,124	9,565	97,960	17,170	80,790
Tadzhik S.S.R.	99,769	13,439	86,330	12,409	978	11,431	87,360	12,461	74,899
Armenian S.S.R.	75,563	8,813	66,750	6,232	741	5,491	69,331	8,072	61,259
Turkmen S.S.R.	74,843	16,278	58,565	10,102	900	99,202	64,741	15,378	49,363
Estonian S.S.R.	33,763	5,787	27,976	1,773	437	1,336	31,990	5,350	26,640

[a]Based on *Itogi . . . 1959 goda: SSSR*, Tables 30, 32, pp.
96–99; Tables 30, 32, in each republic census volume.

TABLE 5. Distribution and percentage of women among state farm workers and collective farmers engaged in predominantly physical labor, January 15, 1959.[a]

Occupation	Total	Females	Females %
Total employed in physical labor...........................	33,893,082	19,742,736	58.3
Heads of livestock and poultry farms.......................	143,097	22,273	15.6
Brigadiers of field brigades...............................	259,136	22,691	8.8
Brigadiers of livestock brigades...........................	74,487	11,761	15.8
Other brigadiers...	262,888	16,499	6.3
Bookkeepers...	30,119	6,198	20.6
Field-team leaders.......................................	156,505	136,509	87.2
Tractor and combine drivers..............................	2,389,292	17,240	0.7
Implement handlers and workers on agricultural machinery.....	150,232	3,070	2.0
Workers in plant breeding and feed production..............	611,267	432,464	70.7
Cattle farm workers......................................	961,463	545,964	56.8
Milking personnel.......................................	1,431,489	1,415,609	98.9
Stablemen and grooms....................................	1,015,292	85,560	8.4
Swineherds..	563,142	513,827	91.2
Herdsmen, drovers, shepherds.............................	753,615	141,011	18.7
Other livestock workers..................................	188,555	62,732	33.3
Poultry workers..	162,153	151,882	93.7
Beekeepers..	79,989	13,582	17.0
Orchard and vineyard workers.............................	106,404	55,337	52.0
Vegetable and melon growers.............................	84,829	67,664	79.8
Irrigators...	19,610	3,015	15.4
Nonspecialized agricultural workers.......................	24,213,821	15,932,948	65.8

[a]Based on *Itogi . . . 1959 goda: SSSR*, pp. 159–60.

appendix
VIII

SEMIPROFESSIONAL AND
PROFESSIONAL OCCUPATIONS

TABLE 1. Number and percentage of women specialists with higher and specialized secondary education employed in the economy, by republic, December 1, 1957, 1960, and 1961.[a]

Republic	Total Higher and Specialized Secondary			Number of Women					
				Higher			Specialized Secondary		
	1957	1960	1961	1957	1960	1961	1957	1960	1961
U.S.S.R.	4,087	5,189	5,547	1,464	1,865	2,015	2,623	3,324	3,532
R.S.F.S.R.	2,578	3,279	3,486	902	1,149	1,236	1,676	2,130	2,250
Ukrainian S.S.R.	759	965	1,031	283	360	387	476	605	644
Belorussian S.S.R.	138	171	185	46	60	65	92	111	120
Uzbek S.S.R.	86	108	117	33	44	48	53	64	69
Kazakh S.S.R.	140	184	205	46	59	67	94	125	138
Georgian S.S.R.	83	94	105	39	44	50	44	50	55
Azerbaidzhan S.S.R.	54	67	71	23	29	31	31	38	40
Lithuanian S.S.R.	42	54	59	15	19	21	27	35	38
Moldavian S.S.R.	36	48	51	12	17	18	24	31	33
Latvian S.S.R.	46	59	65	18	23	25	28	36	40
Kirgiz S.S.R.	28	37	41	10	13	15	18	24	26
Tadzhik S.S.R.	19	25	26	7	9	10	12	16	16
Armenian S.S.R.	30	37	40	13	18	19	17	19	21
Turkmen S.S.R.	19	24	26	6	8	9	13	16	17
Estonian S.S.R.	29	37	39	11	13	14	18	24	25

TABLE 1. Number and percentage of women specialists with higher and specialized secondary education employed in the economy, by republic, December 1, 1957, 1960, and 1961.[a]—continued

Republic	Percentage								
	Total			Higher			Specialized Secondary		
	1957	1960	1961	1957	1960	1961	1957	1960	1961
U.S.S.R.	60	59	59	52	53	53	65	63	63
R.S.F.S.R.	62	61	61	54	55	55	67	65	65
Ukrainian S.S.R.	60	58	57	53	52	52	65	62	61
Belorussian S.S.R.	64	62	62	55	55	54	70	67	67
Uzbek S.S.R.	47	45	45	40	40	41	53	49	49
Kazakh S.S.R.	55	54	54	48	47	47	59	58	59
Georgian S.S.R.	51	49	52	42	41	44	63	60	61
Azerbaidzhan S.S.R.	45	44	44	40	39	40	49	48	49
Lithuanian S.S.R.	62	59	60	52	52	52	69	64	65
Moldavian S.S.R.	61	58	58	51	50	50	67	64	63
Latvian S.S.R.	61	59	60	57	57	57	64	61	62
Kirgiz S.S.R.	52	52	52	44	46	45	58	57	57
Tadzhik S.S.R.	44	44	42	41	38	37	46	48	46
Armenian S.S.R.	49	50	49	41	44	44	58	57	56
Turkmen S.S.R.	45	45	45	37	37	37	51	50	50
Estonian S.S.R.	61	61	60	55	54	54	66	65	64

[a]Absolute figures are expressed in thousands. Based on *Zhenshchina v SSSR* (Moscow, 1960), p. 60; *Zhenshchiny i deti v SSSR* (Moscow, 1961), p. 140; and *Zhenshchiny i deti v SSSR* (Moscow, 1963), p. 121.

TABLE 2. Number and percentage of women in various "mental" occupations, 1926, 1939, and 1959.[a]

Occupation	1926	%	1939	%	1959	%
Total number (including private subsidiary economy).....	–	–	34,102.1	43	47,604.6	48
Total employed in primarily physical labor..............	–	–	29,469.4	45	36,550.2	46
Total employed in primarily mental work..............	717.4	26	4,632.7	34	11,054.5	54
Heads of state, administrative, party, Young Communist League, trade union, co-operative organization, and other social organizations and their structural subdivisions....	5.3	6	54.3	12	100.4	26
Heads of all-Union, republic, *krai, oblast, okrug, rayon,* and city state administrative, party, Young Communist League, trade union, co-operative organs, and other social organizations and their structural subdivisions...	–	–	36.0	15	58.1	25
Heads of primary party, Young Communist League, trade union, and other social organizations..............	–	–	8.4	13	8.1	14
Chairmen and secretaries of executive committees of rural and village Soviets......................	–	–	10.0	7	34.2	33
Heads of establishments (industrial, construction, agricultural, forestry, transport, communications, and their structural subdivisions)........................	1.0	1	46.2	6	118.3	12
Directors, chiefs, and heads of establishments.........	–	–	16.1	7	35.6	12
Shop, section (*prolet*), workshop, and division chiefs....	–	–	14.7	9	54.2	15
Engineering-technical personnel.......................	–	–	360.4	22	1,650.2	39
Engineers and chief engineers.......................	0.9	2	32.8	13	268.4	32
Model builders, draftsmen.........................	–	–	48.3	46	165.7	56
Foremen (technical personnel)......................	–	–	24.9	9	182.4	24
Technicians (excluding agro-zootechnicians and veterinary technicians)...............................	–	–	56.5	21	230.5	45
Laboratory personnel (excluding wage worker laboratory personnel)	–	–	123.9	79	376.6	86
Film mechanics.................................	–	–	2.0	5	19.8	12
Coal-mining foremen	–	–	2.2	2	16.2	20
Railroad transport technical personnel (excluding those indicated above)...............................	–	–	6.2	11	27.7	28
Agronomists, zootechnicians, veterinary personnel, and foresters..	–	–	40.3	14	164.5	34
Agronomists, zootechnicians.......................	–	–	31.7	18	114.8	41
Veterinary doctors...............................	–	–	3.2	16	13.3	30
Veterinary technicians and *feldshers*.................	–	–	4.2	5	25.6	23
Foresters, forest assessors.........................	–	–	1.2	7	10.8	25
Medical personnel...................................	115.7	58	549.5	81	1,517.1	89
Chief doctors and other heads of public health institutions...................................	1.2	31	6.5	39	23.0	52
Doctors..	21.8	40	74.6	61	265.5	79
Dentists..	8.8	79	11.7	84	26.2	83
Feldshers, midwives...............................	32.4	54	109.5	72	306.1	84
Pharmacists.....................................	–	–	27.0	93	56.3	95
Nurses...	–	–	177.7	99	689.5	100
Nursery directors and training personnel..............	–	–	117.5	100	120.1	100
Scientific personnel, teachers, and training personnel......	–	–	829.9	53	1,904.4	67
Scientific personnel, higher educational institution teachers, heads of scientific research institutions.........	2.9	21	34.9	31	120.2	38
Teachers in primary, 7-yr., and all secondary educational institutions and courses (including heads of primary schools)......................................	217.8	63	657.6	55	1,467.0	73
Physical culture and sports teachers and instructors.....	–	–	4.1	14	28.7	27
Children's homes and kindergarten heads and training personnel, boarding school personnel..............	–	–	124.0	93	262.2	95
Literary and press personnel......................	–	–	16.6	29	47.6	46
Writers, journalists, editors, proofreaders, technical editors, designers................................	–	–	7.3	69	20.8	82

TABLE 2. Number and percentage of women in various "mental" occupations, 1926, 1939, and 1959.[a]—*continued*

Occupation	1926		1939		1959	
		%		%		%
Cultural-enlightenment personnel.....................	–	–	141.4	50	317.0	69
Library heads, librarians, directors of theaters, cultural and rest parks, museums, personnel of club institutions, and other cultural-enlightenment personnel....	–	–	65.8	33	100.3	45
Art personnel......................................	–	–	41.3	29	59.4	31
Artists, producers................................	–	–	23.9	42	29.1	45
Composers, conductors, musicians..................	–	–	6.0	14	8.1	18
Painters, sculptors...............................	–	–	7.6	23	15.7	24
Juridical personnel................................	1.3	5	8.3	13	25.7	33
Judges, procurators...............................	–	–	2.7	14	5.4	23
Lawyers, legal consultants, and other juridical personnel.	–	–	5.6	13	20.3	36
Communications personnel...........................	–	–	179.6	68	372.3	78
Radio-telegraphers...............................	–	–	4.1	26	15.1	25
Telegraphers.....................................	–	–	39.6	73	67.2	94
Telephone operators..............................	–	–	100.4	95	169.3	97
Trade, public dining, procurement, supply, and sales personnel..	44.0	13	507.1	31	1,380.0	61
Sales personnel, heads of departments and divisions of stores, pavilions, stalls, buffets....................	154.0	23	407.9	57	994.7	85
Planning and recordkeeping personnel..................	–	–	1,246.0	40	2,499.5	71
Economists, planners, statisticians, bookkeepers, tally clerks, cashiers..................................	–	–	182.2	65	363.5	88
Office (correspondence) personnel.....................	–	–	378.0	77	497.4	93
Personnel of communal establishments and personal services...	–	–	64.9	32	147.1	53
Barbers, manicurists..............................	–	–	45.9	40	83.3	60
Agents and expediters.............................	–	–	23.4	13	53.5	37

[a]Absolute figures are expressed in thousands; *parentheses*, estimates; –, data not available. Calculated from *Itogi . . . 1959 goda: SSSR*, Table 48, pp. 167–70; *Zhenshchiny i deti v SSSR* (Moscow, 1961), pp. 114–19; and *Zhenshchiny i deti v SSSR* (Moscow, 1963), pp. 94–99.

Table 3. Number of women scientific workers, 1947–64.[a]

Position	1947	1950	1952	1955	1956	1957	1958	1959	1960	1961	1962	1963	1964
Total........................	51.3	59.0	65.7	81.6	87.0	93.7	101.4	111.1	128.7	150.0	177.7	204.8	230.2
With academic titles.........	18.7	16.6	17.5	18.7	19.7	22.3	23.7	25.4	26.3	28.0	38.0	41.4	42.9
Academicians, corresponding members, professors................	0.5	0.5	0.5	0.6	0.6	0.6	0.7	0.7	0.7	0.8	0.9	0.9	1.0
Dotsents and senior research workers.........	6.0	6.7	7.4	9.2	9.8	10.4	10.5	11.2	12.0	12.7	14.4	15.6	16.7
Dotsents...................	2.9	3.2	3.7	4.8	5.1	5.4	5.5	5.8	6.2	6.7	7.3	8.0	8.8
Senior research workers.......	3.1	3.5	3.7	4.4	4.7	5.0	5.0	5.4	5.8	6.0	7.1	7.6	7.9
Junior research workers and assistants......	12.2	9.4	9.6	8.9	9.3	11.3	12.5	13.5	13.6	14.5	22.7	24.9	25.2
Total without academic titles......	32.6	42.4	47.2	62.9	69.3	71.4	77.7	85.7	102.4	122.0	138.7	163.4	187.3

[a] Including teachers and workers in higher educational institutions. Figures are expressed in thousands and are as of October 1 except for 1963 and 1964 which are as of November 1. Based on *Zhenshchiny i deti v SSSR* (Moscow, 1963), p. 129; *Vysshee obrazovanie v SSSR* (Moscow, 1961), p. 212; *Kul'turnoe stroitel'stvo SSSR* (Moscow, 1956), p. 251; *Narodnoe khoziaistvo SSSR v 1958 godu* (Moscow, 1959), p. 844; *Narodnoe khoziaistvo SSSR v 1962 godu* (Moscow, 1963), p. 583; *Narodnoe khoziaistvo SSSR v 1963 godu* (Moscow, 1965), p. 590; and *Narodnoe khoziaistvo SSSR v 1964 godu* (Moscow, 1965), p. 700.

appendix
IX

WOMEN SCIENTISTS AT UNIVERSITIES

AMONG THE WOMEN scientists at Moscow State University is Professor Valentina Iveronova, who has been head of the department of general physics since 1931. She was born in 1908, the daughter of a professor. After graduating from Moscow State University in 1930, she began teaching and doing research there, received her candidate degree in 1936 and her doctorate in 1947, and became professor in 1948. She is known for her studies in X-ray structural analysis and is the author of more than forty works. She has been decorated with the "Badge of Honor" for her scientific and pedagogical activity.

Klavdiia Topchiieva is dean of Moscow State University's department of chemistry. She was born in 1911 and worked on her parents' farm before taking a job in the mechanical workshops of a chemical plant as an ordinary worker. In 1934 she graduated in chemistry from Moscow University and took a postgraduate course in physical chemistry. In 1937 she received her candidate degree and was appointed a lecturer in the department of physical chemistry. In 1942 she was made an associate professor and in 1954, a year after receiving her doctorate, she was appointed professor. She has written more than thirty scientific works.[1]

At Leningrad State University, Anastasiia Yakubchik, a former peasant woman, heads the division of polymers. In 1936 the U.S.S.R.

Academy of Sciences granted her a doctor's degree in chemistry for her scientific work, and in 1940 she was made a professor. She is co-author with S. V. Lebedev on a method on which the Soviet synthetic rubber industry is based. She has made the training of highly skilled chemists her special concern. She has written and published more than fifty scientific works.

The head of the department of medieval history at the same university is Alexandra Liublinskaia, who has been teaching and doing research for more than twenty years. She received her doctorate in 1951. She has written more than thirty works, has trained many historians, and is an active social worker.

Professor Zinaida Razumovskaia, who is a doctor of biology, heads the department of microbiology at Leningrad State University. She is the author of more than thirty works. Like many other Soviet women scientists, she comes of peasant stock.

Professor Vera Kamysheva-Elpat'evskaia, who is a doctor of geology and mineralogy, heads the department of paleontology at Saratov University. The daughter of a clergyman, she graduated from Saratov University in 1924. In 1948 she earned her doctor's degree. She has written and published several major studies in geology and hydrogeology and is also scientific adviser to the paleontological group of the Saratov Oil Trust.[2]

---

[1]Galkin, *The Training of Scientists in the Soviet Union* (Moscow, 1959), p. 130.

[2]*Ibid.*, p. 131.

Another accomplished woman at Saratov University is Maria Bobrova, who heads the program in world literature. The daughter of a Donbas coalminer, she began her career as a school mistress in Lugansk on completing secondary school in 1926. She successfully combined teaching with studies at the Don Institute of Education, followed by a postgraduate course. When the war broke out, she volunteered for service at the front and was decorated with several medals. After the war she was awarded the candidate degree in 1946. Later she became an associate professor and, after working on her doctoral dissertation on Mark Twain at Moscow University in 1954–56, received her doctoral degree and became a professor. She has published more than twenty papers in her field.[3]

Felitsiana Vergunas, the daughter of a Polish railway man, graduated from Tomsk University in 1931, and a year later she took postgraduate courses at the Siberian Physico-Technical Institute. She then started teaching and doing research at Tomsk University. In 1937 she became a candidate in physics and mathematics and in 1954 received her doctorate. She now heads the division of general physics at Gorky University.[4]

Mariia Grekhova is deputy director for scientific work at the Gorky Physico-Technical Institute and simultaneously holds an academic post at Gorky University. She graduated from Moscow State University in 1924, after which she taught there and simultaneously took up postgraduate studies. In 1936 she became a doctor of physics and mathematics and in 1938 was appointed professor. She has published more than fifty works in the electronics of superhigh frequencies.[5]

---

[3]*Ibid.*, pp. 131–32.

[4]*Ibid.*, pp. 129–30.
[5]*Ibid.*, p. 130.

appendix

X

METHOD OF MAKING ARTICLE COUNTS

AN ATTEMPT was made to select important and representative journals in each field for which the percentage of women was known. *Vysshee Obrazovanie v SSSR* (Moscow, 1961), p. 66, gives the percentage of women specialists with a higher education employed in the economy. A. Ia. Sinetskii, *Professorsko-prepodavatel'skie kadry vysshei shkoly SSSR* (Moscow, 1950), p. 139, gives the percentage of women on the staffs of higher educational institutions.

The sample (based upon names which have unambiguous male or female endings) was made from issues of the journals for 1940, 1950, 1960, and sufficient surrounding years to increase the sample to a significant size. Articles of an editorial or historical character were excluded in the sample of scientific and technical journals so that some minimum scholarly standard of scientific merit was presumably met by those included. This does not rule out the possibility, however, that the average quality of the contributions by men might differ from that of women.

There were also sampling problems. The least of these was adjusting for multiple authorship. In instances where two, three, four, or more authors were listed, fractional credit was given to each author who was unambiguously male or female. It is interesting to note a trend toward multiple authorship, especially in a field such as physics, and a tendency for women to appear more frequently than men as multiple authors.

More important was the question of the representativeness of the sample. It is not possible to ascertain the sex of every contributor, since only certain family names tell us unambiguously whether the bearer is a male or female. Therefore a considerable proportion of contributors could not be included in the sample. To the extent that our sample is representative of the total population, this is not a serious problem, but the names yielding unambiguous results are primarily Slavic, which might bias the sample in favor of women, since the role of women in scholarship is smaller in the non-Slavic portion of the population.

Some empirical tests of the representativeness of the sample were made which indicate that as the sample size is increased to 100 or more contributions, the proportion of males and females tends to converge on the total population value. These tests were made by comparing the actual proportion of male and female zoologists in a handbook giving full names, including the patronymic, with the proportion indicated by the family name alone in the instances where the indication of sex was unambiguous. If the latter sample included as many as 100 names it was found to provide a good indication of the population value. As a result, a sizable sample of contributors to professional journals was made in every instance where it was feasible. Nevertheless, more extensive sampling, if time and resources permitted, would be desirable.

304

A list of the journals employed in making the various samples is included below:

Engineering:
  Electrical
    Elektrichestvo
  Mining
    Gorny zhurnal
  Mechanical
    Stanki i instrument
    Vestnik mashinostroeniia
  Civil
    Promyshlennoe stroitel'stvo
  Chemical
    Khimicheskaia promyshlennost'
    Neftianoe khoziaistvo
  Transportation
    Sotsialisticheskii transport
    Zheleznodorozhyni transport
Agriculture, agronomy, zootechnology, veterinary medicine, and forestry:
  Agronomy
    Sovetskaia agronomia
    Vestnik Akademii sel'skokhoziaistvennykh nauk—doklady (in 1940 *Doklady Vsesoiuznoi Akademii sel'skokhoziaistvennykh nauk*)
    Zemledelie
  Veterinary medicine
    Sovetskaia veterinariia
Economics, statistics, and trade:
  Economics
    Planovoe khoziaistvo
    Mirovoe khoziaistvo
    Voprosy ekonomiki
  Statistics
    Vestnik statistiki
Law
    Sovetskoe gosudarstvo i pravo
Medicine (excluding dentistry)
    Akademii meditsinskikh nauk SSSR—vestnik
    Klinicheskaia meditsina
    Sovetskaia meditsina
Physics and mathematics
    Izvestiia Akademii nauk SSSR—seriia matematicheskaia
    Zhurnal eksperimental'noi i teoreticheskoi fiziki

Zhurnal prikladnaia matematika i mekhanika
Zhurnal tekhnicheskoi fiziki
Chemistry
    Zhurnal obshchei khimii
Biology
    Botanicheskii zhurnal
    Zhurnal obshchei biologii
    Zoologicheskii zhurnal
Geology
    Izvestiia Akademii nauk SSSR—seriia geologicheskaia
    Sovetskaia geologiia
Physical culture
    Fizkultura i sport
Geography
    Izvestiia Akademii nauk SSSR—seriia geograficheskaia i geofizicheskaia
    Izvestiia gosudarstvennogo Russkogo geograficheskogo obshchestva
    Izvestiia vsesoiuznogo geograficheskogo obshchestva
History
    Iztoricheskii zhurnal
    Voprosy istorii
Philology
    Iazyk i myshlenie
    Trudy otdela drevne—Russkoi literatury
    Uchenye zapiska instituta Slavianovedenia
    Voprosy iazykoznaniia
    Voprosy literatury
Arts
    Iskusstvo
    Sovetskaia arkhitektura
Pedagogy
    Izvestiia Akademii pedagogicheskikh nauk RSFSR
    Narodnoe obrazovanie
    Sovetskaia pedagogika
    Srednee spetsial'noe obrazovanie
    Vestnik vysshei shkoly
Social-political and philosophy
    Bol'shevik
    Kommunist
    Partinaia zhizn'
    Pod znamenem Marksizma
    Voprosy filosofii

Bibliography

Non-Russian-Language Books, Monographs, and Chapters in Books

ACADEMY OF SCIENCES OF THE UZBEK REPUBLIC, *Academy of Sciences of the Uzbek SSR,* ed. by Kh. F. Fazilov. Tashkent, Publishing House of the Academy of Sciences of the Uzbek Republic, 1958, 156 pp.

ALBERT, ETHEL M., "The Roles of Women: Questions of Values," *The Potential of Woman,* ed. by Seymour M. Farber and Roger H. L. Wilson. New York, McGraw-Hill Company, Inc., 1963, pp. 105–15.

ALT, HERSCHEL, AND ALT, EDITH, *Russia's Children.* New York, Bookman Associates, 1959, 240 pp.

ASHBY, SIR ERIC, *Scientist in Russia.* New York, Penguin Books, 1947, 252 pp.

BEREDAY, GEORGE Z. F., BRIDEMAN, WILLIAM W., AND READ, GERALD H. (eds.), *The Changing Soviet School.* Cambridge, Mass., Riverside Press, 1960, 514 pp.

BEREDAY, GEORGE Z. F., AND PENNAR, JAAN (eds.), *The Politics of Soviet Education.* New York, Praeger, 1960, 219 pp.

BERGSON, ABRAM, AND KUZNETS, SIMON (eds.), *Economic Trends in the Soviet Union.* Cambridge, Mass., Harvard University Press, 1963, 392 pp.

BILSHAI, VERA, *The Status of Women in the Soviet Union.* Moscow, Foreign Languages Publishing House, 1957, 106 pp.

BRACKETT, JAMES W., "Demographic Trends and Population Policy in the Soviet Union," in Joint Economic Committee of the United States Congress, *Dimensions of Soviet Economic Power.* Washington, D.C., Government Printing Office, 1962, pp. 556–69.

CARR, E. H., *The Bolshevik Revolution, 1917–1923.* New York, The Macmillan Co., 1952–53, 3 vols.

CENTRAL ADMINISTRATION OF ECONOMIC AND SOCIAL STATISTICS OF THE STATE PLANNING COMMISSION OF THE U.S.S.R., *Socialist Construction in the U.S.S.R.* Moscow, Soyuzorgouchet, 1936, 538 pp.

CENTRAL STATISTICAL BOARD OF THE U.S.S.R. COUNCIL OF MINISTERS, *Cultural Progress in the U.S.S.R.: Statistical Returns.* Moscow, Foreign Languages Publishing House, 1958, 326 pp.

————, *Forty Years of Soviet Power in Facts and Figures.* Moscow, Foreign Languages Publishing House, 1958, 319 pp.

————, *National Economy of the U.S.S.R.: Statistical Returns.* Moscow, Foreign Languages Publishing House, 1957, 230 pp.

————, *Women and Children in the USSR: Brief Statistical Returns.* Moscow, Foreign Languages Publishing House, 1963, 196 pp.

CHAUNCEY, HENRY, *Interviews with Soviet Educators on Recent Developments and the Current Status of Education in the U.S.S.R.* Mimeographed report, Princeton, Educational Testing Service, 1965, 236 pp.

CONANT, JAMES BRYANT, *The American High School Today: A First Report to Inter-*

ested Citizens. New York, McGraw-Hill Book Company, Inc., 1959, 140 pp.

———, *The Education of American Teachers.* New York, McGraw-Hill Book Company, Inc., 1963, 275 pp.

———, *Slums and Suburbs: A Commentary on Schools in Metropolitan Areas.* New York, McGraw-Hill Book Company, Inc., 1961, 147 pp.

DEWAR, MARGARET, *Labor Policy in the U.S.S.R., 1917–1928.* Royal Institute of International Affairs, London and New York, Chatham House, 1956, 286 pp.

DEWITT, NICHOLAS, *Education and Professional Employment in the U.S.S.R.* National Science Foundation, Washington, D.C., Government Printing Office, 1961, 856 pp.

———, *Soviet Professional Manpower.* National Science Foundation, Washington, D.C., Government Printing Office, 1955, 400 pp.

DODGE, HOMER L., AND DODGE, NORTON T., *Notes on Visits to Educational Institutions in the U.S.S.R., April 20 to May 21, 1955.* Mimeographed report, Cambridge, Mass., 1955, 161 pp.

DODGE, NORTON T., "Recent Trends in the Training of Soviet Secondary School Teachers," in *The Politics of Soviet Education,* ed. by George Z. F. Bereday and Jaan Pennar. New York, Frederick A. Praeger, Inc., 1960, pp. 144–63.

———, *The Utilization of Women in Soviet Science and Technology, Report A.* Mimeographed report, College Park, Md., 1963, 117 pp.

———, *The Utilization of Women in Soviet Science and Technology, Report B.* Mimeographed report, College Park, Md., 1963, 23 pp.

———, *The Utilization of Women in Soviet Science and Technology, Report C: Data on the Role of Women in the Academy of Sciences of the U.S.S.R. and Union Republics.* Mimeographed report, College Park, Md., 1963, 29 pp.

DOUGLAS, WILLIAM O., *Russian Journey.* Garden City, N.Y., Doubleday & Co., 1956, 255 pp.

DUNN, ROBERT W., *Soviet Trade Unions.* New York, The Vanguard Press, Inc., 1928, 238 pp.

EASON, WARREN W., *Soviet Manpower, the Population and Labor Force of the U.S.S.R.* Unpublished doctoral dissertation, Columbia University, 1959, 484 pp.

———, "Labor Force," in *Economic Trends in the Soviet Union,* ed. by Abram Bergson and Simon Kuznets. Cambridge, Mass., Harvard University Press, 1963, pp. 38–95.

ENGELS, FREDERICK, *The Origin of the Family, Private Property and the State in the Light of the Researches of Lewis H. Morgan.* New York, International Publishers, 1942, 157 pp.

ENGINEERS JOINT COUNCIL, *The Training, Placement and Utilization of Engineers and Technicians in the Soviet Union.* New York, Engineers Joint Council, Inc., 1961, 101 pp.

FARBER, SEYMOUR M., AND WILSON, ROGER H. L. (eds.), *The Potential of Women.* New York, McGraw-Hill Book Company, Inc., 1963, 328 pp.

FAINSOD, MERLE, *How Russia is Ruled.* Rev. ed., Cambridge, Mass., Harvard University Press, 1963, 684 pp.

FIELD, MARK G., *Doctor and Patient in Soviet Russia.* Cambridge, Mass., Harvard University Press, 1957, 266 pp.

GALKIN, K., *The Training of Scientists in the Soviet Union.* Moscow, Foreign Languages Publishing House, 1959, 204 pp.

GEIGER, HOMER KENT, *The Urban Slavic Family and the Soviet System.* Unpublished doctoral dissertation, Harvard University, 1954, 333 pp.

GORDON, MANYA, *Workers before and after Lenin.* New York, E. P. Dutton & Co., Inc., 1941, 528 pp.

GREAT BRITAIN, BOARD OF EDUCATION, *Education in Russia.* Special Reports on Educational Subjects, Vol. 23, London, His Majesty's Stationery Office, 1909, 569 pp.

A Guide to the Soviet Academies. Rev. ed., May 1961, 103 pp.

HALLE, FANNINA W., *Woman in Soviet Russia.* London, Routledge, 1933, 409 pp.

———, *Women in the Soviet East.* New York, E. P. Dutton & Co., Inc., 1938, 363 pp.

HANS, NICHOLAS, *History of Russian Educational Policy (1701–1917).* New York,

Russell & Russell, Inc., 1964, 255 pp.

———, AND HESSEN, SERGIUS, *Educational Policy in Soviet Russia*. London, P. S. King and Son, Ltd., 1930, 236 pp.

HINDUS, MAURICE, *House without a Roof.* Garden City, N.Y., Doubleday & Co., Inc., 1961, 562 pp.

HUBBARD, LEONARD E., *Soviet Labor and Industry*. London, Macmillan and Co., Ltd., 1942, 315 pp.

INKELES, ALEX, AND BAUER, RAYMOND A., *The Soviet Citizen*. Cambridge, Mass., Harvard University Press, 1959, 533 pp.

INSTITUTE FOR THE STUDY OF THE USSR, *Prominent Personnel of the Academies of Sciences of the USSR and Union Republics*. Munich, Institute for the Study of the USSR, 1963, 71 pp.

JOHNSON, WILLIAM H. E., *Russia's Educational Heritage*. Pittsburgh, Carnegie Press, 1950, 351 pp.

JOINT ECONOMIC COMMITTEE OF THE UNITED STATES CONGRESS, *Dimensions of Soviet Economic Power*. Washington, D.C., Government Printing Office, 1962, 744 pp.

KINGSBURY, SUSAN M., AND FAIRCHILD, MILDRED, *Factory, Family and Women in the Soviet Union*. New York, G. P. Putnam's Sons, 1935, 334 pp.

KORNILOV, ALEXANDER, *Modern History of Russia*. New York, Alfred A. Knopf, 1924, 370 pp.

KOROL, ALEXANDER G., *Soviet Education for Science and Technology*. Cambridge, Mass., The Technology Press of Massachusetts Institute of Technology, 1957, 513 pp.

KORSHUNOVA, Y., AND RUMYANTSEVA, M., *The Rights of Soviet Women*. Moscow, Trade Union Publishing House, 1962, 53 pp.

KRASNOPOLSKII, A., AND SVERDLOV, G., *The Rights of Mother and Child in the U.S.S.R.* Moscow, Foreign Languages Publishing House, 1953, 80 pp.

KULSKI, W. W., *The Soviet Regime*. Syracuse, N.Y., Syracuse University Press, 1954, 807 pp.

LEARY, DANIEL B., *Education and Autocracy in Russia*. Buffalo, N.Y., College of Arts and Sciences, University of Buffalo, 1919, 127 pp.

LEVIN, DEANA, *Soviet Education Today*. New York, J. DeGraff, 1959, 170 pp.

LIASHCHENKO, PETER I., *History of the National Economy of Russia*. New York, Macmillan, 1949, 880 pp.

LORIMER, FRANK, *The Population of the Soviet Union: History and Prospects*. Geneva, League of Nations, 1946, 289 pp.

MACCOBY, ELEANOR E., "Woman's Intellect," in *The Potential of Woman,* ed. by Seymour M. Farber and Roger H. L. Wilson. New York, McGraw-Hill Book Co., Inc., 1963, pp. 24–39.

MACE, DAVID, AND MACE, VERA, *The Soviet Family*. Garden City, N.Y., Doubleday, 1963, 367 pp.

MANNES, MARYA, "The Problem of Creative Women," in *The Potential of Woman,* ed. by Seymour M. Farber and Roger H. L. Wilson. New York, McGraw-Hill Book Co., Inc., 1963, pp. 116–30.

MAYNARD, SIR JOHN, *Russia in Flux*. Abridged ed., New York, The Macmillan Co., 1951, 564 pp.

MEDINSKY, Y., *Public Education in the U.S.S.R.* 4th ed., Moscow, Foreign Languages Publishing House, 1953, 120 pp.

NATIONAL MANPOWER COUNCIL, *A Policy for Scientific and Professional Manpower*. New York, Columbia University Press, 1953, 263 pp.

———, *A Policy for Skilled Manpower*. New York, Columbia University Press, 1954, 299 pp.

———, *Utilization of Scientific and Professional Manpower*. New York, Columbia University Press, 1954, 197 pp.

NATIONAL SCIENCE FOUNDATION, *Women in Scientific Careers,* prepared by Bella Schwartz. Washington, D.C., Government Printing Office, July, 1961, 18 pp.

PARES, SIR BERNARD, *A History of Russia*. 5th ed., New York, Alfred A. Knopf, 1950, 552 pp.

PETROVA, L., AND GILEVSKAIA, S. (eds.), *Equality of Women in the U.S.S.R.* Moscow, Foreign Languages Publishing House, 1957, 362 pp.

PRESIDENT'S COMMISSION ON THE STATUS OF WOMEN, THE, *American Women*. Washington, D.C., Government Printing Office, 1963, 86 pp.

PRICE, GEORGE M., *Labor Protection in Soviet*

Russia. New York, International Publishers, 1928, 128 pp.

RICKOVER, HYMAN G., *American Education, a National Failure.* New York, E. P. Dutton and Co., Inc., 1962, 502 pp.

———, *Education and Freedom.* New York, E. P. Dutton and Co., Inc., 1959, 256 pp.

SCHULZ, HEINRICH E., AND TAYLOR, STEPHEN S. (eds.), *Who's Who in the U.S.S.R.* New York, Scarecrow Press, Inc., 1960, 967 pp.

SCHWARZ, SOLOMON, *Labor in the Soviet Union.* New York, Frederick A. Praeger, Inc., 1952, 364 pp.

SEREBRENNIKOV, G. N., *The Position of Women in the U.S.S.R.* London, Victor Gollancz, Ltd., 1937, 288 pp.

SOSNOVY, TIMOTHY, "The Soviet City," in Joint Economic Committee of the U. S. Congress, *Dimensions of Soviet Economic Power,* Washington, D.C., Government Printing Office, 1962, pp. 325–45.

SOUTER, L. S., AND WINSLADE, R., *Women Engineers in the U.S.S.R.* London, Caroline Haslett Memorial Trust, 1960, 28 pp.

STALIN, J., *Problems of Leninism.* Moscow, Foreign Languages Publishing House, 1940, 667 pp.

TIURIN, S. P., *From Peter the Great to Lenin: A History of the Russian Labor Movement with Special Reference to Trade Unionism.* London, P. S. King and Son, Ltd., 1935, 217 pp.

UNESCO, *Access of Women to Higher Education.* United Nations, Jan. 28, 1958, 67 pp.

U.S. BUREAU OF THE CENSUS, *Comparison of U. S. and U.S.S.R. Employment in Industry: 1939–1958,* prepared by Murray S. Weitzman. Washington, D.C., Government Printing Office, 1963, 70 pp.

———, *Estimates and Projections of the Population of the U.S.S.R. and of the Communist Countries of Eastern Europe, by Age and Sex.* Washington, D.C., Government Printing Office, April, 1964, 143 pp.

———, *The Magnitude and Distribution of Civilian Employment in the U.S.S.R.: 1928–1959,* prepared by Murray S. Weitzman and Andrew Elias. Washington, D.C., Government Printing Office, 1961, 193 pp.

———, *Projections of the Population of the U.S.S.R., by Age and Sex: 1964–1985,* prepared by James W. Brackett. Washington, D.C., Government Printing Office, 1964, 45 pp.

———, *The Soviet Statistical System: Labor Force Recordkeeping and Reporting,* prepared by Murray Feshbach. Washington, D.C., Government Printing Office, 1960, 151 pp.

———, *The Soviet Statistical System: Labor Force Recordkeeping and Reporting since 1957,* prepared by Murray Feshbach. Washington, D.C., Government Printing Office, 1962, 99 pp.

———, *United States Census of Population, 1960: Detailed Characteristics.* Washington, D.C., Government Printing Office, 1963, 823 pp.

U.S. BUREAU OF LABOR STATISTICS, *Principal Current Soviet Labor Legislation: A Compilation of Documents.* Report No. 210, Washington, D.C., Government Printing Office, 1962, 135 pp.

U.S. DEPARTMENT OF HEALTH, EDUCATION AND WELFARE, SOCIAL SECURITY ADMINISTRATION, *A Report on Social Security Programs in the Soviet Union.* Washington, D.C., Government Printing Office, 1960, 157 pp.

VUCINICH, ALEXANDER, *The Soviet Academy of Sciences.* Hoover Institute Studies, Series E, Institutions, No. 3, Stanford, Calif., Stanford University Press, 1956, 157 pp.

WEITZMAN, MURRAY S., FESHBACH, MURRAY, AND KULCHYCKA, LYDIA, "Employment in the U.S.S.R.: Comparative U.S.S.R.-U.S. Data," in Joint Economic Committee of the United States Congress, *Dimensions of Soviet Economic Power.* Washington, D.C., Government Printing Office, 1962, pp. 591–667.

WOLFLE, DAEL, *America's Resources of Specialized Talent.* Report of the Commission on Human Resources and Advanced Training, New York, Harper & Bros., 1954, 332 pp.

ZARECHNAK, GALINA V., *Academy of Medical Sciences of the USSR: History and Organization, 1944–1959.* Public Health

Monograph No, 63, Washington, D.C., Government Printing Office, 1960, 48 pp.

ZINOVYEV, M., AND PLESHAKOVA, A., *How Illiteracy Was Wiped Out in the U.S.S.R.* Moscow, Foreign Languages Publishing House, n.d., 101 pp.

VOZTRIKOVA, A. M., "A Születési Mozgalom, a Házasságkötések és a Család Viżsgálata a Szovjetunióban," *Demografia*, No. 4 (1962), 537–45.

WHITESIDE, ELENA, "For Soviet Women: A 13-Hour Day," *The New York Times Magazine* (Nov. 17, 1963), 28 ff.

YANOWITCH, MURRAY, "Soviet Patterns of Time Use and Concepts of Leisure," *Soviet Studies*, No. 1 (July, 1963), 17–37.

Non-Russian-Language Articles

BROWN, EMILY CLARK, "A Note on Employment and Unemployment," *Soviet Studies*, No. 3 (Jan., 1961), 231–39.

DODGE, HOMER L., AND DODGE, NORTON T., "Russia Gains over the U. S. in Educating Scientists," *U. S. News and World Report* (Sept. 16, 1955), 96–104.

EASON, WARREN W., "The Soviet Population Today," *Foreign Affairs* (July, 1959), 598–606.

FAKIOLAS, R. E., "Work Attendance in Soviet Industry," *Soviet Studies*, No. 4 (April, 1963), 365–78.

FOREIGN BROADCAST INFORMATION SERVICE, "Sociologists Reveal Labor Turnover Factors," *Daily Report: U.S.S.R. and East Europe* (July 28, 1964), 6–10.

GRUNFELD, JUDITH, "Women's Work in Russia's Planned Economy," *Social Research*, IX, No. 1 (Feb., 1942), 22–45.

"Marriage—Grounds for Firing a Woman?" *Soviet Woman*, No. 5 (May, 1960), 12.

"Meet Ten Women Ministers," *Soviet Woman*, No. 1 (Jan., 1957), 6–7.

OSIPOV, S. A., "Flowering Gardens," *Soviet Women*, No. 4 (April, 1960), 11.

PARRISH, JOHN B., "Professional Womanpower as a Soviet Resource," *Quarterly Review of Economics and Business* (Autumn, 1964), 55–61.

PETROVA, V., "After-School Centre for Children," *Soviet Woman*, No. 12 (Dec., 1950), 17–19.

ROOF, MICHAEL K., "Soviet Population Trends," *Eugenics Quarterly* (Sept., 1961), 123–34.

STAVSOVA, HELEN, "How Russian Women Won the Right to Higher Education," *Soviet Woman*, No. 4 (July, Aug., 1946), 49–50.

Russian-Language Books, Monographs, Chapters in Books, and Major Serials

ABRAMOVA, A. A., *Okhrana trudovykh prav zhenshchin v SSSR*. Moscow, Gosudarstvennoe izdatel'stvo iuridicheskoi literatury, 1954, 69 pp.

———, "Razvitie zakonodatel'stva ob okhrane truda zhenshchin," in *Novoe v razvitii trudovogo prava v period mezhdu XX i XXII s"ezdami KPSS*, ed. by N. G. Aleksandrov. Moscow, Izdatel'stvo Moskovskogo universiteta, 1961, pp. 136–60.

Akademiia khudozhestv Soiuza SSR. Moscow, no publisher, 1964, 58 pp.

AKADEMIIA MEDITSINSKIKH NAUK SSSR, *Spravochnik na 1964 god*. Moscow, Izdatel'stvo "Meditsina," 1964, 220 pp.

AKADEMIIA NAUK KAZAKHSKOI SSR, *Akademiia nauk Kazakhskoi SSR*. Alma-Ata, Izdatel'stvo Akademii nauk Kazakhskoi SSR, 1961, 18 pp.

AKADEMIIA NAUK SSSR, *Akademiia nauk soiuznykh respublik—spravochnik na 1957–1958 gody*. Moscow, Izdatel'stvo Akademii nauk SSSR, 1957.

———, *Akademiia nauk soiuznykh respublik—spravochnik na 1962 g*. Moscow, Izdatel'stvo Akademii nauk SSSR, 1962, 615 pp.

———, *Akademiia nauk SSSR—spravochnik na 1960 god*. Moscow, Izdatel'stvo Akademii nauk SSSR, 1960, 461 pp.

———, *Akademiia nauk SSSR—spravochnik na 1962 god*. Moscow, Izdatel'stvo Akademii nauk SSSR, 1962, 417 pp.

————, *220 let Akademiia nauk SSSR, uchastniku iubileinoi sessii Akademii nauk SSSR*. Moscow, no publisher, 1945, 120 pp.

————, *Nauchnye kadry v SSSR*, ed. by A. V. Topchiev. Moscow, Izdatel'stvo Akademii nauk SSSR, 1959, 303 pp.

————, *Spravochnik: 1725–1925, dlia uchastnikov prazdnovaniia dvukhsotletnogo iubileia Akademii nauk*. Leningrad, Izdatel'stvo Akademii nauk SSSR, 1925, 74 pp.

————, *Spravochnik kalendar' na 1940 god*. Moscow, Leningrad, Izdatel'stvo Akademii nauk SSSR, 1940, 245 pp.

————, *Spravochnik svedeniia po Akademii nauk SSSR na 1929 god*. Leningrad, Izdatel'stvo Akademii nauk SSSR, 1929, 26 pp.

————, INSTITUT EKONOMIKI, *Osobennosti i faktory razmeshcheniia ostraslei narodnogo khoziaistva SSSR*, ed. by Iu. G. Feigin *et al.* Moscow, Izdatel'stvo Akademii nauk SSSR, 1960, 696 pp.

————, ZOOLOGICHESKII INSTITUT, *Zoologi Sovetskogo Soiuza, spravochnik*. Moscow, Leningrad, Izdatel'stvo Akademii nauk SSSR, 1961, 292 pp.

AKADEMIIA PEDAGOGICHESKIKH NAUK RSFSR, *Spravochnik na 1958 god*. Moscow, Izdatel'stvo Akademii pedagogicheskikh nauk RSFSR, 1958, 212 pp.

————, *V pomoshch' rabotnikam shkol-internatov, dokumenty i materialy*. Moscow, Izdatel'stvo Akademii pedagogicheskikh nauk RSFSR, 1956, 112 pp.

AKADEMIIA STROITEL'STVA I ARKHITEKTURY SSSR, *Spravochnik na 1962 god*. Moscow, Gosudarstvennoe izdatel'stvo literatury po stroitel'stvu, arkhitekture i stroitel'nym materialam, 1962, 294 pp.

ALEKSANDROV, N. G. (ed.), *Novoe v razvitii trudovogo prava v period mezhdu XX i XXII s''ezdami KPSS*. Moscow, Izdatel'stvo Moskovskogo universiteta, 1961, 333 pp.

ARUTIUNIAN, IU. V., *Mekhanizatory sel'skogo khoziaistva v 1929–1957 gg. (formirovanie kadrov massovykh kvalifikatsii)*. Moscow, Izdatel'stvo Akademii nauk SSSR, 1960, 342 pp.

————, *Sovetskoe krest'ianstvo v gody Velikoi otechestvennoi voiny*. Moscow,

Izdatel'stvo Akademii nauk SSSR, 1963, 460 pp.

BAIKOVA, V. G., DUCHAL, A. C., AND ZEMTSOV, A. A., *Svobodnoe vremia i vsestoronnoe razvitie lichnosti*. Moscow, Izdatel'stvo "Mysl'," 1965, 272 pp.

BELONOVSKAIA, G. P., "Khimiia—cheloveku," in *Zhenshchiny goroda Lenina, sbornik*, ed. by E. A. Giliarova *et al.* Leningrad, Lenizdat, pp. 326–32.

BOLGOV, V. I., *Vnerabochee vremia i uroven' zhizni trudiashchikhsia*. Novosibirsk, Redaktsionno-izdatel'skii otdel Sibirskogo otdeleniia AN SSSR, 1964, 136 pp.

BOL'SHAIA SOVETSKAIA ENTSIKLOPEDIIA, *Ezhegodnik Bol'shoi Sovetskoi entsiklopedii, 1957*. Moscow, Gosudarstvennoe nauchnoe izdatel'stvo, "Bol'shaia Sovetskaia entsiklopediia," 1957, 648 pp.

————, *Ezhegodnik Bol'shoi Sovetskoi entsiklopedii, 1960*. Moscow, Godsudarstvennoe nauchnoe izdatel'stvo, "Bol'shaia Sovetskaia entsiklopediia," 1960, 613 pp.

————, *Ezhegodnik Bol'shoi Sovetskoi entsiklopedii, 1962*. Moscow, Gosudarstvennoe nauchnoe izdatel'stvo, "Bol'shaia Sovetskaia entsiklopediia," 1962, 623 pp.

BRAGINSKII, B. I., *Proizvoditel'nost' truda v sel'skom khoziaistve (metodika ucheta i planirovaniia)*. Moscow, Sel'khozizdat, 1962, 432 pp.

DAVIDOVICH, V. G., *Planirovka gorodov*. Moscow, Izdatel'stvo Ministerstva kommunal'nogo khoziaistva RSFSR, 1947, 315 pp.

DEINEKO, M. M. (ed.), *Spravochnik direktora shkoly i sbornik postanovlenii, prikazov, instruktsii i drugikh rukovodiashchikh materialov o shkole*, 2nd ed., Moscow, Uchpedgiz, 1955, 513 pp.

Deputaty Verkhovnova Soveta SSSR, shestoi sozyv. Moscow, Izvestiia, 1962, 528 pp.

DUBINSKAIA, OL'GA DANILOVNA, *Prava i obiazannosti chlenov kolkhoza*. Moscow, Vsesoiuznoe obshchestvo po rasprostraneniia politicheskikh i nauchnikh znanii, Moskovskoe oblastnoe otdelenie, 1957, 47 pp.

GALKIN, K. T., *Vysshee obrazovanie i podgotovka nauchnykh kadrov v SSSR*. Moscow, Gosizdat "Sovetskaia Nauka," 1958, 175 pp.

GOSPLAN SSSR, *Itogi vypolneniia pervogo*

piatiletnego plana razvitiia narodnogo khoziaistva SSSR. Moscow, Gosplanizdat, 1935, 279 pp.

————, *Vsesoiuznaia perepisi naseleniia 1926 goda,* tom XXXIV, *Soiuz Sovetskikh Sotsialisticheskikh Respublik,* Moscow, Izdatel'stvo plankhozgiza, 1930, 226 pp.

————, *Vsesoiuznaia perepisi naseleniia 1926 goda:* tom LI, *Soiuz Sovetskikh Sotsialisticheskikh Respublik.* Moscow, Leningrad, Gosudarstvennoe sotsial'no-ekonomicheskoe izdatel'stvo, 1931, 244 pp.

GOSUDARSTVENNAIA ORDENA LENINA BIBLIOTEKA SSSR IMENI V. I. LENINA, *Bibliografia dissertatsii: Doktorskie dissertatsii za 1941–1944 gg.* Moscow, 1946, 183 pp.

————, *Bibliografia dissertatsii: Doktorskie dissertatsii za 1945 g.* Moscow, 1947, 104 pp.

INSTITUT MARKSIZMA-LENINIZMA PRI TsK KPSS, *Trinadtsatyi s"ezd RKP(b)—stenografieheskii otchet.* Moscow, Gosudarstvennoe izdatel'stvo politicheskoi literatury, 1963, 883 pp.

KAPLUN, S., *Zhenskii trud i okhrana ego v Sovetskoi Rossii.* Moscow, Gosudarstvennoe izdatel'stvo, 1921, 228 pp.

KARNAUKOVA, E. S., "Ispol'zovanie trudovykh resursov v kolkhozakh," in *Puti povysheniia proizvoditel'nosti truda v sel'skom khoziaistve SSSR,* ed. by E. S. Karnaukova and M. I. Kozlov. Moscow, Izdatel'stvo "Nauka," 1964, pp. 51–84.

————, and KOZLOV, M. I. (eds.), *Puti povysheniia proizvoditel'nosti truda v sel'skom khoziaistve SSSR.* Moscow, Izdatel'stvo "Nauka," 1964, 392 pp.

KAZANTSEV, N. D., PAVLOV, I. V., AND RUSKOL, A. A. (eds.), *Kolkhoznoe pravo.* Moscow, Gosudarstvennoe izdatel'stvo iuridicheskoi literatury, 1955, 383 pp.

KLIMOV, N., *Rabochii den' v obshchestve stroiashchem kommunism.* Moscow, Izdatel'stvo sotsial'no-ekonomicheskoi literatury, 1961, 142 pp.

KOMAREVSKAIA, V., LUZGINA, V., AND SHATSKII, V., "Ispol'zovanie i material'noe stimulirovanie sel'skokhoziaistvennogo truda v raionakh Bratskotaishetskogo promyshlennogo uzla," in *Ispol'zovanie trudovykh resursov v sel'skom khoziaistve SSSR,* ed. by I. A. Borodin. Moscow, Izdatel'stvo "Nauka," 1964, pp. 202–12.

KOMAROV, V. E., *Ekonomicheskie osnovy podgotovki spetsialistov dlia narodnogo khoziaistva.* Moscow, Izdatel'stvo Akademii nauk SSSR, 1959, 208 pp.

KORSHUNOVA, E., AND RUMIANTSEV, M., *Prava Sovetskikh zhenshchin.* Moscow, Profizdat, 1960, 92 pp.

KOTOV, F. I., *Problemy truda i zarabotnoi platy v period perekhoda k kommunizmu.* Moscow, Ekonomizdat, 1963, 336 pp.

Kuda poiti uchit'sia, spravochnik dlia postupaiushchikh v vysshie i srednie spetsial'nye uchebnye zavedeniia (tekhnikumy, uchilishcha, shkoly) Moskvy i Moskovskoi oblasti v 1960 godu. Moscow, Izdatel'stvo "Moskovskaia pravda," 1960, 126 pp.

LAPTEV, I. D., *Material'noe stimulirovanie razvitiia kolkhoznogo proizvodstva.* Moscow, Izdatel'stvo Akademii nauk SSSR, 1963, 327 pp.

LEBEDEVA, V., *Okhrana materinstva i mladenchestva v Sovetskoi trudovoi respublike.* [Bound with, and catalogued under, Kaplun, Sergei Il'ich, *Zhenskii trud i okrana ego v Sovetskoi Rossii.*] Moscow, Gosudarstvennoe izdatel'stvo, 1921, 76 pp.

LENINGRADSKII ORDENA LENINA GOSUDARSTVENNYI UNIVERSITET IMENI A. A. ZHDANOVA: NAUCHNAIA BIBLIOTEKA IMENI M. GOR'KOGO, *Dissertatsii, zashchishchennie v Leningradskom ordena Lenina Gosudarstvennom Universitete imeni A. A. Zhdanova v 1934–1954 gg.* Leningrad, Izdatel'stvo Leningradskogo Universiteta, 1955, 256 pp.

LISHCHINA, E., "Podgotovka spetsialistov," in *V edinom stroiu,* ed. by G. D. Kostromarov. Moscow, Moskovskii rabochii, 1960, pp. 316–24.

MALYSHEV, I. S. (ed.), *MTS vo vtoroi piatiletke.* Moscow, Leningrad, Gosplanizdat, 1939, 132 pp.

MINISTERSTVO IUSTITSII RSFSR, *Kodeks zakonov o brake, sem'e i opeke RSFSR.* Moscow, Gosudarstvennoe izdatel'stvo iuridicheskoi literatury, 1950, 137 pp.

MINISTERSTVO KUL'TURY RSFSR, GOSUDARSTVENNAIA ORDENA LENINA BIBLIOTEKA SSSR IMENI V. I. LENINA, *Katalog kandidatskikh dissertatsii, postupivshikh v Biblioteku imeni V. I. Lenina.* Vol. 1, Moscow, 1956, 198 pp.

————, *Katalog kandidatskikh dissertatsii, postupivshikh v Biblioteku imeni V. I. Lenina.* Vol. 2, Moscow, 1957, 224 pp.

————, *Katalog kandidatskikh dissertatsii, postupivshikh v Biblioteku imeni V. I. Lenina.* Vol. 3, Moscow, 1958, 203 pp.

————, *Katalog kandidatskikh dissertatsii, postupivshikh v Biblioteku imeni V. I. Lenina.* Vol. 4, Moscow, 1957, 135 pp.

————, *Katalog kandidatskikh dissertatsii, postupivshikh v Biblioteku imeni V. I. Lenina i Gosudarstvennuiu Tsentral'nuiu Nauchnuiu Meditsinskuiu Biblioteku: v 1-m polugodie 1957 goda.* Moscow, 1958, 171 pp.

————, *Katalog kandidatskikh dissertatsii, postupivshikh v Biblioteku imeni V. I. Lenina i Gosudarstvennuiu Tsentral'nuiu Nauchnuiu Meditsinskuiu Biblioteku: vo 2-om polugodie 1957 goda.* Moscow, 1958, 188 pp.

————, *Katalog kandidatskikh i doktorskikh dissertatsii, postupivshikh v Biblioteku imeni V. I. Lenina i Gosudarstvennuiu Tsentral'nuiu Nauchnuiu Meditsinskuiu Biblioteku: v 1-m polugodie 1958 goda.* Moscow, 1959, 212 pp.

————, *Katalog kandidatskikh i doktorskikh dissertatsii, postupivshikh v Biblioteku imeni V. I. Lenina i Gosudarstvennuiu Tsentral'nuiu Nauchnuiu Meditsinskuiu Biblioteku: vo 2-om polugodie 1958 goda.* Moscow, 1959, 291 pp.

————, *Katalog kandidatskikh i doktorskikh dissertatsii, postupivshikh v Biblioteku imeni V. I. Lenina i Gosudarstvennuiu Tsentral'nuiu Nauchnuiu Meditsinskuiu Biblioteku: v 1-m polugodie 1959 goda.* Moscow, 1959, 291 pp.

————, *Katalog kandidatskikh i doktorskikh dissertatsii, postupivshikh v Biblioteku imeni V. I. Lenina i Gosudarstvennuiu Tsentral'nuiu Nauchnuiu Meditsinskuiu Biblioteku: vo 2-om polugodie 1959 goda.* Moscow, 1960, 296 pp.

————, *Katalog kandidatskikh i doktorskikh dissertatsii, postupivshikh v Biblioteku imeni V. I. Lenina i Gosudarstvennuiu Tsentral'nuiu Nauchnuiu Meditsinskuiu Biblioteku: v 1-m kvartale 1960 goda.* Moscow, 1960, 196 pp.

————, *Katalog kandidatskikh i doktorskikh dissertatsii, postupivshikh v Biblioteku imeni V. I. Lenina i Gosudarstvennuiu Tsentral'nuiu Nauchnuiu Meditsinskuiu Biblioteku: vo 2-om kvartale 1960 goda.* Moscow, 1960, 188 pp.

————, *Katalog kandidatskikh i doktorskikh dissertatsii, postupivshikh v Biblioteku imeni V. I. Lenina i Gosudarstvennuiu Tsentral'nuiu Nauchnuiu Meditsinskuiu Biblioteku: v 3-m kvartale 1960 goda.* Moscow, 1961, 241 pp.

————, *Katalog kandidatskikh i doktorskikh dissertatsii, postupivshikh v Biblioteku imeni V. I. Lenina i Gosudarstvennuiu Tsentral'nuiu Nauchnuiu Meditsinskuiu Biblioteku: v 4-m kvartale 1960 goda.* Moscow, 1961, 263 pp.

————, *Katalog kandidatskikh i doktorskikh dissertatsii, postupivshikh v Biblioteku imeni V. I. Lenina i Gosudarstvennuiu Tsentral'nuiu Nauchnuiu Meditsinskuiu Biblioteku: v 1-m kvartale 1961 goda.* Moscow, 1961, 263 pp.

————, *Katalog kandidatskikh i doktorskikh dissertatsii, postupivshikh v Biblioteku imeni V. I. Lenina i Gosudarstvennuiu Tsentral'nuiu Nauchnuiu Meditsinskuiu Biblioteku: vo 2-om kvartale 1961 goda.* Moscow, 1961, 262 pp.

————, *Katalog kandidatskikh i doktorskikh dissertatsii, postupivshikh v Biblioteku imeni V. I. Lenina i Gosudarstvennuiu Tsentral'nuiu Nauchnuiu Meditsinskuiu Biblioteku: v 3-m kvartale 1961 goda.* Moscow, 1962, 267 pp.

————, *Katalog kandidatskikh i doktorskikh dissertatsii, postupivshikh v Biblioteku imeni V. I. Lenina i Gosudarstvennuiu Tsentral'nuiu Nauchnuiu Meditsinskuiu Biblioteku: v 4-m kvartale 1961 goda.* Moscow, 1962, 260 pp.

————, *Katalog kandidatskikh i doktorskikh dissertatsii, postupivshikh v Biblioteku imeni V. I. Lenina i Gosudarstvennuiu Tsentral'nuiu Nauchnuiu Meditsinskuiu Biblioteku: v 1-m kvartale 1962 goda.* Moscow, 1962, 256 pp.

————, *Katalog kandidatskikh i doktorskikh dissertatsii, postupivshikh v Biblioteku imeni V. I. Lenina i Gosudarstvennuiu Tsentral'nuiu Nauchnuiu Meditsinskuiu*

Biblioteku: vo 2-om kvartale 1962 goda. Moscow, 1962, 208 pp.

———, *Katalog kandidatskikh i doktorskikh dissertatsii, postupivshikh v Biblioteku imeni V. I. Lenina i Gosudarstvennuiu Tsentral'nuiu Nauchnuiu Meditsinskuiu Biblioteku: v 3-m kvartale 1962 goda.* Moscow, 1963, 251 pp.

———, *Katalog kandidatskikh i doktorskikh dissertatsii, postupivshikh v Biblioteku imeni V. I. Lenina i Gosudarstvennuiu Tsentral'nuiu Nauchnuiu Meditsinskuiu Biblioteku: v 4-m kvartale 1962 goda.* Moscow, 1963, 255 pp.

———, *Katalog kandidatskikh i doktorskikh dissertatsii, postupivshikh v Biblioteku imeni V. I. Lenina i Gosudarstvennuiu Tsentral'nuiu Nauchnuiu Meditsinskuiu Biblioteku: v 1-m kvartale 1963 goda.* Moscow, 1963, 248 pp.

———, *Katalog kandidatskikh i doktorskikh dissertatsii, postupivshikh v Biblioteku imeni V. I. Lenina i Gosudarstvennuiu Tsentral'nuiu Nauchnuiu Meditsinskuiu Biblioteku: vo 2-om kvartale 1963 goda.* Moscow, 1964, 236 pp.

MINISTERSTVO VYSSHEGO I SREDNOGO SPETSIAL'NOGO OBRAZOVANIIA SSSR, *Spravochnik dlia postupaiushchikh v vysshie uchebnye zavedeniia SSSR v 1961 g.* Moscow, Gosudarstvennoe izdatel'stvo "Vysshaia shkola," 1961, 301 pp.

———, *Spravochnik dlia postupaiushchikh v vysshie uchebnye zavedeniia Soiuza SSR v 1962 g.* Moscow, Gosudarstvennoe izdatel'stvo "Vysshaia shkola," 1962, 140 pp.

———, *Spravochnik dlia postupaiushchikh v vysshie uchebnye zavedeniia SSSR v 1963 g.* Moscow, Gosudarstvennoe izdatel'stvo "Sovetskaia nauka," 1963, 144 pp.

———, *Spravochnik dlia postupaiushchikh v vysshie uchebnye zavedeniia SSSR v 1964 g.* Moscow, Izdatel'stvo "Vysshaia shkola," 1964, 286 pp.

———, *Spravochnik dlia postupaiushchikh v vysshie uchebnye zavedeniia SSSR v 1965 g.* Moscow, Izdatel'stvo "Vysshaia shkola," 1965, 352 pp.

MINISTERSTVO VYSSHEGO OBRAZOVANIIA SSSR, *Vysshaia shkola, osnovnye postanovleniia, prikazy i instruktsii,* ed. by L. I.

Karpov and V. A. Severtsev. Moscow, "Sovetskaia nauka," 1957, 656 pp.

———, *Spravochnik dlia postupaiushchikh v vysshie uchebnye zavedeniia Soiuza SSR v 1956 g.* Moscow, Gosudarstvennoe izdatel'stvo "Sovetskaia nauka," 1956, 248 pp.

———, *Spravochnik dlia postupaiushchikh v vysshie uchebnye zavedeniia Soiuza SSR v 1959 g.* Moscow, Gosudarstvennoe izdatel'stvo "Sovetskaia nauka," 1959, 303 pp.

MINISTERSTVO ZDRAVOOKHRANENIIA SSSR, INSTITUT ORGANIZATSII ZDRAVOOKHRANENIIA I ISTORII MEDITSINY IMENI N. A. SEMASHKO, *Postanovleniia KPSS i Sovetskogo pravitel'stva ob okhrane zdorov'ia naroda.* Moscow, Medgiz, 1958, 339 pp.

MINTS, L. E., *Agrarnoe perenaselenie i rynok truda v SSSR.* Moscow, Gosudarstvennoe izdatel'stvo, 1929, 470 pp.

MOSKOVSKII GOSUDARSTVENNII UNIVERSITET IMENI M. V. LOMONOSOVA, NAUCHNAIA BIBLIOTEKA IMENI A. M. GOR'KOGO, *Doktorskie i kandidatskie dissertatsii, zashchishchennie v Moskovskom Gosudarstvennom Universitete s 1934 po 1954 gg.* Moscow, Izdatel'stvo Moskovskogo Universiteta, 1956, 255 pp.

———, *Doktorskie i kandidatskie dissertatsii, zashchishchennie v Moskovskom Gosudarstvennom Universitete s 1934 po 1954 gg.* 2d ed., Moscow, Izdatel'stvo Moskovskogo Universiteta, 1957, 219 pp.

———, *Doktorskie i kandidatskie dissertatsii, zashchishchennie v Moskovskom Gosudarstvennom Universitete s 1934 po 1954 gg.* 3d ed., Moscow, Izdatel'stvo Moskovskogo Universiteta, 1960, 204 pp.

MOSKOVSKOE OBSHCHESTVA ISPYTATELEI PRIRODY, *Slovar' Russkie botaniki.* Moscow, Izdatel'stvo Moskovskogo obshchestva ispytateli prirody, 1952.

NARODNOI KOMISSARIAT IUSTITSII SSSR, *Kodeks zakonov o trude, s izmeneniiami na 1 Iulia, 1938.* Moscow, Iuridicheskoe izdatel'stvo, 1938, 255 pp.

NAUCHNO-ISSLEDOVATEL'SKII INSTITUT TRUDA, *Voprosy truda.* Vol. IV, ed. by Iu. A. Pisarev. Moscow, Sotsekgiz, 1959, 260 pp.

PASKHAVER, I. S., *Balans trudovykh resursov kolkhozov (voprosy metodologii, metodiki i analiza)*. Kiev, Izdatel'stvo Ukrainskoi Akademii sel'skokhoziaistvennykh nauk, 1961, 364 pp.

PATRUSHEV, V. D., *Intensivnost' truda pri sotsializme*. Moscow, Izdatel'stvo ekonomicheskoi literatury, 1963, 238 pp.

POD"IACHIKH, P. G., *Naselenie SSSR*. Moscow, Gosudarstvennoe izdatel'stvo politicheskoi literatury, 1961, 191 pp.

PRUDENSKII, G. A. (ed.), *Vnerabochee vremia trudiashchikhsia*. Novosibirsk, Izdatel'stvo Sibirskogo otdeleniia Akademii nauk SSSR, 1961, 255 pp.

————, *Vremia i trud*. Moscow, Izdatel'stvo sotsial'no-ekonomicheskoi literatury "Mysl'," 1964, 352 pp.

ROZHIN, V. P., *Nekotorye voprosy pod"ema ekonomiki slabykh kolkhozov*. Moscow, Ekonomizdat, 1961, 183 pp.

RUMIANTSEV, A. M. (ed.), *Rol' zhenshchiny v sovremennom obshchestve*. Prague, Izdatel'stvo "Mir i Sotsializm," 1963, 273 pp.

RUMIANTSEVA, M., PERGAMENT, A., AND GROMOVA, G., *Spravochnik zhenshchiny-rabotnitsy*. Moscow, Profizdat, 1963, 287 pp.

SHISHKIN, N. I. (ed.), *Trudovye resursy SSSR (Problemy raspredeleniia i ispol'zovaniia)*. Moscow, Izdatel'stvo ekonomicheskoi literatury, 1961, 246 pp.

SHMELEV, G. I., *Raspredelenie ispol'zovanie truda v sovkhozakh*. Moscow, Izdatel'stvo "Mysl'," 1964, 143 pp.

SINETSKII, A. IA., *Professorsko-prepodavatel'skie kadry vysshei shkoly SSSR*. Moscow, Gosudarstvennoe izdatel'stvo "Sovetskaia nauka," 1950, 235 pp.

SONIN, M. IA., *Vosproizvodstvo rabochei sily v SSSR i balans truda*. Moscow, Gosplanizdat, 1959, 368 pp.

STRUMILIN, S. G., *Problemy ekonomiki truda*. Moscow, Gosudarstvennoe izdatel'stvo politicheskoi literatury, 1957, 735 pp.

TSENTRAL'NYI STATISTICHESKII KOMITET, *Obshchii svod po imperii resul'tatov razrabotki dannykh pervoi vseobshchei perepisi naseleniia*. Vol. I, St. Petersburg, Statisticheskii komitet, 1905, 268 + 89 pp.

TSENTRAL'NOE STATISTICHESKOE UPRAVLENIE PRI SOVETE MINISTROV ARMIANSKOI SSR, *Sel'skoe khoziaistvo Armianskoi SSR, statisticheskii sbornik*. Erevan, Aipetrat, 1961, 483 pp.

TSENTRAL'NOE STATISTICHESKOE UPRAVLENIE PRI SOVETE MINISTROV KIRGIZSKOI SSR, *Zhenshchina v Kirgizskoi SSR, kratkii statisticheskii spravochnik*. Frunze, Gosstatizdat, 1960, 96 pp.

TSENTRAL'NOE STATISTICHESKOE UPRAVLENIE PRI SOVETE MINISTROV LITOVSKOI SSR, *20 let Sovetskoi Litvy, statisticheskii sbornik*. Vilnius, Gosstatizdat, 1960, 352 pp.

TSENTRAL'NOE STATISTICHESKOE UPRAVLENIE PRI SOVETE MINISTROV MOLDAVSKOI SSR, *Zhenshchina Moldavii, kratkii statisticheskii spravochnik*. Kishinev, Gosstatizdat, 1961, 73 pp.

TSENTRAL'NOE STATISTICHESKOE UPRAVLENIE RSFSR, *Kul'turnoe stroitel'stvo RSFSR, statisticheskii sbornik*. Moscow, Gosstatizdat, 1958, 459 pp.

TSENTRAL'NOE STATISTICHESKOE UPRAVLENIE PRI SOVETE MINISTROV SSSR, *Itogi Vsesoiuznoi perepisi naseleniia 1959 goda: Azerbaidzhanskaia SSR*. Moscow, Gosstatizdat, 1963, 157 pp.

————, *Itogi Vsesoiuznoi perepisi naseleniia 1959 goda: Armianskaia SSR*. Moscow, Gosstatizdat, 1963, 116 pp.

————, *Itogi Vsesoiuznoi perepisi naseleniia 1959 goda: Belorusskaia SSR*. Moscow, Gosstatizdat, 1963, 146 pp.

————, *Itogi Vsesoiuznoi perepisi naseleniia 1959 goda: Estonskaia SSR*. Moscow, Gosstatizdat, 1962, 107 pp.

————, *Itogi Vsesoiuznoi perepisi naseleniia 1959 goda: Gruzinskaia SSR*. Moscow, Gosstatizdat, 1963, 150 pp.

————, *Itogi Vsesoiuznoi perepisi naseleniia 1959 goda: Kazakhskaia SSR*. Moscow, Gosstatizdat, 1962, 202 pp.

————, *Itogi Vsesoiuznoi perepisi naseleniia 1959 goda: Kirgizskaia SSR*. Moscow, Gosstatizdat, 1963, 149 pp.

————, *Itogi Vsesoiuznoi perepisi naseleniia 1959 goda: Latviiskaia SSR*. Moscow, Gosstatizdat, 1963, 106 pp.

————, *Itogi Vsesoiuznoi perepisi naseleniia 1959 goda: Litovskaia SSR*. Vil'nius, Gosstatizdat, 1963, 179 pp.

————, *Itogi Vsesoiuznoi perepisi naseleniia 1959 goda: Moldavskaia SSR*. Moscow, Gosstatizdat, 1962, 104 pp.

————, *Itogi Vsesoiuznoi perepisi naseleniia 1959 goda: RSFSR.* Moscow, Gosstatizdat, 1963, 456 pp.

————, *Itogi Vsesoiuznoi perepisi naseleniia 1959 goda: SSSR (svodnyi tom).* Moscow, Gosstatizdat, 1962, 248 pp.

————, *Itogi Vsesoiuznoi perepisi naseleniia 1959 goda: Tadzhikskaia SSR.* Moscow, Gosstatizdat, 1963, 140 pp.

————, *Itogi Vsesoiuznoi perepisi naseleniia 1959 goda: Turkmenskaia SSR.* Moscow, Gosstatizdat, 1963, 150 pp.

————, *Itogi Vsesoiuznoi perepisi naseleniia 1959 goda: Ukrainskaia SSR.* Moscow, Gosstatizdat, 1963, 210 pp.

————, *Itogi Vsesoiuznoi perepisi naseleniia 1959 goda: Uzbekskaia SSR,* Moscow, Gosstatizdat, 1962, 168 pp.

————, *Kul'turnoe stroitel'stvo SSSR, statisticheskii sbornik.* Moscow, Gosstatizdat, 1956, 332 pp.

————, *Narodnoe khoziaistvo RSFSR v 1960 godu, statisticheskii ezhegodnik.* Moscow, Gosstatizdat, 1961, 572 pp.

————, *Narodnoe khoziaistvo SSSR, statisticheskii sbornik.* Moscow, Gosstatizdat, 1956, 262 pp.

————, *Narodnoe khoziaistvo SSSR v 1956 godu, statisticheskii ezhegodnik.* Moscow, Gosstatizdat, 1957, 296 pp.

————, *Narodnoe khoziaistvo SSSR v 1958 godu, statisticheskii ezhegodnik.* Moscow, Gosstatizdat, 1959, 959 pp.

————, *Narodnoe khoziaistvo SSSR v 1959 godu, statisticheskii ezhegodnik.* Moscow, Gosstatizdat, 1960, 896 pp.

————, *Narodnoe khoziaistvo SSSR v 1960 godu, statisticheskii ezhegodnik.* Moscow, Gosstatizdat, 1961, 943 pp.

————, *Narodnoe khoziaistvo SSSR v 1961 godu, statisticheskii ezhegodnik.* Moscow, Gosstatizdat, 1962, 961 pp.

————, *Narodnoe khoziaistvo SSSR v 1962 godu, statisticheskii ezhegodnik.* Moscow, Gosstatizdat, 1963, 735 pp.

————, *Narodnoe khoziaistvo SSSR v 1963 godu, statisticheskii ezhegodnik.* Moscow, Gosstatizdat, 1965, 760 pp.

————, *Narodnoe khoziaistvo SSSR v 1964 godu, statisticheskii ezhegodnik.* Moscow, Statistika, 1965, 888 pp.

————, *Srednee spetsial'noe obrazovanie v SSSR, statisticheskii sbornik.* Moscow,

Gosstatizdat, 1962, 155 pp.

————, *SSSR v tsifrakh v 1960 godu, kratkii statisticheskii sbornik.* Moscow, Gosstatizdat, 1961, 381 pp.

————, *SSSR v tsifrakh v 1962 godu, kratkii statisticheskii sbornik.* Moscow, Gosstatizdat, 1963, 360 pp.

————, *SSSR v tsifrakh v 1964 godu, kratkii statisticheskii sbornik.* Moscow, Statistika, 1965, 160 pp.

————, *Sel'skoe khoziaistvo SSSR, statisticheskii sbornik.* Moscow, Gosstatizdat TsSU SSSR, 1960, 665 pp.

————, *Vysshee obrazovanie v SSSR, statisticheskii sbornik.* Moscow, Gosstatizdat, 1961, 255 pp.

————, *Zdravookhranenie v SSSR, statisticheskii sbornik.* Moscow, Gosstatizdat, 1960, 272 pp.

————, *Zhenshchina v SSSR, kratkii statisticheskii spravochnik.* Moscow, Gosstatizdat, 1960, 102 pp.

————, *Zhenshchiny i deti v SSSR, statisticheskii sbornik.* Moscow, Gosstatizdat, 1961, 230 pp.

————, *Zhenshchiny i deti v SSSR, statisticheskii sbornik.* 2d ed., Moscow, Gosstatizdat, 1963, 203 pp.

TSENTRAL'NOE STATISTICHESKOE UPRAVLENIE PRI SOVETE MINISTROV TADZHIKSKOI SSR, *Zhenshchina v Tadzhikskoi SSR, kratkii statisticheskii spravochnik.* Stalinabad, Gosstatizdat, 1960, 96 pp.

TSENTRAL'NOE STATISTICHESKOE UPRAVLENIE PRI SOVETE MINISTROV TURKMENSKOI SSR, *Zhenshchina v Turkmenskoi SSR, kratkii statisticheskii spravochnik,* Ashkhabad, Gosstatizdat, 1960, 84 pp.

TSENTRAL'NOE UPRAVLENIE NARODNOKHOZI-AISTVENNOGO UCHETA GOSPLANA SOIUZA, SSR, *Kul'turnoe stroitel'stvo SSSR, statisticheskii sbornik.* Moscow, Leningrad, Gosplanizdat, 1940, 267 pp.

TSENTRAL'NOE UPRAVLENIE NARODNOKHOZI-AISTVENNOGO UCHETA GOSPLANA SSSR, *Sotsialisticheskoe stroitel'stvo.* Moscow, Soiuzorguchet, 1934, 496 + 127 pp.

————, *Zhenshchina v SSSR,* ed. by I. D. Kraval'. 2d rev. ed., Moscow, Soiuzorguchet, 1937, 190 pp.

URLANIS, B. Ts., *Dinamika i struktura naseleniia SSSR i SShA.* Moscow, Izdatel'stvo "Nauka," 1964, 232 pp.

————, *Rozhdaemost' i prodolzhitel'nost' zhizni v SSSR.* Moscow, Gosstatizdat, 1963, 136 pp.

VASILENKO, M. P., *Puti preodoleniia sezonnosti truda v kolkhozakh.* Moscow, Izdatel'stvo "Sovetskaia Rossiia," 1963, 200 pp.

VENZHER, V. G., *Voprosy ispol'zovaniia zakona stoimosti v kolkhoznom proizvodstve.* Moscow, Gosplanizdat, 1960, 320 pp.

VSEROSSISKII TSENTRAL'NOI SOVET PROFESSIONAL'NYKH SOIUZOV, *Kodeks zakonov o trude i deklaratsiia prav trudiashchegosia i eksploatiruemogo naroda.* Moscow, Izdanie Vserossiiskogo tsentral'nogo soveta professional'nykh soiuzov, 1920, 32 pp.

VSESOIUZNAIA KNIZHNAIA PALATA, *Ezhegodnik dissertatsii, 1936 god.* Moscow, Izdatel'stvo Vsesoiuznoi knizhnoi palaty, 1938, 160 pp.

————, *Ezhegodnik dissertatsii, 1937 god.* Moscow, Izdatel'stvo Vsesoiuznoi knizhnoi palaty, 1940, 172 pp.

————, *Knizhnaia letopis': dopolnitel'nyi vypusk.* No. 1, 1964, Moscow, Izdatel'stvo "Kniga," 1964, 297 pp.

————, *Knizhnaia letopis': dopolnitel'nyi vypusk.* No. 2, 1964, Moscow, Izdatel'stvo "Kniga," 1964, 264 pp.

————, *Knizhnaia letopis': dopolnitel'nyi vypusk.* No. 3, 1964, Moscow, Izdatel'stvo "Kniga," 1964, 200 pp.

————, *Knizhnaia letopis': dopolnitel'nyi vypusk.* No. 4, 1964, Moscow, Izdatel'stvo "Kniga," 1964, 238 pp.

VSESOIUZNAIA KOMMUNISTICHESKAIA PARTIA (BOL'SHEVIKOV), *XVII S"ezd Vsesoiuznoi kommunisticheskoi partii (b), stenograficheskii otchet.* Moscow, Partizdat, 1934, 716 pp.

VSESOIUZNAIA ORDENA LENINA AKADEMIIA SEL'SKOKHOZIAISTVENNYKH NAUK IMENI V. I. LENINA, *Spravochnik.* Moscow, Sel'khogiz, 1958, 125 pp.

Russian-Language Articles

ARUTIUNIAN, IU. V., AND DANILOV, V. P., "Svod otchetov kolkhozov strany za period otechestvennoi voiny," *Istoricheskii arkhiv,* No. 6 (Nov.-Dec., 1962), 19–68.

BABYNIN, B., "Trudovye ressursy kolkhozov i ikh ispol'zovanie," *Problemy ekonomiki,* No. 2 (1940), 67–74.

BELIAEV, E., et al., "Izuchenie biudzheta vremeni trudiashchikhsia kak odin iz metodov konkretno-sotsialogicheskogo issledovaniia," *Vestnik Leningradskovo universiteta, Seriia ekonomiki, filosofii i prava,* Vypusk 4, No. 23 (1961), 96–110.

BRONSHTEIN, E., "Blizhaishie perspektivy zhenskogo truda," *Na planovom fronte,* No. 11 (1932), 48–54.

CHEREVKOV, K., "Pervye russkie zhenshchiny —inzhenery," *Ogonek,* No. 46 (Nov., 1956), 13.

CHERNETSKII, O. E., "Organizatsiia raboty po snizheniiu abortov," *Sovetskoe zdravookhranenie,* No. 6 (1961), 20–22.

CHUDINOVA, M. G., "V detskikh sadakh Iakutii," *Doshkol'noe vospitanie,* No. 4 (Apr., 1946), 37–38.

CHUFAROVA, G., "O rezhimakh truda i otdykha pri dal'neishem sokrashchenii rabochego vremeni," *Biulleten' nauchnoi informatsii, trud i zarabotnaia plata,* No. 9 (Sept., 1961), 10–16.

FILIPPOVA, L. D., "Iz istorii zhenskogo obrazovaniia v Rossii," *Voprosy istorii,* No. 2 (Feb., 1963), 209–18.

GABRIELIAN, T., "Doshkol'noe vospitanie v Sovetskoi Armenii za 25 let," *Doshkol'noe vospitanie,* No. 7 (July, 1946), 29–31.

GALKIN, K. T., "Iz istorii attestatsii nauchno-pedogogicheskikh kadrov," *Vestnik vysshei shkoly,* No. 9 (Sept., 1957), 44–48.

GIMMEL'FARB, S., "Likvidatsiia bezrabotnitsy v SSSR i problema kadrov," *Problemy ekonomiki,* No. 4–5 (Apr.-May, 1931), 23–56.

GLADYSHEV, A. N., "Reservy rabochei sily v gorodakh Sibiri," *Izvestiia Sibirskogo otdeleniia Akademii nauk SSSR,* No. 11 (1962), 11–17.

"Gotovit'sia k priemu uzhe sevodnia," *Vestnik vysshei shkoly,* No. 1 (Jan., 1961), 3–6.

GROMOVA, G., "Sovetskie zhenshchiny v upravlenii gosudarstvom," *Sovety deputatov trudiashchikhsia,* No. 5 (Nov., 1957), 21–25.

GUREVICH, S., AND GUREVICH, I., "O statisticheskikh sbornik mestnikh organov narodnokhoziaistvennogo ucheta," *Planovoe khoziaistvo*, No. 3 (1940), 117–24.

"K smotry doshkol'nykh uchrezhdenii sela," *Doshkol'noe vospitanie*, No. 8 (August, 1964), 26.

KALASHAIKOV, A., AND PEGOV, A., "O rasshirenii seti detskikh doshkol'nykh uchrezhdeniiakh v gor. Moskve na 1963–1965 gody, reshenie ispolnitel'nogo komiteta Moskovskogo gorodskogo Soveta deputatov trudiashchikhsia ot 21 Fevralia, 1963 g., No. 915," *Biulleten' ispolnitel'nogo komiteta Moskovskogo gorodskogo Soveta deputatov trudiashchikhsia*, No. 7 (Apr., 1963), 5–8.

KORSHUNOVA, E., "Zhenskii trud v SSSR," *Sotsialisticheskii trud*, No. 2 (Feb., 1961), 36–46.

KOZHEVINA, A., "Doshkol'noe vospitanie v Udmurtskoi ASSR za gody Sovetskoi vlasti," *Doshkol'noe vospitanie*, No. 3 (Mar., 1947), 37–41.

KUZNETSEV, I., "O chem rasskazali inspektora," *Doshkol'noe vospitanie*, No. 3 (Mar., 1964), 11–12.

LAVROVA, I. G., "Russkie zhenshchiny-khirurgi," *Meditsinskaia sestra*, No. 12 (1956), 27–28.

MASLOV, P., "Vnerabochee vremia v usloviakh perekhoda ot sotsializma k kommunizmu," *Voprosy ekonomiki*, No. 12 (Dec., 1961), 59–70.

———, "Vremia v bytu," *Novy mir*, No. 10 (Oct., 1960), 157–65.

MEL'NIKOV, V., "K dal'neishemu uluchsheniiu trudovykh uslovii," *Sotsialisticheskii trud*, No. 11 (Nov., 1959), 68–76.

OLSHANSKII, V., "Operatsia na konkretno-sotsialogicheskie issledovaniia (zametki sotsialoga)," *Partinaia zhizn'*, No. 15 (1963), 55–60.

ORLIKOVA, E., "Sovetskaia zhenshchina v obshchestvennom proizvodstve," *Problemy ekonomiki*, No. 7 (1940), 106–22.

———, "Zhenskii trud v SSSR," *Planovoe khoziaistvo*, No. 10 (Oct., 1939), 107–20.

PADEZHNOV, I., "Bol'she domov dlia malen'kikh detei," *Doshkol'noe vospitanie*, No. 2 (Feb., 1963), 33–35.

PETROSIAN, G. S., "O ratsional'nom ispol'zovanii vnerabochego vremeni trudiashchikhsia," *Voprosy ekonomiki*, No. 4 (June, 1963), 32–41.

POPOVA, N., "Zhenskii trud v SSSR," *Sotsialisticheskii trud*, No. 3 (Mar., 1957), 3–14.

PRUDENSKII, G., "Voprosy ucheta vnerabochego vremeni," *Voprosy ekonomiki*, No. 4 (Apr., 1959), 84–90.

RATNER, EVGENII, "Step' shirokaia," *Znamia*, No. 7 (1963), 112–55.

ROMIN, I., "Zhenshchina strany sovetov," *Kommunist*, No. 4 (Mar., 1960), 67–73.

ROZDIALOVSKAIA, V., "Zaniatiia grazhdan SSSR po dannym perepisi naseleniia 1959 goda," *Vestnik statistiki*, No. 3 (Mar., 1961), 3–12.

RUDAKOVA, I., "O chem rasskazali inspektora," *Doshkol'noe vospitanie*, No. 3 (Mar., 1964), 9–10.

SADVOKASOVA, E. A., "Nekotorye sotsial'no-gigienicheskie aspektu izucheniia aborta (po materialam spetsial'nogo issledovaniia v riade gorodov i sel'skikh mestnostei RSFSR za 1958–59 gg.)," *Sovetskoe zdravookhranenie*, No. 3 (Mar., 1963), 45–50.

SHMELEV, G., AND LADENKOV, U., "Ispol'zovanie zhenskogo truda v kolkhozakh," *Ekonomika sel'skogo khoziaistva*, No. 10 (Oct., 1962), 28–34.

SHUBKIN, V. N., "Vybor professii v usloviiakh kommunisticheskogo stroitel'stva," *Voprosy filosofii*, No. 8 (1964), 18–28.

"Sovkhozy—detskii sad," *Doshkol'noe vospitanie*, No. 3 (Mar., 1964), 1–3.

"Statisticheskie materialy," *Vestnik statistiki*, No. 8 (Aug., 1963), 91–92.

"Stroit' bol'she detskikh sadov luchshe vospityvat' detei," *Doshkol'noe vospitanie*, No. 1 (Jan., 1963), 1–2.

USTIUZHANINOVA, E. R., "Detskie kolkhoznye ploshchadki," *Doshkol'noe vospitanie*, No. 5 (May, 1947), 1–5.

———, "Sotsialisticheskaia pomoshch' Sovetskomu krest'ianstvu," *Doshkol'noe vospitanie*, No. 4 (Apr., 1948), 1–5.

VINOGRADOVA, N. I., "Doshkol'noe vospitanie v 4-i Stalinskoi piatiletke," *Doshkol'noe vospitanie*, Nos. 9–10 (Sept.-Oct., 1946), 1–5.

"Vnimanie i zabotu doshkol'nomu vospitaniiu

v derevne," *Doshkol'noe vospitanie,* No. 3 (Mar., 1963), 1–3.

VOLKOVA, E. I., "30 let doshkol'nogo vospitaniia," *Doshkol'noe vospitanie,* No. 10 (Oct., 1947), 8–19.

ZABLUDOVSKAIA, E. D., "Pervye zhenshchiny-vrachi v Rossii," *Meditsinskaia sestra,* No. 10 (1964), 25–30.

"Zhenshchina v SSSR," *Partinaia zhizn,* No. 4 (Feb., 1960), 58–61.

"Zhenshchiny sovetskogo soiuza," *Srednee spetsial'noe obrazovanie,* No. 3 (Mar., 1960), 2–9.

"Zhenshchiny sredi sovetskoi elity," *Sotsialisticheskii vestnik, sbornik,* No. 1 (Apr., 1964), 70–76.

Russian Newspapers and Journals Cited Directly

Ekonomicheskaia gazeta
Izvestiia
Izvestiia narkomtruda
Kazakhstanskaia pravda
Kommunist Tadzhikistana
Krasnaia zvezda
Meditsinskiy rabotnik
Narodnoe khoziaistvo Kazakhstana
Partinaia zhizn'
Pravda
Sovetskaia etnografiia
Sovetskaia Kirgiziia
Sovetskaia Rossiia
Turkmenskaia iskra
Vestnik statistiki

INDEX

Q

Women in the Soviet Economy
by
Norton T. Dodge

typesetter: Monotype Composition Company
typefaces: Times Roman
printer: Universal
paper: Perkins and Squier White Smooth Offset
binder: Moore and Company
cover material: Columbia Riverside Linen